IFIP Advances in Information and Communication Technology

459

Editor-in-Chief

Kai Rannenberg, Goethe University Frankfurt, Germany

Editorial Board

IFIP – The International Federation for Information Processing

IFIP was founded in 1960 under the auspices of UNESCO, following the First World Computer Congress held in Paris the previous year. An umbrella organization for societies working in information processing, IFIP's aim is two-fold: to support information processing within its member countries and to encourage technology transfer to developing nations. As its mission statement clearly states,

> IFIP's mission is to be the leading, truly international, apolitical organization which encourages and assists in the development, exploitation and application of information technology for the benefit of all people.

IFIP is a non-profitmaking organization, run almost solely by 2500 volunteers. It operates through a number of technical committees, which organize events and publications. IFIP's events range from an international congress to local seminars, but the most important are:

- The IFIP World Computer Congress, held every second year;
- Open conferences;
- Working conferences.

The flagship event is the IFIP World Computer Congress, at which both invited and contributed papers are presented. Contributed papers are rigorously refereed and the rejection rate is high.

As with the Congress, participation in the open conferences is open to all and papers may be invited or submitted. Again, submitted papers are stringently refereed.

The working conferences are structured differently. They are usually run by a working group and attendance is small and by invitation only. Their purpose is to create an atmosphere conducive to innovation and development. Refereeing is also rigorous and papers are subjected to extensive group discussion.

Publications arising from IFIP events vary. The papers presented at the IFIP World Computer Congress and at open conferences are published as conference proceedings, while the results of the working conferences are often published as collections of selected and edited papers.

Any national society whose primary activity is about information processing may apply to become a full member of IFIP, although full membership is restricted to one society per country. Full members are entitled to vote at the annual General Assembly, National societies preferring a less committed involvement may apply for associate or corresponding membership. Associate members enjoy the same benefits as full members, but without voting rights. Corresponding members are not represented in IFIP bodies. Affiliated membership is open to non-national societies, and individual and honorary membership schemes are also offered.

More information about this series at http://www.springer.com/series/6102

Shigeki Umeda · Masaru Nakano
Hajime Mizuyama · Hironori Hibino
Dimitris Kiritsis · Gregor von Cieminski (Eds.)

Advances in Production Management Systems

Innovative Production Management Towards Sustainable Growth

IFIP WG 5.7 International Conference, APMS 2015
Tokyo, Japan, September 7–9, 2015
Proceedings, Part I

 Springer

Editors

Shigeki Umeda
Musashi University
Tokyo
Japan

Masaru Nakano
Keio University
Kanagawa
Japan

Hajime Mizuyama
Aoyama Gakuin University
Kanagawa
Japan

Hironori Hibino
Tokyo University of Science
Chiba
Japan

Dimitris Kiritsis
EPFL
Lausanne
Switzerland

Gregor von Cieminski
ZF Friedrichshafen AG
Friedrichshafen
Germany

ISSN 1868-4238   ISSN 1868-422X   (electronic)
IFIP Advances in Information and Communication Technology
ISBN 978-3-319-37425-3   ISBN 978-3-319-22756-6   (eBook)
DOI 10.1007/978-3-319-22756-6

Printed on acid-free paper

Springer International Publishing AG Switzerland is part of Springer Science+Business Media
(www.springer.com)

Preface

Modern companies in industrially advanced countries face the low growth of the global economy. Every enterprise makes various efforts to survive in such a severe management environment. Mass production style has disappeared, and manufacturers must provide goods that the customer favors when the customer wants them.

Organizations today cannot do it alone. Most modern enterprises depend on the collective efforts of a group of trading partners to stretch a supply chain from the raw material supplier to the end customer. A trading partner in this context means any external organization that plays an integral role in the enterprise and whose business fortune depends wholly or partly on the success of the enterprise. This includes factories, contract manufacturers, sub-assembly plants, distribution centers, wholesalers, retailers, carriers, freight forwarder services, customer broker services, international procurement organizations, and value-added network services. Building such resilient global value-chains is needed.

Current enterprises also face global environment issues. Saving energy, reduction of industrial waste, and reutilization of natural resources are required in all operational stages to realize environmentally friendly production and logistics systems. Modern manufacturing enterprises should cope well with such issues as enterprise management responsibilities.

This book collects suggestions of leading researchers and practitioners from all around the world, including conceptual frameworks of new approaches, developments of novel technologies, and case studies of practical issues. The book comprises five main categories, including specific subtopic themes as follows:

- Collaborative networks

  - Collaborative tools in production management
  - Collaborative design
  - Distributed systems and multi-agent technologies
  - ICT for collaborative manufacturing
  - Innovation for enterprise collaboration
  - Collaborative information networks
  - Performance measurement and benchmarking
  - B2B, B2C

- Globalization and production management

  - Inventory management in large supply chains
  - Global supply chain systems
  - Mass customization
  - Social and cultural aspects of global supply chains

- Worldwide procurement
- Logistics and distribution management

• Knowledge-based production management

- Computational intelligence in production management
- Intelligent manufacturing systems
- Knowledge engineering
- Knowledge-based PLM
- Production planning and control
- Scheduling
- Automatic learning systems
- Modeling and simulation of business and operational processes
- Supply chain simulation
- Social networks for manufacturing
- Virtual factory
- Agile and flexible manufacturing systems

• Project management, engineering management, and quality management

- Closed loop design
- Highly customized products and services
- Quality management
- QFD
- Six-sigma
- New products development
- Engineering management
- Engineering and management education

• Sustainability and production management

- Eco-design and eco-innovation
- Energy efficiency in manufacturing
- Green manufacturing
- Life cycle assessment
- Remanufacturing
- Disassembly and recycling
- Sustainable supply chains
- Sustainability in global supply networks
- Smart factory

The papers in this book were peer reviewed and presented at the advanced production management systems conference – APMS 2015 – which was held in Tokyo, Japan, September 7–9, 2015. The conference was supported by Working Group 7 of Technical Committee 5 of the International Federation for Information Processing called Advances in Production Management Systems (APMS) and was hosted by Musashi University, Tokyo, Japan.

There were 185 full paper submittions, and 163 of them were accepted through peer review. Thus, the acception ratio is about 88 %. As the book editors, we would like to thank all the contributors for the high-quality presentation of their papers. We would also like to thank the members of the international Program Committee for their work in reviewing and selecting the papers.

June 2015

Shigeki Umeda
Masaru Nakano
Hajime Mizuyama
Hironori Hibino
Dimitris Kiritsis
Gregor von Cieminski

Organization

Conference Chair

Shigeki Umeda   Musashi University, Japan

Co-chairs

Masaru Nakano   Keio University, Japan
Dimitris Kiritsis   EPFL, Switzerland
Gregor von Cieminski   ZF Friedrichshafen AG, Germany

International Scientific Committee

Chair

Masaru Nakano   Keio University, Japan

Members

Erlend Alfnes   NTNU, Norway
Sergio Cavalieri   University of Bergamo, Italy
Stephen Childe   University of Exeter, UK
Hyunbo Cho   Pohang University of Science and Technology, Korea
Byoung-Kyu Choi   KAIST, Korea
Gregor von Cieminski   ZF Friedrichshafen AG, Germany
Catherine Da Cunha   Ecole Centrale de Nantes, France
Heidi Carin Dreyer   NTNU, Norway
Christos Emmanouilidis Knowledge, Communication and Information
                         Technologies, Greece
Peter Falster   Technical University of Denmark, Denmark
Jan Frick   Stavanger University, Norway
Marco Garetti   Politecnico di Milano, Italy
Samuel Gomes   UTBM, France
Bernard Grabot   ENIT, France
Gideon Halevi   Hal Tech Ltd., Israel
Hans-Henrik Hvolby   Aalborg University, Denmark
John Johansen   Aalborg University, Denmark
Susanne Altendorfer   Montan Universität, Austria
  Kaiser
Tomasz Koch   Wroclaw University of Technology, Poland
Boonserm Kulvatunyou   NIST, USA
Andrew Kusiak   University of Iowa, USA

Jan-Peter Lechner	First Global Liaison, Germany
Ming K. Lim	University of Derby, UK
Hermann Lödding	Technical University of Hamburg-Harburg, Germany
Marco Macchi	Politecnico di Milano, Italy
Magali Bosch-Mauchand	Université de Technologie de Compiègne, France
Kai Mertins	Knowledge Raven Management GmbH, Germany
Ilkyeong Moon	Seoul National University, Korea
Dimitris Mourtzis	University of Patras, Greece
Gilles Neubert	EMLYON Business School, France
Jinwoo Park	Seoul National University, Korea
Henk-Jan Pels	Eindhoven University of Technology, The Netherlands
Vittaldas V. Prabhu	Pennsylvania State University, USA
Jens O. Riis	Aalborg University, Denmark
David Romero	Mexico
Paul Schoensleben	MTEC, Switzerland
Riitta Smeds	Aalto University, Finland
Vijay Srinivasan	NIST, USA
Kenn Steger-Jensen	Aalborg University, Denmark
Volker Stich	FIR Forschungsinstitut für Rationalisierung Aachen, Germany
Stanisław Strzelczak	Warsaw University of Technology, Poland
Marco Taisch	Politecnico di Milano, Italy
Klaus-Dieter Thoben	Universität Bremen, Germany
Mario Tucci	Universitá degli Studi di Firenze, Italy
Bruno Vallespir	University of Bordeaux, France
Iveta Zolotová	Technical University of Košice, Slovakia
Abdelaziz Bouras	Qatar University, State of Qatar

Local Committee

Members

Eiji Arai	Osaka University, Japan
Susumu Fujii	Kobe University, Japan
Hiroyuki Hiraoka	Chuo University, Japan
Ichiro Inoue	Kyoto Sangyo University, Japan
Toshiya Kaihara	Kobe University, Japan
Fumihiko Kimura	Hosei University, Japan
Keiji Mitsuyuki	Denso, Japan
Yasuyuki Nishioka	Hosei University, Japan
Seishi Ono	Nezu Foundation, Japan

Program Committee

Chair

Hajime Mizuyama   Aoyama Gakuin University, Japan

Co-chair

Hironori Hibino   Tokyo University of Science, Japan

Members

Nobutada Fujii   Kobe University, Japan
Koji Iwamura   Osaka Prefecture University, Japan
Eiji Morinaga   Osaka University, Japan
Tomomi Nonaka   Aoyama Gakuin University, Japan
Mizuho Sato   Keio University, Japan
Takayuki Tomaru   Keio University, Japan
Akira Tsumaya   Kobe University, Japan

Doctoral Workshop

Chair

Hironori Hibino   Tokyo University of Science, Japan

Co-chair

Marco Macchi   Politecnico di Milano, Italy

International Advisory Board

Dimitris Kiritsis   EPFL, Switzerland
Vittal Prabhu   Penn State University, USA
Bernard Grabot   University of Toulouse, INP-ENIT, France

Contents – Part I

Globalization and Production Management

Knowledge Based Production Management

Sustainability and Production Management

Contents – Part II

The Practitioner's View on "Innovative Production Management Towards Sustainable Growth"

The Role of Additive Manufacturing in Value Chain Reconfigurations and Sustainability

Operations Management in Engineer-to-Order Manufacturing

Cloud-Based Manufacturing

**Ontology-Aided Production - Towards Open and Knowledge-Driven
Planning and Control**

**Product-Service Lifecycle Management: Knowledge-Driven Innovation
and Social Implications**

Collaborative Networks

Power and Trust: Can They Be Connected in an Interorganizacional Network?

Walter C. Satyro[1(✉)], Jose B. Sacomano[1], Renato Telles[2], and Elizangela M. Menegassi de Lima[1]

[1] Postgraduate Program in Production Engineering, Paulista University-UNIP, Rua Dr. Bacelar, 1212, Sao Paulo, SP 04026-000, Brazil
{satyro.walter, jbsacomano}@gmail.com,
menegassi@unipar.br
[2] Postgraduate Program in Administration, Paulista University-UNIP, Rua Dr. Bacelar, 1212, Sao Paulo, SP 04026-000, Brazil
rtellesl@gmail.com

Abstract. Studies on interorganizational networks tend to be dense in their different aspects such as structural characteristics, nature of the links and transactional content, but light on power in networks. The purpose of this paper is to study a possible correlation between power and trust in an interorganizational network. Using quantitative methodology based on a survey sample made in 29 food companies that belong to a Brazilian food association, it was possible to statistically correlate power and trust in this network. The findings can be of importance to present what aspects the companies in this network pay more attention to: power, trust and their relationship, and to present a methodology that can be reproduced for the studies of power in networks. As a characteristic of empirical studies in networks, the temporal transversality of the nature of the sample does not allow generalizations.

Keywords: Power · Networks · Trust · Methodology · Quantitative

1 Introduction

Due to the great complexity of the modern days, the competition and the interdependency between the organizations, some of them do not operate isolated, but in strategic alliances, including suppliers, customers and even competitors, when they exchange raw materials, products, services, and develop technology, services and products in partnership. Such strategic alliance was called interorganizational networks [1].

A new range of studies was opened to analyze the interorganizational networks under a wide variety of approaches, mainly in its structural characteristics, nature of the links and transactional content, when trust, commitment and cooperation were usually studied, leaving power in networks as an obscure variable with a few studies [2].

There are still gaps in the academic studies in knowledge on power in networks [3, 4], that would require more researches [2].

© IFIP International Federation for Information Processing 2015
S. Umeda et al. (Eds.): APMS 2015, Part I, IFIP AICT 459, pp. 3–10, 2015.
DOI: 10.1007/978-3-319-22756-6_1

Politics and power involve the organizations in a process of giving and receiving, difficult to be unveiled [5], as in the interactions between people there are social exchanges, and with it, power emerges [2].

Power is so relevant in interorganizacional networks that it should constitute one of the four theoretical mechanisms of its analysis. The other ones are: access to resources, trust and signaling [6].

Studies on networks tend to be dense in matters such as trust and negotiation, but exceptionally light on themes such as power and domination among their members [2].

The aim of this research is to correlate power and trust, using quantitative approach, in the interorganizacional network subject of this study, and to analyze the results. The findings can be of importance to show what the companies in this network pay more attention to: power, trust and their relationship, for future researches in this area.

2   Literature Review

This chapter aims to provide an overview of power in interorganizational networks and trust.

2.1   Power in Interorganizational Networks

Power can shape and reshape the networks as their actors are always interacting; and from these interactions, interests arouse, when actors tend to fight for power to themselves, or to stop the power of others, and that can change the structure and patterns of the network, showing its dynamics, in opposite to the idea of a perennial position of the networks structure [7].

The changes in networks can be positive or negative, depending on the relationship between the organizations that compose the network: their gains and loss, advantages or disadvantages, time and energy to keep the relationships in the networks, and others [8].

Each actor in the network represents an individual organization that keeps its own independency. Organizations can have different interests, and when it is difficult to reach an understanding in the networks, conflicts can arouse, when the harmony can be difficult to maintain and the network can reach a collapse [9–11].

In interorganizational networks both conflicts and cooperation are present [12], so it is necessary to consider power in all its dimensions, as well as the human beings search for power to reach their dreams, hopes, interests … [4].

It is difficult to provide a taxonomy of power, due to the many windows power opened to observe the daily life [13–15], with each author seeing power through different approaches. In Table 1 it can be seen some authors and their different approaches.

The concept of power used in this research was of the conscious submission [17] as in Table 1, when power varies from control to influence of the network.

Table 1. Different approaches on power in networks (Source: adapted [16])

Concept of power	Basic idea	Authors	Year
Collective changes	Movement of material goods for the community, lived under the sign of spontaneity	Mauss	1925
Collective purpose	Actors from a given community must perform actions legitimized by their society	Parson	1968
Exercise	Power manifests itself associated with relationships, regardless of ownership or legitimacy	Foucault	1979
Interdependency	Power as the basis for regulation of relations between actors of networks - formal and informal governance	Powell	1983
Group agglutinative	Power groups the individuals by their position of way of communication in their social interactions	Luhmann	1997
Base for network analysis	Variable conditional on the level of analysis of the decision to be adopted in the research (dyad, ego or network)	Zaheer et al. [6]	2010
Conscious submission	Actors in networks analysis benefits and efforts to stay in the network and consciously submit to power – that varies from control to influence.	Telles et al. [17]	2014

2.2   Trust

Trust can be defined as the understanding that the other actors of the network will take the right attitude, no matter the consequences, in result of the compromise that is being generated by the longtime of interaction among the actors of the network [18]; that reflects the reputation and value of each agent within the network [19].

3   Methodology

This work uses a descriptive research as the main objective is to study a phenomenon (power) in a specific population (network), with a nuance of exploratory research [20]. The approach will be quantitative as the purpose is to stablish a statistical relation between power and trust in networks [21].

3.1   Planning the Research

To operationalize the research, here follows how it was planned.

Sample. This study was performed at a network of a Brazilian food association, composed of 44 associated companies. This association had 12 years of activity in a very competitive market, and this made it special for the research. The actors chosen had more than one year of association and were up to 60 km far from the association head office. The sample of the research was composed of 29 food companies (66 % of the total).

Strategy of Research. For data collection it was chosen a sample survey [22] with the application of a printed questionnaire that was delivery on hands to the each actor – that represents the company in the food association -, in their own companies, for immediate fulfilling.

For this research 729.7 km were covered to perform the interviews that lasted about 1 h, each one.

The questionnaire was divided in three parts.

In the first part it was asked to inform the companies in the network that the interviewed actor used to keep in touch more frequently (to get information, advices, experience change, …). After that, it was asked to provide a grade – from 0 % (minimum) to 100 % (maximum) of the influence that the already named company (more frequently contacted) exerted over the interviewed actor, as shown in Table 2.

Table 2. First part of the questionnaire. (Source: adapted [16])

Name of the company in the network more contacted	Name of the actor more contacted	Grade of influence of this actor/company in your decisions (%)										
1°		0	10	20	30	40	50	60	70	80	90	100
2°		0	10	20	30	40	50	60	70	80	90	100
3°		0	10	20	30	40	50	60	70	80	90	100
…		0	10	20	30	40	50	60	70	80	90	100

In the second part of the questionnaire it was asked to the interviewed actor to mark in a Likert scale of 5 points, where 1 point corresponds to "Disagree completely" and 5 points represents "Agree completely", five assertions about power in networks and two about trust in networks, as shown in Table 3.

Table 3. Second part of the questionnaire. (Source: adapted [16])

Nr.	Assertion	Disagree completely	Disagree partially	Neither agree nor disagree	Agree partially	Agree completely
		①	②	③	④	⑤

Assertions about power that got correlations in the survey:

11. Everybody can speak their minds in the Association.
14. Even with conflicts it is possible to be heard in decision-making meetings in the Association.

Assertions about trust that got correlations in the survey:

18. I trust in the Association (members of the association as a whole) guidelines.
19. I trust in the Board guidelines.

In the third part of the questionnaire it was asked to the interviewed actor to freely talk about how he/she saw the food association, and along the speech, it was tried to observe if what the actor was talking was coherent with what was marked in the first and second parts of the questionnaire for check [23].

Analysis. For analysis, the questionnaires that resulted from the survey of the 29 food Brazilian companies were divided in four stratums, accordingly to the medium of the grades they received based on the results of Table 1, as presented in Table 4.

Table 4. The sample was divided in four stratums for power and trust analysis. (Source: adapted [16])

Stratum	Medium grade resulted from Table 1
Low power	1.5–2.5
Regular power	2.6–5
Satisfactory power	5.1–7.5
High power	7.6–10

Ten actors were excluded for receiving grade zero, and two more for refusing to fulfil Table 1.

It was used the IBM SPSS Statistic v. 21 to verify the Pearson's correlation coefficient between the six assertions of power and the two of trust (Table 3) for each stratum in separate.

4   Results

Here follows the analysis of the Pearson's correlation of the assertions that were significant in the research.

In the stratum "low power", the power to speak his mind in the association is correlated to the trust the actor has in the members of the association as a whole.

The stratum "regular power" showed that the power to speak their mind in the association is correlated to the trust the actor has in the members of the Board of Directors.

In the stratum "satisfactory power", the power to speak their mind in the association is correlated to the trust the actor has in the members of the association as a whole, or in the members of the Board of Directors.

By the other side, the stratum "high power" showed that the power to be heard during decision-making meetings in the association is correlated to the trust the actor has in the members of the association as a whole, or in the members of the Board of Directors.

The statistical values are shown in Table 5.

Table 5. Pearson sample correlation observed between power and trust in the survey.

Stratum	Pearson sample correlation coefficient (r)	Level of significance (p) (for two tailed test)
Low power	1.00	0.000
Regular power	0.98	0.014
Satisfactory power	0.98	0.038
	0.98	0.038
High power	0.92	0.028
	1.00	0.00

4.1   Validation of the Findings

For validation of the results, it was compared for each stratum, the degree of importance the assertion that reached the acceptable Pearson correlation coefficient between power and trust, was of importance to the group that composed each stratum, as follows in Table 6.

Table 6. Comparison of the relative importance that the power assertion – that reached the acceptable Pearson correlation coefficient – has to the group.

Stratum	Relative importance of the power assertion to each group
Low power	75 %
Regular power	50 %
Satisfactory power	100 %
High power	75 %

This comparison was not made with trust, because it has just two assertions, so both could be considered of significance.

As the assertions that reached the Pearson correlation between power and trust reached a considered level of importance, the correlation between power and trust can be confirmed.

5   Conclusions

It was made a survey in 29 Brazilian companies of a food network to analyse power and trust among their members.

It was found that power and trust point to be correlated in this study of interorganizational network.

The stratums: "low power", "regular power" and "satisfactory power" value the power to speak their minds in the Association.

The stratum "high power" values the power to be heard in decision-making meetings in the Association.

As power increases, the stratum with greater power ("satisfactory" and "high power") is divided in correlating power based on the trust of members of the Board, and based on the members of the Association as a whole.

There is not a common vision of power and trust among the members of the network under study, what can show the different interests members have in this network, what can cause conflicts to be overcome by their members, pointing that power can shape and reshape the networks as their actors are always interacting [7].

As a limitation of this research, the survey portrays a cross-section, figuring a moment in the life of the network which may not reflect the way power and trust are usually connected in this network.

As a characteristic of empirical studies in networks, this temporal cross-section of the sample nature does not allow generalizations.

Future researches were suggested in other networks, using the same methodology developed here, to confirm the findings and to study in deep the consequences of the connections between power and trust as appointed here.

References

1. Gulati, R.: Alliances and networks. Strateg. Manage. J. **19**(4), 293–317 (1988). (Special Issue: Editor's Choice)
2. Giglio, E.M., Pugliese, L.R., Silva, R.M.: Análise dos conceitos de poder nos artigos brasileiros sobre redes. Revista de Administração da UNIMEP **10**(3), 51–69 (2012)
3. Finne, M., Turunen, T., Eloranta, V.: Striving for network power: the perspective of solution integrators and suppliers. J. Purchasing Supply Manage. **21**, 9–24 (2015)
4. Lacoste, S., Johnsen, R.E.: Supplier-customer relationships: a case study of power dynamics. J. Purchasing Supply Manage. (In press, 14 Jan 2015)
5. Mintzberg, H., Ahlstrand, B., Lampel, J.: Safari de estratégia – um roteiro sobre a selva do planejamento estratégico, 2nd edn. Bookman, Porto Alegre (2010)
6. Zaheer, A., Gozubuyuk, R., Milanov, H.: It's the connections: the networks perspective in interorganizational research. Acad. Manage. Perspect. **24**(1), 62–77 (2010)
7. Nohria, N.: Is a network perspective a useful way of studying organizations? In: Nohria, N., Ecles, R. (eds.) Networks and Organizations: Structure, Form, and Action. Harvard Business School, Boston (1992)
8. Pesämaa, O.: Development of relationships in interorganizational networks: studies in the tourism and construction industries. These (Doctorate in Administration) – Department of Administration of Business and Negotiation and Social Sciences, Division of Industrial Organization, Luleä University of Technology, Strömsund, Sweden, pp. 1–304 (2007)
9. Lopes, F.D., Baldi, M.: Redes como perspectiva de análise e como estrutura de governança: uma análise das diferentes contribuições. RAP – Revista de Administração Pública **43**(5), 1007–1035 (2009)
10. Park, S.H., Ungson, G.R.: Interfirm rivalry and managerial complexity: a conceptual framework of alliance failure. Organ. Sci. **12**(1), 37–53 (2001)

11. Sheng-Yue, H., Xu, R.: Analyses of strategic alliance failure: a dynamic model. In: International Conference on Management Science and Engineering – ISTP 2005, pp. 966–973. Harbin Institute of Technology proceedings, Russia (2005). http://www.docstoc.com/docs/111016299/Avoid-Failure-When-Entering-the-Chinese-Market. Accessed 27 Jan 2014
12. Dubois, A., Hakansson, H.: Relationships and activity links. In: Ebers, M. (ed.) The Formation of Inter-organizational Networks. Oxford University Press, New York (2002)
13. Galbraith, J.K.: Anatomia do poder, 4th edn. Pioneira, São Paulo (1999)
14. Cecílo, L.C.O., Moreira, M.E.: Disputa de interesses, mecanismos de controle e conflitos: a trama do poder nas organizações de saúde. Revista de Administração Pública – RAP/EBAPE/FGV **36**(4), 587–608 (2002)
15. Dallari, D.A.: Elementos de teoria geral do Estado, 32nd edn. Saraiva, São Paulo (2013)
16. Satyro, W.C.: A questão do poder na dinâmica das redes interorganizacionais. Dissertation, Master in Administration, Paulista University – UNIP (2014)
17. Telles, R., Giglio, E.M., Satyro, W.C.: Proposta de uma linha conceitual de poder em estudos sobre redes. In: Proceedings of XVII SEMEAD, São Paulo (2014)
18. Granovetter, M.: The impact of social structure on economic outcomes. J. Econ. Perspect. **19**(1), 33–50 (2005)
19. Haus, T., Palunko, I., Tolic, D., Bogdan, S., Lewis, F.L., Mikulski, D.G.: Trust-based self-organising network control. IET Control Theor. Appl. **8**(18), 2126–2135 (2014)
20. Hair Jr., J.F., Babin, B., Money, A.H., Samouel, P.: Fundamentos de métodos de pesquisa em administração. Bookman, Porto Alegre (2005)
21. Gil, A.C.: Como elaborar projetos de pesquisa, 5th edn. Atlas, São Paulo (2010)
22. Creswell, J.W.: Projeto de pesquisa: métodos qualitativos, quantitativos e misto, 3rd edn. Artmed, Porto Alegre (2010)
23. Yin, R.K.: Estudo de caso: planejamento e métodos, 4th edn. Bookman, Porto Alegre (2010)

Relationships and Centrality in a Cluster of the Milk Production Network in the State of Parana/Brazil

Elizangela M. Menegassi Lima[1]([⊠]), Jorge G.A. Pona[2],
Jose B. Sacomano[1], João Gilberto Mendes dos Reis[1],
and Debora S. Lobo[2]

[1] Post-Graduate Program in Production Engineering,
Paulista University-UNIP, São Paulo, Brazil
menegassi@unipar.br, jbsacomano@gmail.com
[2] Post-Graduate Program in Regional and Agricultural Development,
State University of the West of Parana – UNIOESTE, Cascavel, Brazil

Abstract. The objective of this research is to evaluate the relationships of the network formed by the important milk cluster in the city of Umuarama, State of Parana (PR)/BRAZIL, using the Social Network Analysis (SNA) focusing on the collective gains and competitive advantages of this cluster. The methodology used was qualitative and quantitative. Questionnaires were applied to the network for the characterization of the existing relationships between them, and also to present the analysis of network measures using the UCINET software and the graphics schemes of networks. It was found that this milk production network appears to be diffuse, and that there are few solid relationships, which have no central coordination; the network did not present governance relationships nor a defined empowerment with significant transaction costs relationships. The relevance of this paper is to present a procedure of study in networks that can be reproduced in future researches.

Keywords: Clusters · Networks · Simultaneous networks · Relationship · Milk

1 Introduction

The advent of globalization and the internationalization of the economy made the competitive advantages be seen as essential to the business management [1–3]. Therefore, studies are needed to clarify new forms of regional operations in niche markets, due to their increasingly competitiveness, creating sustainable competitive advantages in that niche.

This process requires the actors to implement a development policy and seek new concepts of organization of products and services in micro and macroeconomic terms, to favors a more flexible structure supported by new technologies [2, 4].

One of these new technologies used to increase the competitiveness of organizations is the approach by the concepts of Business Networks, mainly regarding the relationships between the actors and the centrality of the network [4].

© IFIP International Federation for Information Processing 2015
S. Umeda et al. (Eds.): APMS 2015, Part I, IFIP AICT 459, pp. 11–19, 2015.
DOI: 10.1007/978-3-319-22756-6_2

However, the large number of actors involved makes it difficult to conduct a study of the agents' role in the structure of these networks. Thus, some studies have been developed by analyzing the company networks from the perspective of social networks using softwares such as UCINET and NetDraw [5].

The studies of Roy and Sarkar [6] proposed a method to rank the stock indices from across the globe using social network analysis approach; Söylemezoglu and Doruk [4] clearly confirm that the clustering approach has positive results in regional development and also values the cluster.

The aim of this study is to evaluate the network relationships of the milk production network, using Social Network Analysis (SNA) in the city of Umuarama-PR/BRAZIL, focusing on the collective gains and competitive advantages for the cluster of milk producers in the city.

For this, a survey was applied to agents of the milk production network through an analysis of the simultaneous networks (physical, value and business) [7], in three dimensions: relationship, governance and distribution of power and cost transaction. It is inferred that, when the relationships between the actors of a network are dense, the cluster becomes more competitive, allowing a local and regional growth.

2 Theoretical Background

2.1 Networks Analysis

In the relationships that occur within the organization between their individuals, it can be argued that the interactions between the various types of actors are understood and studied by the analysis of the theory of companies networks [8–12].

The concept of business network is shown as a collection of individuals or organizations connected through relationships of various kinds, and that a network consists of nodes and links (lines or edges) that connect the nodes based on bilateral relations between two actors [13].

In a network there is a central actor joining many other actors not connected to each other that helps to lead the actions of the group. This centrality describes the degree of the position where the individual can be found in this network. It is noteworthy that many are the quantitative indicators that measure and reflect the power of the actors [4, 13, 14].

The centrality emphasizes the positive effects of dense and consistent ties in a regulatory environment. Such ties facilitate trust and cooperation between individuals, and in return, provide benefits, such as information and knowledge sharing.

The existence of structural holes in a network represents business opportunities, in which an actor can join to complete the network [11, 15, 16]. A network can be characterized for its general structure and by the way it establishes the links between the actors. A business network is dense when the maximum of information takes place between the actors. On the contrary, the business network is considered diffuse when the relations between the actors are weak [17].

2.2 Networks Companies

In the study of the key attributes of companies networks it can be considered the existence of three sub networks that interact with each other, called Simultaneous Networks. These networks are divided into (a) physical network, (b) value network and (c) business network, as can be seen in Fig. 1 [7].

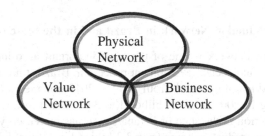

Fig. 1. Simultaneous networks (Source: adapted [7])

The physical network is responsible for the activities or delivery functions of raw material supplies; from suppliers to the places of their effective use, it is there that the physical production of goods and/or services can be checked.

The value network is the place where occurs the alternative development activities to obtain the conditions for meeting the needs that customers consider important.

The actors of value networks are companies with areas of projects connected with the achievement of a particular item of value, such as universities, research centers, among others.

		Dimensions of the Milk Production Network		
		Relationship	Governance and Power Distribution	Transaction Costs
The simultaneous networks	Physical	Enable the free flow of products, services and information.	Enable the reduction in operating costs by creating a more favorable working environment.	Are reduced in a cooperation environment due to the confidence of the members.
	Value	Enable greater access to information and innovations to support the activities of the agent.	Enable efficiencies gains and make clear the network value creation processes.	More efficient operations and more credibility between the partners; generate lower transaction costs.
	Business	Enables a better understanding between the agents and joint works for the network performance.	Enables more partnerships and more agility in decision making, identifying new opportunities, generating business.	Transparency, credibility and trust generate advantages in the search for new partnerships.

Fig. 2. Conceptual research model (Source: adapted [7])

The business network is composed of agents that assess or measure the needs dictated by a given market; it is meant to discover them and pass on to their business partners; it should develop commercial activities, and is responsible for implementing activities that facilitate customer access to products and services [7, 8, 18].

In this study it was proposed a conceptual model of simultaneous networks, whose dimensions are shown in Fig. 2.

2.3   The Milk Production Network in Brazil and in the State of Parana

The milk production network is one of the most important agro-industrial activities, and in the economic and social development process in Brazil it has an important role, given that milk production in Brazil, from 2009 to 2013 obtained a percentage growth of 17.67 %, starting in 2009 from 29 billion l to 34 billion l in 2013.

The milk production in the state of Parana/Brazil has increased year after year; for example, in 2009 the production came from 3.3 billion l, reaching 4.3 billion l in 2013, a percentage growth of 30.19 %. Compared with the national growth, the state of Parana stood out greatly, as shown in Table 1.

Table 1. Evolution of milk production. (Source: adapted [19])

Year	Brazil Quantity (1,000 l)	Parana state Quantity (1,000 l)	%
2013	34,255,236	4,347,493	12.69 %
2012	32,304,421	3,968,506	12.28 %
2011	32,091,012	3,819,187	11.90 %
2010	30,715,460	3,595,775	11.71 %
2009	29,112,024	3,339,306	11.47 %

While all domestic production grew 51,436 billion l, the production in Parana grew more than 1 billion l, which means that 19.60 % of the national production growth between the years 2009 and 2013 were from Parana.

The milk production network in the state of Parana presents distinct aspects from the producing regions. For example, in the southern state, in the cities of Carambei, Castro, Palm and Arapoti (Ponta Grossa's region), some dairy cattle are among the best in the country, with the average yield in the region of about 4,000 l/cow/year; however, in these regions it is not uncommon to come across properties that hit the mark 8,000–10,000 l/cow/year.

3   Methodology

The study was conducted in the city of Umuarama, located in southern Brazil, in northwestern Parana region.

It was chosen a case study with descriptive approach with quantitative and qualitative methodology [16], using a survey research that is more appropriate for this type of approach [8, 13, 14].

The agents considered active participants in the milk production network are called:

- [AG1] Cooperatives - Cooperatives of farmers operating in the city of Umuarama, headquartered in this city or not;
- [AG2] industry and trade of machinery and equipment - milking equipment and other technologies used in the management of dairy cattle, operating in the study region, directly or through resellers;
- [AG3] industry and animal feed trade and veterinary products - supply of feed for dairy cattle nutrition and veterinary products for animal health of dairy cattle, in the study region;
- [AG4] milk producers (with herd of considered dairy breeds) – producers of cow milk, with properties located in the city of Umuarama - PR, which have herd of considered dairy breeds;
- [AG5] EMBRAPA – Brazilian federal agency of agricultural research, which seeks to develop technologies for agricultural production;
- [AG6] SEAB/EMATER - State government agency that looks for the management and collection of information about the operations performed in the market of the state (regulatory body) and extension member (technology transfer and technical assistance), that operates providing technical and managerial support to producers in the region;
- [AG7] universities - higher education units that prepare professionals to work in agribusiness (especially Agronomy, Veterinary, Food Engineering, Food Technology and Management), mainly those operating in the region (UNIPAR and UEM);
- [AG8] industries for processing and dairy - intermediate industry, which operates processing the fresh products produced by the farmer, turning them into finished products for final consumption;
- [AG9] commercial banks and credit unions - private or public financial agents, who work in the milk production network, and provide credit to its various links;
- [AG10] IAPAR - State Institute of Agricultural Research, active in agricultural research and technological development of the municipality;
- [AG11] producer associations - milk producers associations operating in the city of the study.

To collect data, questionnaires and interviews with participants in the milk network agents in the city of Umuarama – PR were made. The data were tabulated and it was attributed a value of 1 (one) when a particular agent relationship was appointed by the respondent, and attributed 0 (zero) when a particular agent relationship was not appointed by the respondent, forming with this an analysis matrix.

The tabulated data were processed using the software UCINET to compute various metrics of interest for network analysis patterns and relationships [5, 9, 13].

4 Results and Discussion

4.1 Relationship Dimension

The first dimension by which the production network has been examined is the Relationship Dimension [RD], as can be seen in Fig. 3.

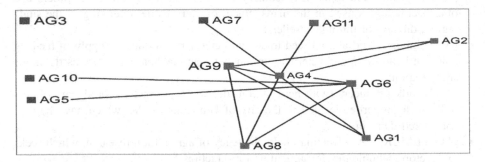

Fig. 3. Relationship dimension network

In Fig. 3 the data analysis showed that the physical network is represented by the agents AG1, AG2, AG4 and AG8. The nodes AG3, AG5, AG7 and AG10 represent the value network, but may also belong to the physical network. The nodes AG6, AG9 and AG11 indicate the business network and may also be a participant of the physical network and of the value network.

The analysis showed that only AG4, AG6 and AG9 had significant factors in the relationship dimension, so the others are not the focus of consistent relationships.

This configuration shows that the network focuses its relationships at key points, but they fail to prioritize agents that could help in the development of the sector in the region, such as universities, dairy and producer association and industries.

The calculated density of this network was approximately 0.26; so, the physical network in the relationship dimension is considered diffuse [13, 17], what indicates that they are unprepared to reach the goal of a free flow of goods, services and information.

4.2 Governance and Distribution of Power Dimension

To demonstrate the adequacy of factor analysis [20] it was used the MOK (Meyer-Olkin Kaiser) test and the Bartlett's test of sphericity to study the governance and distribution of power dimension [GDPD].

The results showed that the relationship matrix performed wholly void, composed only of zeros, that is, without relationships, suggesting that the network is not being managed, and none of the concurrent networks is being governed in order to develop the sector as a whole.

As the relationship dimension has performed diffuse, the governance and distribution of power dimension performed similarly diffuse, as one is linked to the other.

4.3   Transaction Costs Dimension

The transaction costs dimension [TCD] has an important analysis parameter in relationships related to agribusiness. Figure 4 shows this dimension in the milk production network.

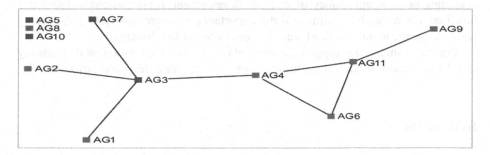

Fig. 4. Networks in transaction costs dimension

Through the network graph analysis in the transaction costs dimension, the agents [AG3], [AG11] are part of the physical network and of the value network, simultaneously, and the agents [AG6], [AG9] are simultaneously part of the value network and of the business network.

The agent [AG3] with four significant ties of relationships shows that this agent is of greater impact in the transaction costs. This indication may be due to the purchase and handling of veterinary products.

The agent [AG6] is related to this dimension due to regulatory issues and supervision exerted by the SEAB. The dairy market is a regulated market by the Brazilian Federal laws.

The questionnaires applied to the financial institutions that represent the agent [AG9] indicate a significant relationship of transaction costs with the agent [AG11]. Another important result showed that the farmers also point the agent [AG11] as focus of the relationship in this dimension.

5   Conclusions and Outlook

The analysis carried out in the simultaneous networks (physical, value and business) have shown unexpectedly that the current configuration of the existing relationship network in this production network is inadequate to promote collective gains and competitive advantages to its agents. Even making the analysis for three different dimensions they confirmed the lack of solid relationships to promote coordination of significant collective actions that could lead to a reduction of transaction costs and to collective gains for the participants in the milk production network, showing a diffuse network.

However, the research, and in particular the analysis of the relationship dimension, indicated significant ties - centrality indicators - in three agents, namely: milk producers, EMATER/SEAB, and financial institutions, representing respectively the production, the regulation and propagation of knowledge, and the finance and credit in the production network.

The connection between the three agents shows that they may be responsible for the beginning of a strategic policy of sectorial development, if encouraged to fulfill this function. The research reaffirms also the importance of integration among the supply network agents, in an organized way for better competitive benefits.

For future studies it is suggest the study of other networks, focused on their density and determination of continuous improvement factors using this same procedure.

References

1. Tilahun, N., Fan, Y.: Transit and job accessibility: an empirical study of access to competitive clusters and regional growth strategies for enhancing transit accessibility. Transp. Policy **33**, 17–25 (2014)
2. Porter, M.: Location, competition, and economic development: local clusters in a global economy. Econ. Dev. Q. **14**, 15 (2000)
3. Huggins, R., Izushi, H.: Competition, Competitive Advantage and Clusters: The Ideas of Michael Porter, pp. 1–328. Oxford University Press, Oxford (2011)
4. Söylemezoglu, E., Doruk, O.T.: Are clusters efficient for the relation between milk production and value added per capita in regional level? An empirical assessment. Procedia Soc. Behav. Sci. **150**, 1277–1286 (2014)
5. Borgatti, S.P., Everett, M.G., Freeman, L.C.: Ucinet for Windows: Software for Social Network Analysis. Analytic Technologies Borgatti, Harvard (2003)
6. Roy, R.B., Sarkar, U.K.: Identifying influential stock indices from global stock markets: a social network analysis approach. Procedia Comput. Sci. **5**, 442–449 (2011)
7. Ferdows, K.: Making the most of foreign factories. Harvard Bus. Rev. **75**, 73–88 (1997)
8. Hahn, M.H., Lee, C., Lee, D.S.: Network structure, organizational learning culture, and employee creativity in system integration companies: the mediating effects of exploitation and exploration. Comput. Hum. Behav. **42**, 167–175 (2015)
9. Spear, S.E.: Reducing readmissions to detoxification: an interorganizational network perspective. Drug Alcohol Depend. **137**, 76–82 (2014)
10. Grandori, A., Soda, G.: Inter-firm networks: antecedents mechanisms and forms. Organ. Stud. **16**(2), 183–214 (1995)
11. Granovetter, M.: Economic action and social structure: the problem of embeddedness. Am. J. Sociol. **91**(3), 481–510 (1985)
12. Williamson, O.E.: The Nature of the Firm: Origins, Evolution, and Development. Oxford University Press, Oxford (1991)
13. Mohammadi, H.K., Hosseinzadeh, M., Kazemi, A.: Women's position in intra organizational informal relationship networks: an application of network analysis approach. Procedia Soc. Behav. Sci. **41**, 485–491 (2012)
14. Shao, J., Zhang, J., Guo, B.: Research on the influencing factors of customer referral behavior based on social network -application in the catering industry. J. High Technol. Manage. Res. **25**, 163–171 (2014)

15. Williams, T.: Cooperation by design: structure and cooperation in interorganizational networks. J. Bus. Res. **58**, 223–231 (2005)
16. Wäsche, H.: Interorganizational cooperation in sport tourism: a social network analysis. Sport Manage. Rev. (2015)
17. Lazzarini, S.G.: Empresas em rede. Cengage Learning, São Paulo (2008)
18. Fusco, J.P., Sacomano, J.B.: Alianças em redes de empresas. Arte and Ciência, São Paulo (2009)
19. IBGE - Instituto Brasileiro de Geografia e Estatísticas. http://www.ibge.gov.br. Accessed 10 Mar 2015
20. Gujarati, D.N.: Econometria Básica. Makron Books, São Paulo (2000)

Extended Administration: Public-Private Management

Yacine Bouallouche, Catherine da Cunha$^{(\boxtimes)}$, Raphael Chenouard,
and Alain Bernard

LUNAM Université, Ecole Centrale de Nantes,
IRCCyN UMR CNRS 6597, 1 Rue de la Noë, Nantes, France
{yacine.bouallouche,catherine.da-cunha,
raphael.chenouard,alain.bernard}@ec-nantes.fr

Abstract. In a difficult economic context, the control of public efficiency and the steering of public investment in the private sector are of paramount importance. Here we focus on the evaluation of public-private partnerships efficiency regarding key performance indicators relating to quality of service and financial cost. Computational results on a case study validate the potential of discrete-event simulation for the clothing function in the French army. Initial and final steps are simulated, but also transition steps.

Keywords: Extended administration · Public-private partnership · Simulation · Network performance

1 Context

The economic crisis and the budgetary rigor that followed had many consequences (Fig. 1). In Europe it drove the States to diminish their expenses and reduce the number of public servants. Yet one of the levers to boost the economic recovery was to inject public money in sectors that would allow the most pay back in terms of innovation, employment, and public value. Both objectives can be obtained when externalizing previous state realized mission to private tiers. In France the public budget that is re-injected in the private economy to maintain public value mission represents 10 % of global GDP [1]. Furthermore the lever effect is then of 1 to 5 (depending on the sector) [2]. The main challenge is then to use this great opportunity to overcome the economic crisis by optimizing the public-private relationships. The resulting network of actors forms a extended administration.

The economic recovery plans are not limited to programs of public work (by nature one-time and limited to construction) but also a real sustainable investment of public found in the private economy. The European Commission [4] proposed 3 indicators to estimate the added value of expenses:

© IFIP International Federation for Information Processing 2015
S. Umeda et al. (Eds.): APMS 2015, Part I, IFIP AICT 459, pp. 20–26, 2015.
DOI: 10.1007/978-3-319-22756-6_3

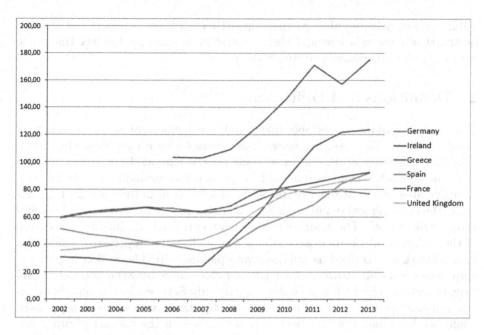

Fig. 1. General government gross debt (Percentage of GDP) [3]

- Do the expenses have a political nature?
- Do tey offer a payback at the European level?
- Do they enable to meet their objective (efficiency)?

In France, a major difficulty is that most investments are done by regions or cities [2]. National directives have little impact, yet a successful example at the national level could play the role of a good practice to follow. Like the Canadian "Program Review" [5] and many other programs conducted by OECD countries and inspired by the New Public Management (NPM) [6], the French General Revision of Public Policies aims at:

- focalizing the State on its sovereign functions,
- doing better and cheaper,
- creating and developing intern and extern providers.

Faced with the limits of the NPM, several countries have begun to amend the reforms inspired by NPM. The French General Revision of Public Policies (GRPP) was deleted and replaced by the Modernization of Public Action (MPA). If the spirit of reform changes, the goal remains the same: reduce the operating costs of administrations. In addition, the MPA has do deal with the legacy of the NPM. The previous reforms have caused fragmentation of public value chains, leaving a legacy of multiple public and private organisms engaged in public services [7]. The production and service networks should combine the strengths of public and private actors to enable the 3 phases of the relationship: shift from public only to private-public partnership (PPP), PPP management but also the destruction of the relationship either to re-integrate the function into the public area or to choose another private provider.

2   Definitions and Difficulties

This context requires the establishment and management of networks to deliver public services. The resulting network of actors forms a extended administration that can relies on the advance made on the extended enterprise domain. A public network is composed of public organizations autonomous in their management although controlled by the state and/or local authorities. In this network, the management of interactions is difficult because its structure is by definition legally "split". The complexity rises in an extended administration because of the inclusion of private organizations. The inclusion of a private organization in a network is described as public-private partnership. The notion of partnership here covers all forms of openings and close links between the public and private sectors. The PPP is a "lasting partnership between legally separate entities pursuing private and public aims and objectives, which, taken separately, could not be achieved with efficiency and economy in the context of programs, projects or operations of general interest, common good or public service" [8]. A literature review and discussions with different actors of the public sectors, we identified three categories of problem with public-private networks

- The public-private partnership performance evaluation;
- The partnership relationship management throughout its life cycle;
- The public-private network management as a whole, to ensure that the local performance is not achieved at the expense of overall performance.

3   Modeling and Managing

The actual interaction between the State and the potential Private partners takes the form of invitation to tender and corresponding responses. The invitations to tender expose the expectations in term of services and also the contractual commitments in terms of creation of public value (e.g. local supply and employment). The responses present the estimated price and some implementation solutions. Yet as for today there is no tool that enables the quantitative comparison based on objective simulation.

4   Use Case: Clothing in the French Army

4.1   Context

In France the clothing function for the civil servants represents a market of 650M€per year, the French army itself stands for 150M€per year [9]. Table 1 presents some key figures in 2012.

Table 1. Key figures in 2012 [10]

Headcount of the users	300 000
Headcount of the public clothing	1 600 people
network civil servants	1 300 Full time equivalent
Warehouses	6 in France
Defense bases (France and abroad)	90
Value of the stocked items	800 M€

4.2   As Is Modeling

Today, the clothing function is operated by public servants see Fig. 2. The procurement is done at a national level, items being furnished by suppliers (often abroad in low cost countries). The replenishment is done on a temporal basis, volumes negotiated for several years based on forecasting.

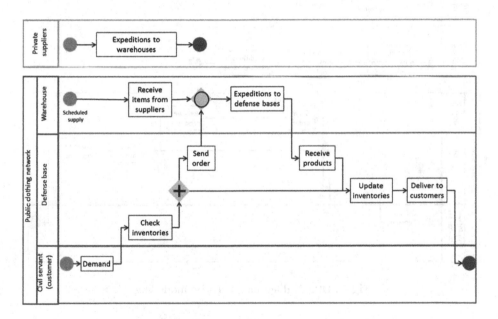

Fig. 2. BPMN diagram for As-Is Modelling

The storage is done on 6 warehouses, each of them responsible for several defense bases both in France and abroad (in fixed bases and special operations' bases). When a customer (member of the armed force) need an item he/she goes to its defense base supply shop and receive the required item, in the best case immediately and the worst case within days. Local inventories in defenses bases are managed on a base stock policy.

This operating policy is quite effective on a customer view, level of service and time of service are evaluated as more than satisfying. Yet the operating costs are important (cf. 4.1). The objective of the French government is to reduce both the employment cost and the inventory cost. For instance, there is more than 2 years of inventory held in the 6 warehouses for some items like socks. In this context a proposition is to create a private public network to operate the clothing service.

4.3   To Be Modeling

The proposed scenario is to externalize the purchasing and warehousing function for the non-specialized items (high-tech and strategically items such as deminers' vests will remain in the public management). The private provider will manage the interaction with the items' suppliers and answer the demand from the defense bases, see Fig. 3.

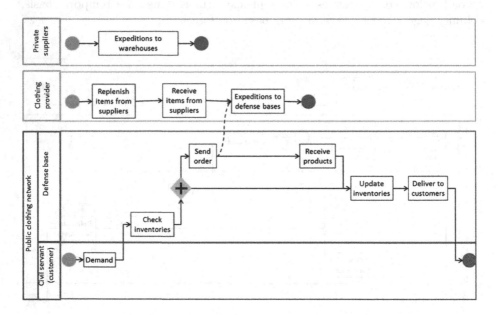

Fig. 3. BPMN diagram for To-Be modelling

The public value generated by the service provider will be guaranteed per contract, with indicators including insertion of disabled employees, employment of target cities inhabitants.

4.4   Computational Results

Using the python SimPy library[1], we modeled and simulated the As-Is scenario (step 0) and the transition shift to the To-Be PPP (progressive shutting down

---

[1] https://simpy.readthedocs.org/en/latest/.

of the 6 public warehouses: step 1 to 6) using discrete event processes. At each
transition step, the private provider increases its activity to answer the bases'
needs. This modelling aimed at evaluating the impact in terms of service level for
the customers (defense civil servants) and eventually re-assess the replenishment
policies in the defense bases.

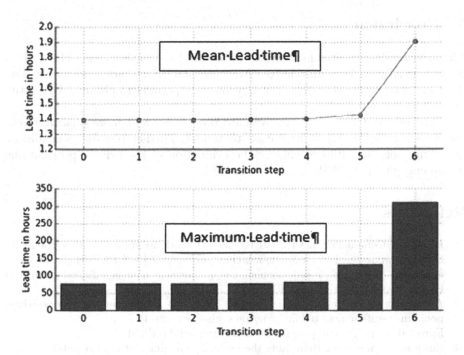

Fig. 4. Simulation results

The simulation encompasses the 90 bases and 6 warehouses. The number of
items required reaches 2 million for each step, each having a time window of a
year.

Figure 4 presents 2 performance indicators: average lead time (curve) and
maximal lead time (sticks) for the different steps of the shift. The lead time
highlights the quality of service for the army civil servants i.e. the time between
the order and the reception of the goods. This time is conditioned not only by
the availability of the items but also by the availability of civil servants for the
clerical tasks, the packing, the shipping and delivering of the items.

It is interesting to note that if the replenishment policy of the bases remains
the same the average lead-time remains acceptable moving form 1.4 h to 1.9 h.
The maximal lead times correspond to a situation when the defense base needs to
replenish its stock to answer the civil servant demand. In this case the lead time
is multiplied by 4, but this evolution occurs only in steps 5 and 6 when defense
bases abroad shift from public to private provider. The increases is maintained,

mostly because to the delivery policy of the PPP agreement, the private partner being committed by contract to ship the items within days of demand reception.

Regarding the HR indicators, the shutting down of public warehouses enable the immediate redeployment of public clothing network civil servants and on the long term their non-replacement.

5   Conclusion

The first results presented here enable us to verify that a simulation of a PPP is possible even with little knowledge of the internal private actor activities. The representation of the contractual obligation only permits to obtain KPI for the public service.

This new tool will enable to evaluate objectively and more quantitatively the response to the public invitation to tender. Further research will aim at including more activities to enlarge the evaluation of the private propositions before engaging in a PPP.

References

1. European Commision: LIVRE VERT sur la modernisation de la politique de l'Union européenne en matière de marchés publics /GREEN PAPER on the modernisation of EU public procurement policy Towards a more efficient European Procurement Market- COM/2011/0015 (2011)
2. Assemblée des communautés de France: Assises de l'investissement: propositions pour un investissement public levier de croissance (2014)
3. Eurostat. http://ec.europa.eu/eurostat. Accessed April 2015
4. European commission: Reforming the budget, changing Europe - A public consultation paper in view of the 2008/2009 budget (2007)
5. Bourgon J.: Program Review, the Government of Canada's Experience Eliminating the Deficit, 1994–1999: A Canadian Case Study. Centre for international Governance Innovation (2009)
6. Osborne, D., Gaeblert, T.: Reinventing Government: How the Entrepreneurial Spirit is Transforming the Public Sector. Plume, New York (1993)
7. Lévesque, B.: Social in novation in governance and public management systems: towards a new paradigm. In: Moulaert, F., McCallum, D., Mehhmood, A., Hamdouch, A. (eds.) Social Innovation: Collective Action Community Learning and Transdisciplinary Research. Edward Elgar Publishers, Cheltenham, UK (2012)
8. Mazouz, B., Facal, J., Viola, J.-M.: Public-private partnership: Elements for a project-based management typology. Project Manage. J. 39(2), 98–110 (2008)
9. Ministère Français de l'Economie et des Finances: Guide Gestion de la fonction habillement dans le secteur public-Groupe d'étude des marchés d'habillement et de textile (GEM-HT) (2012)
10. Roger, G., Dulait, A.: Projet de loi de finances pour 2013: Défense: préparation et emploi des force, Commission des affaires étrangères, de la défense et des forces armées (2013)

Intelligent and Accessible Data Flow Architectures for Manufacturing System Optimization

Roby Lynn, Aoyu Chen, Stephanie Locks, Chandra Nath, and Thomas Kurfess$^{(\boxtimes)}$

The George W. Woodruff School of Mechanical Engineering,
Georgia Institute of Technology, Atlanta, GA 30309, USA
{roby.lynn, achen75, slocks, kurfess}@gatech.edu,
nathc2@asme.org

Abstract. Many traditional data acquisition (DAQ) systems are expensive and inadaptable – most rely on traditional closed-source platforms – thus limiting their usefulness for machine tool diagnostics, process control and optimization. In this study, three different intelligent data flow architectures are designed and demonstrated based on consumer grade off-the-shelf hardware and software. These architectures allow data flow between both open- and closed-source platforms through multiple wired and wireless communication protocols. The proposed architectures are also evaluated for machine tool diagnostics and monitoring of multiple machine tools in manufacturing systems. To realize cloud-based manufacturing, real time sensor data are collected and displayed on remote interfaces, smart devices and a cloud/global data platform via the Internet. Findings reveal that such cyber physical system (CPS)-based manufacturing systems can effectively be used for real time process control and optimization.

Keywords: Intelligent manufacturing · Machine communications · Data flow · Machine diagnostics · Productivity

1 Introduction

Nowadays, in advanced high-tech manufacturing systems, much attention is given to big data analytics for better process control and optimization. When multiple machines and devices are involved in complex manufacturing systems for a single part to be produced, information has to be transferred between these components to enable efficient system operation. In such a case, CPS-based digital manufacturing can enable better process control by realizing an open accessible data flow and exchange between devices [1, 2]. Although high performance DAQ systems are available that can enable these process improvements, many of these systems are found to be both inaccessible and inadaptable due to their cost and reliance on closed-source platforms. In addition, the sensors used in most of these systems are hard wired, resulting in inflexibility.

Within digital manufacturing, a few data flow architectures have been proposed to realize data acquisition and cloud storage [3–5]. Some research were conducted to

© IFIP International Federation for Information Processing 2015
S. Umeda et al. (Eds.): APMS 2015, Part I, IFIP AICT 459, pp. 27–35, 2015.
DOI: 10.1007/978-3-319-22756-6_4

address the data accessibility limitations of the standard machine diagnostics approach by integrating a data flow architecture [6]. Shen *et al.* presented a concept of iShop-Floor—an intelligent shop floor based on the Internet, web, and agent technologies supported by Java and XML [7]. The generic architecture makes the system respond quickly to shop floor changes and customer demands. However, the Java based communication between agents limits the hardware platform. Also, the Java applets' user interface decreases the flexibility of data manipulation. Wang also proposed a cloud-based approach to distributed process planning based on machine and resource availability [8]. Xu *et al.* designed an economic wireless sensor network system for structural health monitoring using off-the-shelf hardware [9]. This approach is novel, but is not able to transmit raw sensor data in real-time and the user must manually collect it from the system for later analysis.

Thanks to the maker movement, the limitations of the previously performed works in industrial data flow can be addressed by employing readily available and affordable high performance consumer-grade microcontrollers, sensors and wireless communication modules. While the computing power available on these platforms is limited, it can be harnessed to perform data analysis on the device itself before the data are relayed on to a cloud-based storage system. Many of these hardware platforms are open-source, and can thus be easily modified to adapt in evolving production environments. The simple connectivity of this hardware can enable the development of a novel DAQ system that is interconnected and able to share data across platforms and facilities. Additionally, the accessibility of this hardware could allow for increased adoption by manufacturers for whom traditional DAQ systems were either unusable due to their inadaptability or inaccessible due to their cost. However, the construction of an intelligent data flow architecture using these widely available components has yet to be formulated in modern manufacturing systems.

The objective of this research is to design and evaluate intelligent, accessible, and low-cost industrial data flow architectures for manufacturing system control and optimization. In this paper, three different architectures are designed using high performance consumer-grade hardware and software systems that allow data flow between both open- and closed-source platforms. A cloud-based manufacturing system is demonstrated using multiple wired and wireless communication protocols. These architectures are also evaluated for machine tool diagnostics and monitoring of multiple machine tools in manufacturing systems.

2   Data Flow System Architectures

Collaborative manufacturing and real-time data collection and analysis are of great interest in the emerging CPS field. The overall purpose of the data flow system architecture presented below is to enable collaborative analysis and optimization by making manufacturing process data from different machine tools widely available. Three different data flow system methodologies are constructed and evaluated: (1) MTConnect network, (2) wireless distributed sensor network, and (3) sensor-MTConnect hybrid network. This collection of wireless protocols, various processor architectures, and sensor types demonstrates that the architecture is portable between all platforms. In this section, all system architectures are discussed with construction methodology, capabilities, limitations, and a case study in the machining environment.

2.1 MTConnect Network

System Architecture. Aconnectivity concept to a piece of manufacturing equipment is created using MTConnect and a National Instruments (NI) myRIO field-programmable gate array (FPGA) device. MTConnect – a communication protocol for data acquisition from CNC machine tools – is implemented as a web service, enabling any web browser to access the machine tool's data output via a wired or Wi-Fi router. The myRIO is connected to the local wireless network and used to generate HTTP requests that are sent to the machine tool. The MTConnect-based data flow architecture system is presented in Fig. 1. The myRIO processes the MTConncet data from the machine tool and presents them on a display.

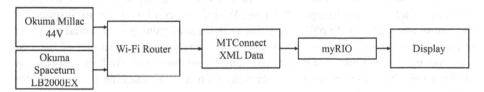

Fig. 1. MTConnect data flow

Case Study: Process Condition Monitoring. The MTConnect implementation allows for access to spindle speed, spindle motor power output, axis positions and axis servo power outputs of machine tool(s). These data are gathered from two machine tools simultaneously: an Okuma Millac M44V and an Okuma Spaceturn LB2000EX.

Local Interface. The axis loads and positions from the machine tools are graphed and displayed to the user on a computer display as shown in Fig. 2. The visualization of these data allows manufacturers to quickly and easily monitor and obtain an intuitive idea of the process state, the tool-work relative position, and the machining process parameters.

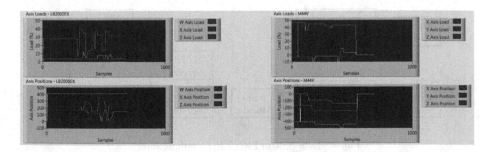

Fig. 2. MTConnect front panel

Mtconnect Capabilities and Limitations. The MTConnect protocol provides manufacturers with a simple yet powerful way to access data collected by their machine tools. Because the protocol is implemented as a web service, it is easily accessible to any device that is connected to the machine network. Due to the protocol's reliance on the machine controller for the data, both the update speed and the number of available data are limited. For example, most CNC machine tools do not include accelerometers in their spindles to monitor vibration, and thus these data are not available from MTConnect. Additionally, the data update speed is set by the controller and therefore it may not be fast enough for some applications. For the Okuma machine tools utilized in this implementation, the maximum data update rate is 1 Hz; this may be too slow to enable real-time data analysis using MTConnect data alone.

2.2 Distributed Wireless Sensor Network

System Architecture. Two related configurations are created to demonstrate the distributed wireless sensor architecture: one relies on ZigBee and Wi-Fi, while the other relies on Bluetooth Low Energy (BLE) and Wi-Fi. The configurations are inspired by the internet-of-things (IoT) philosophy that is nowadays gaining widespread adoption in both industrial and consumer applications. To increase the accessibility of the system, consumer grade microcontrollers and sensors are employed. Both demonstrations of the architecture use an accelerometer placed on a CNC machine tool to monitor vibration.

The first construction of this architecture uses a PIC32MX board, a Microchip Wi-Fi module and Digi's 802.14 XBee radios. The PIC32MX is used to gather accelerometer data via the ZigBee link and transmit them via Wi-Fi to a receiving device. This implementation highlighted the use of multiple wireless networking standards that can be chained together to create a coherent data pathway. The connection diagram of the PIC32 implementation is presented in Fig. 3. The PIC32 serves to receive the accelerometer data and package it so that it can be interpreted by the server PC after flowing through the Wi-Fi connection; the PC then renders the data to users through the HTTP server. The NFC tag is used by networked smart devices to access the HTTP server: the IP address of the server is written to the tag, and devices access the page through a mobile browser after reading from the tag.

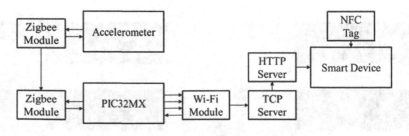

Fig. 3. Data flow in PIC32 IoT configuration

This architecture is then reconfigured using different communication methods and illustrates the use of a different device, the NI myRIO. By replacing the PIC32 with a myRIO device and swapping the ZigBee chips for BLE chips, a new system with the same capabilities as the ZigBee and PIC32 system is established. Once again, the system uses only consumer grade off-the-shelf components and illustrates the ease of connectivity offered by current technologies.

Case Study: Machine Crash Detection. The wireless sensor network is employed to monitor the vibration generated by the spindle that arises from a crash of a CNC machine tool. By monitoring the accelerometer output, normal spindle operation can be distinguished from a machine crash or other emergency condition.

Local Interface. Due to the increasing prevalence of Wi-Fi networks, 802.11g was chosen as the backbone network type for data flow for the wireless sensor system. To increase the accessibility of the data from a variety of connected devices, a dynamic webpage was created that was compatible with both standard and mobile browsers.

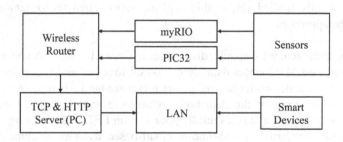

Fig. 4. Dynamic webpage data flow

The webpage was created using HTML5, JavaScript and the JavaScript Data-Driven Documents (D3) library. The D3 library is responsible for rendering the graph of sensor data coming from the networked microcontrollers. The overview of this data flow architecture is shown in Fig. 4. Because the webpage is hosted on the local network, it is visible to other connected smart devices. This interface is easily accessed by smart devices by exploiting the quick tap-and-go abilities of an RFID communication link. When a user wants to view process data from a particular machine tool, they only need to tap an NFC-capable device on the tag to access the dynamic webpage.

Cloud-Based Remote Data Interface. To demonstrate the wide availability of these data, they are streamed to an active cloud data visualization tool via the Internet where they are accessible from any device. This interface utilized Google Docs' spreadsheet environment to visualize incoming sensor data. A TCP server was written in C# that received the sensor output stream from the PIC32 microcontroller and parsed it into individual readings. The Google Data API for .NET was then invoked within the C# server program to communicate with a Google spreadsheet. While not as responsive as the local webpage, the Google Doc implementation proved that these data can be accessible from anywhere using an internet-enabled device.

Capabilities and Limitations. The wireless sensor network described above is useful in production environments where data availability and quick implementation are critical; however, because the system relies heavily on the relatively weak computing power of standard microcontrollers, the data throughput is limited. For this reason, the wireless sensor network may not be suitable for applications in which high-frequency data analysis must be performed in real-time.

2.3   Sensor-MTConnect Hybrid Network

System Architecture. The spindle is a key component for a CNC and its sudden break down usually causes a huge loss of productivity. Using a real-time data acquisition system, diagnostics can be performed on a CNC machine tool to evaluate the health of the spindle to avoid this productivity loss. This implementation demonstrates the usefulness of a distributed sensor approach combined with the MTConnect protocol. Machine diagnostics based on the combination of external sensors and MTConnect have not been fully studied yet, so this implementation attempts to demonstrate the novelty of the approach.

The data flow architecture for spindle diagnostics is shown in Fig. 5. An accelerometer, a power meter, and MTConnect data are combined together and processed by an NI myRIO. Both the accelerometer and the power meter are hard wired to the processor to demonstrate the concept of the data flow architecture and the effectiveness of the diagnostic method. The diagnostics result appears as an FFT pattern. Using JavaScript, the data can be transferred in real-time to cloud-based dynamic documents such as Google Docs to enable further analysis on remote systems.

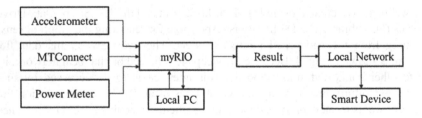

Fig. 5. Spindle diagnostics data flow

Case Study: Machine Tool Spindle Diagnostics. Accelerometers are attached to the spindle housing of an Okuma Millac M44V to assess and diagnose the health of the spindle. From the vibration data of the accelerometer, a fast Fourier transform (FFT) is performed to provide information related to critical elements of the spindle, including the spindle bearings, which are typical components that fail due to lifecycle fatigue or a severe crash scenario [10]. Accelerometer signals have certain well defined characteristics, such as their fundamental frequency, as well as certain harmonics that are integer multiples of the fundamental frequency. Other well documented characteristics include bearing related frequencies or so-called bearing tones, such as the ball pass frequency on the rollers and the races [11]. A record of a healthy spindle FFT is calculated and stored for the spindle at various spindle operational frequencies for comparison purposes. Spindle health degradation is monitored by comparing the record of the initial healthy spindle to the vibration of the current spindle.

Local Interface. It should be noted that the current system does not have a permanent human interface device. By allowing the workers to use their pre-existing smart devices or by providing them with tablets, the cost of having a full computer and display at each machine can be eliminated. The local interface can be transmitted to the cloud if desired, making the operation of this system truly global. If standard communication protocols such as MTConnect, Bluetooth and Wi-Fi are employed, updating the systems to employ the latest interface technology will be as easy as updating one's smartphone. Finally, while the communication for this system is one way, in the future, two way communication may be implemented that integrates the machine controller into automatic test cycles based on a pre-set time or system conditions.

Spindle Diagnostics Capabilities and Limitations. The spindle diagnostics example illustrates the flexibility and ease with which data from manufacturing systems can be processed and monitored by the data flow architecture. The fusion of MTConnect and discrete sensors helps to increase the diversity of available data. Based on time and frequency domain analysis, a malfunction of the spindle can be detected. Messages can be transmitted to alert operators and maintenance and scheduling personnel to take further actions. Data can be shared on smart devices or to remote PCs through local networks or the cloud via the Internet.

3   Discussion

This intelligent data flow architecture demonstrates that multiple configurations exist which can be employed to create a data pathway between sensors and data users. In the distributed wireless sensing approach, low-cost sensors and computing platforms can be deployed to monitor machine tools on the shop floor. This system is accessible to any machine tool operator because it is both affordable and easy to implement. When combined with Google Docs, the wireless sensor data can be shared between facilities and used for collaborative manufacturing. This system is unique in that it relies on accessible and easily deployable consumer grade hardware; thus, widespread adoption in smaller facilities is more likely.

While dedicated computer displays were employed in the preceding implementations to present both raw and analyzed data to users, they are not required in order to realize these data flow architectures. As smart devices such as phones and tablets become more affordable and widespread, it is reasonable to expect that all personnel working in a given manufacturing facility would carry such a device. As such, the dedicated displays can be eliminated and each smart device can serve as a separate display for its owner. These personal displays would allow for a limitless number of users to view one set of data at a time; if the data were stored in the cloud, these data could be accessed from anywhere. Cyber-security concerns present problems that must be solved in order to advance this concept, but this has been proven to be possible by several successful cloud-based storage services that exist today.

The implementation of a reconfigurable data flow architecture, such as the ones presented above, would be highly adaptable to changes on the shop floor and would require only simple software updates (which can be performed remotely) to alter system behavior. A reconfigurable system would allow manufacturers access to any process or machine data that they want to analyze, which eliminates costly and time-consuming hardware setups. As the speed of data acquisition and analysis can increase with these reconfigurable systems, and if cloud-based storage and processing are integrated, real-time collaborative manufacturing and control begin to look like a reality. This globalization of these manufacturing data would accelerate the pace of process development and optimization, leading to increased productivity, higher sustainability, and lower costs for all participating parties.

4 Conclusions

In this study, three different intelligent and accessible data flow architectures are designed and implemented for manufacturing systems. Conclusions are as follows: (i) The MTConnect protocol was shown to be compatible with the myRIO and useful data were successfully gathered and presented, (ii) A distributed wireless sensor approach was shown using two different computing platforms – PIC32 and myRIO, (iii) A cloud-based data platform was implemented with the wireless sensor approach to demonstrate that the collected data are available globally, and (iv) A real-time spindle diagnostics application was developed using the myRIO to demonstrate sophisticated analysis that can be performed with the data acquired using one of these architectures.

References

1. Rajkumar, R., et al.: Cyber-physical systems: the next computing revolution. In: 2010 47th ACM/IEEE Design Automation Conference (DAC) (2010)
2. Wang, L., et al.: Current status and advancement of cyber-physical systems in manufacturing. J. Manuf. Syst. **36** (2015)
3. Karnouskos, S., et al.: A SOA-based architecture for empowering future collaborative cloud-based industrial automation. In: IECON 2012 - 38th Annual Conference on IEEE Industrial Electronics Society (2012)
4. Tao, F., et al.: Cloud manufacturing: a computing and service-oriented manufacturing model. J. Eng. Manuf. **225**(10), 8 (2011)
5. Wang, X., Xu, X.: ICMS: a cloud-based manufacturing system. In: Li, W., Mehnen, J.(eds.) Cloud Manufacturing, pp. 1–22. Springer, London (2013)
6. Milfelner, M., et al.: An overview of data acquisition system for cutting force measuring and optimization in milling. J. Mater. Process. Technol. **164–165**, 8 (2005)

7. Shen, W., et al.: iShopFloor: an internet-enabled agent-based intelligent shop floor. IEEE Trans. Syst. Man Cybern. **35**(3), 11 (2005)
8. Wang, L.: Machine availability monitoring and machining process planning towards cloud manufacturing. CIRP J. Manuf. Sci. Technol. **6**(4), 11 (2013)
9. Xu, N., et al.: A wireless sensor network for structural monitoring. In: Proceedings of the 2nd International Conference on Embedded Networked Sensor Systems, p. 12 (2004)
10. Li, Y., et al.: Adaptive prognostics for rolling element bearing condition. Mech. Syst. Sig. Process. **13**(1), 103–113 (1999)
11. Billington, S.: Sensor and machine condition effects in roller bearing diagnostics (Masters Thesis) (1997). http://hdl.handle.net/1853/17796

Social Network Analysis on Grain Production in the Brazilian Scenario

Lúcio T. Costabile[1(✉)], Oduvaldo Vendrametto[1],
Geraldo Cardoso de Oliveira Neto[2], Mario Mollo Neto[3],
and Marcelo K. Shibuya[1]

[1] Graduate Program in Production Engineering, Paulista University-UNIP,
Dr. Bacelar St. 1212, São Paulo, Brazil
luciotc@terra.com.br

[2] Graduate Program in Production Engineering, Nove de Julho University -
UNINOVE, Francisco Matarazzo Avenue, 612, São Paulo, Brazil

[3] Graduate Program in Production Engineering, São Paulo State University
"Júlio de Mesquita Filho", Tupã, São Paulo University-UNINOVE, Francisco
Matarazzo Avenue, 612, São Paulo, Brazil

Abstract. This article provides study of the 2012/2013 grain harvest of federal units of Brazil in relation to the following factors: planted areas, productivity, and production, which assist producers in agricultural planning. The research method used for data collection was the documentary and exploratory data analysis using the software Ucinet® for social networks. The findings indicate that the Midwest has the largest area planted in soybean per thousand/ha, demonstrating the opportunity for producers to develop new crops. In production in thousand/ton, the Midwest region also excelled in soybeans, showing the possibility for producers to seek new techniques for planting. The southern has the highest productivity of the rice grain per kg/ha, contributing to the producer having the best land use and resource optimization.

Keywords: Network analysis · Centrality · Grains · Geographic regions

1 Introduction

Brazil is one of the largest economies in the world and in this context contributes significantly to agribusiness, standing as one of the largest producers and exporters of grain. With the advance of incentives, the country's agriculture has been increasing in the production and export of grains, mainly soybeans, corn, rice [1, 2] and wheat [3]. The country's federal units have undergone changes in recent years. Factors such as the emergence of new technologies, research development, and new planting techniques have emerged [3]. In this context, it is necessary to plan agricultural production, considering the use of machinery and equipment and manpower for operation [4]. The soybean is one of the agricultural products with highest production and participation in Brazilian agriculture [5]. Rice production provides satisfactory results in the Brazilian agribusiness, due to the cultivation of rice [6] and adoption of new techniques and specialized machinery [7]. On the production of corn, Brazil ranked third, as a major

S. Umeda et al. (Eds.): APMS 2015, Part I, IFIP AICT 459, pp. 36–44, 2015.
DOI: 10.1007/978-3-319-22756-6_5

exporter [8]. Regarding the wheat crop, production exceeded expectations for planted area, resulting in a reduction in imports [3].

A literature search on grain production in Brazil found the need of agricultural production planning to minimize risk and achieve better financial return [4]. In this context, it is necessary to invest in new technologies to provide the development of new techniques in the Brazilian agricultural sector. These new technologies include, for example, the study of geographic variables (soil, atmosphere, and temperature) of each region to improve handling and increase productivity [5], intensification of technologies for a grain storage process to reduce loss [9], introduction of incremental changes in rice planting to contribute to increased productivity [6], and the analysis of the influence of rice as the ability to influence [7] the economy of a region. There was a lack of research related to social network analysis at a national level to measure the relationship between the network actors (regions and types of grains) to assist the producer in the planning of agricultural production. The analysis included data extracted from the following variables: areas planted per hectare, yield, and production [10]. In this context, for effectiveness in grain production, new forms of agricultural planning can be performed based on the centrality of the network, i.e., other technological applications in terms of resources and enhancement techniques can be employed in regions with the highest centrality. The degree of centrality measures the number of links between actors in the network, allowing inclusion of the strategic position of each actor [11]. From this emerged the following research question, which grain has the greatest impact on Brazilian Agriculture in relation to the planted area, yield per hectare, and production per ton? To answer this question, we chose to analyze Social Networks. These structures can be defined by the reciprocal relationship between independent, but economically interdependent, agents, aimed at cooperation to achieve common or complementary goals [12–14]. The structure of the network and the position of the actors can affect the functions of the organization and their skills in generating value [15]. Connectivity, which is the ability to link each individual network, can be represented by the intensity and frequency of communication between the actors [16]. The most common representations of networks are those in which the nodes represent actors and ties, allowing transfer of information [17]. We can classify the links/bonds by their intensity, denoting absent, weak, and strong ties [18].

Thinking of the research question, this study aims to assess which of the grains and regions of the 2012/2013 harvest had greater impact on the Brazilian agribusiness in relation to the acreage productivity per hectare and production per ton. This can help producers with agricultural planning and will present the factors that influence the culture of grains. Our assessment was done using Ucinet®. By applying network analysis with relational matrices, and the visual analysis of graphs of these same networks, it allowed the finding of new indicators, other than those offered by traditional statistical analysis with specific focus on the degree of centrality.

2 Methodology

This article presents an exploratory research study through a literature review using the keywords: grain production and agribusiness, in databases: Science Direct, Proquest, Ebsco, Capes, and Scielo. Data collection was conducted through research in a

Table 1. Mapping of crop – planted area, production and productivity

Federal Units	Planted area – million hectares (mm/ha)				Production – thousands of tons (m/t)				Productivity – kilogram per hectare (kg/ha)			
	Soyabean	Corn	Rice	Wheat	Soyabean	Corn	Rice	Wheat	Soyabean	Corn	Rice	Wheat
North	833	560	320	0	2537	1624	965	0	3045	2898	3011	0
Northeast	2329	2450	604	0	6915	5375	1043	0	2696	2194	1727	0
South	9604	4438	1238	1817	28705	24699	9125	4245	2989	5565	7369	2336
Southeast	1735	2178	45	53	5082	12274	135	162	2828	5633	3002	3036
Midwest	12738	5133	201	24	39389	27962	658	68	3092	5447	3269	2750

Source: CONAB (2012/2013)

regulatory government agency of the Brazilian agricultural sector called the National Supply Company (Companhia Nacional de Abastecimento - Conab). Using these sources, we mapped the crops of grains under study for a period related to the cultivated area, including yield per hectare and production in thousand tons, for the harvest of 2012/2013 in the federal units of Brazil, as shown in Table 1.

For the creation of the crop mapping, we used matrix and graphical analysis of the data provided to look at the relationship between the individuals in the network. For this, we used social network analysis software (Ucinet®), developed in the laboratories Analytic Technologies at the University of Greenwich. This methodology allows the mapping of networks of federal units with the respective values of area, yield, and production per hectare.

The values obtained from literature surveys are included in generated files in the Windows operating system notepad, thus building the files of type ".vna" (visual network analysis) required for implementation and enforcement in Ucinet® software. The processes result in the values of the degree of centrality of interaction of the actors within the network [19].

The general degree of centrality is composed of the input degree of centrality and by the output degree of centrality, and these depend on the relative direction of flow. The sum of relations that an actor has with other actors is the output degree centrality, and the sum of relations that the other actors have with a particular actor is the input degree of centrality [20]. An actor is locally central, if it has a large number of connections to other points. It is globally central, if it has a significant strategic position in the network as a whole [11]. The centrality of degree is measured by the number of ties that an actor has with other actors in a network [21].

Generally, for software available for network analysis, as used in this research with the Ucinet® and Netdraw® module, the data is provided by relational matrices (socio-matrices in the language of sociologists), which can be viewed through graphs. The graphic display alone can offer new information and insights for researchers [21, 22]. This function was used via the Netdraw® module accompanying Ucinet® to enable the visualization of networks based on the ".vna" files generated.

The corresponding graphs of Planted area networks, Productivity, and Production, are generated with Netdraw®, and the images obtained are marked by relationships of higher intensities and their respective directions. Likewise the actors are indicated (highlighted with discs in red) with its expanded size (larger diameter) based on their relative centrality, in order to visually indicate the actors with greater power or influence, and participation in the network by means of larger diameter.

The design of centralities in accordance with the indications [23], obeyed the software, application of the following Eq. 1:

$$C_G(v_k) = \sum_{j=1}^{n} w_{kj} \tag{1}$$

Where:

C_G = Degree of centrality;
v_k = Node of the net to be considered;
$j =$ Number of nodes;
w_{kj} = Number of adjacent nodes;

and, w_{kj} if there is a link between the nodes vk e vj.

After visualizing the data for analysis and the corresponding graphical behavior in the networks under study, it is possible to obtain the patterns of the actor's behavior and to transcribe this data to relational matrices (also known as sociometric matrices), which are necessary for the data analysis by the chosen analysis program, Ucinet®.

3 Results and Discussion

After data entry, the actors were processed using UCINET® software. The data represents areas planted in million hectares, productivity in kilograms per hectare, and production in thousands of tons of soybeans, corn, rice and wheat, in the Brazilian states of the Midwest, South, Northeast, Southeast, and North, and their relationships, represented by the values of participation of each grain which resulted in the interaction of the actors within the network.

Planted Area. The graph of the corresponding network acreage was developed in Netdraw® (Fig. 1) and it shows the centrality of the network and the positional

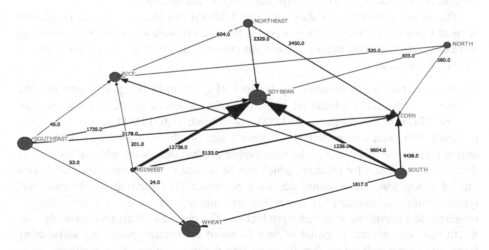

Fig. 1. Representation of the corresponding network acreage, crops, and regions represented by Ucinet® software and its Netdraw® module.

indicators and intermediary actors. The results indicate that the Midwest and South regions have the highest densities (or most significant trade links) between the actors in the network, i.e., greater participation among the federal units in areas planted on millions of acres, confirming what was collected in the literature review, with 12,738 million/ha of soybeans planted in these areas, 5,133 million/ha of maize, 201,000/ha of rice, and 24,000/ha of wheat. Soy has the highest centrality in the relationship, due to new technologies, research development, and economic changes in the [4] region. On the international scene, Brazil appears as the largest soybean supplier to China and the United States.

The results obtained by Ucinet® found that the OutDegree is the level of output, representing the share of each federal unit. The Midwest revealed 18,096 million hectares of planted areas; followed by the southern region, with 17,097; the Northeast, 5,383; Southeast: 4,011; and North, 1,713. The InDegree represents the degree of entry, or the quantities of areas planted with beans with their respective values in million hectares, considering all regions, resulting in soybeans for 27,239; corn, 14,759; rice, 2,408; and wheat, 1,894. The actor "soy" has the highest degree of entry, with the Midwest region 12,738,000/ha, Southeast 1,735 million/ha, South 9,604,000/ha, Northeast 2,329 million/ha, and North 833,000/ha, totaling 27,239 million hectares. The highlight is the Midwest region, which has the highest level of output, i.e., is the main actor who has the highest participation of areas planted in million hectares in the country. This share is characterized due to research for adaptation of new crops for fertile soils, such as cotton, soybean, wheat, corn, etc [5]. It is noteworthy that the increase of planted areas is due to the new planting techniques, improved communications, and the significant consumer market in the Southeast region, which has contributed to the increase in commercial agriculture development [5].

We found that the average degree of centrality of the relationship between the actors of the network was measured at 14,298 % for output values, and 24,392 % for the input values, which indicates that power is distributed over the network heterogeneously both for input relationships and output relationships.

The values obtained also show that the Midwest has the largest area of planted areas in million hectares, and the prospect is that the Midwest will continue to invest in increasing planted areas, mainly in soybean cultivation, which showed growth during the last three decades.

Production. The results obtained by Ucinet® (Fig. 2) in OutDegree, found that the Midwest was the most substantial at 68,077,000/t, followed by the southern region, with 66,774,000/t, Northeast: 13,333,000/t; Southeast: 17,651,000/t, and North: 5.126 million/t. The results show that the Midwest and South, have the highest levels of output and are the main actors who have higher productions thousand/t and have more developed techniques for planting, which can be studied by the regions with the lowest rate of production. These techniques were presented [7] regarding the different soil types, climate, availability of water for agriculture, land use, and technological resources that contribute to increase production. The research [4] also mentions that the South has great genetic potential of new forms of cultivation, producing satisfactory levels of commercialization, directly impacting the profitability of agribusiness.

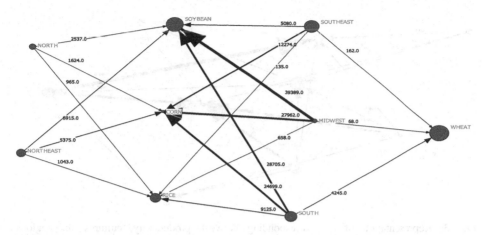

Fig. 2. Representation of the corresponding network production, cultures and regions represented by Ucinet® software.

The actors' (representing the grain) InDegree accounted for soybeans: 82,626, corn: 71,934, rice: 11,926, and wheat: 4,475. Soy has the highest degree of entry, most notably in the Midwest: 39,389,000/t; South: 28,705,000/t; Northeast: 6,915 million/t; Southeast: 5,080,000/t; and North: 2,537,000/t, for a total production of 82,626 million/t. General indicators of the network and their descriptive statistics related to the production per thousand/t denoted the state of network centrality output was measured as 17,523 %, and the degree of input centrality was 22,717 %.

These figures show that power is distributed over the network heterogeneously both for input relationships and output relationships. However, with regard to the levels of output, it is observed that there is a higher concentration to the power of the regions center -west and south, which are, as highlighted earlier, the largest producers. But, one should also highlight, the areas are very disparate from each other as well as the productivity of the regions focused on in the study.

Productivity. In Fig. 3, using calculations applying the processing with the software, the results indicate via the analysis of OutDegree, that the southern region has the highest level of output (18,259 kg/ha), followed by the Southeast (14,599 kg/ha), Midwest (14,558 kg/ha), North (8954 kg/ha) and Northeast (6617 kg/ha). It is noteworthy that in the South, the rice grain represents the largest production (7,369,000/t), followed by maize (5565 kg/ha), soybean (2989 kg/ha) and wheat (2336 kg/ha). In relation to InDegree analysis, we found that corn grain is the most representative (21,737 kg/ha), followed by rice (18,378 kg/ha), soybean (14,750 kg/ha) and wheat (8122 kg/ha). This finding is corroborated by [4] due to favorable conditions for growing. The southern region has attracted several companies in the agribusiness sector for research, use of new technologies, and new inputs correcting soil deficiencies for planting.

The degree of overall centrality of network output was measured in 21,489 % and the degree of input centrality was 28,126 %. The figures show that the network has low power relations between the actors in the case of the degrees of output, which indicates

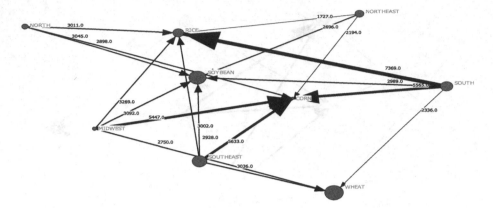

Fig. 3. Representation of the corresponding network productivity, cultures and regions represented by Ucinet® software.

that there is no balanced participation of regions for the production as a whole. This can be seen in the lower contribution of North and Northeast. However, the product that stood out in this case was the highest input degree of centrality, the corn, and its production was strongly influenced by good production in all federal units participating in the study.

The largest production in thousands of ton was presented in the South concerning the growth of planted areas, alternative crops, adoption of new management systems appropriate to the soil, use of technology, tax breaks, and donations of new land for planting. This stands out because the participating regions provide areas with large differences in their size and production per ton varies greatly between states.

4   Conclusions

With the use of the social network analysis technique, we found that the Midwest region showed the highest share of areas planted in million hectares in the country, followed by the South region, with the soybean receiving the largest investment, and presenting the largest participation in the growth of cultivated areas. This analysis can help producers based on cultivating the soil with the help of research and new techniques of planting, as well as new forms of financing. For example, the producers of the region with the lowest degree of centrality (North) could develop new crops in the region.

The Midwest region was found to have the highest production in thousand/t, followed by the South, with the largest share of soybeans, corn, and rice, because of the resources used in cultivation. In pursuit of increased production, this result will allow direct producers to better understand the planting techniques. For example, regions with lower production volume can intensify these factors to increase their crops.

The southern region aims to be the leading region with higher grain yield kg/ha, with the emphasis on the grains of rice and corn, taking advantage of climate conditions, and human and technological resources of the region. The results indicate to producers the need for better use of soil, seed selection, and the best use of natural resources in the region, because with this, other regions could contribute to the grain productivity at a national level. For example, the Midwest, the leader in planted areas and production, is not the most important in productivity per hectare, indicating that the increase in productivity is related to better land use and resource optimization, leading to better crop yield. A limitation of this research is the use of a documentary exploratory research approach. For future research regions with less centrality could be explored to propose new incentives and agricultural practices to increase productivity.

References

1. WTO : Trade policy review. http://www.wto.org/english/tratope/tpre/s212-04e.doc. Accessed 08 Nov 2008
2. USDA United States Department of Agriculture: Production, supply and distribution. www.fas.usda.gov/psdonline. Accessed 6 Mar 2013
3. CONAB: Companhia Nacional de Abastecimento. Situação da Armazenagem no Brasil. www.conab.gov.br. Accessed 10 Apr 2006
4. Osaki, M., Batalha, M.O.: Optimization model of agricultural production system in grain farms under risk, in Sorriso, Brazil. Agric. Syst. **127**, 178–188 (2014)
5. Pontes, H.L.J., Carmo, B.B.T., Porto, A.J.V.: Problemas Logísticos na Exportação Brasileira da soja em grão. Revista Eletrônica Sistemas Gestão **4**, 155–181 (2012). (Niterói)
6. Nitzke, J.A., Biedrzicki, A.: Terra de Arroz. http://www.ufrgs.br/Alimentus/terradearroz/producao/pd_ecossistemas_sim.htm. Accessed 8 Feb 2012
7. Vieira, A.C.P., Bruch, K.L., Watanabe, M., Yamaguchi, C.K., Neto, R.J., Bolson, E.A.: A influência das inovações no campo: as cultivares produzidas na Região Sul Catarinense no Brasil. Revista Espacios **33** (2012)
8. Ferraz, J.P.S., Felício, P.E.: Production systems – an example from Brazil. J. Meat Sci. **84**, 238–243 (2010)
9. Tefera, T., Kananpiu, F., Groote, H., Hellin, J., Mugo, S., Kimenju, S., Beyene, Y., Boddupalli, P.M., Shiferaw, B., Banziger, M.: The metal silo: an effective grain storage technology for reducing post-harvest insect and pathogen losses in maize while improving smallholder farmers' food security in developing countries. CropProtection **30**, 240–245 (2011)
10. CONAB: Companhia Nacional de Abastecimento. Acompanhamento da Safra Brasileira – Grãos 2012/13. www.conab.gov.br. Accessed 10 Mar 2014
11. Scott, J.: Social Network Analysis. Sage Publications, Thousands Oaks (2000)
12. Powwel, W.: Neither market not hierarchy: network forms of organization. Res. Organ. Behav. **12**, 295–336 (1990)
13. Williams, T.: Cooperation by design: structure and cooperation in inter organizational networks. J. Bus. Res. **5**(867), 1–9 (2002)
14. Borgatti, C.R.: A social network view of organizational learning. Manage. Sci. **49**, 432–445 (2003)
15. Lazzarini, S.G.: Empresas em rede. Cengage Learning, São Paulo (2008)
16. Borgatti, C.R., Li, X.: On social network analysis in a supply chain context. J. Supply Chain Manage. **45**, 5–22 (2009)

17. Krackhardt, D., Hanson, J.R.: Informal networks: the company behind the chart. Harvard Bus. Rev. **4**, 104–111 (1993)
18. Granovetter, M.: Getting a Job: A Study of Contacts and Careers, 2nd edn. University of Chicago Press, Chicago (1995)
19. Borgatti, S.P., Everett, M.G., Freeman, L.C.: Ucinet for Windows: Software for Social Network Analysis. Analytic Technologies, Harvard (2002)
20. Velazquez, A.O.A., Aguilar, G.N.: Manual Introdutório à Análise de Redes Sociais – Medidas de Centralidade: Exemplos práticos com UCINET 6.109 e NetDraw 2.28. http://www.aprende.com.pt/fotos/editor2/Manual%20ARS%20[Trad].pdf. Accessed 3 Feb 2005
21. Wasserman, S., Faust, K.: Social Network Analysis: Methods and Applications. Cambridge University Press, Cambridge (1994)
22. Iacobucci, D.: Graphs and matrices. In: Wasserman, S., Faust, K. (eds.) Social Network Analysis: Methods and Applications. Cambridge University Press, Cambridge (1994)
23. Emirbayer, M., Goodwin, J.: Network analysis, culture and the problem of agency. Am. J. Sociol. **99**, 1411–1454 (1994)

Innovation and Differentiation Strategies Integrating the Business Strategies and Production in Companies Networks

Francisco José Santos Milreu[1,2,3(✉)], Pedro Luiz de Oliveira Costa Neto[1], Sergio Luiz Kyrillos[1,4], José Barrozo de Souza[1,5], and Marcelo Shibuya[1]

[1] Paulista University-UNIP, Dr. Bacelar St. 1212, São Paulo, Brazil
milreu@uol.com.br
[2] School Engineering, São Caetano do Sul Municipal University - USCS,
Goias Ave. 3400, São Caetano do Sul, Brazil
[3] School Engineering, Santo André Fundation - FSA,
Principe de Gales Ave. 821, Santo André, Brazil
[4] School Engineering, São Paulo Federal Institute - IFSP,
Pedro Vicente St. 625, São Paulo, Brazil
[5] School Engineering, Espírito Santo Federal Institute of Education,
Science and Technology - IFES, Vitória Ave. 1729, Vitória, Brazil

Abstract. This study presents an overview of the business and production strategies with a focus on innovation and differentiation strategies as main factors for competitiveness in companies networks (NetC), developed through a qualitative and exploratory approach with data from multiple sources in interviews with the automotive industry business managers from suppliers in Stamping, Forged and Machined segment of São Paulo, in which the participation of governance of corporation as a key element for the success of NetC was highlighted, bringing competitive advantages by acquired know-how, promoting the strengthening and consolidation among partners, developing productive sets as many focuses of action, as well as providing shorter delivery times and order fulfilment, enabling the standardisation of programs and growth of social capital among the involved companies.

Keywords: Companies networks · Business strategies · Production strategies · Innovation · Differentiation strategies

1 Introduction

In the way organisations are being structured in NetC, which occurs almost as paradigm shift, corporate strategies do not exhaust the dimensions of analysis, which means that managers have to resort to multiple research sources to compose an alternative that best suits the needs of their operations.

Productive organisations are each time more concerned with the positive or negative impacts on the strategic plan of operations, plus the reflection of the development of its activity in the social environment as a player in the network.

In business activities, especially in the manufacturing area, there is a great dependence on factors linked to the production, because the movement of goods and

© IFIP International Federation for Information Processing 2015
S. Umeda et al. (Eds.): APMS 2015, Part I, IFIP AICT 459, pp. 45–52, 2015.
DOI: 10.1007/978-3-319-22756-6_6

services should pursue objectives aligned to the needs of adding both values and sustainable economic outcomes.

On the other hand, the fall of consumer markets barriers and political changes have built different economic blocs, as globalisation, allowing the growing impact of new players from different competitive dimensions and local and global interests, stokes competition.

For companies, in order to adequate to this competitive environment, there are options for integration into production networks, considering the demands of the environment and the market.

The purpose of this paper is to identify in the Stamping, Forged and Machined segment of São Paulo innovative and strategic attributes that provide integration between business strategies and production in the studied productive networks.

2 Bibliographic Review

2.1 Governance of Corporations

The theme of the governance role in corporations, considering the business strategies and production, involves several actors participating in NetC and [1] defines it as a set of delivery mechanisms of a social system and organised actions taken towards ensure security, prosperity, coherence, order and continuity of the system.

The rules for governance act systemically in corporations, in the market, in society and in government agencies, each with its established rules and seeking balance regarding its goals, aimed at interaction between the parties and the systemic inter-dependence as stated in [2] regarding the theoretical approaches that address the governance theme in six different areas: the agency theory, the stewardship theory, the theory of resource dependence, democratic perspective, stakeholder theory and the theory of managerial hegemony.

So, these theoretical perspectives emphasise what each of them understands as being the role for the development of governance, their responsibilities and nature of its intervention in the organisation.

This ability to expand and enhance the results through the simultaneous efforts of all members of a system at a higher level, which is the sum of the individual results of the parties, is called synergy, a basic feature of a organisation when seen by the systemic approach.

Therefore, this governance corresponds to the administration forms of this system that best meet the wishes of the majority of the people involved, generating sound management of development and thus highlighting the importance of this concept of organization that values the effects of dynamic interaction of the corporation with other market players, which represents key aspect to their competitiveness.

2.2 Competitive Strategy

Regarding strategies, [3] define it as a global set of decisions and actions that place the organisation in its environment and aim the accomplishment of its long term goals.

At the same time, [4] say strategy is an integrated set of commitments and actions, which aims to explore the core competencies and achieve competitive advantage.

As every strategy has a goal, prior to the adoption of measures, to which it applies and demonstrates a common understanding of the vision and strategic mission of the company, what is seen is that organisations develop and exploit core competencies in many different functional areas to implement their strategies.

Reference [5] postulates that the competitive strategy is associated with the search of a favourable position in the competitor environment, which competitive advantages originate from the set of activities that the company performs in design, production, marketing and product logistics and support by setting what the author calls the value chain, which in turn fits into a larger stream of activities, the value system, which includes suppliers, distributors and customers.

For [5], the activities are related by links and thus open up the opportunity for obtaining a competitive advantage from the management of such links.

2.3 Operations Strategy

Regarding operations, [6] define it as a set of objectives, policies and self-imposed restrictions which together describe how the organisation has tried to manage and develop all the resources invested in operations, in order to run better (and possibly redefine) their mission, guiding in the school of strategic planning, through a formal process and from top to bottom that covers the strategic, tactical and operational levels.

From the perspective of strategic planning, operations strategy is a functional strategy and therefore should promote support to the competitive strategy, given the fact that the elements that make up the production system have to be designed to achieve certain ends and perform certain tasks. So, different competitive strategies may require different configurations of the production system, which for [7], the industrial production systems represent the transformation of inputs into outputs, with inherent value.

Thus, it is necessary to systemically study the internal processes of manufacturing, so that we can decisively prevent the incidence of failures, encourage improvements in the efficiency of operations and better use of the inputs.

2.3.1 Strategic Planning and Production Control

To plan, to control and to produce mean to unite the productive organisation in order to obtain an integrated work in all the chain, structured to simplify the activity and to eliminate time on unnecessary activities.

As the manufacturing systems to [8] represent the set of interrelated elements (human, physical and management procedures) that are designed to generate final products, whose commercial value exceeds the total costs incurred to get them, the PPC system needs to properly inform the current situation of the availability of resources and make decisions about what, when, how and with which resources to work in order to produce goods and services.

Planning involves design and formalisation of future activities and aspirations, being essential to have controls and the possible adoption of correction strategies to the materialisation and confirmation of the plans.

2.4 Competitiveness

Competitiveness is the characteristic or ability of an organisation to fulfil its purposes more successfully than other competing organisations, which is based on the ability to meet the needs and expectations of customers or citizens that they serve according to their specific mission, for which the company has been created.

Reference [5] states that companies achieve of competitive advantage through innovation initiatives, that addresses it in the broadest sense, encompassing new technologies and new ways of doing things and perceive a new basis for competition or find better ways to compete in an old fashion manner.

2.5 Innovation and Business Networks

Innovation comes from knowledge and, according [9], it represents a process of creating new possibilities through the combination of different perceptions that results in the search for technologies, markets or actions of competition. Therefore, innovation, integrated in business networks, according to [10] offers a favourable environment for strategic intelligence activities, generation of new knowledge, internal and external information related to the existing experience and skills in the organisation, what contributes to innovation processes environments.

To [5], innovation is manifested in new product designs, new production processes, in new marketing approaches or new training methods. It always requires investments in skill and knowledge, as well as physical assets and reputation of brands.

Considering this theoretical framework and to support this article, the model showed in Fig. 1 and developed by [11] links the business strategy, production and PPC in companies networks. This model has evolved into the profile expressed through the governance of corporations, involving business strategies and operations strategies, and arises from the business network with business strategies directing the actions in network operations.

3 Methodology

According to [12], inductive process of analysis can be used in case studies to verify the trend of relations between two or more phenomena, with instruments and ways of data collection in multiple cases and inclusion of academic literature.

In this study, as the goal was in the search of affirmatives, it was considered the qualitative and exploratory approach, gathering data from multiple sources through a research with 47 managers of the automotive chain companies that deal with suppliers related to Stamping, Forged and Machined segment in São Paulo, involving various verifications, detailed in [11], structured in the model developed in Fig. 1 and contemplating innovation and differentiation strategies integrating business and production strategies in companies networks, providing meaningful results for the players.

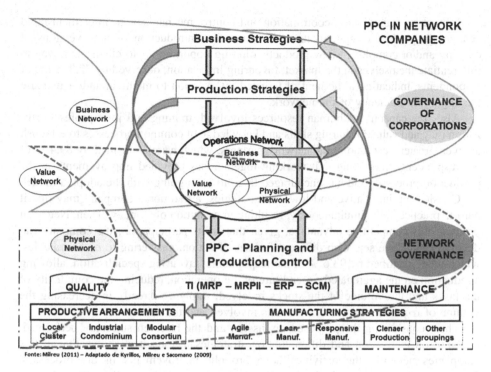

Fonte: Milreu (2011) – Adaptado de Kyrillos, Milreu e Sacomano (2009)

Fig. 1. PPC in NetC. Source: author based on conceptual map [11]

4 Summary of Observations in the Studied Cases

Current models cannot provide answers to complex agreements between companies that are organised in networks - which have established deep functional relationships – to the demands promoted by an organised society and the changes that have occurred on governance in recent times.

According to [13], making intra and intercompanies governances is an ability to govern relations including class interests and ways of understanding them, which interfere in hierarchy and control aspects, contracts and monitoring, motivation based on trust and loyalty, reflecting on intended targets and conditions of alliances, which are based on dependent cooperation. The process of governance in NetC has the ability to guide the course of a business unit maintaining interfaces with the stakeholders involved.

In the pursuit of success, aiming the competitiveness of organisations, competent management, coupled with the high degree of trust and commitment, lead to the achievement of goals.

These groups of suppliers become strategic in the development of this network of companies, meeting the demands with quality, production capacity, supply costs and capacity for innovation, exchanging information and updating their production processes seeking to innovate in processes and develop new opportunities of products and/or services.

It must be maintained a coordination and control mechanisms to implement rapid changes in product design, in its mix, in the fast introduction of new versions of existing and/or completely new products, offering opportunities to clients as a way to differentiate themselves in the market, favouring innovation, observed by 72.3 % the of respondents, indicating a moment of targeted intervention to maintain and/or increase the aggregate efficiency of the network.

Also, the capacity of human resources involved, training and joint professionalization may add value in sharing skills and knowledge of common processes to establish an even greater trust among the network partners, which were confirmed by 89.4 % of the respondents, indicating that working together has provided improvements in the production processes and has encouraged them to keep going with the adopted model.

Considering innovative and low cost strategies, a traditional company may find it hard to practice both simultaneously, resulting in an option of strategy. Then, NetC can promote this competitive advantage, given that in its participation, the company can develop productive sets with different focuses of action, answering to both strategies, which were identified by 93.6 % of the respondents, favouring specialisation, allowing a reduction on the aggregated expenditure of the operation, reducing the complexity of the tasks and the volume of the stocks involved, implying directly in decreasing the volume of required investment, the costs involved and the final price.

Thus, considering the proposed discussion and the research summary performed, focusing on innovation and differentiation strategies factors, it is shown that in this companies network, the activities have brought improvements in the processes, favouring differentiation, obtaining competitive advantages, as well as strengthening and consolidating relationships on the network through the governance of corporations, an effective tool for network management.

5 Conclusions and Recommendations

A thoughtful look to the satisfaction of the customers served by the NetC also deserves attention, focusing on shorter lead times and order fulfillment on the dates and amounts requested, innovating in the relationship.

Learning and the dissemination of the techniques used by the network participants, combining their skills and using the acquired know-how, can provide a competitive advantage for the NetC in addition to the standardisation of programs combining quality, sharing internal standards and certifications to meet international standards, differing themselves in their business.

Another important factor that can be considered is the economic gain to the accumulation of social capital among the companies involved, because the bonds relating to alliances and trust promotes the strengthening and consolidation of activities among the partners, thereby inhibiting opportunistic actions and facilitating development of innovation processes.

Finally, several proactive triggered actions, considering the proposed arguments, show the competitive priorities and innovation and differentiation factors.

Given the dynamic environment in which companies operate, the movement of goods and services pursues the objectives aligned to the needs of adding both value and economic sustainable outcomes with the use of competitive advantage by integrating business strategies in the context of corporations' governance with the operations strategies. In this sense, companies involved in the network must necessarily rethink their corporate strategies and use the strategic attribute sets for its network integration, innovation and thus they will be competitively differentiated in the market.

Some issues need to be part of this integrated environment prospects of NetC, thus demonstrating the effective participation of governance, and so, one of the contributions of this paper focuses on the possibility and feasibility of studying the competitive advantages when opting for functional strategies to set answers to the above questions, confronting standards required with reality, with the scenarios that can be built considering, obviously, the feedback from the market, reducing costs, diminishing response time for production, facilities availability, workforce training, systems and technology availability, among many other determining factors for companies that are part of the networking environment.

Some issues must be part of the prospection in this integrated environment of companies networks, demonstrating the effective participation of governance. Thus, one of the contributions of this article focuses on the possibility and feasibility of studying the competitive advantages when opting for functional strategies to indicate answers to the questions above, comparing requested standards in terms of the set reality with the scenarios that can be built considering, obviously, market feedback, cutting costs, reducing response time for production, available facilities, workforce training, available systems and technology among many other determining factors for companies inserted in the networking environment.

References

1. Milani, C.R.S.: Governança global e meio ambiente: como compatibilizar economia, política e ecologia. In: Fundação Konrad-Adenauer Stiftung. Pesquisas: Governança Global – Reorganização da política em todos os níveis de ação. São Paulo, 16 (1999)
2. Cornforth, C.: The governance of public and non-profit organisations. What do boards do? In: Routledge Studies in the Management of Voluntary and Non-profit Organizations, London (2003)
3. Slack, N., Chambers, S., Johnston, R.: Administração da produção. Atlas, São Paulo (2002)
4. Hitt, M.A., Ireland, R.D., Hoskisson, R.E.: Administração estratégica. Pioneira Thomson Learning, São Paulo (2003)
5. Porter, M.E.: On competition: estratégias competitivas essenciais. Campus, Rio de Janeiro (1999)
6. Hayes, R.H., Pisano, G.P., Upton, D.M., Wheelwright, S.C.: Operations, Strategy and Technology, Pursuing the Competitive Edge. Wiley, New York (2004)
7. Sipper, D., Bulfin, R.L.: Production: Planning, Control and Integration. Mc Graw Hill, New York (1997)
8. Maccarthy, B.L., Fernandes, F.C.F.: A multi-dimensional classification of production systems for the design and selection of production planning and control systems. Prod. Plan. Control 11(5), 481–496 (2000)

9. Tidd, J., Bessant, J., Pavitt, K.: Gestão da Inovação (Tradução: Elizamari Rodrigues Becker et al.). Bookman, Porto Alegre (2008)
10. Faggion, G.A., Balestrin, A., Weyh, C.: Geração de Conhecimento e Inteligência Estratégica no Universo das Redes Interorganizacionais. Revista Inteligência Empresarial, número 12 (Julho 2002)
11. Milreu, F.J.S.: Estratégias, fatores e atributos para a estruturação do Planejamento e Controle da Produção em Redes de Empresas. São Paulo, 2011. Tese de Doutorado Engenharia de Produção – Universidade Paulista. Orientador Professor José Benedito Sacomano
12. Yin, R.K.: Estudo de caso, planejamento e métodos. Bookmam, São Paulo (2001)
13. Noteboom, B.: Inter-Firm Alliances – Analysis and Design. Routledge, London (1999)

Platform-Based Production Development

Towards Platform-Based Co-development and Co-evolution of Product and Production System

Jacob Bossen[✉], Thomas Ditlev Brunoe, and Kjeld Nielsen

Department of Mechanical and Manufacturing Engineering, Aalborg University,
Aalborg, Denmark
jbo@m-tech.aau.dk

Abstract. Platforms as a means for applying modular thinking in product development is relatively well studied, but platforms in the production system has until now not been given much attention. With the emerging concept of platform-based co-development the importance of production platforms is though indisputable. This paper presents state-of-the-art literature on platform research related to production platforms and investigates gaps in the literature. The paper concludes on findings by proposing future research directions.

Keywords: Platform-based co-development · Platform-based production development · Integrated product development

1 Introduction

Over the years, modularising products has been seen as means for increasing the efficiency of product development, products in general as well as the manufacturing process. The research field is documented intensively within the research field of Mass Customization, and methods for product modularisation, product family design, and product platform design have been developed under such names as Modular Function Deployment, Product Family Master Plan [5], and Extended Product Family Master Plan. One of the key outcomes of using these methods is awareness of a product architecture i.e. the structured mapping of functional elements in the product, the mapping of functional elements to physical components, and specification of interfaces among product elements. The common elements in an architecture can be considered to constitute a platform that may enable cost effective reuse across products if properly designed [2]. Competitive market conditions demand products manufactured with the lowest possible cost, and hence a need for a more holistic understanding of the product realisation process must be incorporated in the architectures. In other words, the product must not only be designed for the consumer, it must also be designed for manufacturing [8], and this creates a need for integrated product development and concurrent engineering.

One emerging concept that seeks to extend integrated product development is called platform-based co-development and co-evolution of product and production system [15] (later referred to as platform-based co-development). The intention is to use one common platform for both product and production development or align the

© IFIP International Federation for Information Processing 2015
S. Umeda et al. (Eds.): APMS 2015, Part I, IFIP AICT 459, pp. 53–61, 2015.
DOI: 10.1007/978-3-319-22756-6_7

product and production platforms. Thus, the communality that constitutes the platform is more complex than just considering common product parts.

This paper presents a review of literature in the research field of platform-based co-development and identifies gaps in literature. To frame the paper, the following two research questions are used: *(1) which research exists concerning platform-based co-development, and (2) how can this be classified in order to identify gaps?* The paper concludes on the two research questions by arguing for future research directions within the field of production platforms and platform-based co-development.

2   Method

The literature identified for this study is found by searching the databases of Web-Of-Science, SpringerLink, ScienceDirect and Scopus in a combination of block searching and pearl growing. The search string was defined rather broadly with exact search phrases relating to production platform development, and combined with specific terms that relates to production development. Exact phrases used was for instance "Process Platform*", "Manufacturing Platform", "Production Platform", "Platform-based development", and specific terms used was for instance "Manufacturing", "Production" and "Design". If available by the search engine, filtering according to the research field and keywords was done to limit the number of search hits. In total 13 keywords were used such as "Platform development", "Platform approach", "Platform-based" and "Platform strategy".

2.1   Classification

A classification is created for differentiating focus in the identified literature. Due to space limitations of this paper, the citations selected to present state-of-the-art is though not exhaustive. They rather serve as an illustration of one part of the classification, and thus as an illustration of the type of focus appearing in state-of-the-art literature related to production platforms and platform-based co-development. The full classification distinguishes between research focus, application focus and research maturity but only research focus is considered for this paper. This focus is elaborated below.

Regarding research approach, studies can be differentiated by their origin in either problem base or theory base, which influence the research approach [9]. Both approaches give academic contribution, but the former does it in the sequence of (1) analysis (i.e. exposure of structure, causality, empirical knowledge), (2) diagnosis and (3) synthesis (i.e. generation of solutions, assessment of consequence and selection) [9]. The latter gives academic contribution by (1) synthesising on theory (i.e. building structure, internal consistency etc.), (2) propose models and (3) conducting theory analysis (i.e. validity, usefulness, external consistence etc.) [9]. Seen from a viewpoint of Design Science, the output of research is artefacts that are classified into constructs, models, methods and instantiation but not necessarily all of them in each contribution [19]. This study relates research approach and research output in the literature classification by considering literature focusing in construct, model and

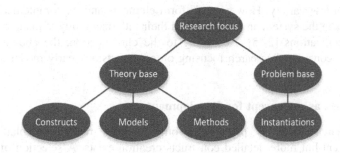

Fig. 1. Illustration of classification used for differentiating literature

method creation as theory based research, whereas literature focusing on instantiation is considered to be research within a specific problem base (Fig. 1).

3 State-of-the-Art

3.1 What Is a Platform?

The platform as a term is not new and has been used in several contexts with several meanings. This study focuses on product and production development, and in that perspective Baldwin and Woodward [2] report use of the platform term as early as the 16th century with meaning as 'a design, a concept, and idea; (something serving as) a pattern or model'. In more recent time, several platform definitions have been proposed in the area of product development research such as "*collection of assets that are shared by a set of products, including components, processes, knowledge, as well as people and relationships*" [18], or "*set of subsystems and interfaces developed to form a common structure from which a stream of derivative products can be efficiently developed and produced*" [13]. The common way of grasping product platforms is however component/part communality, but some definitions do hence also include other aspects such as technology, people and relationships. Thus, production aspects—such as production technology, process, operations, and resources—may also set the foundation for identifying or designing platforms. Such kind of platforms is referred to as production platforms [17]. In fact, studies show that the basic principle of platforms is the same across research fields [2]. This is referred to as the *architecture of platforms* and more specifically …"*platform architecture displays a special type of modularity, in which a product or system is split into a set of components with low variety and high reusability, and another set with high variety and low reusability*" [2]. The first set is the platform and the second is argued to have no generic name but can be referred to as 'the complements' of the platform [2]. Research related to product development has however called the first set of components *Standard design* and classified the compliments into *Design unit, Future design unit* and *Future std. design* [5]. Even though the basic principle of a platform seem similar, the two examples above show minor differences since one argue that platforms consist of standard modules and hence no variety, whereas the other is less unambiguous and states that a platform consist of modules with low variety. However, platform elements and its complements are distinct modules in the system architecture, and their interoperability is made possible via interface specifications [2, 5]. According to the classification, the above studies of platforms are considered research focusing on constructs and early model creation.

3.2   Platform as a Concept for Development

Similar research focus is present in other studies related to platform-based co-development but more detailed constructs creation exists. A selection of this literature is reviewed below.

Three evolution paths of relevancy towards executing platform-based co-development are identified with starting point in dedicated co-development i.e. (1) *product platform based co-development* (only product platforms), (2) *production platform-based co-development* (only production platforms) and (3) *platform-based co-development* (utilising both product and production platforms) [14]. Dedicated co-development is considered as traditional development of product and production system with some degree of collaboration, but without the use of platform thinking [15]. The opposite approach that encourages such co-development is the traditional engineering which is also referred to as *Over-the-wall-engineering* and *Sequential engineering*. Platform-based co-development can hence be considered as an integrated product development approach that can be ranked alongside or as a branch of concurrent engineering where cross-functional work and information sharing is in focus. An important purpose in co-development processes is to create and intelligently visualise boundaries and capabilities for product and production system design such that variety is only present where it is desirable and acceptable [10].

One aspect of platform-based co-development is product platforms for product family development. This aspect is relatively well-studied and Jiao et al. [8] present a heavily cited collection of research conducted in this field. Regarding the production aspect of platform-based co-development specific definitions on production platforms has not been identified in the study for this paper, but Johannesson [10] emphasize the fact that product and production are co-equal systems, and hence such definition will have significant similarities or be equal to the product platform definitions just presented. Term-wise platform-based co-development was first coined by Michaelis [16] and later elaborated [15], but the research can in principle be traced back to the product platform definition by Meyer and Lehnerd [13]. This definition advocate co-development since communality is not necessarily limited to product information but also include support for product realisation information, and hence support for reuse of production system assets. This is consistent with Johannesson [10] who emphasize importance of reusing assets by means of product and production platforms.

Research on *Process Platform* is considered research encouraged by the inclusion of production aspect in product platform development, and hence something that relates to a production platform. Conceptually Process Platforms was coined in Jiao et al. [7], and later the term was elaborated by e.g. Zhang [25]. The literature identified on process platform is focused around—but not limited to—generic product and process structures, generic routing, generic planning and generic variety representation

[20]. For instance Zhang and Rodrigues [24] used a tree unification approach to create an algorithm for identifying generic process elements in known production system data. The algorithm was tested on industry data that contained 30 different process trees with operations and operations precedence for production of vibration motors. From these 30 process trees, 13 basic process trees were identified and merged into one generic process tree. With the perception of platforms reviewed above, such generic process tree constitutes a platform and the remaining processes can be considered as compliments of the platform. The narrow scope of the algorithms does though not support a complete identification of production platform elements, but rather—as indicated by the name—identification of a process platform.

3.3 Representation and Methodologies for Platform Development

An important aspect of Platform-based co-development is communication through models and visualisation techniques [10] (later referred to as representation). By considering identified literature on representation according to the classification (Fig. 1), then this literature can be considered to focus on model and method creation. Representative selections of this literature are reviewed below.

A part of the research identified on representation focus on platform as concept i.e. conceptual models formulated according to basic constructs, definitions, relationships, and functionalities [21]. Other research deals with representation techniques for a platform design methodology with various scopes and degrees of abstraction on co-development [12, 24]. This indicates that platform design in a co-development process must have focus on different co-development aspects, different abstraction and different detail levels.

Baldwin and Woodward [2] presented three basic representation techniques that can be used to investigate relationships between variables of any types of platform i.e. Graph representation, Design-Structure-Matrix and layer maps. Graph representation is for instance used in the tree unification algorithm [24], and layer maps are used for communicating product platform elements in [5]. Such visual representation of relationships for identification of possible platform elements is in this sense considered tools for platform design and hence something serving as support for methodologies.

Furthermore, dynamic models are proposed to represent relevant processes and their behaviour [21], and can generally be classified into visual diagrammatic process language and programming process modelling [21]. The latter in itself is reported to have strong limitations in readability and comprehensibility [21] and hence not a relevant for co-development alone. The dynamic models are for instance used for process platform configuration [23].

In the area of product development, Harlou [5] has managed to enable visualisation of product data and structure for easy product family development and evolution. The research covers both constructs, models, methods and applications, which is operationalised in the tool called "Product Family Master Plan". The tool builds on "Theory of Domains" and the "Chromosome model" created by Andreasen et al. [1] for visualisation of the product composition, and to structure relevant product development information into three views (Customer view, Engineering view and Part view). The customer view decomposes functions as perceived by the customer, needed in the product, which are related to engineering organs (Engineering View) and physical parts of the product (Part View). The composition structure for each view is referred to as a "Part-of" and is combined with a classification-like approach called the "Kind-of". Later research extended this tool to cover production information [11]. Some researchers argue however that these models lack support for production system design [15], and hence also co-development. One argument is that these modelling and visualisation approaches combine the existing product structure and manufacturing process—and thereby address the production of the product—but not the design of the production system itself. The models do thus not completely support co-development of product and production system development, but they provide an elegant way of model existing functional elements and relate them to other existing product modelling domains. Hence, the tool model the architecture AS-IS but does not provide TO-BE.

Other research seeks with similar approach to overcome the representation challenge by using a so-called Configurable Component framework [12, 15]. Configurable Component is an object-oriented modelling technique that can be used as building blocks to model technical systems [3]. One central part of a Configurable Component is a function means tree that can capture the intention of the designed technical solutions. Initially the framework was intended to the product domain, but later research has proposed to use it in an integrated model for co-development [14, 15]. The integrated model by Michaelis [14] presents with a relatively high abstraction level both product and production system in three domains (i.e. function, solution and component domain), and related them to each other through a production process domain. The production process domain is here fabrication operations and assembly operations, which is referred to as *operations for integration of features* and *operations for integration of parts*. The research based on Configurable Component and the chromosome model from above origins from design of Theory of Technical Systems created by Hubka and Eder [6].

Although not based in Theory of Technical Systems, other research on representation techniques exist related to platform-based co-development. Zhang et al. [22] propose for instance an object-oriented language that is based on Unified Modelling Language to represents a process platform. In this work, the author emphasizes that not only platform structural information is represented but also product and process knowledge (in form of selection and planning rules). Later this research has been extended to the dynamic Object-Oriented Visual Diagrammatic Modelling Language presented in Zhang [21]. Petri-nets have also been studied as a dynamic modelling language for process platform-based production configuration [23].

4 Discussion on Research Gaps

The state-of-the-art literature reviewed above found focus in literature on constructs and representation techniques with various scope and abstraction level. Regarding design methodologies building on profound constructs and representations models, much literature is identified on product platform development. However, regarding production platforms only methodologies with limited scope exist. Some of them cover method development and instantiation [24] but build on narrow constructs and models.

Hence, the current literature lacks maturity for a comprehensive method creation on production platform development.

Literature identified on production platforms seems clustered in two groups. The review indicates that some research has strong base in design of Theory of Technical Systems and have focus pointed at creating constructs and representation which are refined through industry case studies [12, 15]. In such research, communication through visualisation is given importance. Other literature indicates focus on simple constructs but seeks to analyse them with comprehensive mathematical representation models which are validated and used for optimisation with industry data [23, 25].

Since the optimal design of a production system involves many complicated considerations, one can argue that such challenges are not possible to solve with only mathematical optimisation. One of the reasons is that the solution space to consider becomes large for even simple product designs because of entangled relations between product and production system. For example, designing assembly systems requires consideration on product design, assembly sequence, assembly system configuration, assembly line balancing etc. Furthermore, the life cycle of factory related elements are usually longer than the product life cycle, and will require the solution to be dynamic for coping with e.g. fluctuation in demand, capabilities etc. [4].

5 Conclusion

Some of the findings from this study are that constructs, models and methods on production platform design and platform-based co-development are rather weakly defined in literature. Comprehensive conceptual studies have been made with either focus on constructs and models, or models and methods, but these studies must be aligned and put into context of industrial problems. Hence, there is a need for a reference model giving holistic understanding of production platforms to enable creation of methodologies for co-development. Such research would put forward a "language" for discussing platform-based production development and platform-based co-development.

Different engineering disciplines are utilised for fully defining and designing a production platform in industry context, and hence communication of data is an important aspect. Diagrammatic languages that visualise needed data on different abstraction levels and details levels is important and must be investigated further. We envision such research can enable creation of information models for use in co-development tools.

Algorithms for identifying communality and relations were identified in the review. We consider this as an important preparation task since normally new design concepts build on previous knowledge, and hence communicating existing and potential commonalty may be a good input to make platform design process manageable. The current algorithms are though narrow in scope, and we suggest that case-studies must conducted to investigate which types of communality that are relevant to search for i.e. which kind of communality is value adding for specific companies, industries, geographical locations etc.

References

1. Andreasen, M.M., Hansen, C.T., Mortensen, N.H.: The structuring of products and product programmes (1996)
2. Baldwin, C.Y., Woodard, C.J.: The architecture of platforms: a unified view. In: Gawer, A. (ed.) Platforms, Markets and Innovation, p. 19. EE Publishing, UK (2009)
3. Claesson, A.: A Configurable Component Framework Supporting Platform-Based Product Development. Chalmers University of Technology, Gothenburg (2006)
4. ElMaraghy, H.A., Wiendahl, H.P.: Changeability - an introduction. In: ElMaraghy, H.A. (ed.) Changeable and Reconfigurable Manufacturing Systems, pp. 3–24. Springer, London (2009)
5. Harlou, U.: Developing product families based on architectures: contribution to a theory of product families. In: ORBIT (2006)
6. Hubka, V., Eder, W.E.: Theory of Technical Systems: A Total Concept Theory for Engineering Design, vol. 1, p. 291. Springer, Berlin (1988)
7. Jiao, J., Zhang, L., Pokharel, S.: Process platform planning for mass customisation production. Int. J. Mass Customisation 1, 237–259 (2006)
8. Jiao, J., Simpson, T.W., Siddique, Z.: Product family design and platform-based product development: a state-of-the-art review. J. Intell. Manuf. 18, 5–29 (2007)
9. Joergensen, K.A.: A selection of system concepts (2000)
10. Johannesson, H.: Emphasizing Reuse of Generic Assets Through Integrated Product and Production System Development Platforms. Springer, Berlin (2014)
11. Kvist, M.: Product family assessment (2010)
12. Levandowski, C., Michaelis, M.T., Johannesson, H.: Set-based development using an integrated product and manufacturing system platform. Concurrent Eng. 22, 234–252 (2014)
13. Meyer, M.H., Lehnerd, A.P.: The Power of Product Platforms: Building Value and Cost Leadership. Free Press, New York (1997)
14. Michaelis, M.T., Johannesson, H., ElMaraghy, H.A.: Function and process modeling for integrated product and manufacturing system platforms. J. Manuf. Syst. (2014)
15. Michaelis, M.T.: Co-development of Products and Manufacturing Systems using Integrated Platform Models. Chalmers University of Technology, Gothenburg (2013)
16. Michaelis, M.T.: Co-development of Products and Manufacturing Systems-Applying a Configurable Platform Approach. Chalmers University of Technology, Gothenburg (2011)
17. Nielsen, O.F.: Continuous platform development. DTU Management Engineering, Department of Management Engineering, Technical University of Denmark, Lyngby (2010)
18. Robertson, D., Ulrich, K.: Planning for product platforms. Sloan Manage. Rev. 39, 19–32 (1998)
19. Vaishnavi, V., Kuechler, W.: Design science research in information systems. Accessed 23 Oct 2013 (2004)
20. Wang, L., Fu, X., Zhong, S.: Generalized process family modeling based on process platform, pp. 183–196 (2013)
21. Zhang, L.: Modelling process platforms based on an object-oriented visual diagrammatic modelling language. Int. J. Prod. Res. 47, 4413–4435 (2009)

22. Zhang, L., Jiao, J., Helo, P.T.: Process platform representation based on unified modelling language. Int. J. Prod. Res. **45**, 323–350 (2007)
23. Zhang, L.L., Rodrigues, B.: A petri net model of process platform-based production configuration. J. Manuf. Technol. Manage. **24**, 873–904 (2013)
24. Zhang, L.L., Rodrigues, B.: A tree unification approach to constructing generic processes. IIE Trans. **41**, 916–929 (2009)
25. Zhang, L.L.: Process platform-based production configuration for mass customization (2007)

Developing a Collaborative Framework for Mapping and Managing Key Drivers of Future Value Creation Based on Intangible Assets

Stephane Pagano[✉] and Gilles Neubert

EMLYON Business School - UMR5600,
23, Avenue G. de Collongue, 69134 Ecully, France
{Pagano,GNeubert}@EM-Lyon.com

Abstract. Companies, their suppliers and networks of partners need to be aligned to fulfill the strategy to deliver the value and adapt rapidly whatever challenge arises. To be resilient, companies and their networks have to build ecosystems in a systemic thinking. To help firms achieving this, we propose a methodology based on "value drivers" that allows the mapping, the analysis and the management of intangible assets, and the way they are activated through a multi perspective and a multi stakeholder framework.

Keywords: Value creation · Collaborative networks · Resilient SC · Ecosystem · Intangible assets · Stakeholders

1 Introduction

In a rapidly changing environment, companies have to face many challenges while the competitive and technological environment keeps evolving at a fast pace: Globalization of markets through trade agreements and communication technologies, consumers' maturity and power of influence; strong trend towards a service-focused and dematerialized economy. Today's value chains consist of globally spread stakeholders, production processes, global distribution and retail channels. As part of the procurement process, the purchasing function is a hub upstream the Supply Chain that plays a fundamental role both in term of value creation and adaptation of the business models of the companies.

Our research objective is to construct a dictionary of resources at work in processes, seen here as drivers of performing relationships, by mapping their importance and role in the interactions taking place in the processes. Our applied research proposition is to build tools for the management of value creation in the buying and supply-chain processes integrating multiple stakeholders and multiple perspectives.

The paper is organized as follow: after the introduction, the second part reviews essential concepts underlying the stakes for the sustainability and the performance of firms' supply chain, the third part presents our framework approach and gives some details on our research and propositions. The fourth part concludes on findings, expected contributions and future operational outputs.

© IFIP International Federation for Information Processing 2015
S. Umeda et al. (Eds.): APMS 2015, Part I, IFIP AICT 459, pp. 62–69, 2015.
DOI: 10.1007/978-3-319-22756-6_8

2 Context

2.1 Value and Value Creation

Value is a multi-perspective concept that extends beyond the limits of the firm. With globalization and technological innovation, value is delivered through dynamic networks or chains of interconnected firms or supply chain. This raises the question on how a particular relationship helps a firm creating value in terms of offerings, and what factor(s) are essential to successfully establish a particular relationship [1]. The strategic models of Value Creation based on arms-length confrontation with suppliers has led many companies on a short term value creation path, which meant value destruction for many suppliers and their economic ecosystem, impacting their entire value chain and their stakeholders.

2.2 Corporate Social Responsibility

There's an increasing pressure to consider the environmental and social aspects in purchasing policies: expectations are rising from stakeholders such as customers, the general public, NGOs, and governments who now hold companies responsible, not only for their own actions, but also all the partners within the supply chain [2–5]. CSR advocates the idea that companies need to change their business models and value propositions, actually creating value not only for themselves, but also for a larger number of stakeholders. Since 1930, the stakeholder theory poses the question of the definition of the objectives of firms, arguing about shareholders value or about sharing value with partners. Porter and Kramer recently introduced the idea of Shared Value [6]. Over the last decade, many authors [7–9] called for an urgent renewal of the strategic objectives of firms, towards financial success, but taking into account the actual needs of the communities where they operate or have an impact.

2.3 Collaboration and Risks Mitigation

Usual strategies based on competitive advantage [10, 11] can't last. To address this issue, firms have investigated other domains: process optimization to save resources, flexibility, changes in relationship with other partners to secure exclusive access to suppliers. These developments impact the complexity and importance of purchasing decisions [12–14]. Supplier management is a key issue in supply chain performances and this reflects in a continuing growth of publications [15–18]. Since suppliers can represent up to 90 % of firms turnover, the potential impact of inappropriate portfolio management of suppliers can seriously impact the value of a company. Firms also interconnected with their societal, natural and economic environment [19] because it's from these that depend their competitiveness: trained employees, infrastructures, communications, political stability. The state of the global environment therefore impacts the firms activity, operational costs, the availability of the resources, and the value of the firms viewed by the stakeholders. These risks are putting a high pressure on companies that need to adapt rapidly to innovative or disruptive situations.

2.4   The Role of Intangible Assets

The way value is generated lies in the way physical and intellectual resources are managed and activated. Companies are looking for durable and sustainable strategic resource to acquire and maintain competitive advantages. This is why knowledge management should be completely integrated [11, 20, 21]. The importance of knowledge in the success of firms has already been described [22, 23] specifically the role of intangible assets in providing sustainable competitive advantage [24, 25]. Though there is an abundant literature in economy and management on intangibles assets [26], we think that there is still a great work to do to operationalize intangible assets management, moreover in operations and supply chain management.

2.5   Conclusion

We see the complexity of supply chain and value chain configuring when it comes to describe how intangibles assets such as human competencies, organizational knowledge and behavioral characteristics deployed by interacting individuals, departments and organizations achieve each stakeholder's values, expectations and perspective. The "life" of projects and processes such as buyer-supplier relationship can be as complex as a human based interaction between organizations and services can be, because it greatly relies on organizational and personal "qualities" of the actors on both sides of each relation (buyers, vendors, and other stakeholders involved).

As value creation has many meanings, we see the limits of closed-off reasoning and the potential of widening the perspectives of firms through a paradigm shift: stakeholders, environment and future generations no longer being expandable when building sustainable business models and value creation strategies. This requires considering internal organization of the firm, its networks of connections and partners, its tangible and intangible assets and the notions of capital and investment [27].

3   Approach and Empirical Method Development

Firms need to adopt a multi-perspective approach on the supplier selection and management: purchasing process and supply chain play a strategic role, which must go beyond optimization of processes, and take into account the temporal dimensions of the ROI (short, mid and long term) and the management of intangibles.

Measure, management and value creation in the firm are spread over time and must take into account the stakeholders. To ensure the longevity of the firm, the following dimensions and perspective must be included in the processes:

- The time horizon of the firms' strategies;
- Value creation/destruction for the firm and its ecosystem;
- Actual place of intangible assets as drivers of competitiveness and value creation.

To achieve this, we are constructing on an approach by value "enablers" or "drivers" for future value creation [28], mapping intangible assets, processes and stakeholders through events that will generate new value proposition (Fig. 1) and eventually economic value and performance for the firm.

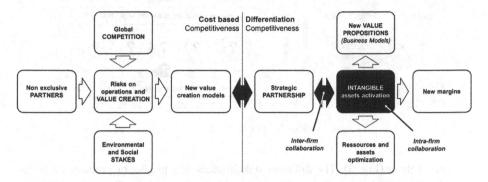

Fig. 1. Placing intangible assets at the heart of renewed value propositions.

3.1 Ground of the Research

The global research ground for our projects is based on three companies which offered participating buyers teams for initial explorations. Later on two firms offered a long standing participation for the conduct of the full research, currently ongoing, through long standing projects involving transversal teams.

3.2 Connecting the Intangibles

To map and understand interactions and flows beyond the specifics of each situation (project, company, process, industry etc.), instead of trying to provide predefined items, we focused on building a generic methodology to analyze and manage value creation in the processes, objectively linking the activation of intangible assets to value creation. The applied output can be used by managers to follow projects and processes along their lifetime, and comprises four main phases: A consistency strategy analysis; the identification of key drivers; the selection of key performance indicators and the construction of dashboards.

The heart of the methodology is to analyze the drivers represented by intangible assets (human capital, relational capital, structural capital) and connect them with the process to achieve value proposition and delivery made to the clients.

To do so, we need to clarify what happens in what we call a fuzzy box (Fig. 2) where players activate processes and stakeholders to achieve objectives and create value. Key steps here are to identify *helping* events occurring during the life of the project to evaluate the role and contribution of intangibles assets, and *breaking* events to capitalize on experience and construct feedback.

3.3 Mapping Value Created/Destroyed and Stakeholders' Impact

We have elaborated an interactive tool that allows the mapping, contextualization and linking of the stakeholders, their interactions and the value created or destroyed for

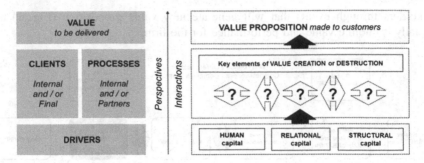

Fig. 2. The fuzzy box.

each one of them (Fig. 3). The different stakeholders of a project or process are listed twice: Underneath the time line, each stakeholder has its own timeline to position the source of helping and breaking events. Above the timeline, the same stakeholders are listed with once again their own timeline to position the different impacts of the events: value created or destroyed, assets created.

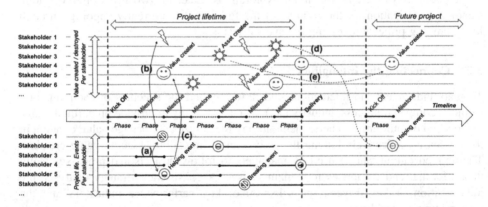

Fig. 3. Visual canvas, mapping events, value and stakeholders' interactions.

Helping and breaking points of the projects' life are positioned on the timelines. The interaction of the events (a) are visually mapped. When an event is positioned, it is possible to map the value destruction caused by the breaking event (b) and the value created for each helping event (c). Causes and consequences are spread over time and can generate positive or negative impact on different horizons: short, medium and long. Hence, assets created during one project can be identified as a significant source of a helping event in a future project (d), or directly create value (e).

This is a capital notion we want to document because assets mobilized in one project are probably the result of a previous investment, just like assets generated in the current project can be drivers of future value, a concept that is at the core of our research work. This can have a significant impact on the affectation of costs and value in industries, because every production line is analyzed through return on investment.

3.4 Empirical Validation of the Method

To validate the method and the tools we have organized a workshop with a team from each of the firms. The objectives of the workshop were to validate the methodology, and to verify the ease of appropriation of the method and the tools, knowing that the concepts and approaches used by the tools were quite far of the everyday operations and scope of the participants.

All the team members found easy to list the stakeholders, to map the helping and breaking events, to connect the values generated, even though these values were outside of direct economic results, and to point value destructions for the different stakeholders. A very significant result is that the method offered the possibility to identify and map the ripple effects of the outcomes of a given project, allowing the affectation of more value to the global outcome of a project due to previously unaccounted dissemination to other projects. Comments were here that the method offered unsuspected outputs: some assets generated are reusable and thus multiplying their effects and value while remaining unaccounted or miss-affected. Value generated by one team could be capitalized by third parties without recognition of the original creators. Some assets generated by one project could be integrated in an innovative Business Models not foreseen before.

The results showed that the buyers and the managers of the purchasing departments easily grab the approach and tools, both to build a reflexive dialogue on past experiences, where they try to identify solutions to achieve better performances, but also to elaborate a decisive argumentation to promote the strategic role of the purchasing function. All participants noted that the method could be used as a knowledge management tool to communicate the history of a project, to illustrate the history of the relationship with a supplier, allowing the understanding of the factors, namely human related, that were decisive along the projects phases.

4 Conclusion and Future Works

Our approach to integrate in the same framework different types of value (i.e. economic, monetary but also market, image, competencies, organizational skills etc.) was validated. The method and tools allow the objectivization of the different values created or destroyed, and of the future values that will eventually be generated with the intangible assets activated or created. Very formalized processes can alter the adaptive capacities of companies and networks, building the case for the ability to build transversal qualitative approach of relationships and information sharing, all these heavily relying on the intangible assets of companies.

The ability for firms to adapt, reconfigure and respond, greatly relies on the capacity of the different stakeholders involved to collaborate and mutually adjust to each-others, diffuse information and realign. All this relies almost exclusively on the very own capacities of the actors involved thus illustrating the central importance of intangible assets. This research builds meaningful methods to track, document and manage intangibles assets in response to internal or external pressure on value creation.

Expected outputs are tools to: analyze the strategy of the firm, how it is translated along the supply chain; identify and take into account all the stakeholders; map, contextualize and link the stakeholders, their interactions and the value created or destroyed for each one of them. These deliverables are being developed and refined through field work. They describe, operationalize and value intangible assets, not in the book value of the firms, but in the future value they can generate or destroy. Other outputs are being developed in field now such as knowledge management tools.

Among scientific contributions, we expect this research will contribute to Resource-Based View theory, to Knowledge Management, to Sustainable Supply Chain and to Supply Chain performance.

Acknowledgements. The authors would like to thank THESAME and the PEAK program: member companies of the program, the F2I, funding structure of the UIMM, the UDIMERA, the Research Division of the Regional Council of Rhône-Alpes, and the General Council of Haute-Savoie.

References

1. Srivastava, V., Singh, T.: Value creation through relationship closeness. J. Strateg. Mark. **18**, 3–17 (2010)
2. Jiang, B.: The effects of interorganizational governance on supplier's compliance with SCC: an empirical examination of compliant and non-compliant suppliers. J. Oper. Manage. **27**, 267–280 (2009)
3. Kovács, G.: Corporate environmental responsibility in the supply chain. J. Clean. Prod. **16**, 1571–1578 (2008)
4. Goebel, P., Reuter, C., Pibernik, R., Sichtmann, C.: The influence of ethical culture on supplier selection in the context of sustainable sourcing. IJPE Sustain. Dev. Manuf. Serv. **140**, 7–17 (2012)
5. Igarashi, M., de Boer, L., Fet, A.M.: What is required for greener supplier selection? A literature review and conceptual model development. J. Purchasing Supply Manage. **19**, 247–263 (2013)
6. Porter, M.E., Kramer, M.R.: Creating shared value. HBR **89**, 62–77 (2011)
7. Hughes, J., Weiss, J.: Simple rules for making alliances work. Harvard Bus. Rev. **85**, 122–131 (2007)
8. Murphy, P.: Shareholders first? Not so fast. HBR **87**, 126–127 (2009)
9. Ready, D.A., Truelove, E.: The power of collective ambition. Harvard Bus. Rev. **89**, 94–102 (2011)
10. Porter, M.E.: Competitive Advantage: Creating and Sustaining Superior Performance: with a New Introduction, 1st edn. Free Press, New York (1998)
11. Barney, J.: Firm resources and sustained competitive advantage. J. Manage. **17**, 99 (1991)
12. De Boer, L., Labro, E., Morlacchi, P.: A review of methods supporting supplier selection. Eur. J. Purchasing Supply Manage. **7**, 75–89 (2001)
13. van Weele, A.J.: Purchasing & Supply Chain Management: Analysis, Strategy, Planning and Practice. Cengage Learning, Andover (2010)
14. Oshri, I., Kotlarsky, J., Willcocks, P.L.P.: The Handbook of Global Outsourcing and Offshoring. Palgrave Macmillan, New York (2011)
15. Ho, W., Xu, X., Dey, P.K.: Multi-criteria decision making approaches for supplier evaluation and selection: a literature review. Eur. J. Oper. Res. **202**, 16–24 (2010)

16. Cao, M., Zhang, Q.: Supply chain collaboration: impact on collaborative advantage and firm performance. J. Oper. Manage. **29**, 163–180 (2011)
17. Wu, C., Barnes, D.: A literature review of decision-making models and approaches for partner selection in agile supply chains. J. Purchasing Supply Manage. **17**, 256–274 (2011)
18. Chai, J., Liu, J.N.K., Ngai, E.W.T.: Application of decision-making techniques in supplier selection: a systematic review of literature. Expert Syst. Appl. **40**, 3872–3885 (2013)
19. Porter, M.E., Kramer, M.R.: The competitive advantage of corporate philanthropy. Harvard Bus. Rev. **80**, 56–69 (2002)
20. Drucker: Coming of the New Organization. Harvard Business School Reprint (1988)
21. Grant, R.M.: The knowledge-based view of the firm: implications for management practice. Long Range Plan. **30**, 450–454 (1997)
22. Drucker, P.F.: Long-range planning-challenge to management science. Manage. Sci. **5**, 238–249 (1959)
23. Penrose, E.T.: The Theory of the Growth of the Firm. Oxford University Press, Oxford (1995)
24. Hall, R.: A framework linking intangible resources and capabiliites to sustainable competitive advantage. Strateg. Manage. J. **14**, 607–618 (1993)
25. Hall, R.: The strategic analysis of intangible resources. Strateg. Manage. J. **13**, 135–144 (1992)
26. Sveiby, K.-E.: Methods for measuring intangible assets. http://www.sveiby.com/articles/IntangibleMethods.htm. Accessed 16 May 2014
27. Parung, J., Bititci, U.S.: A metric for collaborative networks. Bus. Process Manage. J. **14**, 654–674 (2008)
28. Marr, B., Schiuma, G., Neely, A.: Intellectual capital - defining key performance indicators for organizational knowledge assets. Bus. Process Manage. J. **10**, 551–569 (2004)

Key Performance Indicators for Integrating Maintenance Management and Manufacturing Planning and Control

Harald Rødseth[✉], Jan Ola Strandhagen, and Per Schjølberg

Department of Production and Quality Engineering,
Norwegian University of Science and Technology, Trondheim, Norway
{harald.rodseth,ola.strandhagen,
per.schjolberg}@ntnu.no

Abstract. Based on current research and industrial experience, it is found to be a challenge with "silos" where an asset with several disciplines have poor collaboration and result in sub-optimised outcome in production. A structured approach to tackle this situation is through the concept of Integrated Planning (IPL). The purpose of this article is through literature study to identify relevant KPIs within both of the disciplines Manufacturing, Planning & Control (MP&C) and Maintenance Management. As a result, Overall Equipment Effectiveness (OEE) is used in both of the disciplines and throughput time is an essential KPI in MP&C. Finally, a KPI structure which integrates MP&C and Maintenance Management is developed in this article.

Keywords: Key Performance Indicators (KPIs) · Manufacturing Planning & Control · Maintenance Management

1 Introduction

In industry it has been identified a need for improving the integration between the different disciplines, and has in Oil & Gas industry been labelled as Integrated Operations (IO) [20]. In particular, an own research programme called "Center for Integrated Operations in the petroleum industry" has defined IO as integration of people, organisations, work processes and information technology to make smarter decisions [7]. In order to operationalise IO it is crucial to also integrate all the planning disciplines in O&G industry into an Integrated Planning (IPL) concept [19]. The challenge for operating IPL is that the different domains in an organisation function more often than not as separate "silos" [19, 20]. This phenomena occurs in an organisation where an asset with several disciplines and departments performs activities which affects each other [21]. However, due to poor collaboration between these disciplines and departments, the result in production is rather sub-optimised. This challenge is also apparent in manufacturing industry with several challenges found in a literature study [18]. The main finding was that the Manufacturing Planning and Control (MP&C) system is today not well integrated with maintenance planning system. Even worse is that maintenance is only considered on a tactical and operation level in manufacturing, leaving out maintenance for strategic decisions in the organisation. Despite these challenges, initiatives in production exist to integrate production and maintenance.

© IFIP International Federation for Information Processing 2015
S. Umeda et al. (Eds.): APMS 2015, Part I, IFIP AICT 459, pp. 70–77, 2015.
DOI: 10.1007/978-3-319-22756-6_9

Such an example is Lean Production which includes the maintenance concept Total Productive Maintenance (TPM). According to Shah and Ward [23], TPM is of relevance in order to achieve high level of equipment availability. However, TPM also aims at maximizing the equipment effectiveness not only through increased availability in terms of preventing breakdowns, but also reduction of speed losses and quality defects occurring from process activities [1]. In this article the disciplines Maintenance Management, MP&C is evaluated within IPL.

From a maintenance perspective, lack of IPL may have several unfortunate impacts, such as increased maintenance backlog due to unplanned maintenance activities [25], sub-optimal prioritizing of activities and unnecessary production downtime [20], and Enterprise Resource Planning (ERP) systems which has not integrated the maintenance function into production planning [18].

An essential approach for successfully operationalise IPL is applying suitable Key Performance Indicators (KPIs) [2]. In fact it is argued that plans need to be coupled with a mechanism which can monitor the effectiveness of the plan and the progress in order to take corrective actions when needed [2]. Today, there exist vast sources of literature within KPIs for providing terminology, purpose and operation and identification of them [6, 8, 12, 15, 16]. A KPI is defined by Eckerson [8] to be *"a metric measuring how well the organisation or an individual performs an operational, tactical or strategic activity that is critical for the current and future success of the organisation"*. This definition is also aligned in Maintenance management where KPI is described by Palmer to be a metric which is determined by the company to be particularly important [16]. Furthermore, Palmer also describes a metric to be an indicator or measure of maintenance performance. In both of the disciplines Maintenance Management and MP&C, KPIs are essential for decision making. In Maintenance Management an own standard of KPIs has been developed, covering economic, technical and organisational KPIs [6]. Examples of an economic maintenance KPI would be the ratio between preventive maintenance cost and total maintenance cost. Furthermore, in MP&C KPIs such as throughput time is essential and is measured as manufacturing throughput time per part (MTTP) [10].

This article evaluate through a literature study existing KPIs for both Maintenance Management and MP&C. Furthermore, the common KPI for these disciplines are identified and structured as a set of KPIs.

The remainder of this article is structured as follows; in Sect. 2 existing KPIs within both Maintenance Management and MP&C is investigated. Further in Sect. 3 an integrated set of KPIs are proposed for Maintenance Management and MP&C. Finally, concluding remarks are drawn in Sect. 4.

2 Key Performance Indicators in Maintenance and Manufacturing

2.1 Identification and Evaluation Within Maintenance Management

Within Maintenance Management, several maintenance KPI and structural frameworks exist [6, 17, 26, 28, 31]. A specific standard for maintenance KPIs have been established, denoted as EN-NS 15341 [6]. From a Maintenance Management perspective, this standard is of relevance when outlining maintenance objectives and KPIs [13]. The overall aspect of this standard is shown in Fig. 1. The indicator level divides the indicators into application for the plant production (level 1), production line (level 2) and the specific equipment (level 3). Moreover, the indicator group is divided into economic, technical and organisational groups.

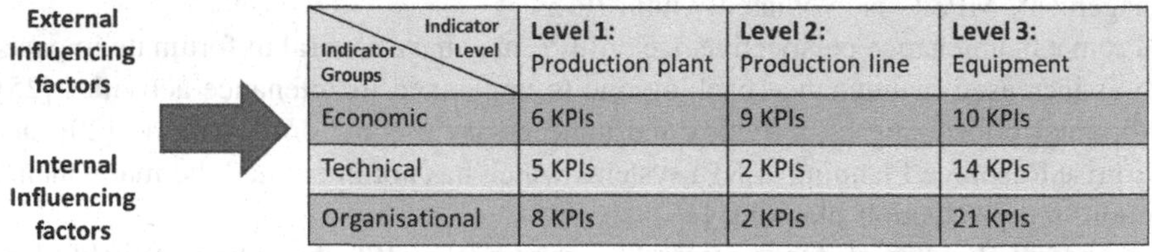

External Influencing factors	Indicator Groups Indicator Level	Level 1: Production plant	Level 2: Production line	Level 3: Equipment
	Economic	6 KPIs	9 KPIs	10 KPIs
Internal Influencing factors	Technical	5 KPIs	2 KPIs	14 KPIs
	Organisational	8 KPIs	2 KPIs	21 KPIs

Fig. 1. Structure of maintenance KPIs in NS-EN 15341 adapted from [6].

This standard has also been evaluated in the context of Value-driven maintenance [27]. The authors propose here a dedicated level 0 in the KPI structure which are the most essential indicators to prioritize for implementation. Some of KPIs has also been selected as KPIs within World Class [22] and is presented in Table 1. The selection of these KPIs is based on expert judgement from both academia and industry. When these KPIs have reached a specific target, the companies are considered to be a company which practice World Class Maintenance (WCM). A proposed definition of WCM is inspired by Wiremans expression "best maintenance practice" [30] where WCM then is defined as *"the maintenance practices that enable a company to achieve a competitive advantage over its competitors in the maintenance process"*.

Table 1. Maintenance KPIs in world class maintenance adapted from Schjølberg and Baas [22].

No.	Maintenance KPI	Description of KPI
1	Total maintenance cost/asset replacement value	Describes if the company has too high maintenance costs
2	Average inventory value of maintenance materials/asset replacement value	Is used to evaluate if the inventory value of maintenance is too large
3	Time for preventive maintenance/total time for maintenance	Indicates the time portion of preventive maintenance
4	Total maintenance cost/total turnover	Describes the cost of maintenance compared of the turnover of the company
5	Time for critical corrective maintenance/total time for maintenance	Indicates the time portion for critical corrective maintenance
6	Planned and predictive time for maintenance/total time for maintenance	Describes the amount of time in maintenance organisation used for proactive work in terms of planned and predictive maintenance
7	Actual operation time/required operation time	This indicator shows the operational availability in production
8	Overall equipment effectiveness (OEE)	OEE = Availability rate * Performance rate * Quality rate

The maintenance concept Total Productive Maintenance (TPM) has influenced this list with the OEE indicator. This indicator is the most central KPI in TPM and was introduced by Nakjima [14] and is endorsed today through establishments of both industry standard [5] and user guide [11]. In fact, based on a thorough literature study performed by Simões *et al.* [24], OEE was ranked to be number 2 out of 37 maintenance performance measures applied in the maintenance organisation. Furthermore, OEE is regarded to be an essential KPI in Asset Management which is a new concept for WCM. In fact, it is dedicated as an asset indicator for strategic, tactical and operational purpose [29]. OEE measures time losses in production in terms of the six big losses which comprise machine breakdown (1), waiting (2), minor stoppages (3), reduced speed (4), scrap (5) and rework (6) [11]. In addition it is important to include a KPI which is leading in nature and measure the maintenance process instead of the maintenance outcome. A proposed leading maintenance KPI is % maintenance work order with due date compliance [2]. A decrease of this KPI can indicate a future machinery breakdown, reduced speed in production and defects and will therefore be a leading KPI for OEE.

2.2 Identification and Evaluation Within Manufacturing Planning and Control

Within MP&C specific KPIs have been developed for MRP which measures issues such as lateness, mean tardiness and percent tardy [9]. However, these KPI are mostly relevant for MRP and more generic KPIs should be applied. A comprehensive list of KPIs within MP&C is presented in Table 2 for this purpose. The selection of these KPIs is based on existing indictors applied in lean production [12]. In addition throughput time should be of high importance within MP&C. This is also supported as an important KPI by Olhager and Selldin [15] who measure the performance of speed in production. Alfnes *et al.* [3] also endorse throughput time who consider both production flow and work in progress to be areas within operations of excellence. The reason to endorse throughput time as an essential KPI within MP&C, is based on evaluating the flow perspective of products in manufacturing. If the throughput time decreases of the products, the faster will the customer pay for the finished goods. In addition OEE will sustain a machine perspective where the machine adds more value to the customer. This KPI will also be of importance in MP&C as well as it is regarded one of the most important KPIs within WCM.

3 Towards Integrated KPIs

For MP&C the throughput time (MTTP) is of importance. Some studies have been performed of reducing the throughput time [4, 10]. In particular in Johnson's study [10] indicates the importance of maintenance in reducing the throughput time. When consider OEE, issues in terms of reduction of setup time (waiting time loss), scrap and rework (scrap), time in operation (reduced speed) and processing variability through improving preventive maintenance (machine breakdown) was identified in this study.

When comparing the KPIs from MP&C in Table 2 and Maintenance Management in Table 1 OEE is one KPI applied in both of these disciplines. In order to construct

Table 2. Important KPIs within MP&C

No.	KPI for MP&C and source	Explanation
1	Dock to dock (DTD) [12]	Is measured by counting the total inventory, including raw materials, Work-in-process and finished goods, and dividing bye the average rate of products shipped
2	First time through (FTT)	% of total units that pass through the value stream on the first pass without rejected
3	Floor space (savings) [12]	Area of space of production, including among others, space for raw material, work-in-process, and finished goods inventories
4	On-time shipment [12]	% of the scheduled customer orders volumes actually shipped on schedule
5	WIP-to-SWIP [12]	(Total inventory on the cell)/standard cell inventory
6	OEE [12]	Described in previous section
7	Sales per person [12]	Calculated as sales amount divided by the number of people in the value stream
8	Average cost per unit [12]	Is described by all the costs of the value stream for the week and dividing by the quantity of units shipped to customers within in a time period
9	Throughput time [10]	The length of time from when material enters a production facility until it exits

KPIs which are integrated for MP&C and Maintenance Management, it is therefore proposed to combine the KPIs OEE and MTTP. In addition it is proposed to have one KPI from each discipline. From Maintenance Management the KPI % maintenance work order with due date compliance. Since OEE influence the MTTP, % maintenance work order with due date compliance can indicate a future increase of MTTP. From MP&C a leading KPI should also be applied.

A summary of the KPI structure for leading and lagging KPIs for the diciplines MP&C and Maintenance Management is shown in Fig. 2.

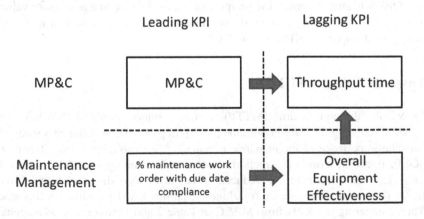

Fig. 2. Structure of leading and lagging KPIs for MP&C and Maintenance Management

A proposed approach for operationalising this concept should be based on more integrated use of the company's maintenance management model and material requirements planning. The maintenance department might experience too low amount of maintenance work order with due date compliance, i.e. too high maintenance backlog. If the maintenance plan itself is not poor, this leading KPI should be communicated to MP&C in order to update the MRP calculations. In addition, it should also be considered to reduce today's throughput time in order to improve the maintenance backlog. Furthermore, The OEE indicator should be used for root cause analysis where time used for maintenance or even the need for maintenance activities can be reduced. This could also improve the maintenance backlog and the throughput time. Even though this type of improvement work is taking place in today's WCM companies, the KPI structure should be considered as an important support tool where the effects and the awareness of IPL is better documented.

4   Concluding Remarks

This article has through a literature study both in MP&C and Maintenance Management identified both the common KPI OEE and established a relationship with leading and lagging KPIs and has been developed as a KPI structure. The expected result of the KPI structure will not only result in reduced throughput time, but also improved coordination between maintenance management and MP&C. From a maintenance perspective, this will e.g. lead to better understanding of why the maintenance backlog level in short term should not be reduced in order to achieve high throughput time. In long-term this should also lead to awareness for MP&C why the throughput time should be temporary reduced in order to allow for reducing the maintenance backlog and over time increase the throughput time. Further research will require several case studies in manufacturing companies that will further evaluate and improve this KPI structure.

References

1. Ahuja, I.P.S., Khamba, J.S.: Total productive maintenance: literature review and directions. Int. J. Qual. Reliab. Manage. 25(7), 709–756 (2008)
2. Al-Turki, U.M., Ayar, T., Yilbas, B.S., Sahin, A.Z.: Integrated Maintenance Planning in Manufacturing Systems. Springer, Cham (2014)
3. Alfnes, E., Dreyer, H., Strandhagen, J.: The operations excellence audit sheet. In: Koch, T. (ed.) Lean Business Systems and Beyond. IFIP – The International Federation for Information Processing, vol. 257, pp. 129–141. Springer, US (2008)
4. Barker, R.C.: Development of demand pull type control methods: the design of block action production control methods to reduce throughput time and improve supply chain synchronization. Prod. Plan. Control 12(4), 408–417 (2001)
5. BLOM OEE Industry Standard. Blom Consultancy (2003)
6. CEN NS-EN 15341: Maintenance - Maintenance Key Performance Indicators (2007)

7. Center I Annual Report 2013 - Center for Integrated Operations in the petroleum industry (2013)
8. Eckerson, W.W.: Performance Dashboards, Measuring, Monitoring, and Managing Your Business. Wiley, Hoboken (2006)
9. Enns, S.T.: MRP performance effects due to lot size and planned lead time settings. Int. J. Prod. Res. **39**(3), 461–480 (2001)
10. Johnson, D.J.: A framework for reducing manufacturing throughput time. J. Manuf. Syst. **22** (4), 283–298 (2003)
11. Koch, A., Oskam, A.: OEE for the Production Team: the Complete OEE User Guide. FullFact, Lieshout (2007)
12. Maskell, B.H., Baggaley, B.: Practical Lean Accounting: a Proven System for Measuring and Managing the Lean Enterprise. Productivity Press, New York (2011)
13. Meland, O., Rødseth, H.: Maintenance management models - A crucial tool for achieving a world-class maintenance function? In: 11th International Probabilistic Safety Assessment and Management Conference and the Annual European Safety and Reliability Conference 2012, PSAM11 ESREL 2012, June 25–June 29, 2012, Helsinki, Finland, 2012. Probablistic Safety Assessment and Management (IAPSAM), pp. 191–200 (2012)
14. Nakajima, S.: Introduction to TPM: Total Productive Maintenance. Productivity Press, New York (1988)
15. Olhager, J., Selldin, E.: Manufacturing planning and control approaches: market alignment and performance. Int. J. Prod. Res. **45**(6), 1469–1484 (2007)
16. Palmer, D.: Maintenance Planning and Scheduling Handbook. McGraw-Hill, New York (2013)
17. Parida, A., Kumar, U.: Maintenance performance measurement (MPM): issues and challenges. J. Qual. Maintenance Eng. **12**(3), 239–251 (2006)
18. Powell, D., Rødseth, H.: ICT-enabled integrated operations: towards a framework for the integration of manufacturing- and maintenance planning and control. Paper presented at the Advances in Production Management Systems: Sustainable Production and Service Supply Chains, Penn State University, 9–12 Sept 2013 (2013)
19. Ramstad, L.S., Halvorsen, K., Wahl, A.M.: Improved coordination with integrated planning: organisational capabilities. society of petroleum engineers. Paper prepared for presentation at the SPE intelligent energy conference and exhibition held in Utrecht, The Netherlands, 23–25 March 2010
20. Rosendahl, T., Hepsø, V.: Integrated Operations in the Oil and Gas Industry. Business Science Reference, Hershey (2013)
21. Rødseth, H., Schjølberg, P.: The importance of asset management and hidden factory for integrated planning. Adv. Mater. Res. **1039**, 577–584 (2014)
22. Schjølberg, P., Baas, C.: Kartlegging av vedlikehold og driftssikkerhet i norsk industri 2002, vol NTNU 200302. Instituttet, Trondheim (2003)
23. Shah, R., Ward, P.T.: Defining and developing measures of lean production. J. Oper. Manage. **25**(4), 785–805 (2007)
24. Simões, J.M., Gomes, C.F., Yasin, M.M.: Reviews and case studies a literature review of maintenance performance measurement a conceptual framework and directions for future research. J. Qual. Maintenance Eng. **17**(2), 116–137 (2011)
25. Sleire, H., Brurok, T.: Opportunity based maintenance in offshore operations. In: Condition Monitoring and Diagnostics Engineering Management COMADEM 2009 (2009)
26. Sondalini, M.: Useful key performance indicators for maintenance (2005)
27. Stenström, C., Parida, A., Kumar, U., Galar, D.: Performance indicators and terminology for value driven maintenance. J. Qual. Maintenance Eng. **19**(3), 222–232 (2013)

28. Vaisnys, P., Contri, P., Beith, M.: Benchmarking study of maintenance performance monitoring practices. Summary report. In: European Commission. Office for Official Publications of the European Communities, Luxembourg (2007)
29. Van der Lei, T., Herder, P., Wijnia, Y.: Asset Management: The State of the Art in Europe from a Life Cycle Perspective. Springer, Netherlands (2012)
30. Wireman, T.: Maintenance Management and Regulatory Compliance Strategies. Industrial Press, New York (2003)
31. Wireman, T.: Developing Performance Indicators for Managing Maintenance. Industrial Press, New York (2005)

ERP Evaluation in Cloud Computing Environment

Valdir Morales[1(⊠)], Oduvaldo Vendrametto[1],
Samuel Dereste dos Santos[1], Vanessa Santos Lessa[1],
and Edivaldo Antonio Sartor[2]

[1] Graduate Program in Production Engineering, Paulista University-UNIP,
São Paulo, Brazil
{valdir_morales, samuel_dereste}@yahoo.com.br,
oduvaldov@uol.com.br, vlessa@terra.com.br
[2] Instituição Faculdade de Informática e Adm. Paulista – FIAP,
São Paulo, Brazil
edivaldo@tjsp.jus.br

Abstract. With the evolution of the Internet many services before running on a local network, they moved to the cloud environment. As an example, the ERP Local migrating to the Cloud environment. This concept provides a new way of using IT resources. This research aims to evaluate the use of ERP in the Cloud Computing environment observing its advantages and disadvantages, as well as to identify its real applicability in the market, using as references the global survey by Gartner and an applied survey with IT experts on Internet services in Brazil. Based on these two studies it is possible to mitigate risks in the Local ERP migration to the ERP Cloud.

Keywords: ERP · Cloud computing · System · Market

1 Introduction

Upon the Internet arrival, changes began to happen more frequently and with a smaller time interval. Many companies seek new technological tools for decision-making processes with greater efficiency. Within the market alternatives, Cloud Computing emerges as a service available to organizations, in collaboration with organizational strategy.

Systems before located in the organizational environment, according to the company's strategy, can now be relocated to this new cloud service.

As an object of research, ERP is already established in organizations where it provides better process control, monitoring, informing, and enabling top management to have an increased visibility about the results.

Organizations usually keep information systems within their organizational environment, but with this new technology of Cloud Computing, one can envision a greater flexibility and at the same time be less dependent on the enterprise computational environment by decentralizing the workload capacity to the cloud.

Among the ERP objectives are included the integration of automation systems and their vital activities, such as manufacturing, human resources, finance and supply chain

© IFIP International Federation for Information Processing 2015
S. Umeda et al. (Eds.): APMS 2015, Part I, IFIP AICT 459, pp. 78–84, 2015.
DOI: 10.1007/978-3-319-22756-6_10

management [1]. The information generated from this process serves to support organizational decision-making processes.

The ERP solution is considered a business application, enabling the interconnection of data, processes and functional areas from an organization, providing a graphical interface so the user can manage such information [2].

The Enterprise Resource Planning (ERP) is seen as a strategic information and a tool to face competitors and to allow corporations to improve productivity [3]. Organizations implement ERP to gain visibility into business processes in a dynamic environment [2].

The expansion of the Internet and business led to a conceptual change in which the services performed on a desktop computer migrated to the internet providers [4].

The characteristics of cloud computing are: it is sold on demand; the service is managed by the provider; users can determine the amount of service to be taken; and users can log on to the network from any computer in the world [5].

A comprehensive definition is given by the National Institute of Standards and Technology, that states: "Cloud computing is a model for enabling ubiquitous, convenient, on-demand network access to a shared pool of configurable computing resources (e.g., networks, servers, storage, applications, and services) that can be rapidly provisioned and released with minimal management effort or service provider interaction" [5].

Cloud computing is a new way to provide information technology (IT) services for individuals and organizations. Its adoption is driven by availability, flexibility and agility [6].

Cloud computing offers a new computing paradigm that provides IT as a service. Service models (IaaS, PaaS, SaaS) provides a basis for understanding cloud computing and its capabilities [7].

IaaS - Infrastructure as a Service - the computing environment is provided as requested by the customer, as if it were rented, so the customer does not have to worry about maintenance costs or to upgrade the hardware used on the basis because the cloud environment is being used [7].

PaaS - Platform as a Service Cloud – the customers' capacity to move to cloud applications, designed and developed by themselves using certain programming language and tools provided by the supplier [7].

SaaS - Cloud Software as a Service - the consumers have the possibility to use an application that is not installed on their personal computer, just accessing the Internet [7].

Through this new scenario, there are questions between the use of local form ERP or in the Cloud.

2   Materials and Methods

2.1   Survey Procedure

Global companies conducted an exploratory research with reference to the research firm Gartner data in order to assess the world stage as the use and trends of Cloud Computing.

Gartner Research had a global character with 89 respondents. Respondents were distributed geographically: 33 were from North America, 36 from EMEA (Europe, the Middle East, and Africa), 13 from the APAC (Asia Pacific Region) and five from Latin American countries (two of them did not provide details of their location). There were companies in the service and manufacturing segments.

It is shown Ten Myths of Cloud Computing, data from Gartner [8]. Next, we highlight the local ERP characteristics confronting it with the Cloud environment.

It was also developed a survey applied to about sixteen IT specialists in Brazil aiming to identify the stage of Internet service providers in Brazil, with the following questions: (1) Do you consider that broadband providers meet the SLA (Service Level Agreement) standards? (2) Do you consider that broadband providers meet the connection speed expectations contracted? (3) What are the aspects to be observed for migrating from an ERP site to Cloud Computing?

To obtain feedback on the technical feasibility of a possible change to the Cloud ERP.

3 Results and Discussion

3.1 Research Summary

The worldwide market for ERP has a large competition in several segments, the companies market share that sell ERP shows a significant revenue: SAP 24 % U$ 26.6 billion, Oracle 12 % U$ 3.07 billion, Sage 6 % U$ 2.1 billion, Infor 5.8 % U$ 1.49 billion, Microsoft 5 % U$ 1.28 billion, Other 41.2 [9].

What makes shows the ERP market as promising and expanding in the most several segments, stimulating employment new technologies.

There is a long way to go by migrating from Local ERP to Cloud ERP and there is a paradigm shift, because not all businesses have full compliance with this emerging concept. Gartner magazine published a report on the 10 Myths of Cloud Computing, and described shows below [8]:

1. Addresses that changing to the Cloud Computing (CC) technology is always related to money. Only 14 % of companies choose to work with CC for cost reduction reasons.
2. You will have a Cloud Computing technology and everything will work well. The demands and the strategy for this decision-making should be analyzed.
3. The cloud should be used for everything. Not all the available service will indeed adherence.
4. The CEO decides the cloud strategy.
5. We need to understand if CC is a strategy or just a natural sale. The cloud strategy must be aligned with business objectives in order to meet multiple responses for investment.
6. The cloud is less secure than the local capacity of organizations. It depends on the suppliers to meet security standards.
7. Cloud is not for critical use mission. For certain segments it fits perfectly.
8. Cloud corresponds to Data Center. Which services should be taken to cloud.

9. Migrating to the cloud means automatically obtaining all features of the Cloud. Cloud computing has attributes and unique features, including scalability and elasticity, service based (and selfservice) Internet technologies are used, as it is shared (and uniform) and measured by use.
10. Virtualization = Private Cloud. Virtualization is commonly used enabling technology for cloud computing. However, it is not the only way to implement cloud computing.

Observing the 10 Myths of Cloud Computing presents the fundamental aspects such as relevance of the business, adhering to provide services in the Cloud, the organization's strategic alignment to use the new computing environment in order to contribute to the success of CC.

The benefits of cloud computing for users consists of: providing access to various applications without the need for installation on computers; applications can be accessed anywhere from any computer; avoiding the costs of hardware and software, using only what is necessary [5]. According to the Gartner research, cost is not always the relevant factor to opt for Cloud Computing.

The Gartner global survey reiterates the scenario about the decision-making to migrate to Cloud Computing [10]. In Fig. 1, a degree of uncertainty among opting for the new technology was identified, with about 30 % of the participants choosing to keep the technology of the local ERP in their own organization, while 17 % did not know, which shows lack of visibility planning and a timid tendency to make changes in a medium to long term period.

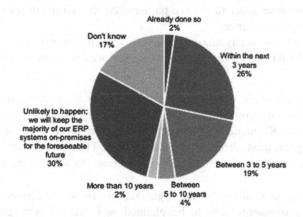

Fig. 1. Decision-making to migrate to Cloud Computing.

The most common disadvantages of cloud computing are related to the users identity and data security, because the shared environment generates a margin of doubt, another critical point that touches the supplier's security model and the loss of physical control of the environment [11].

As Gartner research, there is a percentage between 40 and 100 % of failing the changes in manufacturing sector companies, because the use of ERP by departments such as MRP (Material Resource Planning) and PCP (Production Planning Control) require availability in information systems [10]. Although it is already being strongly used in the Communications and Services, Government and Education segments, the best insight for the next three years stands out in the Communication and Service segment.

The choice of not migrating to Cloud Computing in the manufacturing segment may be related to operations involved within the Organization because the ERP operation basically focuses on the following functions: Demand (Demand Forecast), Production (Planning and Control), Displacement (Data Transition, Shift Movement Material, Quality Control, Inventory) [12].

The Gartner research shows that for companies whose revenue is less than 10 million dollars, plans to implement it during the next 3 years varies around 70 % while for companies with revenues exceeding 10 billion there is a more cautious attitude to move to cloud computing [10]. Thus, we can say that for small to medium-sized companies there is a need or strategy to change the paradigm in hardware investment and maintenance. This aspect can bring out that for large corporations, new technology goes through a maturation process but it do not let explicit the risk issue.

Observing the Cloud Computing scenario, it was developed a comparison to the Local ERP in order to establish the different characteristics of computer environments. The following differences are listed below:

1. There is a need to invest in infrastructure such as hardware, software, database and networks in the local environment.
2. Since ERP is in the organization's environment, adjustments can flow more naturally and quickly.
3. Several departments and stakeholders are involved; people have a degree of knowledge because either they have participated in its implantation or they have experienced system change.
4. It depends exclusively Organization's investments in security in the local.
5. On the Local ERP, being critical or not, the services work to meet the company's demands.

The topics cited above make clear the needs of each environment, providing an insight into the use of resources and their strategies. Thus, a survey was applied.

The success of ERP implementation depends on various types of integrations, such as processes, organization, data and applications [3]. Thus we can say that a synergy between people, processes and technology is necessary to achieve the critical success factor.

The ERP plays a vital role in the organization. Therefore changes such as corrections and improvements need to be planned and verified with greater certainty before entering the production environment, since the investment in hardware and software is highly critical [13].

The first question addressed in the survey applied is about the broadband access providers in Brazil that you use (or have used). Do you consider they meet the SLA (Service Level Agreement) standards? The responses obtained were as follows: Totally Agree 6.3 %, Agree 6.3 %, neither agree nor disagree 12.5 % Disagree 62.5 % Strongly Disagree 12.5 %. Thus, it can be said: observing the availability criteria to keep the service in the air, if a company had total dependence on Internet providers and required some maintenance, it faced major disruptions.

This aspect is of paramount importance and shocking to opt for a location shift to ERP Cloud. The availability criterion in the IT field, should always be assessed and rated to not damage the provision of services with users.

Cloud Computing allows greater flexibility to the user through high-speed Internet, highlighting the use of the remote service and the low commitment of the use of hardware and software [14]. Based on this, the second question of the applied survey is whether the providers meet the connection speed expectations contracted from the broadband.

The scenario was as follows: 0 % totally agree, 18.8 % agree, 0 % neither agree nor disagree, 68.8 % disagree, 12.5 % totally disagree. Based on this scenario, the internet speed question highlights that the level of dissatisfaction is latent based on the service offered, showing weaknesses regarding the necessary infrastructure.

The following scenario can be envisioned with Cloud Computing as opinions posed by experts:

- Before opting to migrate, it is required to mitigate the risks, identifying criteria to apply a methodology for decision-making. Alternatively, the Analytic Hierarchy Process (AHP) method allows better visibility.
- The business must grip on CC in the types of services that will be available; otherwise, it will be more feasible to keep the ERP at the new location.
- The hybrid solution (cloud services and some local services) initially shows the most cautious decision enabling to measure what should in fact be made available in the cloud.
- In case of a disaster in an organization, the data would be secure in a cloud environment.
- The security that was controlled by the organization's computing environment is decentralized to the IT providing company, with a need for trust in the services provided.

The hybrid cloud environment combine cloud services public and private allowing require extra capacity to a cloud public for temporary workload peaks [15]. The hybrid solution is cautious in decision making and what kind of services can be allocated in Local mode or in the Cloud.

Cloud Computing provides best results in the management of scalable hardware and software resources, optimizing the work, increasing the performance of implementation of computational tools [16].

Thus, alternative methods were presented in order to channel efforts as a suggestion for improving the selection and applicability of Cloud Computing environment.

4   Conclusions

The development of this research allowed to reveal that cloud computing is in a maturing stage, not everything that is currently being done in the local environment of an organization is exactly in accordance with the cloud environment. There is a conceptual change in the aspect of using the new technology. The real needs of an organization that leads to cloud computing should be identified in order to achieve an effective decision-making, assessing critically the adhesion of technology for business.

References

1. Razmi, J., Sangari, M.S., Ghodsi, R.: Developing a practical framework for ERP readiness assessment using fuzzy analytic network process. Adv. Eng. Softw. **40**(11), 1168–1178 (2009)
2. Candra, S.: ERP implementation success and knowledge capability. Procedia Soc. Behav. Sci. **65**, 141–149 (2012)
3. Wu, W.-W.: Segmenting and mining the ERP users' perceived benefits using the rough set approach. Expert Syst. Appl. **38**(6), 6940–6948 (2011)
4. Cheng, F.-C., Lai, W.-H.: The impact of cloud computing technology on legal infrastructure within internet—focusing on the protection of information privacy. Procedia Eng. **29**, 241–251 (2012)
5. Bose, R., Luo, X., Liu, Y.: The roles of security and trust: comparing cloud computing and banking. Procedia Soc. Behav. Sci. **73**, 30–34 (2013)
6. Stieninger, M., Nedbal, D., Wetzlinger, W., Wagner, G., Erskine, M.A.: Impacts on the organizational adoption of cloud computing: a reconceptualization of influencing factors. Procedia Technol. **16**, 85–93 (2014)
7. Ferreira, O., Moreira, F.: Cloud computing implementation level in portuguese companies. Procedia Technol. **5**, 491–499 (2012)
8. GARTNER Inc. The Top 10 Cloud Myths. http://www.gartner.com/smarterwithgartner/the-top-10-cloud-myths/. Accessed 18 Feb 2015
9. Infográfico Mercado de ERP 2013. http://portalerp.com/destaques/1299-infografico-mercado-de-erp-2013. Accessed 03 March 2015
10. GARTNER Inc. Survey Analysis: Adoption of Cloud ERP, 2013 Through 2023. https://www.gartner.com/doc/2656317/survey-analysis-adoption-cloud-erp. Accessed 24 Jan 2014
11. Mezgár, I., Rauschecker, U.: The challenge of networked enterprises for cloud computing interoperability. Comput. Ind. **65**(4), 657–674 (2014)
12. Kandananond, K.: A roadmap to green supply chain system through enterprise resource planning (ERP) implementation. Procedia Eng. **69**, 377–382 (2014)
13. Law, C.C.H., Chen, C.C., Wu, B.J.P.: Managing the full ERP life-cycle: considerations of maintenance and support requirements and IT governance practice as integral elements of the formula for successful ERP adoption. Comput. Ind. **61**(3), 297–308 (2010)
14. Pardeshi, V.H.: Cloud computing for higher education institutes: architecture, strategy and recommendations for effective adaptation. Procedia Econ. Finance **11**, 589–599 (2014)
15. Garrison, G., Wakefield, R.L., Kim, S.: The effects of IT capabilities and delivery model on cloud computing success and firm performance for cloud supported processes and operations. Int. J. Inf. Manag. **35**(4), 377–393 (2015)
16. Oliveira, T., Thomas, M., Espadanal, M.: Assessing the determinants of cloud computing adoption: an analysis of the manufacturing and services sectors. Inf. Manag. **51**(5), 497–510 (2014)

Co-operative Production Planning: Dynamic Documents in Manufacturing

Steinar Kristoffersen(✉)

Møreforsking Molde AS and Molde University College,
Postboks 2110, 6402 Molde, Norway
steinar.kristoffersen@himolde.no

Abstract. This case study describes the manufacturing of advanced, high-value maritime vessel equipment as an opportunistic, dynamic, knowledge-needy and collaborative process, in which planning and construction is closely integrated, rather than as a repeatable physical assembly that takes place in phases, for each of which planning is pre-hoc and pre-emptive. We assert that this is one reason that the anachronistic perspective of "documents as documentation", contributes to actors' conflicting views of their project. This paper examines these difficulties, offers a theoretical examination and design implications for next generation industries to consider.

Keywords: Design and manufacturing in a collaborative setting · Engineer-to-order (ETO) · Lean documentation · Quality · IT support for industry

1 Introduction

Many enterprises in high-income countries are bound to struggle with higher production costs than those of many less-mature, yet ambitious economies. Straight competition on identical terms is impossible. Hence a succession of process re-construction efforts has been launched in high-cost countries [1]. Most reformation programs bring together existing schemes, such as *lean*, mass customization and ETO (engineer-to-order), concurrent engineering and front-end loading [2, 3]. There has been little improvement, however. Traditionally bureaucratic and vertically integrated manufacturing, with centralized planning, scheduling, and control mechanisms are not sufficiently flexible for this type of production and product-mix [4]. We find suggestions in the literature that hard problems of process planning and manufacturing control in a dynamic, distributed portfolio may possibly be solved using agent technology [4], expert systems [5] or case-based reasoning [5], etc. However, experience shows us that most businesses rely on simple software, such as spread sheets and text editors, email and databases for their manufacturing management support. As a consequence, multiple perspectives on planning, evaluation and the economy of the project arise, which reduces manageability. *This paper's objective is to explicate this practice and initiate a road map ahead that may alleviate the situation.*

In the domain that pertains to this paper ratio of labor to value-creation has been relatively stable since the seventies [6], which might imply that our industry's "high

© IFIP International Federation for Information Processing 2015
S. Umeda et al. (Eds.): APMS 2015, Part I, IFIP AICT 459, pp. 85–92, 2015.
DOI: 10.1007/978-3-319-22756-6_11

value-creation knowledge networks" (cf. [7]) are less efficient than we believe. This might have to be improved shortly.

2 Research Problem

The ability to be flexible and respond favorably to change orders is a distinguishing characteristic of the so-called "engineer-to-order" industries [8]. However, when extraneous factors such as a fall in the oil price comes into play, it turns out that this edge becomes very blunt, indeed, as customers start demanding that "flexible costs" regardless, are made "off-the-shelf". In the current paradigm, outsourcing to low-cost countries possible has contributed to make this possible as well as profitable [9]. However, when the same performance become universally available, customer do not wish to pay a premium for tradition [10]. Hence, a next step up and forward is required for European industries to survive in global competition [11].

We believe that poorly understood documentation practices have contributed to reduce innovation of the current situation. Outsourcing as a "division of labor" has often been based on insufficient specifications, incomplete planning or inaccurate estimation techniques [12], which may be hard to change, essentially, but the situation is exacerbated when documents are presented as objectively describing the state of affairs, whilst in reality they are interacted with as a type of agent [13].

Any detached and extraneous description is bound to be out of synch, inconsistent and erroneous, but this is not a problem unless it is poorly handled [14]. Members of an organization purposefully create different documents describing the same phenomena. If conflicts occur, however, the exposition of them in a technical perspective only [15], is not sufficient. Current digitization of production processes hide the co-existence of multi-perspective documentation and when retrieved, purport that they are equivalent representation of a phenomena. That is, as we shall demonstrate in this paper, when the trouble begins.

This paper proposes to treat documentation as "perspective elements". It may seem like a paradox that it thus rejects the objectivity of "documents as labels" in favor of a subjective, constructionist view of "documents in actor-networks", but in the transformation of our industry to a 4.0-type "internet of things", this is, we believe, exactly what is needed. Operationally, as well, we aim to demonstrate that this approach can be modelled using object-oriented techniques [16].

3 Research Methodology

This study is based on ethnographic and participative research in one company. It is of course always a challenge to generalize from single case studies. However, the rich experience, which have been gained from taking part in more than 10 project meetings, in addition to phone calls/discussions and document exchanges per meeting and finally to contribute with findings, ideas and as a discussion partner in a project, do give a solid grounding for qualitative, theoretical reasoning. This research methodology, admittedly, does look broadly and pragmatically on what constitutes "data" for research purposes [17]. It represents, however, a well-known foundation for qualitative research [18].

4 Investigation Results in *a Crane Company* (ACC)

The company that we have studied makes small and mid-sized (up to ca. 50 metric tons) cranes and handling systems, which can operate on depths down to 4000 meters. Typically, the cranes are used to place and recover underwater unmanned robots or excavators, that dig tranches, connect cables and pipes, etc., which are necessary infrastructure to support the oil and gas industry offshore.

Early projects in ACC were commonly termed "prototypes" and the current process is seen as one of increasing standardization. From the sales division's point of view, the predictability of the cost situation is crucial. They have to defend the price to the customer as well as the margins internally, towards their role as a profit centre in a group consisting of many engineering-oriented companies in a diverse concern.

The market connections are made locally, although the customers themselves already operate internationally and many have subsidiaries worldwide. Inevitably, as the business grows, so does the network and sales, which are made independently of geography.

There are clearly many rational reasons to outsource industrial production from high-cost countries, which are usually near to the affluent market and its ambition to innovate, to low-cost countries offshore, which cannot market and sell their skills in an integrated and packaged product. Repetitive or at least voluminous, man-hour intensive and burdensome parts of the manufacturing process, will still be decisive parts of large-scale industrial projects. The solution for ACC has been to stop doing manufacturing and specialize instead on sales, design, engineering, integration and commissioning. Steel work, therefore, is outsourced. Engines and pumps are procured, as is the control system and drives. Electrical systems design, however, is mainly carried out locally.

The following recount explains the procedure of contracting and building an ETO offshore crane, together with its multifarious documentation practices.

4.1 The Go-Ahead Decision

After initial contact with a customer and preliminary information exchange concerning the scope of the project, the VP of the offshore division calls a go-ahead board meeting to make the decision about bidding. The ambition has to be commercially sound, which in this context means a solid 15 % margin on the total cost of sales.

The decision is tricky, since there are many variables, especially connected to the ratio of value created through labour vs. procurement. For many suppliers to the offshore industry, it has been treated as a common fact that outsourced and procured parts of a project typically constitute 80 % of the value created. If the parts were standardized or easily available, the decision to build a 1 million GBP crane, if it comprised 800 000 GBP of parts and only 200 000 of management and engineering work at home, to produce a profit of 150 000 would be relatively transparent, albeit hard to achieve. It is, however, neither the case that the first 800 000 are risk-free, nor that the 200 000 in "knowledge work" are fixed, predictable or even particularly "manageable" as we shall show below. We put forward that one of the reasons is the way in which documents are used as documentation, paradoxically a role for which they seem wholly unsuited.

4.2   Assertions About a Procurement-Centric Process

The market situation is dynamic, with oil prices governing much of what the customers on the one hand know or think they need and are willing to pay, on the other. One aspect of the current conjunctures is that the pioneering spirit of the oil & gas sector, which has dominated for the past 15 years, have created a steady increase in demand for capacity, i.e., ships, cranes, rigs and therefore engineering work volume connect to the production of steel units and structures. Sales, design and engineering, on the other hand, which we have called knowledge work, is crucial to every project, but this intellectual capacity is rather more "flexibly available" in a way that steel work is not.

First assertion: Affluent economies educate technical engineers and accountants steadily. They take well-paid, salaried jobs mainly, which in the welfare state-models in Europe entail relatively little risk. Therefore, although companies think they struggle to find the best people and certainly would have liked to have to pay them less, they are not strongly limiting factors.

Second assertion: Pertaining somewhat to the nature of intellectual capacity as a non-limiting factor as well, is the inherent ability of knowledge work, especially in the consulting nature that dominates the market in an upward conjuncture, to be available at "super capacity", or in another less euphemistic term, over-booked. This entails that the design team might quite simply not be as available as the project needs them, due to other competing and sometimes conflicting assignments.

Third assertion: As the physical labour and manipulation of materials, which require production facilities and workshops have been "offshored", the threshold of establishing competing businesses is low. Typically, consultants, engineers and sales staff need only a laptop and a mobile phone, before they are can operate. This means that a profitable area of operation will soon be saturated with equally skilled and motivated actors, who put commercial pressure on each other.

Together these observations mean that there is much demand in the "front end" (from customer trough sales and design), whose conceptual products cannot easily be met by simply turning up the intensity of supplies from factories that make physical goods. Engineering is the bridge between design and procurement, and its interface to the factory means that it often ends up being a bottle-neck. When all projects are "urgent" and many offer to take them on, the middle-tier components suppliers, which are ETO, becomes a victim of customers who can always go elsewhere and suppliers who know that the ETO-companies inevitable come back to them, because there is no other easily available alternatives. Thus, when prices are transparent in an international market (everybody can call and get a quote), downwardly static and upwardly mobile, as a consequence there is no profit easily won for the ETO companies in terms of putting a margin on top the goods that they buy.

Fourth assertion: There are a growing number of designers and engineers who due to the specialized and reductionist nature of the distributed manufacturing processes do not have any hands-on experience with production as such. Hence, they depend on their own suppliers for integration and feedback on the designs they have made. Drawings are frequently incomplete or erroneous, at least in the perspective of what may be manufactured in a streamlined fashion.

Fifth assertion: When physical production facilities, such as ship yards, welding stations, rollers and forges are physical limiting production factors, at the same time as optimism is creating a drive to invest in new project (a trend that has turned, just recently, but never influenced this case), investors may want to put money into projects just to get them going, and secure their slot on the production conveyor belt, as it were. During the year or so that an advanced offshore or seismic vessel is under production, thus, it may be modified many times due to change of demand, new ideas or owners and the plans for future contracts, which have still to be negotiated. This is the business opportunity and uniqueness indicator of the ETO as well, and probably the main reason they are even still in business. They can and will change their designs to accommodate new requests and change orders from the customer in a way that larger set-ups abroad have not been able to.

5 The Ubiquitous Spreadsheet

In all stages, front-end as well as back-end reporting, the company relies on spreadsheets in various formats and designs (numbered below as (i)–(viii)). The sales people use it to create (i) *a preliminary parts + work overview*, to indicate how much of a margin the project may be able to fetch in terms of profit margins. This is also used to produce an offer to the customer. The *go-ahead-decision* (ii) revises and expands the simple set-up, with the (iii) offer made to the customer as a "ceiling" idea of how much the cost of parts plus work and margins should be.

This is where the first observable set of opportunistic-dynamic strategies connected to documents (as-such) become manifest. The first document (i) is created as the technical division feeds in experienced-based numbers of the number of hours and thus the cost, of the engineering, integration and commissioning. The numbers are still uncertain, because the exact organization of activities within each of these functional areas is variable according to which sub supplier is going to be picked. This is not known for certain at this stage. Some suppliers include the work needed to do the FAT (Factory Acceptance Test) and others do not. Some turn out to need a lot of support from the engineering team. With margins like we have indicated, of (in the order of) 100 000 GBP (which corresponds to 1000 h from a budget of work that typically sums of to 3000 h), this is a vulnerable situation. Depending on the sub supplier alternatives that exist, therefore, several variants of this "go-ahead" spreadsheet (ii) are created. During the discussions (and certainly before), variables are adjusted and tuned in order to see if it is at all possible to create viable project. If it is accepted, a bid is made (iii), and hopefully won.

The accounting budget (another spreadsheet (iv), Fig. 1), eventually pasted into or attached with a formal letter) is then made and passed on to cost centre management, in order for them to know what to expect from the project. This is the most formal so far, and it represents the official view of the cost and risk of the project, and finally, the profit it is going to offer to the company.

The project manager, on the other hand, in parallel with this process, has already started looking at specifically which sub suppliers are willing, capable and available to offer the best combination of work capacity, skills, courage and physical location of the

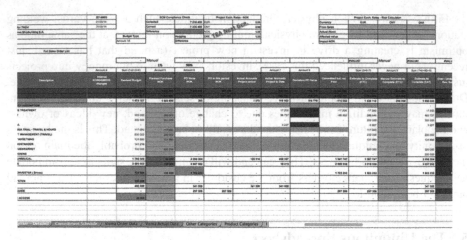

Fig. 1. Final sales/profit calculations of ACC for project P

company and their facilities. In addition, they usually need to have validated (pre-qualified) working relations with the customer as well. This spreadsheet variant (v) is worked out in close collaboration with the procurement officer responsible for the project. Next, one spread sheet is created to account for the orders that are placed of parts, with currency risk, volumes and discounts analysed and accounted for (vi). This spreadsheet, which is an export from the accounting system (part of the company's ERP (Enterprise Resource Planning) system) may have thousands of lines, for which generally a "Pareto-principle" of 20/80 applies: The 20 topmost-% accounts for 80 % of the cost. In the same format, but separately, parts confirmed and delivered are accounted for (vii). Finally, accounting keeps track of the hours worked (viii).

The result is that 6–8 different spreadsheets in two to three different formats and systems account for overlapping information, and is used in parallel by people who are working in the same project put from different points of responsibility.

6 Digital Manufacturing: A Concept for Dynamic Design

Design in most senses is clearly already dynamic. Its processes and outcomes can and will be changed. It is forward moving and creative. Hence it is also open-ended and expansive. "Front-end loading" relies on the assumption that all current and future dimensions can be fully explored and dealt with. Usually, they cannot.

Design captures experiences and evaluates previous drafts. The trouble is that when they are embedded into design, this new design rationale tends to be forgotten [19]. Hence, when the next problem of a similar kind is addressed, designers tends to start from the original "template", which is either completely from scratch or an anticipation of needs, which is lacking recent practical experiences that might have been embedded.

Therefore, we suggest challenging the current notion of design, which entails going from idea to product, by "inverse conceptualization", which would be to start from finished, well-known and functional products, which are the re-engineered step-by-step, in a backwards fashion, through all previous versions, releases *and* assembly steps, in a collaborative and problem-solving process. Clearly this cannot replace "standard design", but may complement it.

Another design-approach might be to start from a library of exceptions, deviations and previous recoveries, to look for enhancements and extensions. Products for re-engineering as well as exceptions and experiences might be documented in an advanced, branch-oriented and snapshot-preserving version management system (similar to *GitHub*) for software.

This way of working dynamically and experience-based with design should aim to move the decoupling point as far along the production timeline as possible. There is no real product designed until it has been built. Similarly, documents should be seen as representations of ambition and a decision-making *agenda*, rather than snapshots of complete state. Documents are not managed, instead they manage, fit, force and frame processes. Each data element ought then to be versioned and new snapshots made every time one is requested. The planning and control of manufacturing may thus become a data-driven dynamic design science.

Acknowledgments. The financial support of VRI Møre & Norway is appreciatively acknowledged, as well as the willingness of ACC to explore this set of ideas within a project that first and foremost aimed at reducing the cost of building cranes. We would especially like to thank managers, engineers and administrators in ACC who spent extra time in meetings and dialog with the author and other researches.

References

1. Ekstedt, E.: A new division of labour: the "projectification" of working and industrial life. In: Moreau, M.-A., Negrelli, S., Pochet, P. (eds.) Building Anticipation of Restructuring in Europe, pp. 31–54. Peter Lang, Bruxelles (2009)
2. King, J.P., Jewett, W.S.: Robustness Development and Reliability Growth: Value Adding Strategies for New Products and Processes. Pearson Education, Boston (2010)
3. Rocha, H.M., de Souza, C.N.A., dos Santos Filho, D.F.: Mass customization enablement through lean design & set-based concurrent engineering application. J. Oper. Supply Chain Manag. **7**(2), 124–139
4. Shen, W., et al.: Applications of agent-based systems in intelligent manufacturing: an updated review. Adv. Eng. Inform. **20**(4), 415–431 (2006)
5. Choy, K.L., Lee, W., Lo, V.: Design of an intelligent supplier relationship management system: a hybrid case based neural network approach. Expert Syst. Appl. **24**(2), 225–237 (2003)
6. Froud, J., et al.: Financialization across the Pacific: manufacturing cost ratios, supply chains and power. Crit. Perspect. Acc. **25**(1), 46–57 (2014)
7. Camarinha-Matos, L.M., Afsarmanesh, H.: Collaborative networks: value creation in a knowledge society. Knowl. Enterp. IFIP **207**, 26–40 (2006)
8. Grabenstetter, D.H., Usher, J.M.: Developing due dates in an engineer-to-order engineering environment. Int. J. Prod. Res. **52**(21), 6349–6361 (2014)
9. Hummels, D.: Transportation costs and international trade in the second era of globalization. J. Econ. Perspect. 131–154 (2007)

10. Venkata, S., et al.: What future distribution engineers need to learn. IEEE Trans. Power Syst. **19**(1), 17–23 (2004)
11. Brettel, M., et al.: How virtualization, decentralization and network building change the manufacturing landscape: an industry 4.0 perspective. Int. J. Mech. Ind. Sci. Eng. **8**(1), 37–44 (2014)
12. Dwivedi, Y.K., et al.: IS/IT project failures: a review of the extant literature for deriving a taxonomy of failure factors. In: Dwivedi, Y.K., Henriksen, H.Z., Wastell, D., De', R. (eds.) Grand Successes and Failures in IT. Public and Private Sectors, pp. 73–88. Springer, Berlin (2013)
13. Christensen, L.R., Bjorn, P.: Documentscape: intertextuality, sequentiality, & autonomy at work. In: Proceedings of the 32nd Annual ACM Conference on Human Factors in Computing Systems. ACM (2014)
14. Massey, C., Lennig, T., Whittaker, S.: Cloudy forecast: an exploration of the factors underlying shared repository use. In: Proceedings of the 32nd Annual ACM Conference on Human Factors in Computing Systems. ACM (2014)
15. Sun, D., et al.: Creative conflict resolution in realtime collaborative editing systems. In: Proceedings of the ACM 2012 Conference on Computer Supported Cooperative Work. ACM (2012)
16. Iivari, J.: Object-orientation as structural, functional and behavioural modelling: a comparison of six methods for object-oriented analysis. Inf. Softw. Technol. **37**(3), 155–163 (1995)
17. Twidale, M.B., et al.: Quick and dirty: lightweight methods for heavyweight research. In: Proceedings of the Companion Publication of the 17th ACM Conference on Computer Supported Cooperative Work & Social Computing. ACM (2014)
18. Crabtree, A., et al.: Ethnomethodologically informed ethnography and information system design. J. Am. Soc. Inf. Sci. **51**(7), 666–682 (2000)
19. Engelbart, D.C.: Toward high-performance organizations: a strategic role for groupware. In: Proceedings of the GroupWare (1992)

Collaborative Supplying Networks: Reducing Materials Management Costs in Healthcare

Lorenzo Tiacci[✉] and Chiara Paltriccia

Dipartimento di Ingegneria, Università degli Studi di Perugia,
Perugia, Italia
lorenzo.tiacci@unipg.it,
chiara.paltriccia@studenti.unipg.it

Abstract. Materials and inventories management is becoming a more and more important subject in the health care sector, because of its impact on efficiency, and quality of services provided. This study is focused on the inventory management and the service of surgical instruments reprocessing related to the operating room. The aim is to analyse which benefits may produce the combination of two different factors: the implementation of the RFId technology along the supply chain and the cooperation thorough a long-term collaborative-networked organization of the supplying companies. The first factor, named 'RFId effect', allows implementing a Continuous Review policy, instead of the Periodic Review policy normally utilized. The second factor, named 'Network effect', gives to supplying companies the possibility to share transportation costs. The model is inspired by a real case study of a long-term collaborative network of supplying companies in the health care sector that operates in central Italy. A numerical experiment shows that combining the RFId and Network effects may bring to a relevant reduction of expected costs.

1 Introduction

Providing health services with high quality standards and containing public expenditure are increasingly important objectives to be achieved in the context of public healthcare. Among the solutions adopted to contain healthcare spending, one of the most important trend in the public healthcare sector is to entrust some outsourced services, optimizing performance through a contract. In this way, healthcare managers tried to reduce spending without affecting the quality of service offered [1]. The spread of non-core processes outsourcing in healthcare has become very fast because, being the hospital a set of many departments handling a large number of activities, there is the need to entrust outside the no core ones [2]. Cost effectiveness is important even for activities that have greater impact on the hospital core business; among those, there is the surgical instruments reprocessing process, which is considered to be a potential area for important cost savings [3]. van de Klundert et al. [4] studied the logistic activities between the central sterilization service department and the operating theater. These activities affect total costs faced by the operating block. Hospitals that outsource these types of activities are still very few.

© IFIP International Federation for Information Processing 2015
S. Umeda et al. (Eds.): APMS 2015, Part I, IFIP AICT 459, pp. 93–101, 2015.
DOI: 10.1007/978-3-319-22756-6_12

Inventory management of drugs and medical devices is also become a very important argument for hospital management. Many medical organizations reorganized their logistics in order to contain costs and ensure quality in services provided [5].

This paper investigates a new outsourcing model for the management of the operating room materials, inspired by a real case study of a network of enterprises born in Central Italy, in the Umbria Region. The network is based on the VDO network model [6] and provides the supplying of all the consumables for the operating room and the reprocessing service of surgical instruments. The network business model provides the implementation of the RFId technology for the automatic and continuous monitoring of hospital's inventories, and for the total traceability of all the materials utilized during surgeries. Through reading tags, stickers on which one can transcribe information on circuits, it is possible to have remote tracking. Inventory tracking becomes easier than ever and many other probable applications of RFId technologies have been proposed [7]. As evidenced by Sarac et al. [8] this technology may improve the potential benefits along the supply chain reducing inventory losses, increasing efficiency and speed of the processes involved and improving information accuracy.

The integrated service, provided by the network as a single entity, includes: (1) surgical instruments sterilization service; (2) provision of sets of surgical instruments for surgical procedures; (3) provision of disposable non-woven materials, such as surgical drapes, masks, gloves, caps, gowns; (4) provision of disposable surgical devices, such as suture threads, syringes, video-laparoscopic devices; (5) provision, control and maintenance of medical equipment.

The specific characteristic of the case study, with respect to traditional models of materials management, consists in the implementation of the RFId technology, and in the long-term strategic cooperation between the supplying companies. Aim of the work is to provide a model to evaluate the effect of these two key factors on total operational costs.

2 The Model

This case study refers to a stable network of companies located in central Italy, in the region of Umbria. The network provides an integrated set of services for the operating room. The network, named Sanitanet, is composed of five companies: four of them are companies already operating as single suppliers in the healthcare sector, while the fifth one is a University Spinoff in the field of collaborative networks management. For the purpose of the present work, we consider in the model just two of the five companies (Company A and Company B).

Company A provides a 'pay per use' service of sterile surgical instruments kits. These single-use kits are specifically designed for each surgery. This company owns all the surgical instruments composing the kits and reprocesses them in its own plant outside the hospital. At the beginning of each day, the company brings all the surgical kits needed for the daily planned surgery to the hospital. At that time, it withdraws the kits utilized the day before to reprocess them at its plant.

Company B provides non-woven surgical protective drapes for patients, operators and furniture (beds, trolleys, etc.). The supplied materials include masks, gloves, caps, gowns and drapes. All these items are packaged as single-use 'custom pack', specifically designed for each surgery type. Thus, each custom pack provides all the necessary materials for a single surgery. The company periodically delivers its supplies, based on orders placed by the hospital staff every month.

As already mentioned, the specific characteristic of the case study consists in: (1) the implementation of the RFId technology; (2) the long-term strategic cooperation between the supplying companies. We will refer to these two key factors with the terms 'RFId effect' and 'Network effect' respectively. The impact of these two factors on the Expected Total Relevant Costs (ETRC) will be evaluated through an analysis of scenarios. In the next sections we will formalize the 'Network effect' and the 'RFId effect'.

Notation

i: different products line
Q_i order quantity of item i [units]
D_i mean annual demand of item i [units/year]
A: cost per shipment for Company B without the network effect [€/roundtrip]
A' cost per shipment for Company B with the network effect [€/roundtrip]
r: inventory carrying charge [€/€/year]
v_i unit variable cost of item i [€/unit]
k_i safety factor for item i

2.1 Network Effect

The Network effect allows companies to share setup costs, which substantially correspond to transportation costs. We assume that cost per shipment is proportional to the Euclidean distance covered for the shipment. Companies A and B may share some part of the way to the hospital. In particular, Company B can take advantage of the daily frequency of the shipment of Company A.

In this case, the lower distance that can be covered in a roundtrip is equal to the perimeter of the triangle (see Fig. 1) formed by the Hospital (point H), Company A (point A), and Company B (point B). Thus, when the two companies cooperate as a network, the shipment trip will always start from, and finish at, Company A plant, due to the necessity to bring back the utilized kits from the hospital. The round trip will consist of:

- load of sterile kits at Company A plants
- trip from Company A to Company B

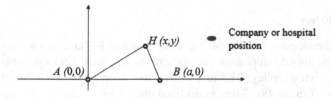

Fig. 1. Schematic position of companies and hospital

- load of packs from company B
- trip from Company B to the Hospital for the delivery of kits and packs
- trip from the Hospital to Company A to bring back utilized kits

To estimate the savings achievable through the network effect, the cost per shipment related to the network configuration have to be compared with cost per shipment when companies act individually. The condition for evaluating the convenience of the network collaboration is that $(AB + AH + BH < 2BH + 2AH)$. In this relation, the first term represents the total length of the round trip in a network collaboration. The second term describes the total distance travelled by the two companies, if they work individually. The relation can be simplified in the following way: $AB < BH + AH$. As the sum of two sides of a triangle is always greater than only one side, the last relation is always verified. This implies that working as a network always allows reducing cost per shipment.

The total savings SV achievable under the 'network effect' will be proportional to $SV = 2BH + 2AH - (AB + AH + BH)$. From a Network perspective, this reduction of shipment cost can be entirely assigned to Company B. Indeed, it is noteworthy that shipment cost does not affect the replenishment policy of Company A, which is obliged to ship the required quantities on a daily basis. On the contrary, a reduction of shipment cost could determine a variation of the optimal quantity shipped by Company B. In fact, the optimal reorder quantity for each item i is equal to the Economic Order Quantity $EOQ = \sqrt{2A \cdot D/v \cdot r}$. So if the shipment cost A drops to A' when the network effect is present, the optimal order quantities of each item also decrease. In this view, as the Company B shipment cost without the network is equal to $A = 2BH$, A' can be estimated as: $A' = A - SV = 2BH - [2BH + 2AH - (AB + AH + BH)] = BH + AB - AH$. Thus, it is possible to define the 'Network coefficient' λ as the ratio between A' and A, with $0 \leq \lambda \leq 1$:

$$\lambda = \frac{A'}{A} = \frac{1}{2} + \frac{AB - AH}{2BH} \tag{1}$$

λ depends from the mutual positions of Company A, Company B and the Hospital.

In summary, when the scenario provides the network effect, the cost per shipment will be equal to λA, and consequently, if a continuous review policy is adopted, reorder quantity Q_i will be calculated as:

$$Q_i = \sqrt{2\lambda A \cdot D_i / v_i \cdot r} \tag{2}$$

2.2   RFId Effect

Among the advantages related to the implementation of RFID technology, we consider: (1) to avoid incomplete shipments, misplacements and theft; (2) to possibly implement a continuous review policy. The first benefit has been modelled using the study by Ustundag and Tanyas [9]. They considered that RFID technology implementation

Table 1. Error rates of non-RFId and RFId integrated systems

Technology	α (%)	β (%)	γ (%)	δ (%)
Non RFID	2	0.2	0.5	0.3
RFID	0	0.2	0	0

eliminates item losses caused by theft, incorrect positioning and incomplete shipments. Only damages that can occur during transportation cannot be avoided. This effect can be considered using the following four coefficients: α (incorrect positioning), β (damage), γ (theft) and δ (incomplete shipment). They represent the error rates related to the corresponding causes. Table 1 shows the values, derived from the experimental study of Ustundag and Tanyas [9], that has been assumed in our study.

As far as the second benefit is concerned, the conceptual model assumes that without the implementation of the RFId technology a periodic review policy is adopted, while the RFId effect allow implementing a continuous review policy. In the following subsections, the description of both policies is carried out.

Periodic Review – No RFId Effect. Without the RFID effect, Company B actually adopts a periodic review policy (R, S), with a review period R equal to 2 weeks, which is common for all the four items. This type of policy is very common in healthcare [10], and it is often adopted when it is not possible to have an automatic monitoring of the warehouse. Indeed, if the inventory has to be checked manually, it is usually preferred to limit the number of times the checking activities have to be performed. Furthermore, if the orders are placed on a periodic basis, different items can be incorporated in the same shipment in order to save on transportation costs. For each item i, the order-up to level S_i and the safety stocks SS_i are calculated respectively as: $S_i = SS_i + D_i (R + L)$; $SS_i = k_i \sigma_{(R+L)i}$, where $\sigma_{(R+L)i}$ is the standard deviation of demand during $R + L$, and k_i is the safety factor. The safety factor k_i is determined by imposing a specified service level required by the customer. Given the critical function of the supplied items, the required service level is high. We assumed a value of $P = 99.9$ % of demand satisfied immediately from the shelf ('fill rate'). From this condition, the value of k_i can be calculated in the considering the following function [11]:

$$G_u(k_i) = \frac{(1 - P)D_i R_i}{\sigma_{(R+L)i}} \tag{3}$$

where $G_u(\cdot)$ is the loss probability function, equal to:

$$G_u(k) = \int_k^\infty (u - k)\phi(u)\, du = \phi(k) - k(1 - \Phi(k)) \tag{4}$$

$\phi(k)$ being the unit normal density function, and $\Phi(k)$ the corresponding distribution function. From the value of $G_u(k_i)$, calculated from (3), it is possible to determine the value of k_i using the tabular form of Eq. (4).

Continuous Review – RFId Effect. When RFID technology is implemented, Company B can apply a continuous review policy (s, Q). In this case the optimal order quantity Q_i, for each item i, is calculated through the Economic Order Quantity (EOQ):

$$Q_i = EOQ_i = \sqrt{2AD_i/v_i r} \tag{5}$$

Note that, if the network effect is simultaneously present, the network coefficient λ has to be considered to calculate order quantities using Eq. (2), because A decrease to $A' = \lambda A$. The reorder-point s_i and safety stocks SS_i are calculated in this case through: $s_i = SS_i + D_i\,L$; $SS_i = k_i\,\sigma_{(L)i}$, where $\sigma_{(L)i}$ is the demand standard deviation during the lead time L. To find the values of the safety factors k_i that allows us to reach the fill rate $P = 99.9\ \%$, it is necessary to calculate the loss function as (see [11]):

$$G_u(k_i) = \frac{(1-P)Q_i}{\sigma_{(L)i}} \tag{6}$$

Then the value of k_i can be determined using the tabular form of Eq. (4).

2.3   Scenario Analysis

Four different scenarios will be compared on the basis of the annual Expected Total Relevant Costs (*ETRC*), which is considered composed by four components: replenishment costs, holding costs, RFId implementation costs, and costs related to thefts and misplacements. The total annual costs related to RFId implementation has been estimated by summing the periodic amortization payment, related to hardware and software investments, and the annual costs of the 'one use' UHF tags, and it is equal to 4434 [€/year] (the detailed costs are omitted due to space limitation). The impact of thefts on the *ETRC* is calculated considering a cost equal to the value of each item stolen. The cost of items misplaced is considered equal to item value only when item are expired and cannot be used if they are found. In the model it is assumed that the 50 % of misplaced items expires before the finding, and a cost equal to the value of the item is considered; the other 50 % is considered utilizable and for this reason it does not represent a cost.

The four scenarios considered are described in the following.

Scenario 'AS IS'. In the 'as is' scenario neither the 'Network effect' nor the 'RFId effect' are present. Thus, the companies operate individually, Company B utilizes a periodic review policy, with a cost per shipment equal to A, where the products line share the same shipment. *ETRC* can be estimated through:

$$ETRC = \frac{A}{R} + \sum_i \left(\frac{D_i \cdot R}{2} + k_i \cdot \sigma_{(R+L)i} \right) \cdot v_i \cdot r + \sum_i \left(\frac{\alpha}{2} + \gamma \right) D_i \cdot v_i \tag{7}$$

In (7), the first term corresponds to replenishment costs, the second one to carrying costs, and the last one approximate costs associated to thefts and misplacements.

Scenario 1 – Network Effect. Company A and B belong to the same network. Company B still adopts a Periodic Review policy, but it is possible to share the cost per shipment with Company A. Thus, *ETRC* can be estimated through (7) by substituting the shipment cost A with $A' = \lambda A$.

Scenario 2 – RFID Effect. In this scenario, the companies still operates individually, but Company B implements a continuous review policy, which is enabled by the RFId implementation. The cost per shipment between Company B and the Hospital is still equal to A, because it is not shared. Each shipment contains only one product line, due to the different times each product line reaches the respective reorder point. In this case, there are no costs related to thefts and misplacements, while the annual cost related to RFId implementation is considered:

$$ETRC = \sum_i A \frac{D_i}{EOQ_i} + \sum_i \left(\frac{EOQ_i}{2} + k_i \cdot \sigma_{(L)i}\right) \cdot v_i \cdot r + C_{RFId} \tag{8}$$

Scenario 3 – Network + RFId Effects. The Network effect and the RFId effect are simultaneously present. Thanks to RFId technology Company B can implement a continuous review policy. At the same time, each time a product line reaches the reorder point, the corresponding shipment can be shared with Company A, thanks to the network effect. Thus, $ETRC$ can be estimated through Eq. (8) by considering a shipment cost equal to $A' = \lambda A$, instead of A. Note that even the optimal quantities EOQ_i are affected by the decrease of the shipment cost (see Eq. (5)).

3 Numerical Experiment and Discussion

The values utilized in the experiments are related to a hospital placed in a city in the south of the Umbria region, in Italy: cost per roundtrip between Company B and the Hospital $A = 50$ [€], network coefficient $\lambda = 0.1158$, inventory carrying charge $r = 0.25$ [€/€/year], lead time $L = 2$ days, required service level (demand satisfied directly from the shelf) $P = 99.9$ %. The annual demand data of the four item lines considered are related to the surgeries done in the hospital during the year 2012. Each product line represents a specific surgical discipline custom pack of non-woven drapes. Demand is assumed to be exponentially distributed, and the annual average values D_i and the value v_i of each item are reported in Table 2.

The value of k_i for both the periodic and the continuous review policies have been derived using the procedures described in Sect. 5. Table 3 shows the results related to the numerical experiment. In scenario 1, by virtue of the option of cooperating as a network, there is the possibility for Company B to share shipment costs with Company A, which supplies the hospital on a daily basis. This is of course preferable with

Table 2. Data related to the 4 product lines

Product line	Description	Average demand [units/year]	Item value [€/unit]
1	Surgery	560	208
2	Otorhinolaringologist	20	198
3	Orthopaedics	673	220
4	Obstetrician e genecology	454	247

Table 3. Results of the numerical experiment

Scenarios data				Annual costs					
Scen.	RFId effect	Network effect	Repl. policy	Unitary shipment cost	Transp. costs [€/y]	Holding costs [€/y]	RFId invest. [€/y]	Thefts mispl. [€/y]	ETRC [€/y]	Saving
AS IS	NO	NO	(R, S)	A	595	6700	–	4568	11863	/
1	NO	YES	(R, S)	λA	69	6700	–	4568	11337	4.4 %
2	YES	NO	(s, Q)	A	2817	3466	4434	–	10717	9.7 %
3	YES	YES	(s, Q)	λA	969	1766	4434	–	7170	39.6 %

respect to the AS IS scenario, because holding costs remain unchanged, and transportation costs are reduced by a factor equal to λ. Results related to scenario 2 show that, even in absence of the network effect, the implementation of the RFId technology makes the adoption of a continuous review policy more convenient. This is due to two reasons: firstly, the RFId annual investment is lower than the annual costs related to thefts and misplacements. Secondly, the parameters of the continuous review policy (s and Q) are optimized for each product line, while in the periodic review policy the review period R is the same for all product lines and it is imposed by the hospital organization ($R = 1$ month). In scenario 3, the effect obtainable combining the RFId technology with networked cooperation among enterprises is evaluated.

The reduction achievable in terms of *ETRC* is notable, reaching almost the 48 % with respect to the AS IS scenario. It is noteworthy that the interaction of the two effects brings to a cost reduction higher than the sum of the savings obtainable when the two effects are applied separately. This is due to the fact that the Network Effect, by allowing decreasing the cost per shipment, has a much more great impact on policies with frequent of shipments (s, Q) then on policies with low number of shipments (R, S). Thus, only the simultaneous adoption of the RFId technology and the collaborative network model allows maximizing the expected savings.

4 Conclusions

In the paper a methodology to evaluate possible savings of a new business model of collaborative supply network in the healthcare sector is described. The case study show that an integrated supplying service for the operating room can be less expensive than traditional models, while maintaining an adequate service level to the patient. In fact, the presence of RFId technology allows the implementation of a continuous review policy, which is known to reduce the uncertainty period with respect to periodic review policies. Consequently, relevant savings related to holding costs are achievable. At the same time, the collaborative network of suppliers allows sharing transportation costs. In this way, the costs connected to shipments, which are typically higher in continuous review policy, are limited.

It is reasonable to assume that the economic benefits achievable in reality may increase as the number of different products handled and the number of companies involved increase. In fact, when there are more than four products considered in this work, it is correct to assume that, even by adopting a continuous review policy, the replenishment instant may be the same for more products simultaneously. In the same way, shipment costs can be lowered even in the case where more than two companies are considered, by optimizing the routing from Company A to the Hospital.

In order to generalize the results obtainable by the proposed approach, future improvements consists in performing a sensitivity analysis on the parameters that can have a direct influence on total costs, starting from the network coefficient λ. Finally, a discrete event simulation model could be designed to accurately evaluate the impact of thefts and misplacement on real costs and service level, in order to better quantify the benefits connected to RFId implementation.

References

1. Roberts, V.: Managing strategic outsourcing in the healthcare industry. J. Healthc. Manag. **46**, 239–249 (2001)
2. Baffo, I., Confessore, G., Liotta, G., Stecca, G.: A cooperative model to improve hospital equipments and drugs management. In: Camarinha-Matos, L.M., Paraskakis, I., Afsarmanesh, H. (eds.) PRO-VE 2009. IFIP AICT, vol. 307, pp. 43–50. Springer, Heidelberg (2009)
3. Reymondon, F., Pellet, B., Marcon, E.: Optimization of hospital sterilization costs proposing new grouping choices of medical devices into packages. Int. J. Prod. Econ. **112**, 326–335 (2008)
4. van de Klundert, J., Muls, P., Schadd, M.: Optimizing sterilization logistics in hospitals. Health Care Manag. Sci. **11**, 23–33 (2008)
5. de Vries, J.: The shaping of inventory systems in health services: a stakeholder analysis. Int. J. Prod. Econ. **133**, 60–69 (2011)
6. Saetta, S., Tiacci, L., Cagnazzo, L.: The innovative model of the virtual development office for collaborative networked enterprises: the GPT network case study. Int. J. Comput. Integr. M **26**, 41–54 (2013)
7. Choi, T.M.: Pre-season stocking and pricing decisions for fashion retailers with multiple information updating. Int. J. Prod. Econ. **106**, 146–170 (2007)
8. Sarac, A., Absi, N., Dauzere-Peres, S.: A literature review on the impact of RFID technologies on supply chain management. Int. J. Prod. Econ. **128**, 77–95 (2010)
9. Ustundag, A., Tanyas, M.: The impacts of radio frequency identification (RFID) technology on supply chain costs. Transport. Res. E-Log. **45**, 29–38 (2009)
10. Nicholson, L., Vakharia, A.J., Erenguc, S.S.: Outsourcing inventory management decisions in healthcare: models and application. Eur. J. Oper. Res. **154**, 271–290 (2004)
11. Silver, E.A., Pyke, D.F., Peterson, R.: Inventory Management and Production Planning and Scheduling. Wiley, Hoboken (1998)

Collaborative Knowledge for Analysis Material Flow of a Complex Long Stud Using Multiple Stoke Cold Heading

Suthep Butdee[1](✉) and Uten Khanawapee[2]

[1] Department of Production Engineering, Faculty of Engineering,
King Mongkut's University of Technology North Bangkok, Bangkok, Thailand
stb@kmutnb.ac.th
[2] Department of Mechanical Engineering Technology, College of Industrial
Technology, King Mongkut's University of Technology North Bangkok,
Bangkok, Thailand
ukp@kmutnb.ac.th

Abstract. Productivity Improvement is one of the most important strategies for every enterprise. Head cold forging is a widely common production process which can achieve economical processes and less energy consumption. Die is the major key of the forging process but how to perform an effective design, needs several years of experiences or using engineering tools for assistance. This paper proposes the collaborative die design and analysis by combining engineering methods and industrial experts to correct problems and to validate a new and complex design. DEFORM is used to investigate suitable parameters by guidance from the expert. One of the classical problem in the head cold forging is to make a small long complex stud. It is found from simulation that a five step of punch with suitable taper angle is the most effectiveness.

Keywords: Collaborative knowledge · DEFORM · Complex long stud head forging · Analysis material flow

1 Introduction

Cold forging aims for producing net and near-net-shape parts, such as shafts, axles, bolts, gears and so on, using room temperature. Products in different shapes and sizes are formed by high speed and high pressure processes with tool steel or carbide dies which are able to increase the hardness, yield, and tensile strengths. Cold heading is used for making screw production. It transforms wire into the designed shapes by die and punch cavities. Die is one of critical components of such processes. The force of the blow creates enough pressure to cause the metal to flow outward into a die cavity. The head or upset portion of the part is larger in diameter than the original billet. It commonly deforms aluminum, carbon and alloy steels. Presently, cold forging can produce ±0.025 mm of tolerance. The process is applied for producing nuts, bolts, screws, rivets, and other fasteners. Complex shapes of products require multi-step of cold heading or combine with other processes. Consequently, the blows may be struck, with the billet moving through a sequence of dies. Extrusion is one of the effective

© IFIP International Federation for Information Processing 2015
S. Umeda et al. (Eds.): APMS 2015, Part I, IFIP AICT 459, pp. 102–109, 2015.
DOI: 10.1007/978-3-319-22756-6_13

process applied to assist the cold forging for creating the ratio of head to shank size beyond the normal cold heading capability. Cold heading shape design can be single blow headers or double blow headers. The single blow headers are the simplest and fastest process. They can produce hundreds of pieces per minute but are limited to minor shank extrusion and simple head shapes using a single stroke machines which a wire roll is sheared in a die, struck one blow, and ejected. The process type is suitable for the material lends itself easily to upsetting. Hard materials are deformed by double blows. The first punch delivers the metal flow. The shape is completed with the second blow. Double stoke headers are necessary when the diameter of the head is more than two sizes. The large heads of a nut needs multi-die machines and multiple step cold heading process. Multi-station or progressive headers are used, when many strokes are required for more complicated contours dies [1].

In our work recently, university-industrial collaboration is preferable to Thai-government policy. In production engineering department and department of tool and die are concentrated on material flow analysis using DEFORM, a commercial software. Different types of products, processes and material flow of cold and hot forging are captured for knowledge. It is rarely used and validated even on the real-time problem solving. In this case of research study, collaborative works of specialist CAE lab engineer and industrial die design expert team are on-line discussing via a suitable social media platform that will be explained in a next section. Industry has received more and more complex and hard shapes of products. The paper proposes and discusses an analysis of material flow for a long stud via a line environment. Such product needs a multi-stoke machine together with progressive die and punch. DEFORM, is applied to solve problem of material flow in a particular shape, size, and its tolerances. The knowledge of die and punch design has been built in the library before being used and routinely updated by both sides. A collaborative design process is created via a common social network on their own smart mobile phones. Therefore, A LINE network is created in group in order to share knowledge and ideas. Including some parts of solving solutions before they have been stored in the database library.

2 Related Works and Problems

This section presents previous works which relate to our paper and defines scope of study. Im et al. [2] presented computer aided process design in cold-former forging of ball joint using a forging simulator and a commercial CAD software. The forging sequence design and its detail design are generated interactively from a design database, knowledge-based rules and basic laws. The simulation technique is used for verification. Die set design and die manufacturing information are generated automatically. Such techniques can improve productivity. Kim and Im [3] proposed an expert system for multi-stage cold-forging process design with a re-designing algorithm. The system consists of a user interface, a system shell, a material data-base, and a design rule-base. The system developed is able to reduce trial-and-error by design engineers in determining forging parameters. Stephen and Vollertsen [4] presented a laser-based micro upsetting process which takes advantage of scaling effects to optimize the conventional multi-stage upsetting. In conventional process, it is risk of bulking and cracks, whereas the laser-based process separate treatment process between the upsetting steps omitted. MaCormack and Monaghan [5] proposed the FEA of cold forging die using two and three dimensional models using DEFORM. The result showed contact and friction. Finding that the highest stress concentration occurred within the body of the tool and not along the contact surface. Weroński et al. [6] explained research of upsetting ratio in forming processes on a three slides forging press. Hussain et al. [7] proposed a study on cold forging die design using different techniques. Danno et al. [8] proposed multi-stage cold forging of thin-walled components. The case studies were conducted through FE simulation and experiments. The result showed that the process was effective to reduce the forming load and improve flow in the forming of two kinds of thin aluminum alloy components with multi thickness. Ku et al. [9] proposed multi-stage cold forging and experimental investigation for the outer race of constant velocity joints. Joun et al. [10] presented an application-oriented finite element approach to forging die structural analysis. Stress on tools and work pieces are the critical problems in cold forging processes which may cause fatigue cracks. Several experimental and numerical have been studied on the fracture and estimations of service life of forging tools. However, little research is on the complex stud analysis using tool steel and hard steel. It rarely presented collaborative sharing knowledge between university and industry in aspect of real time and on-line. The next section explains the collaborative model.

Industrial knowledge is indispensable context for improving productive and competitive enterprises. Particularly in the area of tools and die design because it needs many years of learning by their own experiences. In addition, different areas requires alter knowledge and know-how. In the aluminum extrusion die design requires a specific knowledge together with global collaborative working group [11–14]. Knowledge is able to manage in different types. Case-based reasoning is well known and suitable for industrial knowledge because it can learn knowledge more from the previous experience comparing theory general basic knowledge and adapt to fit to solve new problems quickly [15–17]. Knowledge management plays an important role of an advanced enterprise. Basically, knowledge can be explicit and implicit but need to capture and store in a well-structure system. Capitalization knowledge is a critical part of knowledge management [18–21].

3 Collaborative University and Industry System

In some areas of cold forging design needs a lot of experience in order to improve productivity, quality and efficiency. Presently, customers can easily link to global sourcing and need a manufacturer to response satisfactory and competitively in aspects of cost and time. This paper proposes a creative model which collaborate among involving workforces. They are design knowledge engineer, advisor and industrial knowledge designer via a common social media, LINE tool. Problems comes to industrial design department all the time of working day, and it is time consuming to solve such problems. It routinely uses narrow scope of experience. The company's need is to improve productivity and increase more competitiveness by sharing problems and solutions. Figure 1 shows the collaborative design system which composes of

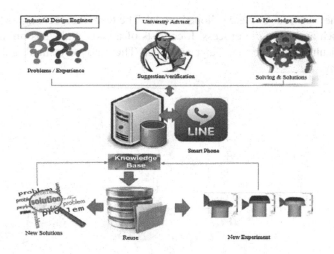

Fig. 1. Collaborative knowledge design system

three main players; the industry design engineer, the university advisor and the lab knowledge engineer. They are all participants via LINE environment. The problem-solving procedures and solutions are stored in the knowledge base which can be useful as a reference and future use on both sides. The lab knowledge engineer can perform a new experiment shortly, whereas the industry design engineer can trial a new process whenever the production line is available.

Figure 1 shows the collaborative knowledge design system. It is the simplest communication media system using LINE which popular in Thailand. New specific problems (products) coming from customer which are different from the previous parts are posted in the LINE group linked to every member on their smart phones. The LINE is interfaced to the knowledge base library which attracts the useful knowledge in a certain format. The solution is divided into two categories; real-time and storage. Some experience problems can be provided directly by specialists whereas the other some need time to analysis. Storage knowledge is retrieved from library. Some new solution which is invested from diary performance will be recorded in the new solution part of the memory. On the other hand, the new experiment which existed from the lab will store the new experiment part. Both parts of memory are linked to the knowledge base library (KBL). However, the KBL requires an effective management to share and not share information. It is defined as public and private sections.

4   Experimental Study

The case study selected to show how problems can be solved by collaborative model. A long small complex stud using 1035 (S35C). The present facing problem is that the material has blended because of the length of work-piece. The collaborative team is discussed and agreed that the process should be increased one more step of deforming. Process change causes risk of failure and take more time to solve problems. Fortunately, the collaborative method can reduce the risk and time saving. The session presents the new process of the developed model. The team members agree to start with the three punch and three die process. It consists of a body and steps on the head and tail. The difficulty areas are the chafer and fillet. They are very small and have close tolerances (Fig. 2).

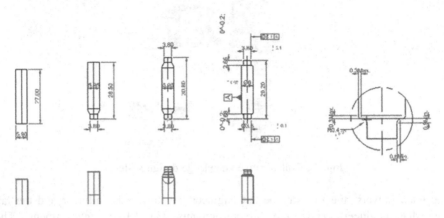

Fig. 2. Example of a long small complex stud heading part

DEFORM of CAE is taken into account for the three punch and three die process analysis. The parameter assigned for heading speed is 300 m/s and fiction coefficient is 0.08. The first experiment on the 150th step. The heading process is stopped. It is because a shock size reduction. The design expert suggests that heading step should be increased. The knowledge engineer takes the five punch and five die process with the concave size reduction.

The Fig. 3 illustrates the result of the second experiment. The flashing problem still occurs in the third die of the 301st step. The expert further suggests that the second die should be modified to increase more area on the straight line of material flow as well as to increase taper area.

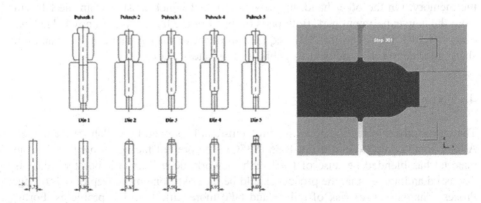

Fig. 3. The second experiment of using the five punch and five die process

Figure 4 shows the third experiment of using five punch and 5 die process with the first modification. It is found that the billet could not go through. It occurs a flashing problem in the third die. The collaborative team is then agrees to modify as an opening die. The billet is formed to become tapers on both sides. The second die is modified by increasing on the straight flow line to support the billet.

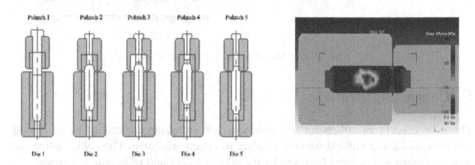

Fig. 4. The five punch and five die with the first modification

Figure 5 shows the result of the forth experiment. It is still having flashing problem on the fifth die. The expert suggests that the punch 2 and punch 4 should be modified. The angle must be reduced smaller than the former in order to improve a better flow inside the third die. In addition, the straight line area must be extended to protect distortion.

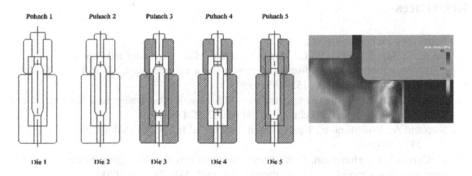

Fig. 5. The five punch and die process with the second modification

Figure 6 shows the final modification which the second and third die are modified. The second die should be a very small angle of orifice whereas the fourth die must have very long straight line area in order to support the billet while is flowing through the whole die.

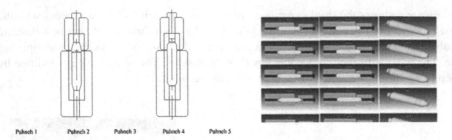

Puhnch 1   Puhnch 2   Puhnch 3   Puhnch 4   Puhnch 5

Fig. 6. The final modification and its result

5 Concluding Remarks

The new concept of collaborative knowledge for analyzing material flow of a long complex stud using multi stoke cold heading has been presented. The cold heading die process design is discussed followed by the related works and problems statement. The collaborative industrial design is also expressed. The proposed development system is shown. A selected case experiment study is presented. A small long complex stud is experimented and investigated the best result from the collaborative team. It is only the fifth time of trial on the DEFORM software and can achieve a well-result to guide the industrial design engineer. This method impacts productivity and is less time consuming to reach an effective design and manufacturing.

References

1. http://www.nickelinstitute.org/
2. Im, C.S., Suh, S.R., Lee, M.C., Kim, J.H., Joun, M.S.: Computer aided process design in cold-former forging using a forging simulator and a commercial CAD software. J. Mater. Process. Technol. **95**(1999), 155–163 (1999)
3. Kim, H.S., Im, Y.T.: An expert system for cold forging process design based on a depth-first search. J. Mater. Process. Technol. **95**(1999), 262–274 (1999)
4. Stephen, A., Vollertsen, F.: Upset ratio in laser-based free form heading. Phys. Procedia **5**, 227–232 (2010)
5. MaCormack, C., Monaghan, J.: A finite element analysis of cold forging dies using two and three dimension models. J. Mater. Process. Technol. **118**, 286–292 (2001)
6. Weronski, W.S., Gontarz, A., Pater, Z.: Research of upsetting ratio in forming processes on a three – slides forging press. JAMME **17**(1-2) (2006)
7. Hussain, K., Samad, Z., Othman, A.R., Salman, A.N.J., Basruddin, I.A., Hakim, S.S.: A study on cold forging die design using different techniques. Mod. Appl. Sci. **3**(3), 143–154 (2009)
8. Danno, A., Berner, S., Fong, K.S., Yap, W.T.: Multi-stage cold forging of thin-walled components. Procedia Eng. **81**, 407–412 (2014)
9. Ku, T.W., Kim, L.H., Kang, B.S.: Multi-stage cold forging and experimental investigation for the outer race of constant velocity joints. Mater. Des. **49**(2013), 368–385 (2013)

10. Joun, M.S., Lee, M.C., Park, J.M.: Finite element analysis of presented die set in cold forging. Int. J. Mach. Tools Manuf. **42**(2002), 1213–1222 (2002)
11. Tichkiewitch, S., Butdee, S., Marin, P.: Knowledge management for the design of dies in aluminum extrusion process. In: The Proceeding of 2002 International CIRP Design Seminar (2002)
12. Butdee, S., Noomtong, C., Vignat, F., Thomann, G.: Methodology of knowledge library management for concurrent cooperative design. In: Proceeding of the 24th International Manufacturing Management, vol. 2, pp. 711–718 (2007)
13. Pimapunsri, K., Butdee, S., Tichkiewitch, S.: Industrial knowledge management using collaborative knowledge acquisition in a consultancy project. J. Achievements Mater. Manufact. Eng. **31**, 803–809 (2008)
14. Pimapunsri, K., Tichkiewitch, S., Butdee, S.: Collaborative negotiation between designers and manufacturers in the wood furniture industry using particleboard or fiberboard. In: The 15th CIRP International Conference Design (2008)
15. Janthong, N., Brissaud, D., Butdee, S.: Knowledge-based adaptable design to support customer-oriented production system of industrial equipment. In: The 42nd CIRP Conference on Manufacturing Systems (2009)
16. Janthong, N., Brissaud, D., Butdee, S.: Combining axiomatic design and case-based reasoning in a design methodology of mechatronics. In: The Proceeding of 2009 CIRP Design Conference (2009)
17. Butdee, S., Noomtong, C., Tichkiewitch, S.: Collaborative aluminum profile design to adaptable die process planning using neural networks. Key Eng. Mater. **443**, 207–212 (2010)
18. Hirunyasiri, V., Butdee, S.: Knowledge synthesis using multichannel of media in the case study of integrated circuit industry. KMUTNB Int. J. Appl. Sci. Technol. **6**(1), 67–79 (2013)
19. Butdee. S.: Case-based formulation to knowledge capitalization for plastic injection mold design. In: IEEE IEEM, pp. 934–939 (2010)
20. Butdee, S., Tichkiewitch, S.: Global Product Development, pp. 491–496. Springer, Berlin (2011)
21. Numthong, C., Butdee, S.: The knowledge based system for forging process design based on case-based reasoning and finite element method. KMUTNB Int. J. Appl. Sci. Technol. **5**(2), 45–54 (2013)

Globalization and Production Management

Leagility in a Triad with Multiple Decoupling Points

Joakim Wikner(✉), Jenny Bäckstrand, Fredrik Tiedemann,
and Eva Johansson

Jönköping University, Jönköping, Sweden
{joakim.wikner, jenny.backstrand, fredrik.tiedemann,
eva.johansson}@ju.se

Abstract. Leagility is a strategic concept that represents a combination of lean and agile. Lean is assumed to be a cost-based strategy that is appropriate in a forecast-driven context upstream of the customer order decoupling point (CODP). Agile is the corresponding flexibility-based strategy in a customer-order-driven context downstream of the CODP. Competitive advantage is based on that the position of the CODP is aligned with the market requirements. In a dyad setting this alignment can be realized with relative ease but in a triad setting it becomes more complicated if both supply actors pursue a leagile strategy. If lean based purchasing faces an agile based delivery strategy or the opposite, where agile based purchasing faces a lean based delivery strategy, the interface is misaligned. In this paper, four interface configurations are identified and empirical examples of each are given based on a case study.

Keywords: Leagility · Lean · Agile · Lead-time · Supplier relations · Decoupling points

1 Introduction

Lean and agile are two strategies that have attracted considerable interest in both practice and in the literature. Lean has been considered as emphasizing efficiency and how to perform a value stream in the most cost efficient way possible [1]. Ford and Toyota are seen as originators of this approach but over the years the approach has disseminated into many industries and a vast array of companies. As a reaction to this efficiency based approach, the agile strategy was suggested as an alternative that in a more explicit way embraces IT enabled virtual organizations [2]. In addition, the capability to serve individual customers was emphasized for the agile strategy and this requires a higher level of flexibility which is in contrast to the Heijunka approach to levelling that is at the core of lean. The lean and agile approaches are applicable to individual companies as well as more complex multi actor supply chains since each strategy suggests a homogenous and integrated design of all actors in the network. In the late 90's, the two strategies were combined in different ways and the most refer-enced is the leagile strategy that is a design employing lean and agile in tandem [3].

Employing lean and agile in tandem is manageable within a dyad setting where one company applies a leagile strategy in order to both act in a flexible way towards its

© IFIP International Federation for Information Processing 2015
S. Umeda et al. (Eds.): APMS 2015, Part I, IFIP AICT 459, pp. 113–120, 2015.
DOI: 10.1007/978-3-319-22756-6_14

customers and at the same time having a cost focus upstream. However, when it comes to a triad setting, i.e. three actors in a sequence [4] corresponding to a direct supply chain [5], the applications of a leagile strategy is less straight forward. There is a risk of misalignments at the interfaces between the actors in the triad due to the different strategies applied. If the companies are unaware of this complexity related to the actor interfaces, the potential advantages of employing a leagile strategy may not be realized. The purpose of this paper is thus to describe the different types of actor interfaces that can be identified when a leagility strategy is employed by the two supply actors in a triad. Consequently, the contribution is the identification of interface alignments and interface misalignments when the two consecutive supply actors act individually.

Next, leagility is investigated in the original context of a dyad and some key characteristics are outlined. Thereafter, leagility is put into a supply chain context of a triad and two types of interface alignment and two types of interface misalignment are identified. Finally, the four types of interfaces are illustrated by case examples and some ideas for further research are outlined.

2 Leagility in a Dyad Context

The concept of leagility was first defined by Naylor et al. [3] and they suggested that the decoupling point [6] is a key construct when combining lean with agile. The decoupling point is also referred to as the customer order decoupling point (CODP) by e.g. Giesberts and van der Tang [7]. A key property of the CODP was identified by Shingō [8] and was termed the P:D ratio [9] which is based on the relation between the two strategic lead-times: the cumulative Product lead-time (P) and the requested Delivery lead-time (D). In some cases the product lead-time has been referred to as the Supply lead-time (S), see e.g. Bäckstrand and Wikner [10], to emphasize that the lead-time of all supply activities should be included, and S is hence used in this paper.

These two strategic lead-times (S and D) are illustrated in Fig. 1 where the dyad with the focal actor (FA) and the customer actor (CA) is the unit of analysis. The CA requests a product with the delivery lead-time D_{FA} from the FA and all activities at FA during the D_{FA} are customer-order-driven. The CODP is positioned based on the D_{FA} and differentiates activities based on forecast from activities based on customer order.

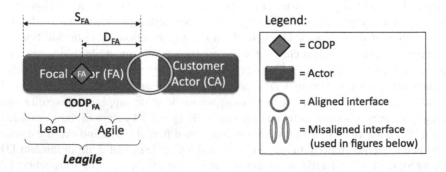

Fig. 1. Leagility in a dyad

The CODP is illustrated by a diamond in Fig. 1 in line with Wikner [11]. The FA has a supply lead-time S_{FA} to supply the product to CA and if $S_{FA} > D_{FA}$ there is not enough time available during D_{FA} to supply the product and hence the FA must initiate supply before the customer order is known and this is referred to as supply to forecast, which is also known as forecast-driven activities. Naylor et al. [3] observed that the characteristics of forecast-driven activities are similar to several lean characteristics and concluded that upstream from the CODP, a lean approach is appropriate with its focus on cost efficiency through level flow in terms of volume and mix. Downstream from the CODP, the customer order is known and already in the original work on agility by Goldman and Preiss [2] it was pointed out that an agile strategy is appropriate for customer-order-driven activities where flexibility is key. This provided the third building block (in addition to CODP and lean) in the definition by leagility, see e.g. Wikner [12]. The interface between the FA and the CA is indicated by a circle in Fig. 1 and by definition this interface is balanced, i.e. the leagility applied by the FA is aligned with the requirements of the CA, since the CODP is positioned based on the lead-time D_{FA} which reflects the market requirements. In subsequent figures, an unbalanced interface is indicated with two separate ellipses.

3 Leagility in a Triad Context

The triad consists of a CA that is the final customer in the triad and the supply is represented by two actors in sequence, where the FA is responsible for supplying the CA and a supplier actor (SA) is responsible for supplying the FA. The triad context thus represents a higher level of complexity than the dyad, in the sense that there are two supply actors involved in the supply network. We investigate the impact of the CA on both the FA and the supplier of the FA (i.e. the SA) and in this context the triad is the most simple, and still relevant, supply chain structure to use. A triad is investigated to avoid unnecessary complexity and still maintain the fundamental characteristics of a supply chain. The triad has the cumulative supply lead-time of $S_{SA} + S_{FA}$. If the two supply actors (SA and FA) were integrated, they would basically correspond to one actor. But, in most cases, the integration is limited and each actor has one CODP each, which is a case of multiple decoupling points, see e.g. Sun et al. [13].

In such a fragmented triad setting it is possible to identify two configurations where there are misalignments at the interface between the SA and the FA and two configurations where the interfaces are aligned. Alignment is here defined as when the two sides of the interface between SA and FA have the same competitive priorities in terms of cost or flexibility. Alignment hence corresponds to when lean is facing lean at the interface (Fig. 2) or when agile faces agile (Fig. 4). In addition, two misalignment configurations where lean is interfaced with agile are identified, see Figs. 3 and 5.

3.1 Leagility in a Triad: Interface Alignment 1

The first configuration is when the FA purchases materials based on forecast and the SA is forecast-driven and delivers from stock. This means that at the interface both the

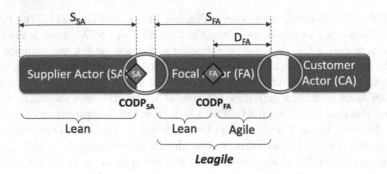

Fig. 2. Interface alignment 1: Cost-Cost

SA and the FA are lean-oriented and cost focus hence meets cost focus. This configuration is referred to as interface alignment 1 and is illustrated in Fig. 2 where the CODP of the FA ($CODP_{FA}$) is positioned internal to the FA. This corresponds to that all activities except purchasing can be customer-order-driven and hence the delivery lead-time is shorter than the supply lead-time of the FA ($S_{FA} > D_{FA}$). The SA is forecast-driven with the CODP ($CODP_{SA}$) positioned at the end of the SA and it delivers from stock. The delivery lead-time to FA from the SA is here assumed to be zero ($D_{SA} = 0$).

3.2 Leagility in a Triad: Interface Misalignment 1

In the configuration alignment 1, above, the $CODP_{SA}$ is positioned at the end of the SA. In the configuration in Fig. 3 the $CODP_{SA}$ is instead positioned upstream from the FA interface (i.e. $D_{SA} > 0$). Still, the FA is purchasing based on a forecast of future orders from the CA, i.e. purchasing to stock (i.e. $S_{FA} > D_{FA}$). However, the SA performs its last activities as customer-order-driven, which means that at the interface the SA is agility oriented but the FA is lean oriented. This is referred to as interface misalignment 1 where flexibility focus meets cost focus and indicated with two ellipses in Fig. 3.

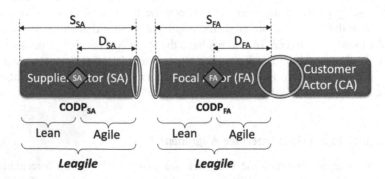

Fig. 3. Interface misalignment 1: Flexibility-Cost

3.3 Leagility in a Triad: Interface Alignment 2

The second configuration with alignment is when the FA is purchasing based on customer order from the CA (i.e. purchase to order, $S_{FA} \leq D_{FA}$) and the SA is performing some activities based on customer order from the FA (i.e. $D_{SA} > 0$). Both sides of the interface between SA and FA are thus agility oriented with flexibility focus, see Fig. 4. Note that it is not necessary for the two CODPs to be positioned at the same place within the SA, they could be positioned separately due to e.g. the bill of material of the item provided by the SA. This would result in a partial misalignment with limited sense business wise but could still exist for technical reasons.

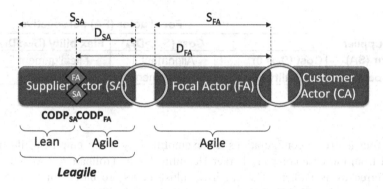

Fig. 4. Interface alignment 2: Flexibility-Flexibility

3.4 Leagility in a Triad: Interface Misalignment 2

The fourth configuration is based on Interface alignment 2 where the two CODPs were positioned at the same place within the SA. However, in this case, the SA is forecast driven and hence the $CODP_{SA}$ is positioned at the end of SA (i.e. $D_{SA} = 0$) as shown in Fig. 5. As a consequence, lean at the SA side is facing agile at the FA side resulting in a misalignment. Note that this could be the consequence of limited information sharing between the two supply actors since even though the FA has the delivery lead-time of D_{FA}, where $S_{FA} \leq D_{FA}$, this information is not known by the SA which thus has selected a forecast-driven approach.

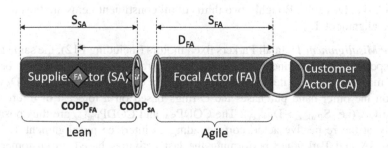

Fig. 5. Interface misalignment 2: Cost-Flexibility

4   Examples of the Four Interface Configurations

Table 1 provides a structured summary of the four configurations outlined above. The first column of Table 1 represent configurations where purchasing is based on forecast. The two cases in the second column represent configurations where purchasing is customer-order-driven. The first row represents delivery from finished goods inventory by the SA and the second row that the SA performs some customer-order-driven activities before the actual delivery is performed.

Table 1. Four interface configurations

Supplier actor (SA) perspective		Focal actor (FA) perspective	
		Cost ($S_{FA} > D_{FA}$)	Flexibility ($S_{FA} \leq D_{FA}$)
	Cost ($D_{SA}=0$)	Alignment 1	Misalignment 2
	Flexibility ($D_{SA}>0$)	Misalignment 1	Alignment 2

The four interface configurations are exemplified by using empirical illustrations gathered from the case company Parker Hannifin AB in Trollhättan, Sweden (henceforth referred to as Parker). The empirical illustrations are based on a deeper case analysis presented in [4, 14]. Parker is part of Parker Hannifin Corporation, which is a global leader in 'Motion and Control Technologies'. Parker manufactures heavy-duty hydraulic pumps and motors with fixed and variable displacement. The product family F12, in the fixed motors segment, is sold both as a standard product and as a customized product and is used to exemplify the four interface configurations in terms of four scenarios. Parker is acting as the FA in the examples below, and hence "Parker" is used instead of "FA" as the index. For the standard F12, the requested delivery lead-time from the CA (D_{Parker}) positions the $CODP_{Parker}$ within Parker (Figs. 2 and 3), while the D_{Parker} for the customized F12 positions the $CODP_{Parker}$ upstream from Parker and within the SA (Figs. 4 and 5).

Interface Alignment 1: The F12 is assembled from 30 items and out of these items four are made in-house and 26 are purchased [4]. Out of all the purchased items 19 are purchased based on forecast (i.e. $S_{Parker} > D_{Parker}$) where 18 of them are made-to-stock by the SA (i.e. $D_{SA} = 0$). Roughly two thirds of all constituent items are thus related to Interface alignment 1.

Interface Misalignment 1: In all Parkers fixed motors (including F12), the same type of Parker specific O-ring is included, regardless of product variant. The SA for these O-rings manufactures this item based on a customer order from Parker (i.e. $D_{SA} > 0$). Parker on the other hand purchases the O-rings based on a forecast of future orders from the CA (i.e. $S_{Parker} > D_{Parker}$). The $CODP_{SA}$ and $CODP_{Parker}$ are thus positioned internally at the respective actor, corresponding to interface misalignment 1. Hence, both the SA and Parker are performing the last activities based on customer order respectively. However, Parker identified this misalignment and later changed this scenario to alignment 1, by replacing the customized O-ring with a standard O-ring stocked by the SA.

Interface Alignment 2: One of Parkers more strategic items, a shaft, is purchased and manufactured based on customer order from the CA (i.e. $S_{Parker} \leq D_{Parker}$) as it is customized. The customization also affects the SA and, under the assumption that customization is not performed on speculation, the $CODP_{SA}$ and the $CODP_{Parker}$ are positioned at the same place, i.e. inside the SA (i.e. $D_{SA} > 0$). This scenario therefore corresponds to interface alignment 2 where the two decoupling points are positioned within the SA. Note that Parker is delivering to customer order from the CA and that SA is delivering based on customer order from Parker. Both these CODPs are however positioned at the same place in the triad.

Interface Misalignment 2: The conic roller bearings used in F12 are standard items for Parker since they are used for every F12 regardless of product variant. Parker purchases this item based on customer order from the CA, positioning the $CODP_{Parker}$ internally at the SA (i.e. $S_{Parker} \leq D_{Parker}$). However, the SA delivers this item from stock (i.e. $D_{SA} = 0$), positioning the $CODP_{SA}$ at the end of the SA. Hence, the supply lead-time S_{Parker} is shorter than the delivery lead-time (D_{Parker}) for F12. The SA could have manufactured this item based on a customer order from Parker but has decided to manufacture this item based on forecast. This scenario therefore corresponds to interface misalignment 2.

5 Conclusions and Further Research

Leagility is usually approached in a dyadic setting where the CA's requirements are considered (at FA) in terms of the requested delivery lead-time. By including a third actor (the SA), a triad perspective is obtained and as we have shown this leads to additional complexity due to the two actor-interfaces. The strategic lead-times S and D of the actors, and consequently the position of the CODPs, have a critical impact on how to balance cost with flexibility at the actor interfaces. The examples presented above point to that the two aligned interface strategies are preferable to the misaligned strategies, but a more detailed investigation of other cases will need to be performed to provide empirical support for the properties of the four identified interface configurations and on preferred transitions between the configurations. In this leagility context it would also be interesting to investigate the impact on financial performance. Furthermore, the theory needs to be extended to also cover a more detailed discussion on internal properties of the SA and FA and in particular how the CODPs can be positioned at different internal positions. Also the impact of different levels of customization in relation to the agile strategy needs to be analyzed.

Acknowledgement. This research has been performed in collaboration with six companies in the projects KOPeration and KOPtimera. The projects are funded by the Swedish Knowledge Foundation (KKS), Jönköping University and the participating companies. In particular the authors would like to express their gratitude to Parker Hannifin in Trollhättan, Sweden.

References

1. Womack, J.P., Jones, D.T.: Lean Thinking: Banish Waste and Create Wealth in Your Corporation. Simon & Schuster, New York (1996)
2. Goldman, S., Preiss, K. (eds.): 21st Century Manufacturing Enterprise Strategy: An Industry-Led View. DIANE Publishing, Collingdale (1991)
3. Naylor, J.B., Naim, M., Berry, D.: Leagility: integrating the lean and agile manufacturing paradigms in the total supply chain. Int. J. Prod. Econ. **62**, 107–118 (1999)
4. Bäckstrand, J.: A method for customer-driven purchasing: aligning supplier interaction and customer-driven manufacturing. School of Engineering. Jönköping University, Jönköping (2012)
5. Mentzer, J.T., DeWitt, W., Keebler, J.S., Min, S., Nix, N.W., Smith, C.D., et al.: Defining supply chain management. J. Bus. Logistics **22**, 1–25 (2001)
6. Hoekstra, S., Romme, J. (eds.): Integral Logistic Structures: Developing Customer-Oriented Goods Flow. Industrial Press, New York (1992)
7. Giesberts, P.M.J., van der Tang, L.: Dynamics of the customer order decoupling point: impact on information systems for production control. Prod. Plann. Control **3**, 300–313 (1992)
8. Shingō, S.: Study of Toyota Production System From Industrial Engineering Viewpoint. Japan Management Association, Tokyo (1981)
9. Mather, H.: Attack your P: D ratio. In: Proceedings from the 1984 APICS Conference (1984)
10. Bäckstrand, J., Wikner, J.: Time-phasing and decoupling points as analytical tools for purchasing. In: Proceedings from the IEEE International Conference on Industrial Engineering and Engineering Management Bangkok, Thailand (2013)
11. Wikner, J.: On decoupling points and decoupling zones. Prod. Manuf. Res. **2**, 167–215 (2014)
12. Wikner, J.: Supply chain management strategies in terms of decoupling points and decoupling zones. In: Grabot, B., Vallespir, B., Gomes, S., Bouras, A., Kiritsis, D. (eds.) Advances in Production Management Systems. IFIP AICT, vol. 438, pp. 371–378. Springer, Heidelberg (2014)
13. Sun, X.Y., Ji, P., Sun, L.Y., Wang, Y.L.: Positioning multiple decoupling points in a supply network. Int. J. Prod. Econ. **113**, 943–956 (2008)
14. Hedén, E., Tiedemann, F.: How to Improve the Inbound Flow of a Manufacturing Company: Analyzing and Refining the Customer-Driven Purchasing Method. Jönköping University, Jönköping (2014)

Information System as a Tool to Decrease the Economic Distortion in Trade Metrology

Bruno A. Rodrigues Filho[1,3], Mauricio E. Silva[1],
Cláudio R. Fogazzi[1], Marcelo B. Araújo[2,3],
and Rodrigo F. Gonçalves[3(✉)]

[1] National Institute of Metrology, Quality and Technology - INMETRO,
Duque de Caxias, Brazil
bafilho@inmetro.gov.br
[2] Federal Institute of Education, Science and Technology - IFSP,
São Paulo, Brazil
[3] Paulista University - UNIP, São Paulo, Brazil
rofranco@osite.com.br

Abstract. In economy, the amount of money due to an error of a measuring instrument used in trade is described as the economic distortion and this asymmetry is higher as the error involved. Repaired measuring instruments are responsible for a significant part of instruments used in the market. In Brazil, they are responsible for 64.8 % of fuel dispensers and 21.1 % of non-automatic weighing instruments used in trade, and they are subject to greater distortion once issues as impartiality and independence are involved in metrological control of these measuring instruments. In this study, an information system strategically aligned to legal control of measuring instruments was developed to map and identify repaired measuring instruments. Since the system implementation in 2012, an increase of 27.6 % is observed in after repair verifications of fuel dispensers and 104.8 % for non-automatic weighing instruments, contributing to decrease economic distortion in trade.

Keywords: Economics · Legal metrology · Market asymmetry · Information technology

1 Introduction

Legal metrology is a specific field in the science of measures, where regulations are applied on measurements, determining required characteristics and methods in measuring instruments that are relevant to a measure. Regulations change according to each country necessity however they are usually applied, in metrology, to instruments where trade, health and safety are involved [1].

Specifically in trade, the consumers have no means to check the amount of goods that is being traded, leading to an unfair competition as well as to consumer's protection issues [2], consequently leading to a lack of confidence undermining the relationship between consumers and suppliers. The impact of measuring instruments can be significant to a country, affecting a significant part of its Gross Domestic Product (GDP) [3]. The economic impact of measuring in trade can be realized in

© IFIP International Federation for Information Processing 2015
S. Umeda et al. (Eds.): APMS 2015, Part I, IFIP AICT 459, pp. 121–128, 2015.
DOI: 10.1007/978-3-319-22756-6_15

studies carried out in USA in 1996 that showed that measures represent the amount of 54.5 % of the GNP [4], and more recently in the United Kingdom where goods which value is based on a measure represented £622 billion in 2002 [2]. Impact studies have also presented that an average of 0.1 % error in measures would represent 0.05 % of GDP [5]. The substantial impact of measurements in the GDP of a country demonstrates the importance of developing tool to improve legal metrology control.

The legal control of measuring instruments is the tool used in legal metrology to maintain under control this asymmetry, using verifications and surveillance activities to keep these errors according to established in regulations.

This market asymmetry, i.e. the economic distortion between what is being traded and the measurement indicated by an instrument, indicates the monetary unit attached to an error in a measuring instrument [6]. In the macro economic scenario this indicator allows to obtain the amount of money under uncertainty due to measuring errors. This distortion is considerate one of the causes that can fail a market, where increasing accuracy of the metrology system increases the economic return [7], so an efficient way to decrease the economic distortion is vital to improve a nation economy. Moreover, the main aspect of the economic distortion indicator is to be a monetary representation of measuring errors, allowing comparisons among countries.

Repaired measuring instruments represent a significant number of instruments used in trade, as an example, in Brazil, 276,464 fuel dispensers were repaired in 2013, representing 64.8 % of total and 21.1 % of the 1,401,510 non-automatic weighing instruments in use [8]. The repaired instrument is an important part of the legal metrology control because when an instrument in the marked is repaired, its metrological performance is affected and a complementary verification, defined as after repair verification is necessary to attest if the errors are according to regulations, keeping the market under control. The commercial relationship involving repaired measuring instruments involves impartiality and independence issues once a body responsible for the repair evaluates its own service.

In order to decrease the economic distortion in trade due to repaired measuring instruments the present study aims to implement an information system align strategically to be used as a tool to decrease this asymmetry in repaired measuring instruments under the legal metrology control.

2 The Control of Measures in Trade

In most countries, metrology is centralized in a National Metrology Institute (NMI), responsible for regulation in legal metrology and maintenance of the national standards and laboratorial infrastructure to dissemination of traceability [1].

The activities to control the measuring instruments can be divided in three different levels [9]:

- Type approval an initial verification – Type approval comprehends the compliance of instrument features according to the regulations, before its production; and initial verification represents the assessment of the instrument, according to its legal requirements, after it is manufactured. Both are conducted before the instrument is put in the market.

- Periodic and after repair verification – Regulated measuring instruments are verified regularly in the market to attest the continuous attendance of the instrument to the legal requirements. After a repair, the instruments are also verified, once it may cause influence over its performance, affecting its reliability.
- Surveillance – This level represents the control of instrument in use in the market applied to identify frauds and misuses of regulated measuring instruments.

These actions in legal metrology are named as the legal metrological control activities and must be conducted in order to keep the reliability of measures in trade.

The NMI can delegate the verification and repair activities to notified bodies to either private or public bodies, as in France, where verifications are carried out by both public and private notified bodies [10] and in Brazil where verifications are executed exclusively by public bodies [11].

Another relevant aspect that must be pointed regards the repairs performed in measuring instruments by notified bodies. There are two approaches regarding a repair in a measuring instrument: the body responsible for the repair conducts the verification; or the NMI carries out the verification after the repair is executed. In the first case, there is a lack of impartiality once the body verifies its own repair. In the second situation despite after repair verification carried out by a third independent body, the measuring instrument is still in use right after the repair for an indeterminate period. This period depends on the infrastructure of the NMI to perform the after repair verification as soon as possible. Also, it is not possible to predict when or where a repair is going to be demanded. This aspect is vital to countries with large territories.

3   Information Systems

Information systems (IS) were introduced in organizations mainly to support managers [12]. The concept of an information system involves not only technical aspects of a system as the software or hardware, but also all the information flow, i.e. data and human resources [13].

The aspects of developing an information system are wider than developing software or a platform as it also incorporates human, administrative and organization aspects [14].

Strategy is also a significant component of success to implant an information system inside an organization. The misalignment between the organizations and IS strategies may lead to the inefficiency of the IS when compared to its full potential [15]. Consequently, to have full benefits of an efficient information system, the organization should be strategically aligned to the information system to be implemented [16].

Regarding the insertion of IS inside an organization, development of data process can be divided into six stages: initiation (I); contagion (II); control (III); Integration (IV); data administration (V); maturity (VI). The managing action to the progress of the IS starts with the initiation of the system within the organization passing throw contagion, control, integration, data administration concluding in the maturity stage. According to this model, the first stage represents the initialization of the system inside the organization, the users are not concerned about the system and the control is considered lax. As the system evolves inside the firm, in stage three (control), the management moves from the computer management to data resources management. In the final stage of growth, the system application is considered mature and the managements are focused on information flow [17].

In addition, the IS when properly lined up to the strategic requirements of the organization contributes to innovation [18].

4 Methodology

The system used to control repaired measuring instruments was incorporate in a specific website named PSIE - Portal de Serviços do Inmetro nos Estados (Platform of Services of Inmetro in States, literally). For simplicity, the system will be called hereinafter PSIE. The platform can be accessed in the link http://servicos.inmetro.rs.gov.br, and allowed to identify the location and the technical specifications of repaired measuring instruments. The authors were involved in establishing the requirements to the system according to legal metrology requirements in Brazil, coordinate the programmers' team, as well as to analyze the results in order to verify its impact in the after repair verifications.

In order to initiate a mandatory activity in legal metrology, a regulation development is necessary. Thus the project was divided into three well-defined steps:

- Step 1. Launching the system as voluntary for fuel dispensers in August 2012, in order to identify possible problems;
- Step 2. Developing and implementing regulation for bodies that execute repairs in fuel dispensers, issued in January 2013;
- Step 3. Expanding the regulation (to be issued in 2015) to notified bodies that provide repairs to measuring instruments used in trade (non-automatic weighting instruments, taximeters, length measuring instruments, and measuring systems for gaseous fuel).

The control of repaired fuel dispenser was set as a priority due to fraud events related to this instrument [19]. It would also be used as a test case to point out failures in the system, allowing improvements to the system to be applied to other instruments. Despite the regulation to be issued in 2015, the system is available since January 2013 as voluntary to non-automatic weighing instruments (NAWI).

No comparisons to other countries were conducted, once similar studies were not available, according to systematic literature review carried out in the legal metrology control [20].

4.1 Strategy Alignment

In order to develop the system that will monitor repaired measuring instruments used in trade, the strategic alignment between Inmetro (National Institute of Metrology, Quality and Technology), the Brazilian NMI, and the system was explored. Inmetro strategic guidelines are available for consult in the link: http://www.inmetro.gov.br/english/institucional/index.asp.

According to Inmetro strategy, the system has been developed to meet the necessities in metrology regarding competitiveness, fair competition and consumers' protection since its main objective is to decrease the economic distortion due to increase of after repair verification.

4.2 Using the Platform

When a bodied is notified by the NMI to be responsible for repairs in measuring instruments, it gets, for each technician, a unique password to access the platform. After a repair, the technicians have a five days deadline to inform the specifications of the repair, measuring instrument information, and address in the platform (as serial number, ID, number of type approval certificate and sealing marks). This deadline period was chosen due to regional aspects of Brazil, once it is a continental country and internet connection problems may occurs in remote regions.

The bodies responsible for verifications conduct after repair verifications using the information provided by the notified body, as well as the surveillance over the usage of the platform by the notified bodies.

5 Results and Discussion

A three level curve was obtained, where first level (A) represents the understanding and initialization of the system followed by a fast growth (second level) as the use of the system becomes more frequent (B), and finally a stabilized behavior where the number of repair fluctuates around an average (C). According to the six stages of processing growth, first level (A) of curve in Fig. 1 can be interpreted as stage I, which means the initialization of the system. Step two (B) is related to stage II and III as PSIE use proliferated and regulation was implemented. In step three (C), the curve stabilizes and

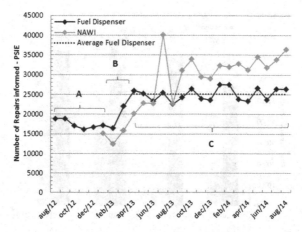

Fig. 1. Repairs informed to the PSIE by notified bodies for fuel dispensers from August 2012 to December 2014.

integration of repairs and after repairs verification is implemented representing stage IV. Data managing and full use of the system, including not only repairs in fuel dispensers would represent stages V and VI, and are next step to be achieved by the PSIE. The organization in this case can be interpreted as a composition of the National Metrology Institute and bodies responsible for repairs.

Figure 1 shows the number of repairs informed to the PSIE for fuel dispensers. The first level (A) can be observed from August (2012) - February (2013), second level (B) from February–April (2013) and third level (C) after April (2013), where repairs float around an average of 25,050.

For NAWI, a fast growth of the curve is not observed, regarding its voluntary use until 2015. A Pearson correlation coefficient $\rho = 0.6713$ characterizes the curve as still in the first level (A). A fast growth, similar to fuel dispenser repair, is expected during 2015 due to mandatory aspects of the PSIE to NAWI.

In 2012 (August–December) 87,740 repairs in fuel dispensers were informed in PSIE, in 2013 276,464 (January–December) repairs were informed and finally in 2014 that number increased to 315,013. For non-automatic weighing instruments, 295,624 repairs were informed in 2013 (January–December) and from January to December 2014 it increased to 405,668. A superior number of repairs in NAWI are expected when compared to fuel dispenser since 1,384,825 verifications were executed in NAWI compared to 363,803 in fuel dispensers, in 2014.

The number of after repair verifications in fuel dispensers and NAWI is exhibited in Fig. 2.

For fuel dispensers, an increase from 57,598 to 71,913 (24.8 %) comparing 2012 to 2011 and from 71,913 to 80,273 (11.6 %) in after repair verifications comparing 2013 to 2012. In 2014 it decreased from 80,273 to 73,551 is observed due to external aspects, once periodic verifications decreases 17.22 % as well. However, since the system implantation, comparing 2014 to 2011, an expansion from 57,598 to 73,551 (27.6 %) is observed for after repair verifications for fuel dispensers.

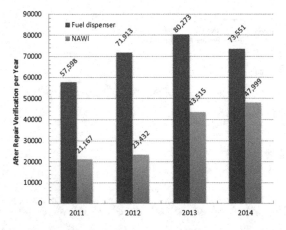

Fig. 2. After repair verification for fuel dispensers and non-automatic weighing executes from 2011 to 2014.

Regarding after repair verification in NAWI, a growth from 23,432 to 43,515 (85.7 %) comparing 2013 to 2012, and a growth to 47,999 (10.3 %) comparing 2014 to 2013. However, as the PSIE was implemented as voluntary in 2013, an increase 104.8 % from 2012 to 2014 is contemplated in NAWI.

As a consequence of after repair verifications, 6,300 fuel dispensers and 4,417 NAWI (considering accuracy class III and IV, up to 1,500 kg capacity) were rejected and were withdrawn of use in 2014.

6 Conclusions

The system presented in this study has shown an important tool to legal metrological control. After the implementation of PSIE, in 2012, an abrupt increase of 24.8 % was observed in after repair verification in fuel dispensers comparing to 2011. And an increase of 27.6 % is observed comparing 2014 to 2011.

Legal aspects were also a vital component to PSIE to succeed. It can be observed since the performance of the system has not shown the same efficacy to non-automatic weighing instruments when compared to fuel dispensers mainly because the PSIE is not mandatory to NAWI however a significant growth of 104.8 % in after repair verification in observed from 2012 to 2014.

The impact to the consumers can be realized in the 6,300 fuel dispensers and 4,417 NAWI rejected and withdrawn from market in 2014. Despite this significant result, a stable number of repairs to NAWI are still desirable. However, it can be interpreted that the system has been vital to this result.

Strategic alignment of PSIE to legal metrology, incorporating legal aspects in the regulation was also an important goal for the system, once three well-defined steps can be observed after the system implantation. Also, according to the six stages of growth of data processing in an organization, in this case an organization is composed of the NMI and bodies responsible for repairs, it can be conclude that the system is between stages III and IV, where proliferation and data processing are in course.

Finally, due to the increase of after repair verifications, inaccurate instruments are withdrawn from the market, consequently decreasing the economic distortion in the commerce. Once measuring instruments used in trade are according to regulation, they lead to fair competition, consumer's protection, contributing to the economic development.

It can be concluded that the PSIE has achieved its main objective since the increase of after repair verifications is responsible for decrease economic distortion once an abrupt growth is verified in after repair verifications for fuel dispensers. For NAWI this behavior has not been observed, mainly because of voluntary use of PSIE, However, a similar performance is expected after 2015.

Acknowledgement. The authors acknowledge the support of INMETRO, which enabled us to carry out this research.

References

1. De Silva, G.M.S.: Development of metrology in developing economies. OIML Bull. **XLVII**, 13–20 (2006)
2. Sanders, R.: Why do we regulate measuring instruments used for trade. OIML Bull. **LII**, 13–15 (2011)
3. Carstens, S.: AFRIMETS (Intra–Africa metrology system). OIML Bull. **LI**, 5–10 (2010)
4. Ardianto, R.: A way to stimulate public awareness. OIML Bull. **LII**, 33–38 (2012)
5. Birch, J.: Economic and social benefits of legal metrology. OIML Bull. **XLV**, 10–13 (2004)
6. Birch, J.: Benefit of legal metrology for the economy and society - a study for the international committee of legal metrology. In: International Organization of Legal Metrology - OIML, Paris, France (2003)
7. Swann, P.: The Economics of Metrology and Measurement. National Measurement Office, UK (2009)
8. Rodrigues Filho, B.A., Silva, M.E., Gomes, L.C., Soratto, A.N., Gonçalves, R.F.: Enhancements of the legal metrological control in Brazil due to after repair verification. In: 9th International Symposium "Metrologia 2014" Proceedings, p. 8, Havana, Cuba (2014)
9. Klenovsky, P.: Legal metrological control over measuring instruments in use: current situation. OIML Bull. **XLVII**, 22–33 (2006)
10. Lagauterie, G.: The evolution of the metrological control of measuring instruments in France. OIML Bull. **XLV**, 25–31 (2004)
11. Silva, P.P.A., Réche, M.M.E., Silva, M.E.: The legal metrology Brazilian model. Presented at the XVIII IMEKO World Congress - Metrology for a Sustainable Development, Rio de Janeiro, Brazil (2006)
12. Gupta, Y.P.: Management information systems planning: analysis and techniques. Technovation **9**, 63–81 (1989)
13. Alter, S.: Information Systems: A Management Perspective. Addison-Wesley Publishing Co., Reading (1992)
14. Keen, P.G.W.: Information technology and the management theory: the fusion map. IBM Syst. J. **32**, 17–38 (1993)
15. Henderson, J.C., Venkatraman, N.: Strategic alignment: leveraging information technology for transforming organizations. IBM Syst. J. **32**, 4–16 (1993)
16. Luftman, J.N., Lewis, P.R., Oldach, S.H.: Transforming the enterprise: the alignment of business and information technology strategies. IBM Syst. J. **32**, 198–221 (1993)
17. Nolan, R.L.: Managing the crises in data processing. Harv. Bus. Rev. **57**, 115–126 (1979)
18. Yang, M.L., Wang, A.M.-L., Cheng, K.C.: The impact of quality of IS information and budget slack on innovation performance. Technovation **29**, 527–536 (2009)
19. Brandão, P.: Contramedidas de hardware y software sobre el fraude de alta tecnología al Surtidor de combustible bajo el alcance de Metrología Legal. In: 9th International Symposium "Metrologia 2014" Proceedings, p. 8, Havana, Cuba (2014)
20. Rodrigues Filho, B.A., Gonçalves, R.F.: Legal metrology, the economy and society: a systematic literature review. Measurement **69**, 155–163 (2015)

Consumer Attitudes Toward Cross-Cultural Products in Convenience Stores: A Case Study of Japanese Food in Thailand

Supimmas Thienhirun and Sulin Chung[(⊠)]

Industrial Engineering and Management, Graduate School of Decision Science and Technology, Tokyo Institute of Technology, Tokyo 152-8550, Japan
{thienhirun.s.aa, chung.s.aa}@m.titech.ac.jp

Abstract. Recently, cross-cultural products are distributed to various countries. In Thailand, Japanese products are popular, especially food. Most of Thai people normally consume Japanese food in restaurants and street markets. On the other hand, Japanese food in convenience stores is not sold well comparing to Japan. In order to increase the sales of cross-cultural products, a case study of Japanese food has been conducted in order to understand consumer culture and behavior. Therefore, this research has investigated the attitudes and factors affected on decision making towards consuming Japanese food. Firstly, one-to-one interview is conducted to reveal consumer perception and behavior. Secondly, conjoint analysis is used to figure out importance values from consumer point of view.

Keywords: Cross-cultural · Japanese food · Convenience store

1 Introduction

When the world becomes globalization, the barrier across national boundary has been reduced. Various kinds of cross-cultural products are exported to other countries in order to expand business and introduce its own culture. Currently, ASEAN is one of growing markets that foreign investors are interested, especially, consumer goods. From the statistical survey across ASEAN countries, Thailand is classified as a promising market among other countries, the market size is large and has high potential of market growth rate [1]. Furthermore, around 30 % of Thai population in 2015 will belong to the group of medium to high income people which account for 20.63 million. These people are the main target who can afford cross-cultural products which are sold more expensive than local products. Therefore, selling cross-cultural products in Thailand tends to increase.

Due to the city life, people's lifestyle has been shifted from home-cooking to eating out. Therefore, the number of consumers who eat outside has been increased. With the popularity of Japanese trend, various kind of Japanese food are sold in restaurants and café, especially at the center of the city. Many campaigns and promotions are launched to boost up sales. Likewise, convenience stores also adapt Japanese strategies and launch campaigns related to Japanese mascots such as Hello Kitty and Doraemon.

© IFIP International Federation for Information Processing 2015
S. Umeda et al. (Eds.): APMS 2015, Part I, IFIP AICT 459, pp. 129–135, 2015.
DOI: 10.1007/978-3-319-22756-6_16

Recently, different kinds of Japanese foods and sweets are already available on shelf for consumers. Recently, in some branches of convenience stores in Bangkok has started offer made-to-order Japanese meals such as Udon, Katsudon and Chicken Teriyaki with a few seats inside the stores [2]. Therefore, consumers can sit and eat inside the provided area in a store for 24 h.

Even though Japanese food has become more popular in Thailand, Japanese food in convenience stores is not yet well recognized. Therefore, this paper has investigated the consumer attitudes toward Japanese food and identified the key factors of Japanese ready-to-eat food in order to increase the sale in convenience stores.

2 Cross-Cultural Research

Cross-cultural refers to the difference in cultures. Each country has unique or traditional culture which belongs to a specific group and passes from one generation to another generation by learning [3]. Hofstede and Minkov further stated in the dimensions of national cultures that some countries have different culture although they located in the same continent. For example, in Asia, Japan leans to individualism while Thailand leans to collectivism. From 1970 to present, many papers related to cross-cultural study between customer attitude and behavioral comparison have been published [5, 6]. The study of factors affected purchasing of new food comparing between U.K. and Chinese consumers showed that healthy and food quality were revealed as the primary factors for both countries [7]. Besides, in the study of predicting consumer's aesthetic taste for cultural products, the researchers found that consumers who are past oriented trend to prefer cultural product of old generation [8]. Thus, making these group of consumers adapt to cross-cultural products might be a challenging issue. Cross-cultural products can be referred as the products come from other countries that have different cultures. However, these products might be made in originated countries or other countries but still represent the culture from origins. For example, Onigiri, the traditional Japanese rice ball wrapped with dry seaweed is sold widely in various countries but consumers still perceive this product originated from Japan [4]. When the products are not fitted with consumer culture, it leads to the loss in business. For example, Walmart, a big retailer in U.S. used to cooperate with 7–11 in Japan and had introduced some products such as tomato sauce and Jam to Japanese consumers. However, these products were not sold well because the size of tomato sauce (1,000 ml.) is too big and the taste of Jam is too sweet for Japanese consumers [9]. In addition, characteristics of Japanese consumer might be different from U.S. consumers as they put more emphasis on small packaging and product quality more than low-price products. In addition, when environment and situation change, consumer preferences have changed as well [10].

3 Trend of Japanese Food in Retail Store in Thailand

Typically, retail stores can be classified as traditional and modern retailing. In Thailand, modern retailing is accounted for approximately 40 % of retail market [1]. This type includes supermarkets, hypermarkets, department stores, shopping malls and

Table 1. Comparing purchase frequency and available Japanese products between traditional and modern retailing (adapted from Kawazu [1]; data collected from October to November 2011)

Thailand	Traditional Retailing			Modern Retailing				
	Fresh food market	Nearby traditional store	Grocery store	Super market	Hyper market	Department store	Shopping mall	Conve nience store
Purchase frequency	11.0	6.7	15.7	3.2	3.2	1.9	2.0	16.4
Available product	F*	None	S*, D*	F, RTE, S, D	F, RTE, S, D	All	All	RTE, MTO*, S,D

F: Fresh materials imported from Japan such as seafood and vegetables

RTE: Ready-to-eat Japanese foods refer to food which is packed in a package.
The customers can open and eat it immediately or/and warm it before eating.
MTO: Made-to-order Japanese foods refer to food which is cooked after customer ordering
S: Japanese snacks and desserts
D: Drink category such as Japanese Green tea and Hokkaido milk
Remark * means a product is available in some branches.

convenience stores. On the other hand, traditional retailing includes fresh food markets, nearby traditional small stores and grocery stores. In urban areas, majority are small retail stores due to the high land price, while in rural areas the stores are larger. Comparing among modern retailing types in Table 1, convenience stores revealed the highest percent rate of use with the approximate purchase frequency 16.4 times per month among others. Furthermore, classification of Japanese products for each location has been shown including fresh ingredients, ready-to-eat foods, made-to-order foods, snacks and drinks. With the culture and lifestyle, traditional retail stores often sell Thai products rather than cross-cultural products. However, only snacks and drinks are available in some branches of grocery stores around city areas. In fresh food market, only some places sell fresh ingredients from Japan to the customers such as sweet potato, saba and salmon. For modern retailing group, department store and shopping mall normally sell all 5 types of Japanese products. However, supermarket and hypermarket do not offer made-to-order Japanese food, while it is available in some branches of convenience stores.

In Thailand, especially Bangkok, various kind of Japanese restaurants in department stores are opened nowadays which are mostly recognizing brands from Japan where focused on healthy and fresh cuisine. Recently, as convenience stores in some branches offer similar products as sold in Japan such as bento box and made-to-order Japanese meals, the sales of the stores have been increased but not as high as in Japan.

4 Survey of Consumer Attitudes Toward Japanese Food in Thailand

In this research, the data were gathered by using interview method. 34 people who worked and lived in Bangkok areas were interviewed one by one for approximately 20 min because only branches of convenience in Bangkok sell made-to-order and ready-to-eat Japanese food. The outline of interview was mainly divided into 4 sections; (1) made to order food and (2) ready to eat food in convenience stores, (3) made to order food and (4) ready to eat food in other places except convenience stores. Firstly, participants were briefly explained about the outline of the interview. After that the participants were asked whether they get familiar with Japanese food or not in order to classify participant background. Moreover, before conducting this survey, pilot test had been done to figure out the problem during the interview which lead to an improvement of the interview question and outline structure.

In each section of the interview, the participants were asked to write about 3 things related to the topic about Japanese food in different places if they have tried it before. For example, "Write down 3 things when thinking about made-to-order Japanese food in convenience stores". However, if participants never try it, they will not be requested to answer this question. In addition, they were asked about what kind of Japanese food they eat, where and when they normally had Japanese food. In the last part of the interview, 9 cards from conjoint analysis related to ready-to-eat Japanese food had been shown to the participants and let them rank the most to the least preferable card themselves. Conjoint analysis is the popular method used in market research to identify the key attributes from customer viewpoint [11]. Therefore, in this research 4 attributes were selected in which each attribute has 3 levels as presented in Table 2. The examples of the card are presented in Fig. 1.

Table 2. Attributes in conjoint analysis

Attribute / Level	Price	Taste	Design	Calories
1	Low (10-30 Baht)	Japanese	Clear plastic	Less (<400 Kcal)
2	Medium (31-50 Baht)	Thai	Letter	Medium (401-800 Kcal)
3	High (51-70 Baht)	Mixed	Colorful picture	High (>801 Kcal)

No. 3

Price: 31-50 Baht
Taste: Thai e.g. Tom-yum-kung onigiri, Chili paste onigiri
Design: Colorful with picture
Calories: less (Less than 400 Kcal)

No. 7

Price: 51-70 Baht
Taste: Thai and Japanese e.g. Tom-yum salmon Ramen, Salmon spicy salad onigiri
Design: Letter on plastic package
Calories: less (Less than 400 Kcal)

(a)   (b)

Fig. 1. Examples of conjoint cards (a) adapted from http://www.catdumb.com, (b) adapted from www.quitecurious.com

5 Result and Discussion

From the interview, majority of participants consumed made-to-order Japanese food every month. Most of them explained that Japanese food was quite expensive. Therefore, they normally ate it on occasion with family or friends at Japanese restaurants around both city areas and in department stores. However, some of participants who really love Japanese food mentioned that they ate it every week. Around 70 % of participants ate made-to-order Japanese food for dinner after work and for lunch or dinner during weekend because they had plenty of time to enjoy meals at the restaurants. Approximately 50 % of participants have tried ready-to-eat Japanese food at street markets while 35 % purchased at supermarkets. Most of them consumed it for lunch and dinner but seldom ate it because they perceived it was not fresh and tasty. Besides, they mentioned that the quality of the product was not good. Similar to the result of ready-to-eat Japanese food in convenience stores, the participants claimed it did not look tasty. They explained further that consuming ready-to-eat food was not good for their health because they thought that it contained preservative and was not fresh. Therefore, only 40 % of participants bought ready-to-eat Japanese food at convenience stores mostly in the afternoon and at night when they were really hurry. Lastly, as convenience stores in Thailand recently launched made-to-order Japanese food, the result revealed that less than 10 % of participants tried it in which most of them ate it for breakfast and lunch. Some participants did not know that the convenience stores offer made-to-order Japanese food and in Bangkok due to only a few branches of convenience stores sell this products. However, participants who knew but did not try it because they thought that the food might not be tasty and expensive comparing to made-to-order Thai food in street markets and canteens.

After asking participants about the first 3 things when thinking about made-to-order Japanese food in other places except convenience stores, 35 words were collected. The most frequent mentioned words were sushi, sashimi, salmon, tasty and expensive as shown in Fig. 2. For ready-to-eat Japanese food in convenience stores and other places, most of the participants wrote about onigiri, sushi and convenience. As a few participants tried made-to-order Japanese food in convenience stores, only 2 repeated words were collected, katsudon and udon. This result showed that most of the participants recognized sushi and sashimi as representative made-to-order Japanese food in the restaurants and street markets which quite expensive. In contrast, katsudon and udon were written because the participants might try these made-to-order food in convenience stores. Besides, onigiri and convenience were the most mentioned word about ready-to-eat Japanese food regardless of any location.

The result of conjoint analysis showed that the taste was the most important value among other attributes, followed by design, price and calories (Table 3). Furthermore, card number 7 as shown in Fig. 1 had the highest total utility of 6.303 ($Y_7 = 5.078 - 0.118 + 0.784 + 0.284 + 0.275$). With this result, ready-to-eat Japanese food sold in convenience stores should be emphasized on the taste of the product in order to match with Thai preference. This result is corresponding with the study of customer perception about chain restaurants in Bangkok, in which taste was the second concerned attributes apart from the convenience location [12]. The taste of Japanese

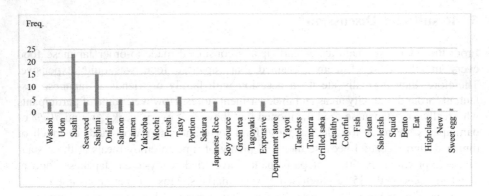

Fig. 2. The frequency of mentioned words about made-to-order Japanese food in other places except convenience stores

and Thai flavor was found as the highest utility score. In contrast, the product with Thai flavor only was not preferable because the participants were able to find it on street market and in office canteen. Besides, some participants preferred authentic Japanese taste because it was hard to find traditional Japanese cuisine in Thailand. For packaging, the letter label on a transparent packaging was preferred to leave space for showing product inside. The participants mentioned that when the product was made with a good taste and they could see the ingredients inside a package with a nice label, they preferred to buy it. The price and calories were revealed in the same direction, the less number of calories and price was preferred. Also, majority of participants also mentioned that the ready-to-eat food should be fresh and does not contain preservative.

Table 3. Importance value from conjoint analysis

	Important values
Taste	27.799
Design	24.932
Calories	23.066
Price	24.203

6 Conclusion

This research presents attitudes of consumer toward cross-cultural product, Japanese food in convenience stores. From this study, the important factors when consumers make a decision to buy Japanese food related to intrinsic values including freshness, taste and health. The result from conjoint analysis for ready-to-eat food showed both taste and design were precedence over others which was analogous with the result from past literature reviews [7, 12]. Besides, one cultural reason that Thai consumers did not commonly purchase Japanese food in convenience stores in Bangkok related to collectivism. Most of consumers normally eat with friends and family at the restaurants or canteen while only a few seats available in convenience stores. In a contrast, Japanese are individualism which means consumers tend to eat individually. As this study limited participants only in Bangkok, the future research will focus on a large nationwide survey and applying choice architecture tools to influence consumer to consume more Japanese food in convenience stores.

References

1. Kawazu, N.: Consumer Trends and Expansion of Retail Markets in Growing ASEAN Economies, pp. 6–13. Nomura Research Institute, Tokyo (2013)
2. Easybiznezz. http://www.easybiznezz.com
3. Hofstede, G., Hofstede, G.J., Minkov, M.: Culture and Organization: Software of the Mind. McGraw Hill, New York (2010)
4. Stack Exchange. http://japanese.stackexchange.com
5. Guerrero, L., et al.: Consumer-driven definition of traditional food products and innovation in traditional foods. A qualitative cross-cultural study. Appetite **52**, 345–354 (2009)
6. Nagashima, A.: A comparison of Japanese and U.S. attitudes toward foreign products. J. Mark. **34**, 68–74 (1970)
7. Eves, A., Cheng, L.: Cross-cultural evaluation of factors driving intention to purchase new food products- Beijing, China and south-east England. Int. J. Consum. Stud. **31**, 410–417 (2007)
8. Holbrook, M.B., Schindler, R.M.: Age, sex and attitude toward the past as predictors of consumers' aesthetic tastes for cultural products. J. Mark. Res. **31**, 412–422 (1994)
9. Yoshinobu, S.: Some reasons why foreign retailers have difficulties in succeeding in the Japanese market. In: International Retailing Plans and Strategies in Asia. Haworth Press, New York (2004)
10. Yau, O.H.M.: Consumer Behavior in China: Customer Satisfaction and Cultural Value. Routledge, New York (1994)
11. IBM cooperation: SPSS conjoint **22**, 1–10 (2013)
12. Kessuvan, A., Akanit, R.: The perceived service quality of chain restaurants in Bangkok. In: 12th SARD Workshop, Bangkok, pp. 248–267 (2014)

Logistics Issues in the Brazilian Pig Industry: A Case-Study of the Transport Micro-Environment

Sivanilza Teixeira Machado[1], Irenilza de Alencar Naas[1(✉)],
João Gilberto Mendes dos Reis[1], Rodrigo Couto Santos[2],
Fabiana Ribeiro Caldara[2], and Rodrigo Garófallo Garcia[2]

[1] Postgraduate Studies Program in Production Engineering, Paulista University,
Dr. Bacelar St. 1212, São Paulo, Brazil
sivateixeira@yahoo.com.br, irenilza@gmail.com
http://www.unip.br
[2] Agricultural Sciences Department, Federal University of Grande Dourados,
Rod. Dourados Itahum, Km 12, Dourados, Brazil

Abstract. Inadequate thermal characteristics inside a truck during livestock transport might lead to an important decrease meat quality and increase swine mortality. This study aims to assess the microenvironment characteristics of the pig transportation truck in tropical regions. These characteristics involve air temperature, relative humidity, wind and vehicle speed, and noise level. The present study compares two pig transportation schedules by assessing the ambient and pig surface temperature, and calculating the environmental temperature and humidity index (THI). The surface temperature was recorded using a thermal camera. Results showed that thermal characteristics inside the truck varied between the farm and the slaughterhouse plant ($p < 0.0489$). The unloading process at the slaughterhouse plant impacted the pigs surface temperature ($p < 0.027$) more than the loading management at the farm.

Keywords: Pig transport logistic · Hot weather · Pre-slaughter management

1 Introduction

The key factor in a pre-slaughter logistics chain is the transportation system. The main links of the chain are the farm, transport and slaughterhouse plants. Transportation is essential throughout production. Typically, pigs are sent to the slaughterhouse plant by the farmer through some intermediaries not necessarily well trained in taking good care of the animals [1]. Maximizing the management between each supply chain component will help to minimized losses; therefore, reducing the weight loss in livestock transportation is an essential element in the meat supply chain. The pre-slaughter logistics scheme is presented in Fig. 1.

S.T. Machado—The authors wish to thank the CAPES.

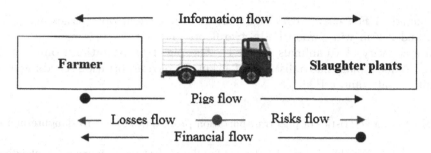

Fig. 1. Pre-slaughter logistics

High air temperatures and humidity impact negatively livestock production and animal welfare [2,3]. The micro-climate inside the truck affects livestock production and animal welfare. Climate changing impact has led to global warming of approximately 1°C in the last 30 years affecting regional hydrological systems and agribusiness including livestock production [2,4]. Brazil is the world fourth-largest pork producer and export [5] and the country is located in a tropical and sub-tropical region. The country swine herd is nearly 40 million heads, and approximately 80 % of the production is concentrated in three main regions South, Southeast and Midwestern of Brazil [6]. High air temperatures and humidity impact negatively livestock production and animal welfare [2,3]. Pre-slaughter logistics exceed the boundaries of the farm, and it involves mostly animal transportation [7,8]. The thermal environment inside the truck lead to a loss in live weight, especially in large animals during long distances [9].

A major problem that farmers and slaughterhouse plants face is to determine the alignment between the slaughterhouse plant capacities with the pre-slaughter logistics, to comply with several issues, including animal welfare [7,10]. Several slaughterhouse plants adopt the pigs transportation at night, due to the incidence of high temperatures during the day [11]. However, slaughterhouse plants production logistics usually imply in receiving the pig loads during the day, generally under the hot weather. At the slaughterhouse plant (final node of the chain), vehicles often have to queue while waiting to unload the pigs. Long queues at the slaughterhouses delivery point often cause problems for drivers and also negatively affect the animal welfare. Brazilian law required a total fasting time up to 24 h [12] and animals under fasting time after above 24 h must be fed. As this condition implies in the extra management of pre-slaughter logistics, it is avoided. Brazilian logistics performance adopts two different ways: (i) animals arrival at night are slaughtered in next morning; and (ii) animals arrival at morning are slaughtered in the afternoon.

Considering that while pigs are transported the truck microenvironment is a critical issue, this study aimed to assess the variation in the truck thermal conditions during two schedules in the afternoon.

2   Methodology

The present study used hybrids finishing pigs from a commercial farm located in Espírito Santo State, Brazil (6°20′4′S, 35°18′33′W). The experiment was conducted in February 2015. Pigs were transported in open truck with 7 m long and 2.45 m wide, wood body, two floors and two compartments per floor with a capacity of 70 animals (Table 1). The pigs transportation from farm to slaughterhouse plant had a distance of 45 km. Two transportation schedules were monitored at 1 and 4 P.M.

Table 1. Characteristics of pigs transportation process from farm to slaughterhouse.

Period (P.M.)	Weight of pigs (kg)	1st floor (kg/m^2)	2nd floor (kg/m^2)	Loading (min)	Journey (min)	Unloading (min)
1:11 at 2:57	123	260.0	246.0	24	75	7
3:45 at 5:18	120	254.1	240.0	18	60	15

2.1   Animals, Pre-slaughter Handling, and Variables Recorded

A total of 140 finishing hybrid pigs (Landrace and Large White) had feed deprivation of six hours. During the loading process, the animals were moving in groups of six pigs. Pigs were moving from the pens to the truck on a hallway with a concrete floor until the wood dock that gave them access to the truck. The difference in the material of floor made the pigs stop in front of the dock. In this occasion, handlers used a kind of rattle to guide pigs inside the truck. The overall stocking density was $250 \, kg/m^2$ [8,10]. Pigs were sprinkled with water before the truck started moving to the processing plants. In the slaughter plant, pigs were unloaded, moving from the truck to the waiting pens. In these pens, the pigs remain a minimum of eight-hour in rest until the slaughter. During the fasting time, the transportation process and the rest the pigs had access only to water for 15 h.

The variables ambient air temperature (AT), relative humidity (RH), wind speed (WS), truck speed (TS) and noise (N), and animals surface temperature (ST) were recorded. A data logger (Testo model 174H) recorded the variations in air temperature and humidity relative inside of truck during pigs transportation. The recording of wind speed and the noise was done using an anemometer (Krestel, Nielsen-Kellerman Co., US) and decibel meter (Testo model 815, Testo Co., Germany). The pigs surface temperature was assessed using a thermal infrared camera (Testo model 875, Testo Co., Germany). The measurements were taken every 5 min [13], during the logistics of the pre-slaughter phase, except the surface temperature that took place during the loading and unloading of animals. The thermal images were taken from the lateral of the truck in randomly select pigs located on the first and second truck floors. The measurement of AT and RH started with loading of the first animal and finished with unloading of the last animal [10]. The measurement of WS, TS and N were taken when the truck started moving from the farm to the slaughterhouse.

2.2   Thermal Environment, Surface Temperature Analysis, and Statistical Method

THI (Eq. 1) allows the assessment of pigs thermal comfort during transportation. The wet bulb temperature was calculated using RH as input in the software Psicrom [14].

The temperature humidity index (THI) was calculated as suggested by [15].

$$THI = 0.45WT + 1.35AT + 32 \tag{1}$$

The average values of ST (°C) were determined by selecting 40 points within the thermal image and using the software Testo Software IRSoft, Version 2.5 adopting the emissivity of the pig skin equal to 0.95.

Data from the data logger were transferred to Excel and analyzed using Statistical Analysis System, version 9.0 [16] by Means and General Linear Models procedures. The THI values were calculated for the region climatic condition and inside studied sites (farm, truck, and slaughterhouse). Means of THI and ST of pigs were tested using T-test adopting a confidence value of 95 %.

3   Results and Discussion

No difference was found between the variables assessed during the pigs transportation process, except to RH ($p = 0.018$). According to the recommended by [17] the THI should be between > 57 and < 62. In the present study, the schedule of pigs transportation during the afternoon is unsuitable for the animals (Table 2).

Table 2. Average values of temperature (AT), relative humidity (RH), temperature and humidity index (THI), wind speed (WS), truck speed (TS) and noise (N) during pre-slaughter logistics.

Period (P.M.)	AT (°C)	RH (%)	THI	WS (m/s)	TS (k/h)	N (dB)
1 : 11 at 2 : 57	36.33	35.75[b]	91.76	0.94	47.0	81.13
3 : 45 at 5 : 18	36.03	41.05[a]	91.85	0.76	40.6	84.46

ab = Means with the same letter do not differ ($p > 0.05$).

The truck micro-environment is determined by AT, RH and WS [13]. However, other variables also affect the truck microenvironment during transportation, such as stocking density, size, weight and age of animals, and vehicle motion. The monitoring procedure showed the variation in temperature and relative humidity during the transportation of pigs in three moments within two periods: loading, journey, and unloading (Fig. 2).

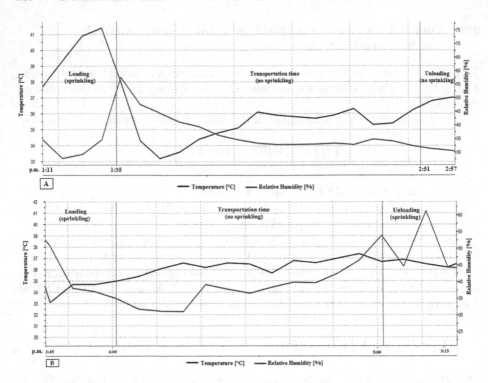

Fig. 2. Monitoring of air temperature (°C) and relative humidity (%) during pigs transportation from the farm to the slaughterhouse from 1:11 to 2:57 P.M. [A]; and from 3:45 to 5:18 P.M. [B].

Despite the variation be similar to both schedules of transportation, in the first transportation during the loading of animals, AT increased in 4.1°C. With water sprinkling during loading AT values inside the truck decreased 8.2°C. ST was not affected by sprinkling, but stress signs in pigs were observed [10]. In the present study, during the pigs transportation process AT increased gradually 2.5°C. During the unloading process AT increase 1°C.

Throughout the second schedule of transportation, AT increased 1.9°C during loading and 1.7°C during the journey. AT inside the truck decreased 0.7°C when water sprinkling of the animals was done before unloading at the slaughter plant. The thermal comfort varied 4.63 between farm and slaughter plant ($p < 0.0489$). The variation can be associated with the transportation process. No difference was found between the sites truck and slaughterhouse. However, truck and slaughter plant show different ambient THI values from the regional ones (Table 3). Such values indicate that both farm and meat processing industry should invest in environment control.

AT and RH are variables responsible for the thermal comfort and welfare of livestock, and they may affect animals ST ($p < 0.0001$), Fig. 3.

Table 3. Temperature humidity index (THI) values for the sites inside the farm, the truck and the slaughterhouse plant.

	Regional	Farm	Truck	Slaughterhouse
THI*	84.88^b	86.75^{ab}	90.92^a	91.38^a

ab = Means with the same letter do not differ ($p > 0.05$).

Finishing pigs have difficulty to dissipate sensible heat, and it worsens when pigs are in heat stress due warm weather. Some action needs to be adopted by the pig supply chain to minimize this issue such as water sprinkling, adoption of forced ventilation, and improvement in the thermal material in the construction of the truck body. Pigs surface temperature increased 0.7°C in the first schedule of transportation and 1.7°C in the second schedule (Table 4). Results agree with the threshold of surface temperature observed by [10] in pigs transported during hot weather (30.1 − 38.7°C).

Loading activities are preceding transportation process and the pigs ST has been affected by region and farm THI. Unloading activities ($p < 0.027$) occurred after transportation, and pigs ST were mostly influenced by the variables microenvironment inside the truck, time of transportation and region climate [9,11]. Also, pigs transported on the second floor of the truck (mean = 40.1) showed a difference of 1.2°C when compare pigs located on the first floor (mean = 38.9). [13] showed an increasing of dead pigs with increase the ST after transportation.

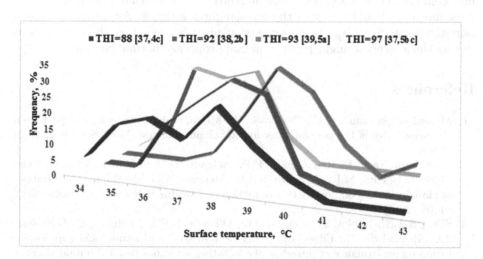

Fig. 3. Effects of temperature humidity index (THI) at pre-slaughter logistics on the surface temperature (ST) of pigs in two-schedules of transportation.

Table 4. Average values of the surface temperature (ST) of pigs during loading and unloading.

Period (P.M.)	Number	Activity	Minimum	Maximum	Average	THI
1 : 11 at 2 : 57	34	Loading	35.1	39.6	37.5^c	95.06^a
	26	Unloading	36.5	40.0	38.2^c	
3 : 45 at 5 : 18	36	Loading	34.4	40.1	37.4^c	91.61^b
	34	Unloading	37.0	43.0	39.1^a	

Number = total of animals assessed per activity.
abc = Means with the same letter do not differ ($p > 0.05$).

4   Conclusions

Transport of livestock requires special care, becoming a challenge logistic issue along the chain. In developing countries, the available transport infrastructure is relatively poor with inappropriate maintenance. Inadequate logistics services are associated not only with product loss but also with the spread of disease at different stages of food supply chain. Although logistics risk in livestock production covers a wider scope, this study focused on the element transportation from the node farm to the node slaughterhouse plant, with the focus on the truck microenvironment.

Adequate environmental control might reduce the effect of the temperature humidity index on pigs surface temperature, leading to increase the animal thermal comfort and welfare. The present study concludes that pigs farmers and pork industry should invest in the pre-slaughter logistics. Adopting the transport the livestock during the morning or at night is needed, as those operations during the afternoon might provide an inappropriate thermal comfort.

References

1. Miranda-de la Lama, G.C., Villarroel, M., María, G.A.: Livestock transport from the perspective of the pre-slaughter logistic chain: a review. Meat Sci. **98**(1), 9–20 (2014)
2. de Alencar Naas, I., Romanini, C.E.B., Salgado, D.D., Lima, K.A.O., do Vale, M.M., Labigalini, M.R., de Souza, S.R.L., Menezes, A.G., de Moura, D.J.: Impact of global warming on beef cattle production cost in Brazil. Scientia Agricola **67**(1), 01–08 (2010)
3. Silva, B.A.N., Noblet, J., Donzele, J.L., Oliveira, R.F.M., Primot, Y., Gourdine, J.L., Renaudeau, D.: Effects of dietary protein level and amino acid supplementation on performance of mixed-parity lactating sows in a tropical humid climate. J. Anim. Sci. **87**(12), 4003–4012 (2009)
4. Intergovernmental Panel on Climate Change: Climate change 2014: synthesis report. Technical report, Intergovernmental Panel on Climate Change, Geneva, (2014). http://www.ipcc.ch/
5. Foreign Agricultural Service: Livestock and poultry: world markets and trade. Technical report, United States Department of Agriculture (2014)

6. Instituto Brasileiro de Geografia e Estatística: Produção da pecuária municipal (2011). http://www.ibge.gov.br
7. de Oliveira, L.M.F., Yanagi Jr., T., Ferreira, E., de Carvalho, L.G., da Silva, M.P.: Bioclimatic mapping of southern Brazilian region for animal and human thermal comfort. Engenharia Agrícola **26**(3), 823–831 (2006)
8. Amaral, A.L., Silveira, P.R.S., Lima, G.J.M.M., Klein, C.S., Paiva, D.P., Martins, F.: Boas práticas de produção de suínos. Technical report, Empresa Brasileira de Pesquisa Agropecuária (2006). http://www.cnpsa.embrapa.br
9. Silva, I.J.O., Vieira, F.M.C.: Ambiência animal e as perdas produtivas no manejo pré-abate: o caso da avicultura e corte brasileira. Archivos de Zootecnia **59**, 113–131 (2010)
10. Kephart, R., Johnson, A., Sapkota, A., Stalder, K., McGlone, J.: Establishing sprinkling requirements on trailers transporting market weight pigs in warm and hot weather. Animals **4**(2), 164–183 (2014)
11. Bench, C., Schaefer, A.L., Rushen, J.P., Passill, A.M., Faucitano, L., Lewis, N., Gonyou, H., Bergeron, R., Widowski, T.: Welfare implication of pig transport journey duration: scientific background of current international standards. Technical report, Agriculture and Agri-Food Canada (2008)
12. BRASIL: Regulamento da inspeção industrial e sanitária de produtos de origem Animal (1952). http://www.agricultura.gov.br
13. McGlone, J., Johnson, A., Sapkota, A., Kephart, R.: Temperature and relative humidity inside trailers during finishing pig loading and transport in cold and mild weather. Animals **4**(4), 583–598 (2014)
14. Roriz, M.: Psicrom 1.0 software Relações Psicométricas (2003)
15. Roller, W.L., Goldman, R.F.: Response of swine to acute heat exposure. Trans. ASAE **12**(2), 0164–0169 (1969)
16. Statistical Analysis System: SAS/STAT 13.2 Users Guide (2014)
17. Leal, P.M., Naas, I.A.: Ambiência Animal, 1st edn. Unicamp, Campinas (1992)

Design of an Integrated Model
for the Real-Time Disturbance Management
in Transportation Supply Networks

Günther Schuh[1], Volker Stich[2], Christian Hocken[2(✉)],
and Michael Schenk[2]

[1] Laboratory for Machine Tools and Production Engineering (WZL),
RWTH Aachen University, Aachen, Germany
[2] Institute for Industrial Management (FIR),
RWTH Aachen University, Aachen, Germany
{christian.hocken,michael.schenk}@fir.rwth-aachen.de

Abstract. In recent years supply chain participants are increasingly suffering the effects of disturbances in transportation supply chains. Both, dynamics in consumer demands and global supply chains lead to a growth in unplanned supply chain events. These can cause from rather manageable disturbances through to complete break-downs of transportation chains, resulting in high follow-up and penalty costs. Consequently, concepts for an efficient supply chain disturbance management are needed, preferably with a real-time identification and reaction to disturbance events. Therefore in the following paper the research results of the German research project Smart Logistic Grids with the focus on designing an integrated model for the real-time disturbance management in transportation supply networks are presented. This includes the introduction of elaborated classification models for disturbances and action patterns as well as an associated costs and performance measurement system. Finally, a procedure model for the disturbance management is presented.

Keywords: Supply chain management · Supply chain disturbances · Supply chain resilience · Supply chain event management · Disturbance management

1 Introduction

The complexity of transportation supply chains is steadily increasing by the rising global cross-linking of production and sales regions. They are increasingly exposed to worldwide occurring disturbances. On the other hand the requirements of in time delivery and supply chain security a rising [1–3].

The complexity of this development affects not only strategic considerations of supply chain participants, but is also a constant component of their daily business. High requirements on all levels, from the supply chain design top-down to the supply chain execution, need to be fulfilled. The supply chains currently show obvious deficiencies in managing disturbances within their transportation networks. One reason for this situation can be deduced by the missing understanding of disturbances and their impacts on the transportation network as well as by the missing assessment and

© IFIP International Federation for Information Processing 2015
S. Umeda et al. (Eds.): APMS 2015, Part I, IFIP AICT 459, pp. 144–151, 2015.
DOI: 10.1007/978-3-319-22756-6_18

application of reaction patterns. Another reason for this deficiency can be found in the shortcoming of applicable supporting ICT systems. Current systems cannot stand up to the increasing requirements, because their functional scope can neither provide the necessary real-time disturbance identification nor returning valuable action patterns with the required excellence [4, 5].

The German research project Smart Logistic Grids is one research example with the focus on overcoming these weak points by designing an integrated model for the real-time disturbance management in transportation supply networks and implementing this model within a software-based disturbance management system [5]. In the following work, the results of the model design are presented. Therefore in the following to chapters, the project itself as well as the methodological approach is described. In the main chapter four the integrated model is presented and finally, an outlook on further research within the project is given.

2 The Project Smart Logistic Grids

The project Smart Logistic Grids aims at developing a system for a cross-company disturbance management as well as ensuring improved information availability and a smooth integration of all supply chain partners. The application focus is on industries with a low production depth, e.g., the automotive industry, which rely on a functioning value-adding network. In these transportation supply chains, disturbances pose a high risk for production strategies such as Just-in-time and Just-in-Sequence [6] (Fig. 1).

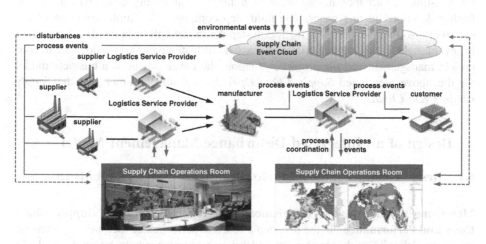

Fig. 1. Vision of the research project smart logistic grids [6]

Therefore, the main targets of the research project are the development of an integrated model for the real-time disturbance management in transportation supply networks as the necessary theoretical basis and its integration into a software-based *Supply Chain Operations Control Center* and *Supply Chain Event Cloud*.

The *Supply Chain Operations Control Center* focuses on the compilation and visualization of disturbances and action patterns, based on real-time data generated by the logistic network. It represents a central control station and generates action patterns for occurring disturbances, based on an elaborated costs and performance measurement system.

A central *Supply Chain Event Cloud* provides therefore processed information where all supply chain partners have access to. Operating this cloud requires the recording of the entire logistic network's conditions at any time. Required information will be collected by integrating entirely real-time data such as RFID and GPS data. Additionally, further information will be used for calculating the network status, e.g., order, weather and traffic data.

3   Methodological Approach and Preliminary Works

The methodological approach for the model design is subordinated to the overall approach of the research project. The project itself is divided into ten work packages which can be subsumed into five main project steps. The first step includes the requirement definition for disturbance management in transportation supply chains, the deduction of use cases for the later field testing and the identification of relevant events and disturbances in supply chains, related action patterns as well as important key performance indicators. The first project step has taken place in close collaboration with the industrial partners of the research project. The second step forms the core part of the project as it focuses on the design of the integrated model for an integrated model for real-time disturbance management in transportation supply chain which will be further described in this paper. The third step comprises the implementation of the model into software, whereas in the fourth step the model will be applied and evaluated in several field tests with industrial partners. The fifth step includes, besides the overall project management and the project evaluation, the development of a business model for the above mentioned *Supply Chain Operations Control Center* and the *Supply Chain Event Cloud*.

4   Design of an Integrated Disturbance Management Model

4.1   Design Elements of the Integrated Disturbance Management Model

Measuring the Impacts of Disturbances and Action Patterns on Supply Chain Costs and Performance. In the first step a cost and performance measuring system for the evaluation of disturbance impacts and action patterns needs to be established. [7] regard therefore the three target figures logistics costs, capital lockup and logistics performance. Capital lockup represents the opportunity costs as a result of committing liquid assets in industry stocks, so that they cannot be invested on the financial market. It is measured as sum of the products of material costs and material units on stock in each time step. As the presented research work is focusing on disturbances and action patterns in transportation supply chains, capital lockup can be neglected, as it is neither affected by the above introduced disturbances nor the corresponding action patterns. Logistics costs result by summing up the costs for production as well as the unit-based stock holding and backorder costs for each time step. Production costs result from the value-adding processing of products. In logistic processes, equivalent costs arise by planning and executing transports, so that in this context, these occurring costs can be defined as process costs. In the context of this project, backorder costs are the most tangible cost values besides the process costs. They are depending on the delivery date deviation and represent follow-up and penalty costs, e.g., using alternative means of transport or contract penalties, caused by a deviation from the agreed delivery date [8].

The logistics performance measures a company's delivery performance that is defined by delivery date deviation between the agreed and actual delivery date. It arises as a result of the total material order quantity and the resulting backlog of unfulfilled order quantities. By contrast to logistics costs and capital lockup, the supply service level evaluates the supply chain performance.

Furthermore, an additional category was introduced to value the ecological impact of effects on the transportation supply chain. Therefore the CO_2 emission has been chosen as an adequate key performance indicator.

The following figure shows the overall measurement system for the integrated model of an adaptable transportation supply chains and provides a manageable assessment tool for disturbance impacts and action patterns (Fig. 2).

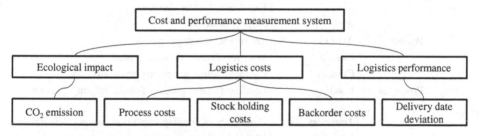

Fig. 2. Measurement system

Modelling Disturbance Reasons and Impacts. Generally, disturbances (both their reasons and impacts) are deduced as a pattern of simple events that means a logical combination of simple events, based on time and place of occurrence. Therefore, a classification model for events in transportation supply chains and a deduction of resulting disturbance types needs to be developed.

For the first classification model the events and their relations are represented using an UML class diagram, which gives the possibility to show different relation types between categories and events.

The developed diagram includes four event levels that become more specific from the upper to the lower level. The first three levels represent categories for aggregating the events, while the fourth level shows actual events. When an attribute applies to all underlying events it is hold in this level. As every event can be described by the occurrence probability, the place and the expected duration (see Fig. 3), all these

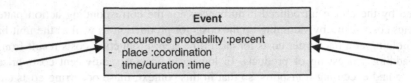

Fig. 3. Event type

attributes are allocated to the top level, which only consists of the general and theoretic event.

Disturbance events can be divided into the categories environment, traffic, politics and process, which form the second level of the diagram. For enhanced transparency and to introduce attributes in a higher level, a third level with further specializations has been included (see Table 1). Meanwhile, the fourth event level shows the actual events.

Table 1. Event classification

Level 1	Level 2	Level 3	Level 4
Event	Environment	Storms	Storm, extreme rain, fog, snow
		Natural disasters	Seismic events, fire (wood)
	Traffic	Train	Traffic disruptions, station closures
		Road	Traffic jam, road works, accident, stoppage
		Sea	Flood, ice, harbor closure
		Air	Airport closure
	Politics	Attacks	Terrorism, sabotage, piracy
		Unrests	War, revolution, rioting, strikes
		Customs	Customs delay, temporary transport ban
	Processes	Loading	Loading failure, picking failure, missing loading aids
		Transport	Deficiency of loading capacities, wrong deliveries
		Material	Material defects, material quantity deviation

As outlined before, disturbances can be described as complex events that result from a combination of the previous described events and the reference to an actual transportation order. Hence, the disturbances are always connected with the transportation order path of the underlying transport network. As a result of the research work the disturbances can be divided in the following five main disturbance archetypes:

- Transportation delay on a supply chain relation (disturbance reason)
- Resource shortfall (good, loading aid, carrier) for a transport (disturbance reason)
- Demolition or damage of transported good (disturbance reason)
- Transport arriving delay in a supply chain node (disturbance impact)
- Transport departure delay in a supply chain node (disturbance impact)

Modelling Action Patterns. Based on the preliminary work of identification of typical action patterns with the project partners an adequate classification for action patterns was elaborated as shown in Table 2.

Table 2. Action pattern classification

Type of disturbance	Action pattern	Activity level					
		Proactive			Reactive		
		Supply chain planning and control level					
		stra	tact	oper	stra	tact	oper
Transportation delay on specific transport relations	Consideration of temporary/permanent disturbances (e.g. road works)	X	X				
	Preliminary customer information			X			X
	Re-scheduling of transportation routes		X	X		X	X
	Detouring disturbed relation /node						X

Therefore in a first step, possible action patterns need to be assigned to the previously defined three disturbance types. Further, the action patterns have been divided in proactive and reactive actions corresponding to the activity level. That means that action patterns can either be used as reactive measures in case of an occurring disturbance or as preventive measure to reduce disturbance occurrences. As a further characteristic for classification, the planning and control level of the specific action pattern in terms of a strategic, tactical or operative measure should be determined.

The application of this classification system for action patterns can be seen in the following table as an excerpt for action patterns corresponding to transportation delay related disturbances.

4.2 Aggregation of the Design Elements into an Integrated Approach for the Disturbance Management in Transportation Supply Chains

Based on the above introduced design elements a comprehensive approach for the disturbance management in transportation supply chains has been elaborated which consists of the following three steps:

1. Disturbance identification
2. Analysing and evaluating the disturbance impacts
3. Preparation and application of action patterns

The *disturbance identification* subsumes real-time data identification from the material flow, the planning system as well as the contextual information, e.g. traffic or weather, in a close and timely proximity of shipments in the network as well as the identification of effects on shipments by quantifying effect relations.

The aim of *analysing and evaluating the disturbance impacts* is to determine a prognosis of delivery date deviations on the next node and eventually inform about the occurrence probability as well as resulting costs.

Depending on the measurement system, different *action patterns* can be proposed. Action patterns normally do not affect the transported resources anymore. Instead, the following transhipment will be rescheduled or the shipment will be transported by a faster mean of transport.

The following figure will therefore show a comprehensive view of the model approach. In this case, based on a real-time disturbance identification the overall delivery date deviation is issued with five days. The model identifies and proposes different action patterns ("Do nothing" vs. "Use faster modality") and indicates the resulting costs and performance values (Fig. 4).

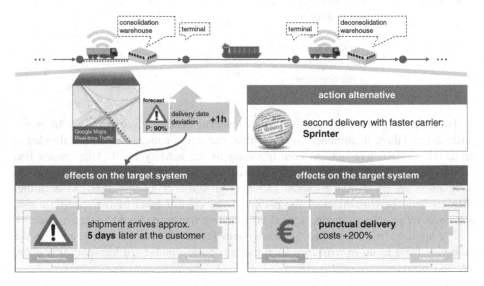

Fig. 4. Example for the integrated disturbance management approach

5 Conclusion and Outlook

The rising vulnerability of globalized supply chains combined with the dynamics in consumer demand patterns lead to increased requirements for coping with supply chain disturbances. Focusing this problem, the presented work shows an eligible design of an integrated disturbance management model for transportation supply chains. It includes classification systems for disturbance events and action patterns as well as a measurement system for valuing both impacts. Finally, these model elements were consolidated in an integrated approach for an efficient disturbance management. All results have been evaluated with the project partners and an extended group of associated industrial companies.

In the further progress of the research project the shown model will be implemented into software based on the existing software PSI*global*©. For the generation of complex disturbance events as described in chapter 4 the Java based rules language Prova is used. Following, the software development the model and software will undergo a multi-level field testing. Starting with tests in an experimental environment based on historical order and disturbance data as far as pilot testing in the daily business of the industrial project partners.

Acknowledgement. The authors would like to thank the Federal Ministry for Economic Affairs and Energy for the kind support within the research project „Smart Logistic Grids" (BMWi; funding code: 19 G 13002C).

References

1. Deloitte: Supply Chain Resilience: A Risk Intelligent Approach to Managing Global Supply Chains, p. 7. Deloitte, New York (2012)
2. The Business Continuity Institute: Supply Chain Resilience 2011 - An International Survey of More Than 550 Organizations from over 60 Countries, Which Considers the Causes and Consequences of Disruption, the Techniques and Approaches to Identify Key Supply Chains, and Methods to Gain Assurance of Resilience Capability. The Business Continuity Institute, Reading (2011)
3. Henke, M., Lasch, R., Eckstein, D., Neumüller, C., Blome, C.: Supply Chain Agility. Strategische Anpassungsfähigkeit im Supply Chain Management, p. 10. Bundesvereinigung Logistik (BVL) e.V., Bundesverband Materialwirtschaft, Einkauf und Logistik e.V. (BME), Bremen (2012)
4. Rice, J.B., Caniato, F.: Building a secure and resilient supply network. Supply Chain Manage. Rev. **7**(5), 22–30 (2003)
5. Schenk, M., Stich, V.: Managing supply chain disturbances–review and synthesis of existing contributions. In: Grabot, B., Vallespir, B., Gomes, S., Bouras, A., Kiritsis, D. (eds.) Advances in Production Management Systems. Innovative and Knowledge-Based Production Management in a Global-Local World, pp. 262–269. Springer, Heidelberg (2014)
6. Prestifilippo, G., Hocken, C., Schmitz, S., Schenk, M.: Smart logistic grids: Entwicklungeines Risikomanagementsystems. Anpassungsfähige multimodale Logistiknetzwerke durch integrierte Logistikplanung und –regelung. Unternehmen der Zukunft **14**(2), 32–34 (2013)
7. Schuh, G., Stich, V.: Produktionsplanung und-Steuerung 1. Grundlagen der PPS. Springer, Berlin (2012)
8. Fischäder, H.: Störungsmanagement in netzwerkförmigen Produktionssystemen. Deutscher Universitäts-Verlag, Ilmenau (2007)

The Responsiveness of Food Retail Supply Chains: A Norwegian Case Study

Heidi C. Dreyer[✉], Natalia Swahn, Kasper Kiil,
Jan Ola Strandhagen, and Anita Romsdal

Department of Production and Quality Engineering,
Norwegian University of Technology and Science, 7491 Trondheim, Norway
heidi.c.dreyer@ntnu.no

Abstract. This paper describes a case study which highlights responsiveness in a Norwegian retail supply chain. The dynamics in the conventional food market is increasing which is seen in online and multichannel shopping concepts, a wide range of campaigns and promotions, and demographic changes. While the conventional food supply chains are designed to handle large product volumes efficiently, this might impact on the responsiveness. This study explores the relation between the responsiveness and demand pattern in Norwegian food retail supply chains, and identifies key principles for the associated planning and control models.

Keywords: Supply chain responsiveness · Food retail supply chain · Case study · Demand variability

1 Introduction

In Norway the conventional food supply chain is serving a dynamic marketplace with a broad range of different consumer segments claiming high service levels and low prices. Consumers look for convenience and alternative ways to buy food, such as online shopping and home deliveries. The complexity of the dynamic market is amplified by the characteristics of food products, e.g. short shelf life, temperature and weather sensitivity, and strong seasonal features (Ivert et al. 2014).

The conventional food supply chain has responded to the market dynamics by developing highly industrial processes. Over the past decades the main supply chain strategy has been to restructure production facilities, warehouses, distribution centres and stores to handle large product volumes efficiently, becoming less responsive as a result (Hübner et al. 2013). However, the need of the supply chains to adapt to rapidly changing market environment is increasing (Thatte et al. 2013). Hübner et al. 2013 point out the misalignment of supply and demand in the retail supply chain and the need for planning and control models in order to coordinate the wide range of decisions.

This study explores the relation between the responsiveness and demand pattern in Norwegian food retail supply chains, and identifies key principles for the associated planning and control models.

© IFIP International Federation for Information Processing 2015
S. Umeda et al. (Eds.): APMS 2015, Part I, IFIP AICT 459, pp. 152–160, 2015.
DOI: 10.1007/978-3-319-22756-6_19

2 Supply Chain Responsiveness and Flexibility

The organization's ability to adjust to market dynamics is one of its core capabilities, and the means to achieve competitive advantage (Bernardes and Hanna 2009; Lee et al. 2004). The key concepts in this respect are responsiveness and flexibility (Reichhart and Holweg 2007). Responsiveness tends to be linked to the changes of behaviour required by the system's external environment. It also includes some time or effort dimension, such as speed of response (Thatte et al. 2013). In this study, responsiveness is defined as a system performance capability to timely change behavior in response to external stimuli. Flexibility, in turn, is defined as an operating characteristic and a system's ability to change status within an existing configuration of pre-established parameters enabling the system to be responsive.

This distinction between internal flexibility and requirements for responsiveness is reflected in Reichhart and Holweg's (2007) conceptual framework where the external factors which require the system to be responsive, and the internal factors, which enable the system's responsiveness, are identified. This perspective of responsiveness presents a comprehensive overview of other relevant literature on the subject, and their work has also been recognized in more recent literature (Bernardes and Hanna 2009). Therefore, it has been operationalized into tangible measures (the study's analytical framework) by supporting literature (Table 1).

The analytical framework specifies the definition of the external and internal factors together with operational measures allowing evaluation of the required responsiveness. *Demand uncertainty* is related to changes in mix and volume. *Demand variability* is related to uncertainty, yet is different since large swings in known demand will still require responsiveness. *External product variety* can directly increase the need for mix responsiveness, potentially increasing demand forecast error. *Lead time* compression increases the need for responsiveness as less time is available to respond to customer orders. Internal factors that enable responsiveness can be separated into operational factors and supply chain integration. *Demand anticipation* and the accurate forecast increases ability to respond to customer requirements. *Manufacturing flexibility* can reduce production lead time and change-over times for products. *Inventory* can both increase and decrease the responsiveness of supply chains. It is linked to customer order decoupling point (CODP). *Product architecture/postponement* determines where CODP is placed, and thus how responsiveness can be achieved. *Information integration* can reduce demand uncertainty and variability by reducing demand amplification and eliminating delays due to slow information flow. *Coordination and resource sharing* reduces demand uncertainty and variability by removing delays and unnecessary activities. *Organisational integration* has a major impact on trust thus affecting a variety of interaction between supply chain members. *Spatial integration and logistics* lead to the reduction of transport lead times and strengthens process coordination and organisational integration by moving supply chain partners physically closer together or implementing infrastructural improvements.

Table 1. Elaboration of external and internal factors (Ivert et al. 2014; Romsdal 2014; Chopra and Meindl 2013; Thatte et al. 2013; van Donk et al. 2008; Reichhart and Holweg 2007; Min et al. 2005).

	Definition	Operational measure
External requirements		
Demand uncertainty	Stems from volume/mix changes in customer demand	Stability in volume; stability in mix; degree of campaigns
Demand variability	Large swings in demand	Stability in volume; seasonality
External product variety	The number of SKUs available to at any point in time	Number of SKUs; service level; change in product portfolio/NPI
Lead time compression	Required or expected response time to fulfil a customer order	Shelf life; delivery time
Internal determinants *Operational factors*		
Demand anticipation	How accurately products are forecasted	Forecast error; safety stock
Manufacturing flexibility	The degree to which operations is capable of changing without compromising throughput time	Ability to handle changes in: volume, mix., deliveries, and product portfolio/NPI
Inventory	Inventories as buffer against demand uncertainty	Inventory allocations and levels
Product architecture/postponement	The postponement of differentiation	Order complexity; CODP; customer base complexity
Internal determinants *Supply chain integration*		
Information integration	Transparency and information availability within the supply chain	Use of information exchange between supply chain partners
Coordination and resource sharing	How processes are coordinated across firm boundaries	Joint problem solving; speed of communication
Organizational integration	Integration of information, monetary and material flow	Type of relationship between partners/level of trust
Spatial integration and logistics	Logistical proximity which reduces lead-times	Infrastructure; physical distribution

3   Methodology

The purpose of the study is to explore the relation between the responsiveness of the food retail supply chains in Norway and the demand pattern. Since it is limited to the retailer perspective, an explorative single case study has been chosen. The strength of the case study methodology is the ability to study in-depth elements and relations in real-life situations which often can be highly complex (Yin 2009), and, by this to explore new phenomena (Eisenhardt 1989). The food retail supply chain of Coop Handel has been selected because its supply chain is comparable to the other retailers. Coop Handel is one of three big Norwegian food retailers: NorgesGruppen (40 %),

Coop Handel (22 %), and Rema (24 %) (Nielsen 2015). The supply chain structure of the retailers is quite similar with a strong wholesaler unit (a combination of centralised and decentralised warehouses) and a trade unit (different stores and concepts).

Data for the case study has been collected and triangulated through interviews, point-of-sales data, orders requirements, insight to internal terms and conditions, and workshops.

4 Coop Handel

Coop is a consumer cooperative, owned by over 100 Norwegian cooperatives. The organization consists of a wholesaler and retailer unit, which together supply 796 stores. The stores are profiled under 5 different concepts, and are supplied either from the central warehouse, from one or several of the regional warehouses or a combination of centrally and regional storage. In the following sections the data from the case study is described and structured according to the framework developed in Sect. 2.

Table 2 shows the uncertainty and variability of demand and the causes (seasonality, market activities, product range and product launches). In Figs. 1 and 2, variation in all the three parts of the supply chain is seen. First, there is a variation between store concepts, time periods and the product mix and volume. Second, Table 2 demonstrates the role of supply uncertainty relative to the quality of raw materials. Third, Table 2 show the lead time compression and the shelf life restrictions impact delivery frequency, though the impact depends on the localization and the size of the store.

Table 2. The external factors in the Coop supply chain

	Supply Chain
Demand uncertainty	*Stores:* Changes in mix and volumes due to campaigns and loyalty card offerings, weather and seasonality. Differs between the five concept stores, store localization and size. Figure 2 illustrates the uncertainty for one of the five concepts. *Wholesaler:* Changes in mix and volumes due to seasonality, campaigns. About 10 % of the products are at any time on campaigns. *Supplier:* Changes in mix and volume. Supply uncertainty due to raw material quality
Demand variability	*Stores:* Demand variability is observed especially in regards to the stores' demand at the warehouse and the warehouse's demand towards the suppliers as seen in Fig. 1. *Wholesaler:* Variability in purchased volume and mix. *Supplier:* Variability in volume and mix
Product variety	*Stores:* Varies. SKU: Coop OBS! – 9.800; Coop Mega – 10.900; Coop Extra – 7.800; Coop Prix – 6.800; Coop Market – 6.800. The service level varies between the SKU's with 97 % on average. *Wholesaler:* About 38.000 SKU. Product are launched 3 times/year. *Supplier:* Varies between some few up to 100
Lead time compression	*Stores:* 2 days lead time. Daily delivery to big and central stores. Min. 3 deliveries/week to other stores. Min. 1/3 of the remaining shelf life left when delivered to the store. *Wholesaler:* 1 day delivery time. Min. 2/3 of the remaining shelf life left when delivered to the wholesaler. *Supplier:* 1 day delivery time

An observation from Table 3 is that volume flexibility in the supply chain is determined by the production and stocking principles (capacity utilization and service level requirements) and the push supply, which is supported by economic incentives (pallet and full load discount). However, the table also shows that when and how products are delivered is decided by the inventory structure (location, CODP and stock level), the fixed transport schedule and the full load requirements which impact flexibility. The broad product range and the number of SKU have a positive impact on mix flexibility. At the same time, ordering principles (AVS, store planogram, transport and delivery frequency) regulate what and when a store is ordering. Figures 1 and 2 show the gap between the consumer demand and store replenishment procedures.

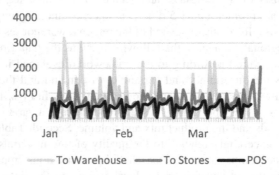

Fig. 1. 'POS' reflects what the demand to the consumers, 'to stores' reflects what have been delivered from the warehouse to the stores, and 'to warehouse' reflects what have been delivered from the suppliers to the warehouse. There is a clear sign of varying demand, especially to the stores and to the warehouse.

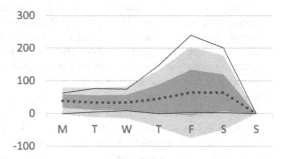

Fig. 2. The dotted line represents an average demand at one store concept for three months. The dark gray area is ±1 stdv., light gray is ±2 stdv., the thin black lines are min. and max. values. Demand uncertainty, especially towards weekends, also observed at other store concepts.

Table 4 shows that there is collaborative fundament for sharing information and for integrating processes in the supply chain, which positively impact the flexibility (transport hub, supplier organization). However, the table also shows a potential for

Table 3. Internal factors in the Coop supply chain

	Supply Chain
Demand anticipation	*Store:* The average shelf level is between A (not under 40 % of sale), B (not under 30 % of sale) or C (not under 10–20 % of sale) products. The goal is an average of 97 % service level. *Wholesaler:* The average stock level is 3 days (max 5–8), but differs with regard to product, season and market. The stock level is used as a buffer for demand variability and uncertainty. Forecast error is not used systematically to adjust parameters. *Supplier:* Use forecasts and historical sales to estimate demand
Manufacturing flexibility	*Store:* Product variety is decided by the store concept. Low mix flexibility. *Wholesaler:* Purchase to stock. Volume flexibility in picking and packing and mix flexibility at the central warehouse because fully automated mix palletizing, but mix flexibility is reduced since orders with full pallets or loads are discounted. Small stores can order a mix crate but achieve no discounts. Fixed delivery schedules (time and date). *Supplier:* Volume flexibility because of make-to-stock production. Limited mix flexibility caused by set up cost and time
Inventory	*Store:* Automated replenishment of dry, frozen and some chilled products. Manually ordering of fruit/vegetables (F&V) based on last period sale, corrected for stock level information and campaign. All products have a min. stock level/push stock. *Wholesaler:* Driven by scale and volume principles. Fixed stock level and stock order-up-to replenishment principles. Yearly volume and discount contracts with suppliers and weekly call-offs. *Supplier:* Stock of raw materials and finished goods
Product architecture/postponement	*Store:* The order size is driven by volume discounts and varies by store concept, localization and size. Min. delivery frequency is 2–3 times/week. Product shelf life varies from a few days to several weeks/months. *Wholesaler:* Product mix flexibility because of the broad product range. CODP: central warehouse, regional warehouse or at the supplier. Decided by type of product and order volume. *Supplier:* Pick and packs to order

sharing information that can improve production and transport planning. It is evident that transport, inventory, replenishment, planning and control, and information and communication technology are integrated in some parts of the supply chain (wholesaler, freight forwarder and store).

Table 4. Supply chain integration in the Coop supply chain

Information integration	The wholesaler and stores shares POS data and stock level information as input to the automatic replenishment system. Campaign information is shared with the stores 2 weeks in advance. Some suppliers receive forecasts 6–8 weeks in advance. Most of the orders are automatically exchanged; portal solution
Coordination and resource sharing	Transport to stores and from F&V suppliers, organized by the wholesaler. Vendor management inventory is implemented for selected suppliers. Collaboration between the suppliers of F&V
Organizational integration	A transport hub coordinates inbound and outbound transport. The wholesaler distributes the majority of the products from suppliers
Spatial integration and logistics	Inventory infrastructure: central and regional warehouses. The transport network: 2–3 freight forwarders and a fixed transport schedule. Automatic warehouse operations (pick by voice), and fully automated mix pallet packaging at the central warehouse. The replenishment system: modules of advanced forecasting and business intelligence. Orders from stores are transmitted through a portal

5 Discussion

The analysis of Coop in the previous sub-section shows the relation between the supply chain responsiveness and demand varies in the food. Demand variability in thefood supply chain can be observed (Fig. 1), which is a similar observation made in other studies such as Ivert et al. 2014 and Romsdal 2014. However, this study additionally shows the demand variability in the different parts of the chain, between the store concepts and time periods. Even though measuring the level of demand variability is outside the scope of the paper, some research literature (Thatte et al. 2013; Olhager 2013) supports our assumption that the variability will become more evident. For the food supply chain, this means that managers should be prepared for handling uncertainty, variability and lead time compression, caused especially by variations in the product shelf life and by broadness of the product range.

The current strategy for dealing with the demand variability is to use inventory and stock levels as a buffer. Products are produced and stored in high volumes and at several locations in the supply chain, which additionally allows the retailers to source, collect and distribute efficiently and achieve product availability. Yearly contracts and discounts determine the total volumes sourced from suppliers and by weekly call-offs based by economic quantities and batch sizes principles impact on the supply chain flexibility (transport schedule, delivery terms and conditions, store planogram). The transport schedule is fixed and set to optimize such criteria as volume, cost, distance, opportunity for return shipment and full pallets. Altogether, these practices impact the order structure. Since there is a discrepancy between the consumer demand pattern and how the store is replenished, and because of the short shelf life of some products, there are reasons for questioning whether the existing strategy is sustainable for achieving overall supply chain responsiveness. To be more responsive and aligned, we suggest that the planning and control models should be developed along the following dimensions:

- Integrated planning between production, inventory and replenishment according to consumer demand pattern
- Advanced models for forecasting and demand scenario simulation
- Control principles for dynamic order management
- Methods for reducing batch size, optimal order quantity and load units
- Differentiated supply chains: by store concept, store size and region
- Information sharing between all actors in the supply chain

6 Conclusion

This study analyses the responsiveness in the food retail supply chain based on a theoretical framework of responsiveness and a case study of a Norwegian retailer. The findings show range of market dynamics and how they are met by a volume, inventory and efficiency strategy. The study also shows that product flow in the supply chain is very much driven be fixed rules and principles designed in order to be efficient and to gain scale benefits which impact on the mix flexibility. Since the shelf life is restricted for many of these products we propose that the strategy should be changed and aligned according to the selling pattern in the store. Since this study is limited to a few products we recommend that future studies include a broader product range.

Acknowledgement. The research is supported be The Research Council of Norway and the Retail Supply Chain 2020 project.

References

Bernardes, E.S., Hanna, M.D.: A theoretical review of flexibility, agility and responsiveness in the operations management literature: toward a conceptual definition of customer responsiveness. Int. J. Oper. Prod. Manage. **29**, 30–53 (2009)

Chopra, S., Meindl, P.: Supply Chain Management: Strategy, Planning, and Operation. Pearson, Boston (2013)

Eisenhardt, K.M.: Building theories from case study research. Acad. Manage. Rev. **14**(4), 532–550 (1989)

Hübner, A.H., Kuhn, H., Sternbeck, M.G.: Demand and supply chain planning in grocery retail: an operations planning framework. Int. J. Retail Distrib. Manage. **41**(7), 512–530 (2013)

Ivert, L.K., Fredriksson, A., Johansson, M.I., Dukovska-Popovska, I., Damgaard, C.M., Kaipia, R., Tuomikangas, N., Dreyer, H.C., Chabada, L.: Sales and operations planning: responding to the needs of industrial food producers. Prod. Plann. Control **26**, 280–295 (2014)

Lee, H.L., Padmanabhan, S., Whang, H.L., Padmanabhan, H.L.: Information distortion in a supply chain: the bullwhip effect. Manage. Sci. **50**, 1875–1886 (2004)

Min, S., Roath, A.S., Daugherty, P.J., Genchev, S.E., Chen, H., Arndt, A.D., Glenn Richey, R.: Supply chain collaboration: what's happening? Int. J. Logistics Manage. **16**, 237–256 (2005)

Nielsen: Daglivarerapporten 2015 (2015)

Olhager, J.: Evolution of operations planning and control: from production to supply chains. Int. J. Prod. Res. **51**, 6836–6843 (2013)

Reichhart, A., Holweg, M.: Creating the customer-responsive supply chain: a reconciliation of concepts. Int. J. Oper. Prod. Manage. **27**, 1144–1172 (2007)

Romsdal, A.: Differentiated production planning and control in food supply chains, p. 16, Norwegian University of Science and Technology, Faculty of Engineering Science and Technology, Department of Production and Quality Engineering (2014)

Thatte, A.A., Rao, S.S., Ragu-Nathan, S.S.: Impact of SCM practices of a firm on supply chain responsiveness and competitive advantage of a firm. J. Appl. Bus. Res. **29**, 499–530 (2013)

Van Donk, D.P., Van Der Vaart, T., Akkerman, R.: Opportunities and realities of supply chain integration: the case of food manufacturers. Br. Food J. **110**, 218–235 (2008)

Yin, R.K.: Case Study Research: Design and Methods, 4th edn. Sage Publications, Thousand Oaks (2009)

Application of Mass Customization in the Construction Industry

Kim Noergaard Jensen[✉], Kjeld Nielsen, and Thomas Ditlev Brunoe

Department of Mechanical and Manufacturing Engineering, Aalborg University,
Fibigerstraede 16, 9229 Aalborg East, Denmark
knj@m-tech.aau.dk

Abstract. This paper is based on the assumption of that Danish companies in the construction industry can benefit from the advantages inherent in the use of Mass Customization.

Mass Customization is a production strategy that focuses on offering customized products, at a low cost. Exploiting of principles in Mass Customization, like standardization of modules, configuration and flexible production, makes it possible using a variety of tools to composing and producing customized products for commercializing at similar conditions as serial produced standard products.

The research contribution of the project is to clarify the situation of "where we are today" and to determine the development potential for the companies, and since it is early days in the project, the statistical material will improve when involving more companies in the workshops.

Keywords: Mass Customization · Construction industry · Increased productivity

1 Introduction

The construction industry employs approx. 25 % of the private workforce in Denmark, and the industry is currently facing a number of challenges, including a lot of burden on costs that makes companies continuously searching for initiatives to reduce production costs to meet competition.

The productivity in the Danish construction industry has doubled since 1966, which is significantly less than the construction industry in other European countries, but also less compared to other sectors in Denmark (Fig. 1).

Increasing industrialization has achieved results in other industries in Denmark in terms of increasing productivity. We interpret increased industrialization as increasing utilization of new technologies for production, streamlining and constant development of production processes and other correlated support processes.

One of the reasons that construction industry having less degree of industrialization is that construction industry, opposite the standardized products that formed the basis for the industrial revolution, is very different and often one-of-a-kind, and therefore it may seem difficult or challenging to streamline and optimize processes as "assembly line production" [1, 3]. However, over the past decades, industrial production has gone

© IFIP International Federation for Information Processing 2015
S. Umeda et al. (Eds.): APMS 2015, Part I, IFIP AICT 459, pp. 161–168, 2015.
DOI: 10.1007/978-3-319-22756-6_20

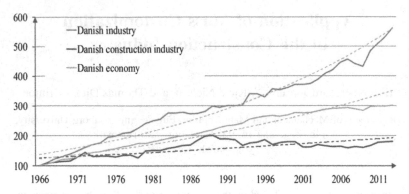

Fig. 1. Labor productivity by industry, unit cost and time (Year (index 1966 = 100, 1966-price level chain figures) [Statistics Bank NATP23])

through a process in which more and more companies are offering customized products [9] "at a price near mass production [1]" under the production strategy called Mass Customization [7]. The construction industry's traditional demand for customization e.g. distinctive architecture, function, quality, timeframe, environment, is difficult to reconcile with traditional industrialization (standardization, mass production). However, Mass Customization characterizes the requirement of flexible products and processes.

In Mass Customization, applied IT tools like automated business process, product configurators, flexible production processes, and product design allows customization where the end customer can choose from millions of product variants and chose the flavor that just matches unique needs for a low price (cost minimization) [5, 7]. These principles are widely and with great success used in e.g. automotive and computer industry [7, 8].

The applied principles behind Mass Customization enable industrial production of customized products [7], and for the construction industry, a great potential may result in applying these principles, as they face the challenge of producing products with high variance and often one-of-a-kind production [5].

Some segments of the construction industry have already implemented parts of Mass Customization where manufactures of windows, doors, kitchen, housing, and bath products for example offering customized products manufactured in a highly automated and flexible production [2, 4].

A current research project has as one of the objectives to increase knowledge and utilization of Mass Customization in Danish construction industries. The objectives are to make Danish companies in the construction industry capable of implementing the principles of Mass Customization leading to increasing industrialization and productivity.

Recent research shows that companies that utilize Mass Customization must have three fundamental capabilities [8]:

1. "Solution Space Development; the ability to identify how customer requirements are different and develop products that can effectively adapt to these individual requirements through the product platforms or modularization"

2. "Choice Navigation; the ability to guide the customer to select or configure the product that matches his requirements"
3. "Robust Process Design; the ability to efficiently to produce a large batch of products at low cost that typically is achieved by using the flexible manufacturing systems"

Furthermore, the objectives of the project are to develop these three capabilities for companies in the construction industry by utilization of Mass Customization. These companies will be able to realize a greater growth potential, as they will be able to meet the needs from their customers faster and at lower cost [6].

This may also lead to, and increase in the ratio of exports in those companies, because development of capabilities focusing on a greater share of the market [6].

In relation to the three capabilities, the project includes for each of the companies the following activities organized as conferences, networking, and workshops [8]:

- Solution Space Development
  - Make a screening of the current product structure to determine to which extent modularization id used and identifying the variety in the product portfolio.
  - Choose areas, e.g. specific parts of products where the company can benefit from using modularization in a short and a long term to gain competitive advantages.
- Choice Navigation
  - Identify opportunities for application of product configuration for sale and specification of products in a sales situation, and
  - To develop prototypes of configurators
- Robust Process Design
  - Analysis of current production processes to identify the potential of automation (business processes and physical production processes) and the use of flexible manufacturing equipment
- General
  - Together with the company, to conduct workshops where the knowledge gained about the tools and methods incorporated on selected specific areas.

The participating companies will during the project gain knowledge and skills in tools and methods to utilize, so after the participation they are able to properly using the tools for Mass Customization.

The innovation potential of the participating companies is to be able to meet the customers demand for unique products cost effectively, by:

- Develop new and more cost-effective business and production processes
- Develop products customized more efficiently than traditional building products.

Apart from the innovation objectives in the project, there are also formulated research objectives. The research objectives are to analyze how companies in the Danish construction industry can typically benefit from utilizing Mass Customization principles. Furthermore, the objective is to identify which specific challenges these companies typically face when implementing Mass Customization, since it is expected by the authors that these challenges are different from those met in the general manufacturing industry. Finally, the objective is to adapt methods for enhancing the performance within Mass Customization, so that they are applicable in the construction industry. This paper addresses the first two research objectives, by discussing the potential in applying Mass Customization and some of the initial challenges.

This paper summarizes the result of two workshops done in corporation with a number of companies that are a part of the supply chain of the construction industry. The workshops are mapping the involved companies according to their current and their expected future position of Mass Customization relative to their competitors, and expectations of their customers.

The innovative contribution for all of the participating companies is to increase the knowledge of tools and methods used for Mass Customization, which leads to increasing productivity. The research contribution is to clarify the situation of "where we are today" and to determine the development potential for the companies.

2   Workshop Approach

The methodology includes a number of companies participating in workshops concerning the following themes of Mass Customization:

- Mapping Mass Customization
- Mapping Product Varity

The findings from the workshops summarizes in Sect. 4 "Results" and the content of the workshops are as described in the following.

2.1   Variety-Volume Mapping of Mass Customization

Each company was at the workshops asked to plot in a coordinate system (shown in Figs. 2 and 3), the following questions:

1. What does our customers expect?
2. Where are the competitors?
3. Map the current position (As-Is). Where are we now?
4. Map the future desirable position (To-Be). Where would we like to be?

3   Workshop Participants

A number of companies have participated in the two workshops, and the companies represent the following types of industries.

A company makes roof tiles, wall bricks and pre-stressed brick beams for the whole market of Northern Europe. By using the technique with pre-stressed bricks, one can produce brick beams for large spans, roofs and brick elements that are not possible by traditional bricks. The company has acquired a number of production facilities placed different places in Denmark. The company makes standard products as well as customized products.

A company has specialized in a new generation of High Performance Precast Concrete, which can achieve minimalistic and elegant design. The precast High Performance Concrete products are unique because they combine the free shape ability of concrete, the strength of steel and a higher durability than both steel and normal concrete. The company is the largest producer of precast Compact Reinforced Composite and one of the world market leaders in structural applications of Ultra High Performance Fiber Reinforced Concretes.

A company makes products for clearing the air, to design, develop and make available kitchen hoods with innovative technology to strive for maximum extraction efficiency with minimum noise levels. The company has been at the forefront of finding the best solutions to any specific ventilation needs. The range of the products is among the most comprehensive available. Regardless of the style of the kitchen or personal preferences, they have a model that will suit the needs for ventilation as well as design.

A company is the world's leading manufacturer of stainless steel machine feet, and the company has an efficient and fully automated machinery, which enables to offer the customers a comprehensive range of machine feet in stainless steel and reinforced polyamide for adjustment, stabilization and vibration control of all types of machinery and equipment. Products are to meet the hygienic requirements applying in Europe and the USA. The company is providing hygienic solutions for machinery and equipment in the food industry and pharmaceutical industry. Flexibility is an important factor in offering customized solutions. It may be of minor adjustments of standard products or a completely different design of the products used on the machines.

A company is a modern sign company, which is a total supplier of designer products in signage solutions, digital signage and Way Showing Services and street furniture, including bike racks, information creation, flags and flagpoles and mailboxes. The company have experience in creating the visual identity for companies, and institutions sending signals to employees, customers, visitors and residents. Among the clients are private companies, business parks, business centers, nursing and senior services, hospitals, education, housing associations, churches and public administration buildings.

A company offers easy and intuitive way finding solutions designed for large buildings and campuses as well as resource booking and visitor management tools. The solutions enable great user experiences in flexible, dynamic indoor environments, and make it easy to book available resources like meeting or conference rooms. The company improves the guest experience in a building marked, as the solutions will welcome the guest, all the way from entrance to he sits comfortably organized in the right meeting room. The company has the headquarters, showroom and development department in Denmark, as well as office and sales department in the US.

A company offers a wide range of doors and parties, and all the doors are available with either painted, laminated or veneered surface. They are making fire protected doors in different categories, and soundproof doors in different audio category.

4 Results

The results of the workshops are presented briefly here.

4.1 Variety-Volume Mapping of Mass Customization for Different Companies

Figure 2 shows the positioning of the different companies according to the questions asked (number 1–4. See Sect. 2.1). The different companies are marked with different colors and an arrow that illustrate the movement from "As-Is" to "To-Be"; meaning "where they are now" and "where they would we like to be in the near future". A precise pattern shows that all of the participating companies see themselves moving towards a higher degree of Mass Customizing in the future, by being able to offer the customers more variants than today. Furthermore, it looks like that everyone consider themselves better than the competitors. Generally, it seems that everyone have a knowledge about what their customers want, even though there is no precise pattern of how each company are positioning the company "As-Is" or "To-Be" relative to the customer need, and the competitors.

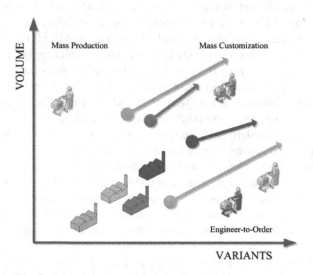

Fig. 2. Mapping the position for the different companies.

4.2 Variety-Volume Mapping Internally in Companies

After analyzing cross-company, if the individual companies had intentions to move towards Mass Customization, it was analyzed whether there was internal agreement on which way the companies should change.

Figure 3 shows for one company the positioning made by different persons within the same company, according to the questions asked (number 3–4, see Sect. 2.1). The different persons are marked with different colors and an arrow that illustrate the individual perception of the company's "As-Is" and "To-Be" position. Even though, there is some variation in opinions, there seems to be a trend showing a movement towards a higher degree of Mass Customizing in the future. However, disagreement on which way the company should move, can be critical for the implementation of a Mass

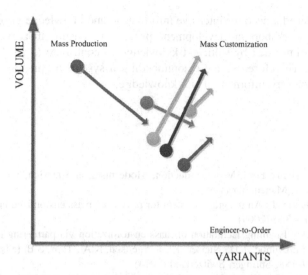

Fig. 3. Map the positioning relative to volume and variants for different persons within the same company.

Customization, as with the implementation of any strategy. Hence, it seems that this particular company will need to align opinions on company strategy in relation to Mass Customization. This picture is general to many of the companies taking part in the project and is thus considered a general tendency within the industry, which must be addressed.

5 Discussion

The results indicate that each company did the mapping differently and personnel within the same company have different perception of how to make the positioning, even though all participants prior to the workshops have gone through the same introduction to Mass Customization philosophy and workshop introduction.

This may be due to many reasons, e.g. individual skills, background, role within the company, knowledge about products, customers, competitors, and knowledge about internal business strategy, and of course different understanding of the workshop.

The innovative contribution for all of the participating companies is as a part of the collaboration during the project to increase the knowledge of tools and methods used for Mass Customization, which leads to increasing productivity. Therefore, by moving towards the "To-Be" position, it will improve the individual company and make small improvements to the Danish construction industry by implementing the principles of Mass Customization to increasing productivity.

The research contribution of the project is to clarify the situation of "where we are today" and to determine the development potential for the companies, and since it is early days in the project, the statistical material will improve when involving more companies in the workshops.

We experienced a need for intensive information and knowledge prior to any Mass Customization workshop or development process to ensure that everyone are in alignment, well informed by sufficient knowledge to contribute to the Mass Customization process. Therefore, we are recommending a systematic process to inform the parties with necessary information and knowledge.

References

1. Batchelor, R.: Henry Ford, Mass Production, Modernism, and Design, vol. 1. Manchester University Press, Manchester (1994)
2. Benros, D., Duarte, J.: An integrated system for providing mass customized housing. Autom. Constr. **18**, 310–320 (2009)
3. Bohnstedt, K.D.: Enabling facilitation of mass customization via partnering in the construction industry. In: Brunoe, T.D., Nielsen, K., Joergensen, K.A., Taps, S.B. (eds.) MCPC 2014. LNIP, pp. 179–188. Springer, Switzerland (2014)
4. Dean, P., Tu, Y., Xue, D.: A framework for generating product production information for mass customization. Int. J. Adv. Manuf. Technol. **38**, 1244–1259 (2008)
5. Dean, P., Tu, Y., Xue, D.: An information system for one-of-a-kind production. Int. J. Prod. Res. **47**, 1071–1087 (2009)
6. Jiao, J., Ma, Q., Tseng, M.M.: Towards high value-added products and services: mass customization and beyond. Technovation **23**, 809–821 (2003)
7. Pine, B.J.: Mass Customization: The New Frontier in Business Competition. Harvard Business School Press, Boston (1993)
8. Salvador, F., De Holan, P.M., Piller, F.: Cracking the Code of mass customization. MIT Sloan Manage. Rev. **50**, 71–78 (2009)
9. Walcher, D., Piller, F.T.: The Customization 500, 1st edn. Lulu Press, Aachen (2011)

A Cybernetic Reference Model for Production Systems Using the Viable System Model

Volker Stich and Matthias Blum[(✉)]

Institute for Industrial Management (FIR), Campus-Boulevard 55, 52074
Aachen, Germany
{Volker.Stich,Matthias.Blum}@fir.rwth-aachen.de

Abstract. Designing viable and integrative production systems is challenging for big companies. Researchers often fail to holistically consider the production system. Thus, the aim of this paper is to propose a holistic approach how the supply chain, the production and shop floor planning intermesh. Hereby a Viable System Model was applied. Standardized communication channels were able to be defined among three entities. In conclusion this newly proposed approach enables companies to reduce necessary stocks, production lead times and manpower allocation. This proposed approach boosts the efficiency of all production planning processes. This in turn translates to decreased stocks, shorter lead times and to more efficient manpower allocation. This holistic approach is a key to success for companies, in particular, in high-wage countries.

Keywords: Cybernetic reference model · Manufacturing execution · Production system · Supply chain · Viable System Model

1 Background

Today, manufacturing companies are increasingly confronted with the influences of a dynamic environment and the ensuing continuously increasing planning complexity [1]: Reduced time to markets, increasing product diversity, and increasingly complex multi-tier and world-spanning supply chains are faced with growing interconnectivity of production machinery, manufacturing execution systems, and enterprise resource planning systems under the term Industry 4.0. The Cluster of Excellence "Integrative Production Technology for High Wage Countries" at RWTH Aachen University addresses these opportunities and challenges and aims at resolving the "polylemma of production" which spans along two dilemmas plan-oriented vs. value-oriented production and scale vs. scope [1].

Within the Cluster of Excellence (CoE) on "Integrative Production Technology for High-Wage Countries" several institutes at RWTH Aachen University are conducting research on fundamentals of a sustainable production strategy. As part of the Cluster of Excellence on "Integrative Production Technology for High-Wage Countries" the sub-project D-1 aims at the goal of developing a self-optimizing production network. By applying instruments of self-optimization it leads to a quicker achievement of an optimal working point under changing input-parameters. A specific focus is on the consideration of human decisions during the production process when elaborating the

© IFIP International Federation for Information Processing 2015
S. Umeda et al. (Eds.): APMS 2015, Part I, IFIP AICT 459, pp. 169–176, 2015.
DOI: 10.1007/978-3-319-22756-6_21

cognitive model. To establish socio-technical control loops, it is necessary to understand how human decisions in diffuse working processes are made as well as how cognitive and affective abilities form the human factor within production processes. Thus a cybernetic based reference model of self-optimizing production management, addressing all levels from the supply chain management to the production cell control, has been developed and detailed building on these earlier results. The model has been concretized by individual elements.

2   Introduction

On a management level, companies are facing a wide range of challenges in the field of customer demand, dynamic environment conditions and quality problems [2]. Companies have to adapt themselves and their processes to dynamic environment conditions like movements in customer demand, reschedules in supply as well as turbulences in networks [3]. Nevertheless, a successful production management is characterized by high process efficiency and a high availability of information. The challenge is to manage negative consequences, such as wrong decisions in the planning processes, caused by poor communication and conventional solution approaches based on centralized planning methods. Conventional planning and control concepts try to tackle these problems by using highly sophisticated and centralized planning methods. These approaches constrain the ability of companies to react quickly and flexibly on internal and external disturbances [4]. This leads to a slower and more inflexible reaction of companies on internal and external disturbances and thus to an increasing gap between reality and intention [5]. To achieve a higher changeability and a better value-orientation of inter- and inner-company PPC processes, it is necessary to replace the present static arrangement of the central-controlled processes [6].

3   Methodological Approach and Preconditions

The structure of the cybernetic reference model is derived from principles of the Viable System Model (VSM). The Viable System Model was evolved by STAFFORD BEER in the 1960s as a management model to support managers dealing with complex management processes. It is built on three main principles: viability, recursivity and autonomy. Viability means that a company must react to internal and external disturbances in an appropriate way, in order to sustain its existence. Recursivity is a principle to structure organizational systems in a self-similar way. Hence, a viable system is a composition of nested systems, which are viable systems, too [6, 7]. In this context, autonomy means that a system can act independently as long as it is in accordance with its meta-systems' rules [8, 9] (Fig. 1).

For realizing these principles, BEER introduced a System consisting of a topology with five subsystems (see Fig. 2).

System 1 reacts to the development of the relevant operative unit's environment and it coordinates itself with the other operative units with the objective of own stability and whole company's stability. System 2 enables the units of System 1 to

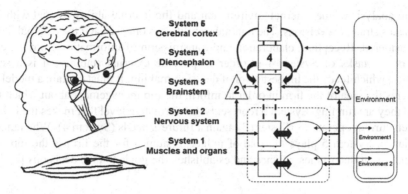

Fig. 1. Structure of the Viable System Model (Source: Beer 1979, p. 319, Malik 2006, p. 84, Gomez 1978, p. 24, Espejo and Harnden 1989, p. 99)

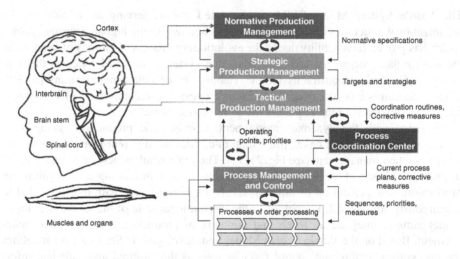

Fig. 2. System structure of the CPM model derived from the VSM

solve their own problems allowing decentralized decision-making and solve conflicts between those units. It also carries out the coordination of the operative units regulatory centers. It is an interface between Systems 1 and 3. System 3 has an overall model which is superior to all Systems 1 and their interactions. The operative overall management system ensures optimization of the whole system. By its direct connections with all subsystems it detects simultaneously and in real time everything that occurs in System 1. It is also notified about activities in System 2. System 3 passes on instructions directly to System 1 via the central command axis. The monitoring and validation of information from the operative units are functions of System 3*.

System 3 realizes the control of the orders that are taken in the current operations. It checks the strategic activities provided by System 4 and converts them into tactical operations. Systems 1, 2 and 3 constitute an autonomic system that regulates internal stability and tries to optimize performance within a given structure and criteria. System 4 does an analysis of the external environment and the internal ability to deal with it. It also makes strategic decisions. The internal stability has only sense if the external factors are considered. Reception, elaboration and transmission of information from the environment are tasks of System 4 in order to provide external stability. It is a set of activities, which feeds the highest level of decision making. It must contain a model that represents the idea of the firm in order to inform the top management about which type of firm they are running. System 5 represents the normative level that makes the balance between current operations (System 3) against future's needs (System 4). When there is no balance, System 5 plays the role of judge. System 5 for the firm is the top management and it determines policies and establishes the goals to take decisions [6, 7, 9].

4   Application of the Viable System Model to Cybernetic Production Management

The Viable System Model (VSM) is, as stated above, serving as a basis for the organizational structure view. It is conceived in analogy to the human nervous system, which has proven its reliability due to the evolutionary process of billions of years to be the most reliably organized and most adaptable system. The VSM specifies the necessary and sufficient constraints for the viability of complex organizations [6, 10]. These constraints can be subsumed as completeness and recursiveness of the system structure. This leads to the requirements of the basic model.

To cope with the dynamic environment, a cybernetic production management reference model has been developed which integrates the different level of production and production management (see Fig. 2) [11]. The main result which has been achieved in previous phases of the project is a cybernetic model structuring a self-optimizing production management on its different levels, capable to cope with dynamics and to continuously adjust itself. In contrast to the international state of the art the developed model aims to integrate all levels and domains of production and production management. Based on the Viable System Model first developed by Stafford Beer it defines the necessary planning and control tasks as well as the required and sufficient information channels for a self-optimizing production management. It serves as a regulatory framework to allocate the planning and decision models within the overall production management context and to derive design requirements.

Based on these results the project addresses now the comprehensive application of self-optimizing planning and control. This implies the integration of self-optimizing control loops on cell level with those addressing the production planning and control (PPC) as well as supply chain and quality management aspects and will lead to an improvement of planning decisions on different levels of the production network.

The Viable System Model provides an adequate structure for consistent integration of trans-disciplinary control loops and their alignment to a super-ordinate target system. It serves as a regulatory framework to allocate the planning and decision models within the overall production management context and to derive design requirements.

To incorporate the different levels of the production systems the levels have been specified. The following figure shows the application of the Viable System Model in production networks and provides an overview of the results of the different levels (see

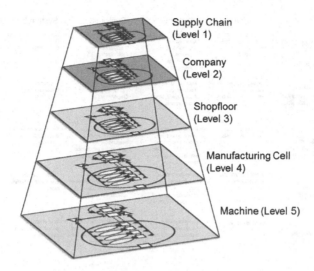

Supply Chain
(Level 1)

Company
(Level 2)

Shopfloor
(Level 3)

Manufacturing Cell
(Level 4)

Machine (Level 5)

Fig. 3. Recursive organizational level of the Viable System Model

Fig. 2). As recursion levels the supply chain, the company, the shopfloor, the manufacturing cell and on the bottom the machine level have been defined for the model. The entire model takes on a recursive structure. Recursiveness means that the structure of the model is the same on each level of observation. Any Viable System Model contains and is contained in another viable system model.

The description of the function of these levels is the central goal of the article at hand and will be shown in the following (see Fig. 3). The figure shows the different levels within the production management and the function of each system in the context of the Viable System Model. To get a more detailed impression of the composition of such a cybernetic based production management model, exemplarily the process and information view for the Supply Chain are described in the following (Fig. 4).

The policy function of a Supply Chain is defined by System 5 and in charge of giving a general respectively a legal framework for the whole Supply Chain. System 5 generates neither know-how nor takes direct action in the Supply Chain. It simply ensures that a balance is maintained between the Supply Chain Control Room (Systems 3 and 2) and for example the Market Analyses (System 4). When an imbalance develops, i.e. Systems 4 predicts high economic growth and System 3 is not capable to cope with this situation, System 5 will take measures (subsidies, laws etc.). By this, System 5 has the power to design the way Supply Chains work without interacting in an operative way. Based on the information System 4 is providing, actions are taken to design the future framework of the Supply Chain.

There are different ways of how the Supply Chain can be affected by its environment or how the Supply Chain can influence it. On the one hand all companies (System 1) can interact with its environment, but only for its own professional expertise. On the other hand System 4 comprises the environments of the separate System 1 and the greater environment. System 4 identifies needs and potential for change, i.e. economic development, new technologies and new markets and transmits

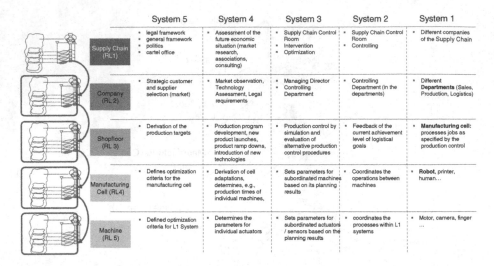

		System 5	System 4	System 3	System 2	System 1
	Supply Chain (RL1)	• legal framework • general framework • politics • cartel office	• Assessment of the future economic situation (market research, associations, consulting)	• Supply Chain Control Room • Intervention • Optimization	• Supply Chain Control Room • Controlling	• Different companies of the Supply Chain
	Company (RL 2)	• Strategic customer and supplier selection (market)	• Market observation, Technology Assessment, Legal requirements	• Managing Director • Controlling Department	• Controlling Department (in the departments)	• Different Departments (Sales, Production, Logistics)
	Shopfloor (RL 3)	• Derivation of the production targets	• Production program development, new product launches, product ramp downs, introduction of new technologies	• Production control by simulation and evaluation of alternative production control procedures	• Feedback of the current achievement level of logistical goals	• Manufacturing cell: processes jobs as specified by the production control
	Manufacturing Cell (RL4)	• Defines optimization criteria for the manufacturing cell	• Derivation of cell adaptations, determines, e.g., production times of individual machines,	• Sets parameters for subordinated machines based on its planning results	• Coordinates the operations between machines	• Robot, printer, human...
	Machine (RL 5)	• Defined optimization criteria for L1 System	• Determines the parameters for individual actuators	• Sets parameters for subordinated actuators / sensors based on the planning results	• coordinates the processes within L1 systems	• Motor, camera, finger ...

Fig. 4. Information transfer between the different levels

the information to System 3. It is also important that the information is exchanged between the separate Systems 4 in the recursion levels. In Supply Chains these tasks are fulfilled by lobbyists to influence the environment, or by Market researchers and associations to collect information. This information is then transferred to System 3 (Supply Chain Control Room) and to other Systems on other recursion levels.

The monitoring and optimization of the various actors in the supply chain is carried out by System 3 and System 2 which represent both together the Supply Chain Control Room. Although, the different companies in the supply chain (System 1) usually are in contact and interact among each other, their behavior is not synchronized. As part of the Supply Chain Control Room System 3 intervenes as necessary and solves conflicts between the companies. To achieve this aim System 3 transfers the information about the operations of the companies into an input-output-matrix and tries to optimize them. The relevant information provides System 2. The aim of System 2 is to coordinate the companies and to avoid oscillations between them. So, System 2 is a system of individual rules and behavior for coordinating operations of the companies. Typical activities of System 2 in the supply chain are for example the rules for joint purchases, the rules for the distribution of parts and the rules for logistical concepts. Furthermore, System 2 is collecting information of the activities such as inventory levels, point of sales data etc., compares the plans to standards and is informing System 3 about deviations to avoid for example the Bullwhip Effect. The gathered information arises from the companies (System 1).

System 1 is directed by the meta-system (System 5-3) and reflects the different companies in the Supply Chain.

In addition, for the other levels of the model (company, shop floor, manufacturing cell and machine) also the functions inside the model have been specified. In order to generate a holistic framework including all levels in the Viable System Model the information transfer will be designed as a relationship model describing the connections between the targets on the different levels of the system.

5 Summary and Further Research

In today's time companies are facing a wide range of challenges. In this paper, the application of Stafford Beer's Viable System Model (VSM) on the production management has been discussed as one way of handling these challenges. It has been used as a basis to build up a holistic framework for a changeable production management system. After introducing the preconditions of the model, we have derived the structural framework of the cybernetic production management from the Viable System Model and specified the functions of the system elements and their interactions.

Further research is needed to substantiate the presented solution principles for the different tasks in order to verify and validate the model's ability to support the design of control loops. Thereby a specific focus should be dedicated to the determination of the input and output values for each of the systems.

Acknowledgements. The presented research is result of the Cluster of Excellence (CoE) on "Integrative Production Technology for High-Wage Countries" funded by Deutsche Forschungsgemeinschaft (DFG). Within the CoE "Integrative Production Technology for High-Wage Countries" several institutes at RWTH Aachen University are conducting research on fundamentals of a sustainable production strategy. The authors would like to thank the German Research Foundation DFG for the kind support within the Cluster of Excellence "Integrative Production Technology for High-Wage Countries".

References

1. Brecher, C. (ed.): Integrative Production Technology for High-Wage Countries. Springer, Heidelberg (2012)
2. Brosze, T., Bauhoff, F., Stich, V., Fuchs, S.: High resolution supply chain management – resolution of the polylemma of production by information transparency and organizational integration. In: Vallespir, B., Alix, T. (eds.) Advances in Production Management Systems. IFIP AICT, vol. 338, pp. 325–332. Springer, Heidelberg (2010)
3. Schuh, G., Stich, V., Brosze, T., Fuchs, S., Pulz, C., Quick, J., Schürmeyer, M., Bauhoff, F.: High resolution supply chain management. In: German Academic Society for Production Engineering (WGP). Production engineering. Springer, Berlin (2011)
4. Meyer, J., Wienholdt, H.: Wirtschaftliche Produktion in Hochlohnländern durch high resolution supply chain management. Supply Chain Manage. III 7, 23–27 (2007)
5. Fleisch, E.: High Resolution Production Management. Wettbewerbsfaktor Produktionstechnik: Aachener Perspektiven, pp. 451–467. Apprimus, Aachen (2008)
6. Beer, S.: Brain of the Firm: the Managerial Cybernetics of Organization. The Penguin Press, London (1972)
7. Malik, F.: Strategie des Managements komplexer Systeme. Ein Beitrag zur Management-Kybernetik evolutionärer Systeme. Haupt, Bern (2006)
8. Beer, S.: The Heart of Enterprise. Wiley, Chichester (1979)
9. Gomez, P.: Die kybernetische Gestaltung des Operations Managements. eine Systemmethodik zur Entwicklung anpassungsfähiger Organisationsstrukturen. Haupt, Bern (1978)

10. Espejo, R., Harnden, R.: The Viable System Model. Interpretations and Applications of Stafford Beer's VSM. Wiley, Chichester (1989)
11. Stich, V., et al.: Viable production system for adaptable and flexible production planning and control processes. In: Proceedings of POMS 20th Annual Conference. POMS, Orlando, Florida, USA (2009)

Knowledge Based Production Management

Manufacturing Digitalization and Its Effects on Production Planning and Control Practices

Siavash H. Khajavi$^{(\boxtimes)}$ and Jan Holmström

Department of Industrial Engineering and Management, Aalto University,
Espoo, Finland
{siavash.khajavi,jan.holmstrom}@aalto.fi

Abstract. Advent of additive manufacturing (AM) as a final-parts production method has the capacity to impact the supply chains radically (The Economist, 2012). This effect extends from raw material procurement to production management and further towards distribution and the final customers. Digitalization of production as for the other industries such as automotive and aerospace reduces the operational complexity, while embedding the complexity in the digital components of the system. For instance, the production planning and control for an AM-enabled manufacturing may be distinctly different compared to conventional production methods. Production routing, loading and scheduling can become simplified as steps of production are combined through AM utilization. Moreover, production dispatching, reporting, inspection and corrective actions require development of novel effective practices. In this paper we investigate the in-depth impact of digital production technologies (e.g. additive manufacturing) on the production management practices. Our methodology is based on conceptual modelling intertwined with case data.

Keywords: Production planning and control · Manufacturing digitalization · Supply chain simplification

1 Introduction

The development of production systems introduced batching methods, standardization of components and stock keeping units to improve the efficiency of the production systems, however the emergence of computers and digitalization of tasks, changed the production methods and visibility of operations by improving the data gathering and sharing methods [7]. Now that the manufacturing machines becoming more and more software based and flexible, the question is do we still need the concepts previously set for the labor managed operations. We see a transition from a full human operated world towards a human-machine operated world within which machines are smarter and embed the know-how. In the new paradigm the order can be accomplished by an autonomous system to reach the outcome.

What we looked into throughout this research is the possible impact of direct digital manufacturing technologies (including additive manufacturing) on the conventional production practices. If the conventional shop floor concepts such as batching, SKUs, and other production planning and control tactics can be necessary for the new

© IFIP International Federation for Information Processing 2015
S. Umeda et al. (Eds.): APMS 2015, Part I, IFIP AICT 459, pp. 179–185, 2015.
DOI: 10.1007/978-3-319-22756-6_22

paradigm of digital smart production. The method is to review the conventional practices point out the costly ones then realize the possibility to omit them through the new tagging and other methods, while using available case studies.

The remainder of this paper is organized as follows: Sect. 2 presents a literature review; Sect. 3 explains the research methodology; and Sect. 4 presents the findings and results of our analysis. This paper ends with conclusions summarizing the research outcomes, and suggestions for future investigation are provided.

2 Literature Review

In this section we briefly review the literature on the two main subjects of this paper which are direct digital manufacturing and production planning and control.

2.1 Direct Digital Manufacturing

Direct Digital Manufacturing (DDM) technologies are a set of novel manufacturing techniques that produce the final parts from a computer aided design (CAD) file. These technologies which started to appear during the 1980s also have been known as additive manufacturing and 3D printing production techniques. In most of these technologies the computer software slices the three dimensional model of the part to very thing two dimensional cross sections and send them one at a time to the printing machines. The machine then utilized various technologies to produce these parts a layer at a time to reach the final geometrical form factor [1, 10].

The application of these CAD based technologies in the beginning was focused on the production of design models and prototypes. However, as the material range expanded and production quality and precision increased the application shifted to functional prototypes and recently final parts. Still there are obstacles to overcome before this method of production can enter the mainstream use and realize a wide application. For instance the cost intensiveness of the production machines as well as raw material, low throughput of the processes, limited range of available material and labour intensiveness of the pre and post production steps are among the most notable issues that need to be addressed [2].

However, DDM has a number of unique characteristics which makes it a very useful manufacturing method for a number of industries even at the current cost levels. DDM enables the production of very small batch size (as small as the batch of one in medical applications) while also removes the design for manufacturing limitations to a high extent. This means the production of very complex parts with moving parts is possible in a single run, which translates to designers' freedom to take advantage of design for performance instead. This is very relevant especially to the aerospace industry which searches for any opportunity to cut weight from the components and increase the fuel efficiency of airplanes. The other important features of this production method are the significant reduction in the amount of raw material waste through the production, the nonexistence of economics of scale (no tooling) and high flexibility for modifications on the fly [1, 9].

As the DDM attracts more attention and investment the new advancements will emerge which may turn it to a common production method for small and medium volume production batches in distributed settings which also has the potential to enable on-shoring of the manufacturing to the world's developed countries and cut the costs of transportation of goods significantly [1]. Therefore we see the urge to study the impact of this technology on various aspect of production management to illustrate the potentials and refute the myths.

2.2   Production Planning and Control

Production planning and control (PPC) are a set of activities which have been designed to make the production and delivery of products more smooth and efficient both time and cost-wise. Planning sets the goals for the production's long, medium and short term goals with regard to product and processes, in order to satisfy the customers' needs on time and uninterrupted. Production control is responsible to check the performance of the organization with regard to its production schedules and deliveries to alert any sign of derailment from the established plans. Moreover, the healthy functioning PPC can keep the inventories in check and customers satisfied through the optimum utilization of labor, material and machinery [7, 8].

Planning, routing, scheduling and loading are the main tasks in the production planning while, dispatching, follow up, inspection and corrective action are the production control practices. Planning is concerned with the processes which are required to be done to enable the production of the product, routing is the task of determining a path for the movement of the production lots in the factory while it is being made. Loading of the works on the machines is related to the capacity utilization of machines. Scheduling which is the last action in the production planning function, determines when and for how long a machine will be occupied with the production of specific parts or batches [8].

Dispatching deals with authorization of machine starts on various jobs based on the routing and scheduling. The action of controlling the start and stop of the works on the machines is called follow-up. Moreover, inspection of products acts as the problem detection method which will be fixed through the corrective actions on planning of the processes [7].

2.3   Literature Gap

The current literature on the impact of DDM on PPC is quite limited and mostly is focused on the utilization of PPC practices also on direct digital manufacturing technologies [2]. However, there is no critical study of the PPC to evaluate the actual necessity of those concepts in the new production management [7]. We tend to address this literature gap through this paper.

3 Method

The methodology chosen for this research is the literature review and use of case studies while available. By doing so we aim to locate and describe the potential changes that are required in the current production planning and control practices as the DDM evolves. The current challenge with studying the DDM technologies is the lack of case data in the low or medium volume production which makes it difficult to study this phenomenon fully. However, by finding cases in somehow similar and currently in use production technologies we can expand our understanding of what might be possible when the existing limitations are removed. However, the prospects are bright as the new wider applications for the DDM is starting to appear which makes it possible for our method to be tested and refined against the facts while they become available.

4 Results

In this section we utilize case analysis and literature to synthesize a potential impact of DDM on the current PPC practices. Cases will be explained and then analyzed for the potential efficiency improvements and lessons learned in production planning and control of the future.

Our first case is an example of a digitalized manufacturing system. The company which is active in the area of custom-made industrial hoses has developed a production system which can be assumed as a digital factory. When the company receives the orders, they directly go to a machine which holds different variants of hoses with various diameters. The machine reads the order and chooses the correct hose by reading the tag on it. Then the ordered length will be cut and the process continues until the whole order batch is ready. While the machine is cutting the hose it also tags it with the correct metal connection ordered for it, which after the completing of the cutting on the production batch will be installed by the operator. Throughout this process the production planning has a shorter routing, simpler scheduling and loading. Moreover in this plant the digitalization has also enabled the possibility of customization on product by product bases. The main advantage of this process also comes from this feature which eliminates the need for stock keeping units as the orders can be manufactured and stocked in single containers with the customers' tags.

In this case the dispatching can also be out-sourced to the machine through the prioritization of each order before sending it to the machine. Then if the machine receives an order with a higher priority it can utilize its capacity to fulfill the newly received one and hold the previous batch until the completion of that. In our case the follow-up process can be done well in advance as the process time can be predicted right after the loading. However, at this point the inspection of the products should be done manually but in the future when the machine can also install the metal end connections to the hose; this can also be done by the digital system. All in all, the digitalization of manufacturing can significantly reduce the need for SKUs on the product bases and also improve order delivery and inventory levels.

In direct digital manufacturing where, the product is manufactured through a CAD file, most of the PPC information can be delivered to the machines and after the production is complete it can be directly delivered to the customer after packaging. The additional value of a direct digital manufacturing will be less complexity in the PPC operations while increases the possibility for customization.

In the second example which is the result of analyzing the Volvo's Kalmar radical automobile assembly plant (Fig. 1). The company tried to revolutionize the production line and switch towards a more worker friendly and group oriented fixed position (the vehicles were carried on electric carriers on the plant floors in various directions reprogrammable by the assembly group). Moreover, by giving the workers a team and a single vehicle at each time, they also tried to make the workers skilled in multiple tasks and provide them with the feeling of responsibility for the product that they are completing. However, while the efficiency of production was improved as the workers got used to their tasks and become comparable with the production line concept, Volvo Company decided to close the Kalmar plant in 1994 [4, 5]. Among the main reason was the fact that group assembly in a single location required kitting of the assembly parts and transferring them to the location of production and to the working team. This was quite a time consuming and complex task which in relatively simpler in the production line concept [5, 6]. However, the kitting process in the future can be done by the autonomous robots, while the production plan is sent to the additive manufacturing machines, located in the plant to produce them according to the daily production plan. Then the robots similar to Kiva system which are in use by Amazon company can directly deliver the parts on a just in time bases to the assembly teams for the installation.

In such scenario, the complexity of kitting and dispatching will be out sourced to the computers and DDM systems and the follow-up as well as the product inspections can be done more carefully and on a timely fashion. Such scenario requires a major

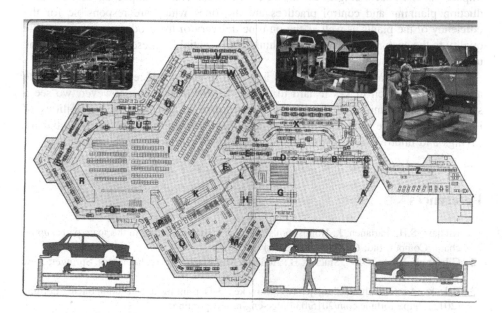

Fig. 1. Volvo Kalmar plant layout

leap in the development of additive manufacturing technologies to enable a reliable and repeatable production method that can also produce the parts quicker and more economically. However, currently AM is suitable for a number of low volume productions such as jet engine components and medical prosthesis production but the push towards more customized products in various industries will make AM necessary for other ones. Also as the level of implementation grows, bigger industrial players consider the potential improvements to their business from direct digital manufacturing technologies and potentially to build a competitive edge, invest in the advancement and finding new applications. This potentially realizes the impact of DDM on production planning and control practices.

5 Conclusions

Although the promise of DDM is strong and revolutionizing for the current manufacturing processes there is a need to understand the current limitations and possibilities. Although the DDM technologies are progressing rapidly, there still are sizable obstacles when it comes to the production throughput, reliability of parts, material range and costs. Having this in mind General Electric Company which is among the biggest and most advanced manufacturing companies in the world has started to manufacture the fuel nozzles of their CFM Leap jet engines using direct metal laser melting (DMLM) additive manufacturing process. And this is just the beginning as they and also other manufacturer of aerospace products are going to use this method for additional parts [3].

In this research we tried to utilize the industrial example to carefully predict the impact of DDM technologies on the PPC practices. That is important because production planning and control practices are the ones which are responsible for the efficiency of the plants as well as the on time delivery of the products with acceptable quality to the customer. Therefore, we think it is essential for these practices to become updated and be as efficient as possible.

The main limitation of this research is rooted in the lack of real world cases in the area of DDM which makes it hard to assess the situation fully. However, we see a significant opportunity for researchers to speculate and spread the possibilities of improvement to the industrial managers that they become aware of the potential for savings and improvements through this novel digital production technology.

References

1. Khajavi, S.H., Partanen, J., Holmström, J.: Additive manufacturing in the spare parts supply chain. Comput. Ind. **65**(1), 50–63 (2014)
2. Gibson, I., Rosen, D.W., Stucker, B.: Additive Manufacturing Technologies. Springer, New York (2010)
3. Zaleski, A.: GE's bestsellnig jet engine makes 3-D printing a core component. Fortune (2015). http://fortune.com/2015/03/05/ge-engine-3d-printing/

4. Sandberg, Å.: Enriching Production: Perspectives on Volvo's Uddevalla Plant as an Alternative to Lean Production. National Institute for Working Life and KTH Royal Institute of Technology, Stockholm, Sweden (2007)
5. Sandberg, T.: Volvo Kalmar - Twice a Pioneer, Enriching Production, Digital Edition, pp. 87–101, Stockholm, Sweden (2007)
6. Engström, T., Jonsson, D., Johansson, B.: Alternatives to line assembly: some Swedish examples. Int. J. Ind. Ergon. **17**(3), 235–245 (1996)
7. Berry, W.L., Whybark, D.C., Jacobs, F.R.: Manufacturing Planning and Control for Supply Chain Management. McGraw-Hill/Irwin, New York (2005)
8. Peterson, R., Silver, E.A.: Decision Systems for Inventory Management and Production Planning, pp. 799–799. Wiley, New York (1979)
9. Holmström, J., Romme, A.G.L.: Guest editorial: five steps towards exploring the future of operations management. Oper. Manage. Res. **5**(1–2), 37–42 (2012)
10. Kruth, J.P., Leu, M.C., Nakagawa, T.: Progress in additive manufacturing and rapid prototyping. CIRP Ann. Manuf. Technol. **47**(2), 525–540 (1998)

Financial Measures and Their Relations to Decoupling Points and Decoupling Zones

Joakim Wikner[⊠]

Jönköping University, Jönköping, Sweden
joakim.wikner@decouplingpoints.org

Abstract. Financial management is concerned with the financial evaluation of activities performed in the supply chain. Each activity has implications on the financial situation but the actual cause-effect relation involved in this context is not always obvious. From a return on investment (ROI) perspective the financial measures revenue, cost, and assets, i.e. investment, are identified. Strategic lead-times have been highlighted in the literature as key components for flow design. Strategic lead-times are thereafter further analyzed and the relations between financial measures and strategic lead-times are outlined. Based on these relations, it is possible to establish a relation between financial measures, and decoupling points and decoupling zones. Subsequently this is shown to also provide a reference to supply chain management strategies as they are defined in the literature.

Keywords: Decoupling points · Strategic lead-times · Financial measures

1 Introduction

Financial measures play a significant role in much decision making at a company level. Money in the bank has for long been a guiding star but as highlighted by e.g. Pierre S. du Pont the actual return obtained on the investment is the key measure. This return on investment (ROI) has since played an important role in the allocation of funds. Money is travelling from activities providing insufficient ROI to relatively more profitable investments and by using the so called DuPont scheme the ROI can be disintegrated into its constituent parts related to the balance sheet and the profit and loss statement respectively. In summary, the balance sheet provides the "investment" of ROI and the profit and loss statement provides the revenues and costs during a period. In short the ROI can be defined as the profit (revenues minus costs) divided by the assets in the balance sheet, which in some cases can be seen as the investment.

Even if Henry Ford once stated that "My idea was then and still is that if a man did his work well, the price he could get for that work, the profits, and all financial matters would care for themselves." [1, p. 44] the relation between "work well" and "profits" is, however, not always that obvious. Henry Ford, as the main owner of Ford, could trust his intuition on this but in most cases this is not possible. Frequently, the owners are not present in the operations, and are many times also not that interested in the operational details. Instead, the owners focus on the ROI of each period. In a stable environment of mass production this approach works well as the system may be

© IFIP International Federation for Information Processing 2015
S. Umeda et al. (Eds.): APMS 2015, Part I, IFIP AICT 459, pp. 186–193, 2015.
DOI: 10.1007/978-3-319-22756-6_23

fine-tuned and compete based on economies of scale. Many companies are however facing a much more dynamic environment where in particular the demand changes rapidly due to for example short product life cycles. But, also supply can be dynamic in the sense that the dynamic demand puts pressure on the supply network to be able to respond to the demand changes. At an operational level these dynamics are much more perspicuous in the sense that the dynamics of demand and supply directly influence the capability of the system. These dynamics are known as the Forrester effect [2] or later the Bullwhip effect [3] and may be mitigated in several ways of which changes to the structure of the supply chain, the reduction of lead-times and simplification of information flows are important. One common theme here is the lead-times of the supply chain. Lead-time management has developed in many directions over the years and is a corner stone of e.g. time-based management [4], lean thinking [5], and decoupling thinking, see e.g. [6, 7]. All these approaches focus on lead-time and efficient use of resources but still the connection between different lead-times and ROI is not that well investigated in the literature. The purpose here is therefore to outline relations between the financial measure of ROI and the key lead-times, i.e. the strategic lead-times.

Next, decoupling layers are outlined and then financial measures are further analyzed followed by an overview of strategic lead-times in the context of decoupling thinking. Finally, the two areas of financial measures and decoupling based on strategic lead-times are combined and some conceptual relations between ROI and strategic lead-times are identified and illustrated in a decoupling framework.

2 The Decoupling Layers

Management in general is a challenging subject and Wikner [7] suggests that three distinct system perspectives can be used to focus on different aspects. At a fundamental level there is a logical perspective where the transformation is in focus (see Fig. 1). This layer is associated with process management which can be divided into a meta level of flow constructs and a higher level of constructs focusing on specific decision categories. The details of the logical perspective are further described in [7]. The physical perspective is based on the fundamental flow logic but employs these constructs in terms of supply chain management strategies where the type of transformation is important and this is further outlined in [8]. Finally, all these transformations must be interpreted in terms of economic consequences where the actual sponsor of the transformation is identified and this is the subject of this paper.

Fig. 1. The three perspectives legal, physical, and logical [7].

3 Financial Measures

As pointed out initially the key fundamental financial measure is return on investment (ROI). ROI can be defined in different ways, depending on what the "investment" represents, but the key point is that the result obtained should be put in relation to the size of the investment. The result is the Profit obtained, from the profit and loss statement, and expressed per time period and referred to as Revenue minus Cost, i.e. Profit = Revenue − Cost. In throughput accounting [9] the ROI is based on the throughput, operating expenses and inventory but the result is the same except for some effects due to allocation to different periods. In addition, the size of the investment is here represented by the Assets in the balance sheet. As a consequence, the ROI can be calculated as: ROI = (Revenue − Cost)/Assets and each of these three components are further elaborated on below. Note that this particular definition of ROI corresponds to return on assets (ROA). But, since the key message here is the significance of the relative property of the measure the more general name ROI is used below.

Revenue is based on income and is defined as the income allocated to different periods. The revenue generating capability of an offering is correlated to the competitiveness of the offering. The competitiveness of the business is thus an important factor for the revenue generating capability. For example, if the market requests customization it usually indicates that the customer can accept some delivery lead-time but also that the business must have flexibility for customization to generate the revenue. Correspondingly, a focus on low price usually indicates that the market can accept a more standardized offering, i.e. a commodity, but then available within a short lead-time. As a consequence, the revenue is dependent on the lead-time facing the customer and the capability of the company to use this lead-time to provide a competitive offering.

Costs are related to expenses and can be categorized in different ways. A frequently used approach is to divide costs into direct and indirect costs. The two key components in direct costs are directly attributed to the cost object and are direct material (DM) and direct labor (DL). Indirect costs are then allocated to the cost objects on some basis that is usually related to direct costs such as resources used during a lead-time.

Assets, as used here, concern both materials and capacity. Materials are related to the expected scenarios such as the expected lead-time for a flow section which will contain a certain amount of material in relation to the lead-time. The other aspect refers to unexpected events and buffers that are introduced to protect against these unexpected events. Capacity is less directly related to lead-times but obviously outsourcing reduces the level of own capacity at the expense of higher costs for direct materials.

4 Financial Measures and Strategic Lead-Times

There are six types of strategic lead-times that are of particular interest here and can be seen as aggregate reflection of certain perspectives of performed activities, see e.g. [7]. On the supply side, the cumulative lead-time (S) is fundamental but also the division of the lead-times into internal (I) and external (E) is important as it refers to the controllability of the activities. In addition, the capability to create customized solutions is related to the customization that could be created based on the properties of the product. These properties can be created certain lead-time before delivery and this is referred to as the supply based adapt lead-time (A_S). The A_S hence represents the capability of the business to provide a customized solution (in the figure it is A_S for item U, hence the notation $A_{S,U}$). On the demand side the requested delivery lead-time (D) is key. However, it is important to note that D is not related to level of customization, but only to how long time before delivery that the customer order is obtained. The distinction between requested customization and standardization is instead covered by the demand based adapt lead-time (A_D). These strategic lead-times (S, I, E, A_S, D, and A_D) are illustrated in the example of Fig. 2. Note that the strategic lead-times, E and I, are unique for each branch of the bill-of-material and that there can be several A_S depending on the properties of the bill-of-material. Next, these strategic lead-times are investigated based on their impact on some financial measures.

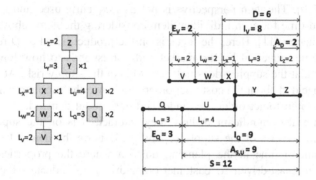

Fig. 2. Example of material-based and lead-time-based bill-of-materials [7].

4.1   External Lead-Time (E) and Internal Lead-Time (I)

External lead-time (E) is defined for each branch of the time phased bill-of-material. E is based on the lead-time that is external to the logical entity and is usually related to purchased material that is considered as direct material cost (DM). Correspondingly, the internal lead-time (I) is based on transformation that is performed on the direct material and is hence related to the direct labor cost (DL).

In addition, I represents the time the item spends in the system, and thus also the value of the item. Consequently, it is related to the amount of material in the system, also referred to as work in process (WIP) inventory. A measure of the extent is provided by Little's formula that tells us that the amount of material in the system is related to the flow rate multiplied by the lead-time, which in this case is I for that item. In a similar manner, E is related to the replenishment lead-time from suppliers and due to both the lead-time and the potential uncertainty in the external lead-time the magnitude of E may impact assets in terms of raw material inventory, c.f. safety lead-times.

Note that this discussion refers to the main impact. From a more general perspective it could be argued that the ratio of E and I indicates the use of external capabilities that may also contribute to impact revenues. This ratio could be altered by e.g. outsourcing parts of the activities. However, these "side effects" are not emphasized here.

In summary, I and E are both important from a cost perspective as well as from an asset perspective. E is related to DM and raw materials inventory, and I impacts the assets in terms of capital tied up in the flow, also known as WIP inventory.

4.2 Supply Lead-Time (S) and Delivery Lead-Time (D)

Both the supply lead-time (S) and the delivery lead-time (D) are important from a risk perspective where S indicates where the provider must start taking a material based supply risk and D is where the supply risk is neutralized in the sense that the provider does not need to speculate any more due to that the customer has made a decision, i.e. released a customer order. S can be defined from a product perspective and from an item perspective. The product perspective refers to the longest cumulative lead-time of the complete product structure. This lead-time was originally referred to as the product lead-time (P) [10]. The item perspective is not as frequently used and represents the cumulative lead-time for each individual item considering the items above the item in the product structure [11]. Here, the focus is on the product based S. D represents the delivery lead-time requested by the market and corresponds to how long before the actual delivery that the supplier does not have to take the supply risk. At this time the customer has decided about the customer order and hence the supplier can perform the transformation to customer order, i.e. under certainty about demand.

S and D are also significant in how they interact. S is on the supply side and represents characteristics of the supply capability. D is on the demand side and represents the point in time in the planning horizon where the properties of demand changes from forecast-driven to customer-order-driven. S indicates the part of the planning horizon with released or firm planned orders in line with the planning time fence (PTF). It represents the time span within which the materials available are constrained. D represents the positioning of the customer order decoupling point (CODP) [12] and also the demand time fence (DTF) and this is where the uncertainty for planning is further reduced. The relation between time fences and S and D is further outlined in [7]. Since S, and in particular S–D, is based on speculation it is also where WIP is most likely to accumulate and impact assets in an additional way.

In summary, D affects the positioning of a key buffer point, the CODP, and as a consequence also capital tied up, i.e. assets. In addition, it is a key lead-time for creating a competitive advantage and thus represents an opportunity for increasing revenues. S is mainly a measure of where material-based speculation needs to be initiated and hence where the preconditions for buffers are initiated at the latest.

4.3 Adapt Lead-Time Based on Demand (A_D) and Supply (A_S)

The adapt lead-time is related to the customization of the product. Basically there are two possible perspectives on customization [13]. The market oriented is the demand based adapt lead-time (A_D) based on the customers' requirements on customization. The second perspective is related to supply and if the product has untapped possibilities for creating customization. This is basically unused potential in the product and is usually related to particular items that provide this opportunity and this adapt lead-time is called supply based adapt lead-time (A_S). The market based customization has obvious potential for increased revenue. For the supply based customization this relation is not as obvious, since it has not been requested by the market, and the potential cost impact is more significant since it e.g. would result in more variants.

In summary, the two types of adapt lead-time both impact revenue but as noted there is also a direct relation to costs for A_S.

4.4   Summary of Financial Measures and Strategic Lead-Times

Three financial measures have been identified based the fundamental definition of return on investment, ROI. As indicated in Fig. 3, the demand based lead-times mainly impact revenues and the supply based mainly impact cost and assets. Revenue is created by the customers and hence the demand based strategic lead-times represent revenue opportunities. The delivery lead-time D is the time the customer waits for delivery and the adapt lead-times are related to customization. The adapt lead-time requested by the market (A_D) also represents the shortest possible delivery lead-time but, if still competitive, a D that extends even further upstream reduces the risk of the supplier and the need for buffers which is a consequence on the asset side.

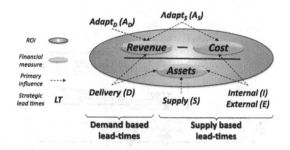

Fig. 3. ROI, financial measures and the strategic lead-times.

The supply-side affects assets most obviously in terms of E (raw-materials inventory) and I (work-in-process inventory). Note that I is related to a logical entity [7] which could involve for example a single site or a network of sites. The key message here is that everything upstream from I would be considered as DM. In addition, there is some impact on assets from D, on the demand side, since the positioning and dimensioning of the CODP buffer is based on properties of D. From an inventory perspective this means that the three strategic lead-times E, I, and D correspond to the three categories of inventory from an accounting perspective, i.e. raw materials inventory, work-in-process inventory and finished goods inventory (which is a special case of CODP inventory). S, finally, also impacts assets from the supply side but it is a separate case as it is not related to one particular class of inventory but it is rather the baseline for when plans must be firmed (c.f. PTF) and hence this indicates a shift to less flexibility to changes in the planning horizon. The strategic lead-times I and E have obvious relation to cost as they are related to the two main categories of direct costs, i.e. DM and DL, and in addition also the allocation of indirect costs since DM and DL are often used as a basis for allocation. E and I also provide some insights on the ratio between DM and DL. The types of activities involved are however not known from a general perspective and the actual magnitude of the costs cannot be observed. Finally, A_S indicates potential future customization offerings and as such it is not only a revenue opportunity but also a source of additional cost if the opportunity is exploited.

5 Financial Measures and the Decoupling Framework

The strategic lead-times can be used in positioning of strategic decoupling points where A_D (A in Fig. 4), D, and I are of particular interest. These three lead-times indicate the position of three strategic decoupling points: Customer order decoupling point (CODP), Customer adaptation decoupling point (CADP), and Purchasing order decoupling point (PODP). These three types of decoupling points are illustrated in Fig. 4 and the corresponding buffer points are illustrated with black triangles. The three financial measures used in ROI are also included in the figure and positioned based on their respective relation to the strategic lead-times, as outlined above and illustrated in Fig. 3.

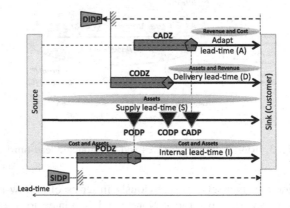

Fig. 4. Financial measures and the decoupling framework.

The three decoupling zones CODZ, CADZ, and PODZ represent a mix of conditions before and after each zone (the Z in the zone acronyms represents Zone) (see e.g. [7]). For example, CODZ is the customer order decoupling zone and is related to a compromise between forecast and customer orders. Two of these zones also represent the condition for positioning of the demand information decoupling point (DIDP) and the supply information decoupling point (SIDP), both related to information transparency. The fundamental framework in Fig. 4 is thoroughly discussed and defined in [7]. In [8] it is shown how eight different supply chain management strategies can be interpreted in terms of a decoupling framework. This is here extended to also involve financial measures. Further research will involve empirical investigation of the relationships between financial measures and strategic lead-times. In particular the companies involved in this research has expressed interest in the measure "cost of lead-time" but as shown here also revenue and assets may play a significant role.

Acknowledgement. This research has been performed in collaboration with five companies in the project KOPtimera. The project is funded by the Swedish Knowledge foundation (KKS), Jönköping University and the participating companies.

References

1. Ford, H., Crowther, S.: My Life and Work. Doubleday, Page (1922)
2. Forrester, J.W.: Industrial dynamics: a major breakthrough for decision makers. Harvard Bus. Rev. **36**, 37–66 (1958)
3. Lee, H.L., Padmanabhan, V., Whang, S.: Information distortion in a supply chain: the bullwhip effect. Manage. Sci. **50**, 1875–1886 (2004)
4. Stalk, G., Hout, T.M.: Competing Against Time: How Time-Based Competition is Reshaping Global Markets. Free Press, New York (1990)
5. Womack, J.P., Jones, D.T.: Lean Thinking: Banish Waste and Create Wealth in Your Corporation, 1st edn. Free Press, New York (2003)
6. Hoekstra, S., Romme, J. (eds.): Integral Logistic Structures: Developing Customer-Oriented Goods Flow. Industrial Press, New York (1992)
7. Wikner, J.: On decoupling points and decoupling zones. Prod. Manuf. Res. **2**, 167–215 (2014)
8. Wikner, J.: Supply chain management strategies in terms of decoupling points and decoupling zones. In: Grabot, B., Vallespir, B., Gomes, S., Bouras, A., Kiritsis, D. (eds.) Advances in Production Management Systems. IFIP AICT, vol. 438, pp. 371–378. Springer, Heidelberg (2014)
9. Goldratt, E.M., Cox, J.: The Goal: A Process of Ongoing Improvement, Rev. edn. North River Press, New York (1986)
10. Shingō, S.: A Study of the Toyota Production System from an Industrial Engineering Viewpoint, Rev. edn. Productivity Press, Cambridge (1989)
11. Bäckstrand, J.: A Method for Customer-Driven Purchasing: Aligning Supplier Interaction and Customer-Driven Manufacturing. School of Engineering, Jönköping University, Jönköping (2012)
12. Mather, H.: Competitive Manufacturing. CRC Pr I Llc, Boca Raton (1999)
13. Bäckstrand, J., Wikner, J.: Time-phasing and decoupling points as analytical tools for purchasing. In: Proceedings from the IEEE International Conference on Industrial Engineering and Engineering Management, Bangkok (2013)

Knowledge and Quality for Continuous Improvement of Production Processes

Marcos O. Morais[1]([✉]), Antônio S. Brejão[1], Pedro L.O. Costa Neto[2],
Helcio Raymundo[2], João Gilberto Mendes dos Reis[2], Oduvaldo Vendrametto[2],
Emerson Abraham[2], Carla C. Parizi[2], Sivanilza Teixeira Machado[2],
and Helton R.O. Silva[2]

[1] Postgraduate Studies Program in Production Engineering, Dr. Bacelar 1212,
São Paulo, São Paulo 04026002, Brazil
marcostecnologia@ig.com.br
[2] UFGD, Dourados, Brazil

Abstract. This work aims to show the scale of the use of tools and concepts for quality management and knowledge. In addition, it seeks the improvement of industrial processes and products, which we also need the conscious and motivated employee participation. Moreover, it seeking their commitment with the changes to be implemented. An illustrative case of application is performed on company of aluminum smelter, with significant results.

Keywords: Organizational change · Process improvement · Knowledge · Quality

1 Introduction

The organizations need to prepare people for the challenges of daily life are far beyond numbers and manage conflicts. It is necessary to rethink, learn and lead forms of sharing among the various types and levels of employees within organization.

Knowledge is created by individuals, and the organization must support employees with creativity and interest, providing them with contexts for knowledge creation, making it concrete. For an organization to remain competitive in the market, knowledge is a key strategic resource [1].

The knowledge management is the collection of processes that govern the creation, dissemination and use of knowledge. Thus, to fully achieve the companies' goals, a new confluence of information technology and administration, a new link between strategy, culture and the organization's information systems are necessary [2]. Figure 1 shows the integration between departments.

The changes that are occurring and those that occur are not seen as mere trend, but permanent changes and favorable to all segments, as organizations have extremely important role also in the professional growth of its employees.

The purpose of this paper is analyze how the kind of knowledge (tacit and explicit) is related to use of tools of quality to continuous improvement in production process.

© IFIP International Federation for Information Processing 2015
S. Umeda et al. (Eds.): APMS 2015, Part I, IFIP AICT 459, pp. 194–201, 2015.
DOI: 10.1007/978-3-319-22756-6_24

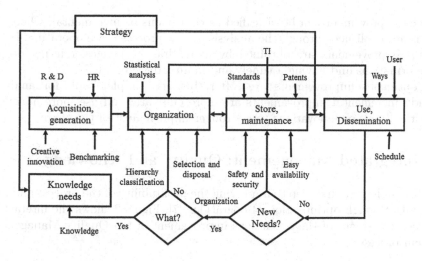

Fig. 1. Model for knowledge management. Source: Adapted [3]

2   Organizational Change

It is configured as organizational change the modification of existing resources patterns, whether is structural, human, strategic or technological, reflecting an a systematic way or parts of the organization [4]. A process of change, to be successful, must be well planned, well publicized, well justified and well executed. It is necessary to take on consideration the climate and the culture of the organization [3].

Everyone in the organization should be aware and willing to carry out these changes, from the lowest organizational level to senior management. Therefore, for change to happen occur, it is necessary that the organizational values and attitudes change at all levels [5]. Actions such as hiring consultants and/or internal and external training help improve and speed the results, starting to promote awareness of the team. Emphasizes that the leader's role is necessary for the implementation of any change [6].

Every change generates mistrust and resistance, since the comfort zones are affected. This resistance is inherent in any process of organizational change. The shift in paradigm becomes one of the points decisive in the success of the change. The cultural issue is a factor that should be treated with due importance by organizations in breaking paradigms, aiming to promote a culture of excellence that should be pursued and developed [6].

3   Process Improvement

The improvement process within organizations becomes very important because it affects all sectors and levels. Improvement is always the order, because perfection, although it should always be purse, is unattainable [3].

The improvement can be classified as continuous or incremental, where the first is accomplished through the analysis of how processes are operating. Incremental improvements are obtained by more drastic changes, offering deeper transformations and having a timely and more intense effect.

Continuous improvements are softer, but use simpler tools for analysis; already incremental improvements are more emphatic and use more advanced statistical tools or innovations to a stronger improvement of the shares.

4   Integrated Management: Quality and Knowledge

Quality tools are a first step to improving the profitability of the process and productivity through optimization of operations [7]. Figure 2 shows the interaction between the stages of the continuous improvement of the Quality Management System process.

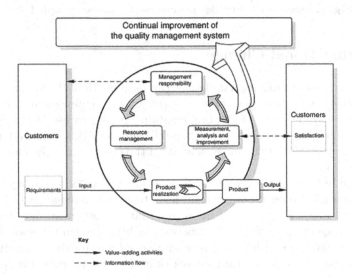

Fig. 2. Continuous improvement of the Quality Management System. Source: [8,9]

The methodology of integrated management was proposed by [10], in order to achieve better organizational results, and is represented by strategic actions, structural, behavioral and operational. The main purpose is the focus of eliminating flaw in the processes to maximize and provide service and products closer to perfection. In support of continuous quality improvements are listed the basic quality tools [3].

5 Quality Tools

For continuous quality improvement are listed the basic quality tools [3]:

- **Check Sheet:** important to ensure that nothing that should be done or checked is forgotten.
- **Histogram:** basic statistical tool of graphic sample description of variables, useful to understand their behavior.
- **Pareto Chart:** as it is represented the items under analysis in descending order of importance (value, frequency, etc.) to prioritize analysis of the most important.
- **Ishikawa Diagram:** or cause and effect, or herringbone, used to identify causes of problems according to their nature.
- **Process Control Chart:** main statistical tool of control processes.
- **Stratification:** used when there is suspected values for different origins of elements.
- **Scatter Diagram:** appropriate to set behavior analysis of two quantitative variables considered simultaneously and evaluate their correlation.
- **Flow Chart:** provides a graphical representation of the interrelationship of all its activities, allowing a better visualization and understanding.

The following tools are also complementary in assisting quality management [11].

- **Brainstorming:** is a group process in which individuals send free form of ideas, in large quantities, without criticism and in the shortest possible time.
- **5W1H or 5W2H:** it is a tool to help structuring action plans from key issues (What ?; Who ?; When ?; Where ?; Why ?; How ?). Although 5W2H adds the issue How much ?, emphasizing the cost of action.
- **5S:** a set of concepts and practices that are the main goals of the organization and rationalization of the work environment. The program refers to five Japanese words beginning with the letter S: seire, seiton, Seiso, Seiketsu and Shitsuke.

6 Knowledge

There are several levels of interaction that can arise within an organization for the development of knowledge that may be relevant in continuous improvement. The knowledge conversion model should be based on the interaction between the tactical knowledge and explicit [11]. Tacit knowledge has a personal quality, subjective, the result of processing information, insights and technical abilities also that integrate the acquired knowledge, or know-how. Explicit knowledge refers to that transmitted into a formal language, systemic, onto a objectively from. Proposes a conversion model of knowledge where the integration of explicit knowledge and tacit knowledge complement each other, as shown in Fig. 3 [12].

Fig. 3. Knowledge Spiral. Source: Adapted [12]

The knowledge spiral contemplates a successive process covering: (a) Socialization: is the process which experiences are shared and tacit knowledge is socialized among individuals; (b) Outsourcing: is the most important conversion model, because it allows the creation of new and explicit concepts through the tacit knowledge that normally are difficult to verbalize; (c) Combination: This process is based on the exchange of explicit information and use paradigms of information technology; (d) Internalization: is the mental absorption of the results of combinations checked in practice, or "learning by doing", returning to the beginning of tacit knowledge and the new working process at an advanced level of knowledge. While most share new mental models, tacit knowledge becomes part of the organizational culture, and by every successful internalisation, the cycle starts again, leading to improvement or innovation. Table 1 combines the main tools of quality and levels of knowledge, as well as its goals and objectives.

Existing tools and techniques in the management of knowledge and quality help define, analysis and measurement to solve problems.

Knowledge management is becoming an important integrator in organizations. Therefore, the implementation and use of systems such as ERP are the focus of studies that aim to address the effects on organizations under the technical and functional perspective [13].

7   Illustrative Case

An application of various ideas outlined in this work was done in an aluminum smelter company during the period of a year. This sets the presence of the action research methodology.

Action research is a type of social research with empirical basis that is designed and carried out in close association with an action or resolution

Table 1. Quality tools and levels of knowledge

Quality tools	Homes	Level
Cause and effect diagram	Identify the relationship between the result and all causes of a problem	Tacit
Pareto chart	Encourage the identification, measurement and the priority of the most important problems of a process	Explicit
Flowchart	Provides the sequences of process steps on easy veining	Explicit
Letter control	Monitor the variability and the problem of a process through charts explicit	Explicit
Check sheet	Enumerate the constant occurrences of a production process at a given time	Tacit
Histogram	Monitoring identification the monitoring of variables of a process	Explicit
Diagram of dispersion	Provide statistics of dependent and independent variables of a process	Explicit
Brainstorming	Detail the perceptions of a particular subject, looking for different opinions from the collective creativity	Tacit
5W2H	Represent and unify the processes, on organizing action plans and statement of Assistant methods to indicators, to a management	Tacit
Stratification	Identify variables from different sources in order to avoid inconsistent analyzes	Tacit
5S	Collaborate in the behavioral modification of employees in order to have a sense of organization keeping the pleasant atmosphere and abolishing waste	Tacit

of a collective problem, which researchers and representative participants of the situation or problem are involved in cooperative mode or participatory [14].

This work was carried out in an aluminum die casting company on the surroundings of São Paulo, which currently has 109 employees over three shifts. It was established by senior management should be prepared a medium-term action plan for the organization to become competitive stand out compared to its competitors. For this, to happen quality management methodologies and knowledge management were used in solving the problems. The main problem listed by managers was the high rate of noncompliance, Fig. 4, caused by not having appropriate method on dealing some of the appointed internally problems and by the clients.

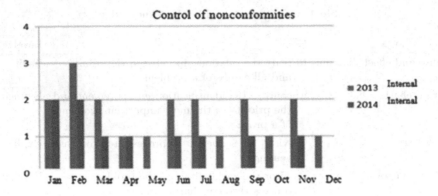

Fig. 4. Control of non-conformities internal

As can be seen in Fig. 4, the comparison between the 2013, with a total of twenty non-conformities and 2014, with a total of ten internal non-compliance where it is possible to see a fifty percent improvement after the implementations suggested by the tools of quality and knowledge management. Figure 5 shows the comparison between 2013 and 2014 for external nonconformities.

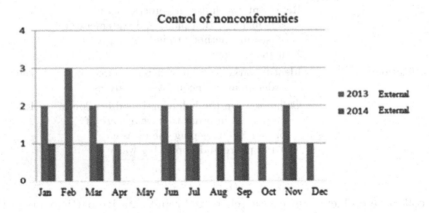

Fig. 5. Control of no external compliance

As can be seen in Fig. 5, 2013 presented a total of eighteen nonconformities, and 2014, showed a total of seven external nonconformities cohere it is possible to see an improvement of sixty-one percent after the suggested tools implementations suggested by the tools of quality management and knowledge management.

8   Conclusion

Over the past few years organizations seek to develop methods to become increasingly competitive and stand out in the market in which they operate, but what is the gain that the implementation of knowledge and quality management tools can generate?

The research carried out in the company in question presented quantitative results and a substantial improvement in the quality, demonstrated by reducing the number of non-internal and external compliance.

The positive results were only possible after the interaction and the commitment of everyone in the organization, shared together the integration of management systems.

With this work we seek to offer a small contribution to organizations and emphasize the relationship of open tools for managing problems and improvements to the organization.

References

1. Choi, B., Poon, S.K., Davis, J.G.: Effects of knowledge management strategy on organizational performance: a complementarity theory-based approach. Omega **36**(2), 235–251 (2008)
2. Texeira Filho, J.: Gerenciando conhecimento: como a empresa pode usar a memória organizacional e a inteligência competitiva no desenvolvimento dos negócios. SENAC, São Paulo (2000)
3. Costa Neto, P.L.d.O., Canuto, S.A.: Administração com qualidade: conhecimentos necessários para a gestão moderna. Bluncher, São Paulo (2010)
4. Wood Junior, T.: Mudança organizacional: aprofundando temas atuais em administração de empresas. Atlas, São Paulo (1995)
5. Duck, J.D.: The Change Monster: The Human Forces that Fuel or Foil Corporate Transformation and Change. Crown Business, New York (2002)
6. Falconi, V.: O verdadeiro poder. INDG, Belo Horizonte (2009)
7. Lobo, R.N.: Gestão da qualidade. Erica, São Paulo (2010)
8. Associação Brasileira de Normas Técnicas: NBR ISO 9001:2008. Sistema de Gestão da Qualidade Requisitos (2008)
9. Eurocontrol: ISO 9001 Certification (2009). https://www.eurocontrol.int
10. Rodrigues, M.V.: Ações para a qualidade: gestão estratégica e integrada para a melhoria dos processos na busca da qualidade e competitividade - planejamento e estratégia. Campus, Rio de janeiro, 4th edn. (2012)
11. Carpinetti, L.C.R.: Gestão da qualidade: conceitos e técnicas. Atlas, São Paulo (2010)
12. Nonaka, I., Takeuchi, H.: The Knowledge-Creating Company: How Japanese Companies Create the Dynamics of Innovation. Oxford University Press, Oxford (1995)
13. Baskerville, R., Pawslowsky, S., McLean, E.: Enterprise resource planning and organizational knowledge: patterns of convergence and divergence. In: International Conference on Information Systems, vol. 20, pp. 396–406. Association for Information Systems, Atlanta (2000)
14. Thiollent, M.: Metodologia da pesquisa-ação. Cortez, São Paulo (2011)

A Logical Framework for Imprecise and Conflicting Knowledge Representation for Multi-agent Systems

Jair Minoro Abe[✉], Nelio Fernando dos Reis, Cristina Corrêa de
Oliveira, and Avelino Palma Pimenta Jr.

Graduate Program in Production Engineering, Paulista University,
R. Dr. Bacelar 1212, São Paulo, SP 04026-002, Brazil
jairabe@uol.com.br,
{nelio.reis.phd,appimenta}@gmail.com,
crisolive@ig.com.br

Abstract. Nowadays multi-agents has established as one of the most important areas of research and development in information technology. Agents are normally involved in cooperative distributed problem and they face frequently with incomplete and/or conflicting information or task. Since more and more concern is attached to agents' teamwork and agents' dialogue, conflicts naturally arise as a key issue to be dealt with, not only with application dedicated techniques, but also with more formal and generic tools. In this semi-expository paper we show that a formal treatment for multi-agent knowledge representation that can represent conflicts and incomplete information is possible through new logical system, namely the paraconsistente logics. We discuss one of such system adding suitable modal operators for knowledge.

Keywords: Multi-agent systems · Conflicts in distributed systems · Multi-agents and logical representation · Paraconsistente logics

1 Introduction

Multi-agent systems have emerged as one of the most important areas of research and development in information technology in the 1990s. Since the theme has received attention of specialists and nowadays a number of research topics has been considered such as cooperative distributed problem solving, mechanism design, auctions, game theory, multi-agent planning, negotiation protocols, multi-agent learning, conflict resolution, agent-oriented software engineering, including implementation languages and frameworks, E-business agents, novel computing paradigms (autonomic, grid, P2P, ubiquitous computing), among innumerous themes.

In this paper we are focused in the problem of conflict resolution among agents. For this task we need a suitable language for represent agent's communication and moreover inference rules to get interest results; in other words we need an underlying logical system to represent agent's interaction.

© IFIP International Federation for Information Processing 2015
S. Umeda et al. (Eds.): APMS 2015, Part I, IFIP AICT 459, pp. 202–210, 2015.
DOI: 10.1007/978-3-319-22756-6_25

Agents' conflicts arise for different reasons, involve different concepts, and are dealt with in different ways, depending on the kind of agents and on the domain where they are considered.

For example,

- incompleteness and uncertainty of the agents' knowledge or beliefs: in dynamic contexts, an agent may have more recent or more complete information than the others, and the differences in the agents' knowledge create knowledge conflicts;
- limited or unavailable resources: not all agents have access to the same resources, thus resulting in resource conflicts;
- differences in the agents' skills and points of view: autonomous and heterogeneous agents have different abilities, or even different preferences, which can cause conflicts if the agents' pieces of information are not comparable, if they come up with different answers to the same questions, or if they are strongly committed to their own preferences.

Up till now, the focus has been much on how to avoid, solve or get rid of conflicts. However, recent research has shown that conflicts have positive effects in so far as they can generate original solutions and be a basis for a global enrichment of the knowledge within a multi-agent system.

Since more and more concern is attached to agents' teamwork and agents' dialogue, conflicts naturally arise as a key issue to be dealt with, not only with application dedicated techniques, but also with more formal and generic tools.

2 Paraconsistent, Paracomplete, and Non-alethic Logics

In what follows, we sketch the non-classical logics discussed in the paper, establishing some conventions and definitions. Let T be a theory whose underlying logic is L. T is called inconsistent when it contains theorems of the form A and $\neg A$ (the negation of A). If T is not inconsistent, it is called *consistent*. T is said to be *trivial* if all formulas of the language of T are also theorems of T. Otherwise, T is called *non-trivial*.

When L is classical logic (or one of several others, such as intuitionistic logic), T is inconsistent iff T is trivial. So, in trivial theories the extensions of the concepts of formula and theorem coincide. A *paraconsistent logic* is a logic that can be used as the basis for inconsistent but non-trivial theories. A *theory* is called *paraconsistent* if its underlying logic is a paraconsistent logic.

Issues such as those described above have been appreciated by many logicians. In 1910, the Russian logician Nikolaj A. Vasil'év (1880–1940) and the Polish logician Jan Lukasiewicz (1878–1956) independently glimpsed the possibility of developing such logics. Nevertheless, Stanislaw Jaskowski (1996–1965) was in 1948 effectively the first logician to develop a paraconsistent system, at the propositional level. His system is known as 'discussive' (or discursive) propositional calculus'. Independently, some years later, the Brazilian logician Newton C.A. da Costa (1929–) constructed for the first time hierarchies of paraconsistent propositional calculi C_i, $1 \le i \le \omega$ of paraconsistent first-order predicate calculi (with and without equality), of paraconsistent description calculi, and paraconsistent higher-order logics (systems NF_i, $1 \le i \le \omega$).

Another important class of non-classical logics are the paracomplete logics. A logical system is called *paracomplete* if it can function as the underlying logic of theories in which there are formulas such that these formulas and their negations are simultaneously false. Intuitionistic logic and several systems of many-valued logics are paracomplete in this sense (and the dual of intuitionistic logic, Brouwerian logic, is therefore paraconsistent).

As a consequence, paraconsistent theories do not satisfy the principle of non-contradiction, which can be stated as follows: of two contradictory propositions, i.e., one of which is the negation of the other, one must be false. And, paracomplete theories do not satisfy the principle of the excluded middle, formulated in the following form: of two contradictory propositions, one must be true.

Finally, logics which are simultaneously paraconsistent and paracomplete are called *non-alethic logics*.

3   A Logical Framework for Representing Impreciseness, Conflicts and Paracompleteness

We present, in this section, the multimodal predicate calculi Mτ, based on annotated logics extensively studied by Abe [1, 4, 6, 13] and multimodal systems considered in [7, 8, 9, 10, 11, 12].

The symbol $\tau = <|\tau|, \leq, \sim>$ indicates some finite lattice with operator called the *lattice of truth-values*. We use the symbol $\leq$ to denote the ordering under which τ is a complete lattice, $\perp$ and $\top$ to denote, respectively, the bottom element and the top element of τ. Also, $\wedge$ and $\vee$ denote, respectively, the greatest lower bound and least upper bound operators with respect to subsets of $|\tau|$. The operator $\sim : |\tau| \rightarrow |\tau|$ will work as the "meaning" of the negation of the system Mτ.

The language of Mτ has the following primitive symbols:

1. Individual variables: a denumerable infinite set of variable symbols: $x_1, x_2, \ldots$
2. Logical connectives: $\neg$ (negation), $\wedge$ (conjunction), $\vee$ (disjunction), and $\rightarrow$ (implication).
3. For each n, zero or more n-ary function symbols (n is a natural number).
4. For each $n \neq 0$, n-ary predicate symbols.
5. The equality symbol: =
6. Annotational constants: each member of τ is called an annotational constant.
7. Modal operators: $[]_1, []_2, \ldots, []_n, (n \geq 1), []_G, []_G^C, []_G^D$ (for every nonempty subset G of $\{1, \ldots, n\}$).
8. Quantifiers: $\forall$ (for all) and $\exists$ (there exists).
9. Auxiliary symbols: parentheses and comma.

A 0-ary function symbol is called a *constant*. We suppose that Mτ possesses at least one predicate symbol.

We define the notion of *term* as usual. Given a predicate symbol p of arity n and n terms $t_1, \ldots, t_n$, a *basic formula* is an expression of the form $p(t_1, \ldots, t_n)$. An *annotated atomic formula* is an expression of the form $p_\lambda(t_1, \ldots, t_n)$, where λ is an annotational constant. We introduce the general concept of *(annotated) formula* in the standard way. For instance, if A is a formula, then $[]_1A$, $[]_2A$, ..., $[]_nA$, $[]_GA$, $[]_G^CA$, and $[]_G^DA$ are also formulas [7].

Among several intuitive readings, an atomic annotated formula $p_\lambda(t_1, ..., t_n)$ can be read: *it is believed that $p(t_1, ..., t_n)$'s truth-value is at least λ.*

Definition 1. Let A and B be formulas. We put $A \leftrightarrow B = _{\text{Def.}} (A \to B) \wedge (B \to A)$ and $\neg^*A =_{\text{Def.}} A \to ((A \to A) \wedge \neg(A \to A))$. The symbol '$\leftrightarrow$' is called *biconditional* and '$\neg^*$' is called *strong negation*.

Let A be a formula. Then: $\neg^0A =_{\text{Def.}} A$, $\neg^1A =_{\text{Def.}}\neg A$, and $\neg^kA =_{\text{Def.}} \neg(\neg^{k-1}A)$, ($k \in N$, $k > 0$). Also, if $\mu \in \tau$, $\sim^0\mu =_{\text{Def.}} \mu$, $\sim^1\mu =_{\text{Def.}} \sim\mu$, and $\sim^k\mu =_{\text{Def.}} \sim(\sim^{k-1}\mu)$, ($k \in N$, $k > 0$). If A is an atomic formula $p_\lambda(t_1, ..., t_n)$, then a formula of the form $\neg^kp_\lambda(t_1, ..., t_n)$ ($k \geq 0$) is called a *hyper-literal*. A formula other than hyper-literals is called a *complex formula*.

The postulates (axiom schemata and primitive rules of inference) of $M\tau$ are the same of the logics $Q\tau$ [1] plus the following listed below [7], where A, B, and C are any formulas whatsoever, $p(t_1, ..., t_n)$ is a basic formula, and λ, μ, μ_j are annotational constants.

(M1) $[]_i(A \to B) \to ([]_iA \to []_iB)$, $i = 1, 2, ..., n$

(M2) $[]_iA \to []_i[]_iA$, $i = 1, 2, ..., n$

(M3) $\neg^*[]_iA \to []_i\neg^*[]_iA$, $i = 1, 2, ..., n$

(M4) $[]_iA \to A$, $i = 1, 2, ..., n$

(M5) $\frac{A}{[]_iA}$, $i = 1, 2, ..., n$

(M6) $[]_GA \leftrightarrow \wedge_{i \in G}[]_iA$

(M7) $[]_G^CA \to []_G(A \wedge []_G^CA)$

(M8) $[]_{\{i\}}^DA \leftrightarrow []_iA$, $i = 1, 2, ..., n$

(M9) $[]_G^DA \to []_{G'}^DA$ if $G' \subseteq G$

(M10) $\frac{A \to []_G(B \wedge A)}{A \to []_G^B B}$

(M11) $\forall x[]_iA \to []_i\forall xA$, $i = 1, 2, ..., n$

(M12) $\neg^*(x = y) \to []_i\neg^*(x = y)$, $i = 1, 2, ..., n$

$M\tau$ is an extension of the logic $Q\tau$. As $Q\tau$ contains classical predicate logic, $M\tau$ contains classical modal logic S5, as well as the multimodal system studied in [7] in at least two directions. So, usual all valid schemes and rules of classical positive propositional logic are true. In particular, the deduction theorem is valid in $M\tau$ ant it contains intuitionistic positive logic.

Theorem 1. $M\tau$ is non-trivial.

Now we introduce a semantical analysis by using Kripke models [3, 5].

Definition 2. A Kripke model for $M\tau$ (or $M\tau$ structure) is a set theoretical structure $K = [W, R_1, R_2, ..., R_n, I]$ where W is a nonempty set of elements called 'worlds'; R_i ($i = 1, 2, ..., n$) is a binary relation on W such that it is an equivalence relation. I is an interpretation function with the usual properties with the exception that for each n-ary predicate symbol p we associate a function $p_I:W^n \to |\tau|$.

Given a Kripke model K for the language L of Mτ, the *diagram* language $L(K)$ is obtained as usual.

Definition 3. If A is a closed formula of Mτ, and $w \in W$, we define the relation $K,w \Vdash A$ (K,w *force* A) by recursion on A:

1. If A is atomic of the form $p_\lambda(t_1, ..., t_n)$, then $K,w \Vdash A$ iff $p_I(K(t_1), ..., K(t_n)) \geq \lambda$.
2. If A is of the form $\neg^k p_\lambda(t_1, ..., t_n)$ ($k \geq 1$), $K, w \Vdash A$ iff $K,w \Vdash \neg^{k-1} p_{\sim\lambda}(t_1, ..., t_n)$.
3. Let A and B formulas. Then, $K,w \Vdash (A \wedge B)$ iff $K,w \Vdash A$; $K,w \Vdash B$; $K,w \Vdash (A \vee B)$ iff $K,w \Vdash A$ or $K,w \Vdash B$; $K,w \Vdash (A \rightarrow B)$ iff it is not the case that $K, w \Vdash A$ or $K,w \Vdash B$;
4. If F is a complex formula, then $K,w \Vdash (\neg F)$ iff it is not the case that $K,w \Vdash F$.
5. If A is of the form $(\exists x)B$, then $K,w \Vdash A$ iff $K,w \Vdash B_x[i]$ for some i in $L(K)$.
6. If A is of the form $(\forall x)B$, then $K,w \Vdash A$ iff $K,w \Vdash B_x[i]$ for all i in $L(K)$.
7. If A is of the form $[]_i B$ then $K,w \Vdash A$ iff $K, w' \Vdash B$ for each $w' \in W$ such that $wR_i w'$, $i = 1, 2, ..., n$

Definition 4. Let $K = [W, R_1, R_2, ..., R_n, I]$ be a Kripke structure for Mτ. The Kripke structure K *forces* a formula A (in symbols, $K \Vdash A$), if $K,w \Vdash A$ for each $w \in W$. A formula A is called Mτ-*valid* if for any Mτ-structure K, $K \Vdash A$. A formula A is called *valid* if it is Mτ-valid for all Mτ structure. We symbolize this fact by $\Vdash A$.

Theorem 2. Let $K = [W, R_1, R_2, ..., R_n, I]$ be a Kripke structure for Mτ. Then

1. If A is an instance of a propositional tautology then, $K \Vdash A$
2. If $K \Vdash A$ and $K \Vdash A \rightarrow B$, then $K \Vdash B$
3. $K \Vdash []_i(A \rightarrow B) \rightarrow ([]_i A \rightarrow []_i B)$, $i = 1, 2, ..., n$
4. $K \Vdash []_i A \rightarrow []_i []_i A$, $i = 1, 2, ..., n$
5. $K \Vdash []_i A \rightarrow A$, $i = 1, 2, ..., n$
6. If $K \Vdash A$ then $K \Vdash []_i A$, $i = 1, 2, ..., n$

Theorem 3. Let K be a Kripke model for Mτ and F a complex formula. Then we have not simultaneously $K,w \Vdash \neg F$ and $K,w \Vdash F$.

Theorem 4. Let $p(t_1, ..., t_n)$ be a basic formula and $\lambda, \mu, \rho \in |\tau|$. We have $\Vdash p_\perp(t_1, ..., t_n)$; $\Vdash p_\lambda(t_1, ..., t_n) \rightarrow p_\mu(t_1, ..., t_n)$, if $\lambda \geq \mu$; $\Vdash p_\lambda(t_1, ..., t_n) \wedge p_\mu(t_1, ..., t_n) \rightarrow p_\rho(t_1, ..., t_n)$, where $\rho = \lambda \vee \mu$

Theorem 5. Let A and B be arbitrary formulas and F a complex formula. Then:
$\Vdash ((A \rightarrow B) \rightarrow ((A \rightarrow \neg^* B) \rightarrow \neg^* A))$; $\Vdash (A \rightarrow (\neg^* A \rightarrow B))$; $\Vdash (A \vee \neg^* A)$; $\Vdash (\neg F \leftrightarrow \neg^* F)$; $\Vdash A \leftrightarrow \neg^* \neg^* A$; $\Vdash \forall x A \leftrightarrow \exists x \neg^* A$; $\Vdash (A \wedge B) \leftrightarrow \neg^*(\neg^* A \vee \neg^* B)$; $\Vdash \forall A \leftrightarrow \exists x \neg^* A$; $\Vdash \forall x A \vee B \leftrightarrow \exists x(A \vee B)$; $\Vdash A \vee \exists x B \leftrightarrow \exists x(A \vee B)$.

Corollary 5.1. In the same conditions of the preceding theorem, we have not simultaneously $K \Vdash_\neg A$ and $K \Vdash A$. The set of all formulas together with the connectives $\wedge, \vee, \rightarrow$, and $\neg$ has all properties of the classical logic.

Theorem 6. There are Kripke models K such that for some hyper-literals A and B and some worlds w and $w' \in W$, we have $K,w \Vdash \neg A$ and $K,w \Vdash A$ and it is not the case that $K, w' \Vdash B$.

Proof. Let $W = \{\{a\}\}$ and $R = \{(\{a\},\{a\})\}$ (that is $w = \{a\}$) and $p(t_1, \ldots, t_n)$ and $q(t'_1, \ldots, t'_n)$ basic (closed) formulas such that $I(p) \equiv \top$ and $I(q) \equiv \bot$. As $\top \geq \top$, it follows that $p_\top(t_1, \ldots, t_n) \geq \top$. Also, $\top \geq \sim\top$. So, $p_I \geq \sim\top$. Therefore, $K,w \Vdash p_\top(t_1, \ldots, t_n)$ and $K,w \Vdash p_{\sim\top}(t_1, \ldots, t_n)$. By condition 2 of Definition 3, it follows that $K,w \Vdash \neg p_\top(t_1, \ldots, t_n)$. On the other hand, as it is false that $\bot \geq \top$; it follows that it is not the case that $q_I \geq \top$, and so, it is not the case that $K,w \Vdash q_\bot(t'_1, \ldots, t'_n)$. $\square$

Theorem 7. For some systems $M\tau$ there are Kripke models K such that for some hyper-literal formula A and some world $w \in W$, we don't have $K,w \Vdash A$ nor $K, w \Vdash \neg A$.

Corollary 7.1. For some systems $M\tau$ there are Kripke models K such that for some hyper-literal formulas A and B, and some worlds $w, w' \in W$, we have $K,w \Vdash \neg A$ and $K, w \Vdash A$ and we don't have $K,w \Vdash B$ nor $K,w \Vdash \neg B$.

The earlier results show us that there are systems $M\tau$ such that we have "inconsistent" worlds, "paracomplete" worlds, or both.

Now we present a strong version these results linking with paraconsistent, paracomplete, and non-alethic logics.

Definition 5. A Kripke model K is called *paraconsistent* if there are basic formulas $p(t_1, \ldots, t_n)$, $q(t_1, \ldots, t_n)$, and annotational constants $\lambda, \mu \in |\tau|$ such that $K,w \Vdash p_\lambda(t_1, \ldots, t_n)$, $K,w \Vdash \neg p_\lambda(t_1, \ldots, t_n)$, and it is not the case that $K,w \Vdash q_\mu(t_1, \ldots, t_n)$.

Definition 6. A system $M\tau$ is called *paraconsistent* if there is a Kripke model K for $M\tau$ such that K is paraconsistent.

Theorem 8. $M\tau$ is a paraconsistent system iff $\#|\tau| \geq 2$.

Proof. Define a structure $K = [\{w\}, \{(w, w)\}, I]$ such that $\begin{cases} q_I = \bot \\ p_I = \mathrm{T} \end{cases}$

It is clear that $p_I \geq \top$, and so $K \Vdash p_\top(t_1, \ldots, t_n)$. Also, $p_I \geq \sim\top$, and, so $K \Vdash p_{\sim\top}(t_1, \ldots, t_n)$, or $K \Vdash \neg p_\top(t_1, \ldots, t_n)$. Also, it is not the case that $q_I(t_1, \ldots, t_n) \geq \bot$, so it is not the case that $K, w \Vdash q_\bot(t_1, \ldots, t_n)$. $\square$

Definition 7. A Kripke model K is called *paracomplete* if there are a basic formula $p(t_1, \ldots, t_n)$ and an annotational constant $\lambda \in |\tau|$ such that it is false that $K,w \Vdash p_\lambda(t_1, \ldots, t_n)$ and it is false that $K,w \Vdash \neg p_\lambda(t_1, \ldots, t_n)$. A system $M\tau$ is called *paracomplete* if there is a Kripke models K for $M\tau$ such that K is paracomplete.

Definition 8. A Kripke model K is called *non-alethic* if K are both paraconsistent and paracomplete. A system $M\tau$ is called *non-alethic* if there is a Kripke model K for $M\tau$ such that K is non-alethic.

Theorem 9. If $\#|\tau| \geq 2$, then there are systems $M\tau$ which are paracomplete and systems $M\tau'$ that are not paracomplete, $\#|\tau'| \geq 2$.

Corollary 9.1. If $\#|\tau| \geq 2$, then there are systems $M\tau$ which are non-alethic and systems $M\tau'$ that are not non-alethic, $\#|\tau'| \geq 2$.

Theorem 10. Let U be a maximal non-trivial maximal (with respect to inclusion of sets) subset of the set of all formulas. Let A and B formulas whatsoever. Then if A is an axiom of $M\tau$, then $A \in U$; $A \wedge B \in U$ iff $A \in U$ and $B \in U$; $A \vee B \in U$ iff $A \in U$ or $B \in U$; $A \rightarrow B \in U$ iff $A \notin U$ or $B \in U$; If $p_\mu(t_1, ..., t_n) \in U$ and $p_\lambda(t_1, ..., t_n) \in U$, then $p_\rho(t_1, ..., t_n) \in U$, where $\rho = \mu \vee \lambda$; $\neg^k p_\lambda(t_1, ..., t_n) \in U$ iff $\neg^{k-1} p_{\sim\lambda}(t_1, ..., t_n) \in U$. If A and $A \rightarrow B \in U$, then $B \in U$; $A \in U$ iff $\neg^* A \notin U$. Moreover $A \in U$ or $\neg^* A \in U$. If A is a complex formula, $A \in U$ iff $\neg A \notin U$. Moreover $A \in U$ or $\neg A \in U$. If $A \in U$, then $[]_i A \in U$.

Proof. Let us show only 3. In fact, if $p_\mu(t_1, ..., t_n) \in U$ and $p_\lambda(t_1, ..., t_n) \in U$, then $p_\mu(t_1, ..., t_n) \wedge p_\lambda(t_1, ..., t_n) \in U$ by 2. But it is an axiom $p_\mu(t_1, ..., t_n) \wedge p_\lambda(t_1, ..., t_n) \rightarrow p_\rho(t_1, ..., t_n)$, where $\rho = \mu \vee \lambda$. It follows that $p_\mu(t_1, ..., t_n) \wedge p_\lambda(t_1, ..., t_n) \rightarrow p_\rho(t_1, ..., t_n) \in U$, and so $p_\rho(t_1, ..., t_n) \in U$, by 6.

Given a set U of formulas, define $U/[]_i = \{A | []_i A \in U\}$, $i = 1, 2, ..., n$. Let us consider the canonical structure $K = [W, R_i, I]$ where $W = \{U | U$ is a maximal non-trivial set$\}$ and the interpretation function is as usual with the exception that given a n-ary predicate symbol p we associate the function $p_I : W^n \rightarrow |\tau|$ defined by $p_I(\overset{\circ}{t}_1, ..., \overset{\circ}{t}_n) =_{def.} \vee\{\mu \in |\tau| | p_\mu(t_1, ..., t_n) \in U\}$ (such function is well defined, so $p_\perp(t_1, ..., t_n) \in U$). Moreover, define $R_i =_{Def.} \{(U, U') | U/[]_i \subseteq U'\}$. $\square$

Lemma 1. For all propositional variable p and if U is a maximal non-trivial set of formulas, we have $p_{pI(\overset{\circ}{t}_1, ..., \overset{\circ}{t}_n)}(t_1, ..., t_n) \in U$.

Proof. It is a simple consequence of the previous theorem, item 5. $\square$

Theorem 11. For any formula A and for any non-trivial maximal set U, we have $(K, U) \Vdash A$ iff $A \in U$.

Proof. Let us suppose that A is $p_\lambda(t_1, ..., t_n)$ and $(K, U) \Vdash p_\lambda(t_1, ..., t_n)$. It is clear by previous lemma that $p_{pI(\overset{\circ}{t}_1, ..., \overset{\circ}{t}_n)}(t_1, ..., t_n) \in U$. It follows also that $p_I(\overset{\circ}{t}_1, ..., \overset{\circ}{t}_n) \geq \lambda$. It is an axiom that $p_{pI(t1, ..., tn)}(t_1, ..., t_n) \rightarrow p_\lambda(t_1, ..., t_n)$. Thus, $p_\lambda(t_1, ..., t_n) \in U$. Now, let us suppose that $p_\lambda(t_1, ..., t_n) \in U$. By previous lemma, $p_{pI(t1, ..., tn)}(t_1, ..., t_n) \in U$. It follows that $p_I(t_1, ..., t_n) \geq \lambda$. Thus, by definition, $(K, U) \Vdash p_\lambda(t_1, ..., t_n)$. By Theorem 10, $\neg^k p_\lambda(t_1, ..., t_n) \in U$ iff $\neg^{k-1} p_{\sim\lambda}(t_1, ..., t_n) \in U$. Thus, by Definition 3, $(K, U) \Vdash \neg^k p_\lambda(t_1, ..., t_n)$ iff $(K, U) \Vdash \neg^{k-1} p_{\sim\lambda}(t_1, ..., t_n)$. So, by induction on k the assertion is true for hyper-literals.

The other cases, the proof is as in the classical case. $\square$

Corollary 11.1. A is a provable formula of $M\tau$ iff $\Vdash A$

4 Concluding Remarks

It is quite interesting to observe the role of conflict within a multiagent system, i.e. how this system may evolve thanks to, despite, or because of conflicts. Such concept receives different 'interpretations' or characterizations depending on of the domain considered. Some considerations regarding to it

- It is easier not to be in conflict than to be in conflict. The former may mean that the agents are not even interacting. The latter supposes that the agents are within the same context.
- incompleteness and uncertainty of the agents' knowledge or beliefs: in dynamic contexts, an agent may have more recent or more complete information than the others, and the differences in the agents' knowledge create knowledge conflicts;
- limited or unavailable resources: not all agents have access to the same resources, thus resulting in resource conflicts;
- differences in the agents' skills and points of view: autonomous and heterogeneous agents have different abilities, or even different preferences, which can cause conflicts if the agents' pieces of information are not comparable, if they come up with different answers to the same questions, or if they are strongly committed to their own preferences.
- When two agents (in this case, e.g. two robots) a conflict does not seem to be necessarily symmetric: conflict (a, b) does not imply conflict (b, a). When two robots roam in a 2D space for instance, the notion of spatial conflict appears only at the time when a robot attempts to move to the location of the other robot. But the latter does not see this conflict.
- Are conflicts useful? The answer depends on the problem. To be useful, a conflict must be observed. For example, if an agent think about a solution and ask for two other agent's (experts) for an opinion and they have contradictory opinions, the former agent can decide, for instance, consult a third agent.
- What we learn from a conflict depends on the situation. Learning is possible if agents are aware of the conflict.
- Conflicts are positive in certain cases, e.g. they may create specific behaviours, create competition, or stimulate inference.

Up till now, the focus has been much on how to avoid, solve or get rid of conflicts. However, recent research has shown that conflicts have positive effects in so far as they can generate original solutions and be a basis for a global enrichment of the knowledge within a multiagent system. Thus this work is a contribution in this direction, showing, for instance that it is unnecessary to try to avoid conflicts; on the contrary with a logical knowledge representation of conflicts we can manage mathematically them and so it is possible to understand better the nature of them [2].

References

1. Abe, J.M.: Fundamentos da lógica anotada (Foundations of annotated logics). Ph.D. thesis, University of São Paulo, São Paulo, p. 135 (1992) (in Portuguese)
2. Abe, J.M.: Some aspects of paraconsistent systems and applications. Logique et Anal. **15**, 83–96 (1997)
3. Cresswell, M.J.: Intensional logics and logical truth. J. Philos. Logic **1**, 2–15 (1972)
4. Akama, S., Abe, J.M.: Many-valued and annotated modal logics. In: Proceedings of IEEE 1998 International Symposium on Multiple-Valued Logic (ISMVL 1998), pp. 114–119 Fukuoka, Japan (1998)

5. Cresswell, M.J.: Logics and Languages. Methuen and Co, London (1973)
6. Da Costa, N.C.A., Abe, J.M., Subrahmanian, V.S.: Remarks on annotated logic. Zeitschr. f Math. Logik und Grundlagen d. Math. **37**, 561–570 (1991)
7. Fagin, R., Halpern, J.Y., Moses, Y., Vardi, M.Y.: Reasoning About Knowledge. The MIT Press, London (1995)
8. Fischer, M.J. and Immerman, N.: Foundation of knowledge for distributed systems. In: Halpern J.Y. (ed.) Proceedings of the Fifth Conference on Theoretical Aspects of Reasoning about Knowledge, pp. 171–186. Morgan Kaufmann, San Francisco (1986)
9. Lipman, B.L.: Decision theory with impossible possible worlds. Technical report working paper, Queen's University (1992)
10. McCarthy, J.: Ascribing mental qualities to machines. Technical report CRL 90/10, DEC-CRL (1979)
11. Parikh, R., Ramamujan, R.: Distributed processing and the logic of knowledge, pp. 256–268. In: Parikh, R. (ed.) Proceedings of Workshop on Logics of Program (1985)
12. Rosenschein, S.J.: Formal theories of AI in knowledge and robotics. New Gener. Comput. **3**, 345–357 (1985)
13. Sylvan, R., Abe, J.M.: On general annotated logics, with an introduction to full accounting logics. Bull. Symbolic Logic **2**, 118–119 (1996)

Production Planning in Intra-organizational Network – A Study Under the Point of View of Annotative Paraconsistent Logic

Fabio Papalardo[✉], Fabio Romeu de Carvalho, Jose B. Sacomano,
and Jayme Aranha Machado

Post-Graduate Program in Production Engineering,
Paulista University-UNIP, São Paulo, Brazil
{Fabio.Papalardo, fabio.eng.unip}@gmail.com

Abstract. Competitiveness among enterprises, acting within global sustainability, has resorted to several types of administration in order to keep companies in the vanguard of the market. One of the most efficient types of administration is effective Planning, in such a way as to perform a task at the minimum time required and the lowest possible cost. Planning has become ever so complex, due to the innumerable demands from technology and market. A relevant aspect of Planning is that the sectors that influence it, whether productive or not, compound a chain of influences that will determine either success or failure of such Planning. One manner to tackle a network matrix analysis is by Para-consistent Logic, a mathematical model that does not follow Classic Logic. It was then possible to verify the efficacy of this model of Planning analysis, as a method to be used and studied and subsequently adopted and used.

Keywords: Planning · Networks of Companies · Paraconsistent logic

1 Introduction

The globalization phenomenon has brought into the market ever more so the competitiveness among companies and countries, and, in order to maintain sustainable management, new administration models are necessary.

Innovative companies need agile action towards products and services in order to respond quickly and explore new conditions. This agile action, however, must be systematic [1].

At the industrial area, further to the development of new equipments and new technologies, the administration of Production Planning has become much more complex to face demands from market and new technologies.

One of the ways of analyzing this aspect is under the point of view of Networks of Companies; specifically, as far as Production Planning the analysis is done, an Intra-organizational Network.

Within an organization, and among organizations, there must be resource and knowledge channels, and these can be studied as a network [2].

The study of resource channels can be analyzed in various manners, always keeping in mind that an intra-organizational network has its matrix aspect, as a

© IFIP International Federation for Information Processing 2015
S. Umeda et al. (Eds.): APMS 2015, Part I, IFIP AICT 459, pp. 211–218, 2015.
DOI: 10.1007/978-3-319-22756-6_26

company's sectors or departments do form among themselves a matrix network of interdependency.

Analysis resources, like Statistics, Matlab, Ucinet and others, have been studied for a wider vision of Production Planning.

In this work we shall introduce Annotative Paraconsistent Logic in order to visualize a scenery that presents all sectors involved in the industrial process, so to permit efficient Planning, as well as Control aspects to make sure that all planned requisites are kept during production.

2   Theoretic Foundation

2.1   Production Planning

The most important aspect of the context of development and maintenance of a control and planning production system perhaps is the continual change at the competition approach, and such changes should occur from the technological to the strategic and the legal areas [3].

Along with technological development and a wide range of market strategies, as well as alterations of pertinent legislation due to globalization, Production Planning becoming ever more complex, as the number of variables increases systematically and some of these variables may be subject to alteration or even beyond assessment.

Independently of the type of manufacture or manufacturing system, Planning is an essential factor to the success of the task. Traditional systems, as ERP and others are no longer sufficient for a safe and effective planning. Various ERP projects draw into tangible and intangible developments, considerable in different areas, and to attain competitive advantages for organizations; nevertheless there are several histories of failures as companies use ERP [4].

Therefore, new thinking manners, new organizational formats and new logic reasoning must be implemented in order to keep a company competitive as it operates inside an ever changing universe.

2.2   Company Network

One way of planning and analyzing an organization is to look at it as it were a network, that is, where sectors or departments involved in the production process are seen as actors of this task.

The notion of network organization implies the need to rethink the limits of a sector separately, emphasizing the importance of the several types of relationship it has with other actors and institutions [5].

The connection or influence that a sector or actor applies into another must be taken into consideration, so that it is possible a more global view of the process, instead of a static vision of each department by itself.

Obviously each sector receives and exerts different influence over another. The network study defines as central, the department or actor under scrutiny, and proceeds to identify how the other sectors receive and exert influence over it.

In this work, Planning is considered as central to a network, and the actors are: Sales; Product Project; Industrial Engineering or Processes; Production; Quality; Purchasing and Planning, the central agent.

The intensity of relationship between actors is called "density" and it shows the degree of influence of a sector over another. The assessment of density is important to quantify the network.

Networks inside an organization and between organizations must work as a channel of resources and knowledge. It has been found out that the proprieties of regional clusters show marked differences, which intensify as the size of the network increases. It also became evident that companies connect themselves in different modules; therefore network activity must focus on different modules, in order to support the development of networks [2].

The network performance, as far as the flux of resources and knowledge, can be improved by adding connections inside an organization [6].

Meaningful role in these relationships is the strengthening of the links of experience and knowledge of the central. Added knowledge affects positively the company's competitiveness [7].

2.3 Paraconsitent Logic

In order to analyze an inter-organizational network company, we shall adopt a non classical logic, the so called paraconsistent logic.

Operations in models that tolerated the presence of inconsistencies are vital to uphold solutions of particular designs [1].

In annotated paraconsistent logic, one proposition A can be expressed by a matrix $(\mu; \lambda)$, where μ is the degree of belief A and λ is the degree of disbelief that is, A. Let us consider the maximum degree as one (1) and the minimum as zero (0). Therefore, a proposition A can be expressed by symbol "p", denoting $upp_A(1; 0)$, that is, the grade of belief maximum and a grade of non belief minimum; on the other hand, the denial of A can be expressed by the symbol $\neg p_A(0; 1)$, and reflects, by definition $\neg p_A(0; 1) \leftrightarrow p_A(1; 0)$.

In paraconsistent logic may be evidence with degree of belief or disbelief different from the maximum (one), or the minimum (zero), i.e., there may be belief and disbelief in a proposition A. Placed in a Cartesian diagram, with the degree of belief in x-axis and the y-axis in disbelief, all the notes are a unit square (Fig. 1 left side), where are highlighted the extreme points and the point (0.6, 0.2). Importantly, the sum of two parameters μ and λ will not always be 1 (one) as common sense would indicate, since the degrees of belief and disbelief may be independent of each other, for example, a belief factor can be favorable to time execution of a task, and their degree of disbelief can be affected in relation to the delivery time from a vendor.

Therefore we can have extreme situations in which $p_A(0; 0)$ or also $p_A(1; 1)$. In the first case, there is no evidence of belief or non belief, that is, there are no available information and this extreme situation we call "undetermined". The other case we have evidence of maximum belief and, at the same time, evidence of maximum non belief, which we cal "inconsistent". The above extreme cases along with the concepts of

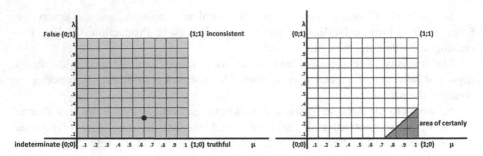

Fig. 1. Cartesian diagram

classical logic – in it we call $p_A(1; 0)$ "Truthful", as the evidences of belief are maximum and non belief are minimum, and the negative of it $p_A(0; 1)$ we call "False", as it denies the Truthful. One point may be closer or more distant from the extremes. It gives us a visual idea of the trend: Truthfulness, Falsity, Inconsistency or Indetermination. Of course the ideal is to have an affirmation the closest possible to the extreme point $p_A(1; 0)$ – Truthful. So, is defined the "Degree of Certainty": it indicates where we are positioned in relation to the ideal $p_A(1; 0)$. The degree of certainty is defined by the equation $H = \mu - \lambda$. Graphically, the degree of certainty is expressed by a line in the graphic.

This is an example that we will use in our methodology. $H = 0,7$. Many combinations may result in $H = 0,7$, that is, $p_A(1; 0,3)$ or $p_A(0,9; 0,2)$ or $p_A(0,8; 0,1)$ or $p_A(0,7; 0)$ and many others.

For the analysis of this work will be considered the region of the unit square, defined by $M \geq 0.7$, called certainly region (Fig. 1 right side).

3 Methodology

The present investigation involved structured interviews with specialists in the areas of Sales, Product Project, Fabrication Processes, Manufacturing, Quality, Purchasing and Planning. The company that was selected is an industry of capital goods, producer of drilling equipment and fluids pumping. Any product is usually "customized", and this is determinant that each product is manufactured just once. Consequently, Planning is essential for low cost and minimum production time, as there is no possibility of improving planning for next production. Interviews were conducted with specialists of managerial rank, one of each area, except the production, for which we interviewed two specialists. Such was necessary because this department is the most sensible to variations of the planning sector, and that is the reason to obtain two opinions of the production area. The criterion adopted for analysis is that each specialist answered questions always through a matrix $(\mu; \lambda)$ and added notes explaining reasons why he had indicated the degrees of belief or non belief. Data was organized in a table. The results indicated by specialists from the same area, in this case, the production, were considered through the disjunction criterion ($\vee$), where, $p_1(\mu_1; \lambda_1) \vee p_2(\mu_2; \lambda_2) \rightarrow p_{1\ or\ 2}(\mu_{max}; \lambda_{min})$. Results from specialists of different areas were considered through the conjunction criterion ($\wedge$), where, $p_1(\mu_1; \lambda_1) \wedge p_2(\mu_2; \lambda_2) \rightarrow p_{1\ or\ 2}(\mu_{mim}; \lambda_{max})$ [8].

The minimum degree of certainty chosen for this work was H = 0,7. Observing the Fig. 2 it appears that the area corresponding to the real area (or certain favorable), we verify that the area in the certainty zone is the area of a triangle 0,3 × 0,3/2, that is a surface of 0.045; graphic total area is the surface of a square 1 × 1, or a surface of 1. The percentage of the certainty area as related to the total surface is $1 - (0.045/1) = 0.955$ and the certainty is 95.5 %, and this is a good number as far as planning is concerned. It is worthy to mention that for more restricted values above 0,7 the costs for the functioning of the network can be very high.

		Sales		Product Project		Processes		Production		Quality		Purchasing		PPC	
		Expert 1		Expert 2		Expert 3		Inter Expert		Expert 6		Especilista 7		Expert 8	
		μ	λ	μ	λ	μ	λ	μ	λ	μ	λ	μ	λ	μ	λ
Sales	Program trends	1	0	0,8	0,2	0,8	0,3	0,8	0,2	0,8	0,3	1	0	0,9	0,3
Product	Benchmarking	0,8	0,3	1	0	0,8	0,2	0,8	0,2	0,8	0,3	0,8	0,2	1	0
Project	Detailed Description	1	0	1	0	1	0	1	0	1	0	1	0	1	0
Processes	Method	0,8	0,3	0,8	0,2	1	0	1	0	0,8	0,2	0,8	0,2	1	0
	Equipment	0,8	0,2	1	0	1	0	1	0	0,8	0,2	0,7	0,3	1	0
Production	Lay Out	0,8	0,2	0,8	0,2	0,8	0,2	0,8	0,2	0,8	0,2	0,9	0,2	0,8	0,2
	Training	0,8	0,3	0,9	0,2	0,8	0,2	1	0	0,8	0,3	0,8	0,3	0,8	0,2
	Kan Ban	0,8	0,2	0,7	0,3	0,8	0,2	0,8	0,2	0,7	0,3	0,8	0,2	0,8	0,2
Quality	Quality System	0,8	0,2	0,8	0,4	0,8	0,2	0,8	0,2	0,8	0,3	0,8	0,2	0,8	0,1
	Statistic Process Control	0,8	0,2	0,8	0,2	0,8	0,2	1	0	0,9	0,3	0,9	0,2	0,8	0,2
Purchasing	Just In Time	0,9	0,2	0,8	0,3	0,8	0,2	1	0	0,8	0,2	1	0	1	0
	PPC	0,8	0,2	0,8	0,2	0,8	0,2	0,8	0,2	0,8	0,2	1	0	0,8	0,2

Fig. 2. Results disjunction criteria

The question brought up was: "How do you classify the condition of the analyzed item?"

The analyzed items were determined by all the consulted specialists through non structured interviews in order to determine the influences of each department over the Planning, considered as the center of the intra-organizational network in this study.

For a better assessment, each particular question was divided into three parts, each corresponding an interval of the degree of certainty: within the target $0,7 \leq H \leq 1$ (a); with relative degree of acceptance $-0,7 \leq H \leq 0,7$ (b); with no acceptance at all $-1 \leq H \leq 0,7$ (c), as we can see in the following list of statements:

Sales: - "*Program Trends*": Stable (a); Increase (b); Decrease (c)
Project Product: - "*Benchmarking*": Very Competitive (a); Somewhat Competitive (b); Hardly Competitive (c)/"*Detailed Description*": High Level Complexity (a); Medium Level Complexity (b); Low Level Complexity (c)
Processes: - "*Method*" and "*Equipment*": Modern and Up to Date (a); not so Modern (b); old (c)
Production: - "*Lay Out*": Functional (a); Not so Functional (b); Difficult to handle and operate (c)/"*Training*": Periodic Training Program (a); Eventual Training Program (b); No Training Program (c)/"*Kan Ban*": Installed (a); Installation in Progress (b); No Kan Ban (c)
Quality: - "*Quality System*": Installed (a); Installation in Progress (b); No Quality System (c)/"*Statistic Process Control*": Installed (a); Installation in Progress (b); No Quality SPC (c)
Purchasing: - "*Just in Time*": Installed (a); Installation in Progress (b); No JIT (c)
Planning Production Control: - "*PPC*": Agile – Quite efficient (a); medium (b); slow off poor performance (c)

Once completed the research, the marks determined by μ and λ were plotted on the graphic. The set of points permits a graphic idea of the network. The total influence of the 12 factors considered is indicated as the gravity center of the network; each point is a knot in a net and the gravity center is the resultant effect of the knots or the center of them [8].

To each knot was assigned the same importance; therefore there are no different values (weights) to add to a knot in order to calculate the gravity center. In case a knot exerts influence of a different weight over the gravity center, a weighted average must be calculated. In this case, the arithmetic mean was also calculated and it did coincide with the weighted average. Therefore, we come up with the global results and hence the present scenario for the sector of Planning.

4 Result and Discussion

After the research the results were found, and according to the disjunction criterion $(\vee)$ among specialists of the same area – Production, we have $p_{1prod}(\mu_1; \lambda_1) \vee p_{2prod}(\mu_2; \lambda_2) \rightarrow p_{1ou\ 2} (\mu_{max}; \lambda_{min})$:

According to the conjunction criterion, among specialists of different areas, we have (Fig. 3):

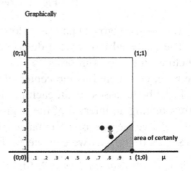

				Network Inter Expert	
				μ	λ
Sales	Program trends			0,8	0,3
Product	Benchmarking			0,8	0,3
Project	Detailed Description			1	0
Processes	Method			0,8	0,3
	Equipment			0,7	0,3
	Lay Out			0,8	0,2
Production	Training			0,8	0,3
	Kan Ban			0,7	0,3
Quality	Quality System			0,8	0,3
	Statistic Process Control			0,8	0,3
Purchasing	Just In Time			0,8	0,2
	PPC			0,8	0,2
Gravity Center (PPC)				0,80	0,25

Fig. 3. Center of gravity scenario

The Center of Gravity, the total effect of the knots, or the center of gravity of the network, comes up as $p_{plan}(0,80; 0,25)$.

It was verified that the center of gravity is not in the region of the desired, as it is not on the region of certainty.

As the objective of Planning is to determine a scenario that makes sure that the task will be performed, individually each factor of lesser certainty was re-analyzed, in order to come up with the global result desired by Planning, that is, right on the area where $H \geq 0,7$.

The chosen factors were Training, KanBan, Quality System, SPC. These factors were chosen based on the notations and comments presented by the specialists when answering the questions.

The Training that had the matrix $p_{train}(0,8; 0,3)$, was based on eventual training programs, which, although not leading to a 100 % certainty, can be effective as far as the workforce involved in Production. New matrix $p_{train} (0,9; 0)$.

KanBan had a matrix $p_{kan}(0,7; 0,3)$; the system analyzed was in the installation process, it was only partially installed. As the installation experience was being positive, total installation was decided. New matrix $p_{kan}(1; 0)$.

The Quality System had a matrix $p_{qual}(0,8; 0,3)$; it was a system in the installation process; it was installed only partially. As the installation experience was positive; it was totally installed. New matrix $p_{qual}(1; 0)$.

SPC which had a matrix $p_{spc}(0,8; 0,3)$ was also being installed, with the same characteristics of the two other items; total installation was decided. The factors chosen for modification in order to achieve the desired result were based on the criteria of lower investment to achieve a combination of μ and λ. In this work was done using the comparison of the most critical items.

New matrix $p_{spc}(1; 0)$.

Other factors, for example, Equipments, also had a low matrix of certainty $P_{equip}(0,7; 0,3)$: it was considered poorly updated; however a decision to bring it up to date would demand a considerable investment and a long installation period – the decision was not to improve this item. Revised planning altered items (Figs. 4 and 5).

Production	Training		0,8	0,3	0,9	0,1
	Kan Ban		0,7	0,3	1	0
Quality	Quality System		0,8	0,3	1	0
	Statistic Process Control		0,8	0,3	1	0

Fig. 4. Revised planning

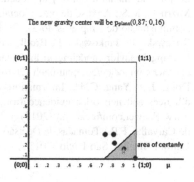

The new gravity center will be $p_{plan}(0,87; 0,16)$

			Network	
			Inter Expert	
			μ	λ
Sales	Program trends		0,8	0,3
Product	Benchmarking		0,8	0,3
Project	Detailed Description		1	0
Processes	Method		0,8	0,3
	Equipment		0,7	0,3
	Lay Out		0,8	0,2
Production	Training		0,9	0,1
	Kan Ban		1	0
Quality	Quality System		1	0
	Statistic Process Control		1	0
Purchasing	Just In Time		0,8	0,2
	PPC		0,8	0,2
Gravity Center (PPC)			0,87	0,16

Fig. 5. Revised center of gravity scenario

5 Conclusion

Paraconsistent logic offers a tool for analysis, which, through the concept of inter-organizational network, guides for attaining the desired scenario, even when some factors or premises are not ideal.

Even when the present scenario does not reach the desired objectives, a re-evaluation may lead to changes, through the adjustment of a few items, thus obtaining a scenario within the expected indicators.

It is important to notice that the questions that were brought up are based on the control of premises, that is, planning is only well managed when the execution of its parameters are being controlled.

In the next paper, we will research the reanalysis of factors for the modification of an actual scenario, using paraconsistent logic and presenting it through a mathematical frame.

Still on this line of thought, we shall research how paraconsistent logic can be used for Production Control, and together with the present work, we intend to present Planning and Production Control according to this logic.

References

1. Ernst, N.A., Borgida, A., Juretac, I.J., Mylopoulos, J.: Agile requirements engineering via paraconsist reasoning. Journal homepage: www.elsevier.com/locate/infosys (2014)
2. Kajikawa, Y., Takeda, I., Matsushima, K.: Multiscale analysis of interfirm networks in regional clusters. Technovation **30**, 168–180 (2010)
3. Vollmann, T.E., Berry, W.L., Whybark, D.C., Jacobs, F.R.: Sistemas de planejamento e controle da produção. Bookman, Porto Alegre (2006)
4. Asla, M.B., Khalilzadeh, A., Youshanloue, H.R., Mood, M.M.: Identifying and ranking the effective factors on selecting enterprise resource planning (ERP) system using the combined Delphi and Shannon Entropy approach. Procedia Soc. Behav. Sci. **41**, 513–520 (2012)
5. Mizruchi, M.S.: Análise de redes sociais: avanços recentes e controvérsias atuais. Revista de Administração de Empresas **46**(3), 10–15 (2006)
6. Rózewski, P., Jankowski, J., Bródka, P., Michalski, R.: Knowledge workers' collaborative learning behavior modeling in an organizational social network. Journal homepage: www.elsevier.com/locate/comphumbeh (2015)
7. Dong, J.Q., Yang, C.-H.: Information technology and organizational learning in knowledge alliances and networks: evidence from U.S. pharmaceutical industry. Journal home page: www.elsevier.com/locate/im (2015)
8. de Carvalho, F.R.: Tomadas de Decisão com Ferramentas da Lógica Paraconsistente Anotada. Editora Blucher, São Paulo (2011)

Mass Customization: Industrial Production Management in Companies Network

Sergio Luiz Kyrillos[1,2], José Benedito Sacomano[1], Fábio Papalardo[1(✉)],
Francisco José Santos Milreu[1], and José Barrozo de Souza[1]

[1] Graduate Program in Production Engineering, Paulista University-UNIP, Dr. Bacelar St. 1212,
São Paulo, Brazil
fabio.eng.unip@gmail.com
[2] School Engineering, São Paulo Federal Institute – IFSP, Dr. Pedro Vicente St. 625,
São Paulo, Brazil
kyrillos@ifsp.edu.br

Abstract. The goal of this report is to analyse how the mass customization manufacturing strategy is being incorporated by a metal-mechanic company that deals with steel drawing. To sustain the research basis regarding the evaluate data, a case study based on research-action methodology was applied. Customisable goods go through the same production processes as regular products, given the fact that the raw material allows flexibility. Nevertheless, customisable goods are made regarding specific mechanical properties and unique profiles, as rounded with specific diameters, or specials, these coming from laminated bars. This entrepreneur vision seeks to integrate the manufacturing process alterations to as down the line as possible. Customers require products that are not always ready to buy in the necessary quantities and different patterns in steel distribution centres, which have regulations to obey before despatch.

Keywords: Business networking · Mass customization · Production

1 Introduction

In this empiric study, the strategic aspects of production and manufacturing are studied from the architecture of companies networks. Under this view, we may conclude that humans, through innovative work and production organisations structures, have become productive entities. We justify this research for the fact that there is a great need to structure the operations and production strategic management model. There are huge gaps in the necessities of production organisations leaderships on conducting the business in the most competitive way as possible.

With that in mind, it becomes relevant for this proposed study to pursue the goal of a management procedure capable of contributing with the production managers of network companies, besides helping to improve the existent production management. In which way can mass customization (MC) be managed and applied in a metal-mechanic industry? What are the inductive requirements to the occurrence of MC on a Production Planning & Control (PPC) strategic model in companies network (NetC)?

© IFIP International Federation for Information Processing 2015
S. Umeda et al. (Eds.): APMS 2015, Part I, IFIP AICT 459, pp. 219–225, 2015.
DOI: 10.1007/978-3-319-22756-6_27

The case study, as it shall be proven, will assure that the implementation of MC – an evolution in the way of organising work and production – brings competitive vantages to the productive process.

2 Bibliographic Review

According to [7] the industrial production system, understood as the 'the group of physical, humane and management procedure elements, designed on a inter-related manner' generating products with aggregated value that surpass the their expenditures, conducting the organization to success.

Due to the intensification of the competition on a global scale, there is a rampant search to aggregate value do the products, as to adequate the productive system to the buyer's necessities besides the pursue of customers' loyalty. The term MC first appeared in 1987 with Stanley Davis in his work "The Perfect Future". MC is understood as the manufacturing system capable of offering personal goods and/or services in large scale, with similar cost of those standard products. Another definition to MC refers to the "ability to offer products and services individually designed to each customer through a highly agile, flexible and integrated system with mass production costs" [3]. According [4] has proposed a PPC based on Manufacturing Management Strategical Paradigms (MaMSPs) and MC should represent a distinctive feature as a competitive advantage and the supply chain must support the demands.

NetC seek to relate the technological level and the productive capacity interacting and offering to the customer a range of products. Actors inserted in a NetC are supporters, supposed to perform business negotiations seeking to bring goods and services nearer the final customer. In a network of companies there is cooperation among the companies and also the collaboration to pursue objectives that wouldn't be accomplished independently. Networks are not a new concept to business. In fact, ever since businesses seeking profit have appeared, cooperative efforts were made to develop products together, and allow valuable support and services to one another. This involves raising the competitiveness, reducing costs, stimulating new business opportunities, reaching for great vantages, gaining velocity in the process and satisfactorily answering customers' needs. NetC PPC contains activities focused in the collective character result, organising efforts to conduce to sucess chain. Companies that develop rapid answer to high quality and personalised products demand shall have competitive advantage [5]. *Latu sensu*, PPC, refers to the production management of goods and services that will be available in future opportunities. The production is the focus of the activities constituted by management structures that stimulate the cooperation inside the company and from company to company.

In this sense is Necessary to integrate flexible technologies to the needs of actors within a reasonable period. These assumptions require new forms of work and organisation in this modern society. Manufactures, particularly agile manufacturing, require designs with integrated and interdependent systems prioritizing interfaces between people, machines and between people and machines. Manufacturing processes have sought to respond with increasing speed to their markets as compared to the responses obtained twenty years ago. This evolution took place due to the rapidly changing economy to a global process in which characteristics can often be expressed in highly complex models. The so-called "competitiveness" is the answer that businesses seek in order to remain at the forefront their markets [2]. Manufacturers throughout the world are facing major new challenges, including shorter product life cycles and increasing competition. The MC is a option to fight that cases. Companies strive to rationalize engineering design, manufacturing, and support processes and to produce a large variety of products at lower costs, modularity is becoming a focus [8]. Reference [10] analyzed and showed a provides a guidelines for managers regarding how to strategically adjust their systems and investments to exploit the complementarities and synergies among the practices for MC development.

3 Methodology and Case Study

3.1 Company Info

Seeking earning more attractive profits and moving away from the traditional format of obtaining margin, which is based on economies of scale, it was noticed a consumer niche products that are not always available in warehouses of iron and steel distributors. Consumers looking for products that can meet their expectations regarding the manufacturing of mechanical parts and components of machines with different applications and constructive characteristics. These are willing to pay higher prices for products made of steel and when subjected to plastic deformation change their mechanical properties depending on the severity of the forming process, the submission of the same to thermal intermediaries or thermochemical treatments.

The search for suppliers that meet the required technical specifications and in adequate quantities has been noticed that within the companies. In steel network chain it is possible to implementation of drawing lines with different profiles (square, round, hexagonal, special cross-sections). A relevant and motivating fact to the implementation of MC refers to the involvement of direct customers as well as customers of those who may not be the end users of the products or services of the transaction throughout the production chain. The operations that interfere with the formation of NetC - permeated by suppliers, for suppliers of suppliers, clients and customers of customers - create supply chains and bring suppliers flow of goods to customers, while the links in this network send manufacturing orders and requests. The two-way traffic - with goods and information following in opposite directions - has been accentuated causing significant changes in production processes including outsourcing the production of components, flexible manufacturing and intensive use of information technology. Thus, instabilities of economic and financial order contributed to erode mass production systems and highlight new conditions companies moulded contours inserted in the global market.

3.2 The Process of Steel Drawing, and Competition Analysis

Wire-drawing consists in making the wire rod (raw material: rods obtained by hot rolling) is forced to pass (by tensile stress) through a calibrated orifice (ring). This is a mechanical forming process by plastic deformation; a common procedure for producing steel wires. Changing the calibrated orifice of the die allows the shaping of different profiles. The drawing process the achievement of wires with controlled diameters and well-defined mechanical properties. In traction banks, it is possible to stretch bars to make special profiles.

Using the current concept of MC, it is clear that in a globalised world - extremely consumerist and utilitarian - all 'ends' tend to have short durations, since the goods have high and induced obsolescence, being the new manufactures the means that are used to other 'ends'. In the high performance parts manufacturing segment, from drawn steel, the material used in addition to meeting specific technical features should allow the identification of very rigid mechanical properties and surface finish (polished drawn, rectified, peeled).

The maintenance of close contact between the commercial area of drawbenches with customers allows the construction of a communication channel which significantly eliminates losses with materials that do not meet requirements relating to the production process. This interface avoids waste, creates savings in project and process, reduces processing time and parts and increases the production. Three factors interfered in the studied manufacturing for it to undertake efforts to implement differentiated lines from this strategic model of manufacturing management.

1. Reliability in the organization information technology system and organised partner network that delivers a information flow.
2. Implementation of a manufacturing system based on the flexibility of the existing lines to enable direct materials for the drawing of steel with different diameters, mechanical properties and profiles, so that there is no idle capacity in processing lines.
3. PPC strongly committed to the time dimension, since it is unacceptable for an activity to add cost at the expense of added value.

For those who observe this case casually, this research ends here. However, transformations of economic order and character management involving production chains, can push into the abyss companies unable to accept the need to serve customers seeking flexibility and functionality order to optimize the performance of their products and see their needs met in terms of price and facilitation of production processes.

In this sense, there is a need to consider the whole post production network once you understand everything you comprehend why customers and suppliers act the way they act. This results from the fact that the competitive advantages, such as reducing costs, reprogramming production processes, increased productivity and profitability will be a consequence of a customized service. Another factor that arises from that is that when we identify our relevant nodes in the network, we will have the key to understanding the PPC in enterprise networks. To obtain relevant data and to justify the implementation of mass customisation in a company in the manufacturing segment, we seek factors present in process capable to tailor high production process, low cost, integration and flexibility in the chain.

Making use of the theory, to improve aspects of reality, and combining aspects of theory to practical application the problem involving this article has been treated by Competitive Analysis Methodology and Technology - CAMT - which focuses on developing better conditions to the production units, as regards the organization of production; [1] note that "assumptions related to the development and implementation of CAMT sending organizational competitiveness (focusing on individual companies) and inter-organizational (which deals with inter-company networks)". The application of the methodology CAMT follows the guidance of the action-research from [9] it capture information that can combine the concepts "theory-application" for validation in practice.

4   Case Analysis and Discussion

The strategy for the MC to the case in question begins by a market research of the company products that are already being produced (with changes to existing ones) and new ones (from the specific raw material).

Sales compile the projection of traded items. After, PPC and Finances prepare the budget for production and costing, and together seek to optimize results with the shortest time (value addition and receiving cash in the shortest time possible) all based on the quantities of products to be produced considering the installed capacity; from then, the detail process is triggered, which is enabled by the engineering for existing products with the necessary changes or new products that are produced from the acquisition of raw material (wire rod/rolled bars) obtained from steel companies or its distributors.

Considering the modeling expressed in Fig. 1 below, it is understood that a PPC designed under the form of network involves the most fundamental economic principles, should predict and provide those involved in supply chains so that all those present agents are understood as productive entities that contribute to the strengthening of the network operations, making the business network to be viable through the value network that has a physical network as basic support.

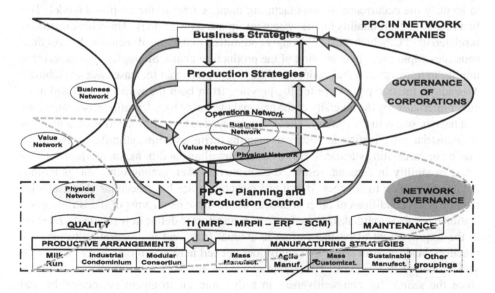

Fig. 1. PPC in NetC. Source: Authors based on conceptual map [6]

The latter - the physical network - is indeed where the productive activities have been actualised. It gives priority to the interrelationship of the inputs flow, capital and technologies that enable the acquisition on the format, on time, in the right quantity, at the opportunity and in the place required by customers. The governance of the corporation (solid line capsule) involves several decisions to be made into a productive character development and from it decisions with increasing complexity can arise.

The governance of the network (grey dash line capsule) involves the management of the physical network with the required specification of production methods, adequacy of the facilities, product quantity and compatible equipment. This requires a management that is involved with the PPC. In Fig. 1 we can see that the MC is a procedure able to support the development in screen. Each organization has a private communication itself to the manifestation of how the tasks are carried out within the complex relationships that make up the organizational structure.

5   Conclusions and Recommendations

The finding of a distinct market acquisition of specific products was the promoter to implant a structured management on the MC associated to deficiency of competitors in meeting the needs performance parts manufacturers generated opportunities to draw-benches. In order to become customizable, the company in question has sought to delay most of the drawn production processes. The PPC seeks to integrate to sales on the most downstream.

Considering the time dimension and performing a thorough analysis of the logistics flow efficiency in the organisation. The aim is to fill orders able to add value by standardizing products considered basics and slowing the manufacturing of items ordered for specific latter applications. In order to make the MC possible inductors requirements are to identify the occurrence of manufacturing management in the proposed model. The first relates to the reliability on the system information technology. The other dimension is related to PPC, which must be strongly committed to the time dimension. Excess time generates capital loss in every link of the production chain. Strategically management implies in transforming the productive time in resources that increase cash availability. Nowadays, the companies are feeling pressure from both the world market and also, either internally, by the diversity of the national market or by international organizations that have business in the country. These movements led to the introduction of new forms of industrial organization in Brazilian manufacturing systems, stimulating the questioning of the existing standards. However, the Brazilian conditions, such as high interest rates, instability in demand, restricted consumer market, among other things require greater adaptation to changes. Brazil and our companies have peculiar characteristics regarding the conditions of other countries where these new forms of industrial organization have also emerged. This study of MC is an effort to define new standards, relevant to the improvement of business of an individual firm, and its integration to network practiced business processes. This study does not end here; it is the basis for others who seek to analyze PCP in NetC. The picture showed in this work was classified as complex, since the search for competitiveness in a dynamic environment permeated by and intensified by global competition demands requires: business reflection, environment context analysis and intellectual daring, all simultaneously. The study deals with the MC strategy from the perspective of PPC in NetC as identified in the conceptual map shown in Fig. 1. This way of conceptualizing the PPC differs from the conventional PPC concepts based, including the understandings of Make to Order (MTO) and Engineering to Order (ETO).

References

1. Barbosa, F.A., Sacomano, J.B., Porto, A.J.V.: Metodologia de análise para redes interorganizacionais: competitividade e tecnologia. Revista Gestão e Produção **14**, 411–423 (2007). São Carlos, SP
2. Boer, W., Fusco, J.P.A.: Produtividade x valor agregado na manufatura: Uma revisão da literatura. Revista Brasileira de Tecnologia Agroindustrial **2**(1), 35–48 (2008). Ponta Grossa, PR
3. Da Silveira, G., Borenstain, D., Fogliatto, F.S.: Mass customization: literature review and research directions. Int. J. Prod. Econ. **72**, 1–13 (2001)
4. Godinho Filho, M., Fernandes, F.C.F.: Manufatura ágil e customização em massa: Conceitos, semelhanças e diferenças. R. Adm. **41**(1), 81–95 (2006). São Paulo, SP
5. Iacocca Institute. Mass Customization. Office of International Affairs Iacocca Institute Professional Education at Lehigh University (2009). http://www.iacocca-lehigh.org/. Accessed 19 Jan 2015
6. Kyrillos, S.L.: Fatores determinantes para o planejamento e controle da produção em redes de empresas: Estudo exploratório em unidades de negócios do segmento metal-mecânico. Tese (doutorado). Programa de Pós-graduação em engenharia de produção. Universidade Paulista, SP (2011)
7. Maccarthy, B.L., Fernandes, F.C.F.: A multi-dimensional classification of production systems for the design and selection of production planning and control systems. Prod. Plann. Control **11**(5), 481–496 (2000). London
8. Shaik, A.M., Rao, V.V.S.K., Rao, C.S.: Development of modular manufacturing system - a review. Int. J. Adv. Manuf. Technol. **76**, 789–802 (2015). Springer, Verlag-London
9. Thiollent, M.: Pesquisa-ação nas organizações. Atlas, São Paulo (2007)
10. Zhang, M., Zhao, X., Qi, Y.: The effects of organizational flatness, coordination, and product modularity on mass customization capability. Int. J. Prod. Econ. **158**, 145–155 (2014). Elsevier, BV

A Heuristic Approach for Integrated Nesting and Scheduling in Sheet Metal Processing

Tatsuhiko Sakaguchi$^{(\boxtimes)}$, Hayato Ohtani, and Yoshiaki Shimizu

Toyohashi University of Technology, Toyohashi, Aichi, Japan
{sakaguchi,shimizu}@me.tut.ac.jp, otani@ise.me.tut.ac.jp

Abstract. In recent years, sustainable and agile manufacturing is aimed at in many manufacturing industries. Reducing the waste of raw materials and managing the production schedule are important factors for such manufacturing. Nesting is an activity designing a cutting layout while scheduling is one managing operational procedures. Noting such nesting and scheduling in sheet metal processing, we need to consider those simultaneously for increasing the entire efficiency. This is because there often occurs a trade-off between them. To resolve such problem, we previously proposed an integrated method of nesting and scheduling. In order to enhance the scheduling ability that was insufficient in our method, this study extends the idea through a heuristic approach. Actually, we apply a local search to update the initial schedule which is decided by EDD based dispatching rule and manage it in terms of the criteria referring to the bottleneck process. Computational experiment is provided to validate the effectiveness of the proposed method.

Keywords: Scheduling · Nesting · Dispatching rule · Bottom left algorithm · Sheet metal processing

1 Introduction

In recent years, manufacturing industries face with increase in raw material cost and diversification of customer needs. In order to provide various products in shorter lead-time and at low price, therefore, it is essential to facilitate highly efficient production planning and operation. From this aspect, this study proposes a heuristic approach for integrating nesting and scheduling in sheet metal processing. In the sheet metal processing, parts cut from sheet metals are processed in an order of bending, welding and assembling processes. The decision of cutting layout is called nesting. In such processing, nesting and scheduling are the important factors to achieve the manufacturing goal in an effective manner. So far, they have been considered separately in each management sector.

To work with the problem, we particularly notice a trade-off between nesting and scheduling due to the differences of objective and property referring to each process. A cutting layout must be decided so as to reduce the waste of materials as much as possible. Hence, the objective of nesting is to minimize the waste

© IFIP International Federation for Information Processing 2015
S. Umeda et al. (Eds.): APMS 2015, Part I, IFIP AICT 459, pp. 226–234, 2015.
DOI: 10.1007/978-3-319-22756-6_28

of raw materials. On the other hand, to provide products in a short time, the operation sequence should be decided by optimizing schedules for all manufacturing processes. So the objective of scheduling is to minimize the make-span or total tardiness. Moreover, while the efficiency of nesting can be affected by the result of scheduling, in turn, scheduling will be affected by the result of nesting. Thus, though nesting and scheduling are different problems essentially, we know those problems should be considered simultaneously to increase the efficiency of entire manufacturing activity.

Under such understanding, we have proposed an integrated method of nesting and scheduling [1]. In our method, we firstly decide the schedule by using a dispatching rule on the basis of Earliest Due Date (EDD). After that, according to the operation sequence obtained by scheduling, we decide the cutting layout by applying Bottom Left (BL) algorithm. By this procedure, we can obtain the suitable cutting layout that considers the schedule of the following processes. However, the quality of such scheduling is not high due to a particular characteristic of schedule for sheet metal processing. Thereat, we need to decide a schedule by considering a fact that the bending process often becomes bottleneck. In this study, therefore, we attempt to extend our previous method in order to enhance the quality of scheduling or scheduling ability. Specifically, we apply a local search to update the initial schedule and manage it in terms of the criteria referring to the bottleneck process.

2   Problem Description [2]

2.1   Decision of Cutting Layout

In sheet metal processing, parts are cut from a rectangular sheet metal by using a turret punch press or a laser beam machine. In order to reduce a waste material, parts are assigned in a sheet metal as many as possible. This assignment operation is called nesting. Nesting is a spatial layout problem which decide where a part is located without overlapping with already-located parts within a rectangular sheet metal. Generally, the shape of parts is irregular, and the thickness typically varies between 1 and 10 mm. For simplicity, in this study, we assume the following conditions.

1. The shape of parts and sheet metals is filled rectangle.
2. Thickness of parts and sheet metal is constant.

Under the above conditions, we can solve the nesting problem as a two dimensional bin packing problem [3]. We formulate the nesting problem as follows.

$$Minimize \sum_{k \in K} k\delta_k \qquad (1)$$

Subject to

$$\sum_{k \in K} \gamma_{i,k} = 1, \quad \forall i \in I \tag{2}$$

$$0 \leq x_i \gamma_{i,k} \leq (W - w_i)\gamma_{i,k}, \quad \forall i \in I, \forall k \in K \tag{3}$$

$$0 \leq y_i \gamma_{i,k} \leq (L - l_i)\gamma_{i,k}, \quad \forall i \in I, \forall k \in K \tag{4}$$

At least one of the next four inequalities holds for every pair i and i'.

$$(x_i + w_i)\gamma_{i,k} \leq x_{i'}\gamma_{i',k}, \quad \forall k \in K \tag{5}$$

$$(x_{i'} + w_{i'})\gamma_{i',k} \leq x_i \gamma_{i,k}, \quad \forall k \in K \tag{6}$$

$$(y_i + l_i)\gamma_{i,k} \leq y_{i'}\gamma_{i',k}, \quad \forall k \in K \tag{7}$$

$$(y_{i'} + l_{i'})\gamma_{i',k} \leq y_i \gamma_{i,k}, \quad \forall k \in K \tag{8}$$

where,

δ_k: 0-1 variable. If k^{th} sheet is used, set $\delta_k = 1$. Otherwise, 0

$\gamma_{i,k}$: 0-1 variable. If part i is assigned to k^{th} sheet, set $\gamma_{i,k} = 1$. Otherwise, 0

l_i: Length of part i

w_i: Width of part i

L: Length of sheet metal

W: Width of sheet metal

x_i: x-coordinate of bottom left corner of part i

y_i: y-coordinate of bottom left corner of part i

k: Sheet number ($k = 1 \cdots K$)

i: Part number ($i = 1 \cdots I$)

Equation (1) represents the objective function that tries to minimize the number of sheet metals. Equation (2) means that all parts should be assigned to either sheet metal. Equations (3) and (4) mean that all parts must be placed into the sheet metal. Equations (5)–(8) means that no two parts overlap.

2.2 Scheduling Problem in Sheet Metal Processing

The sheet metal processing is basically schedules as a flow shop. The processes are composed of punching, bending, welding and assembling. All parts are processed

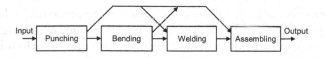

Fig. 1. Process sequence of sheet metal processing

in each process in the same order, though some parts can skip some of the following processes as shown in Fig. 1.

In punching process, a set of parts is cut from a sheet metal. This set is determined according to the cutting layout. Some parts cut from sheet metals are processed in bending process. In bending process, each part is bent respectively by using a press brake. After that, a set of parts are sent to welding or are assembling process. Though bending process is able to process every part independently, in welding and assembling processes multiple parts must be gotten ready for processing. This causes unbalance of workload due to the length of waiting times, and bending process likely becomes bottleneck. In this study, we solve the total tardiness minimization problem under the following conditions.

1. Product is consisted of one or more parts.
2. Every product has a different due date.
3. Every part is processed at one or more processes.
4. Required process for each part is predetermined.
5. Each process has one or more machine, but the machine assignment for each part is predetermined by process plan.
6. Processing time of each operation is predetermined.
7. In bending process, machine can process at most one part at a time.
8. In punching, welding and assembling processes, the parts are allowed to be processed simultaneously.
9. Welding and assembly operations may start only after all operations of parts to be combined have been completed.

2.3   Relation Between Cutting Layout and Schedule

As mentioned in Sect. 1, there exists a certain trade-off relation between nesting and scheduling. Let us consider that the parts of the different products having different due date are assigned to a same sheet metal in order to reduce the waste of raw material. If the part with a strict due date is assigned to the last sheet metal in the processing order, this product may not satisfy the due date. On the other hand, when only the parts having same due date are assigned to a sheet metals, a waste area which no parts are assigned may become large. Therefore, nesting and scheduling are considered simultaneously in order to increase the efficiency of entire manufacturing activity.

As mentioned already, we solve a nesting problem as a two dimensional bin packing problem. A lot of algorithms have been proposed for solving this problem. Lodi et al. [3] surveyed classical approximation algorithms, recent heuristic and metaheuristic method and exact enumerative approaches. Baker et al. [4] proposed Bottom Left (BL) algorithm. In this algorithm, according to the pre-determined assignment priority, rectangles are placed from bottom left corner.

On the other hand, there also exists a lot of studies dealing with a schedul-ing problem. The scheduling problem of sheet metal processing is similar to the two-stage assembly scheduling problem which is a generalization of the two-machine flowshop problem. Potts et al. [5], for example, applied the compact vector summation technique for finding approximation solutions for this prob-lem. Allahverdi and Al-Anzi [6] proposed a Particle Swarm Optimization (PSO) and Tabu search heuristics for solving this problem with respect to Maximum lateness.

However, these studies solved only a nesting problem or a scheduling problem, but did not solve both of them simultaneously. Chryssolouris et al. [7] proposed a rule base decision-making approach for combined problem of scheduling and nesting. Since this paper concerns with a textile industry, only a cutting process is considered in scheduling. Verlinden et al. [8] proposed a integrated production planning model for sheet metal processing, aiming at creating feasible groupings of parts. However, this study does not decide the position of parts in sheet metal.

3   Integrated Nesting and Scheduling Method

3.1   Entire Procedure

Basic concept of the proposed method is summarized as follows. First, the min-imum required number of sheet is estimated. According to this estimated value, the scheduling problem is solved next by applying EDD based dispatching rule. Then the layout of the parts in the sheet metal is decided. We use BL algorithm to determined the position of each part. In our study, an assignment priority of BL algorithm is determined in accordance with the ascending order of starting time of operations. After that, the initial schedule is modified by applying local search. We explain the detail of local search procedure in the next section. The proposed nesting-scheduling is performed according to the following steps.

Step1: Estimation of minimum processing time for punching process

Required minimum processing time for punching process is calculated by the following equation.

$$ft_{punch} = \left\lceil \frac{\sum_{i \in I} l_i w_i}{LW} \right\rceil \times pt_{punch} \qquad (9)$$

where,

ft_{punch}: Estimated minimum processing time for punching process

pt_{punch}: Processing time of punching process for one sheet metal

$\lceil \rceil$: Ceiling function

Step2: Creation of initial schedule by applying dispatching rule

EDD based dispatching rule is applied to all processes except for the punching process in order to create the initial schedule. The operation sequence of punching process cannot be decided because the actual required number of sheet metal is not determined before nesting. Therefore, we use an estimated minimum processing time for punching process calculated by Step1 as a completion time for this process.

Step3: Decision of cutting layout by using BL algorithm

The cutting layout is decided sequentially according to the pre-determined order of priority. It is set as follows based on the priority criterion in terms of the schedule of the bending process.

1. Earliest starting time of operation
2. Earliest finishing time of operation
3. Earliest due date
4. If the above are all equivalent, select part randomly

In addition to the above rule, we consider the following exception to increase the nesting efficiency. When the part with the next priority cannot be assigned to the present sheet, we allow assigning the part from the ones with the lower priority in turn.

Step4: Improvement of initial schedule by applying local search

The operation sequence of punching process is determined according to the actual required number of sheet metal, which is obtained by the nesting result. After that, in order to improve the initial schedule, the operation sequence of bending process is modified by applying local search.

3.2   Local Search for Improving Initial Schedule

As mentioned in Sect. 2.2, bending process often become a bottleneck in sheet metal processing. While every part is processed independently in bending process, a set of parts has to be processed simultaneously in welding and assembling processes. Therefore, in welding and assembling processes, processes cannot be started until every necessary part will arrive there. The length of waiting time is affected by the operation sequence of bending process. In order to minimize the total tardiness, therefore, it becomes effective if the operation sequence of bending process is determined by considering the combination of parts. Under such understanding, we improve the initial schedule by applying local search. The operation sequence of bending process is modified according to the following steps.

Step1: Recognition of bottleneck operations

Bottleneck operations are extracted from all operations in bending process. We define bottleneck operation as the last operation to process the same product in bending process.

Step2: Exchange of operation sequence

For each bending machine, the position of neighboring sets of operations is exchanged. Where, a set of operations is defined as the successive operations

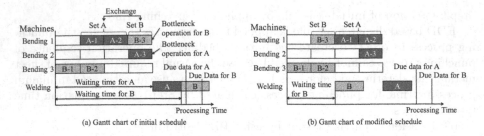

Fig. 2. Example result of local search

to process same product. The neighboring sets is exchanged only when the relation between neighboring sets do not violate the following criteria.

– A forward set of operations includes a bottleneck operation.
– After exchanging, each finishing time of operation in set of operations is later than that of bottleneck operation.
– After exchanging, each starting time of operation in set of operations is earlier than the finishing time of its punching operation.
– Processes for neighboring sets of operations are different. (In other words, an exchange is performed only when a process of both sets is welding, or assembling.)

These steps are iterated until no set of operations can be exchanged.

Figure 2 shows an example of local search. This figure represents a Gantt chart. The rectangles with same capital letter represent the operations of same product. In this case, operation B-3 at bending machine 1 and operation A-3 at bending machine 2 are bottleneck operation. In the initial schedule (a), product B cannot satisfy due date. However, by exchanging the position of set A and set B at bending machine 1, the welding operation of B can start earlier. As a result, product B can satisfy due date.

4   Computational Experiments

In order to validate the effectiveness of the proposed method, we carried out 5 different case studies whose conditions are shown in Table 1. In this table, a skip rate is the ratio showing how many parts skip each process. Other computational conditions are summarised as follows. Where, the number of parts and the processing time are set randomly between figures in parentheses.

– Number of machines: Punching 1, Bending 5, Welding 2, Assembling 2
– Number of products: 10
– Number of parts: [3, 7] for each product
– Processing time: [1, 100]

Table 1. Skip rate for each case

Case number	1	2	3	4	5
Skip rate for bending [%]	0	50	0	0	50
Skip rate for welding [%]	0	0	50	0	50
Skip rate for assembling [%]	0	0	0	30	30

Table 2. Result of experiments

Case number	1	2	3	4	5
Total tardiness (Initial schedule)	8159	2977	8236	4212	7953
Total tardiness (After local search)	**7290**	2977	**7656**	**4089**	**7893**

In order to verify the effectiveness of proposed local search, we compared the total tardiness of initial schedule which is determined by only EDD based dispatching rule. Table 2 shows the result of scheduling. We were able to obtain shorter total tardiness except for case 2, by the proposed method. In case 2, we were not able to improve total tardiness. The skip rate for bending process is high in this case. In other words, the number of operations in bending process is small in this case. Thus the candidates for exchanging position of operation became smaller than other cases. However, we were able to reduce total tardiness by 3–11 % in all other cases.

In addition, the number of sheet metal was 52 for every case. The proposed local search modifies only the operation sequence of bending process. Therefore, the number of sheet metal never increases.

5 Conclusion

To meet the recent requirements on manufacturing, we have concerned an integrated method of nesting and scheduling in sheet metal processing. Noticing the bending process often becomes a bottleneck, we proposed a heuristic method that applies a local search to enhance the scheduling ability from our previous method. Actually, we took several criteria associated with the bottleneck operation into account so that the position of neighboring sets of operations is exchanged adequately in the proposed local search. In order to validate the effectiveness of the proposed method, we carried out computational experiments.

Acknowledgment. This research was partially supported by the Ministry of Education, Culture, Sports, Science and Technology, Grant-in-Aid, 15K17950, Japan.

References

1. Sakaguchi, T., Murakami, T., Fujita, S., Shimizu, Y.: A scheduling method with considering nesting for sheet metal processing. In: ASME/ISCIE 2012 International Symposium on Flexible Automation, St. Louis, ISFA2012-7197 (2012)
2. Sakaguchi, T., Matsumoto, K., Shimizu, Y.: Study on nesting scheduling for sheet metal processing (Improvement of nesting method by parts reallocation). Trans. JSME (in Japanese) **81**(825), 14-00640 (2015)
3. Lodi, A., Martello, S., Monaci, M.: Two-dimensional packing problems: a survey. Eur. J. Oper. Res. **141**(2), 241–252 (2002)
4. Baker, B.S., Coffman Jr., E.G., Rivest, R.L.: Orthogonal packing in two dimensions. SIAM J. Comput. **9**, 846–855 (1980)
5. Potts, C.N., Sevastjanov, S.V., Strusevich, V.A., Van Wassenhove, L.N., Zwaneveld, C.M.: The two-stage assembly scheduling problem: complexity and approximation. Oper. Res. **43**(2), 346–355 (1995)
6. Allahverdi, A., Al-Anzi, F.S.: A PSO and a Tabu search heuristics for the assembly scheduling problem of the two-stage distributed database application. Comput. Oper. Res. **33**, 1056–1080 (2006)
7. Chryssolouris, G., Papakostas, N., Mourtzis, D.: A decision-making approach for nesting scheduling: a textile case. Int. J. Prod. Res. **38**(17), 4555–4564 (2000)
8. Verlinden, B., Cattrysse, D., Van Oudheusden, D.: Integrated sheet-metal production planning for laser cutting and bending. Int. J. Prod. Res. **45**(2), 369–383 (2007)

Identification of Drivers for Modular Production

Thomas Ditlev Brunoe[(✉)], Jacob Bossen, and Kjeld Nielsen

Department of Mechanical and Manufacturing Engineering, Aalborg University,
Fibigerstraede 16, 9220 Aalborg East, Denmark
tdp@m-tech.aau.dk

Abstract. Todays competitive environment in industry creates a need for companies to enhance their ability to introduce new products faster. To increase ramp-
up speed reconfigurable manufacturing systems is a promising concept, however
to implement this production platforms and modular manufacturing is required.
This paper presents an analysis whether and which module drivers from general
product development can be applied to the development process of a modular
manufacturing system. The result is a compiled list of modular drivers for manufacturing and examples of their use.

Keywords: Production platforms · Drivers · Modular manufacturing

1 Introduction

It is generally accepted that the dynamics of markets of today call for higher product
variety as well as reduced product life cycles compared to just one or two decades ago
[4]. This calls for manufacturing companies to become more efficient in introducing new
products into the production system and ramping up production. As product lifecycles
shorten, it becomes increasingly critical to minimize the investments in establishing and
ramping up production, since the time for return of investment in the manufacturing
system incurs over a shorter period than previously. For this reason, reuse of parts of or
reuse of entire production systems becomes increasingly relevant, as this is one means
to reduce cost of investments related to new product introduction in the manufacturing
system. One way to achieve this, is by implementing a flexible manufacturing system,
a system that consists of generic manufacturing equipment, e.g. CNC mills, which can
perform a wide variety of manufacturing tasks, but is relatively inefficient compared to
a dedicated manufacturing system, which on the other hand has very little flexibility [4].
Introduced as a new class of production systems, reconfigurable manufacturing systems
as introduced by Koren [4] realizes a predefined level of flexibility, but reaches a level
of efficiency near that of dedicated manufacturing systems.

A major enabler for implementing reconfigurable manufacturing systems, as well as
a major enabler for reusing assets between different dedicated manufacturing systems
in a company, or reusing assets from one manufacturing system generation to another
is modularity.

The concept of product platforms is relatively well described in literature, whereas less
literature is to be found concerning production platforms. Product platforms are defined

© IFIP International Federation for Information Processing 2015
S. Umeda et al. (Eds.): APMS 2015, Part I, IFIP AICT 459, pp. 235–242, 2015.
DOI: 10.1007/978-3-319-22756-6_29

differently in literature; however in this paper the definition by Ulrich and Eppinger: "... the set of assets shared across a set of products. Components and subassemblies are often the most important of these assets" is adopted [10]. Modularity is closely related to platforms although fundamentally a different concept. Modularity of a system implies that the system is divided into a number of well-defined modules which each implement well defined functions separately, and the interfaces to each module are as simple as possible and well defined. Other research describes the relation between modularity and platform architecture: *"platform architecture displays a special type of modularity, in which a product or system is split into a set of components with low variety and high reusability, and another set with high variety and low reusability"* [1]. This implies that modularity enables a platform architecture, and thus platform architectures will always be modular, while modular architectures may not always apply platform architectures.

The concepts of modularity and platform architecture have been adopted to the production domain, and labelled production platforms [6, 9] and modular manufacturing. The basic concepts of modularity and platform architecture can be altered directly from products to production however; specific methods for designing manufacturing systems introduced as generic product development modularization methods are not directly applicable. The before mentioned modular manufacturing systems are though depended on a structured co-development and co-evolution strategy with supporting design methodologies.

Platform-based Co-development is essentially a research field within the discipline of concurrent engineering and integrated product development, where cross-functional work and information sharing is in focus. The idea is to create and intelligently visualise boundaries for product and production system design in a co-development process, such that variety is only present where it is desirable and acceptable [8]. Early studies of platform-based co-development had inclusions of production aspects in product platform design [7], hence production system assets can be reused.

After the definition on product platforms [7], the term *Process Platform* was coined conceptual wise [3] to underline the production aspect, and later the term was elaborated in another study [13]. Most of the literatures on process platforms focus around generic product and process structures, generic routing, generic planning and generic variety representation. Even though the process platform literature focuses on both product and process structure, the literature lacks support for co-development where a more holistic view is essential.

Research on modular product development states that in order to achieve the optimal product architecture, different criteria for performing the modularization must be considered and prioritized [2, 5, 10]. These criteria are referred to by some as module drivers [5]. Considering different criteria when modularizing a production system or establishing a production platform is also considered of paramount importance, however in the literature reviewed in this research, no systematic exploration of production platform drivers has been identified.

1.1 Resarch Question and Method

The objective of this paper is thus to contribute to modular production development and the area of production platform development by identifying module drivers in production.

Since module drivers in product development are well described, we will take the approach to evaluate different module drivers from product development and adopt those to a production system context. The research question of this paper is thus: *Which module drivers from product development can be translated into drivers for modules in production systems and production platforms?*

The research question has been addressed by reviewing literature and identifying literature describing module drivers in general product development. Each of the identified drivers is evaluated to determine whether they make sense in terms of using them in a production system context and a new definition is proposed which directly addresses modules in production systems.

The basis for evaluating and formulating the module drivers is primarily the work of Ulrich and Eppinger [10] and Ericsson and Erixon [2], as these two frameworks by far present the most elaborate set of module drivers. As described by Wiendahl et al. [12], production system changeability and thereby also modularity is relevant on multiple levels. These levels are defined as (1) station, (2) Cell, (3) System, (4) Segment, (5) Factory, and (6) Network. Modularity in production systems can be relevant at each level, meaning that e.g. a line can be perceived as a module, just as well as a station or an entire factory can be defined as modules. We would even consider lower levels as candidates for modules, e.g. machines, tools or parts of tools, as suggested by Koren [4]. Hence, the examples given below will refer to various levels in production systems to illustrate the diversity of the concept of modularity in manufacturing.

2   Identification of Drivers

In relation to the method modular function deployment a number of module drivers are proposed [2, 5]. These drivers are outlined below: (1) Module carryover, (2) technology Evolution, (3) Planned product Changes, (4) Different Specification, (5) Variety Styling, (6) Common unit, (7) Process and/or Organization, (8) Separate Testing, (9) Supplier available, (10) Service and Maintenance, (11) Upgrading, and (12) Recycling. Ulrich and Eppinger [10] identified a number of factors which are essential to consider when clustering product functions in chunks, which is their terms for defining the modularity. These factors translate directly into module drivers using the terminology of Ericsson and Erixon [2]. These factors are outlined in the following and are to some extent similar, however this will be addressed in the following and a complete list of module drivers will be presented: (1) Geometric Integration and Precision, (2) Function Sharing, (3) Capabilities of Vendors, (4) Similarity of Design or Production Technology, (5) Localization of Change, (6) Accommodating Variety, (7) Enabling Standardization, and (8) Portability of Interfaces.

In the following, the identified primary module drivers will be described in more detail. To combine the different module drivers identified above, five categories are used: (1) Localization of changes in product, (2) Variety and standardization, (3) Production (4) Service and Recycling (5) Product development.

2.1 Product Development

The module driver geometric integration and precision is relevant in products where certain components need to be very carefully aligned for the product to function. Examples of this include cameras, where the optics and sensors need to be very carefully positioned to function correctly. By integrating such components in the same module, there is a lower risk of quality issues in the finished product, since assembly precision will not be an issue in the final assembly of the product. We consider this driver relevant to production modularity, since e.g. assembly operations in manufacturing need very precise alignment of parts and equipment positioning these parts, e.g. manipulators must be very precisely aligned to function properly, and this would likely promote these different functions to be incorporated in the same module of the manufacturing system. Another module driver is function sharing. This refers to cases where two functions in a product can share some kind of subfunction. This module driver is widely applied in design of electronics, where certain functions may be implemented on the same circuit board to share functions like power supply, a micro-processor or cooling. By sharing a support function, the cost of developing producing that support function is saved and the size of the final product may be reduced. In a manufacturing context an example of function sharing within a module could be a robot welding cell, here considered one module, where two fixtures share one welding robot. In this case, because the fixtures "share" the welding robot, a higher utilisation of the robot can be achieved as one fixture can be loaded while the robot welds on the other fixture. Michaelis provides an industrial example of this [8].

In some product types, the portability of interfaces is an essential module driver. Components which have interfaces which are not easily portable will usually be beneficial to implement in one module. The portability of an interface is defined by how easy it is to place two components with a common interface apart from each other. Some specific types of interfaces are more easily portable than others. For example electrical interfaces are usually more portable than mechanical or force transmitting interfaces. This driver is also considered relevant in production systems, since interfaces between different manufacturing equipment also have different portability. Consider painting and drying operations in a production. These two operations must be located next to each other to minimize transport, as transport of wet paint would damage the paint, due to dust and impurities. Other interfaces are more portable, e.g. data interfaces between a control module and a mechanical machine module.

2.2 Localization of Changes

Module carryover refers to cases where some function in the product is not expected to change for a number of product generations. In these cases it is usually beneficial to cluster this function in a module since this module can be 'carried over' more or less unchanged to later generations of the product [2]. This implies that the cost of developing that module type will not occur in subsequent development projects using the module, leading to reduced development cost.

Technology evolution refers to parts of a product where a change can be expected which is caused by demand for new technology, the presently used technology becomes obsolete or opportunities regarding e.g. new materials are introduced [2]. In manufacturing, this could be e.g. a shift from arc welding to laser welding that requires new equipment, and by isolating the welding equipment in one module, the propagation of change can be contained. Planned product changes are similar to technology evolution, however, what drives these changes in the product is not technology but rather product changes, which are part of a product plan e.g. to provide new functionality to the customer. Although in some cases, this would imply using new technology as described above this is not always the case and the motivation for making the change is fundamentally different. In manufacturing systems, this would translate into changes in production capacity or capability, meaning that some production modules may be defined, e.g. an expensive bottleneck operation, which needs to be upgraded when increased production capacity is required.

The benefits of implementing elements, which are expected to change, either due to technology evolution or due to planned changes, are very similar. By clustering these elements in one or a few modules, the change will be focused in that particular module and thus the rest of the production system may remain unchanged. Assuming that making changes in fewer modules leads to lower cost, clustering elements expected to change will reduce development costs for changing the production system to meet future requirements.

2.3 Variety and Standardization

Although contrasting concepts, in relation to modular products, variety and standardization are closely related. It is widely acknowledged that modular product design is an efficient means to achieve a high product variety at low costs. The reason for this is that a product family designed with interfaces supporting exchange of modules may present the customer with a very large variety by combining even a small number of modules.

Ericsson and Erixon [2] have classified the variety into product specification and styling variety, where product specification refers to the actual functionality of the product, whereas styling only refers to the appearance. Since production equipment is seldom specified in terms of aesthetics, we consider the styling driver irrelevant,

The module driver common unit or enabling standardization is the idea of identifying a function which is required in a number of different products in a product portfolio, developing a module implementing this function and utilize it in all of these products. By doing this, development effort is saved, since the module needs only to be designed once, and economies of scale can be achieved in production with lower unit costs as a result [2, 11].

Considering production systems with multiple similar parallel operations, as for example injection moulding of different plastic parts, it may be beneficial to define a "standard module" consisting of a moulding machine and material feeder and a variety carrying module consisting of moulding forms. In this case, any machine (standard module or common unit) can manufacture any part if combined with the corresponding mould, leading to increased flexibility in planning and increased utilization, compared to dedicated machines. Hence the module drivers for "common unit" and "different specification" are highly relevant in a production system context.

2.4 Production

Establishing modules based on similarity in production technology and testing can greatly reduce the manufacturing costs of a module. Consider a modular product requiring three different production technologies, which is available in three different manufacturing lines. If each module requires different manufacturing technologies, the module would have to be moved between manufacturing lines, increasing the lead time and manufacturing costs. Although similarity in production technology and testing may seem relevant when defining production system modules, this is already covered by the "common unit driver" as the production drivers described in this section refer to the production of the focal system, which in this case is the manufacturing system itself. Hence these drivers would refer to the production of e.g. the machines used in the production, which we consider less relevant when designing a production system. We therefore do not include these drivers.

Vendor capabilities can also be a driver for establishing a module. If the development and manufacturing of certain functions in a product is outsourced to external partners, having those functions implemented in a single or few modules will allow easier specification of interfaces and reduced complexity in the assembly process. Furthermore, certain functions may be available from specialized suppliers as standard modules, which would remove development cost and reduce purchase costs as well. This driver is also considered relevant for manufacturing systems as certain manufacturing operations need highly customized equipment delivered from very specialized suppliers, and focusing this functionality in fewer modules reduces complexity and reduces the number of modules developed by external vendors.

2.5 Service and Recycling

During a products life cycle after it has been sold, a number of factors may also be important to consider when defining modules. For service and maintenance purposes, it may be beneficial to simply replace a defective module rather than repairing it while installed in the product. Related to manufacturing systems this drivers is also considered relevant, as being able to interchange a module with a replacement module once it fails, is preferable compared to stopping the whole production system while repairing the failed component. Examples of this could be replaceable cutting tools for mills or lathes, which can easily be replaced instead of sharpening them while in the machine. Modules may also be defined to allow easy upgrading of a product. Modules allowing upgrades are also relevant in manufacturing systems, however these are already covered by the driver "planned changes", and is therefore omitted from the final set of module drivers.

The extent, to which a product can be recycled, depends to a large degree on how easy it is to disassemble and separate material into fractions. Hence designing modules that support this would increase the recyclability of the product as a whole. While this driver is very important when designing products, because they are manufactured in large numbers, this is less relevant for designing production systems, since usually only one or a few production systems are implemented. Furthermore, the expected lifespan of a production system is much longer than a typical consumer product and hence the recyclability is less important to consider when designing the system, although relevant for the manufacturers of the equipment (robot companies for example), as they manufacture large numbers of each machine.

3 Summary of Results

In the sections above, module drivers from product development have been evaluated, using the criteria whether they are relevant when designing a modular production system on various levels. Each driver identified as relevant is presented in the Table 1 below.

Table 1. Overview of module drivers for modules in a manufacturing system

System development	Geometric integration and precision
	Function Sharing
	Portability of Interfaces
Localization of Changes	Module Carryover
	Technology Evolution
	Planned Product Changes
Variety and Standardization	Common Unit
	Different Specification
Production of Manufacturing Equipment	Vendor Capabilities
Service and Recycling	Service and Maintenance

As presented above, many of the module drivers originally described for product development are relevant for production systems as well. Many of the examples presented above for each module driver are even well known design principles for manufacturing systems currently applied widely in industry. However, by identifying the different drivers and explicitly evaluating how they should be prioritised can be a means towards making decisions about modularising production systems, where it is more likely to focus on the module drivers, which are most beneficial in each specific case, thus leading to a better production system.

4 Conclusion

The drivers for modules in production systems presented in this paper are basically expected benefits of defining module in a certain way, and many of these drivers are contradicting, e.g. you cannot accommodate standardization and variety in the same module. Hence, these drivers should be used in relation to a development method for designing a modular production system. Some methods exist for this and it is the authors' expectation that also product modularization methods, such as Modular Function Deployment of Design Structure Matrix, can be adapted to modular production system development. However, the validation of this will be topic of future research.

The drivers presented in this paper have been identified from literature concerning product development. Hence, we cannot conclude that no other drivers exist for development of manufacturing systems, which do not have a product development equivalent. Hence, the drivers that are unique to production system development are not identified in this paper. This will be a topic of future research.

The results of this research, the set of and description of the drivers is expected to be relevant to academics for future research in modular manufacturing as well as practitioners designing new modular production systems and production platforms.

References

1. Baldwin, C.Y., Woodard, C.J.: The architecture of platforms: a unified view. In: Gawer, A. (ed.) Platforms, Markets and Innovation, p. 19. EE Publishing, Cheltenham (2009)
2. Ericsson, A., Erixon, G.: Controlling Design Variants: Modular Product Platforms. ASME Press, New York (1999)
3. Jiao, J., Zhang, L., Pokharel, S.: Process platform planning for mass customisation production. Int. J. Mass Customisation 1, 237–259 (2006)
4. Koren, Y.: The Global Manufacturing Revolution: Product-Process-Business Integration and Reconfigurable Systems. Wiley, Hoboken (2010)
5. Lange, M.W., Imsdahl, A.: Modular function deployment: using module drivers to impart strategies to a product architecture. In: Simpson, T.W., Jiao, J.R., Siddique, Z., Hölttä-Otto, K. (eds.) Anonymous Advances in Product Family and Product Platform Design, pp. 91–118. Springer, Berlin (2014)
6. Levandowski, C., Michaelis, M.T., Johannesson, H.: Set-based development using an integrated product and manufacturing system platform. Concurrent Eng. 22, 234–252 (2014)
7. Meyer, M.H., Lehnerd, A.P.: The Power of Product Platforms: Building Value and Cost Leadership. Free Press, New York (1997)
8. Michaelis, M.T.: Co-Development of Products and Manufacturing Systems Using Integrated Platform Models. Chalmers University of Technology, Gothenburg (2013)
9. Michaelis, M.T.: Co-Development of Products and Manufacturing Systems-Applying a Configurable Platform Approach (2011)
10. Ulrich, K.T., Eppinger, S.D.: Product Design and Development, vol. 2. McGraw-Hill/Irwin, New York (2011)
11. Ulrich, K., Eppinger, S.D.: Product Design and Development. McGraw-Hill, New York (2003)
12. Wiendahl, H., ElMaraghy, H.A., Nyhuis, P., et al.: Changeable manufacturing-classification, design and operation. CIRP Ann.-Manuf. Technol. 56, 783–809 (2007)
13. Zhang, L.L.: Process platform-based production configuration for mass customization (2007)

Numeric Methodology for Determining the Volumetric Consumption of Hydrated Ethanol in Flex-Fuel Vehicles

Marcelo K. Shibuya[1(✉)], Irenilza A. de Näas[1], and Mario Mollo Neto[2]

[1] Graduate Program in Production Engineering, Paulista University-UNIP, Dr. Bacelar St. 1212,
São Paulo, Brazil
{marcelo.shibuya,irenilza}@gmail.com
[2] UNESP - Campus Tupã, Domingos da Costa Lopes St., Tupã, Brazil
mariomollo@gmail.com

Abstract. The beginning of the manufacturing of the flex fuel vehicles in 2003, gave a new dynamic to fuel demand in Brazil. As the flex-fuel vehicles can be supplied with gasoline, hydrated ethanol or the mixture of the both in any proportion, the decision on which fuel to use occurs at the moment of supply, according to the most advantageous price and the consumer's preference. Considering this scenario, the objective of the present study was to obtain a calculation method to determine the fuel volume used by the flex-fuel vehicle fleet. For this purpose, the fuel conversion in energy units of oil barrels was used. The fuel demand by type of vehicle was obtained through the proportion of the number of vehicles and the distance traveled in the period. The results indicate that there was a behavioral change on fuel consumption by the users of the flex fuel fleet.

Keywords: Ethanol · Flex-fuel vehicles · Fuel demand

1   Introduction

According to [1], in 2014, 3.1 million light vehicles were licensed in Brazil. Out of these 3.1 million automobiles, 95 % are equipped with the flex fuel technology and the remaining 5 % are powered by gasoline or ethanol. It is found in current literature [2, 3] that ethanol consumed by Brazilian vehicles may be anhydrous (mixed with gasoline in the proportion of 20–25 %, depending on the availability and price of biofuel in the market) and the hydrated ethanol. The gasoline mixed with anhydrous ethanol is named by the [4] as gasoline type C.

Brazil is the world's largest producer of ethanol from sugar cane [5], with the advantage that the climate is favorable for planting sugar cane. The biofuel production, concentrated in the Center-South region, favored the introduction and acceptance of the flex-fuel vehicles by consumers, and it is the region that has the largest fleet of automobiles. According to [6], flex-fuel vehicles have been replacing vehicles that are supplied by a single type of fuel (only gasoline or ethanol), enabling owners to choose the fuel with lower price at the gas station pump. This characteristic of the flex-fuel vehicles brings a new scenario in fuel consumption by the fleet of light vehicles in Brazil, as well as difficulties to estimate the fuel volumes consumed by these vehicles.

© IFIP International Federation for Information Processing 2015
S. Umeda et al. (Eds.): APMS 2015, Part I, IFIP AICT 459, pp. 243–250, 2015.
DOI: 10.1007/978-3-319-22756-6_30

In the current literature there are studies showing methods for determining future fuel consumption by using the correlation between the parity of prices between the two fuels and the fraction of hydrated ethanol relative to the total volume of fuel demanded by this fleet [7–9]. However, it lacks in information on the calculation method used to obtain the volume of hydrated ethanol and gasoline C consumed by flex fuel vehicles, based on the total amount of fuel consumed in a given period throughout the fleet.

This study aimed to develop a numerical calculation method for determining the fuel consumption by the flex-fuel vehicle fleet in Brazil. It is proposed to obtain the adequate volume of fuel consumed by the vehicle fleet of flex-fuel allowing studies to analyze the demand for behavior change due to the fuel price.

2   The Evolution of Vehicle Fleet of Flex-Fuel and the Fuel Demand in Brazil

With the introduction of flex-fuel vehicles in Brazil in 2003, there was a significant change in the use of hydrated and anhydrous as propellant fuels. According to [10] and [11], anhydrous ethanol is the most important additive in gasoline and the hydrated ethanol can be used as an alternative fuel in flex-fuel vehicles, capable of being supplied with gasoline C, hydrated ethanol or a mixture of both in any proportion.

Ethanol was introduced in the Brazilian energy matrix in 1975 through the Proalcool program (National Alcohol Program) whose objective was the large-scale production of fuels to replace fossil fuels used to supply the Brazilian fleet of vehicles [11–14]. The launch of the flex-fuel vehicles in 2003 gained rapid acceptance by the automobile owners by eliminating the risk of shortages, as it had happened to the owners of vehicles moved by ethanol in Proalcool time [15]. Besides reducing the oil dependency, the use of ethanol for vehicle supply reduces the emission of particulate matter, carbon monoxide and minimizes problems in the ozone layer [16].

The fleet of light vehicles consists of passenger and light commercial automobiles. Light commercial vehicles are vans and pick-ups [1]. As for supply, light vehicle fleet is composed of three types of engine, that is, with engines powered exclusively by gasoline C, ethanol, and flex-fuel. On the National Atmospheric Emissions Inventory of Road Vehicles, published by [8], it was estimated that the fuel demand of the light vehicle fleet can be estimated by the quantity of vehicles circulating in the fleet, the intensity of use and fuel efficiency. The Eq. 1 shows the relationship between these variables.

$$C_{Vi} = \frac{Q_{Vi} x I_{Vi}}{R_{Vi}} \tag{1}$$

where C_{Vi}: fuel demand for a given type of vehicle, Q_{Vi}: number of vehicles that are effectively circulating in the given fleet, I_{Vi}: use intensity for a given type of vehicle and R_{Vi}: is the fuel efficiency for a given type of vehicle.

The Eqs. 2 and 3 show respectively, the mathematical functions for the fraction remaining vehicles of the fleet [8] and the average age of the vehicles fleet.

$$S(t) = 1 - \exp(- \exp(1, 798 - 0, 137(t)))$$ (2)

$$A_n = \frac{\sum_{i=0}^{n}(V_i x A_i)}{\sum_{i=0}^{n} V_i}$$ (3)

where S(t): remaining vehicles of a given fleet, t: average age of the fleet, A_n: mean age in a specific year, Vi: quantity of vehicles for a given type of fleet, Ai: age of the fleet in a given year.

Replacing gasoline with ethanol at the time of filling will only constitutes an advantage to the consumer if the ratio of the price of biofuel compared to the price of gasoline is less than 70 % [10] and [17]. This price relationship is related to the difference between the calorific values of these fuels. The [18] defines that a cubic meter of hydrated ethanol has $5,096 \times 10^3$ kcal and is equivalent to 3.59 oil barrels, and a cubic meter of gasoline C has $7,106 \times 10^3$ kcal and is equivalent to 5.42 oil barrels.

The Fig. 1 shows the fuel consumption and fleet evolution of light vehicles used in Brazil, comprehending the period from 2003 to 2013.

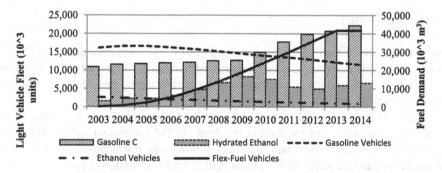

Fig. 1. Fleet of light vehicles and fuel demand in (Source: [1, 4, 8])

The increased consumption of fossil fuels and the reduction of biofuel demand from the year of 2009, showed in Fig. 1, is considered as a phase of stagnation and halt of the sugarcane industry expansion in Brazil [3, 7, 19]. The same authors add that the government intervention in gasoline prices since 2008, in order to combat inflation in the country, contributed to this phase of stagnation, making its marketed price lower than the oil barrel price.

From 2007 to 2013 (Fig. 2), the annual production volumes of gasoline A (gasoline pure without additive), ethanol (including anhydrous and hydrated) and their respective imports indicate that, from the year of 2009 forward, there was an increase in the production and importation of gasoline A, to supply the rise in gasoline C demand by the light vehicle fleet. On the same graph, it is possible to perceive that, from the year of 2010, Brazil starts to import ethanol to supply the domestic demand.

The use intensity of automotive light vehicles, including cars and light commercial is defined by [8]. The present study shows that the distance traveled by a light vehicle in one year varies according to its age. The Eq. 4 defines the mathematical function which expresses the use intensity.

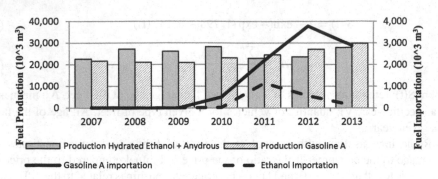

Fig. 2. Gasoline A and ethanol production and importation graph (Source: [4])

$$I_{use} = 19.400 - 600\,(t-1),\ to\ t \geq 1\ or\ I_{use} = 16330x\,t\ to\ t < 1 \tag{4}$$

where I_{use} is the use intensity in km/year and t is the age of the vehicle in year.

3   Methodology

The annual demand for hydrated ethanol and gasoline C were obtained from the data provided by the [4], and the annual quantities of licensed vehicles were obtained from [1]. The study included the determination of the fuels used by flex-fuel vehicles in the period of 2006–2014.

The volumes of hydrated ethanol and gasoline C were convertes into a single unit of calorific value, choosing the for this, the Barrel of Oil Equivalent (BOE). Thus, with the same power measurement unit in volume of the fuels, it was possibility to perform the mathematical operations of both fuels, without the conversions needs.

The annual volumes of gasoline C and hydrated ethanol demanded by the vehicles were calculated by converting the annual volumes of gasoline C and hydrated ethanol in BOE volumes. The total consumption (Ct) of fuels can be expressed by Eq. 5.

$$C_t = C_{VG} + C_{VE} + C_{VF(gas)} + C_{VF(ethanol)} \tag{5}$$

The volumes of fuels supplied by the fleet (Gasoline C or hydrated ethanol) can be further expressed by Eqs. 6–9:

$$C_t = C_{t(G)} + C_{t(E)} \tag{6}$$

$$C_{t(G)} = C_{VG} + C_{VF(gas)} \tag{7}$$

$$C_{t(E)} = C_{VE} + C_{VF(Ethanol)} \tag{8}$$

$$C_{VF} = C_{VF(gas)} + C_{VF(Ethanol)} \tag{9}$$

where C_t: total fuel consumption in a given period; $C_{t(E)}$: total ethanol consumption in a given period; $C_{t(G)}$: total gasoline C consumption in a given period; C_{VG}: total consumption of gasoline C by the fleet of vehicles moved by gasoline; C_{VD}: total consumption of hydrated ethanol by the fleet of vehicles moved by ethanol; C_{VF}: total consumption of fuel (gasoline C e hydrated ethanol) by the flex fuel vehicles; $C_{VF(gas)}$: gasoline fuel consumption by the fleet of flex-fuel vehicles and $C_{VF(ethanol)}$: total ethanol fuel consumption by the fleet of flex-fuel vehicles.

By substituting Eq. 1 on Eqs. 4, 9 is obtained:

$$C_t = \frac{Q_{VG}xI_{Vg}}{R_{VG}} + \frac{Q_{VE}xI_{VE}}{R_{VE}} + \frac{Q_{VF}xI_{Vi}x(1 - E\%)}{R_{VF}} + \frac{Q_{Vi}xI_{Vi}xE\%}{R_{VF}} \tag{10}$$

Considering that the volumes of fuel were expressed in the same unit of energy, it can be considered that the income data in kilometers per unit of BOE for the vehicles powered with gasoline, ethanol and flex-fuel are similar. Thus, it can be defined that the volumes of fuel demanded by the vehicles in the fleet (Eq. 10) is proportional to the amount of fleet vehicles multiplied by its respective use intensity. The volumes of gasoline C and hydrated ethanol consumed by the light vehicle fleet were obtained with the aid of a calculation spreadsheet (Excel).

4   Results and Discussion

Figure 3 shows that from the year of 2011 on the flex-fuel vehicles have become most of vehicle fleet, as reported by [6].

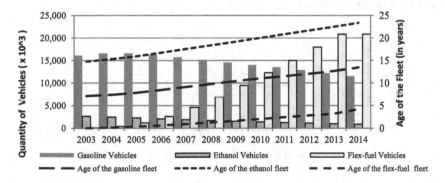

Fig. 3. Variation of the vehicle fleet in circulation in Brazil.

Analyzing the age evolution of the vehicle fleet, calculated by Eq. 3 [8], we can see that the flex-fuel vehicle fleet has the lowest age in 2014 (4.18 years). The gasoline vehicles fleet has the age of 13.45 years and the ethanol vehicles fleet of has 23.36 years. The age of flex-fuel vehicle fleet suggests that these vehicles are responsible for the consumption of a greater share of automotive fuels in Brazil. The results obtained for the fuel consumed by the Brazilian fleet of light vehicles (Fig. 4) were initially calculated in BOE and converted into cubic meters of gasoline C or hydrated ethanol, for their respective fuel supplied to each type of vehicle in the light vehicle fleet.

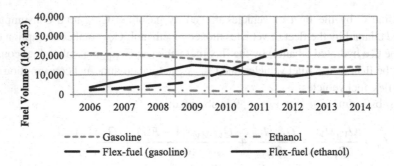

Fig. 4. Fuel consumption by the Brazilian vehicle fleet

A significant increase in the consumption of gasoline C by the flex-fuel vehicles was noticed (Fig. 4). The volume increased from 2.074 million cubic meters in 2006 to 28.787 million cubic meters in 2014. It is also seen an increase in hydrated ethanol consumption by flex-fuel vehicles between 2006 and 2009, and a demand reduction from 2010. These results suggest that the owners of flex-fuel vehicles began to prefer the fossil fuel, against the use of biofuel. These numbers disagrees with other findings [3, 7, 19] which had determined that 2009 was the beginning of stagnating of the sugar-cane industry in Brazil, with the consequences the interruption of the expansion of ethanol plants and the reduction of the biofuel supply. The percentage of gasoline C consumed volume in relation to the total amount of fuel consumed by flex-fuel vehicles had definite change in the fuel demand, such as the increased gasoline C consumption, from 36.7 % in 2006 to 69.8 % in 2014 (Fig. 5).

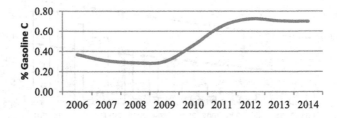

Fig. 5. Percentage of gasoline C consumed by the flex fuel vehicles

The increased consumption of gasoline C and the consequent decrease of the biofuel demand during the study period may have been caused by the artificial maintenance of the gasoline C prices [3, 7, 19] and it can bring two serious consequences to the Brazilian energy sector. The first would be the deepening crisis in the Brazilian ethanol industry, with the closure of ethanol's plants. Referring to [20], from 2009 to 2014, 51 units have closed down their activities, and 18 new units started their operations. It is a negative balance compared to the amount of flex-fuel vehicles, most of the Brazilian light vehicle fleet, released by [19], which enhance the biofuel demand. The second consequence is, if gasoline C consumption rate is maintained at levels similar to the period 2011–2014 (Fig. 5), it might cause a growing need to import this fuel, as disclosed by [4]. Finally, another factor that should not be ignored is the ecologic benefits brought by the use of biofuels, such as the reduction of particulate matter, greenhouse gases including carbon monoxide [16]. The maintenance of these high rates gasoline C use by the flex-fuel vehicles can minimize these benefits and worsen air quality of Brazilian cities.

5 Conclusion

Using the numeric methodology proposed in this study, it was possible to estimate the annual volumes of gasoline C and hydrated ethanol consumed by the flex-fuel vehicle fleet in Brazil. The study covered the period from 2006 to 2014 and allowed to identify changes in the demand for fuels used by flex-fuel vehicles. With the volumes of fuels obtained, the demand (in percentage) curve for gasoline C was determined, where it was possible to identify the change in consumption of the fuel from 2010 forward.

Although there are several causes related to the crisis established in the sugar cane industry, and the consequent change in the fuel demand, it is important to point out that the lack of an energy policy in Brazil may have been their primary factor for the controversial success in the use of flex-fuel vehicles. Maintaining the demand for hydrated ethanol within the same levels of the period of 2006–2010, would bring various benefits to Brazil, such as the return of the Brazilian sugarcane sector growth, job growth in the supply chain, the reduction of oil dependency and finally, the improvement of air quality due to the replacement of fossil fuel by biodiesel. The numeric calculation methodology reported in this study could be used to determine the hydrated ethanol consumption mathematical function on the basis of price parity between hydrated ethanol and gasoline C.

The mathematical function could be used to predict the fuel demand for the light vehicle fleet, allowing it to anticipate the volumes to be consumed, and the make production planning and infrastructure necessary for the supply of such products in the Brazilian fuel market.

References

1. ANFAVEA – Associação Nacional dos Fabricantes de Veículos Automotores, Anuário da Indústria Automobilística Brasileira (2015)
2. Bake, J.D.V.D.W., Junginger, M., Faaij, A., Poot, T., Walter, A.: Explaining the experience curve: cost reductions of Brazilian ethanol from sugarcane. Biomass Bioenergy **33**, 644–658 (2009)
3. Nogueira, L.A.H., Capaz, R.S.: Biofuels in Brazil: evolution, achievements and perspectives on food security. Glob. Food Secur. **2**, 117–125 (2013)
4. ANP - Agência Nacional do Petróleo, Anuário Estatístico 2014. http://www.anp.gov.br/. Accessed Nov 2014
5. Martinez, S.H., Eijck, J.V., Cunha, M.P., Guilhoto, J.J.M., Walter, A., Faaij, A.: Analysis of socio-economic impacts of sustainable sugarcane ethanol production by means of inter-organizational input-output analysis demonstrate of North-East of Brazil. Renew. Sustain. Energy Rev. **28**, 290–316 (2013)
6. Du, X., Carriquiry, M.A.: Flex-fuel vehicle adoption and dynamics of ethanol prices: lessons from Brazil. Energy Policy (2013). doi:10.1016/j.enpol.2013.04.008i

7. EPE – Empresa de Pesquisa Energética. Avaliação do Comportamento dos Usuários de Veículos *Flex-Fuel* no Consumo de Combustíveis no Brasil – Brasília (2013)
8. MMA (Ministério do Meio Ambiente), Inventário Nacional de Emissões Atmosféricas por Veículos Automotores Rodoviários, Brasília/Brasil (2014)
9. Losekann, L., Vilela, T., Castro, G.R., Difusão de Automóveis Flexíveis no Brasil: Sensibilidade ao Preço e Impactos na Emissão de CO_2. Instituto Brasileiro do Petróleo (2012)
10. Freitas, L.C., Kaneko, S.: Ethanol demand under flex-fuel technology regime in Brasil. Energy Econ. **33**, 1146–1154 (2011)
11. BNDES. Bioetanol de cana-de-açúcar: energia para o desenvolvimento sustentável - Rio de Janeiro (2008)
12. Hira, A.: Sugar rush: prospects for a global ethanol market. Energy Police **39**, 6925–6935 (2011)
13. Crago, C.L., Khanna, M., Barton, J., Giuliani, E., Amaral, W.: Competitiveness of Brazilian sugarcane ethanol compared to US corn ethanol. Energy Policy **38**, 7404–7415 (2010)
14. Santos, G.F.: Fuel demand in Brazil in a dynamic panel data approach. Energy Econ. **36**, 229–240 (2013)
15. Stattman, S.L., Hospes, O., Mol, A.P.J.: Governing biofuels in Brazil: a comparison of ethanol and biodiesel policy. Energy Policy **61**, 22–30 (2013)
16. Mollo Neto, M., Vendrametto, O., Walker, R.A.: Is the development of Brazilian biofuel network sustainable? In: International Conference on Advances in Production Management Systems (APMS 2010). Springer, Vienna (2010)
17. Goldemberg, J., Coelho, S.T., Lucon, O., Guardabassi, P.: Brazilian sugarcane ethanol: lessons learned. Energy Police **39**, 6925–6935 (2011)
18. EPE – Empresa de Pesquisa Energética, Conversor de Unidades. http://www.ipeadata.gov.br/. Accessed Nov 2014
19. Milanez, A.Y., Nyko D., Garcia, J.L.F., Reis, B.L.S.F.S.: O déficit de produção de etanol no Brasil entre 2012 e 2015: determinantes, consequências e sugestões de política. BNDES. Rio de Janeiro (2012)
20. UNICA – União da Indústria da Cana de Açúcar; Relatório Final da Safra 2013-2014. http://www.unicadata.com.br/listagem.php?idMn=88. Accessed 12 Feb 2015

Evaluating the Implementation of a Fuzzy Logic System for Hybrid Vehicles as Alternative to Combustion Engine Buses in Big Cities

Emerson R. Abraham[1]([✉]), Sivanilza T. Machado[1], Helton R.O. Silva[1],
Carla C. Parizi[1], João G.M. Reis[1], Helcio Raymundo[1],
Pedro L.O. Costa Neto[1], Oduvaldo Vendrametto[1], Marcos O. Morais[1],
Antônio S. Brejão[1], and Cleber W. Gomes[2]

[1] Postgraduate Studies Program in Production Engineering,
Dr. Bacelar 1212, São Paulo 04026002, Brazil
emerson_abraham@yahoo.com.br
[2] Metodista University,
Alfeu Tavares 149, São Bernardo Do Campo 09641000, Brazil

Abstract. The public transportation in urban centers involve many challenges related to environment. One of these challenges is reduce air and noise pollution in big cities. In São Paulo, for instance, it is estimated that 98 % of the transport are made using buses with combustion engine, which are responsible for greatest part of air and noise pollution. Therefore, it is necessary to develop studies that help change the public transport policies in major cities, favoring the use of electric and hybrid buses. Thus, this paper aims to simulate the use of hybrid bus with fuzzy logic applied to improve the efficiency of this type of system. We made six simulations with MATLAB© software and Fuzzy Logic Toolbox, considering velocity, topography and battery status as input variables. The results showed an effective control of the fuzzy system, with the feasibility of combining this with others experts systems.

Keywords: Hybrid bus · Fuzzy logic · Public transportation · Sustainability · Simulation

1   Introduction

The public transportation in urban centers has been a constant problem for the environment and public health. In Brazil, it has not been different. São Paulo, for example, is the largest city in the country with more than 11 million people and, despite the various strategies used by transportation companies to reduce the air pollution and noise emissions, the level is still high.

A solution to change this scenario was to develop the Ecofrota program by municipality of São Paulo. This program implemented in 2009, requires that all public transportion system in the city use renewable fuel until 2018, reducing the use of fossil fuels at least 10 % per year [1].

© IFIP International Federation for Information Processing 2015
S. Umeda et al. (Eds.): APMS 2015, Part I, IFIP AICT 459, pp. 251–258, 2015.
DOI: 10.1007/978-3-319-22756-6_31

Currently there are three technologies available to the public transportation in São Paulo: bus with conventional combustion engine, electric bus and hybrid bus (combustion plus electric).

Some researchers believe that the hybrid vehicle becomes an interesting alternative because conventional buses have the disadvantage of being highly polluting, while the pure electric vehicle has the disadvantage of having to continually recharge [2] and [3]. Therefore, a hybrid system may provide the benefits of electric power without abandon the combustion engines for some situations.

To establish the feasibility of adopting a hybrid system by the cities and public transportation companies, is necessary to ensure that hybrid buses can respond the same requirements provided by conventional buses. Hence, our study aims to simulate the adoption of a fuzzy logic system to control the hybrid bus and improve its efficiency.

The simulation could be made using different approaches, but we defined adopt the fuzzy logic method because it is an important tool to solve problems in different areas of knowledge and applications.

According to Li et al. as the hybrid vehicle is nonlinear and multivariable, the fuzzy logic is more suitable for the energy management [4]. Moreover, Neffati et al. demonstrated the efficiency of fuzzy logic applied to control hybrid electric vehicles comparing different methodologies. To solve problems in real time the fuzzy logic shows good results [5].

This work was realized using the city of São Paulo as reference. Thus, the data was collected with the São Paulo Transport Company that manage the public transportation systems, and with the company that provide the electric and hybrid systems for buses in operation in the city, the Eletrabus [1] and [6]. The simulation was made with MATLAB© software using the fuzzy logic mode.

2   Hybrid Systems

The hybrid technology uses the combination of two or more sources of energy to feeds the system [6] and [4].

The hybrid system discussed in this work is performed by a electric motor, where the energy comes from a diesel powered engine. In addition, the vehicle has a battery bank that complements the energy available to the electric motor when required; the diesel powered engine recharges the battery bank, that avoid the use of external recharging of batteries. The combustion engine is fixed in rotation, reaching a reduction of smoke emission in 90 % [6]

A hybrid vehicle uses three different types of settings: Series, Parallel-Series and Parallel [3]. In the case of the Eletrabus, responsible for the project in São Paulo city, the hybrid buses follow the parallel configuration [6], Fig. 1.

The advantage of using the parallel system is the flexibility, which allows the system to operate whether a problem occurs in the electric generator, control and inverter, battery bank or the electric motor [3].

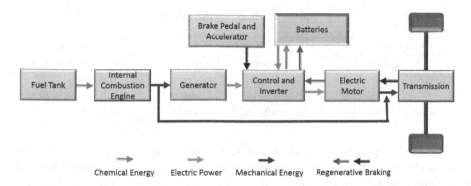

Fig. 1. Parallel hybrid vehicle. Source: adapted from[6]

3   Fuzzy Logic

Fuzzy logic was developed by Lotfi A. Zadeh (1921-) in Berkeley in the 60s. This is a non classical kind of logic that allows intermediate values among False (0) and True (1) [7].

In the real world, there are variables that are vague or uncertain, impossible to be represented by classical logic. Fuzzy logic, enable to work with qualitative values and to infer from these quantitative values [8] and [9].

Zadeh states that there are two main reasons for the use of fuzzy logic, when the information available is too imprecise to justify the use of numbers, and when there is a tolerance for imprecision [8].

The applications of fuzzy logic in information systems began in the 80s. According to Zadeh, some of the first were made by F. L. Smidth to control cement kilns and the Sendai subway system designed by Hitachi [10].

4   Methodology

To answer the objective of this work three variables was considered: velocity, topography and battery status. Currently, Eletrabus uses a controller, as can be seen in Fig. 1, which considers only velocity variable for swapping the system. [6]. We opted to include more variables for two reasons: (i) recommendation of fuzzy logic experts; and (ii) to create a more complex environment to test the potentially of the fuzzy system.

In this study, the main objective was to create a model with the knowledge of experts [9] and make simulations. The interaction of the model with the controller can be discussed in future works.

The fuzzy logic model depends of membership values and basic rules defined by experts. The Table 1 shows the membership values.

Table 1. Membership values

Variables 1	Variables 2	Variables 3
Velocity (Vel)	Topography (Top)	BatteryStatus (Bat)
Slow(S) ($< 20\ km/h$)	Declivity(D)($< 0\ degrees$)	Low(L) ($< 72\%$)
Medium(M) ($18 - 37\ km/h$)	Plane(P) ($-2\ to\ 2degrees$)	Medium(M) ($72\%\ to\ 86\%$)
High(H) ($> 35\ km/h$)	Acclivity(A) ($> 0\ degree$)	High(H) ($> 84\%$)

The next steps were to create 27 rules, each with a specific weight, which represents the possible combinations among the input variables. Applied conjunction (and) among the variables. The possible outputs are: "Batteries", "CombustionEngine" and "Not Applicable", where the last one reflects situations in which the relationship between the variables are not validated. The output values were defined on a scale ranging from 0 to 10, Table 2.

Table 2. Basic rules

N	Input	Output	Weight
1	Vel S and Top D and Bat H =	Batteries	0.5
2	Vel M and Top D and Bat H =	Not applicable	-
3	Vel H and Top D and Bat H =	Not applicable	-
4	Vel S and Top P and Bat H =	Batteries	0.75
5	Vel M and Top P and Bat H =	Not applicable	-
6	Vel H and Top P and Bat H =	Not applicable	-
7	Vel S and Top A and Bat H =	Batteries	1
8	Vel M and Top A and Bat H =	Not applicable	-
9	Vel H and Top A and Bat H =	Not applicable	-
10	Vel S and Top D and Bat M =	Batteries	0.5
11	Vel M and Top D and Bat M =	Not applicable	-
12	Vel H and Top D and Bat M =	Not applicable	-
13	Vel S and Top P and Bat M =	Batteries	0.75
14	Vel M and Top P and Bat M =	Not applicable	-
15	Vel H and Top P and Bat M =	Not applicable	-
16	Vel S and Top A and Bat M =	Batteries	1
17	Vel M and Top A and Bat M =	Not applicable	-
18	Vel H and Top A and Bat M =	Not applicable	-
19	Vel S and Top D and Bat L =	Not applicable	-
20	Vel M and Top D and Bat L =	CombustionEngine	0.5
21	Vel H and Top D and Bat L =	CombustionEngine	0.5
22	Vel S and Top P and Bat L =	Not applicable	-
23	Vel M and Top P and Bat L =	CombustionEngine	0.75
24	Vel H and Top P and Bat L =	CombustionEngine	0.75
25	Vel S and Top A and Bat L =	Not applicable	-
26	Vel M and Top A and Bat L =	CombustionEngine	1
27	Vel H and Top A and Bat L =	CombustionEngine	1

To build the basic rules in MATLAB©, 12 of the 27 combinations were added, where 15 combinations resulting in "Not applicable" were not added because in these cases the actual results are the same value for both "Batteries" and "CombustionEngine". The composition of the inference engine with the input variables, the rules (Hybrid Engine) using Mamdani method, and the output variables using the method (SOM), can be seen in Fig. 2.

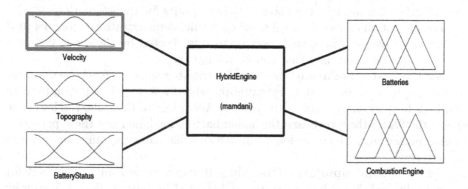

Fig. 2. Inference engine MATLAB

After the construction of the model, we made six simulations on MATLAB©R2014a with addition of the Fuzzy Logic Toolbox: five simulations with data within the specified range of values that meet any of the 12 rules defined in MATLAB©, and 1 simulation based on data within the set of values that do not meet any of the 12 rules defined in MATLAB©. Each simulation produce a representation of the results such as performed in Fig. 3.

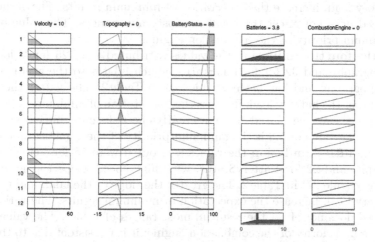

Fig. 3. Graphic resulted from MATLAB© simulations

The analysis presented in the results and discussion section are performed using the graphic resulted of the fuzzy logic simulation.

5   Results and Discussion

The results of these inferences indicate a degree of priority for Batteries or Combustion Engine, ranging from 0 to 10. The use of Mamdani and SOM methods in defuzzification brought the lowest possible results for the simulations.

The allocation of specific weights for each rule, demonstrated a more detailed control of inference. The system performance is effected by the input variables settings and the basic rules that can be refined [11].

For the **first simulation**, the values attributed were 10 for Velocity, 0 for Topo- graphy and 88 for BatteryStatus presented low speed, topography plan and high battery charge (rule 4) in Table 2. According to this rule, the lower the speed, the flatter the terrain and the higher battery load, increase the expectation of minimum result. The value found was 3.8 that indicates the minimum priority of batteries.

For the **second simulation**, the values attibuted were 7 for Velocity, -12 for Topography and 76 for BatteryStatus and showed low speed, slope topography and average battery life (rule 10) in Table 2. According to this rule, the lower the speed, the lower the slope of the land and the higher battery load, increase the expectation of minimum results. The value of 1.2 is the minimum priority of batteries. In this case, the slope of the terrain in 12 degrees affected the result to a low value. This result is consistent, because the weight of the vehicle and the inclination uses the gravity, requiring fewer batteries.

For the **third simulation**, the values attributed were 58 for Velocity, 1.2 for Topography and 22 for BatteryStatus, considering the high speed, flat topography and low battery (rule 24) in Table 2. The flatter the terrain and the lower the battery load, increase the expectation of minimum results. The variation at high speed does not affect the result in most value ranges. The value of 2.8 is the minimum priority of the combustion engine.

For the **fourth simulation** the values attributed were 25 for Velocity, 11 for Topography and 32 for BatteryStatus, which relates to the average speed, slope topography and low battery (rule 26) in Table 2. The flatter the terrain and the lower the battery load, increase the expectation of minimum results. The variation in the average speed does not greatly effect the outcome in most ranges of values. The value of 5.6 is the minimum priority of the combustion engine.

For the **fifth simulation** the values attributed were 55 for Velocity, 12 for Topography and 22 for BatteryStatus, with high speed, slope topography and low battery (rule 27) in Table 2. The greater the slope of the land, and the lower the battery load, increase the expectation of minimum results. The variation at high speed does not effect the result in most ranges of values. The value of 7 is the minimum priority of the combustion engine; it is consistent due to the slope of 12 degrees, which requires more combustion engine to suppress gravity.

For the **sixth simulation**, the values attributed were: 55 for Velocity, 12 for Topography and 92 for BatteryStatus, considering the high speed, slope topography and high battery charge (rule 9) in Table 2. This rule has not been allocated in the database for the simulation, since the combination of its variables are not applied; however the data may occur, which in this case returns the values of 5 for batteries and 5 for combustion engine.

For the 15 rules where the output value is "Not Applicable" rather than prioritize the combustion engine, the inference points to a neutral outcome, allowing other considerations for decision. Moreover, due to the limitations of the fuzzy control [12], these outputs could also be entered as input values to other fuzzy systems or expert systems, such as neural networks. For example, Barzegar et al. studied a hybrid adaptive model, based on a combination of coloured Petri nets, fuzzy logic and learning automata, to efficiently control traffic signals [13].

So, this results and discussions indicated the feasibility of applying the fuzzy logic to control hybrid vehicles.

6   Conclusions and Outlook

The simulation results performed an effective use of the system, apparently showing no flaws or inconsistencies. The system behaved properly according to the rules and the specified values. For the cases that resulted in neutral or equal, the hybrid system could use the combustion engine and batteries (both), or prioritize the use of one in function of other variables. As a suggestion, we recommend using the outputs that returned equal to 5 (sixth simulation) as input values to other systems and new simulations.

This work have presented some limitations, being thus for future works the next steps aim to use SIMULINK on MATLAB© to demonstrate the behaviour of the fuzzy system proposed.

São Paulo like many big cities in the world are suffering with problems of gas and noise emissions and alternatives need to be finding out to reduce or solve these issues. Our studies have indicated the benefits of the use of hybrid systems in public transportation to reduce air pollution and noise emissions.

References

1. SPTRANS: Plano de controle de poluição veicular no município de São Paulo. Secretaria Municipal de Transportes SMT (2011)
2. Choi, H., Oh, I.: Analysis of product efficiency of hybrid vehicles and promotion policies. Energy Policy 38(5), 2262–2271 (2010)
3. Alipour, H., Asaei, B., Farivar, G.: Fuzzy logic based power management strategy for plug-in hybrid electric vehicles with parallel configuration. In: Proceedings of the International Conference on Renewable Energies and Power Quality, Santiago de Compostela, Spain, pp. 28–30 (2012)
4. Li, Q., Chen, W., Li, Y., Liu, S., Huang, J.: Energy management strategy for fuel cell/battery/ultracapacitor hybrid vehicle based on fuzzy logic. Int. J. Electr. Power Energy Syst. 43(1), 514–525 (2012)
5. Neffati, A., Guemri, M., Caux, S., Fadel, M.: Energy management strategies for multi source systems. Electric Power Syst. Res. 102, 42–49 (2013)

6. ELETRABUS: Tecnologia dos Veículos híbridos (2013). http://www.eletrabus. com/hibrido.htm
7. Mendel, J.M.: Reflections on some important contributions made by Lotfi A. Zadeh that have impacted my own research. Scientia Iranica **18**(3), 549–553 (2011)
8. Zadeh, L.A.: Fuzzy logic = computing with words. IEEE Trans. Fuzzy Syst. **4**(2), 103–111 (1996)
9. Rezende, S.O.: Sistemas inteligentes: fundamentos e aplicações. Editora Manole Ltda (2003)
10. Zadeh, L.A.: Fuzzy logic, neural networks, and soft computing. Commun. ACM **37**(3), 77–84 (1994)
11. Taha, M.A., Ibrahim, L.: Traffic simulation system based on fuzzy logic. Procedia Comput. Sci. **12**, 356–360 (2012)
12. Zhou, Y., Ou, S., Lian, J., Li, L.: Optimization of hybrid electric bus driving system's control strategy. Procedia Eng. **15**, 240–245 (2011)
13. Barzegar, S., Davoudpour, M., Meybodi, M.R., Sadeghian, A., Tirandazian, M.: Formalized learning automata with adaptive fuzzy coloured Petri net; an application specific to managing traffic signals. Scientia Iranica **18**(3), 554–565 (2011)

How to Capture Knowledge from Project Environment?

Nada Matta[✉], Xinghang Dai, François Rauscher, Hassan Atifi,
and Guillaume Ducellier

University of Technology of Troyes, Troyes, France
{nada.matta,xinghang.dai,francois.rauscher,hassan.atifi,
guillaume.ducellier}@utt.fr

Abstract. From the beginning, knowledge is a preoccupation of human human preoccupation. A lot of questions are still discussed: what is knowledge? How knowledge is built? How is it represented in mind? How can it be kept? How can it be learned? Our challenge is how to capture design project knowledge related to work episodes and how to extract and represent the deep knowledge belonging to the type of projects and design activities. In this paper, we present an approach that helps to capture knowledge from daily design project environment and to aggregate this knowledge as classifications.

Keywords: Knowledge representation · Design project management · Classification · Project memory

1 Introduction

From the beginning, knowledge is a human preoccupation. A lot of questions are still discussed: what is knowledge? How knowledge is built? How is it represented in mind? How can it be kept? How can it be learned? ... The notion of Knowledge is defined from the antiquity. Platon, for instance, define the thought as the intellectual model of objects. Heraclite went towards the definition of the logos as a triangle in which distinguished thought, from expression, from reality. Saussure defined the base of the semiotic as: a representation of knowledge embedded in an activity is related to a specific symbol [10]. Currently these representations are more and more used to enhance learning from expertise and past experience. So, human who has to recognize concepts in the reference does making sense. Based on this theory, knowledge engineering approaches provide techniques that help to represent expertise as references and enhance learning from these references. We can note especially, knowledge representation using semantic networks. For instance, currently, knowledge sharing (i.e. in semantic web studies) techniques use ontology as guides to share a common sense of a concept in a domain [6]. These techniques are commonly used to represent knowledge in a given domain for a given profession. In our work, we study knowledge produced from a cooperative activity as design projects, in which several actors with different skills and backgrounds work together to reach a given goal. Design project team is a short-lived organization. Moreover, several companies can do projects; actors can belong to different countries. Our challenge is how to capture this type of knowledge related to work episodes and how to extract and

© IFIP International Federation for Information Processing 2015
S. Umeda et al. (Eds.): APMS 2015, Part I, IFIP AICT 459, pp. 259–265, 2015.
DOI: 10.1007/978-3-319-22756-6_32

represent the deep knowledge belonging to the type of projects and design activities. In this paper, we present an approach for capturing knowledge from daily design project environment and aggregating this knowledge as classifications.

2   Design Project Knowledge

2.1   Capturing Knowledge from Design Projects

As we noted above, design projects are currently done in cooperative way. So, expert interviews, Textmining are not adequate to capture the collaborative dimensions of knowledge, which it is produced by interactions between actors. We need to extract knowledge directly from daily work environment. So, we propose to use techniques and tools as proposed on CSCW [9] as support of cooperative activity,. Information and data will be so captured directly from communication, coordination and decision-making support techniques. But, knowledge extracted from daily activity is mainly related as episodic memory, which contribute to build the epistemic knowledge or deep knowledge, in which routines and rules are identified and can be used as heuristics to solve future problems. By keeping track of knowledge during the realization of each project, we obtain a memory of organization projects cases s. These projects will be indexed not only by keywords and by the types of projects but also by main criteria underlined their execution. This indexation must be linked to a typology of projects and problems. Aggregation and classifications of rules must be in order to extract problem solving strategies related to project's typologies and problems (Fig. 1).

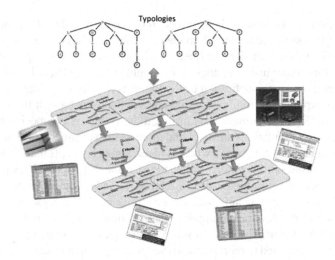

Fig. 1. Project memory architecture

2.2 Representing Design Knowledge as Project Memory

Design project knowledge can be represented in what we call project memory, which can be described as "the history of a project and the experience gained during the realization of a project" [7]. It must consider mainly:

- The project organization: different participants, their competences, their organization in sub-teams, the tasks, which are assigned to each participant, etc.
- The reference frames (rules, methods, laws ...) used in the various stages of the project.
- The realization of the project: the potential problem solving, the evaluation of the solutions as well as the management of the incidents met.
- The decision making process: the negotiation strategy, which guides the making of the decisions as well as the results of the decisions.

Often, there are interdependent relations among the various elements of a project memory. Through the analysis of these relations, it is possible to make explicit and relevance of the knowledge used in the realization of the project.

3 Traceability of Information from Design Projects

Keeping track of information from design projects consists mainly to extract knowledge from several knowledge sources:

- Tools:
  - Project management tools to kept project organizations (tasks, actors, skills, roles, etc.) and project context (budget, delay, planning, etc.)
  - Workflow and documents to capture versioning of results and phases
  - E-mails, wikis to obtain discussions and interactions between actors related to coordination and problem solving.
- Environment:
  - Meetings to capture decision making negotiation and cooperation organizations
  - Actor work-environment to be aware of activities.

In our work, we study traceability of decision meetings and e-mails. So, we develop some techniques in order to capture and structure knowledge from these two information sources.

3.1 Keeping Track of Decision Meetings

Several approaches in CSCW are developed in order to represent design rationale. We can note mainly IBIS and QOC, in which design rationale, named also as the space of design is represented as issues, options and arguments [3]. Other approaches as DRCS and DIPA link decision-making to other elements of the projects like tasks, results and constraints [7]. To represent cooperative activity, we need to link elements from the project context and problem solving. Context is important to enhance learning in an organization. Designer needs to match the context of his problem to past ones in order to understand past related problem solving and use it to solve his problem. Design rationale approaches links decision-making to some aspects of the projects context but it-missed links to project organizations as roles and skills of actors, etc. DYPKM [2] approach recommends keeping track of design rationale from the project context and decision meetings. Structuring information cannot be done directly during the meetings. Also, the meetings animator cannot represent different views of discussions afterward as recommended in several design rationale techniques. Traceability of decision-making has to be done on two steps taking notes during the meetings and structuring notes to define report. Secretary in a meeting has to take notes of discussions in order to keep track of links between these discussions, questions and participants. When writing report, he/she has to distinguish suggestions from arguments and to annotate them by criteria. In order to obtain this type of results and to integrate traceability during an activity, we define a tool «Memory Meeting» [7] that supports collaborative decision-making traceability (Fig. 2). Results are then linked to other project parts using designers' tools like Product Life cycle management tools.

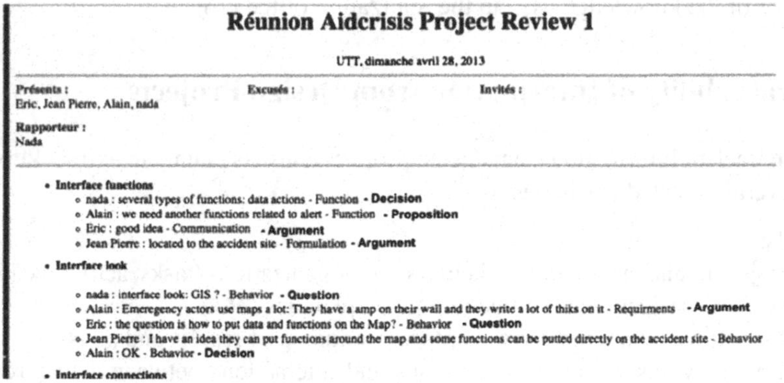
Réunion Aidcrisis Project Review 1

UTT, dimanche avril 28, 2013

Présents : Eric, Jean Pierre, Alain, nada
Excusés :
Invités :

Rapporteur : Nada

- **Interface functions**
  - nada : several types of functions: data actions - Function **- Decision**
  - Alain : we need another functions related to alert - Function **- Proposition**
  - Eric : good idea - Communication **- Argument**
  - Jean Pierre : located to the accident site - Formulation **- Argument**
- **Interface look**
  - nada : interface look: GIS ? - Behavior **- Question**
  - Alain : Emeregency actors use maps a lot: They have a amp on their wall and they write a lot of thiks on it - Requirments **- Argument**
  - Eric : the question is how to put data and functions on the Map? - Behavior **- Question**
  - Jean Pierre : I have an idea they can put functions around the map and some functions can be putted directly on the accident site - Behavior
  - Alain : OK - Behavior **- Decision**
- **Interface connections**

Fig. 2. Example of structured report of decision-making meeting. Information are structured as design rationale methods adding links to actors organization, skills, …

3.2 Keeping Track from Communication

Several approaches study and analyze e-mails as a specific discourse [8]. We note for instance, tagging work. Other works use natural language processing in order to identify messages concerning tasks and commitments. Pragmatics analysis of e-mails uses some of these methods like ngrams analysis. However Techniques studying e-mails, often do not consider the context of discussions, which is important to identify speaker's intention. In this work, we deal with e-mails, extracted from professional projects. So, we mix pragmatics analysis and topic parsing and we link this type of analysis to project context (skills and roles of messages senders and receivers, project phases, and deliverables, etc.) in order to keep track of speakers' intentions. As pragmatics analysis shows [1], there is not only one grid to analyze different types of speech intentions. In project memory, we look for problem solving situations, design rationale, coordination, etc. In this study, we focus on problem solving and we build an analysis grid for this purpose [8].

Firstly, we have to identify the important messages. For that, we have to gather messages in subjects. Then, we can identify the volume of messages related to each subject, related to project phases.

For each message thread (message and answers), we identify:

- Information to be linked to organization: authors, to whom, in Copy
- Information about phases: Date and hour of messages and answers
- Information about product: topic and joined files
- Information about message intention: main speech act.

By linking messages to project organization, we help in making sense of interactions between actors. In fact, the role and skill of messages' senders and receivers help to analyze the role of the message in problem solving and the nature of the content (solution answering a problem, proposition discussions, coordination messages, etc.). In the same way, linking messages to phases help to identify main problems to deal in each phase of the same type of projects. As first work, we focus our speech act analysis on problem solving by identifying request and solution. So, we identify first speech acts that help to localize a request in a message [8]. Request act grid is identified for this aim. In this grid, there are two types: direct request and indirect requests. A direct request may be use an imperative, a performative form, obligations and want or need statements. An Indirect request may use query questions about ability, willingness, and capacity etc. of the hearer to do the action or use statements about the willingness (desire) of the speaker to see the hearer doing X [11].

Then, we study the organization of related messages thread in order to identify the solution proposed (if it exists) to the request (Fig. 3).

From			Sentence elements	Topic	Function
SRA			I put in "Bold", what I need:		Request
	to:	FX	1- *Insurances*		
	cc:	JBl	2- Text without tags Texte in XML files	Code	
FX					Answer
	to:	SRA	I propose to convert: Xpress format in XML		
	cc:	JBl	I can transform it on enriched XML	XML	

Fig. 3. Example of communication analysis results

Knowledge so captured can be stored as examples of projects execution in what we can call a project cases base. Aggregation of routines must be done in order to extract deep knowledge from these cases. We use classification techniques for this aim.

4   Knowledge Discovery by Classification

Low-level data in project memory should be mapped into other forms that might be more compact, more abstract, or more useful [4]. In this section, a classification method to extract knowledge from design project memory will be proposed. In order to generate rules that represent interrelations between concepts or sub-networks, machine-learning techniques are considered. An evaluation of major machine learning techniques (statistical methods, decision tree, rule based method and neural network) is carried out in search for the appropriate algorithm [5]. Our intention is to classify project memory into rule-based knowledge, which leads us to choose a rule-based algorithm ITRULE. It can induce an optimal set of rules from a set of examples [4]. Then project information will be classified according to different views to extract knowledge rules. Here we propose three classification views:

1. Problem-solving view: at a specific project phase, we can classify decision-making process for one particular issue. Solutions that are repetitive will be classified as essential solutions, the solutions that are distinctive will be considered as explorative attempt with its precondition as an explanation.
2. Cooperation view: this classification view allows verifying whether there are parallel tasks that involve cooperative design concerning whole project team. This rule will reveal the influence of concurrent design on project result. i.e. Fig. 4.

Tablet application for product maintenance				
Year	2012		2013	
Phase	Project realization		Project realization	
Project organization	Three sub-groups for each application module (ERP, PLM, Object reconnaissance)	Competence distribution: ERP(computer science) PLM (mechanical design) Object reconnaissance (computer science)	Three sub-groups for each application module (ERP, PLM, object search engine)	ERP(computer science) PLM (computer science, mechanical design) Object search engine (computer science, mechanical design)
Project planning	• 4 working meetings inside each sub-group to validate project specification • A final meeting to simply collect each sub-group's work		• 12 work meetings of whole project team • Sub-group meetings are organized freely	
Result	• Each module has its own database, the application has 3 databases in total • Automatic image recognition increase the cost drastically		• Client-server architecture that requires only one database • Centralized data management	

Fig. 4. Example of classification of management influence. In 2012: 2 groups (mechanics vs. informatics), decision: 4 databases. In 2013: groups are mix. Decision: 1 database.

3. Management view: this classification view will focus on project organization influence on different project memory modules.

5 Conclusion and Perspective

In this paper, we present our work on traceability and structuring of daily knowledge especially from design projects. We present two techniques that help to capture knowledge from decision-making and from communication. We work on defining more techniques in order to capture knowledge from designer's environment (linking to other work on user profiling). Captured knowledge needs to be classified in order to identify routines. Our classifications rules hypothesis needs to be tested in a large number of examples in order to identify ontology of design projects rules.

References

1. Atifi, H., Gauducheau, N., Marcoccia, M.: The effectiveness of professional emails: representations and communicative practices. In: Proceedings of 13th Conference of the International Association for Dialogue Analysis, Dialogue and Representation, Montréal (2011)
2. Bekhti, S., Matta, N.: Project memory: an approach of modelling and reusing the context and the design rationale. In: Proceedings of IJCAI, vol. 3 (2003)
3. Buckingham Shum, S.: Representing hard-to-formalise, contextualised, multidisciplinary, organisational knowledge. In: Proceedings of AAI Spring Symposium on Artificial Intelligence in Knowledge Management, pp. 9–16 (1997)
4. Dai, X., Matta, N., Ducellier, G.: Knowledge classification for design project memory. In: IEEE International Conference on DESIGN, Dubrovnick, pp. 19–22, May 2014
5. Domingos, P.: A few useful things to know about machine learning. Commun. ACM **55**(10), 78–87 (2012)
6. Gruber, T.: Toward principles for the design of ontologies used for knowledge sharing? Int. J. Hum Comput Stud. **43**(5), 907–928 (1995)
7. Matta, N., Ducellier, G.: How to learn from design project knowledge. Int. J. Knowl. Learn. **9**(1/2), 164–177 (2014)
8. Rauscher, F., Matta, N., Atifi, H.: Discovering problem-solving knowledge in business emails, traceability in software design using computer mediated communication. In: IC3 K, Knowledge Management and Information System Conferences, Rome, Oct 2014
9. Schmidt, K., Simone, C.: Coordination mechanisms: towards a conceptual foundation for CSCW systems design. Comput. Support. Coop. Work J. Collaborative Comput. **5**, 155–200 (1996)
10. Saussure, F.: Cours de linguistique générale. Larousse, Paris (1916)
11. Searle, J.R.: Speech Acts. An Essay in the Philosophy of Language. Cambridge University Press, Cambridge (1969)

Reconfigurable Manufacturing on Multiple Levels: Literature Review and Research Directions

Ann-Louise Andersen[(⊠)], Thomas D. Brunoe, and Kjeld Nielsen

Department of Mechanical and Manufacturing Engineering, Aalborg University,
Aalborg, Denmark
ala@m-tech-aau.dk

Abstract. Reconfigurable manufacturing has been widely labelled the manufacturing paradigm of the future, due to its ability to rapidly and cost-efficiently respond to changing market conditions. Manufacturing reconfigurability can be dealt with at various levels of the factory, and includes multiple design and operational issues related to both physical and logical reconfigurations. The purpose of this paper is to review state-of-the-art literature on reconfigurable manufacturing and provide an overview of the current body of research, by assessing which structuring levels of the factory and corresponding research issues that are dealt with. Conclusively, currently unexplored areas and interesting issues that could be addressed in future research are identified.

Keywords: Reconfigurable manufacturing · Reconfigurability · Factory structuring levels · Literature classification · Literature review

1 Introduction

Today's manufacturing companies face challenges that have followed globalization, e.g. the fragmentation and change of customer demands, increased need for customized products, fast developing technologies, and focus on environmental sustainability [30]. In order to remain competitive, manufacturing companies need to develop the ability to design and operate manufacturing systems that can be continuously upgraded and changed, instead of being dedicated and optimized for one specific product model and delivery situation [22, 23]. For that reason, the reconfigurable manufacturing concept has been widely recognized as the manufacturing paradigm of the future [35].

The reconfigurable manufacturing concept was initially introduced in the 90's as an extension of flexible manufacturing, with the goal of combining the efficiency of dedicated manufacturing lines and the functional flexibility of the flexible systems [19]. In this way, the traditional trade-off between efficiency and flexibility is reduced and the issues of flexible manufacturing systems in regards to excess flexibility, low production rate, and low return on investments are avoided [22, 35]. Reconfigurability can generally be defined as the ability to repeatedly change capacity and functionality in a cost-efficient way, in order to meet different demand situations in terms of variation in volume as well as in product characteristics [23]. This ability to change can be achieved at different

© IFIP International Federation for Information Processing 2015
S. Umeda et al. (Eds.): APMS 2015, Part I, IFIP AICT 459, pp. 266–273, 2015.
DOI: 10.1007/978-3-319-22756-6_33

levels, e.g. on system and machine level, and involves multiple aspects of manufacturing enterprises [18]. The purpose of this paper is to review and classify state-of-the-art literature related to the reconfigurable manufacturing paradigm, examine which structuring levels of the factory that are most dealt with, and identify research issues at each level. Moreover, the classification of literature provides the foundation for identifying unexplored areas that could be relevant for future research.

The paper is structured as follows: Sect. 2 presents the methodology applied to collect relevant literature for the review, Sect. 3 briefly introduces reconfigurable manufacturing and the classification framework, while Sect. 4 presents the classification of literature in accordance with the related manufacturing levels. Conclusively, the issues discussed at each level are outlined and viable future research directions are proposed.

2 Literature Review Methodology

The objective of this literature review is to identify major tendencies in current literature on reconfigurable manufacturing, by conducting the following steps: retrieval, exclusion, and classification [14]. In order to identify relevant literature for the review, a rather broad search strategy was applied using Web of Science as the primary search database. The search consists of a topic search with two blocks being "reconfigurable" and "manufacturing" or "production". The time frame was set from 1990 to present day and only papers in English were included. The search was limited to "science technology" as the research domain and the following research areas were included: "operations research", "engineering", and "management science". In addition to the search, experts in the domain were identified through citation records and reference lists, which provided an additional number of papers to the review. In total, approximately 450 papers were initially retrieved, from which only 152 papers were included in the review. The exclusion of papers was based on a qualitative assessment of the following criteria: (a) the reconfigurable manufacturing paradigm should be the central theme or motivation for the research (b) the reconfigurability characteristics (customization, integrability, modularity, convertibility, scalability, diagnosability) are either implicitly or explicitly dealt with in the research.

In order to analyze the selected papers, a classification according six levels of reconfigurability was carried out. These levels correspond to the six structuring levels of factories as proposed by Wiendahl et al. [31]. The papers were classified when a primary level in relation to the research was directly stated or could be identified. Moreover, some of the included papers deal with several levels and are therefore classified in accordance with up to three levels. In total, 24 of the papers were identified as covering multiple levels, where 20 covered two levels and 4 covered three levels. For conciseness, only a minor part of the reviewed papers are included in the reference list of this paper. However, the full research protocol can be provided by inquiry to the authors. In the following section, the concept of reconfigurable manufacturing and the classification framework are presented.

3 Reconfigurability Definition, Characteristics, and Classification Framework

Manufacturing reconfigurability can generally be defined as the ability to repeatedly change capacity and functionality in a cost-efficient way, in order to meet different market situations. This ability to reconfigure efficiently is achieved through the following reconfigurability characteristics: customization, convertibility, scalability, modularity, integrability, and diagnosability [18]. In essence, these characteristics make systems, machines, and enterprises changeable in both capacity and functionality, which is the reason why reconfigurable manufacturing is widely labelled the manufacturing paradigm of the future [35]. Moreover, the reconfigurability characteristics should inherently be embedded in every aspect of reconfigurable manufacturing, e.g. in the planning and control, in the design of the system, and in the machine design in order to realize manufacturing reconfigurability [17]. These different aspects of the reconfigurations are traditionally divided in physical and logical types, where physical reconfigurations involve hard changes in equipment and arrangement of machines and logical reconfigurations involve soft changes such as re-routing and re-planning [31]. Evidently, realizing the vision of reconfigurable manufacturing, in terms of having the exact capacity and functionality needed when needed, involves multiple issues and ability to reconfigure at multiple levels [18]. For instance, system level issues could be the arrangement of physical modules, while on lower levels individual pieces or groups of equipment and machines could be considered [19]. However, reaping the full benefits of reconfigurable manufacturing is widely regarded as a paradigm shift, which inevitably changes at levels beyond what is covered on station and system level [15, 18].

Principally six structuring levels of a manufacturing company can be defined, which are differentiated both from a process and a space perspective and from a product level focus [31, 32]:

- Network: the highest structuring level, which comprises the network of sites that the manufacturing company is embedded in.
- Factory: the level of the plant, covering the building and its infrastructure.
- Segment: the level above the system, which contains all activities involved in manufacturing and making ship-ready products.
- System: the level containing interlinked cells used for manufacturing variants of a part or a product family.
- Cell: the level covering a subsystem of the system, containing groups of work stations and material handling that perform most activities to finish a part.
- Workstation: the lowest structuring level, containing single workstations and machines that add a feature to a work piece.

These structuring levels have in literature been applied to define different classes of changeability in relation to the concept of changeable manufacturing, which is an umbrella term covering all aspects of a manufacturing enterprise that allow for rapid and cost-efficient change in accordance with the environment [12]. In relation to this, reconfigurability is interpreted and defined as a term limited to levels below factory level, whereas agility and transformability are defined as changeability classes for upper levels. However, these changeability classes are not widely used in literature and there is no evidence of consistent use of the terms in relation to the stated levels. The concept of enterprise reconfigurability, which covers the ability of enterprises to adjust the network and form strategic alliances continuously is an example of reconfigurability applied to levels above the segment [6, 18]. Moreover, as the focus of this paper is to investigate current state-of-the-art research on reconfigurable manufacturing, and not research related to all aspects of changeable manufacturing, it is still a pertinent subject to investigate the structuring levels of the manufacturing company in relation to reconfigurability. In other words, the focus of this paper is not on how changeability can be achieved at each level of the factory, but rather how different aspects of reconfigurable manufacturing impact and are dealt with at each level of the factory. This is an interesting research subject, as realizing the benefits of reconfigurable manufacturing as a new production paradigm requires that reconfigurability issues are addressed at various levels of the factory [18]. Thus, it is highly relevant to provide an overview of current research and identify which levels that are addressed widely and more importantly if there are levels that are left comparatively unexplored.

4   Classification of Literature

From the literature retrieval and exclusion process, a total of 152 papers were included in the review and classified in relation to the six structuring levels of the factory. In Table 1, the absolute and relative amount of papers at each level are outlined. Additionally, dominant research issues at each level are indicated and examples of seminal contributions are included as references.

From this classification of literature, it is indicated that research on reconfigurable manufacturing primarily is related to the system and workstation level, with more than two thirds covering the system level and a third covering reconfigurations on work-station level. The system reconfiguration issues are mainly related to logical of soft types of reconfigurations, such as optimal reconfiguration selection or process planning. In contrary, the work-station level deals heavily with physical and hard types of reconfigurations in terms of designing reconfigurable machines. This distinction in research focus across levels supports the proposition by Bi et al. [5], stating that reconfigurability at lower organizational levels mainly is achieved through hardware changes, while reconfigurability at higher levels is achieved through software and control changes.

Another notable result from the classification is the differences between system and cell level, in terms of both research amount and the related issues. At cell-level, a main research issue is how to develop reconfigurable control systems that can control a process that is continuously and physically reconfigured. In many cases, these cell level papers on control systems are also related to the system level, as they demonstrate concepts or methods that are developed ideally for the entire system, but validated at the cell level, e.g. as by Valente and Carpanzano [29]. This logic could also be applied to the issue of developing technologies for seamless integration of machines and devices in the system or cell. A logical conclusion from this is that cell-level papers deal with research issues that are significantly complex and therefore calls for a more narrow scope than the entire system, even though they eventually and in practice must be applied to the entire manufacturing system.

Furthermore, it should be noted, that in the classification, factory and segment level papers are considered as one group. The reason for this is two-fold. First of all, the factory and segment level may not be easily distinguished, as the distinction depends heavily on the relative size of the factory referred to. Additionally, as only few of the reviewed papers cover research on these two levels, it was considered reasonable to regard them as one level. In the following section, the distribution of papers at each of the levels and potential research gaps are discussed, providing the foundation for indicating relevant future research directions.

Table 1. Overview of classified literature

Factory level	No. papers	Research issues
Production network	7 (5 %)	Selecting partners in reconfigurable enterprises [6] External reconfiguration activities [34] High-level planning of reconfigurable enterprises [2] Integration of shop-floor and supply chain [25]
Factory/ segment	7 (5 %)	Reconfigurable factory layouts [4] Transformable factories [32] Assignment of products to systems [13]
System	103 (68 %)	Design of products and product families for RMS design [1] Scalability management [11] Optimal reconfiguration selection [33] Reconfigurability metrics [21] RMS system design [26] Justification models [27] Process planning [3] RMS for exception handling [7] Conceptual RMS research [17]
Cell	14 (9 %)	Plug-and-play technology [10] Cell design principles [24] Reconfigurable control systems [29]
Workstation	45 (30 %)	Design of reconfigurable machine tools [28] Optimal configuration of machine tools [20] Reconfigurable fixtures [8] Reconfigurable inspection [16]

5   Discussion

Only a minor part of the reviewed papers covers research related to higher structuring levels of the factory, which is the plant and the network level. On network level, the few examples of reconfigurability deal primarily with how to achieve agility through continuously reconfiguring the supply chain when a new business opportunity arises. However, this research area lacks an explicit connection to manufacturing reconfigurability and coverage of how changes on shop floor are related to the supply chain structure. Therefore, this literature review indicates a gap in research on supply chain management issues in relation to operating a reconfigurable manufacturing system. Moreover, there is limited indication of research on lower levels acknowledging that reconfigurability on system, cell, or station-level has consequences on activities that happen outside the boundaries of the firm. However, in order to take full advantage of a reconfigurable system, reduce the time for new product introductions, increase product varieties, and quickly adapt to changing market conditions, it appears to be important also to consider the supply chain. Some indications of potential supply chain considerations are provided in current literature, e.g. selecting suppliers based on their type of manufacturing system [9] and issues related to buying or renting machine or tool modules required in a new configuration or selling those that have become obsolete with the reconfiguration [34]. In accordance with this, Chaube et al. [9] indicate that the lack of research on supply chain issues is one of the main problems in the implementation of reconfigurable manufacturing.

A similar gap exists at the factory-level, where research is also rather limited compared to lower levels. One of the primary focuses at this level is the transformable factory, which is a factory that is adaptable in its production and logistical structures, in buildings, and in organizational structures [32]. However, contributions in this area are rather conceptual, which leaves many interesting areas unaddressed, as operating a reconfigurable manufacturing system inevitably has numerous implications and requirements at factory level, in terms of logistical planning, layout planning, and in terms of organizational work structures.

6   Conclusion

Reconfigurable manufacturing has been widely labelled the manufacturing concept of the future, as manufacturers today need to respond quickly and efficiently to changing market conditions. Reconfigurability in manufacturing has been on the research agenda for the last two decades, and covers many different research issues. This paper has investigated which structuring levels of the factory that are currently most dealt with through a classification of literature. Moreover, research issues at each level have been identified, and the findings of the paper support the notion of lower levels primarily discussing physical reconfiguration, while higher levels mostly deal with logical reconfigurations. Additionally, one of the main findings of the classification is that a considerable share of current research is devoted to investigating the lower levels of reconfigurability, which is the system, cell, and station. However, it should be emphasized that doing reconfigurations on shop-floor has numerous implications for the entire factory in terms of its layout, structure, and logistical setup, but also outside the boundaries of the firm. In particular, supply chain management issues related to manufacturing reconfigurations should be a subject to future research, as it is currently left rather unexplored. Therefore, it is necessary that research in the future focuses broadly on the higher level requirements and issues that follow directly from operating a reconfigurable manufacturing system, in order to fully realize its potential in industry as the new manufacturing paradigm.

References

1. Abdi, M.R., Labib, A.W.: A design strategy for reconfigurable manufacturing systems (RMSs) using analytical hierarchical process (AHP): a case study. Int. J. Prod. Res. **41**, 2273–2299 (2003)
2. Argoneto, P., Bruccoleri, M., Nigro, G.L., et al.: High level planning of reconfigurable enterprises: a game theoretic approach. CIRP Ann. Manuf. Technol. **55**, 509–512 (2006)
3. Azab, A., ElMaraghy, H.: Sequential process planning: a hybrid optimal macro-level approach. J. Manuf. Syst. **26**, 147–160 (2007)
4. Benjaafar, S., Heragu, S.S., Irani, S.A.: Next generation factory layouts: research challenges and recent progress. Interfaces **32**, 58–76 (2002)
5. Bi, Z., Lang, S.Y., Verner, M., et al.: Development of reconfigurable machines. Int. J. Adv. Manuf. Technol. **39**, 1227–1251 (2008)
6. Bruccoleri, M., Nigro, G.L., Perrone, G., et al.: Production planning in reconfigurable enterprises and reconfigurable production systems. CIRP Ann. Manuf. Technol. **54**, 433–436 (2005)
7. Bruccoleri, M., Renna, P., Perrone, G.: Reconfiguration: a key to handle exceptions and performance deteriorations in manufacturing operations. Int. J. Prod. Res. **43**, 4125–4145 (2005)
8. Chan, K., Benhabib, B., Dai, M.: A reconfigurable fixturing system for robotic assembly. J. Manuf. Syst. **9**, 206–221 (1990)
9. Chaube, A., Benyoucef, L., Tiwari, M.K.: An adapted NSGA-2 algorithm based dynamic process plan generation for a reconfigurable manufacturing system. J. Intell. Manuf. **23**, 1141–1155 (2012)
10. Chen, H., Fuhlbrigge, T., Zhang, G., et al.: "Plug and produce" functions for an easily reconfigurable robotic assembly cell. Assembly Autom. **27**, 253–260 (2007)
11. Deif, A.M., ElMaraghy, H.A.: Assessing capacity scalability policies in RMS using system dynamics. Int. J. Flex. Manuf. Syst. **19**, 128–150 (2007)
12. ElMaraghy, H.A., Wiendahl, H.P.: Changeability - an introduction. In: ElMaraghy, H.A. (ed.) Changeable and Reconfigurable Manufacturing Systems, pp. 3–24. Springer, London (2009)
13. Gyulai, D., Kádár, B., Kovács, A., et al.: Capacity management for assembly systems with dedicated and reconfigurable resources. CIRP Ann. Manuf. Technol. **63**, 457–460 (2014)
14. Hart, C.: Doing a Literature Review: Releasing the Social Science Research Imagination. Sage Publications, Thousand Oaks (1998)
15. Heisel, U., Meitzner, M.: Progress in reconfigurable manufacturing systems. In: Dashcenko, A.I. (ed.) Reconfigurable Manufacturing Systems and Transformable Factories, pp. 47–62. Springer, Heidelberg (2006)
16. Katz, R.: Design principles of reconfigurable machines. Int. J. Adv. Manuf. Technol. **34**, 430–439 (2007)

17. Koren, Y.: General RMS characteristics. Comparison with dedicated and flexible systems. In: ElMaraghy, H.A. (ed.) Reconfigurable Manufacturing Systems and Transformable Factories, pp. 27–45. Springer, Heidelberg (2006)
18. Koren, Y.: The Global Manufacturing Revolution: Product-Process-Business Integration and Reconfigurable Systems. Wiley, New York (2010)
19. Koren, Y., Heisel, U., Jovane, F., et al.: Reconfigurable manufacturing systems. CIRP Ann. Manuf. Technol. **48**, 527–540 (1999)
20. Liu, W., Liang, M.: Multi-objective design optimization of reconfigurable machine tools: a modified fuzzy-chebyshev programming approach. Int. J. Prod. Res. **46**, 1587–1618 (2008)
21. Maler-Speredelozzi, V., Koren, Y., Hu, S.: Convertibility measures for manufacturing systems. CIRP Ann. Manuf. Technol. **52**, 367–370 (2003)
22. Mehrabi, M.G., Ulsoy, A.G., Koren, Y., et al.: Trends and perspectives in flexible and reconfigurable manufacturing systems. J. Intell. Manuf. **13**, 135–146 (2002)
23. Mehrabi, M.G., Ulsoy, A.G., Koren, Y.: Reconfigurable manufacturing systems: key to future manufacturing. J. Intell. Manuf. **11**, 403–419 (2000)
24. Padayachee, J., Bright, G.: The design of reconfigurable assembly stations for high variety and mass customisation manufacturing. S. Afr. J. Ind. Eng. **24**, 43–57 (2013)
25. Ribeiro, L., Barata, J., Colombo, A.: Supporting agile supply chains using a service-oriented shop floor. Eng. Appl. Artif. Intell. **22**, 950–960 (2009)
26. Rösiö, C., Säfsten, K.: Reconfigurable production system design–theoretical and practical challenges. J. Manuf. Technol. Manage. **24**, 998–1018 (2013)
27. Singh, R., Khilwani, N., Tiwari, M.: Justification for the selection of a reconfigurable manufacturing system: a fuzzy analytical hierarchy based approach. Int. J. Prod. Res. **45**, 3165–3190 (2007)
28. Spicer, P., Yip-Hoi, D., Koren, Y.: Scalable reconfigurable equipment design principles. Int. J. Prod. Res. **43**, 4839–4852 (2005)
29. Valente, A., Carpanzano, E.: Development of multi-level adaptive control and scheduling solutions for shop-floor automation in reconfigurable manufacturing systems. CIRP Ann. Manuf. Technol. **60**, 449–452 (2011)
30. Westkämper, E.: New trends in production. In: Dashcenko, A.I. (ed.) Reconfigurable Manufacturing Systems and Transformable Factories, pp. 15–26. Springer, Heidelberg (2006)
31. Wiendahl, H., ElMaraghy, H.A., Nyhuis, P., et al.: Changeable manufacturing-classification, design and operation. CIRP Ann. Manuf. Technol. **56**, 783–809 (2007)
32. Wiendahl, H., Hernández, R.: The transformable factory–strategies, methods and examples. In: Dashcenko, A.I. (ed.) Reconfigurable Manufacturing Systems and Transformable Factories, pp. 383–393. Springer, Heildelberg (2006)
33. Xiaobo, Z., Jiancai, W., Zhenbi, L.: A stochastic model of a reconfigurable manufacturing system part 1: a framework. Int. J. Prod. Res. **38**, 2273–2285 (2000)
34. Youssef, A.M., ElMaraghy, H.A.: Assessment of manufacturing systems reconfiguration smoothness. Int. J. Adv. Manuf. Technol. **30**, 174–193 (2006)
35. Zhang, G., Liu, R., Gong, L., et al.: An analytical comparison on cost and performance among DMS, AMS, FMS and RMS. In: Dashcenko, A.I. (ed.) Reconfigurable Manufacturing Systems and Transformable Factories, pp. 659–673. Springer, Heidelberg (2006)

Investigating the Potential in Reconfigurable Manufacturing: A Case-Study from Danish Industry

Ann-Louise Andersen[✉], Thomas D. Brunoe, and Kjeld Nielsen

Department of Mechanical and Manufacturing Engineering, Aalborg University,
Aalborg, Denmark
ala@m-tech-aau.dk

Abstract. In today's global manufacturing environment, manufactures must respond to the challenges of quickly adopting new technologies and provide an increasing number of product varieties, while continuously increasing cost-efficiency. Reconfigurable manufacturing systems meet these challenges through rapid and efficient changes in functionality and capacity. The purpose of this paper is to investigate a practical approach for evaluating the potential of reconfigurability in manufacturing companies, through a case-study in Danish industry. In this approach, historical production data is analyzed and focus is explicitly on capacity savings, which makes it applicable for decision support in companies that are in a transition towards becoming reconfigurable.

Keywords: Reconfigurable manufacturing · Reconfigurability · Changeable manufacturing · Reconfigurability potential · RMS potential

1 Introduction

Short product life-cycles, uncertainty in product demand, and pressure for maintaining cost-efficiency are conditions which manufacturing companies need to cope with, in order to remain competitive in today's global market [11]. Therefore, manufacturers need to find solutions for fast adaption of resources to varying market requirements, without significant losses in productivity [4]. The reconfigurable manufacturing system (RMS) is one of the means to this, through its ability to be continuously upgraded and changed, instead of being dedicated and optimized for one specific product model and demand situation [7]. Moreover, as the RMS is designed to contain the exact functionality and capacity needed to produce a given product family, the issues of flexible manufacturing in regards to excess flexibility, low production rate, and low return on investments are avoided [7]. For that reason, the reconfigurable manufacturing concept has been widely labelled the manufacturing paradigm of the future [11].

1.1 Literature Review

Reconfigurable manufacturing meets challenges in the current competitive environment that traditional manufacturing systems are not able to. However, the implementation of

© IFIP International Federation for Information Processing 2015
S. Umeda et al. (Eds.): APMS 2015, Part I, IFIP AICT 459, pp. 274–282, 2015.
DOI: 10.1007/978-3-319-22756-6_34

reconfigurability is still a significantly challenging task with several theoretical and practical problems [6, 8]. Currently, RMS research is widely concerned with optimization techniques for configuration selection, planning and scheduling techniques, and the development of reconfigurable machines. An area that has received only limited attention is the evaluation of RMS potential, even though determining the need for reconfigurability and justifying its investment is one of the first crucial steps in its implementation [1, 3].

In existing research, pre-design evaluations of a RMS is currently carried out through economic justification models. Kuzgunkaya and ElMaraghy [5] present an RMS evaluation model using a fuzzy multi-objective optimization approach incorporating both economic and strategic objectives, such as flexibility and responsiveness. Amico et al. [2] propose a model that compares system alternatives based on traditional net present value and real options analysis. Singh et al. [9] and Abdi and Labib [1] apply fuzzy analytical hierarchy processing logic for the selection of manufacturing systems based on different criteria, such as responsiveness, product cost, operator skill, and convertibility. The common denominator of these contributions is the selection of manufacturing system alternatives based on an economic justification and a quantitative assessment of several different criteria. Despite the significance of these models, their practical applicability can be questioned. First of all, estimating anticipated costs and other quantitative criteria related to each system alternative may represent a highly difficult and time-consuming task in many companies. Secondly, these aforementioned models represent advanced decision support tools and conceptual selection of the best manufacturing system. However, manufacturing system selection also depends heavily on practical considerations, which complicates the use of these models in reality. Moreover, these models do not have explicit focus on the potential of RMS, but rather on justifying its implementation from an economic perspective.

1.2 Research Question

One potential reason for the limited research in how to evaluate RMS potential, may be the difficulty and lack of experience in proving RMS advantages, and the general uncertainty in industry about what reconfigurability actually is [3, 8]. This further emphasizes that when determining the need for reconfigurability in a given company, focus should be on highlighting easily apprehensible aspects and on increasing knowledge of RMS main benefits. However, the aforementioned current approaches to justifying RMS investment do not support this, as they focus heavily on economic evaluation and require much effort to apply, which is unlikely in companies that do not yet fully perceive and understand the real benefits of manufacturing reconfigurability.

Based on these considerations, the following research question is formulated: *how can the potential in reconfigurable manufacturing systems be determined for manufacturing companies using information and data that is readily available and how can the results be interpreted?*

In the following section, the method applied to answering this question and the case-company and related data applied for determining RMS potential is described.

2 Methodology

In order to address the research question stated above, there are two main concerns. The first is the development of a method for evaluating the potential in reconfigurable manufacturing and the second is how to apply it and interpret the results. In order to do this, a case from Danish industry that produces electronic products for a water utility company is applied. This factory produces a large variety of different electronic products that in the latest years have been subject to numerous upgrades. These product generations, both minor and larger, have resulted in completely new and dedicated final assembly lines with no reuse from previous generations of assembly systems. Therefore, this factory is an interesting case for investigating RMS potential, as it exemplifies the traditional approach to manufacturing system design which is dedicated manufacturing lines with decreasing life-time due to rapid product changes.

2.1 Evaluating RMS Potential

Determining the potential in designing and operating a RMS, requires that focus is on the distinguishing feature of the reconfigurable system compared to the dedicated system, which is that its configuration can be changed over time, in order to provide the exact functionality and capacity needed by the market [4]. In order for a system to be reconfigurable, it must possess the characteristics of capacity scalability, function convertibility, and customized flexibility, while modularity, integrability, and diagnosability are supporting characteristics that enables reconfigurability [4]. Therefore, when evaluating RMS potential, focus should be explicitly on these three essential characteristics and the benefits of applying them.

The benefit of scalable capacity is that demand and supply can be matched gradually, thereby avoiding situations with either excess capacity or unmet demand. In contrary, dedicated lines have rigid structures that do not allow for capacity change in accordance with market change, product upgrade, and product maturity curves [4]. The benefit of convertibility is that the life of a RMS is longer than the life of a dedicated line, as it consists of different periods satisfying different demand scenarios, in terms of product variety and product mix. Moreover, as a RMS has customized flexibility, it is able to produce all parts or products within a family. In order to summarize these RMS benefits, the following proposition can be formulated: in a reconfigurable manufacturing setting, capacity is lower than in the situation where products or parts have dedicated systems, as several different product generations and varieties can be produced simultaneously through reconfigurations.

Narrowing attention to this proposition makes it possible to evaluate RMS potential based on the capacity differences between initial dedicated setups and future RMS setups, using readily available historical data on capacities and production output from industrial companies. Nevertheless, evaluating such capacity differences requires both that the actual dedicated setup is analysed and that it is compared to a fictional RMS setup based on the same historical data. Therefore, developing a fictional RMS setup is the key concern in the approach to evaluate RMS potential developed in this paper.

In order to develop a RMS scenario based on actual historical data on production output of different product varieties and product generations, it is presumed that a number of reconfigurable lines are used, which can produce several product generations and varieties simultaneously. Moreover, as each reconfigurable line by definition is modular, the scenario is scalable by adding and extracting lines to the reconfigurable setup. Having a number of reconfigurable lines as the foundation for the reconfigurable scenario, the key task is to distribute the actual historical production output to the RMS lines, thereby dividing the historical data into different configuration periods, which represent the final RMS scenario.

2.2 Data

In order to test this approach to evaluate RMS potential, the aforementioned electronics factory is applied as a case. The foundation for evaluating RMS potential in this case is historical data on production output and capacities of production systems related to a specific electronics product family. More specifically, seven-year production output data from the case-company's ERP system for all varieties and generations within the product family is extracted and used for the analysis. In the seven-year period that is considered here, a total of four product upgrades have occurred resulting in four product generations.

The production area in focus is the final assembly of the electronics products. In this area, production lines are purely dedicated, meaning that all generations are produced on separate lines. Despite the fact that only minor changes have happened between each generation and all variants belong to the same product platform, there is currently no reuse of production equipment. Moreover, there are separate dedicated production lines for product variants within the same generation. In fact, the product family contains two main groups of variants that are sold to different market segments, here denoted as type A and type B. Each product generation contain both groups of variants, besides generation 2 that only contains type B. The two groups of variants have the same overall functionality, but are produced on separate dedicated production lines. Therefore, in the following capacity analysis of the current dedicated setup, these two types will be treated separately.

3 Results

The first step in investigating RMS potential in the case, is to compare actual production output on each production line with the actual available capacity. In Figs. 1 and 2, the results of this analysis are depicted. It is evident that in the seven-year period that was analyzed, the total production capacity far exceeds the actual output. In fact, only a third of the available capacity is used on average for both type A and B equipment. This significant excess in capacity results from inability to gradually scale capacity, but also from having rigid dedicated lines that can only be used for one generation or only a part of the whole product family.

The significant capacity excess in the current dedicated setup indirectly indicates that there is a potential in changing the approach to reconfigurable manufacturing.

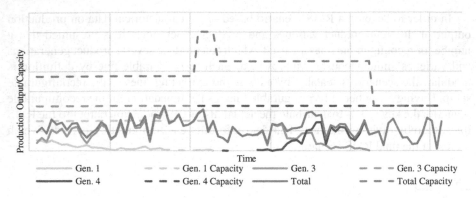

Fig. 1. Analysis of capacity and output of type A generations

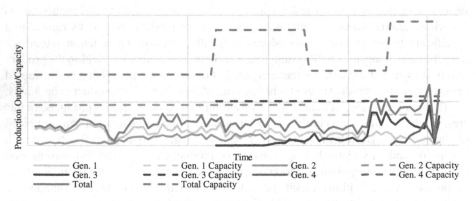

Fig. 2. Analysis of capacity and output of type B generation

However, in order to explicitly evaluate this, the following RMS scenario is developed. In this scenario, the same seven-year historical data is divided into different configuration periods, based on significant changes in demand volume, product phase-outs, or product introductions. In each configuration period, the reconfigurable lines have different setups and the capacity of the overall setup is scalable. Moreover, it is reasonable to include both type A and B groups of variants in the same setup, as RMSs by definition are able to produce a whole product family in contrary to dedicated lines. Therefore, in the scenario it is assumed that a number of RMS lines with fixed capacity is utilized, but that the overall system is scalable by adding and extracting RMS lines. The fixed capacity of the RMS lines and the number of lines is determined in cooperation with the case company.

In order to make the RMS scenario as realistic as possible, the following restrictions have been developed in cooperation with the case-company. First of all, the total capacity of the RMS lines should be sufficient to produce the same output in terms of volume and product types as in the historical data. However, up to two periods in a row with insufficient capacity is allowed, if the previous two months have sufficient capacity for covering the deficit or a RMS line in the same period produced a similar generation and

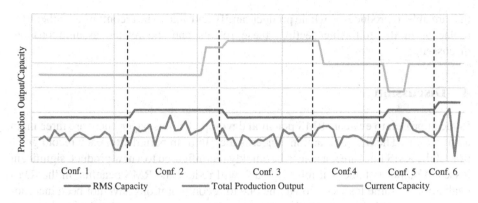

Fig. 3. RMS scenario and comparison of total current and RMS capacity

Table 1. Configuration periods for RMS scenario

Periods	Conf. 1	Conf. 2	Conf. 3	Conf. 4	Conf. 5	Conf. 6
	19 months	18 months	19 months	13 months	10 months	6 months
Line 1	Gen. 1A	Gen. 1A	Gen. 2B	Gen. 3A	Gen. 3B	Gen. 3B
Line 2	Gen. 3A	Gen. 3A	Gen. 4A	Gen. 4A	Gen. 3B	Gen. 3B
Line 3	Gen. 3A	Gen. 3A	Gen. 3A	Gen. 4A	Gen. 4A	Gen. 4A
Line 4	Gen. 1B	Gen. 1B	Gen. 1B	Gen. 1B	Gen. 1B	Gen. 1B
Line 5	Gen. 1B	Gen. 1B	Gen. 1B		Gen. 4A	Gen. 4A
Line 6	Gen. 2B	Gen. 2B		Gen. 3B	Gen. 3B	Gen. 3B
Line 7		Gen. 3A	Gen. 3A + B	Gen. 3A	Gen. 4B	Gen. 4B
Line 8						Gen. 4B

has sufficient capacity. This restriction relates to the fact that some production planning and inventory can be assumed in the RMS scenario, and that both type A and B product can be produced simultaneously. Secondly, it is decided that between two consecutive configuration periods, it is only possible to change functionality of the RMS line from one product generation to the next. This means that it is only possible to change from one generation to the third over more than two configuration periods. This restriction relates to the convertibility of the system, which should match the actual possibilities in the case. In Fig. 3, the resulting reconfigurable scenario and a comparison of total dedicated and RMS capacity are depicted. Table 1 summarizes each configuration of the RMS setup. It is evident that considerable capacity savings will follow from changing the current dedicated lines and applying reconfigurability. In the seven-year period that is analyzed, a capacity reduction of approximately 50 % is possible if the current setup is changed to a reconfigurable setup consisting of up to eight RMS lines. This setup contain only 3 out of 84 periods with a capacity deficit that cannot be satisfied by the above mentioned rules. The capacity reduction results from having manufacturing lines that are able to produce the whole product family and able to be reconfigured rather than replaced. In the following section, these results and the related assumptions are discussed.

4 Discussion

In the approach to evaluate RMS potential developed in this paper, there are three main assumptions. The first assumption concerns the ramp-up period after each reconfiguration. If the RMS lines are not able to be quickly reconfigured to a new product, significant losses in output volume will follow, which will reduce the RMS benefits. In the RMS evaluation, volume losses or downtime due to reconfigurations have not been incorporated, as this would have required more thorough investigations on the changes between generations and the technical aspects of the production conversion. However, in order to further explore RMS potential, it is necessary to investigate systematic ramp-up reduction in the RMS environment. Currently, there are several contributions in research on general problems and performance consequences encountered in the ramp-up period [10]. However, research is limited in regards to ramp-up and the specific challenges in modular and reconfigurable manufacturing systems, which seems like an important future research topic.

The second main assumption is related to the cost and effort of refitting the manufacturing line to new product generations. When potential capacity savings from implementing reconfigurability are indicated above, it is assumed that product generations have sufficient commonality to be treated by the same production processes and equipment. In the specific case, this is a valid assumption due to a minor degree of change between generations that are built on the same product platform. However, when determining RMS potential in further manufacturing cases, this subject should be considered simultaneously.

The third assumption is related to the decision of RMS line capacities. In the case, each line in the RMS scenario have equal and constant capacity, which is determined in cooperation with the case company. However, in reality the decision of system and line capacities is much more complicated and involves levels beyond what is covered in this paper. In other words, the scalability of the entire reconfigurable scenario developed here is achieved simply through adding or extracting RMS lines, while functional convertibility is assumed to be achieved on each line by changing its modules. In reality, reconfigurability can be achieved at numerous levels, e.g. on system, cell, and station level, which means that scalability and convertibility can be realized at more levels than considered in this paper. Therefore, an interesting topic for future research would be to investigate the decision of on which levels to realize reconfigurability and how to effectively determine the capacity of the system.

The approach developed in this paper represents a pre-design activity that can be applied as decision support in companies that are in a RMS transition. The RMS potential is indicated by using historical data, which is considered a useable indicator for future potential. In this regard, it should be emphasized that the development of the RMS scenario is carried out with full predictability in the production output in each period.

Thus, this approach is not intended as a means for configuring future reconfigurable lines, but rather as a means to highlighting performance improvement that could have been achieved through the application of manufacturing reconfigurability. In addition, this approach to evaluate RMS potential do not substitute the economic evaluation models that are present in the current body of RMS research, but rather represents a practical first attempt to evaluate the main RMS benefits.

5   Conclusion

One of the crucial steps in the implementation of reconfigurable manufacturing is the evaluation of its potential in different manufacturing settings. Therefore, the aim of this paper is to investigate a method for determining RMS potential, using data that is readily available in manufacturing companies. The approach to this focuses on potential capacity savings resulting from manufacturing systems where several different product generations and varieties can be produced simultaneously, through reconfigurations. Through a case-study from Danish industry, the approach is applied and historical data on capacities and production output are analyzed, and a reconfigurable manufacturing setup is developed. Moreover, through this approach to evaluating RMS potential, knowledge of reconfigurability is increased in the evaluated manufacturing company, which makes it highly applicable for decisions support in companies that are in a RMS transition.

References

1. Abdi, M.R., Labib, A.W.: Feasibility study of the tactical design justification for reconfigurable manufacturing systems using the fuzzy analytical hierarchical process. Int. J. Prod. Res. **42**, 3055–3076 (2004)
2. Amico, M., Asl, F., Pasek, Z., et al.: Real options: an application to RMS investment evaluation. In: Dashcenko, A.I. (ed.) Reconfigurable Manufacturing Systems and Transformable Factories, pp. 675–693. Springer, Heidelberg (2006)
3. Heisel, U., Meitzner, M.: Progress in reconfigurable manufacturing systems. In: Dashcenko, A.I. (ed.) Reconfigurable Manufacturing Systems and Transformable Factories, pp. 47–62. Springer, Heidelberg (2006)
4. Koren, Y.: The Global Manufacturing Revolution: Product-Process-Business Integration and Reconfigurable Systems. Wiley, New York (2010)
5. Kuzgunkaya, O., ElMaraghy, H.: Economic and strategic perspectives on investing in RMS and FMS. Int. J. Flex. Manuf. Syst. **19**, 217–246 (2007)
6. Malhotra, V., Raj, T., Arora, A.: Evaluation of barriers affecting reconfigurable manufacturing systems with graph theory and matrix approach. Mater. Manuf. Process. **27**, 88–94 (2012)
7. Mehrabi, M.G., Ulsoy, A.G., Koren, Y.: Reconfigurable manufacturing systems: key to future manufacturing. J. Intell. Manuf. **11**, 403–419 (2000)
8. Rösiö, C., Säfsten, K.: Reconfigurable production system design–theoretical and practical challenges. J. Manuf. Technol. Manage. **24**, 998–1018 (2013)

9. Singh, R., Khilwani, N., Tiwari, M.: Justification for the selection of a reconfigurable manufacturing system: a fuzzy analytical hierarchy based approach. Int. J. Prod. Res. **45**, 3165–3190 (2007)
10. Surbier, L., Alpan, G., Blanco, E.: A comparative study on production ramp-up: state-of-the-art and new challenges. Prod. Plann. Control **25**, 1264–1286 (2014)
11. Wiendahl, H., ElMaraghy, H.A., Nyhuis, P., et al.: Changeable manufacturing-classification, design and operation. CIRP Ann. Manuf. Technol. **56**, 783–809 (2007)

Iterative Improvement of Process Planning Within Individual and Small Batch Production

Christina Reuter, Timo Nuyken, Stephan Schmitz, and Stefan Dany[✉]

Laboratory for Machine Tools and Production Engineering (WZL), RWTH Aachen University,
Aachen, Germany
{c.reuter,t.nuyken,st.schmitz,s.dany}@wzl.rwth-aachen.de

Abstract. Present challenges of small batch production are represented by the need to improve time-to-market and the reduction of costs. A promising approach to take up these challenges is the use of highly iterative development processes such as Scrum known from software development. A transfer of these principles to process planning enables the prediction of producibility of customer orders by iteratively learning from manufacturing data of similar jobs from the past. Based on the required data structures described in this paper, work plans for new orders can be generated automatically. The potential of the approach is validated by an industrial example.

Keywords: Computer automated process planning (CAPP) · Production planning · Producibility prediction

1 Challenges in Production Planning Within Individual and Small Batch Production

In projects that WZL of RWTH Aachen University conducted with industrial partners with individual and small batch production, it was found that process planning is time-consuming and the quality of planning strongly depends on the individual level of knowledge of the responsible employee. One way to face these challenges are computer-automated process planning systems. At this point, it became clear that it is very difficult to transfer the process planners' tacit knowledge to computer-aided planning systems.

As "process planning is the link between product design and product manufacturing and re-manufacturing", it is a central lever for reduction of costs and to improve time-to-market [1].

Wiendahl et al. postulate following key enablers for an efficient and flexible generation of process plans [2]: cognitivability, evolvability, adjustability, granularity, automation and ability.

The approach presented in this paper especially focusses on cognitivability and automation ability. Therefore, the aim is to introduce a concept for the iterative improvement of process planning by using data from manufacturing. Data structures that are

© IFIP International Federation for Information Processing 2015
S. Umeda et al. (Eds.): APMS 2015, Part I, IFIP AICT 459, pp. 283–290, 2015.
DOI: 10.1007/978-3-319-22756-6_35

prerequisite for an implementation are explained. Moreover, it is shown how comparative advantages can be generated.

2   Deficiencies of Existing Approaches

In recent years the concept of manual process planning in individual and small batch production has been enhanced by computer-aided approaches. As shown in Fig. 1, Computer-Aided Process Planning (CAPP) systems can be further classified in relation to their degree of automation: Variant process planning, semi-generative process planning and generative process planning [3].

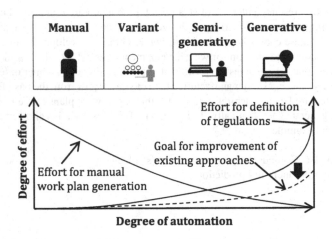

Fig. 1.   Comparison of the described process planning methodologies

Manual process planning implicates the permanent creation of new work plans which are derived from current or former plans. The process planner therefore conducts an analysis based on the specific product features and CAD data [4]. This continual re-creation of work schedules is very time-consuming. Moreover, the degree of standardization suffers because of the great dependency on preferences and expertise of the production planner.

The basic principle of variant process planning has evolved from manual process planning. It includes the allocation of the product range into part families which are based on similarities regarding functionalities, design features or manufacturing processes and comprise similar pre-determined parameters. Each part is related to a unique part family code which contains all the relevant data of the features of the specific family and the corresponding standardized process plan [5].

The classification of part families is challenging due to the great variety regarding features and combined characteristics of a product. The lack of classification of novel products can cause a problem with the creation of work plans under the condition that structural changes occur. Consequently the system has to be re-aligned. This means that variant process planning still depends on the process planners' expertise and knowledge.

The semi-generative process planning extends the variant process planning by the possibility of structural changes based on a master plan which is altered by the required new process operations. It combines variant process planning with an algorithmic procedure which is supported by CAD models, databases, decision trees, knowledge rules and heuristics [6]. Both, variant process planning as well as semi-generative process planning still rely on pre-defined results of earlier planning operations. Moreover, semi-generative process planning systems are not able to cover all part varieties and still depends on operational involvement of the scheduler.

Generative process planning implicates the generation of work plans which are derived from relevant process and product data. This requires knowledge of all relevant information such as restrictions and dependencies as well as transparency over production processes which can be reached by the use of complete and reliable mathematical models. A truly generative process planning system has not been realized yet [6].

Although the effort for manual creation of work plans is constantly minimized by an increasing degree of automation from manual creation of work plans to generative process planning, however, there is still time and effort needed for the definition of rules and regulations.

The initial creation of a set of rules is still possible with great expenses in a static system of production. The real market environment of individual and small batch production is determined by an ever-changing and dynamic system. An exemplary scenario of changing machinery illustrates the consequences of this dynamic. When changing the machinery during the creation of rules and regulations, it is necessary to re-check and adjust the resources again, due to the complexity and interdependency of the existing rules. The additional effort necessary here is similar to the initial definition of the rules. Thus, the initial set of rules and regulations already becomes obsolete during its process of creation. This indicates that for the computer-automated generation of work plans in the individual and small batch production a new approach is crucial.

The goal for the optimization of existing approaches is the reduction of effort for the initial definition and administration of regulations in generative process planning and to enhance planning quality.

3   Approach

The core idea of the presented approach is the iterative use of feedback data from manufacturing in order to improve process planning. According to geometrical, material and functional properties of an individual or small batch product the optimal manufacturing process as well as the optimal machine is identified. Furthermore, standard times for all processes are calculated by using feedback data. As a consequence, the planning quality can be improved und at the same time the planning effort is reduced respectively.

The quality of planning is measured by an appropriate selection of the manufacturing process and machine as well as the accuracy of the calculated standard times. The planning effort in turn is measured by the time required to generate a work plan. It is required that the approach enables a quick response towards customer requests.

Therefore, in an iterative process like it is known from the Scrum method, data from manufacturing is used for an iterative improvement of CAPP. The Scrum method is a framework which is commonly applied in product development processes. It supports solving complex adaptive tasks and enables to productively and creatively deliver goods with the highest possible value [7].

Based on a generic order fulfilment process, there are three core elements of the approach, which are shown in Fig. 2. The core elements are:

1. Iterative improvement of process planning
2. Data management
3. Producibility Prediction.

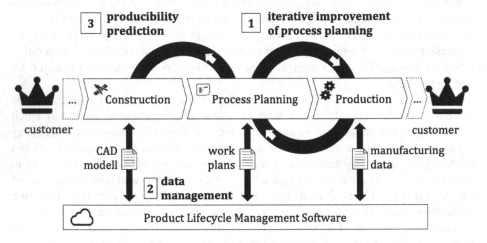

Fig. 2. Concept of iterative improvement of process planning

3.1   Iterative Improvement of Process Planning

In order to improve current CAPP systems, a definition of specifications and rules is necessary. Hereinafter, both are referred to as process planning regulations. These process planning regulations facilitate to model manufacturing technologies and processes virtually. For each manufacturing process specific parameters describing the physical procedure are determined (e.g. cutting speed). Furthermore, maximum product dimensions that can be processed as well as tolerance values have to be defined (e.g. accessible surface roughness in face turning process). All parameters and specifications are stored in a technology database.

Based on geometrical, material and functional specifications of a product and using the process planning regulations, an adequate allocation of manufacturing process and machines is achieved. In contrast to given approaches, the allocation is not done product by product but rather based on generic product specifications. On basis of data from manufacturing, it is possible to identify standard times based on the defined parameters for all manufacturing processes.

To introduce the iterative process, experienced production planners establish initial specifications for each machine and determine initial values for the required parameters. In the second step an initial work plan is created based on the previously defined process planning regulations. Data raised during the production of the first products and batches enables an iterative improvement of the process planning regulations by comparing the planed and realized production plans. In this way, work plans for the same or similar products can be generated easily in the future. Smart algorithms analyze all data from production, cluster production plans according to similar geometrical and functional specification of products and ensure an iteratively improvement of realizing production jobs.

In case an inadequate work plan is generated for a new product with similar material, geometrical and functional specifications as a production job in the past, the approach described above shows the following advantage: In current CAPP systems the regulations have to be reviewed manually in case of inadequate work plans are generated. Firstly, it has to be analyzed why another machine has been used. Secondly, changes in process planning regulations need to be derived and the necessary changes must be implemented. However, by iteratively using manufacturing data to improve process planning, the smart algorithms mentioned above automatically adjust process planning regulations.

Depending on the type of error in the automatic generation of work plans the following types of adjustments are differentiated:

On the one hand, in case the generative creation of a work plan resulted into the right selection of manufacturing processes and machines but there have been deviations regarding the standard times, the consequent corrective measure must be the alignment of parameters in the technology database.

On the other hand, in case the scheduled manufacturing process is not possible due to wrong determinations in the work plan, it is required to update the machine specifications or to introduce additional process planning rules for the specifications of the customer order.

The binding requirements for an iterative improvement are dependent on a sufficient level of detail of manufacturing data. Only if data from production for similar customer orders are collected under consistent conditions such as machine availability, staff availability and utilization of production, they can constitute a basis for optimization of process planning regulations. Hence, only data that has not been raised during a disruption (e.g. failure of machine) in the production can be considered for an iterative improvement of the process planning regulations. Data sets that have been gathered according to these conditions are flagged in the database.

3.2 Data Management

The iterative improvement of production planning requires data from various sources which are stored and administered in a product lifecycle management (PLM) software to ensure a "single source of truth" [1]. The data transferred to the PLM systems in the construction process, in process planning and the production process are shown in Fig. 2.

The classification of products regarding their geometrical specifications is prerequisite for the computer-automated generation of a work plan. The digital model of a product that is crucial to determine its geometric properties is generated during the construction process. This data is stored in the form of a CAD model in the PLM system. Of course, the previously described technology database is also managed by PLM system.

Furthermore, an iterative improvement of process planning is based on data from sensors in production. As described above, only data that has been recorded in comparable situations can be used for the evaluation. Here, sensors in machines and their surrounding can provide a real-time state description of the component and its environment.

Also, the customer order has to be saved in the PLM system. The combination of geometrical specifications of a product and information from the customer order (e.g. batch size) can influence the selection of manufacturing processes and machines.

3.3 Producibility Prediction

By applying the approach it is possible to provide high-quality information upstream the order fulfillment process. This is referred to as "producibility prediction" (see Fig. 2).

A key advantage of a computer-automated process planning is to enable the constructor to review his/her design quickly with respect to feasibility and effort in production. The experience of these feedback loops can be derived into construction guidelines. Based on this feedback and analogous to the iterative improvement of prototypes in product development by applying an iterative process, a construction that meets the requirements can be created easier. Hereby, time-to-market as well as planning costs can be reduced. It is also possible to provide fast feedback about the producibility of a customer request, which also shortens time-to-market and may generate a competitive advantage.

4   Case Study and Validation

The approach is validated with an industrial partner. The company is a leading global manufacturing company for blades, brakes and clutches and offers individual products for forming domains, general mechanical engineering, mobile applications in construction machine industry as well as within the rural economy. The offered product range includes about 40.000 various components, each with up to 70 different variants. As a consequence, the process planning faces a high product variety and the planning quality highly depends on the planner's practical experience.

The validation is realized within two steps: In a first step, the initial situation is documented with regard to planning quality and quality effort. In the second step, the potential of the approach is estimated. The results are summarized in Fig. 3.

Analyzing the results, planning effort can be reduced, reproducibility can be increased and the process planning quality can be improved in a high extent. Experts of industry especially expect a high improvement potential for the calculation of standard times. The planning quality can be considerably enhanced by adjusting the parameters in the technology data base iteratively with the use of an automatically evaluation of data from manufacturing process. Initially, in 75 % of the cases the correct manufacturing method is selected. Taking the new approach for iterative improvement of process

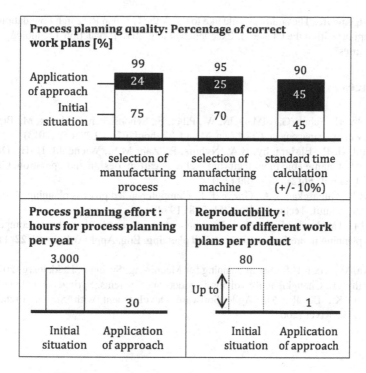

Fig. 3. Initial situation and potential of the approach

planning, the percentage of correct work plans can be increased up to 99 %. The potential for the selection of an adequate manufacturing machine is estimated similarly high. Expenses for the manual creation of work plans can be almost completely eliminated with the approach.

The experts consider reproducibility to be particularly important. By applying the approach, the planning process is independent of the individual expert knowledge of the employee and work plans are a reliable input for Production Planning.

5   Conclusion

The approach of this paper transfers iterative improvement principles known from product development such as Scrum to process planning. It is proposed to use data from manufacturing to enable and improve current CAPP systems. By applying the three elements of the approach, it becomes possible to reduce efforts for process planning and to improve time-to-market. For validation, the approach was discussed with experts from industry to validate its potential.

Further work needs to be done to detail the presented approach: In a next step smart algorithms that are crucial for the iterative improvement of process planning regulations should be developed and detailed. Further research is needed to implement producibility prediction to provide valuable information for the constructor.

Acknowledgement. The authors would like to thank the German Research Foundation DFG for the kind support within the Cluster of Excellence "Integrative Production Technology for High-Wage Countries".

References

1. ElMaraghy, H., Schuh, G., ElMaraghy, W., Piller, F., Schönsleben, P., Tseng, M., Bernard, A.: Product variety management. CIRP Ann. Manuf. Technol. **62**(2), 629–652 (2013)
2. Wiendahl, H.-P., ElMaraghy, H.A., Nyhuis, P., Zäh, M.F., Wiendahl, H.-H., Duffie, N., Brieke, M.: Changeable manufacturing – classification, design and operation. CIRP Ann. Manuf. Technol. **56**(2), 783–809 (2007)
3. Marri, H.B., Gunasekaran, A., Grieve, R.J.: Computer-aided process planning: A state of art. Int. J. Adv. Manuf. Technol. **14**(4), 261–268 (1998)
4. Salehi, M., Tavakkoli-Moghaddam, R.: Application of genetic algorithm to computer-aided process planning in preliminary and detailed planning. Eng. Appl. Artif. Intell. **22**, 1179–1187 (2009)
5. Hazarika, M., Dixit, U.S.: Setup Planning for Machining. Springer, Heidelberg (2015)
6. ElMaraghy, H.: Changing and Evolving Products and Systems. Springer, London (2009)
7. Schwaber, K., Beedle, M.: Agile Software Development with Scrum. Prentice Hall, Upper Saddle River (2002)

Profile of Building Information Modeling – BIM - Tools Maturity in Brazilian Civil Construction Scenery

Samuel Dereste dos Santos[1,2(✉)], Oduvaldo Vendrametto[1],
Miguel León González[2], and Creusa Fernandes Correia[2]

[1] Paulista University-UNIP, Dr. Bacelar St., 1212 São Paulo, Brazil
samuel_dereste@yahoo.com.br, oduvaldov@uol.com.br
[2] Cruzeiro do Sul University-UNICSUL,
Dr. Ussiel Cirillo Ave. 225, São Paulo, Brazil
miguel.leon@uol.com.br, creusa.profmat@gmail.com

Abstract. Building Information Modeling – BIM – tools are gaining, nowadays, great visibility by the possibility of integrated project development. The implementation of BIM tools is gaining space worldwide, including Brazilian scenery. Besides, the degree of tool implementation can vary depending the country, and can show how is the level of projects that are being developed. This paper evaluates the degree of BIM maturity implementation in Brazil's context, to find the differences of BIM software utilization under different projects. The strategy adopted was a technical review focused on periodical papers as well as a case study developed with 16 BIM expert's projects in Brazil. The results shown that Brazil presents an advanced BIM implementation considering BIS - Department of Business Innovations and Skills requirements, with great application in modeling, building installations, infrastructure, and low applicability on development of integrated projects.

Keywords: BIM · CAD · Profile · Maturity

1 Introduction

Building Information Modelling (BIM) has different definitions, with wide aspects considered by experts. It can be defined as the process of generating, storing, managing, exchanging, and sharing information from building process, in an interoperable and reusable way, with the use of a computer generated model to simulate the planning, design, construction and operational phases of a project [1]. The BIM – Building Information Modeling – tools are gaining, worldwide, great importance despite all this qualities for project development in AEC – Architecture, Engineering and Construction – Area. This tool has conceptual differences when compared with other software and permits a project development more efficient [2].

An analysis of the project development history since 1950 shows that the advent of CAD – Computer Aided Design – tools remains the transfer to the computer information that was handmade manipulated. Besides, with software and computer

© IFIP International Federation for Information Processing 2015
S. Umeda et al. (Eds.): APMS 2015, Part I, IFIP AICT 459, pp. 291–298, 2015.
DOI: 10.1007/978-3-319-22756-6_36

popularization starts a process of evolution that changed the type of information manipulated.

Besides all work integration possibilities of BIM tools nowadays, the construction industry worldwide still exhibits a low maturity in BIM use, since no significant changes in the traditional business model accompany the introduction of new tools [2]. The purpose of this study was to evaluate the degree of BIM maturity implementation in Brazil's context, to find the differences of BIM software utilization under different projects. The strategy was based on a technical review focused on periodical papers as well as a study developed with 16 BIM expert's projects in Brazil.

This paper is organized into sections as follows: introduction, technical review, case study, discussion and, finally, results and references.

2 Technical Review

2.1 General Definition

The Building Information Modelling (BIM) can be understood like an IT approach that involves applying and maintaining an integral digital representation of the building information, considering different phases of the project lifecycle, working like a data repository. The common data changed in this environment is geometric data, non-geometric data (parameters), and this information is joined in a virtual reality ambience, that allows research, collaboration, improve data integrity, intelligent documentation, retrieving of building data. All these characteristics allow a high quality process project, thorough an enhanced performance analysis, as well as multidisciplinary planning, verification and coordination [3].

This project model allows reducing design mistakes and increases productivity of construction industry because is being used not only one software, but a family of tools that, in an integrated way, results in an integrated model that have, inside, all the different projects steps and the different types of information joined in the same model. Such, BIM provides an emerging new paradigm for project development and construction management to architecture, engineering and construction industry [4].

The potential of productivity increased by BIM implementation express one consider modification in civil construction production projects. Besides the BIM definition, the need and possibility of project development in integrated and interoperable platforms was yet recognized already in the 1970s. BIM systems can be seen as an evolution of CAD systems through intelligence and interoperable increasing information [4].

When a business implement BIM solutions, there are a substantial impact through all stages of project and construction process. There is an expand of stakeholder collaboration through different steps of project development. However, is necessary a change in business processes, and not only a simple promotion technology. BIM implementation can affect all the processes, and cannot be treated only as a software change [1].

At final, with BIM implementation, is possible to have a more accurate way of working, as a reduction of waste/loses (materials, resources, hour-work, etc.). Besides, the 3 dimensional work allows the development of a better project. Instead, it needs the generation of models in extranet/internet, what makes necessary the utilization of security protocols for information management [1].

2.2 BIM Maturity

The BIM implementation will not occur at the same way in all kind of business. BIM adopters will need to go through a managed process of changing, starting with the internal organization through external suppliers and clients. BIS - Department of Business Innovations and Skills - UK, developed a maturity model defining the levels from 0 through 3 (Fig. 1) to understand software implementation in construction industry. Worldwide, great part of the market is still working with Level 1 processes, and the best in class are experiencing significant benefits in Level 2 [2].

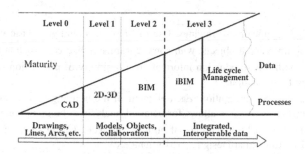

Fig. 1. BIM maturity implementation [2]

According BIS, the BIM evolution can be divided into 4 levels. The level 0 consists in the first CAD applications for project development worldwide. The focus of these applications was bi-dimensional objects, and remains the transfer of handmade projects to computer in all areas, like aeronautics, mechanical and civil construction. The level 1 consists in the first efforts of make bi and tri-dimensional integrated objects, but the objects of this level are difficult to be integrated because they are still vectorized, like CAD previous tools [2].

In the sequence, the level 2 consists in the utilization of BIM first applications. However, the utilization in this phase are still modelling, without integration. At last, the level 3 consists in the application of BIM in an integrated manner, with the project development with different tools.

Others models were developed to understand the BIM implementation. Model Progression Specifications for BIM has been adopted by the American Institute of Architects to address the phase outcomes, milestones, and deliverables, and the idea of assigning tasks on a best person basis. The core was the level of detailing, which describes the steps of the BIM element logical progress. The levels of details ranged from the lowest level (100) of conceptual approximation to the highest level of representational precision (500) (Fig. 2) [2].

Model Progression Specifications (AIA)*				
Level of Detail	100	200	300	400	500
Model Content	Conceptual	Approximate geometry	Precise geometry	Fabrication	As-Built
Design and Cordination	Non-geometric data or line work, areas, volumes, zones etc.	Generic elements shown in three dimensions • maximum size • purpose	Confirmed 3D Object geometry • dimension • capacities • connections	Shop drawing/fabrication • purchase • manufacture • install • specified	
*a portion of table adapted from American Institute of Architects, AIA-E202 element model table.					

Fig. 2. Model progress specifications. Adapted from [2]

2.3   BIM Implementation Stages and Definitions

The evolution of BIM tools can be linked with the type of information manipulated in that phase. According [5], it can be defined by Table 1.

Table 1. BIM stages and definitions. Adapted from [5].

Stage	Definition
2D	First CAD applications drawings. Use of lines, arcs, and geometric vectors
3D	First tri-dimensional objects, with some parameters like construction materials
4D	Models with time-production information. Possibility of production planning using just-in-time solutions
5D	Models with cost-estimation. Each element of the building model has a cost associated with it. It's allows for detailed analysis to be done regarding budgets
6D	Sustainability analysis variables of building projects. LEED - Leadership in Energy and Environmental Design – performance
7D	As-Built. Fundamental part to accurate facilities management. Maintenance planning

The BIM implementation in industry requires the adjustment of variables of working (cooperation between pairs, suppliers), hardware, operators (designers, engineers, architects, collaborators) and client demands. Worldwide, it had not a uniform implementation, where different solutions divide same partners, and it is a great challenge for BIM implementation. To understand these variables in Brazilian Civil Construction scenery, is necessary evaluate the market behavior.

3   Case Study

3.1   Description

To understand the degree of BIM maturity implementation in Brazil, there was made an analysis of works presented by BIM experts of Brazil at "Autodesk University Brazil" in the years 2013 and 2014. In this event, the most important offices shows their BIM experiences developed in Brazil, what made the event one thermometer of how the companies are leading with this technology, and how is the level of BIM software integration in the country.

3.2   Sampling

Sixteen companies was analyzed by their case studies showed on lectures. There was 6.25 % of small companies, 56.25 % of medium companies and 37.5 % of large companies. The business line of the companies were: 37.5 % of companies develop architecture projects and infrastructure works, 18.75 % of the companies works with control and planning production, and 6.25 % with Building Systems (HVAC) (Figs. 3 and 4).

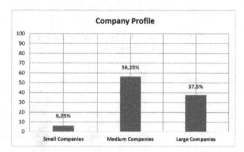

Fig. 3. Company profile

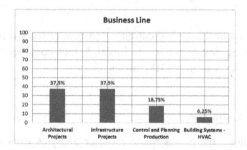

Fig. 4. Business line

3.3   BIS Data Analysis and Classification

Second [2], the BIS made one classification based on levels to define de degree of maturity of BIM tools implementation. The BIS classification consider the scale showed at Table 2. Analyzing the projects and materials available by enterprises, no ones were classified in Levels 0 and 1. About level 2, 37.5 % of the companies were classified in this level because they are using BIM solutions only for modeling, without integration between different instances. So 62.5 % were classified in Level 3 because they were using BIM solutions in a superior instance (Fig. 5).

Table 2. Level Definitions by BIS [2]

Level	Data information	Characteristics
0	CAD	Bi-dimensional information. Vector
1	2D-3D	Tri-dimensional information
2	BIM	Parametric Objects
3	IBIM/lifecycle management	Parametric Objects
		Integrated Data
		Interoperability

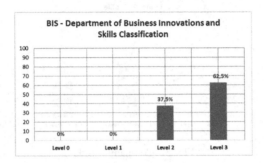

Fig. 5. BIS classification results

A problem resultant of this classification is the generalization made by BIS of how kind of works are being developed inside Level 3, that consider advanced one enterprise that develop projects at high BIM instances.

3.4   Category Data Analysis

To resolve this problem, there was made another analysis dividing the BIM implementation into seven categories, named CAT-01, CAT-02, CAT-03, CAT-04, CAT-05, CAT-06 e CAT-07. The characteristic of each one are listed at Table 3. The objective was understand the differences between BIM implementations in the different enterprises, to know the particularities of each one (Fig. 6).

Table 3. Category BIM classification

Category	Data information	Characteristics
CAT-0	2D	Bi-dimensional information
CAT-1	3D	Tri-dimensional information
CAT-2	BIM	BIM for architectural modeling
CAT-3	i-BIM	Structural analysis
CAT-4	i-BIM	Building systems /HVAC
CAT-5	i-BIM	Thermal and acoustic analysis
CAT-6	i-BIM	Infrastructure projects
CAT-7	i-BIM	BIM integration /interoperability

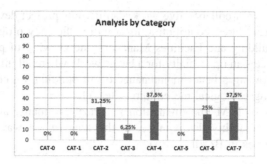

Fig. 6. Category classification results

4 Discussion

The BIM implementation inside a company can get different results depending of the context. BIS classification can indicate the degree of BIM evolution inside a company. The results, according this classification, demonstrated that no enterprises are Level 0 or Level 1, and 37,5 % are Level 2 and 62,5 % are Level 3. These results indicates that great part of companies are implementing BIM tools into an advanced way.

However, the data analysis of Category Classification could shows that no enterprises are using only 2D and 3D solutions, but BIM for modeling (31,25 %), BIM for Structural Analysis (6,25 %), Building Systems (37,5 %) and Infrastructure Projects (25 %). No enterprises are using BIM for thermal and acoustic projects evaluation.

Another important aspect is the low rate of enterprises (37,5 %) using BIM in an integrated way. The great BIM challenge is the possibility of project development in a collaborative job. If the offices in Brazil are not implementing software integration in large scale, the BIM systems values are not full and contributes to a low evolution of the tool in the country.

5 Conclusions

BIM tools were a great change on project development. The study shown that, besides difficulties, the companies are implementing the tool. Considering the BIS classification, the companies are using the BIM tools into an advanced way, signaling that software implementation is accompanying the world context.

Besides, the Category Analysis showed a low application of structural analysis with BIM tools (6,25 %), and a great force in Modeling (31,25 %), HVAC (37,5 %) and Infrastructure (25 %). The Category Analysis also showed that great part of the companies (62,5 %) use BIM tools without instances integration. Companies did not mention the thermal and acoustic analysis.

To professionals, the BIM implementation in AEC industry means a better kind of tool for project development, with could permit the collaborative work, with is very interesting in our actual scenery, where the deadlines are short and changes need to be done in a fastest way. A collaborative work also permits project development without disciplines incompatibilities, contributing for a more efficiency project.

Besides, for Building and Facilities Managers, the growing of projects developed with BIM tools creates an opportunity for a better work, where all information is joined at same model, allowing a better maintenance of all building systems, saving energy and water, becoming ecological the building lifecycle.

The challenges of BIM implementation in Brazil are many, and, the BIM integration with interoperability data can be, in the long run, a way of better project development processes in Brazil context.

Acknowledgment. The authors would like to thank CAPES (Coordenação de aperfeiçoamento de pessoal de nível superior) and Paulista University (UNIP) for the financial support to develop this work.

References

1. Eardie, R., Browne, R., Odeyinka, H., Mckeown, C., Macniff, S.: BIM implementation throughout the UK construction project lifecycle: an analysis. Autom. Constr. **36**, 145–151. doi:10.1016/j.autcon.2013.09.001 (2013). Accessed Mar 2015
2. Porwal, A., Hewage, K.N.: Building information modeling (BIM) partnering frame-work for public construction projects. Autom. Constr. **31**, 203–214. doi:10.1016/j.autcon.2012.12.004 (2013). Accessed Mar 2014
3. Gu, N., London, K.: Understanding and facilitating BIM adoption in the AEC industry. Autom. Constr. **19**, 988–999. doi:10.1016/j.autcon.2010.09.002 (2010). Accessed Mar 2014
4. Miettinen, R., Paavola, S.: Beyond the BIM utopia: approaches to the development and implementation of building information modeling. Autom. Constr. **43**, 84–91. doi:10.1016/j.autcon.2014.03.009 (2014). Accessed Mar 2014
5. Calvert, N.: Why we care about BIM. http://spatialiq.co.nz/index.php/uncategorized/why-we-care-about-bim/. Accessed Mar 2015

Potential of Building Information Modeling – BIM - Tools Inside Brazilian Civil Construction Scenery

Samuel Dereste dos Santos[1,2(✉)], Oduvaldo Vendrametto[1],
Miguel León González[2], and Creusa Fernandes Correia[2]

[1] Paulista University-UNIP, Dr. Bacelar St. 1212, São Paulo, Brazil
samuel_dereste@yahoo.com.br, oduvaldov@uol.com.br
[2] Cruzeiro Do Sul University-UNICSUL,
Dr. Ussiel Cirillo Ave. 225, São Paulo, Brazil
miguel.leon@uol.com.br, creusa.profmat@gmail.com

Abstract. The software utilization in civil construction Brazilian industry has been suffering since the 90's a continuous implementation considering small, medium and large companies. In this scenery, emerged CAD – *Computer Aided Design* –and BIM – *Building Information Modeling* – tools, that have different concepts and operation. The objective is analyze BIM tools potential in Brazilian scenery, stablishing a comparison between the performance of CAD and BIM tools. In order to understand the variables of the subject, was done a technical review focused on most cited authors of the area, as well as a survey, applied to experts of project development in Brazil. The results have shown that BIM tools are more effective than CAD tools considering both basic projects until final projects, and for future challenges, BIM solutions can optimize project process in Brazil's civil construction enterprises.

Keywords: CAD · BIM · Software productivity · Basic projects · Final projects

1 Introduction

The civil construction industry in Brazil has been suffering, since 2006, a great amount of investments that resulted in a great development in this area, since housing construction until infrastructure works. Besides, problems with project development and construction process are very common in this area. When compared with other industries of the country, it is still considered delayed because of work organization, work division, labor, etc [1].

Analyzing the project tools used in this area worldwide, the CAD – Computer Aided Design – software are very common. This family of tool was responsible for the replacement, from clipboard to computer, of the project process in the engineering area. Used in the aeronautics, mechanics and construction, it has made the project process more effective, allowing the utilization of digital files that could be transmitted and edited in a faster way, changing the scenario of project development.

© IFIP International Federation for Information Processing 2015
S. Umeda et al. (Eds.): APMS 2015, Part I, IFIP AICT 459, pp. 299–307, 2015.
DOI: 10.1007/978-3-319-22756-6_37

In the civil construction area, the CAD tools have presented bottlenecks of integration that difficult the evolution in a vector platform. To allow the integration with another software, it is necessary the joint of information that are not possible in this platform. Considered a CAD evolution, emerges the BIM – Building Information Modeling – tools.

The main difference between CAD and BIM tools is the object construction. While CAD are vector information, the BIM models are parametric, which allows the insertion of a different kind of information, like material type, cost, time do produce, codes, etc. Other important characteristic is the possibility of project development in different integrated platforms, what allows different professionals (Architects, Engineers, and Designers) working in a same model real-time, what wasn't possible in CAD platforms.

The BIM technology has been used worldwide, and according to [2, 3], in order to get a successful BIM implementation is necessary the adjustment of projects development variables that need to be carefully studied for a better project performance. In Brazil, the BIM technology have been implemented in some privates and public enterprises like Brazilian Army and Foundation for the Education Development of Sao Paulo State – FDE, in search of better project development routines.

The goal of this paper is to analyses the BIM tools potential in Brazilian scenery, stablishing a comparison between the performance between CAD and BIM tools. The strategy to develop this paper was based on a technical review focused on periodical papers as well as a survey applied of experts of project development in Brazil. This paper is organized into sections as follows: introduction, technical review, case study, discussion, and finally, conclusions and references.

2 Technical Review

2.1 Project Development in Brazil

Project process has been suffering, in Brazil, a big conceptual evolution, that amplify their function in the process. Nowadays projects are very important because they are a font for building process improvement. The importance of project elaboration is growing because it is the major source of improvement of building performance, reducing production costs and occurrence of faults in both product and process, generating an optimization in the implementation activities.

In this stage, the decision-making affects the costs, speed of execution and quality of project. If the right decisions are not taken at this stage, many problems can arise and be solved by different professionals, who are not necessarily qualified, contributing to higher costs and losses [1, 4].

Advances in project development were motivated by various market environmental factors in challenge of greater excellence in costs that could make companies more attractive to customers, who are becoming more rigorous. It can be seen, at Fig. 1, the importance of early stages (viability, conception and project development) for project development. Despite the low initial investment of resources, there is great potential for improving process, reducing the failures and enabling cost reduction.

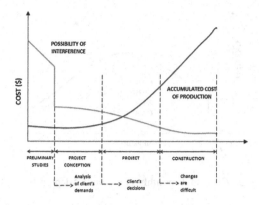

Fig. 1. Investment in projects. Adapted from [4]

According [1], some entrepreneurs in Brazil understand projects like a cost in productive scenery. Great part of the enterprises starts raising money before construction (residential buildings). At this logic, the projects development has been seen like an expense, and the production team solves the problems of construction, that should be resolved before execution, in other words, at construction. A major investment at project development (Fig. 2) allows costs reduction and redistribute de the payments during construction. It is possible because of the mayor variables control and project compatibility.

2.2 CAD Tools

The first applications of computers to assist the engineering steps began in the 1950s, when the Massachusetts Institute of Technology (MIT) started the discussion of CAD technology. CAD systems of this generation were limited to the description of two-dimensional geometric entities, creating and manipulating drawings in monochrome graphics terminals. According [5], these systems has already propitiated advantages such as possibility of sending and receiving drawings by electronic means; management of drawings and information; precision in the design; faster recovery and modification or updating drawings.

During the years 1960–1980, the use of CAD systems has limited the application in large companies such as aerospace and automotive, because of the high costs involved, since software/hardware until qualification of the workforce, which required users with a greater degree of statement. However, at the end of the 90s, with the development of the Windows Operating System, a very robust for applications in PCs, there was a migration of companies that developed their UNIX systems for Windows. This fact has reduced the cost of hardware and the need for highly specialized users. In these first CAD tools, construction elements were the simple junction of geometric entities such as lines, arcs and curves. It was the direct transfer of drawing executed manually on the drawing board to the computer [5].

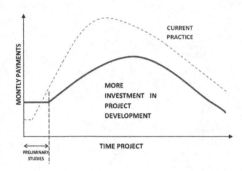

Fig. 2. Costs and monthly payments. Adapted from [4]

Besides all undeniable qualities of CAD implementation on project processes, for AEC – Architecture, Engineering and Construction – area, the CAD tools presented bottlenecks of integration quite difficult to be overcame. The vectorial software architecture became difficult CAD platform integration with other software, and this lack made the emergence of new software.

2.3 BIM Tools

BIM tools can be defined like CAD platforms improvements aiming AEC area. The BIM implementation is the utilization of information systems (IS) in the construction industry. It has been an issue of great importance in order to enhance the effectiveness of construction projects throughout their life cycle and across different construction business function, since construction until utilization [6].

The main difference between BIM and CAD tools is the architecture of the software. The CAD software structure is vectorial while BIM tools are parametric. This characteristic permits the development of collaborative and tridimensional objects, where different professionals can work integrated. The BIM utilization on AEC area can integrate all the whole project process, since conception until construction and operation (Fig. 3) [2].

These tools are used for visualizing and coordinating in the AEC (architecture, engineering and construction) area. By definition, permits avoiding errors and omissions, improves productivity, support scheduling, safety, cost and quality management. It incorporates all the building components, including geometry, spatial relationships, properties and quantities [8, 9].

In general steps, the use of the tool improves an increase of efficiency and precision in project process, reduces the errors with a better information coordination, allows the simulation of some project components, generating of documentation to production, reduces the maintenance costs [9].

The enterprises are implementing BIM tools in their processes but this process are not equal worldwide. In the USA, for example, there is a great government effort for BIM implementation while in Brazil this implementation is happening in some

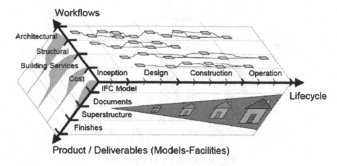

Fig. 3. BIM instances [7]

companies alone. Therefore, to understand the BIM tools potential in front of CAD tools, there was made a case study to discuss about this subject.

3   Case Study

To understand the potential of BIM besides CAD tools in AEC enterprises of Sao Paulo region, in Brazil, there was made an online survey to experts, searching information about, last year:

- Type of projects developed;
- Total area projected;
- Number of professionals involved on project development;
- Total time spent on project development;
- Total time spent by each professional on project development;
- Team experience in software utilization.

This information could permit the establishment of metrics that could define the potential of the tools on project development in Brazilian scenery.

3.1   Sampling

Ten companies of Sao Paulo Region were interviewed, formed by small, medium and large companies. There was 60 % composed by small companies, 30 % by medium and 10 % large ones (Fig. 4).

The types of projects developed by the company are important to show how they are using of technology. To this survey, of respondents, 37.5 % were big buildings projects focusing only architecture, 25 % were little and medium building projects focusing only architecture, and 37 % were infrastructure projects and execution (Fig. 5).

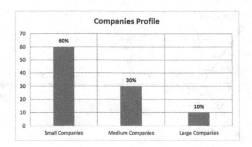

Fig. 4. Companies profile

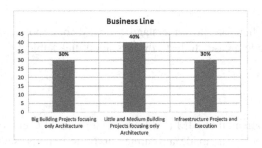

Fig. 5. Business line

3.2   Software Utilization and Users Profile

From respondents, 44 % of the companies uses BIM solutions while 67 % of the respondents uses CAD solutions (Fig. 6). The average experience of the companies using the tools are 10 years to BIM users and 12 years to CAD users (Fig. 7).

3.3   BIM × CAD Productivity Analysis

Having a productivity parameter of the tools, there was made an analysis, in the last 12 months, about the quantity of projects developed by each company, analyzing: number of projects developed, square meters projected, professionals involved in the process and time expended by each designer. This information permitted the analysis of the time spent for square meter projected.

Besides these particularities, the tool utilization can change with particularities of project characteristics in construction area. There was made a comparison between the different project development steps in an enterprise. To initial steps, the designer spent less time and generates gross floor area compared with final projects (for execution) where the level of detailing is more effective. To compare these differences, there was compared the productivity between enterprises.

The results have shown that, to Basic Projects, the BIM users spent 0.44 h for square meter developed while CAD users spent 1.55 h for square meter. To Final

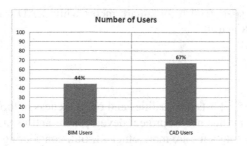

Fig. 6. Users type percent

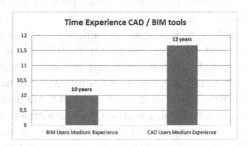

Fig. 7. Time Experience

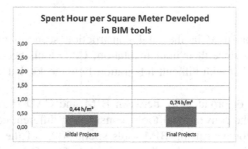

Fig. 8. BIM users

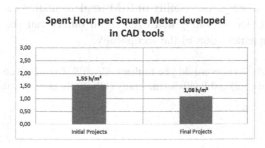

Fig. 9. CAD users

Projects, BIM users spent 0.74 h for square meter while CAD users spent 1.08 h for square meter (Figs. 8 and 9).

4 Discussion

The BIM experts [2, 5–9] lists the qualities and effectiveness in tool utilization, besides they don't establish a difference of project development and its steps. The BIM tools, compared with CAD solutions, are more efficient, but, considering the project step, the differences are significant. The utilization of BIM tools to initial projects spent 0.44 h for each square meter developed against 1.55 h for each square meter in CAD tools. This fact denotes the efficiency of the tool in initial projects, where the time spent for each square meter is lower than other project steps.

To final projects, in both technologies, designers needed to spend more time in activities development, and the time grown up to 0.74 h for each square meter developed by BIM users, and 1.08 h for each square meter developed by CAD users. This consequence of different project instances definitions is not necessary at the initial projects. Even thought, BIM users spent less time than CAD users.

Another aspect to be considered, discussed by the authors cited, is the growing demand of informatics tools integration. BIM tools allows an integration of different project instances, what can permit, in the future, an optimization of the project time production in the final projects.

5 Conclusions

The informatics tools used in the civil construction scenario modified the project process development since their implementation. CAD tools became the project process more effective, but with difficult integration bottlenecks that was broken by BIM tools implementation.

The comparison of productivity between BIM and CAD shows that the first are more efficient than the conventional tools, considering different companies scenarios. Basic projects development using BIM tools spent 30 % of the time used by CAD tools. It can be explained by the modeling facility interface. Otherwise, to final projects, BIM tools spents 68 % of the time spent by CAD tools, what ratify the efficiency of them.

In the Brazilian scenery, the viability of BIM implementation can be guaranteed by the results obtained, demonstrating that even small offices can get good productivity returns with the implementation of the technology.

Acknowledgment. The authors would like to thank CAPES (Coordenação de aperfeiçoamento de pessoal de nível superior) and Paulista University (UNIP) for the financial support to develop this work.

References

1. Peralta, A.C.: Um modelo do processo de projeto de edificações, baseado na engenharia simultânea, em empresas construtoras incorporadoras de pequeno porte. Master Dissertation in Production Engineering. Universidade Federal de Santa Catarina (2002). https://repositorio.ufsc.br/bitstream/handle/123456789/.../188665.pdf. Accessed Mar 2015
2. Migilinskas, D., Popov, V., Juocevicius, V., Ustinovichius, L.: The benefits, obstacles and problems of practical BIM implementation. In: 11th International Conference on Modern Building Materials, Structures and Techniques, MBMST. Science Verse (2013). doi:10.1016/j.proeng.2013.04.097. Accessed Mar 2015
3. Meireles, A.R.: Estratégia para uma integração avançada do BIM no processo construtivo in 3° Seminário BIM – Sinduscon, 24 Mar 2013. http://www.sindusconsp.com.br/envios/2013/eventos/bim/Apresenta%C3%A7%C3%A3o_AntonioMeireles.pdf. Accessed Mar 2015
4. Franco, L.S.: Aplicação de diretrizes de racionalização construtiva para evolução tecnológica dos processos construtivos em alvenaria estrutural não armada. Tese de Doutorado em Engenharia Civil – Escola Politécnica da Universidade de São Paulo, São Paulo (1992)
5. Souza, A.F., Coelho, R.T.: Tecnologia CAD/CAM - Definições e estado da arte visando auxiliar sua implantação em um ambiente fabril. In: XXIII Encontro Nacional de Engenharia de Produção – ENEGEP, 24 Oct 2003. www.abepro.org.br/biblioteca/ENEGEP2003_TR0504_0920.pdf. Accessed Mar 2015
6. Jung, Y., Joo, M.: Building information modelling (BIM) framework for practical implementation. In: Automation in Construction, no. 20, pp. 126–133. doi:10.1016/j.autcon.2010.09.010. Accessed Mar 2015
7. Migilinskas, D., Popov, V., Juocevicius, V., Ustinovichius, L.: The benefits, obstacles and problems of practical bim implementation. In: 11th International Conference on Modern Building Materials, Structures and Techniques, MBMST. Science Verse (2013). doi:10.1016/j.proeng.2013.04.097. Accessed Mar 2015
8. Chen, L., Luo, H.: A BIM-based construction quality management model and its application. In: Automation in Construction, no. 46, pp. 64–73, Oct 2014. doi:10.1016/j.autcon.2014.05.009. Accessed Mar 2015
9. Volk, R., Stengel, J., Schultmann, F.: Building information modeling (BIM) for existing buildings — literature review and future needs. In: Automation in Construction, no. 38, pp. 109–127, Mar 2014. doi:10.1016/j.autcon.2013.10.023. Accessed Mar 2015

Cyber Physical Production Control

Transparency and High Resolution in Production Control

Volker Stich, Niklas Hering, and Jan Meißner[(✉)]

Institute for Industrial Management, RWTH Aachen University,
Campus-Boulevard 55, 52074 Aachen, Germany
{Volker.Stich,Niklas.Hering,Jan.Meissner}@fir.rwth-aachen.de

Abstract. Currently the control of constantly increasing market dynamics and the simultaneously increasing individualization of process chains represent the central challenges for manufacturing companies. These challenges are caused by a lack of transparency in production planning, non-real-time processing of data as well as poor communication between the planning and control level. The research project ProSense addresses this problem and intends to eliminate the current problems in production by developing a high-resolution, adaptive production control based on cybernetic support systems and intelligent sensors. Through the development of a cyber-physical production control as one part of the project, which forms the basis for an innovative self-optimizing advanced planning system, ProSense provides a contribution to accomplish the goals of industry 4.0.

Keywords: Cyber-physical production system · Cybernetic · Production control · Industry 4.0

1 Introduction

The objective of the research project ProSense is the development of a high-resolution, adaptive production control based on cybernetic support systems and intelligent sensors. Focus is on a user-friendly design of control systems, so that human can be optimal supported in the control of production by means of high-resolution data. The cyber physical production system, which provides the framework for a user-friendly production control can be divided into four main tasks. These include the big data acquisition, big data processing, self-optimizing production control system and human-machine interaction (Fig. 1).

The acquisition of big data can be accomplished via simple and inexpensive sensors. In order to ensure a quick and easy interchangeability of these sensor systems, it is necessary to use modular function blocks. These communicate autonomously and act as intelligent units or subsystems. Depending on the level of consideration, it is necessary to adjust the data granularity on demand. This requires uniform interfaces to all IT-Systems to ensure an interoperable capability.

For targeted processing of the collected high-resolution data, these should be kept unchanged in a central database. In this way, high-resolution production data

© IFIP International Federation for Information Processing 2015
S. Umeda et al. (Eds.): APMS 2015, Part I, IFIP AICT 459, pp. 308–315, 2015.
DOI: 10.1007/978-3-319-22756-6_38

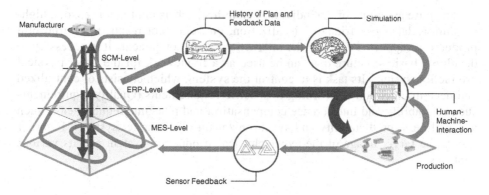

Fig. 1. Target image of the research project ProSense [1]

can be processed appropriate. Based on a standardized data interface, the processed data are then forwarded to a modularly designed production control system.

The third main task is a production control system based on a simulation model. To adapt the simulation model to reality, the real collected data will be used. Subsequently, with the model, different simulation runs are performed which are transferable to the real production. This results in forecasts relating to future meaningful control alternatives, which are then transmitted to the user. The human still retains the task of deciding between the identified control alternatives.

Apart from the validation of meaningful control proposals in particular the interaction between human and control system is very important for the decision support. With the help of an appropriate visualization, relevant decisions can be highlighted and considered simultaneously in an appropriate context. The user will receive an overview of the consequences of his decision and can take on this basis the right decision. With each new proposal, the system relies on the experience from the past. It optimizes itself constantly and gradually improves with the life of the system, the quality of its own control proposals [1].

2   Design of a Cyber Physical Production Control (CPPC)

To develop a cyber physical production control, it is necessary to consider the following points. The control systems must be designed in such a way that they support the human perfectly in control of the production with the help of high-resolution data and their intelligent processing, interpretation and subsequent visualization in order to substantially enhance the efficiency of value-added processes. This leads to increased transparency of the entire manufacturing process control, which will benefit all participating individuals. Due to the provided information the production controller receives a more accurate picture of the status of production and can optimize it in the future. Furthermore, the machine controller better understand why the initiated planning changes are necessary.

The pure assembly of the individual modules such as intelligent sensors, high-resolution data, user-friendly visualization, etc. does not result in a purposeful production support. To ensure the interaction of all components it is necessary to develop a basic structure that can be used as a framework for the cyber physical production system. Its task is to control the system, which consists of centralized and decentralized units according to specific requirements (Quality requirements such as stability and interference compensation and real-time requirements, such as timeliness, predictability and synchronization of the target system). Figure 1 shows the target image of the cyber physical production system and its various subtasks.

2.1 Structure Framework of Production Control

To implement a cyber physical production control, it is necessary to define the basic structure and the regulatory framework of the CPPC. On the premise of controlling complexity, the Viable System Model (VSM) of Beer and the corresponding management model of Versatile Production Systems (VPS) by Brosze is used as a regulatory framework for a cyber physical production control. Structuring principles of the VSM of Beer and the VPS by Brosze are viability, recursiveness and autonomy.

- The principle of viability is the superior of the three design principles. It describes the ability of a system to permanently ensure its institutional continuity over a certain period [2]. Ensuring the viability requires the continued willingness of a company to analyze existing conditions to detect internal or external interferences to react appropriately and if necessary to pursue new goals [3].
- The principle of recursion states, that all viable systems must have the same structure. This means that any viable system consists of several viable systems or is part of a superior viable system [4]. In view of the VSM by Beer this has the consequence that all recursion levels within hierarchical structures are present and that the systems 2, 3, 4 and 5 behave metasystemic in relation to the system 1. At the same time, each system 1 has at the next lower level the same five-stage structure as well as the control mechanisms of the VSM. In combination with the principle of viability the principle of recursivity provides fixed structuring criteria.
- The principle of autonomy addresses the self-design, self-control and self-development of subsystems. In order to enable a correspondingly optimal degree of autonomy, Beer encountered within the VSM the problem with a two-dimensional model. On one hand, the operating units of system 1 can achieve the maximum autonomy and on the other hand, the systems 1 are synchronized with the systems 2–5. Consequently, the systems 1 are not independent, but rather as subsystems of a larger superior system [5].

Figure 2 shows the recursive design of a viable system in relation to the company. The production control system is located on the fourth recursion level and is part of the production system. This in turn is part of a company that integrates itself into the superior supply chain.

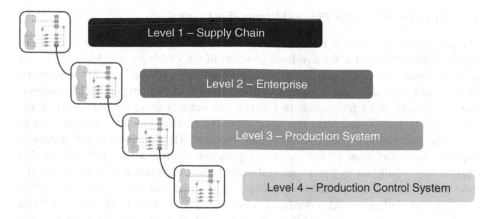

Fig. 2. Recursion levels of an enterprise

2.2 Requirements for the Design of a Cyber Physical Production Control

To the conception of a cyber physical production control, it is necessary to highlight the requirements based on which the new structure will be harmonized. We distinguish between form and content requirements [6].

The content requirements are formulated from the problem and objective of the model structure:

- All entities relevant for production control should be identified and transferred to the VSM structure.
- Any functions of the various production control units and manufacturing entities as well as the significant information flows should be mapped within the Viable System Model.
- Within the model, the instruction and control structures should be designed relating to the VSM mechanisms.
- During the development of the model structure based on the production control system it is necessary to consider, the principles viability, autonomy and recursion of the underlying VSM.

As formal requirements of the established model, the validity, reliability and utility are referred to [6–9]:

- The validity describes the claim of traceability and general applicability.
- The reliability of the results in terms of a similar framework is represented by the reliability.
- In addition, the usefulness of the results must be guaranteed (utility).

With the aim of establishing a cybernetic management model for production control, the functional control structure is transferred to the structure of the Viable System Model and the essential information and referral relationships are designed.

2.3   Structure of a Cyber Physical Production Control

The production control is in the overall model on the fourth recursion level (shown in Fig. 2). This level also has the five-level structure of the Viable System Model. Starting from the main task of the production control 'production of products in the required quantity and at the right time', the metasystem includes all planning and control-related tasks. The entities of production in contrast are defined as operational base units. According to Fig. 3, these are the work areas warehouse, logistics, manufacturing, assembly, maintenance, quality control, and shipment. The definition of the systems 1 requires the compliance of the autonomy principle. In the considered context this requirement is fulfilled by job design and order allocation (system 3) according to the base units which allows autonomous processing of orders for the purpose of superior objectives as well as the self-coordination between the systems 1 (system 2) without regular intervention measures of the metasystem [7]. Relationships between systems 1 and 2 have no hierarchical character. For this reason, the system 2 also belongs to the operational level. With this restriction, the coordination system is defined as a gathering of representatives from all production areas.

The core of the entire system is the operative management (system 3). This role is represented by the production control system, which is used to monitor, to control and to coordinate the production units as well as to guarantee the 'inner stability' of the system. This is supported by the unfiltered information provision of the process monitoring (system 3*). The strategic tasks of the system 4 are executed under consideration of the functional organization in the production planning (work planning and control). The production planning determines planning

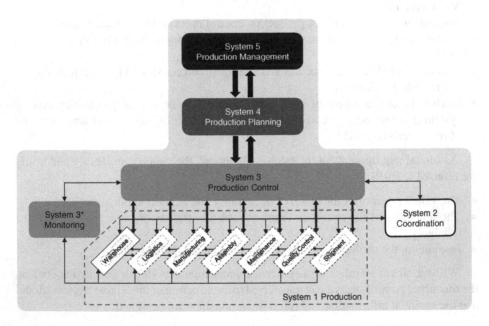

Fig. 3.   Structure of a cyber physical production control

specifications and production programs, taking into account the normative action framework and 'external' conditions. The production management is defined as the normative system 5. This performs the tasks of strategic production management.

Figure 3 shows the various structures of communication between the individual entities. For an optimal use of this structure, functions and targets as well as tasks and input and output variables are defined for all control and operating units. The structure and mechanisms of the viable system model form the framework for the production control and support the coordination and instruction procedures, without limiting the system's autonomy and viability.

3 Guideline for Implementation of the Cyber Physical Production Control

To sustain the efficiency in the production control system, an appropriate guideline for implementation of the cyber physical production control system was developed. This is driven by the application guide of the VPS according to Brosze, which was adapted for the production control [7]. The guideline is divided into three major phases: analysis, mapping and design. All major phases are subdivided in more detail. The adapted application guide is shown in Fig. 4.

Phase 1: Analysis The analysis phase deals with assessment of the actual condition and includes the two steps of project setup and process and structure analysis. At this point, the operational processes of the production planning and control should be considered, which are described both in the VPS as well as in the extended process view of the Aachener PPS model of Schmidt [7, 10].

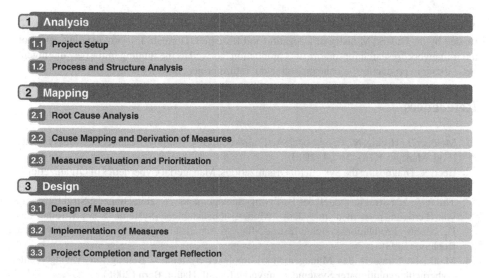

Fig. 4. Guideline for implementation of the cyber physical production control

Phase 2: Mapping Phase 2 focuses the optimization of the production control. Based on the previously identified weaknesses and potential for improvement, the respective causes are identified. The common causes are then clustered and assigned to the problem-solving elements. Finally, the clusters are prioritized with their improvement actions in terms of benefit and cost consideration and placed in an implementation sequence.

Phase 3: Design In the last phase the established measures are designed and operationally implemented. Finally, it is necessary to evaluate the implementation based on pre-defined targets to measure the success of a project and to complete the project.

4   Conclusion and Further Research

In summary it can be stated that the control and execution processes of production are associated with a large amount of information and instruction flow. Each unit of the manufacturing control system has a different kind of skills and responsibilities that must be taken into account in the communication structure and the allocation of tasks concerning the handling of complexity. It is shown that a design of production control according to the approach of viable systems and the consideration of the approach underlying principles of recursion, autonomy and viability supplies the necessary structures and mechanisms to ensure the stability of production and to favor the continuous improvement of processes. Further research is needed in the analysis and integration of appropriate and supportive information and data collection instruments for data transfer. In addition, the planning and control measures for the application of the developed viable production control system together with the communication and referral pathways may be the object of further investigation, so that the requirements are supported by all stakeholders.

Acknowledgement. The research project ProSense is one of the first three industry 4.0 projects, funded by the Federal Ministry of Education and Research (Germany). It provides in context of the framework "research for tomorrow's production" as well as the funding initiative "intelligent networking in production" a contribution to the future project industry 4.0.

References

1. Meißner, J., Hering, N., Hauptvogel, A., Franzkoch, B.: Cyberphysische produktionssysteme. Prod. Manage. **1**(18), 21–24 (2013)
2. Beer, S.: Diagnosing the System for Organizations. Managerial Cybernetics of Organizations. Wiley, Chichester (1985)
3. Thiem, I.: Ein Strukturmodell des Fertigungsmanagements – Soziotechnische Strukturierung von Fertigungssystemen mit dem "Modell lebensfähiger Systeme". Schriftreihe des Lehrstuhls Produktionssysteme/Institut für Automatisierungstechnik, Ruhr-Universität Bochum (1998)
4. Malik, F.: Strategie des Managements komplexer Systeme – Beitrag zur Management-Kybernetik evolutionärer Systeme. 9. unveränd. Aufl. Haupt, Bern (2006)

5. Herold, C.: Einvorgehenskonzept zur Unternehmensstrukturierung – Eine heuristische Anwendung des Modells lebensfähiger systeme. St. Gallen (1991)
6. Nachreiner, F.: Grundlagen naturwissenschaftlicher Methodik in der Arbeitswissenschaft. In: Luczak, H., Volpert, W. (eds.) Handbuch Arbeitswissenschaft. Schäffer-Poeschel, Stuttgart (1997)
7. Brosze, T.: Kybernetisches Management wandlungsfähiger Produktionssysteme. FIR e.V. an der RWTH Aachen (2011)
8. Meier, C.: Echtzeitfähige Produktionsplanung und -regelung in der Auftragsabwicklung des Maschinen- und Anlagenbaus. FIR e.V. an der RWTH Aachen (2013)
9. Kompa, S.: Selbstoptimierende Auftragseinlastung für die kundenindividuelle Serienfertigung. FIR e.V. an der RWTH Aachen (2014)
10. Schmidt, C.: Konfiguration überbetrieblicher Koordinationsprozesse in der Auftragsabwicklung des maschinen- und Anlagenbaus. FIR e.V. an der RWTH Aachen (2008)

Proposing a Standard Template for Construction Site Layout: A Case Study of a Norwegian Contractor

Børge Sjøbakk[✉] and Lars Skjelstad

SINTEF Technology and Society, Industrial Management,
P.O. Box 4760 Sluppen, 7465 Trondheim, Norway
{borge.sjobakk,lars.skjelstad}@sintef.no

Abstract. Having an efficient construction site layout can significantly impact the productivity, cost and safety of a construction project. Construction site layout planning is therefore recognized as a critical step in construction planning by researchers. In literature this is often described as an optimization process where some objectives (e.g. safety, cost savings) are pursued within the constraints of the site and facilities requirements. Such models are usually complex and difficult for practitioners to apply, and usually result in each project having its unique site layout plan. The authors challenge this by proposing a standard layout template that can easily be utilized in planning of multiple construction sites. It is argued that each site should be treated as a factory and that similarity between sites should be pursued due to the nature of the construction industry. The template has been developed in collaboration with a Norwegian contractor, utilizing the action research approach.

Keywords: Construction site layout planning · Standardization

1 Introduction

It is generally agreed that having an efficient site layout can significantly impact the productivity, cost and safety on construction sites [1]. Planning of a site layout involves identification of temporary facilities (TFs) needed to support construction activities, such as barracks, workstations and cranes, and appropriate positioning of the TFs within the boundaries of the construction site [2]. The site layout tries to meet multiple objectives, such as minimizing hazards, travel distance and material handling time and avoiding obstruction of flows of material, equipment and personnel [2, 3]. Usually, all these objectives cannot be met at the same time, and since the early 1970s construction site planning has received much attention from researchers within mathematical optimization [4, 5]. Since then a range of models have been developed to automatically generate optimal layouts for construction sites [6].

In spite of its importance, site layout planning has often been either overlooked or considered to be of less importance by practitioners [7]. Often, site layout objects are located on a first-come first-served basis at the sites [6]. When planned the layout

© IFIP International Federation for Information Processing 2015
S. Umeda et al. (Eds.): APMS 2015, Part I, IFIP AICT 459, pp. 316–323, 2015.
DOI: 10.1007/978-3-319-22756-6_39

is often determined in an ad hoc manner based on various factors, such as rules of thumb, expertise, code of practice and previous experience [8]. Such methods have traditionally been preferred over advanced optimization models by practitioners due to their simplicity [2]. However, a consequence of such approaches is that the site layout is greatly impacted by the preferences of the person responsible for the design of the layout [2].

The authors take the stance that a tool to support practitioners in construction site layout planning should be easy to use, require a minimum of data and promote similarity between different construction sites. The construction site should be viewed as a production plant in that TFs are located in a predefined manner relative to each other, the building and the site. The layout should sufficiently incorporate concerns for travel distances, safety, etc. without requiring vast effort put into the pursuit of an optimal solution. Further, it should be recognizable for employees, vendors and other actors visiting the site to minimize the time used searching for equipment, goods and other facilities. This paper proposes such a tool in the form of a standard template for construction site layout. The template can be used by a contractor (or an architect) to rapidly establish the construction site layout in a consistent and recognizable way, and communicate the layout to relevant actors. It has been developed in close collaboration with a Norwegian contractor.

The remainder of the paper is structured as follows: First, the research method and case company are described. Thereafter, some theoretical background on the construction site layout problem is described. This is followed by a description of the proposed template, including how it was developed together with the case company. Finally, the paper is concluded.

2 Case Description

The research is carried out utilizing the action research method. In action research, the researchers and the problem holder (in this case a Norwegian Contractor) collaborate in solving real life problems while they keep a research interest in mind [9]. This creates a mutual dependence on the researchers' and the problem holder's skills and competences, which in turn generates new knowledge for both parties [9]. The researchers and the problem holder are both partners in a three-year research project related to high performance work systems and efficient industrialized operations in project-based industries in Norway.

The problem holder is a contractor located in the middle of Norway. It mainly carries out construction within commercial building, public works (e.g. schools, culture centers, sports installations) and large-scale housing projects. The company has traditionally focused on carpentry; however, a few years ago it acquired a concrete work company from the same region. In large-scale projects with turnkey contracts the company collaborates with, and coordinates, a number of subcontractors within multiple disciplines, such as HVAC and electrical installation.

The company has developed some standard operating procedures based on lean construction. This is mainly concerned with the Last Planner methodology [10], where trade foremen set up realistic weekly work plans and explore inter-disciplinary dependencies through weekly work planning meetings while keeping the master schedule in mind. Further, the different trades work through the building in a predefined manner; each trade completes its work in a room or section, proceeds to the next one and is succeeded by another trade. This is carried out from the top to the bottom of the building to reduce spillage in completed areas. In this way, the different trades can work in parallel without getting in each other's way.

When starting new projects, the company has traditionally operated with simplistic and static site layouts, if any, often suggested by the architect of the project. Often, the site layout has evolved in a more ad hoc manner, with the first trades at the site (usually concrete work) defining the site layout.

The contractor is often involved in several parallel projects, causing the company to man different sites simultaneously. The company organizes its workforce in several multidiscipline teams, with the size of the teams reflecting experiences with previous projects. For example, the company claims that teams of 6–12 people are optimal for completing the carpentering in an apartment. Yet, lack of material, vacations, injuries etc., necessitates that people move from one site to another from time to time, in order to keep all teams within the preferred size and all projects to meet their due date.

No matter how well planned a single project is, time is spent searching for materials, seeking information, accessing nearest waste-containers etc. Moving personnel between sites and having guest workers on site increases time spent on non-value-adding activities. The need for a standardized site layout was therefore raised by both workers and management.

3   The Construction Site Layout Challenge

Designing a good construction site layout is a challenging task. Available site space is often a limited resource [7], and the site topography and location of fixed facilities within the site often restrict the choice of layout [8]. Within these boundaries required temporary facilities (TFs) should be dimensioned and appropriately positioned in order to achieve smooth and low-cost flow of materials, people and equipment within the site while maintaining safety concerns [2, 3].

In establishing a construction site layout/utilization plan, numerous aspects should be addressed [3, 11, 12]: the site boundary must be identified; required TFs need to be determined based on planned project activities; size needs and other constraints associated with each TF must be established; the relative position of each TF must be decided; and, the timing of the establishment and removal of the TFs during the project must be defined. In practice, however, the construction site layout is often determined on a first-come first serve basis [6], with the detailed site layout being left to the day-to-day scheduling of trade foremen and managers [8]. This can lead to decreased safety and productivity [6], with inappropriate locations often leading to relocation of TFs or extra material handling that could have been avoided [8]. This is especially the case when space is not a limited factor in projects and TFs are located randomly within the site boundaries [11]. According to [2], empirical evidence suggest that the layout is affected by: (1) the role of the person doing it; (2) a person's level of involvement with the project; (3) the personal relationships between individuals making layout decisions and their authority within the organization; (4) a single person choosing among alternative strategies depending on the project's nature.

As construction site layout is an exercise where multiple, often conflicting objectives are pursued within the restrictions of the construction site and project details, it has captured the interest of researchers within mathematical optimization for several decades [4, 5]. Numerous models have been developed to automatically generate optimal layouts for construction sites [6]. The earliest *construction site layout planning* (CSLP) models generated static layouts spanning the entire project duration [4], whereas more recent models typically incorporate concerns for changes over the duration of the construction projects. These are often denoted *dynamic site layout planning* (DSLP) models to distinguish them from static CSLP models [3, 6].

From a research point of view, there are several challenges associated with existing construction site layout models [13]: there is an overweight of static CSLP models; FTs are treated as rectangular blocks (denoted equal-area CSLP models); most of the CSLP research concentrates on improving various optimization algorithms instead of establishing how to select the *best* out of proposed layouts; and, many models are single-objective optimization (SOO) models that fail to incorporate concerns for multiple layout objectives. From practitioners' view, there are several practical shortcomings of these models that make them prefer simple and well-understood models [2]: expertise is required for selecting an appropriate model and formulating each layout problem; the models require a substantial amount of data as input; the models are uneasy to use and alter; and, when substantial simplification is introduced in order to use a model, the results from it may be difficult to interpret.

From the authors' point of view, a large shortcoming of existing models is that they result in each construction project having its own unique site layout [14]. Arguably, the actors on site will be able to move most easily, quickly and safely within the site when the site layout in some way is standardized and recognizable. This especially applies for contractors with several parallel and sequential projects, which are able to reap learning effects from each project and apply in the others. As is evident, tools to support efficient construction site layout design must also be easy and fast to use, in order for practitioners to adapt them. In the next section, such a tool is proposed.

4   Proposing a Template for Construction Site Layout

A lot of research is done within the field of site optimization and lean construction. Still we find that many site optimization methods are too comprehensive to be carried out in construction firms, and also they often rely on a lot of input that is not available with sufficient precision at the time needed. Lean construction has provided valuable input on planning, whilst site layout, 5S, Poka-Yoke and waste in general still needs to be implemented to a larger degree. The proposed model opens for such activities.

Considering aspects that need to be addressed when designing the site layout as a starting point, the following steps were followed in order to develop a standardized site layout to be used as a template for future site layout planning: (1) Identification of temporary facilities (TFs) that should be included in the site layout; (2) establishment of reciprocity between facilities through a closeness rating analysis (CRA); (3) use of the CRA to establish site areas; (4) establishment of relationships between building and site ambit, as well as reciprocal distances between the different areas on site; (5) mapping of the different areas in a generic construction site template. With respect to the latter, the main side of the site, normally the one with road access, was defined and denoted side A. Further, sides B and C, which are secondary in terms of access, were also defined. On large building sites, these sides are often available. Finally, it was decided what must be located on side A, and what might be located on sides B and C (and even D) due to lack of space, improved access to building, or due to different project phases on different sides of a large building.

The TFs include all equipment and locations needed during the construction period. In collaboration with the case company, the following TFs were identified: walkway; barracks; tower crane; power supply; equipment containers; waste containers; entry/exit; material receipt; area for return of goods; inventory; workstation for masonry; parking/ area for emergency vehicles; traffic artery; workstation for plumbing; workstations for others; and, the main entrance of the building. In addition the site might have areas that are not available due to preparation for gardens, parking lots etc., that also is expected to be completed alongside the building itself. These areas are simply considered not available for TFs.

A closeness rating analysis (CRA) was carried out to identify TFs' reciprocal dependencies (Fig. 1). This is a way of rating layout objects against each other with respect to closeness importance, based on considerations such as frequency of inter-action and safety concerns. The rating itself is a matter of team-work. Managers, skilled workers and researchers discussed each intersection in the matrix to get a balanced and compromised first solution. Of course, if experiences over time show disadvantages with the chosen solution, this first designed solution is subject to adjustments. Still, it represents a well-funded first setup. The input to the analysis was derived during a 3 h meeting including sharing of experiences and theory, and discussion before decision.

When going through the results of the analysis, some groups of TFs materialized due to their similar score/pattern in the CRA: (1) *material handling* (material receipt, inventory and area for return of goods); (2) *barracks* (barracks and parking/emergency vehicles); (3) *work stations* (workstations masonry, plumbing and others); (4) *lift* (tower crane); (5) *transportation* (entry/exit and traffic artery); (6) *waste* (waste containers); and (7) *equipment* (equipment containers). By grouping the TFs in such a manner made the analysis more manageable in that it simplified the task and created a sense of over-view. As power supply and walkways are needed on multiple locations, it was decided to leave them out of the analysis and rather draw these up where and when needed.

The next step was to determine how these groups could be distributed over the available site. In doing so, the researchers established a priority chart showing the rela-tionships between the groups of TFs and the distance from the building to the site ambit (Fig. 2).

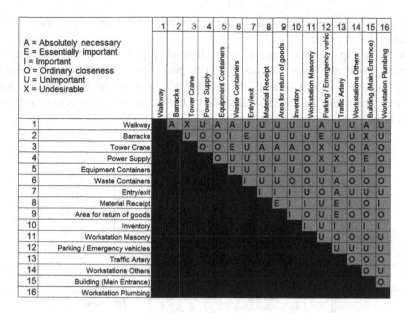

		1	2	3	4	5	6	7	8	9	10	11	12	13	14	15	16
		Walkway	Barracks	Tower Crane	Power Supply	Equipment Containers	Waste Containers	Entry/exit	Material Receipt	Area for return of goods	Inventory	Workstation Masonry	Parking / Emergency vehicles	Traffic Artery	Workstations Others	Building (Main Entrance)	Workstation Plumbing
1	Walkway		A	X	U	A	A	U	U	U	U	U	A	U	U	A	U
2	Barracks			U	O	O	I	E	U	U	U	U	E	U	U	X	U
3	Tower Crane				O	O	E	U	A	A	A	O	X	U	O	A	O
4	Power Supply					O	U	U	U	U	U	O	X	X	O	E	O
5	Equipment Containers						U	U	O	I	U	O	U	I	O	I	O
6	Waste Containers							I	U	U	O	O	U	A	O	O	O
7	Entry/exit								I	I	I	U	O	A	U	U	U
8	Material Receipt									E	I	I	U	E	I	O	I
9	Area for return of goods										I	O	U	E	O	O	O
10	Inventory											I	U	I	I	I	I
11	Workstation Masonry												U	O	O	O	U
12	Parking / Emergency vehicles													U	U	U	U
13	Traffic Artery														O	O	O
14	Workstations Others															O	U
15	Building (Main Entrance)																O
16	Workstation Plumbing																

A = Absolutely necessary
E = Essentially important
I = Important
O = Ordinary closeness
U = Unimportant
X = Undesirable

Fig. 1. Closeness rating analysis for construction site facilities

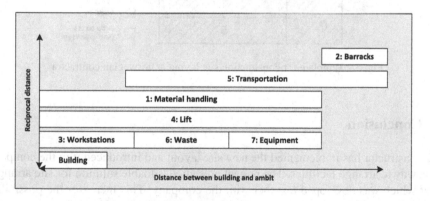

Fig. 2. Priority chart

The next step was to transfer this into a schematic illustration of a construction site, resulting in the proposed template. This was done by analyzing the CRA and the priority chart, and coming up with additional requirements to the layout. For example, the building must be accessible from all sides in terms of a walkway. Further, it is not desirable to spread over multiple sides of the building if there is sufficient space on one side. The traffic artery should force one-directional traffic flow. Power supply need to be a grid on big sites, preferably with access from all sides of the building. Waste-bin access is as important as position of input material. Safety in terms of access to a defined spot with vehicles must not be compromised. Cranes also play an important role in emergency situations if available in the situation. The learnings could then be used to draw a number of possible layouts, from which the project team jointly had to identify the preferred alternative.

Our case-company landed on the layout shown in Fig. 3. If possible, it is considered an advantage with all facilities on one side. This presupposes that cranes can cover both building and the "factory side area". If not, multiple sides should be considered for the site layout. The work therefore also identified what facilities and areas to be moved out to sides B and C in terms of a priority list.

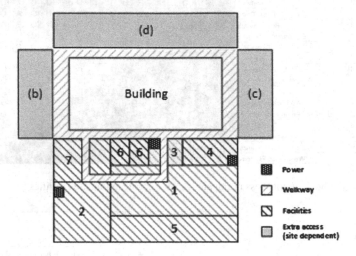

Fig. 3. Template for construction site layout at norwegian contractor

5   Conclusion

The constructor has implemented the new site layout and introduced it in the company as its way to arrange facilities. The project presented a doable solution for site arrangement which was developed together with the company. This increases the possibility for it to be used on a regular basis. At all construction sites a lot of time is spent on searching for materials and tools, and we suggest that this waste is reduced with the suggested model. After experience is gained, adjustments to the first developed layout can be made. A learning curve is expected as the solution is repeated a number of times. Also, between projects similarities allow for easier transfer of people according to needed progress without sacrificing too much time on getting acquainted with the new site. Management should repeat the exercise for different project phases, to build a library of standardized solutions to cover necessary dynamics into the practical solution. The method itself should be part of the company's project execution model. Its simplicity increases its applicability.

A lot of research is done within the field of site optimization and lean construction. Still we find that many site optimization methods are too comprehensive to be carried out in construction firms. Often, they rely on a lot of input that is not available with sufficient precision at the time needed. Lean construction has provided valuable input on planning, whilst site layout, 5S, Poka-Yoke and waste in general still needs to be implemented to a larger degree. The proposed model opens for such activities.

Acknowledgements. This work has been conducted within the project HPWS.no funded by the Research Council of Norway. The authors would like to thank the participants of the projects for providing valuable empirical data.

References

1. El-Rayes, K., Khalafallah, A.: Trade-off between safety and cost in planning construction site layouts. J. Constr. Eng. Manage. ASCE **131**(11), 1186–1195 (2005)
2. Tommelein, I.D., Levitt, R., Hayes-Roth, B.: Site-layout modeling: how can artificial intelligence help? J. Constr. Eng. Manage. ASCE **118**(3), 594–611 (1992)
3. Elbeltagi, E., Hegazy, T., Eldosouky, A.: Dynamic layout of construction temporary facilities considering safety. J. Constr. Eng. Manage. ASCE **130**(4), 534–541 (2004)
4. Elbeltagi, E., Hegazy, T., Hosny, A.H., Eldosouky, A.: Schedule-dependent evolution of site layout planning. Constr. Manage. Econ. **19**(7), 689–697 (2001)
5. Isaac, S., Andayesh, M., Sadeghpour, F: A comparative study of layout planning problems. In: Hajdu, M., Skibniewski, M.J. (eds.) Creative Construction Conference, pp. 272–282, Budapest, Hungary. Diamond Congress Ltd., Budapest (2012)
6. Andayesh, M., Sadeghpour, F.: Dynamic site layout planning through minimization of total potential energy. Autom. Constr. **31**, 92–102 (2013)
7. Tommelein, I., Zouein, P.: Interactive dynamic layout planning. J. Constr. Eng. Manage. ASCE **119**(2), 266–287 (1993)
8. Chau, K.W., Anson, M.: A knowledge-based system for construction site level facilities layout. In: Hendtlass, T., Ali, M. (eds.) IEA/AIE 2002. LNCS (LNAI), vol. 2358, pp. 393–402. Springer, Heidelberg (2002)
9. Greenwood, D.J., Levin, M.: Introduction to Action Research: Social Research for Social Change. Sage, Thousand Oaks (2007)
10. Ballard, H.G.: The Last Planner System of Production Control. The University of Birmingham, Birmingham (2000)
11. Mawdesley, M.J., Al-Jibouri, S.H., Yang, H.: Genetic algorithms for construction site layout in project planning. J. Constr. Eng. Manage. ASCE **128**(5), 418–426 (2002)
12. Zouein, P., Harmanani, H., Hajar, A.: Genetic algorithm for solving site layout problem with unequal-size and constrained facilities. J. Comput. Civil Eng. **16**(2), 143–151 (2002)
13. Ning, X., Lam, K.-C., Lam, M.C.-K.: A decision-making system for construction site layout planning. Autom. Constr. **20**(4), 459–473 (2011)
14. Zolfagharian, S., Irizarry, J.: Current trends in construction site layout planning. In: Construction Research Congress 2014@ s Construction in a Global Network, pp. 1723–1732. ASCE (2014)

Priority Modes of Transport for Soybeans
from the Center-West Region in Brazil

Cristina Corrêa de Oliveira[1(✉)], Danilo Medeiros de Castro[2], Nélio Fernando dos Reis[1],
João Gilberto Mendes dos Reis[1], and Jair Minoro Abe[1]

[1] Graduate Program in Production Engineering, Paulista University, Rua Dr. Bacelar 1212,
São Paulo, SP 04026-002, Brazil
{crisolive,neliojundiai}@ig.com.br
betomendesreis@msn.com, jairabe@uol.com.br
[2] Grande Dourados Federal University, Rodovia Dourados/Itahum, km 12 - Unidade II,
Dourados, 79804-970, Brazil
danilomdecastro@gmail.com

Abstract. Choosing modes of transport for agricultural production involves
uncertainties and decisions that affect logistics costs in the transportation of
grains. This article intends to explain the use of the Paraconsistent Decision
Method based on the Evidential Annotated Paraconsistent Logic Eτ in the decision-making process involving experts in priority modes of transport in Agribusiness logistics. It deals specifically with the distribution and export of soybeans,
the main Brazilian commodity, to the major Brazilian ports, considering the
aspects and features of each mode of transport. Exploratory research was used
and data were collected from questionnaires about the modes of transport. Results
indicate that experts have chosen modes of transport with numeric outputs, where
free costs and payable costs were considered, thereby pointing out the features
that should be taken into account in each mode.

Keywords: Grains · Paraconsistency · Decision-making · Soybean

1 Introduction

Brazil was ranked as the world's eighth largest economy, with a Gross Domestic Product
(GDP) of U$ 2.4 trillion dollars in 2013 [3]. Agribusiness productivity has been
increasing due to the high technology employed, and accounts for 22 % of the Brazilian
GDP [5].

The Center-West Region is the major producing area of soybean complex, with
41,785 thousand tons [5], and accounts for 48 % of the domestic production. Soybeans
are the most important commodity for the Brazilian trade balance. Despite their expressive share in exports, soybeans are a low aggregate-value product and require a well-
performed logistics process that can reduce costs from raw material through exports. In
order to meet the demand, the organizations must evaluate new transportation ways,
whether combining or not modes of transport [10].

© IFIP International Federation for Information Processing 2015
S. Umeda et al. (Eds.): APMS 2015, Part I, IFIP AICT 459, pp. 324–331, 2015.
DOI: 10.1007/978-3-319-22756-6_40

The overall purpose of this work is to employ the Paraconsistent Decision Method (PDM) that allows choosing the mode of transport for soybean distribution from the Center-West Region, considering some factors such as capacity, availability, reliability, periodicity and speed. The specific objectives of this study are deciding upon a tool that might help the decision-making process involving experts from several logistics areas and considering the stakeholders' opinions, and presenting a tool that allows a quantitative evaluation of all items, which results in numerical outputs generated by the model and can be easily understood and compared.

The PDM was developed on the basis of the Evidential Paraconsistent Annotated Logic $E\tau$ (Logic $E\tau$), and its main advantage lies in the fact that input parameters are set according to the experts' thinking structure, thus consolidating a collective logic translated into mathematical expressions.

2   Background

2.1   Paraconsistent, Paracomplete and Non-alethic Logics

In what follows, we sketch the non-classical logics discussed in the paper, establishing some conventions and definitions. Let T be a theory whose underlying logic is L. T is called inconsistent when it contains theorems of the form A and $-A$ (the negation of A). If T is not inconsistent, it is called *consistent*. T is said to be *trivial* if all formulas of the language of T are also theorems of T. Otherwise, T is called *non-trivial*.

When L is classical logic (or one of several others, such as intuitionistic logic), T is inconsistent if T is trivial. So, in trivial theories the extensions of the concepts of formula and theorem coincide. A *paraconsistent logic* is a logic that can be used as the basis for inconsistent but non-trivial theories. A *theory* is called *paraconsistent* if its underlying logic is a paraconsistent logic.

Many logicians have appreciated issues such as those described above. In 1910, the Russian logician Nikolaj A. Vasil'év (1880–1940) and the Polish logician Jan Lukasiewicz (1878–1956) independently glimpsed the possibility of developing such logics. Nevertheless, Stanislaw Jaskowski (1996–1965) was in 1948 effectively the first logician to develop a paraconsistent system, at the propositional level. His system is known as 'discussive' (or discursive) propositional calculus. Independently, some years later, the Brazilian logician Newton C.A. da Costa (1929–) constructed for the first time hierarchies of paraconsistent propositional calculi C_i, $1 \leq i \leq \omega$ of paraconsistent first-order predicate calculi (with and without equality), of paraconsistent description calculi, and paraconsistent higher-order logics (systems NF_i, $1 \leq i \leq \omega$). Another important class of non-classical logics are the paracomplete logics. A logical system is called *paracomplete* if it can function as the underlying logic of theories in which there are formulas such that these formulas and their negations are simultaneously false. Intuitionistic logic and several systems of many-valued logics are paracomplete in this sense (and the dual of intuitionistic logic, Brouwerian logic, is therefore paraconsistent).

Consequently, paraconsistent theories do not satisfy the principle of non-contradiction, which can be stated as follows: of two contradictory propositions, i.e. one of which is the negation of the other, one must be false. In addition, paracomplete theories do not satisfy the principle of the excluded middle, formulated in the following form: of two contradictory propositions, one must be true [1, 2]. Finally, logics that are simultaneously paraconsistent and paracomplete are called *non-alethic logics.*

2.2 Soybean Production

Soybeans, corn and dry beans are the main agricultural products in Brazil. Soybean complex accounts for 49 % of the grain cultivation areas [4]. Soybeans are greatly important because of their use in animal feed and human food industries; and they are the main product exported by the Country [3, 6].

The grain production in Brazil is estimated at 194 million tons spread over 56.9 million ha, i.e. three million tons per hectare. Grain crops achieved the highest productivity rate in recent years, and production is expected to reach 199 million tons in 2015, and 252 million tons in the 2023/2024 season, with a productive area increasing to 67 million ha [5]. The Center-West region has favorable topography and climate conditions, attractive prices, and large areas available for cultivation; and in 2014, it accounted for 48.5 % of the Brazilian production, despite its infrastructure deficiencies.

The transportation of grains can be made through several modes of transport, which are chosen according to the features, extension and benefits of the transport network, including costs of each mode of transport. Brazil's huge geographic area of 8.5 million km^2 must be taken into account, with its 1.5 million km of roads, 28 thousand km of railroads, and 50,000 km of navigable waterways, and four sea ports in the South and Southeast Regions that are used to export soybean grains, which totaled 36.3 million tons in 2014 [11].

Soybeans are the most important commodity in Brazil and account for 14 % of the Brazilian trade balance [7]. The commodity, however, has a low aggregate-value and the choice for modes of transport may affect exports, considering that Center-West producers are between 1,000 and 2,500 km away from the main Brazilian ports - the Port of Santos, located in the State of São Paulo, and the Port of Paranaguá located in the State of Paraná.

2.3 Modes of Transport in Brazil

The modes of grain transportation used in Brazil are waterways, railroads and roads [11, 12], and are distributed according to their ascending order of importance, respectively. Every mode of transport has operating characteristics, particularities, advantages and disadvantages.

The main characteristics of rail transport are the capacity to convey bulk freights with high-energy efficiency, low cost per ton in medium to long-distance conveyances, higher safety and lower risks of accident, robbery or theft when compared to other modes of transport [12]. Low speed and lack of flexibility concerning delivery changes are the main disadvantages of rail transport.

Water transport is advantageous for bulk cargo transportation over the open sea or through the coastline or rivers, and although freight volumes are advantageous, the good performance of this mode of transport depends on climate conditions [10].

Finally, the road transport is flexible for short-distance travels, but costs are highly dependent on fuel prices [13].

In Brazil, logistics costs account for 22 % of the costs of export products. Those costs directly affect the GDP, with their 20 % share, and transportation alone accounts for 56 % of food costs [13]. The study of the modes of transport and the use of tools to elect them demonstrate the high importance of efficient transportation systems for the Brazilian economic development [11, 13].

3   Materials and Methods

This article aims to carry out an applied science research for exploratory purposes, which, according to Zikmund [8], should be carried out to solve doubtful situations or find out business opportunities, and is the first step to any subsequent research. It has a quantitative approach and uses questionnaires about the features and modes of transport. The attributes were defined as literature review. Thus, the characteristics associated to any item of transportation that one should take into account when deciding upon the modes of transport and their financial-economic aspects [9] are listed in Table 1.

Table 1. Features of the modes of transport

Aspects	Features
Capacity	Size of vehicles
	Cargo volume
Availability	Demand
	Services available
Reliability	Delivery changes
	Order fulfillment
Periodicity	Period of time
	Number of travels
Speed	Handling time
	Distance
Costs	Variable cost
	Fixed cost

The development of tools that may help choosing the modes of transport is essential to the organizational strategy, and the evaluation of the performance of transportation services may be used for such purpose [10].

For field research were asked only road modes, rail and waterway, which are systems available for the state of Mato Grosso do Sul, to eight logistics experts engaged in the academic area, in graduate and post-graduate programs, with 4 to 27 years of experience, one of them with fifteen years of experience in productive processes and logistics operations in trade business. The opinions, interests and skills of each of them were taken into account.

We used the Saaty scale [14] ranging from 1 to 9, where one means low importance of a feature and nine means extreme importance of a feature for the mode of transport, with intermediate levels of importance between 1 and 9. Data were normalized by using the same proportion and converting values in the 0 to 1 interval of the PDM, called favorable evidence. The complement rule was employed for contrary evidence.

3.1 Data Analysis

This research consisted of a group decision-making, where two groups were formed according to the time of experience of their members; the first group was formed by experts with up to ten years of experience and the second group was formed by experts with more than ten years of experience in logistics systems. Each expert opinion issued by type of modal, with the degree of favorable evidence for each attribute in Table 1; the degree of contrary evidence was calculated by the complement of favorable evidence, according to Table 2, which shows an excerpt from the original study.

Table 2. Database of specialist's evidences

Aspects	Features	Group > 10				Group <= 10			
		spec 1		spec 2		spec 7		spec 8	
		μ_1	λ_1	μ_2	λ_2	μ_7	λ_7	μ_8	λ_8
Rail	Size of Vehicles	0,88	0,12	0,20	0,80	0,76	0,24	1,00	0,00
	Cargo Volume	0,20	0,80	1,00	0,00	0,88	0,12	0,64	0,36
	Demand	0,76	0,24	0,75	0,25	0,25	0,75	0,90	0,10
	Services Available	0,52	0,48	0,75	0,25	0,20	0,80	0,88	0,12
	Delivery Changes	0,52	0,48	0,64	0,36	0,25	0,75	1,00	0,00
	Order Fulfillment	0,52	0,48	0,54	0,46	0,40	0,60	0,75	0,25
	Period of Time	0,65	0,35	0,75	0,25	0,80	0,20	0,75	0,25
	Number of Travels	0,64	0,36	0,75	0,25	0,75	0,25	0,75	0,25
	Handling Time	0,75	0,25	0,75	0,25	1,00	0,00	0,75	0,25
	Distance	0,64	0,36	0,88	0,12	0,75	0,25	0,77	0,23
	Variable Cost	0,75	0,25	0,64	0,36	0,20	0,80	0,76	0,24
	Fixed Cost	0,20	0,80	0,20	0,80	0,88	0,12	0,75	0,25

The PDM was developed by using the Para-Analyzer based on Logic Eτ, with MIN and MAX operators, where MAX maximizes favorable evidences and minimizes contrary evidences in the group, and the MIN operator minimizes favorable evidences and maximizes contrary evidences between the groups. The use of both operators allows one to determine database inconsistencies [2]. The level of demand depends on the security and confidence in decision-making and the responsibility it entails [2]. The level of demand was set at 0.5 and the global analysis, whose result is equal to the factors' influence, is determined by the weighted average of the factors or features. The global analysis was calculated in duplicate considering only the aspects involved in the mode of transport, without taking into account the costs, indicated by the pink marker, and the global analysis with the costs, indicated in the x form by the green marker. By splitting the global analysis, we aimed to ascertain the influence of costs in the evaluation of the mode of transport.

4 Outcomes of Logic Eτ

The results indicate that the global analysis for water transport is in the central area of the Unit Square in the Cartesian Plane (USCP), which indicates a consensus in the analysis of some features, i.e. demand, delivery changes, order fulfillment, period of time and handling time, because of their low favorable evidence levels for grain transportation, as shown in Fig. 1.

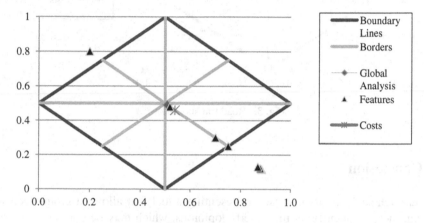

Fig. 1. Water transportation

The global analysis for rail transport is in the truth area, which evidences that it is the most appropriate type for transportation of grains, with all evidences falling in the same area, as shown in Fig. 2.

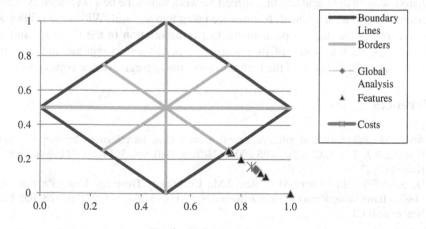

Fig. 2. Rail transportation

The global analysis for road transport, see Fig. 3, is in the truth area, with only two divergent points in the assessment, which is the capacity aspect with its features cargo volume and size.

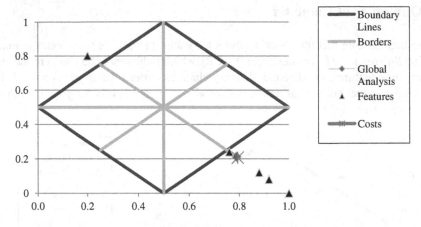

Fig. 3. Road transportation

5   Conclusion

The research achieved its purpose of presenting a tool that allows a group decision-making, thereby quantifying the experts' opinions, which may be contradictory, and detailing the items of each assessment. One may ascertain that costs did not change significantly in the evaluation and helped decision makers choose the mode of transport.

This analysis also supports the modes of grain transportation used in Brazil, given that its waterway network spreads over 50,000 km, which corresponds to 3.3 % of the road network, and its efficient use depends on climate conditions. Despite its reduced extension, with 28 thousand km, the railroad network shows the best favorable evidences for grain transportation when all features are taken into account. With a 1.5 million km network, road is the most popular method of transportation in the Country, and any evaluation should take some of its features, especially cargo volume and size, into account, especially because of the high costs for low aggregate-value commodities.

References

1. Abe, J.M.: Paraconsistent artificial neural networks: an introduction. In: Negoita, M.G., Howlett, R.J., Jain, L.C. (eds.) KES 2004. LNCS (LNAI), vol. 3214, pp. 942–948. Springer, Heidelberg (2004)
2. Da Silva Filho, J.I., Torres, G.L., Abe, J.M.: Uncertainty Treatment Using Paraconsistent Logic - Introducing Paraconsistent Artificial Neural Networks, vol. 211, p. 328. IOS Press, Netherlands (2010)

3. Central Intelligence Agency: The world fact book. https://www.cia.gov/library/publications/the-world-factbook/geos/br.html
4. Brasil, Ministério da Agricultura Pecuária e Abastecimento, Secretaria de Política Agrícola: Cultura de Soja, Brasília (2015)
5. Brasil, Ministério da Agricultura, Pecuária e Abastecimento: Projeções do Agronegócio: Brasil 2013/2014 a 2023/2024 projeções de longo prazo (2014)
6. Brasil, Ministério Desenvolvimento, Indústria e Comércio Exterior, Secretaria de Comércio Exterior: Aliceweb. http://aliceweb.mdic.gov.br/
7. Brasil, Ministério do Desenvolvimento, Indústria e Comércio Exterior: Balança Comercial Brasileira Dados Consolidados (2015)
8. Zikmund, W.G., Babin, B.J., Carr, J.C., Griffin, M.: Business Research Methods, 8th edn. South-Western College Pub, Mason (2009)
9. Junior, I.C.L., de Almeida D'Agosto, M.: Modal choice for transportation of hazardous materials: the case of land modes of transport of bio-ethanol in Brazil. J. Cleaner Prod. **19**, 229–240 (2011)
10. Ballou, R.H.: Gerenciamento da Cadeia de Suprimentos. Bookman, Porto Alegre (2001)
11. Brasil, Ministério dos Transportes: Projeto de Reavaliação de Estimativas e Metas do PNLT (2012)
12. Brasil, Agência Nacional de Transportes Terrestres. http://www.antt.gov.br/index.php/content/view/4971/Caracteristicas.html
13. The World Bank: How to Decrease Freight Logistics Costs in Brazil. The World Bank, Washington, D.C. (2012)
14. Saaty, T.L.: How to make a decision: the analytic hierarchy process. Eur. J. Oper. Res. **48**(1), 9–26 (1990)

Social Network Analysis of a Supply Network Structural Investigation of the South Korean Automotive Industry

Jin-Baek Kim[✉]

Business School, Chung-Ang University,
84 Heukseok-ro Dongjak-gu, Seoul, Korea
jinbaek@cau.ac.kr

Abstract. In this paper, we analyzed the structure of the South Korean auto-motive industry using social network analysis (SNA) metrics. Based on the data collected from 275 companies, a social network model of the supply network was constructed. Centrality measures in the SNA field were used to interpret the result and identify key companies. The results show that SNA metrics can be useful to understand the structure of a supply network. The most significant contribution of this research is that this is the first trial on applying SNA methods to large scale supply networks for an entire automotive industry of a country.

Keywords: Supply chain · Supply network · Social network analysis · The South Korean automotive industry

1 Introduction

Many studies on supply chains investigated linear relationships between supplying and buying companies, by adopting the perspective of hierarchical value chains. However, the companies constituting a supply chain usually belong to supply chains of other companies and commonly have relationships with other companies. Hence, by adopting a network perspective on supply chains or considering supply networks rather than supply chains, one can better understand the supply chain structure of a company or an industry [4, 9, 13–15, 17].

Social network analysis (SNA) methods have been used to study the structure of societies and to identify important entities in a society. If supply chains are modeled as a network, then SNA methods can be useful tools for analysis. Borgatti and Li [2] argued that SNA concepts are particularly useful to identify the patterns of inter-firm relationships in a supply network that lead to competitive advantages through the diffusion of information and management of material flows. Choi and Kim [6] pointed out that SNA methods can complement the traditional perspective on supply chain by capturing the complexity needed to understand a company's strategy or behavior.

Although the potential has been recognized [1–3], there are still relatively few empirical studies on real-world supply networks using SNA methods [11]. One reason for that is the difficulty in obtaining comprehensive information on supply chain relationships among companies, which is necessary to construct a complete social

© IFIP International Federation for Information Processing 2015
S. Umeda et al. (Eds.): APMS 2015, Part I, IFIP AICT 459, pp. 332–339, 2015.
DOI: 10.1007/978-3-319-22756-6_41

network. Another reason is because SNA methods are oriented to analyzing societies not companies working in the supply chain. Social network analysis theory and the way of interpreting results in sociology cannot be directly applied to the supply chain context. In this study, we used data from Korean Auto Industries Cooperative Association (KAICA) to construct a social network representing the supply network structure of the South Korean automotive industry. The KAICA is a non-profit organization, founded in 1962, to develop the South Korean automotive industry. Most major companies in auto parts and components manufacturing industries operating in Korea are KAICA members. The KAICA collects data every year from its members on their major customers. The data used in this paper is customer information from 275 member companies of KAICA for 2013.

The constructed supply network was analyzed based on centrality metrics. Kim et al. [11] proposed a theoretical framework that links widely used social network metrics to supply network constructs based on the insight earned from case-based interpretations [5]. One conclusion from that study is that the framework can both supplement and complement case-based analysis of supply networks. However, the conclusion was based on an application to small scale supply networks (less than 50 companies) of a part of an automotive supply chain(final assembly). In this study, a relatively large scale supply network (close to 400 companies) was constructed and analyzed, based on social network analysis metrics. A more comprehensive supply network model provides an opportunity to further validate the theoretical framework but also creates challenges in applying the theory. In this study, we focused on validating and extending the theory, although we referred to Kim et al. [11]'s framework to interpret SNA metrics in the supply networks.

2 About the South Korean Automotive Industry

As of 2013, there are five major auto makers producing cars in South Korea. They are Hyundai Motor, Kia Motor, Korea GM, SsangYong Motor, and Renault-Samsung Motors. In 2013, the Hyundai-Kia Motor Group produced 3.451 million cars, which corresponds to 76 % of total cars produced in South Korea [10]. GM Korea, Ssang-Yong, and Renault-Samsung accounted for 15.1 %, 6.4 %, and 6 %, respectively, of domestic automobile production. The number of cars produced and sold in South Korea by these five companies is shown in Fig. 1. As can be seen, all five auto makers produce more than they sell in South Korea and thus export cars overseas.

Hyundai and Kia Motor have supply chains that are vertically integrated by companies belonging to the group. Key suppliers of Hyundai and Kia Motor are Hyundai Mobis, which provides key module and system components, Hyundai Dymos supplying power train components; Hyundai Powertech supplying transmission components; Hyundai Wia supplying engine and transmission components; and Hyundai Steel providing steel material. These Hyundai-Kia Motor Group companies are under the command of a group chairman.

GM Korea, which was formerly Daewoo Motors, has been owned by GM since 2002, while Korea Development Bank (KDB) who participated in the restoration of the bankrupt company also owns 17.02 % of the shares. The ownership of SsangYong

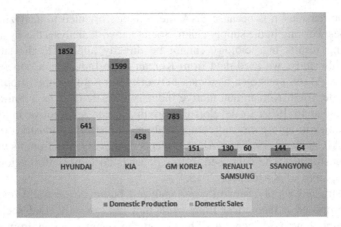

Fig. 1. Domestic production and sales by auto makers in South Korea as of 2013 (thousand units) [10]

Motor has changed hands many times, originally from the Ssangyong Group to the Daewoo Group (1997), and to SAIC (2002). Since 2011, the Mahindra Group is the majority shareholders (72.85 %) of SsangYong Motor. SsangYong's strength has been in the SUV segment and historically had close ties with technologies and supply chains of Daimler AG. Renault-Samsung Motors was originally founded by the Samsung Group in collaboration with Nissan Motor in 1995. Since 2000, it is a part of the Renault Group, which owns 79.88 % share of Renault-Samsung Motors. Samsung Credit Card Co. also owns a 19.9 % share of Renault-Samsung.

3   Analysis of the South Korean Automotive Supply Network Using Social Network Analysis Metrics

When building a social network model, relationships between entities may be modeled as directed or undirected links. Kim et al. [11] suggested that directed links are useful to describe material flows, whereas undirected links are helpful when examining contractual relationships or information flow. In this study, the supply network was modeled as both directed and undirected networks, and was investigated to understand the material flows and information flows in the supply network.

The constructed supply network was analyzed using Gephi 0.8.2, an open source software for social network analysis. The visual representation of the supply network can be seen in Fig. 2. That graph is composed of 395 companies, including 285 KAICA member companies and their customers who may or may not be KAICA members.

As stated in the previous section, the auto makers play central roles in the South Korean automotive industry. Among the first tier suppliers of the auto-makers, technology and capital intensive parts, such as engine and power train components are provided by the large-sized companies of a group, and parts requiring precision engineering, such as casted/forged parts, are supplied by medium-sized independent companies having

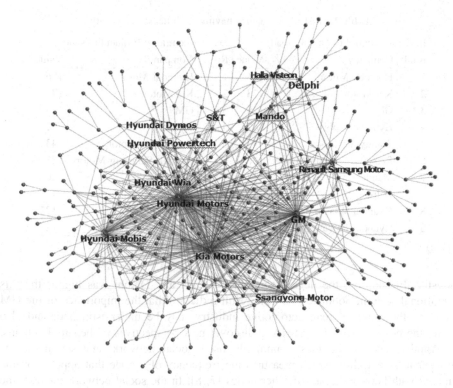

Fig. 2. Visual representation of the South Korean automotive industry supply network

close ties with auto-makers. The second-tier suppliers providing commodity like parts, such as iron rods, bolts, nuts, etc., are usually independent small- and medium- sized companies. Such a hierarchical structure can be ascertained from Fig. 2.

An interesting observation is that Hyundai Mobis, a module component supplier, is as distinctive as the auto-makers. Hyundai Mobis plays a key role in the Hyundai-Kia Motor Group and is recognized as the key driver of productivity and innovation. The graph seems to reflect this reality. Mando and Delphi, key module and system component manufacturers for Hyundai-Kia and GM, respectively, also have high visibility in the graph. This is also a reflection of the reality that auto makers have moved toward module-based production.

One of the most commonly used social network analysis metrics is degree centrality, which measures the number of direct ties to a node. Degree centrality can be interpreted as operational load and influential scope [2, 11]. The degree centrality results of both directed and undirected networks were similar, as summarized in Table 1. Companies that showed a high degree centrality were mostly auto-makers or part manufacturers belonging to the Hyundai-Kia Motor Group. Kim et al. [11] argued that companies having high degree centrality in undirected network are the ones having strong influence on others. Considering the influence of Hyundai-Kia Motor Group on the South Korean automotive industry, this argument seems to be validated and the result shows the degree of power concentration in the South Korean automotive

Table 1. List of companies having high degree centrality

In-degree centrality (supply load)			Degree centrality (influential scope)		
Rank	Company	Value	Rank	Company	Value
1	Hyundai Motor	196	1	Hyundai Motor	196
2	Kia Motor	173	2	Kia Motor	173
3	GM	125	3	GM	125
4	Hyundai Mobis	67	4	Hyundai Mobis	72
5	Ssangyong Motor	43	5	Ssangyong Motor	43
6	Renault-Samsung Motors	28	6	Renault-Samsung Motors	28
7	Mando	14	7	Mando	20
8	Delphi	12	8	Hyundai Wia	14
8	Hyundai Wia	12	9	Delphi	12
8	Hyundai Powertech	12	9	Hyundai Powertech	12
			9	Hyundai Dymos	12

industry. In addition, the degree centrality of GM and Delphi was higher than its operational scale in South Korea. This result indicates that the importance of the GM group in the South Korean automotive industry may be under-estimated; and also shows the possibility of using SNA to discover new perspectives in the supply chains.

Another one of the most commonly used social network analysis metrics is betweenness centrality, which measures the frequency of a node that appears on the shortest path between a pair of other nodes [7, 8]. In the social network context, the betweenness is interpreted as the degree of gate-keeping that a node does for the other nodes.

The results of betweenness centrality were different in directed and undirected network, as can be seen in Table 2. In the directed network model of supply network, two major first-tier suppliers of the Hyundai-Kia Motor Group, Hyunidai Mobis and

Table 2. List of companies having high betweenness centrality

Between-ness centrality in directed network (operational criticality)			Between-ness centrality in undirected network (relational mediation)		
Rank	Company	Value	Rank	Company	Value
1	Hyundai Mobis	228.0	1	Hyundai Motor	30088.4
2	Mando	52.5	2	Kia Motor	19725.3
3	Hyundai Dymos	40.3	3	GM	19075.0
4	S&T Dynamics	21.2	4	Hyundai Mobis	7488.1
5	Halla Visteon Climate Control	18.2	5	Renault-Samsung Motors	5583.5
6	Daewon	11.5	6	Mando	3720.6
7	Magna Powertrain Korea	10.8	7	Hanjoo Metal	3477.0
8	Namyang Industries	9.0	8	Ssangyong Motor	3128.4
9	Central	8.5	9	Hyundai Dymos	2422.6
10	Yura Tech	6.0	10	Delphi	2393.9

Mando, showed the highest betweenness centrality. Companies with high betweenness centrality in the directed network model were key manufacturers of various parts, such as S&T Dynamics (powertrain components), Daewon Indusrty (car seat), Namyang Industry (steering and braking system), Central (steel rods), Yuratech (spark plugs), Halla-Visteon (climate control system), and Magna Powertrain Korea (pumps). Some of these companies (e.g. Halla-Visteon, Magna Powertrain Korea) were large-sized companies whereas others are medium sized companies.

In an undirected network model, the list of companies with high between-ness centrality was similar to the companies having high degree centrality. Kim et al. [11] argued that betweenness centrality in directed network indicates operational criticality, whereas betweenness centrality in undirected network is related to the role of mediating relations. When applying that argument to a result, the operational criticality argument for directed network seems to be validated, whereas the relational mediation argument appears to need further verification and refinement. In addition, the result suggests that in automotive supply network, key parts and suppliers are widely distributed to various parts beside key module components.

In terms of the number of units produced in South Korea, GM's proportion (15.1 %) of the South Korean automotive industry is greater than SsangYong (6.4 %) and Renault-Samsung (6 %) but is significantly smaller than Hyundai-Kia (76 %). However, in terms of degree centrality and betweenness centrality, GM's significance in the South Korean automotive supply network seems to be more than what is suggested by the number of produced units [10]. SssangYong and Renault-Samsung are similar in terms of the number of produced units. However, SsangYong showed higher between-ness centrality than Renault-Samsung in the directed network model, whereas Renault-Samsung's between-ness in the undirected network was higher than Ssang-Yong's. Based on the theoretical framework of Kim et al. [12], that fact can be interpreted to mean SsangYong is more operationally critical than Renault-Samsung, whereas Renault-Samsung has a greater potential to connect separated groups of suppliers. This new insight seems to make sense, yet it needs further investigation.

Closeness centrality, calculated by the average of the minimal length to the other nodes, is also one of the most commonly used social network analysis metrics [7, 8]. Nine companies displayed high closeness centrality in the supply network are shown in Table 3. These companies can be classified into the following three types: (1) auto

Table 3. List of companies having high closeness centrality (undirected network)

Rank	Company	Value
1	Hyundai Motor	1.9
2	Kia Motor	2.0
3	GM	2.2
4	Hyundai Mobis	2.3
5	Mando	2.4
5	Continental Automotive Electronics	2.4
7	Taeyang Metal	2.5
7	Youngsin Metal	2.5
7	Youngshin Precision	2.5

manufacturers (Hyundai, Kia, GM), (2) key module suppliers (Hyundai Mobis, Mando), and (3) companies providing commodity like products (Continental Automotive Electronics, Taeyang Metal, Youngsin Metal, Youngshin Precision) to many companies. Kim et al. [11] argued that companies with higher closeness centrality are those who can act autonomously and navigate freely across the network to access resources in a timely manner. This result confirms that those kinds of companies seem to be independent. But it seems what allows the companies to access information and resources is not just closeness but the nature of the relationships with key companies.

4 Conclusion

It is difficult to obtain knowledge on an industry structure and dynamics through an analysis focusing on individual companies. Using the SNA approach to analyze the supply network, it was possible to better understand the structure of the South Korean automotive industry. This study confirms the potential of the SNA approach as applied to supply network studies. However, it should be noted that prior domain knowledge, as well as SNA-based analysis, on the industry helped in reaching an understanding. In this sense, the SNA methods seem to be useful in confirmatory as well as exploratory studies.

One limitation of this paper is the data. As stated earlier, most major South Korean companies in the automotive industry were included in the data. However, many South Korean companies are suppliers for overseas companies and the complete supply network of those overseas companies was not included in the data that were analyzed. Considering the trend of rapid globalization, the structure and operation of the companies belonging to overseas supply networks may affect the structure and operations of the South Korean companies. Also, because some companies that are primarily in other industries, such as electronics, are not members of Korean Auto Industries Cooperative Association (KAICA), they are not included in the supply network, which was analyzed in this research. Considering the trend of the IT-automobile convergence, the analysis may have missed some important IT companies that are critical to automotive industry.

Another limitation of this research stems from the characteristics of SNA methodologies. Important aspects of business relationships, such as intensity of relationships and scale of transactions, are hard to model as social networks. This research regarded those relationships as all being equal. Of course, by modeling the relationship this way, it is possible to obtain a new perspective from the analysis. However, especially from the practitioner's perspective, this may be considered as a significant barrier to applying the SNA to real industry examples. As Park [15] pointed out, SNA methods are not robust against sampling. Unlike typical statistical analysis where samples are generally independent, entities in the social network are all linked with each other and affect the result of analysis. Hence, to obtain unbiased results, the complete network needs to be modeled and analyzed.

The biggest contribution of this research to the literature is that this is the first trial on applying SNA methods to large-scale supply networks and the entire automotive supply chains of a country. Despite the limitations stated above, by building a relative large social network model containing most major South Korean automotive companies and by using a previously validated framework for the interpretation of SNA metrics in the supply network context, we believe that the results of this study have credibility.

In this study, the focus was on analyzing the overall South Korean automotive industry. As for future research, comparative research on the supply networks of Hyundai Motor and Kia Motor and other companies will be performed. A comparison of the South Korean automotive companies and Japanese automotive companies may also be an interesting future research topic.

References

1. Autry, C.W., Griffis, S.E.: Supply chain capital: the impact of structural and relational linkages on firm execution and innovation. J. Bus. Logistics **29**(1), 157–174 (2008)
2. Borgatti, S.P., Li, X.: On social network analysis in a supply chain context. J. Supply Chain Manage. **45**(2), 5–21 (2009)
3. Carter, C.R., Ellram, L.M., Tate, W.: The use of social network analysis in logistics research. J. Bus. Logistics **28**(1), 137–169 (2007)
4. Choi, T.Y., Dooley, K.J., Rungtusanatham, M.: Supply networks and complex adaptive systems: control versus emergence. J. Oper. Manage. **19**(3), 351–366 (2001)
5. Choi, T.Y., Hong, Y.: Unveiling the structure of supply networks: case studies in Honda, Acura, and DaimlerChrysler. J. Oper. Manage. **20**(5), 469–493 (2002)
6. Choi, T.Y., Kim, Y.: Structural embeddedness and supplier management: a network perspective. J. Supply Chain Manage. **44**(4), 5–13 (2008)
7. Everett, M.G., Borgatti, S.P.: The centrality of groups and classes. J. Math. Sociol. **23**(3), 181–201 (1999)
8. Freeman, L.C.: Centrality in social networks: conceptual clarification. Soc. Netw. **1**, 215–239 (1979)
9. Harland, C.M., Lamming, R.C., Zheng, J., Johnsen, T.E.: A taxonomy of supply networks. J. Supply Chain Manage. **37**(4), 21–27 (2001)
10. KARI (Korea Automotive Research Institute), 2014. Korean Automotive Industry (2014)
11. Kim, C., Jo, H.J., Jeong, J.H.: Modular Production and Hyundai Production System: The Case of Hyundai MOBIS, Economy and Society, vol. 92, pp. 351–385 (2011). (Korean Manuscript)
12. Kim, Y., Choi, T.Y., Yan, T., Dooley, K.: Structural investigation of supply networks: a social network approach. J. Oper. Manage. **29**, 194–211 (2011)
13. Kim, W.S.: Effects of a trust mechanism on complex adaptive supply networks: an agent-based social simulation study. J. Artif. Soc. Soc. Simul. **12**(3), 4 (2009)
14. Lamming, R.C., Johnsen, T.E., Zheng, J., Harland, C.M.: An initial classification of supply networks. Int. J. Oper. Prod. Manage. **20**(6), 675–691 (2000)
15. Park, S.J.: Social network analysis for smart business. KORMS 2011 Spring Conference Tutorial (2011)
16. Pathak, S.D., Day, J.M., Nair, A., Sawaya, W.J., Kristal, M.M.: Complexity and adaptivity in supply networks: building supply network theory using a complex adaptive systems perspective. Decis. Sci. **38**(4), 547–580 (2007)
17. Surana, A., Kumara, S., Greaves, M., Raghavan, U.N.: Supply chain network: a complex adaptive systems perspective. Int. J. Prod. Res. **43**, 4235–4265 (2005)

ACD Modeling of Homogeneous Job Shops Having Inline Cells

Hyeonsik Kim, Byoung K. Choi$^{(\boxtimes)}$, and Hayong Shin

Department of Industrial and Systems Engineering, KAIST,
Daejeon, Republic of Korea
{hyeonsik.kim, bkchoi, hyshin}@kaist.ac.kr

Abstract. In an electronics fabrication line, processing devices are arranged as a network of *inline cells*. Recently, the use of simulation has evolved into *online simulation*, which is used in simulation-based operational management, from the traditional *offline* analysis of facility layout and dispatching rules. An online simulation starts with the *current state* of the manufacturing facilities at any point of time. This paper presents a systematic procedure for building activity cycle diagram (ACD) models of homogeneous job shops having inline cells. In order to demonstrate the effectiveness of the proposed approach, an ACD model was developed for a simple homogeneous job shop having bi-inline cells and a dedicated simulator was also developed.

Keywords: Production simulation · Activity cycle diagram · Homogeneous job shop · Inline cell · Online simulation

1 Introduction

In an electronics fabrication line (Fab), such as a flat panel display (FPD) production line [1] or a semiconductor fabrication line [2], processing devices are arranged as a network of inline cells. An *inline cell* consists of a small number of processing devices and an inner conveyor system that carries individual work-pieces through the processing devices along the conveyor belt [2]. Unlike a table-type machine that processes one work-piece at a time, an inline cell processes a batch of work-pieces simultaneously: each work-piece is loaded at its loading port with an *inter-loading time* (called *takt time*) and travels through the inline cell for a duration of *flow time* to be unloaded at the unloading port. Inline cells in a Fab are usually grouped into a number of *stations* (called *inline stockers* in a FPD Fab or *bays* in a semiconductor Fab) and they are connected by an *automated material handling system* (AMHS) in which cassettes containing individual work-pieces (e.g., glasses or wafers) are transported in the Fab.

The inline cells are largely classified into two types: *bi-inline cells* and *uni-inline cells*. This classification is based on whether the work-pieces are loaded and unloaded in the same port: In a bi-inline cell, work-pieces are loaded at a *loading port* (called the *in-port*) and are unloaded at a separate *unloading port* (called the *out-port*) of the cell; in a uni-inline cell, work-pieces are loaded and unloaded at the same port (called the *in/out-port*). A new (unfinished) work-piece is loaded from a 'new' cassette in the cell; a finished work-piece is unloaded from the cell into an empty cassette. Figure 1 shows

© IFIP International Federation for Information Processing 2015
S. Umeda et al. (Eds.): APMS 2015, Part I, IFIP AICT 459, pp. 340–347, 2015.
DOI: 10.1007/978-3-319-22756-6_42

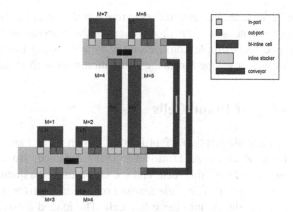

Fig. 1. Layout of a portion of a hypothetical FPD Fab

a portion of a (hypothetical) FPD Fab in which all the inline cells are of bi-inline type. There are eight bi-inline cells (PH: photo-lithography; ET: etching; CLN: cleaning; DEP: deposition) grouped into two stations (i.e. inline stockers). The two stations are connected by a pair of uni-directional conveyors. This kind of job shop consisting of the same type of equipment is referred to as a ***homogeneous job shop***. A job shop consisting of mixed types of equipment is referred to as a *heterogeneous job shop*.

Recently, the use of a simulation has evolved into the day-to-day operational management of facilities, from the traditional *offline* analysis of facility layout and dispatching rules [3–5]. *Online simulation* is used in simulation-based operational management. An online simulation starts with the *current state* of the manufacturing facilities at any point of time [6], and it provides the stakeholders with the ability to evaluate the capacity of the facility for new orders and unforeseen events, and to predict the expected delivery times and changes in operations [4].

Many commercial simulation packages have been introduced to simulate a production system. ASAP (AutoSched AP™) is one of the most popular tools for production simulation [7–9]. More recently, ManPy, a semantic-free open-source discrete-event simulation package, was also used in developing a job shop simulator [10]. However, a simulator implemented with a simulation package generally has less flexibility than one implemented based on a well-defined formal modeling tool such as an *event graph* or *activity cycle diagram* (ACD) [11]. Indeed, the event graph is widely used in modeling and simulation of job shops. Notable examples include event graph modeling of a homogeneous job shop with bi-inline cells [12] and event graph modeling of a heterogeneous job shop with inline cells [13]. However, these event graph models are not suitable for an online simulation because representing the current state of a real system as the initial state of the event graph model is difficult.

This paper presents a systematic procedure for building ACD models of homogeneous job shops having inline cells. *Parameterized ACD* (PACD) [11, 14] is used to build the models of the homogeneous job shops. Compared to the event graph modeling approach [12, 13], the ACD modeling approach presented in this paper has some distinctive advantages: The ACD model is (1) easier to build and validate, (2) more intuitive so that a layman can understand the model more easily, and (3) suitable for online simulation because the current state of a real job shop can easily be reflected in the model. In order to demonstrate the effectiveness of the proposed approach, a PACD model was developed for a simple homogenous job shop having bi-inline cells and a dedicated simulator was developed to make simulation runs with input data.

2 ACD Modeling of Inline Cells

Figure 2 is a schematic description of bi-inline cells in FPD Fab. It is used as a reference model from which an ACD model is to be obtained. An arriving cassette *enters* the *cell queue* (Q) of the inline cell, and the cassettes in the queue are *loaded* on the *in-port* (PI) if there is room. The *glass loading* operation is performed by the *track-in robot* (TI) to load the glasses into the inline cell. The loaded glasses are *processed* until they reach the end of the line where the *glass unloading* operation is performed by the *track-out robot* (TO), which puts the finished glasses into an empty cassette on an *out-port* (PO). When the unloading cassette becomes full, it is removed so that an empty cassette can be *supplied*. A cassette that is emptied at the loading section should also be removed to make room for the next arriving cassette.

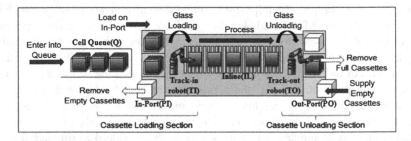

Fig. 2. Reference model of bi-inline cells in FPD Fab

Figure 3 shows an ACD model of the bi-inline cell given in Fig. 2. The activities in Fig. 2 are modeled as regular activities (solid-line rectangle) in the ACD model:

– Enter (for 'enter into queue' in Fig. 2) with activity time t_E (inter-arrival time);
– LoadPI (load a cassette on In-Port) with t_{LPI} (time for loading a cassette at In-Port);
– LoadG (glass loading) with t_L (time for loading all glasses in a cassette);
– ProcessFG (process the 1st glass of a cassette) with t_E (inter-arrival time).
– UnloadG (glass unloading) with t_{TIO} (track-in/out time for a cassette of glasses);
– SupplyEC (supply empty cassettes) with t_{SEC} (time for supplying empty cassette).

The ACD model contains a *computation activity* (dotted-line rectangle) and an *instant activity* ('thin' rectangle) as well. A *regular activity* has a time delay value denoting the activity duration. A *computation activity* is used for computing variables without time delay. The table in Fig. 3 shows detailed computation actions for the

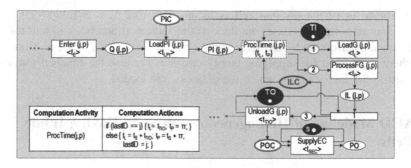

Fig. 3. ACD model of the bi-inline cell in Fig. 2

computation activity ProcTime (If the job type of the current cassette differs from the last cassette id lastID, a set-up time t_S is added). An instant activity denotes an event such as the start of an activity. There are two parameters in the ACD model, j for job type and p for processing step.

Queues in the ACD model are classified into four types: *Entity queue* (solid line circle) for the number of entities, *resource queue* (intaglio circle) for the number of available resources, *capacity queue* (double-line circle) for the number of available seats, and *instant queue* (small circle) in which tokens do not stay.

- Entity queues are Q (cassettes in the cell queue), PI (cassettes in the In-Port), IL (cassettes in the inline), and PO (empty cassettes in Out-Port);
- Resource queues are TI (track-in robot), TO (track-out robot), and S (empty-cassette supplying system);
- Capacity queues are PIC (capacity or available slots in the In-Port), POC (available slots in the Out-Port), and ILC (available slots in the inline).

Let N_{PI}, N_{IL}, and N_{PO} denote the capacities of In-Port, Inline and Out-Port, and then the following relations should hold: $N_{PI} = PI + PIC$; $N_{IL} = IL + ILC$; $N_{PO} = PO + POC$.

Figure 4 shows an ACD model of a uni-inline cell where the *regular* queue PU is the number of cassettes in the in/out port region of the uni-inline cell and the *capacity* queue PUC denotes the number of available ports in the in/out port region. The token in the *resource* queue TIO is used either by the LoadG activity or by the UnloadG activity (LoadG has a higher priority).

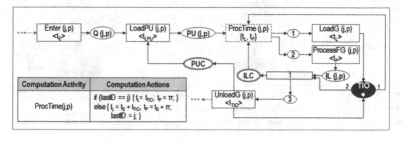

Fig. 4. ACD model of a uni-inline cell

The behavior of a uni-inline cell is identical to that of a bi-inline cell, except loading and unloading of glasses are done at the same port and track-in and track-out operations are performed by the same robot (track-in/out robot). Also, in a uni-inline cell, there is no need for supplying empty cassettes because the finished glasses are unloaded to the cassette from which the glasses were loaded.

3 ACD Modeling of Homogeneous Job Shop Having Inline Cells

This section describes how to build an ACD model of a homogeneous job. Figure 5 shows an ACD model of a job shop consisting of a number of bi-inline cells and a material handling system. The bi-inline cell model of Fig. 3 is parameterized with parameter 'b' and then connected to the ACD model of the material handling system to obtain a *parameterized* ACD (PACD) model of the homogeneous job shop.

In the material handling part of the PACD model, arriving cassettes are generated and stored in the entity queue FQ by the Generate activity based on the Release Plan. A bi-inline cell is selected for the generated cassette at the *computation activity* FindNext according to the Route Data. The transporting time t_T from the current location 'b' to the target bi-inline cell 'b_N' is then computed at the computation activity TransTime referring to the data in the Layout Master Data. Finally, the cassette is transported to the target cell by the regular activity Transport. A cassette containing glasses processed at an inline cell is also stored in FQ, and then it is routed to the next inline cell by the Transport activity or disposed by the Dispose activity if it has completed all the processing steps.

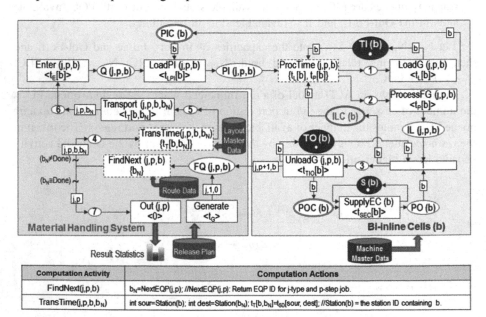

Computation Activity	Computation Actions
FindNext(j,p,b)	b_N=NextEQP(j,p); //NextEQP(j,p): Return EQP ID for j-type and p-step job.
TransTime(j,p,b,b_N)	int sour=Station(b); int dest=Station(b_N); t_T[b,b_N]=t_{SO}[sour, dest]; //Station(b) = the station ID containing b.

Fig. 5. Parameterized ACD model of a homogeneous job shop having bi-inline cells

The upper diagram in Fig. 6 shows an example of the *current state* of a bi-inline cell. There are seven cassettes with glasses and one empty cassette in the diagram: three cassettes in Q, one in PI, two in IL, and so on. The cassette in PI, for example, contains glasses of type-1 (j = 1) waiting for the 5th processing (p = 5). Currently, both robots are idle (TI = 1, TO = 1). The current state data of the bi-inline cell 'b' can be summarized as shown in the *Current State Table* in the middle part of Fig. 6.

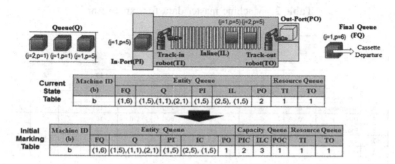

Current State Table	Machine ID (b)	Entity Queue					Resource Queue	
		FQ	Q	PI	IL	PO	TI	TO
	b	(1,6)	(1,5),(1,1),(2,1)	(1,5)	(2,5), (1,5)	2	1	1

Initial Marking Table	Machine ID (b)	Entity Queue				Capacity Queue			Resource Queue	
		FQ	Q	PI	IC	PO	PIC	ILC	POC	TI	TO
	b	(1,6)	(1,5),(1,1),(2,1)	(1,5)	(2,5), (1,5)	1	2	3	1	1	1

Fig. 6. Procedure for initializing state of bi-inline cell #b from current state

Finally, the *Initial Marking Table* shown at the bottom of Fig. 6 can be constructed automatically from the *Current State Table*. Each entry in the *capacity queue* column is computed by subtracting the number of cassettes from the capacity value in the queue (e.g., PIC = 3 – |PI| = 3 – 1 = 2). The ability to obtain the initial marking values from the current state data of the Fab makes it easier for the ACD model to be used in an *online simulation* for real-time operation management.

If the bi-inline cell part of the PACD model in Fig. 5 is replaced by a PACD model of uni-inline cell (See Fig. 4), we obtain a homogeneous job shop having uni-inline cells. Further, if we connect both the bi-inline PACD model and uni-inline PACD model to the same material handling model of Fig. 5, we can obtain a PACD model of a heterogeneous job shop.

4   Implementation

This section presents the results of implementing a dedicated simulator executing the PACD model (See Fig. 5) of a homogeneous job shop having bi-inline cells. The development of the dedicated simulator has been explained in detail in the literature [11]. The dedicated simulator implemented in C# language is posted at http://www.vms-technology.com/ (Publication menu). The simulator is set to start with an empty system (i.e., all initial markings in the entity queues are set to zero) for the sake of simplicity, which makes it an offline simulator. However, if we set the initial markings to real-time WIP values, it becomes an online simulator.

Tables 1 and 2 show the route data and machine master data, respectively, for a homogeneous job shop having bi-inline cells (See Fig. 1). In the experiment, 140 cassettes are released at time 0: 10 cassettes of type-2 jobs (glasses), 20 cassettes of type-1 jobs, 70 cassettes of type-2 jobs, and 40 cassettes of type-1 jobs.

Table 1. Route data for experiment

	Step-1 (p=1)	Step-2 (p=2)	Step-3 (p=3)	Step-4 (p=4)	Step-5 (p=5)	Step-6 (p=6)	Step-7 (p=7)	Step-8 (p=8)	Step-9 (p=9)	Step-10 (p=10)	Step-11 (p=11)	Step-12 (p=12)	Step-13 (p=13)	Step-14 (p=14)	Step-15 (p=15)	Step-16 (p=16)	Step-17 (p=17)	Step-18 (p=18)	Step-19 (p=19)	Step-20 (p=20)
Type-1 (j=1)	{1,2}	{3,4}	{5,6}	{7,8}	{1,2}	{3,4}	{5,6}	{7,8}	{1,2}	{3,4}	{5,6}	{7,8}	{1,2}	{3,4}	{5,6}	{7,8}	-	-	-	-
Type-2 (j=2)	{1,2}	{3,4}	{5,6}	{7,8}	{1,2}	{3,4}	{5,6}	{7,8}	{1,2}	{3,4}	{5,6}	{7,8}	{1,2}	{3,4}	{5,6}	{7,8}	{1,2}	{3,4}	{5,6}	{7,8}

Table 2. Machine master data for experiment

Machine ID (b)	Description	Time Data						Capacity Data		
		Enter time (tE[b])	Load-to-inport time (tLPI[b])	Total track-in/out time (tTIO[b])	Flow time (τπ[b])	Setup time (tS[b])	Supply time (tSEC[b])	In-port (pi[b])	Out-port (po[b])	Inline (n[b])
1	Cleaning-01	0	0	90	180	0	10	1	2	2
2	Cleaning-02	0	0	90	180	0	10	1	2	2
3	Deposition-01	0	0	99	280	0	10	1	2	2
4	Deposition-01	0	0	99	280	0	10	1	2	2
5	Photo-01	0	0	144	800	120	10	2	2	5
6	Photo-02	0	0	144	800	120	10	2	2	5
7	Etching-01	0	0	99	360	0	10	1	2	3
8	Etching-02	0	0	99	360	0	10	1	2	3

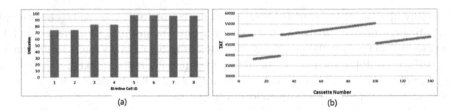

(a)　　　　　　　　　　　　　　　　　　(b)

Fig. 7. (a) Utilization for bi-inline cells, (b) turn-around time for cassette distribution

The simulation results are presented in Fig. 7. Figure 7(a) shows the utilization rate of each bi-inline cell. Notice that the pairs of identical machines have the same utilization rates; this is expected because a machine selection rule of 'smallest-queue-length' was used. Trends of increasing TAT (turn-around-time) also can be observed, indicating that the Fab is becoming congested as more cassettes are released. The disconnections (drops and jumps) in TAT curve Fig. 7(b) are the results of job type changes.

5　Summary and Conclusions

This paper presents a systematic procedure for building and initializing an ACD model of a homogeneous job shop with inline cells. First, the ACD models of a bi-inline cell and a uni-inline cell are presented. Second, the ACD models of the bi-inline cell and a simplified material handling system are combined to form a PACD model of a homogeneous job shop having inline cells. Finally, the initial marking values for initializing the model are obtained from the current state data of the Fab. The resulting PACD model was verified with a dedicated simulator using sample input data. This model can be implemented within a production simulator, which can be used in an online simulation for real-time operation management. In order to develop a more realistic model, further study is required to accommodate a heterogeneous job shop consisting of different types of inline cells with detailed AMHS.

Acknowledgement. The research was supported by the NRF of Korea grant funded by the Korean Government (NRF-2013R1A1A2062607) to which the authors are grateful.

References

1. Jang, Y.J., Choi, G.H.: Introduction to automated material handling systems in LCD panel production lines. In: 2006 International Conference on Automation Science and Engineering, pp. 223–229. IEEE (2006)
2. Lee, J.H.: A study on equipment modeling method for simulation based semiconductor Fab scheduling. M.S. thesis, Department of Industrial and Systems Engineering, KAIST (2007)
3. Park, B.C., Park, E.S., Choi, B.K., Kim, B.H., Lee, J.H.: Simulation based planning and scheduling system for TFT-LCD Fab. In: 2008 Winter Simulation Conference, pp. 1262–1267. IEEE (2008)
4. Heilala, J., Montonen, J., Järvinen, P., Kivikunnas, S., Maantil, M., Sillanopää, J., Jokinen, T.: Developing simulation-based decision support systems for customer-driven manufacturing operation planning. In: 2010 Winter Simulation Conference, pp. 3363–3375. IEEE (2010)
5. Frantzén, M., Ng, A.H.C., Moore, P.: A simulation-based scheduling system for real-time optimization and decision making support. Robot. Comput. Integr. Manuf. **27**, 696–705 (2011)
6. Hanisch, A., Tolujew, J., Schulze, T.: Initialization of online simulation models. In: 2005 Winter Simulation Conference, pp. 1795–1803. IEEE (2005)
7. Pool, M., Bachrach, R.: Productivity modeling of semiconductor manufacturing equipment. In: 2000 Winter Simulation Conference, pp. 1423–1427. IEEE (2000)
8. Potti, K., Gupta, A.: ASAP applications of simulation modeling in a wafer Fab. In: 2002 Winter Simulation Conference, pp. 1846–1848. IEEE (2002)
9. Gan, B.P., Liow, L.F., Gupta, A.K., Lendermann, P., Turner, S.J., Wang, X.: Analysis of a borderless Fab using interoperating autosched AP models. Int. J. Prod. Res. **45**(3), 675–697 (2007)
10. Olaitana, O., Geraghty, J., Young, P., Dagkakis, G., Heavey, C., Bayer, M., Perrin, J., Robin, S.: Implementing ManPy, a semantic-free open-source discrete event simulation package, in a job shop. In: 8th International Conference on Digital Enterprise Technology, pp. 253–260, Procedia CIRP 25 (2014)
11. Choi, B.K., Kang, D.: Modeling and Simulation of Discrete-Event Systems. Wiley, Hoboken (2013)
12. Song, E., Choi, B.K., Park, B.: Event graph modeling of a homogeneous job shop with bi-inline cells. Simul. Model. Pract. Theory **20**(1), 1–11 (2012)
13. Kang, D., Kim, H., Choi, B.K., Kim, B.H.: Event graph modeling of a heterogeneous job shop with inline cells. In: 2014 Winter Simulation Conference, pp. 2156–2167 (2014)
14. Choi, B.K., Kang, D., Lee, T., Jamjoom, A.A., Abulkhair, M.F.: Parameterized ACD and its application. ACM Trans. Model. Comput. Simul. **23**(4), 24:1–24:18 (2013). Article No. 24

A Computer-Aided Process Planning Method Considering Production Scheduling

Eiji Morinaga[1]([✉]), Hiroki Joko[1,2], Hidefumi Wakamatsu[1], and Eiji Arai[1]

[1] Division of Materials and Manufacturing Science, Osaka University, Suita, Japan
{morinaga,hiroki.joko,wakamatu,arai}@mapse.eng.osaka-u.ac.jp
[2] Tokyo Institute of Technology, Meguro, Japan

Abstract. Process planning plays an important role as a bridge between product design and manufacturing. Computer-aided process planning (CAPP) has been actively discussed in this half century, and numerous works have been conducted. To meet recent strong requirements for realizing agile manufacturing, a set of flexible process planning methods have been developed. Those methods dealt with process planning only for one product and generate the optimal plan which achieves the shortest total machining time. However, in real manufacturing, multiple workpieces are machined with multiple machine tools in the same period, and pursuing the shortest machining time for each workpiece may result in poor productivity. This research aims to enhance those methods from the point of view of total productivity. Selection of the optimal process plan in the conventional methods and production scheduling were merged and then formulated as a 0-1 integer programming problem. This method was applied to a simple example and its potential was shown.

1 Introduction

Process planning deals with selection of necessary manufacturing processes and determination of the sequence in which they are applied to convert product design data into a real product. Since it plays an important role as a bridge between product design and manufacturing, computer-aided process planning (CAPP) has been a topic of discussion in this half century and numerous works have been conducted [1].

Due to recent diversified and changeable customers' needs, there is a need to realize agile manufacturing [2] that is capable of immediately adapting to changes in the manufacturing situation, that is, flexible manufacturing systems need to be realized. This need is also being addressed in research related to CAPP [3]. This research aimed to develop autonomous machine tools that require no NC programming and can flexibly adapt to changes in the manufacturing situation, and a flexible process planning method for rough milling was proposed. This method consists of four main steps—(i) decomposing the total removal volume (TRV) through the application of decomposition rules to transform it into sets of machining primitive shapes (MPSs), (ii) converting each of the MPS sets to a set of machining features (MFs) by determining a machining sequence for

© IFIP International Federation for Information Processing 2015
S. Umeda et al. (Eds.): APMS 2015, Part I, IFIP AICT 459, pp. 348–355, 2015.
DOI: 10.1007/978-3-319-22756-6_43

each set of MPSs and recognizing each MPS as an MF, (iii) executing rough operation planning by applying a tool selection rule and a case-based reasoning system for cutting condition decisions, and (iv) extracting the optimal set of MFs to achieve the shortest machining time with information on the machining sequence and the utilized tools as the optimal process plan. With this method, process plans are generated and then the optimal plan is selected. Therefore, when the manufacturing situation changes, it is possible to quickly provide a new optimal plan by executing steps (iii) and (iv). Several enhancements have been made to this method for enabling extraction of a better set of MFs [4], for taking multi-axis milling and reducing computational complexity [5], and for improving computational efficiency [6].

All of these methods deal with process planning to create one product using a single milling machine. However, in real manufacturing, multiple workpieces are machined with multiple machine tools in the same period, and pursuing the optimal plan without consideration of total production may result in poor productivity. This paper presents an enhanced method considering this point. The selection problem of the optimal process plan in the conventional methods and production scheduling problem are merged, and selection of a set of the optimal process plans from the productivity point of view is formulated as a 0-1 integer programming problem.

This paper is organized as follows. The next section provides an outline of the conventional method [6]. Section 3 describes integration of the selection of the optimal process plans for multiple products and the production scheduling problem, and provides formulation of the integrated problem as a 0-1 integer programming problem. This method is applied to a simple example in Sect. 4, and Sect. 5 presents our conclusion.

2   Outline of Conventional Flexible CAPP Method

This section provides an overview of the conventional method [5,6], which will be improved considering production scheduling in Sect. 3. In this method, it is assumed that all the surfaces of a workpiece and the product are parallel to the xy, yz or zx plane of an orthogonal coordinate system and the tool approaches the workpiece along one of these axes (Fig. 1), since this method is for rough machining. Process planning is performed by the following six steps:

1. TRV extraction
   The total removal volume (TRV), which is defined as the volume to be eliminated from a workpiece to obtain the product shape, is calculated by subtracting the product shape from the workpiece shape (Fig. 2).
2. Concavity-based division
   A cutting plane is generated at a concave part of the TRV contour, and then the TRV is divided by that plane. This process is iterated until cutting planes are generated for all concave parts, and the TRV is finally converted into a set of machining primitive shapes (MPSs). The type of the MPS set depends

on the generation direction and sequence of the cutting planes. Therefore, multiple sets of MPSs can be produced from one TRV (Fig. 3).

3. Machining sequence and direction assignment
   For each of the MPS sets, the machining direction (Fig. 1) for each MPS and the machining sequence for those MPSs are considered.

4. MF recognition
   The machining directions and sequence assignment in the previous step makes it possible to regard each MPS as a machining feature (MF) based on the number of its "open faces" and the relationship between its vertices and edges. For each set of MPSs, multiple sets of MFs are generated depending on the direction and sequence (Fig. 4).

5. Process plan generation
   For each of the MF sets, a tool to be used for each MF is selected from a given set of available tools by applying a given rule, and the machining condition for the MF is decided by a case-based reasoning system [7]. This operation generates, for each MPS set, sets of MFs including information about the machining sequence, the machining directions, and the tools to be used—that is, a process plans is generated.

6. Evaluation
   For each process plan of each MPS set, the total machining time $\overline{T}$ is estimated using the following equations:

$$\overline{T} := \sum_{i=1}^{n} T_i + T_{tool}C_{tool} + T_{dir}C_{dir} \tag{1}$$

$$T_i := \frac{V_i}{D_{ia}D_{ir}F_i}, \tag{2}$$

where T_i and V_i stand for the machining time and the volume of MPS i, D_{ia} and D_{ir} are the depth of cut in the axial and radial directions of the tool used for the MPS, F_i is the feed speed of the tool, T_{tool} and T_{dir} are the times required for tool change and direction change, and C_{tool} and C_{dir} are the number of tool changes and direction changes, respectively. The plan that achieves the shortest total machining time is selected as the optimal process plan for the MPS set by the full search [5] or mathematical optimization framework [6]. After performing this operation for all MPS sets, the estimated total machining times for the optimal plans are compared with each other. The optimal plan for which the estimated total machining time is the shortest is ultimately output as the optimal process plan for the TRV.

In real manufacturing, multiple workpieces are machined by using multiple machine tools in the same period generally. If this method is applied to those workpieces, the optimal plan is generated for each of them. However, the set of the optimal plans would not be truly optimal from the point of view of manufacturing systems, since multiple workpieces cannot be machined by a machine at the same time. Therefore, it is desirable to integrate process planning by this method with production scheduling.

Fig. 1. Definition of machining directions.

Fig. 2. TRV extraction.

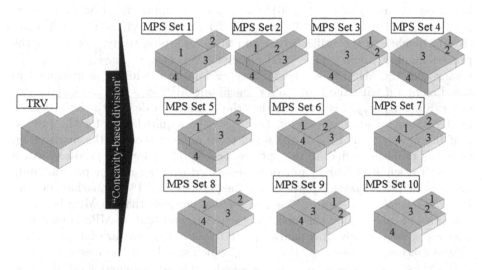

Fig. 3. Sets of MPSs extracted from the TRV. The numbers in each set are the identification numbers for the MPSs.

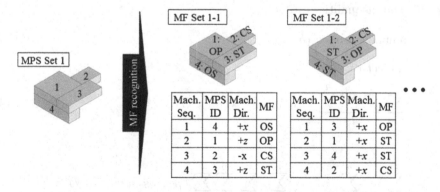

Fig. 4. MF recognition for an MPS set. Strings in each set stand for feature types ("CS", "OS", "OP", and "ST" stand for "closed slot", "open slot", "open pocket", and "step", respectively).

3   Flexible CAPP Method Considering Production Scheduling

This section provides formulation of the integrated problem of the optimal plan selection and production scheduling as a 0-1 integer programming problem. Two 0-1 variables $x_{jvS_{n_j}\cdots S_1 dt}$ and $z_{jpm\delta}$ are introduced, where $j \in \mathcal{J} := \{1, \ldots, J\}$ and $v \in \mathcal{V} := \{1, \ldots V\}$ stand for the ID number of product and MPS set of the product, respectively, and n_j represents the total number of MPSs. S_k is the ID number of the MPS that is machined after machining other $k - 1$ MPSs, and S_1 takes its value in $\mathcal{N}_j := \{1, \ldots, n_j\}$. S_k, $k \geq 2$ takes a value in $\{0\} \cup \mathcal{N}_j$, $k \geq 2$, and $S_{\tilde{k}} = 0$, $\forall \tilde{k} > k$ means that only the first k MPSs has been machined. $d \in \{1, \ldots 6\}$ stands for machining direction $(1 : \ +x;$ $2 : \ -x; \cdots 6 : \ -z)$. $t \in \mathcal{T} := \{1, \ldots T\}$ and $m \in \mathcal{M} := \{1, \ldots, M\}$ are the ID number of the utilized tool and machine, respectively, $p \in \mathcal{N}_j$ is the process number, and $\delta \in \{1, \ldots, \Delta\}$ represents a period. $x_{jv0\cdots0S_kS_{k-1}\cdots S_1 dt} = 1$ means that the MPS S_k of the MPS set v for the product j is machined in the direction d with the tool t after machining MPS S_1, S_2, $\ldots$, S_{k-1} in this order. Similarly, $z_{jpm\delta} = 1$ means that the machine m deal with the process p of the product j at the period δ. Let τ_{jp} is the required time for the process p of the product j and T_m is the set of tools implemented on the machine m, then the problem of finding the optimal process plans for the products which achieve the smallest makespan can be described as a 0-1 integer programming problem by the following equations and inequalities (3)–(18). Equations (4) and (5) and inequalities (6) and (7) assure, for any product, that an MPS is always machined at each turn of the machining sequence and that an MPS is machined only once, respectively. Inequalities (8)–(10) and (11)–(13) are for preventing invalid machining sequences. $P_{jvS_{n_j}\cdots S_1 dt}$ which stands for the machining time of the MPS specified by $x_{jvS_{n_j}\cdots S_1 dt}$ is calculated in advance and is set to a huge value if the machining is infeasible. Equation (14) including $P_{jvS_{n_j}\cdots S_1 dt}$ merges the CAPP problem with the scheduling problem whose constraints are given by Eq. (15) and inequalities (16)–(18).

$$\text{minimize:} \ \max_{j,p,m,\delta} \{\delta \cdot z_{jpm\delta}\} \tag{3}$$

subject to:

$$\sum_{v=1}^{V} \sum_{S_1=1}^{n} \sum_{d=1}^{6} \sum_{t=1}^{T} x_{jv0\cdots0S_1 dt} = 1, \ \forall j \in \mathcal{J} \tag{4}$$

$$\vdots$$

$$\sum_{v=1}^{V} \sum_{\substack{S_n=1 \\ S_n \neq S_{n-1}, \cdots S_1}}^{n} \cdots \sum_{\substack{S_2=1 \\ S_2 \neq S_1}}^{n} \sum_{S_1=1}^{n} \sum_{d=1}^{6} \sum_{t=1}^{T} x_{jvS_n\cdots S_2 S_1 dt} = 1, \ \forall j \in \mathcal{J} \tag{5}$$

$$\sum_{v=1}^{V} \sum_{S_1=1}^{n} \sum_{d=1}^{6} \sum_{t=1}^{T} x_{jv0\cdots0S_1 dt} \leq 1, \ \forall j \in \mathcal{J} \tag{6}$$

$$\vdots$$

$$\sum_{v=1}^{V}\sum_{S_n=1}^{n}\cdots\sum_{S_2=1}^{n}\sum_{S_1=1}^{n}\sum_{d=1}^{6}\sum_{t=1}^{T}x_{jvS_n\cdots S_2S_1dt}\leq 1,\ \forall j\in\mathcal{J} \tag{7}$$

$$\sum_{d=1}^{6}\sum_{t=1}^{T}\left(x_{jv0\cdots 0S_1dt}+\sum_{S_k=1}^{n}\cdots\sum_{\substack{\tilde{S}_1=1\\ \tilde{S}_1\neq S_1}}^{n}x_{jv0\cdots 0S_k\cdots\tilde{S}_1dt}\right)\leq 1,$$
$$\forall k\in\mathcal{N}\backslash\{1\},\ \forall j\in\mathcal{J},\ \forall v\in\mathcal{V},\ \forall S_1\in\mathcal{N} \tag{8}$$

$$\sum_{S_1=1}^{n}\sum_{d=1}^{6}\sum_{t=1}^{T}\left(x_{jv0\cdots 0S_2S_1dt}+\sum_{S_k=1}^{n}\cdots\sum_{\substack{\tilde{S}_2=1\\ \tilde{S}_2\neq S_2}}^{n}x_{jv0\cdots 0S_k\cdots\tilde{S}_2S_1dt}\right)\leq 1,$$
$$\forall k\in\mathcal{N}\backslash\{1,2\},\ \forall j\in\mathcal{J},\ \forall v\in\mathcal{V},\ \forall S_2\in\mathcal{N} \tag{9}$$

$$\vdots$$

$$\sum_{S_{n-2}=1}^{n}\cdots\sum_{S_1=1}^{n}\sum_{d=1}^{6}\sum_{t=1}^{T}\left(x_{jv0S_{n-1}\cdots S_1dt}+\sum_{S_n=1}^{n}\sum_{\substack{\tilde{S}_{n-1}=1\\ \tilde{S}_{n-1}\neq S_{n-1}}}^{n}x_{jvS_n\tilde{S}_{n-1}S_{n-2}\cdots S_1dt}\right)$$
$$\leq 1,\ \forall j\in\mathcal{J},\ \forall v\in\mathcal{V},\ \forall S_{n-1}\in\mathcal{N} \tag{10}$$

$$\sum_{S_1=1}^{n}\sum_{d=1}^{6}\sum_{t=1}^{T}\left(x_{jv0\cdots 0S_1dt}+\sum_{\substack{\tilde{v}=1\\ \tilde{v}\neq v}}^{V}\sum_{S_2=1}^{n}x_{j\tilde{v}0\cdots 0S_2S_1dt}\right)\leq 1,\ \forall j\in\mathcal{J},\ \forall v\in\mathcal{V} \tag{11}$$

$$\sum_{S_1=1}^{n}\sum_{d=1}^{6}\sum_{t=1}^{T}\left(x_{jv0\cdots 0S_1dt}+\sum_{\substack{\tilde{v}=1\\ \tilde{v}\neq v}}^{V}\sum_{S_3=1}^{n}\sum_{S_2=1}^{n}x_{j\tilde{v}0\cdots 0S_2S_1dt}\right)\leq 1,$$
$$\forall j\in\mathcal{J},\ \forall v\in\mathcal{V} \tag{12}$$

$$\vdots$$

$$\sum_{S_1=1}^{n}\sum_{d=1}^{6}\sum_{t=1}^{T}\left(x_{jv0\cdots 0S_1dt}+\sum_{\substack{\tilde{v}=1\\ \tilde{v}\neq v}}^{V}\sum_{S_n=1}^{n}\cdots\sum_{S_3=1}^{n}\sum_{S_2=1}^{n}x_{j\tilde{v}0\cdots 0S_2S_1dt}\right)\leq 1,$$
$$\forall j\in\mathcal{J},\ \forall v\in\mathcal{V} \tag{13}$$

$$\sum_{\delta=1}^{\Delta}z_{jpm\delta}=\sum_{v=1}^{V}\sum_{S_p=1}^{n}\cdots\sum_{S_1=1}^{n}\sum_{d=1}^{6}\sum_{t\in T_m}P_{jv0\cdots 0S_p\cdots S_1dt}x_{jv0\cdots 0S_p\cdots S_1dt},$$
$$\forall j\in\mathcal{J},\ \forall p\in\{1,\ldots,n_j\},\ \forall m\in\mathcal{M} \tag{14}$$

$$\tau_{jp} = \sum_{\delta=1}^{\Delta} \sum_{m=1}^{M} z_{jpm\delta}, \ \forall j \in \mathcal{J}, \ \forall p \in \{1, \dots, n_j\} \tag{15}$$

$$\frac{1}{2} \sum_{\delta=1}^{\Delta-1} \sum_{m=1}^{M} \delta \left| z_{j(p+1)m(\delta+1)} - z_{j(p+1)m\delta} \right| - \frac{\tau_{j(p+1)}}{2} + 1$$

$$\geq \frac{1}{2} \sum_{\delta=1}^{\Delta-1} \sum_{m=1}^{M} \delta \left| z_{jpm(\delta+1)} - z_{jpm\delta} \right| + \frac{\tau_{jp}}{2}, \ \forall j \in \mathcal{J}, \ \forall p \in \{1, \dots, n_j - 1\} \tag{16}$$

$$\sum_{j=1}^{J} \sum_{p=1}^{n} z_{jpm\delta} \leq 1, \ \forall m \in \mathcal{M}, \ \forall \delta \in \{1, \dots, \Delta\} \tag{17}$$

$$\sum_{m=1}^{M} z_{jpm1} + \sum_{m=1}^{M} z_{jpm\Delta} + \sum_{m=1}^{M} \sum_{\delta=1}^{\Delta-1} \left| z_{jpm(\delta+1)} - z_{jpm\delta} \right| \leq 2,$$

$$\forall j \in \mathcal{J}, \ \forall p \in \{1, \dots, n_j\} \tag{18}$$

4   Case Study

The proposed method was applied to a very simple example, since the total number of variables is generally huge. Two products ($J = 2$) of very simple shape (Fig. 5) for which two MPS sets ($V = 2$) with two MPSs ($n_j = 2$) are generated (Fig. 6) are produced by using two machines ($M = 2$). Three tools ($T = 3$) described in Table 1 was assumed. The length of a period was set to 400[sec] to reduce the number of variables, and Δ was set to 40. The calculation was carried out with a generic workstation (Dell Precision T7400, Intel Xeon E5430 2.66 GHz, 20 GB RAM) and the optimization was performed with a commercial solver (IBM ILOG CPLEX Optimization Studio 12.6). The calculation time was 3.9[sec]. The results by the conventional and proposed methods are shown in Tables 2 and 3, respectively. Shorter makespan could be achieved by the proposed method.

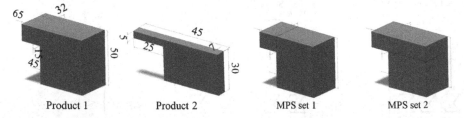

Product 1   Product 2   MPS set 1   MPS set 2

Fig. 5. TRV of assumed products. The numbers show dimensions of them in mm.

Fig. 6. MPS sets for product 1. The numbers are the identification numbers for the MPSs (MPS sets for product 2 are similar to these sets.).

Table 1. Available tools.

Tool ID	Tool type	Diameter [mm]	The number of cutting edge	Breadth of cutting edge [mm]	Machine ID
1	End mill	4	2	12	1
2	End mill	8	2	18	1
3	End mill	10	4	21	2

Table 2. Gantt chart obtained by the conventional method.

Period	1	2	3	4	5	6
Machine 1			2-2			
Machine 2	2-1	2-1	1-1	1-1	1-2	1-2

Table 3. Gantt chart obtained by the proposed method.

Period	1	2	3	4	5	6
Machine 1	2-1	2-1	2-1	1-2	1-2	
Machine 2	1-1	1-1	1-1	2-2	2-2	

5 Conclusion

The conventional flexible CAPP method has been enhanced considering total productivity in production of multiple products. Selection of the optimal process plan in the conventional method and production scheduling were integrated and formulated as a 0-1 integer programming problem. This formulation was applied to a simple example and its potential was proven. The size of the integrated problem is generally huge and the proposed method cannot be applied to a real problem. This point will be discussed in a future work.

Acknowledgement. We thank MAZAK Foundation for its financial support.

References

1. Isnaini, M.M., Shirase, K.: Review of computer-aided process planning systems for machining operation – future development of a computer-aided process planning system –. Int. J. Auto. Tech. **8**, 317–332 (2014)
2. Sanchez, L.M., Nagi, R.: A review of agile manufacturing systems. Int. J. Prod. Res. **39**, 3561–3600 (2001)
3. Nakamoto, K., Shirase, K., et al.: Automatic production planning system to achieve flexible direct machining. JSME Int. J., Ser. C **47**, 136–143 (2004)
4. Hang, G., Koike, M., et al.: Flexible Process Planning System Considering Design Intentions and Disturbance in Production Process, Mechatronics for Safety, Security and Dependability in a New Era. Elsevier, Philadelphia (2007)
5. Morinaga, E., Yamada, M., et al.: Flexible process planning for milling. Int. J. Auto. Tech. **5**, 700–707 (2011)
6. Morinaga, E., Hara, T., et al.: Improvement of computational efficiency in flexible computer-aided process planning. Int. J. Auto. Tech. **8**, 396–405 (2011)
7. Nagano, T., et al.: Expert system based on case-based reasoning to select cutting conditions (in Japanese). J. Japan Soc. Precis. Eng. **67**, 1485–1489 (2001)

Clustering Human Decision-Making in Production and Logistic Systems

Christos Tsagkalidis[1](✉), Rémy Glardon[1], and Maryam Darvish[2]

[1] Laboratory for Production Management and Processes, Swiss Federal Institute of Technology at Lausanne (EPFL), 1015 Lausanne, Switzerland
{christos.tsagkalidis,remy.glardon}@epfl.ch
[2] Faculté des Sciences de l'Administration, Université Laval, Québec, Canada
maryam.darvish.1@ulaval.ca

Abstract. Human decisions play an essential role in Operations and Supply Chain Management. However, these decisions are rarely integrated in simulation models of Production and Logistic Systems. One main reason for this fact is the strong dispersion of human decisions among a population, as well as the variability of a single individual's decision over time. This work presents an experimental study of a human decision consisting in the dynamic selection of suppliers in a well-controlled laboratory environment. The analysis of the results obtained on a large population shows that individual decision behaviors can be grouped into representative clusters typifying different decision behaviors. The results obtained from this study opens up the prospect to significantly reduce the number of decision models required to simulate Production and Logistic Systems including human decisions and could also allow categorizing human decision behavior based on a set of known criteria.

Keywords: Decision-making · Behavioral operations management · Cluster analysis

1 Introduction

A review of papers published in the field of operations management reveals that behavioral operations defined as *"the study of human behavior and cognition and their impacts on operating systems and processes"* (Gino and Pisano 2008) has gained considerable attention during the past few years. One stream of behavioral supply chain studies tries to identify the causes of instabilities within the supply chains using laboratory experiments and reveal some behavioral assumptions that are commonly held true in normative supply chain literature. Following Sterman (1989) a majority of the research on the behavioral causes of the bullwhip effect is using the Beer Distribution Game (BDG), which mimics a linear supply chain consisting of four echelons of retailer, wholesaler, distributor and factory. Studies show how the bullwhip effect could be reduced; shorter lead-times (Steckel et al. 2004), sharing point of sale data (Croson and Donohue 2003) and inventory information (Croson and Donohue 2006) have shown to be important in reducing the overall supply chain cost. The role human factors play in supply chain decision-making is also investigated; overreaction to

© IFIP International Federation for Information Processing 2015
S. Umeda et al. (Eds.): APMS 2015, Part I, IFIP AICT 459, pp. 356–364, 2015.
DOI: 10.1007/978-3-319-22756-6_44

backlogs (Oliva and Gonçalves 2005), the role of trust on the inventory replenishment decision (Kaboli et al. 2012), the role and impacts of power in distribution channels (Guru et al. 2014) are very well studied.

To understand human behavior, the research in behavioral operations tends to study the aggregated behavior; Croson and Donohue (2006) pinpoint the need for more theoretical research analyzing the behavior at the individual level but much of the literature ignores the individual differences. Furthermore, the integration of human decision behavior in simulation models cannot efficiently be performed on an individual level, without identification and modeling of representative behaviors. Accordingly, the main goal of this study is to investigate if and how individual decision-behaviors can be adequately grouped in representative clusters. To this end, a controlled experimental environment, a participatory simulation platform is implemented. More specifically, the human decision studied in this work consists in dynamically allocating the market demand to three competing supply chains in accordance with their delivery performances.

2 Experimental Procedure and Methodology

2.1 Experimental Procedure

The use of participatory simulation as the experimental framework is chosen, as it is known to provide a stable and controlled environment (Katok 2011) that allows reliable observations and eliminates most of the external perturbations (Guru et al. 2014). In this study, a participatory simulation platform developed at Université Laval, Québec, Canada, called XBG-platform, is used (Montreuil et al. 2008) which mimics the dynamics of inventory replenishment in a decentralized, linear, four echelon supply chain. The chosen experimental set-up is illustrated in Fig. 1. It is composed of three competing supply chains delivering products to a continental distributor that must satisfy the volatile market demand. The four echelons of each supply chain are operated by software agents. The human agent plays the role of the continental distributor; his/her decision consists of continuously allocating the market demand to the three supply chains. This decision is modeled by an algorithm called Demand Modulation Algorithm (DMA) that simulates the buyer's decision-making behavior by including the effects of perception, subjective judgment and memory, through a set of 11 parameters (Tsagkalidis 2014). Thus, each individual behavior can be characterized by a vector of 11 parameters (Individual Decision Behavior Vector, IDBV) acquired by best fitting the algorithm to the obtained experimental results (human agent behavior). The inputs of the

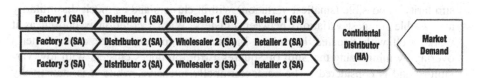

Fig. 1. Structure of the experimental set-up (SA, software agent; HA, human agent)

DMA are 3 quantitative parameters (Delivery performance, Order refusal, Order cancellation). The DMA outputs are the shares of the demand allocated to each of the three supply chains. The computation takes into account behavioral aspects such as asymmetry of the reaction to good or bad performances (i.e. gain or loss of trust in the supplier).

The experiment lasts approximately 40 min, which is equivalent to a 3.5-month business horizon. Through an experimental campaign, 278 individual results; i.e. 278 IDBVs have been acquired and stored, providing a statistically significant sample. Furthermore, information about possibly relevant individual characteristics of each human agent is also stored for later use.

The set of 278 IDBVs is used for the clustering process that aims at building groups (clusters) of individuals having similar decision behaviors within a given cluster and dissimilar between different clusters. The number of possible clusters is not defined a priori but results from the clustering process.

2.2   Methodology

The methodology consists of 4 main steps: (1) experiment with 278 individual human agents, (2) determination of the 278 IDBV through fitting of the DMA, (3) clustering of the 278 IDBV into k clusters, (4) determination of the representative behavior of each cluster (centroid coordinates) that leads to definition of k Cluster Decision Behavior Vectors (CDBV), (5) study of possible relations between clusters and individual human agent characteristics. It must be noted that the optimal number of clusters k is not known in advance.

2.3   Clustering Procedure

The clustering is conducted using SPSS (version 16) from IBM Company. The initial step is the definition of the clustering procedure. Generally two different approaches are available: hierarchical and non-hierarchical clustering. In the current case, as the number of clusters is not known beforehand and the data size is relatively small, a hierarchical, agglomerative clustering procedure is chosen. This means that the process starts by considering each individual as a single cluster and proceeds with a progressive merging process. The main steps are as follows:

- **Selection of distance measurement and clustering algorithm.** The Square Euclidian Distance criterion (Hair et al. 1995, Grimm et al. Grimm and Yarnold 2000) is chosen for similarity measurement between cases and is implemented for all variables. The Ward's method (Ward 1963) is selected as the clustering algorithm. This criterion creates clusters characterized by variables having as much similarity as possible (smallest variation) within clusters and as much dissimilarity as possible (biggest variation) between clusters. Ward's criterion is chosen as it works well with Squared Euclidean Metrics, attempts to reduce each cluster's overlay by minimizing the Sum of Squares Error, produces clusters with low variability and is considered to be computationally intensive, while it is statistically simple (Murtagh and Legendre 2014).

- **Determination of the number of clusters.** The optimal number of clusters represents a critical issue in a hierarchical, agglomerative clustering process. Two indicators are used to support the determination of the cluster number: the fussion coefficient from the agglomeration schedule and the dendrogram.
- **Output of clustering analysis.** In each cluster, each human agent is defined by the 11 parameters of the IDBV and a set of individual characteristics. The following results are finally obtained as an output of the clustering process: (1) Representative behavior of each cluster (11 centroid coordinates, CDBV), (2) Standard deviation of the 11 parameters within the cluster, (3) percentage of each individual characteristics within the cluster.

3 Results of the Clustering Analysis

As stated above, the decision behavior is characterized by the IDBV. Not all 11 parameters have the same significance concerning the clustering process; two of the parameters are constant in the DMA and four show non-significant variations among human agents. Consequently, the clustering process is based on 5 relevant parameters (see Sect. 3.1) of the IDBV.

The number of clusters that leads to a maximum value of the fussion coefficient is found to be $k = 3$ or 4. Additionally, the use of dendrogram indicates the choice of a value $k = 3$. The main characteristics of the main 3 clusters are indicated in Table 1. The CDBVs and the standard deviations of the parameters within clusters are not provided here, as their single values do not have much significance.

Table 1. Final cluster size and characteristics

Cluster	Cluster population	Population percentage
1	62	22.3 %
2	29	10.4 %
3	187	67.3 %
Total	278	100 %

3.1 Cluster Population Characteristics

Based on previous experience and the typology of the experiment participants, the population is characterized by the following criteria:

- **Master Study Field.** Table 2 indicates the frequency of the Master study field per cluster. In all 3 clusters the ratio of population not holding a master degree is still significant (13.8–21 %). Furthermore, it can be noticed that almost half of the population in cluster 1 owns a master in supply chain management, while this ratio is much lower in clusters 2 and 3. Finally, cluster 3 is singled out by a large population ratio (total 28.3 %) with Master in Business or Basic sciences, this ratio is much lower in clusters 1 and 2 (4.8 %, 13.8 %).

Table 2. Master study field

Cluster		Engineering	Life Sciences	Business and Economics	Basic Sciences	Supply Chain	None	Total
1	Count	12	4	3	0	28	13	62
	% cluster population	19.4 %	6.5 %	4.8 %	0.0 %	45.2 %	21.0 %	100.0 %
2	Count	9	0	2	2	3	4	29
	% cluster population	31.0 %	0.0 %	6.9 %	6.9 %	10.3 %	13.8 %	100.0 %
3	Count	51	10	24	29	9	29	187
	% cluster population	27.3 %	5.3 %	12.8 %	15.5 %	4.8 %	15.5 %	100.0 %
Total	Count	72	14	29	31	40	46	278
	% cluster population	25.9 %	5.0 %	10.4 %	11.2 %	14.4 %	16.5 %	100.0 %

- **Familiarity with simulation platforms.** Cluster 1 is characterized by a large population ratio having previous experience with simulation platforms in general (58.1 %) and with the XBG-platform in particular (24.2 %) as shown in Table 3. On the contrary, the ratio of the population with general simulation platform experience drops too much lower values in clusters 2 and 3 (17.2 %, 20.9 %) and the ratio with XBG-experience is even lower (3.4 %, 5.9 %).

Table 3. Familiarity with simulation platforms in general and XBG in particular

Cluster		Familiarity with simulation platform in general		Familiarity with XBG-simulation platform		Total
		Yes	No	Yes	No	
1	Count	36	26	15	13	62
	% cluster population	58.1 %	41.9 %	24.2 %	21.0 %	100.0 %
2	Count	5	24	1	11	29
	% cluster population	17.2 %	82.8 %	3.4 %	37.9 %	100.0 %
3	Count	39	148	11	88	187
	% cluster population	20.9 %	79.1 %	5.9 %	47.1 %	100.0 %
Total	Count	80	198	27	112	278
	% cluster population	28.8 %	71.2 %	9.7 %	40.3 %	100.0 %

- **Acquaintance with supply chain management.** Participants' prior knowledge of SCM is considered important, as due to the experimental set-up, phenomena typical of supply chains are expected. The results presented in Table 4 reveal that the highest population ratio with SCM experience is to be found in cluster 1 (75.8 %) and the lowest in cluster 3 (50.8 %), cluster 3 being close to cluster 2 (55.2 %).

Table 4. Acquaintance with supply chain management

Cluster		Familiarity with supply chain management		Total
		Yes	No	
1	Count	47	15	62
	% cluster population	75.8 %	24.2 %	100.0 %
2	Count	16	13	29
	% cluster population	55.2 %	44.8 %	100.0 %
3	Count	95	92	187
	% cluster population	50.8 %	49.2 %	100.0 %
Total	Count	158	120	278
	% cluster population	56.8 %	43.2 %	100.0 %

Table 5. Working experience in general and in logistics or procurement in particular

Cluster		Working experience in general (years)			Working experience in logistics and procurement			Total
		None	1–5	>5	None	1–5	>5	
1	Count	15	30	17	27	26	9	62
	% cluster population	24.2 %	48.4 %	27.4 %	43.5 %	41.9 %	14.5 %	100.0 %
2	Count	5	15	9	18	6	5	29
	% cluster population	17.2 %	51.7 %	31.0 %	62.1 %	20.7 %	17.2 %	100.0 %
3	Count	48	107	32	143	22	22	187
	% cluster population	25.7 %	57.2 %	17.1 %	76.5 %	11.8 %	11.8 %	100.0 %
Total	Count	68	152	58	188	54	36	278
	% cluster population	24.5 %	54.7 %	20.9 %	67.6 %	19.4 %	12.9 %	100.0 %

- **Working experience.** As shown in Table 5, roughly 25 % of the population in clusters 1 and 3 has no working experience, while this ratio is lower for cluster 2 (17.2 %). However, cluster 1 is also characterized by the lowest population ratio (43.5 %) without any specific working experience in logistics and procurement; this ratio is the highest for cluster 3 (76.5 %). About specific working experience in logistics or procurement, the difference between the three clusters becomes more evident. Cluster 1 presents the highest population ratio with experience (total 56.4 %), cluster 2 a medium value (37.9 %), and cluster 3 the lowest ratio (total 23.6 %).

Table 6. Synthesis of the cluster population characteristics

		Cluster 1	Cluster 2	Cluster 3
Cluster Population		62	29	187
a) Master study field	Engineering	L	H	
	Business & Economics	L		H
	Supply Chain	H		L
	None	H	L	
b) & c) Familiarity with simulation platforms	In general	H	L	
	XBG platform	H	L	
d) Familiarity with SCM	yes	H		L
e) & f) Working experience	In general		H	L
	Logistics & procurement	H		L
Lowest population ratio	L			
Highest population ratio	H			

3.2   Cluster Population, Synthesis

The main features of the three clusters are summarized in Table 6, according to the most significant population characteristics described above. These results indicate that cluster 1 contains a medium size population (62 members) with the strongest background in SCM, logistics and simulation. Thus, it groups the participants with the closest and strongest knowledge about decision-making issues in Supply Chain. Cluster 2, with the smallest population (29 members) is characterized by the largest population ratio with background in engineering and general working experience. Finally, cluster 3 is by far the largest with 67.3 % of the total population (187 members). It is characterized by the least familiarity with SCM professional experience and the largest population ratio with a business and economics education.

4   Discussions and Conclusion

The objective of this work is to study the possibility of grouping human decision-behavior in clusters to simplify the integration of decision-making processes in Supply Chain simulation models. The human decision investigated in this work continuously allocates the market demand to 3 competing supply chains. An experimental campaign is performed using a participatory simulation platform with continuous time scale. The experiment is run with a statistically significant sample of 278 human participants.

Each human decision-maker (agent) is characterized using a vector (IDBV) of 11 parameters obtained by best fitting a decision algorithm developed in a previous study (Tsagkalidis 2014). These experimental results (3058 single values) constitute the database used for a clustering process that aims at identifying typical and representative decision-behaviors. A hierarchical clustering procedure that uses the Square Euclidian Distance criterion as similarity measurement is chosen. Clustering is performed according to Ward's clustering algorithm.

A solution with three clusters arises from the clustering process. They are characterrized by their population size and their centroid, an 11-parameter vector called Cluster Behavior Decision Vector (CDBV) that represents the average decision-behavior of the cluster population.

Each human agent is further described by a set of individual characteristics. A first attempt at identifying links between clusters, i.e. typical decision-behavior, and individual characteristics leads to some preliminary conclusions. They show in particular that previous knowledge and experience in Supply Chain Management appears to have a significant influence on the decision-making behavior. Similarly, an engineering education with no professional experience seems to lead to another specific decision behavior. According to the current results, these two categories appear to build specific groups that single out from the majority of participants characterized by low professional experience and no or weak previous knowledge in SCM.

A further extension of this work is to study how experience influences the decision process as previous limited observations seem to indicate a more random and nervous reactions from less experienced people. The relations between cluster average decision behavior (CDBV) and financial performances in the experiment would also bring interesting conclusions concerning a possible economically optimal decision behavior. Finally finding possible links between individual characteristics and decision behavior constitutes the ultimate goal of this general field of research. Once these relations are identified, they could be validated by reversing the experiment; i.e. by selecting participants belonging a priori to a cluster and verifying if they do behave according to the expectations.

References

Croson, R., Donohue, K.: Impact of POS data sharing on supply chain management: an experimental study. Prod. Oper. Manage. **12**, 1–11 (2003)

Croson, R., Donohue, K.: Behavioral causes of the bullwhip effect and the observed value of inventory information. Manage. Sci. **52**, 323–336 (2006)

Guru, R.R.D., Kaboli, A., Glardon, R.: The effect of coercive power on supply chain inventory replenishment decisions. In: Grabot, B., Vallespir, B., Gomes, S., Bouras, A., Kiritsis, D. (eds.) Advances in Production Management Systems, Part II. IFIP AICT, vol. 439, pp. 230–237. Springer, Heidelberg (2014)

Hair, J., Joseph, F., Anderson, E., Tatham, R., Ronald, L., Black, W.C.: Multivariate Data Analysis: With Readings, 4th edn. Prentice-Hall Inc, Upper Saddle River (1995)

Gino, F., Pisano, G.: Toward a theory of behavioral operations. Manuf. Serv. Oper. Manage. **10**, 676–691 (2008)

Grimm, L.G., Yarnold, P.R.: Reading and Understanding More Multivariate Statistics. American Psychological Association, Washington (2000)

Kaboli, A., Cheikhrouhou, N., Darvish, M., Glardon, R.: An experimental study of the relationship between trust and inventory replenishment in triadic supply chain. In: Proceedings of the POMS World Conference (2012)

Katok, E.: Using laboratory experiments to build better operations management models. Found. Trends Technol. Inf. Oper. Manage. **5**(1), 1–86 (2011)

Murtagh, F., Legendre, P.: Ward's hierarchical agglomerative clustering method: which algorithms implement ward's criterion? J. Classif. **31**(3), 274–295 (2014)

Oliva, R., Gonçalves, P.: Behavioral causes of demand amplification in sypply chains: "satisficing" policies with limited information cues. In: Proceedings of the 2005 System Dynamics Conference, pp. 118–119 (2005)

Steckel, J.H., Gupta, S., Banerji, A.: Supply chain decision making: will shorter cycle times and shared point-of-sale information necessarily help? Manage. Sci. **50**, 458–464 (2004)

Sterman, J.D.: Modeling managerial behavior: misperceptions of feedback in a dynamic decision making experiment. Manage. Sci. **35**, 321–339 (1989)

Tsagkalidis, C.: Study of human decision behavior for the operational selection of suppliers in a competitive framework using a participatory simulation platform. Master Thesis, EPFL (March 2014)

Ward, J.H.: Hierarchical grouping to optimize an objective function. J. Am. Stat. Assoc. **58**(301), 236–244 (1963)

Standardization, Commonality, Modularity:
A Global Economic Perspective

Clément Chatras[1] and Vincent Giard[2(✉)]

[1] Renault S.A.S., Technocentre, 1 avenue du Golf, F78084 Guyancourt, France
clement.chatras@renault.com
[2] PSL, Paris-Dauphine University, LAMSADE-UMR 7243 Place
de Lattre de Tassigny, Paris, France
vincent.giard@dauphine.fr

Abstract. This paper deals with the problem of simultaneous standardization of a set of modules and of multiple sets of components that may be combined in these modules. The aim is to minimize future costs. The components and modules, whether already existing or yet to be created are not related to pre-determined BOMs. The problem takes into account coupling constraints between components because not all components included in a module may be coupled (coupling restriction), although some of the restrictions can be lifted through "junction components". Our approach is readily implemented and significantly improves decisional consistency when compared to the standardization approaches that deal with the problem in isolation as opposed to globally. It also matches the level of detail used in large organizations for forecasting purposes. This approach is illustrated with a real case study of great dimension.

Keywords: Standardization · Management of diversity · Optimization · Product design · BOM definition

1 Introduction

Standardization is a process aiming to rationalize the definition of a set of components with different functional features that are used to satisfy a number of needs of similar nature (Rutenberg 1971, Fisher et al. 1999, Dupont and Cormier 2001, Perera et al. 1999, Baud-Lavigne et al. 2012…). We call these components 'alternative components (ACs)' and related sets 'set of alternative components (SAC)'. In general, when this process is in place, a SAC already exists and can be completed by a set of components that are still in the pre-development, study phase. The functional features of the related ACs are of the same nature as that which currently define the needs to which demand is associated. The proposed rationalization exercise generally results in reducing the number of components as well as the expenses committed to satisfy the needs. Standardization, therefore, is key to improving competitive advantage, particularly in the context of mass production. In practice, the combination of different SACs is limited by technical restrictions that affect the efficiency of models that standardize each SAC separately. We propose a solution to lift some of these restrictions and the related interfacing issues between two ACs through what we call "junction components".

© IFIP International Federation for Information Processing 2015
S. Umeda et al. (Eds.): APMS 2015, Part I, IFIP AICT 459, pp. 365–375, 2015.
DOI: 10.1007/978-3-319-22756-6_45

Modules are particular components that combine elementary ACs belonging to multiple SACs. Modules may exist physically and be delivered to an assembly plant, or virtual and be set up at the production line. Standardization, therefore, can occur at module level, with "alternative modules (AMs)" being selected from a set of AMs (SAM). The modules match needs that we call "services" while the different kinds of needs are called "alternative services (ASs)". These represent the diversity of combinations of functions delivered to customers via such devices as web configurators. The set of ASs must be covered by the relevant SAM. By introducing modules one is able to use the sales forecasts usually prepared at AS, aggregated level. This level of aggregation moreover is adequate to make reliable forecasts down to AC level, where most of the cost saving opportunities are.

A particular AC can be mounted on several AMs, thus creating a commonality, from which valuable economies of scale may be derived. In this context, standardization must be handled jointly at AM and AC level, it being understood that AC demand stems from demand for the relevant AMs. This aspect is all the more valuable as demand forecasts may be limited to an aggregate level and as, in the approach we use, the BOMs for the AMs remain to be defined. The simultaneous optimization of SAM and component SACs standardization is the first contribution of our paper. Its other contribution relates to the cost savings opportunity. We shall show that the cost-benefit analysis enabled by the model covers both the time horizon and spatial dimensions.

Our paper opens with a review of literature on standardization as circumscribed to the relevant scope (Sect. 2). This shall highlight a number of gaps that our model proposes to close. The next section shall present our model which builds on the work described in the literature we reviewed and enables a simultaneous standardization of AMs and their component ACs to be performed (Sect. 3). We end the paper with a quantified case study and a conclusion.

2 Literature Review

Our article is geared to standardization models and we therefore reviewed papers proposing prescriptive methods to reduce diversity. Accordingly, our analysis excludes both papers dealing with diversity management methods as well as descriptive papers (Martin and Ishii 2002; Fonte 1994; Sered and Reich 2006; Perera et al. 1999).

We reviewed research into ways of standardizing components, modules or both. Our definition of modules is compatible with that expounded in the body of reference literature (Ulrich 1995; Sanchez and Mahoney 1996; Baldwin and Clark 1997; Dahmus et al. 2001...). We are not seeking to define an optimal modular architecture, a matter we consider settled, but rather to define AM diversity in a way that is relevant for any particular SAM. We found two distinct approaches in the prescriptive research surveyed.

- That of the school of research focusing on postponed differentiation. Here, the set of SACs and their ACs is known and the question is to find the optimal level of AM diversity (where AMs are seen as groups of components) to be managed

(Swaminathan and Tayur 1998; Agard and Tollenaere 2002; Rai and Allada 2003; Agard and Penz 2009; Baud-Lavigne et al. 2012; Agard and Bassetto 2013). These papers address quality and assembly time rather than cost reduction issues. In this case, the make-up of SACs used to build the modules is predetermined and not open to amendment through introduction of new ACs. This approach therefore appears to be quite remote from the multi-level standardization approach we chose.

- In the second school of research, that founded by Renard (1973), the starting point is a set of needs and of a set of components suitable to meet them. Here, the onus is on determining the corresponding diversity at the lowest cost for this set to be used and therefore produced (Rutenberg 1971; Dupont and Cormier 2001; Fisher et al. 1999; Lamothe et al. 2006; Giard 1999, 2001; Chatras and Giard 2014). This question can be posed at any phase of the life cycle of a product or set of products. Here, the aim is to find the best compromise between the cost of excessively diverse solutions tuned to a wide variety of needs and the cost of a single, over-performing solution, capable of meeting all needs. The definition of a SAC is sometimes implicit in the literature (Rutenberg 1971; Dupont and Cormier 2001; Lamothe et al. 2006) as it is not linked to the definition of any function used to define needs and components. Where the SAC is explicit, it is defined either through a single function (Renard 1973; Fisher et al. 1999) or through several functions (Giard 1999, 2001). From an operational standpoint it is clear that defining components through multiple functions is both more efficient for analytical purposes and for the purposes of defining the input data for the optimization model.

Some authors on standardization as it is defined in our introduction have attempted to standardize several interdependent SACs simultaneously (Rutenberg 1971; Dupont and Cormier 2001; Lamothe et al. 2006). But they did not propose to introduce "junction components" to lift some of the coupling restrictions and so further streamline costs. Moreover, none of these articles include a simultaneous analysis of standardization at two levels of the BOM to deal with the overall diversity of a SAM and of its component SACs as the first step of an approach that can have several levels. The approach that we develop aims to fill the gap through a model readily useable by business actors to directly and easily integrate all of the technical constraints and junction components capable of lifting some of them.

The determination of demand through ACs is a major stake for the model as it is crucial to the solution (Fisher et al. 1999; Baud-Lavigne et al. 2012). Approaches that fail to take demand into account in the target function thus appear not to be entirely relevant from an economic standpoint (Renard 1973; Agard and Tollenaere 2002; Agard and Penz 2009). All of the other approaches rely on volume or percentage by type of need. Our model improves the definition of demand used for economic analysis in three important respects: first by lending consistency to the demand to be satisfied by the AMs and the ACs without reference to any predetermined BOM. Here the BOM actually stems from the optimization exercise. Second, recourse to modules uses an aggregate level of forecasting similar to that produced by sales departments. Third but not least, not only does it take into account demand but also demand change and life cycle dynamics as well as the emergence of new future needs.

Additionally, the fact that the model is capable of integrating the time horizon, an essential feature of strategic choices, enables it to account for both existing and future needs (Fisher et al. 1999). Our recommendation diverges slightly from that by Lamothe et al. (2006) (only paper to have explicitly taken time into account in the target function). To conclude this literature review, we note that our approach is in line with part of the body of research and introduces a number of substantial improvements.

3   Formulation of the Standardization Problem

Our description of the problem is a two-stage process. We begin by a quick analysis (Sect. 3.1) of the models our approach actually extends. This will enable us to discuss a few important concepts as well as introduce our analytical approach. We go on (Sect. 3.2) to fully develop our model against a general context. One can find a table of notations by using the link in Sect. 4.

3.1   The Single SAC Standardization Model

Renard (1973) appears to be the first author to have streamlined the number of ACs required to meet multiple demands. A single functional characteristic f is used to specify the need to be satisfied by an AC and a single technical characteristic q of the AC is taken into account; in the case studied by Renard, q is the diameter of cable and f is the maximum traction the cable can sustain before breaking. Through an experimental study, f is described by a monotonous increasing function of q. Renard proposes to define variety arbitrarily, by breaking up the possible values for f into a fixed number of ranges whose upper limits are subject to geometrical growth. One may criticize this approach in three respects, all of which are actual shortcomings of a number of current ISO standards: it uses a single functional characteristic of continuous nature; one has no reason to determine a priori the optimal number of ACs; the definition of the number of ranges and their boundaries is not based on any economic criteria since demand and costs are not part of the reasoning.

An explicit reference to several functional features and economic criteria is proposed by Giard (1999, 2001). The selected features may be quantitative (weight, torque...) or qualitative (reference to a standard...). Table R cross-referencing ACs ($c = 1..C$) and functional features ($f = 1..F$) of these ACs, either existing or under study can be drawn up, with item R_{fc} corresponding either to a numeric value or to a qualitative attribute (see tables below). The inclusion of ACs in the study phase refers to a perception of future needs, useful in substantiating the conclusions of the selection process. In order to harmonize the terminology used, we consider in this paragraph that an AS is directly satisfied by an AC, since we consider a single BOM level. To each AS s ($s = 1..S$) is associated demand d_p, these ASs actually corresponding to the breakdown of demand. An AS is satisfied by a single AC, which is justified in the absence of production constraints, by the fact that we should use the most cost-efficient AC to satisfy an AS, with any mix leading to a cost increase. On the other hand, an AC can satisfy several ASs. The analysis of these ASs is based on the same functional AC features with quantitative features corresponding to value ranges and qualitative features to the list of acceptable attributes. Table S describes ($\rightarrow S_{sf}$) the conditions for AC eligibility. The combination of tables R and S information serves to draw up the table of Booleans A indicating whether the AC c meets ($A_{cs} = 1$) or not ($A_{cs} = 0$) the specifications of AS s. To optimize the selection of the ACs to be used, we introduce binary variable $x_{cs} = 1$ if AC c is used to satisfy service s; and of course, this variable is only relevant where $A_{cs} = 1$. The constraint $\sum_c x_{cs} = 1$ guarantees that each AS shall be satisfied by a single AC. Total AC c demand is written $\sum_s d_s \cdot x_{cs}$. The function of cost to be kept down refers to AC production costs. If one only uses direct variable costs w_c, the target function is $\sum_c w_c \cdot \sum_s d_s \cdot x_{cs}$ The cost function developed by Giard (1999, 2001) in this formulation of the problem is more complex: it is a monotonous increasing function, which is partly linear. This enables the inclusion of new AC study and investment fixed costs stemming from development of new CAs while in their pre-launch, study phase. It also enables the inclusion of any positive or negative synergy effects induced by production of several ACs at a particular site (Table 1).

Table 1. Example of functional definition of 10 ACs, 14 ASs and the Boolean matrix resulting from the cross-referencing of these definitions

R_{fc} — Actual functional characteristic f

	$f=1$ Power (hp DIN)	$f=2$ Climate 1:Temp 2:Cold	$f=3$ CO$_2$ (g/km)	$f=4$ Wheight (in kg)	$f=F=5$ Euro.X
$c=1$	75	1	90	160	5
$c=2$	90	1	105	160	5
$c=3$	90	1	90	160	6
$c=4$	110	1	110	170	5
$c=5$	110	2	110	170	5
$c=6$	120	2	110	170	5
$c=7$	130	1	120	200	5
$c=8$	150	1	160	180	5
$c=9$	130	2	140	200	5
$c=C=10$	130	2	120	170	6

S_{pf} — Required functional characteristic f

	$f=1$ Power (hp DIN)	$f=2$ Climate 1:Temp 2:Cold	$f=3$ CO$_2$ (g/km)	$f=4$ Wheight (in kg)	$f=F=5$ Euro.X	Demand (10^3)
$p=1$	≥ 65	1	≤ 92	≤ 163	≥ 5	60
$p=2$	≥ 80	1	≤ 107	≤ 160	≥ 4	40
$p=3$	≥ 90	1	≤ 108	≤ 171	≥ 5	20
$p=4$	≥ 90	1	≤ 93	≤ 160	≥ 6	20
$p=5$	≥ 90	1	≤ 104	≤ 170	≥ 6	90
$p=6$	≥ 105	1	≤ 115	≤ 175	≥ 5	52
$p=7$	≥ 110	1	≤ 110	≤ 186	≥ 5	49
$p=8$	≥ 110	2	≤ 135	≤ 200	≥ 4	8
$p=9$	≥ 115	1	≤ 143	≤ 185	≥ 4	40
$p=10$	≥ 115	1	≤ 125	≤ 205	≥ 5	12
$p=11$	≥ 130	1	≤ 150	≤ 200	≥ 5	5
$p=12$	≥ 150	1	≤ 160	≤ 180	≥ 4	92
$p=13$	≥ 130	2	≤ 185	≤ 220	≥ 4	26
$p=P=14$	≥ 130	1	≤ 125	≤ 170	≥ 6	2

A_{cp} — Alternative Component

	$c=1$	$c=2$	$c=3$	$c=4$	$c=5$	$c=6$	$c=7$	$c=8$	$c=9$	$c=C=10$
$p=1$	1	1								
$p=2$		1	1							
$p=3$		1	1							
$p=4$			1							
$p=5$	1									
$p=6$				1	1	1	1			
$p=7$				1	1	1				
$p=8$					1	1				1
$p=9$						1				1
$p=10$							1	1		1
$p=11$								1	1	1
$p=12$								1		
$p=13$									1	1
$p=P=14$										1

This approach, however, present three important limitations that we address under Sect. 3.2: first the SACs are supposed to be independent but this is not realistic (Chatras and Giard 2014); moreover, defining needs and, therefore, demand at component level is very difficult in practice; finally, these approaches largely ignore the spatial (logistical chain) and temporal aspects (demand change and possible launch of new components) in the cost function.

3.2 Formulation of Joint Standardization of a SAM and Its Component SACs

The originality of our extended model lies in the simultaneous selection of AMs and their component ACs to satisfy the requirements of a set of ASs. In our proposed model, Boolean variables are linked to these decisions (Sect. 3.2.1). The way in which both the time horizon and spatial dimensions are factored into the coefficients of the target function is described under Sect. 3.2.2 below.

3.2.1   The Basic Model

Our formulation uses four kinds of sets: ASs, ACs and SACs complemented by another set, discussed below, so as to include the junction components required to couple two ACs from two different sets in the absence of any suitable interface.

- The set of *alternative services* includes S ASs, subscripted by s. d_s is the Demand for service s.
- The set of *alternative modules* includes **M** AMs, subscripted by m. Some AMs may not meet the needs of some ASs. The Boolean parameter a_{sm} takes a value of 1 where AM m is suitable to meet demand for AS s, and the value 0, if it does not. An AM may satisfy several ASs. Since the needs for an AS are met by a single AM, the number of AMs selected in the solution cannot exceed S. The fixed cost f_m corresponding to the development and investment expenditure for the selected AM m is then added to the formula as well as its direct variable production cost, g_m.
- One distinguishes **K** sets of *alternative components* (SACs), subscripted by k ($k = 1..K$). SAC k includes C_k alternative components ($c_k = 1..C_k$). The choice of AC c_k from SAC k is associated to a fixed cost $w_{c_k}^k$, corresponding to development and investment expenditure, plus direct variable production cost $v_{c_k}^k$. Where one has to factor in two SACs simultaneously, subscripts k_1 and k_2 are used. An AM always includes an AC drawn from each SAC. The same AC can be mounted in multiple AMs and some ACs cannot be mounted on certain AMs. The Boolean parameter $b_{mc_k}^k$ takes a value of 1 where AM m can comprise AC c_k from the SAC, and 0, if it does not.

Let x_{sm} be a *decision variable* that corresponds to the demand for the AM m selected for the purpose of the AS s. This variable is only utilized if AS s can be provided through module m ($\rightarrow a_{sm} = 1$). Service s is met by an AM, as enforced by constraint (1).

$$\sum_{m=1}^{m=M} x_{sm} = d_s, \forall s = 1..S \tag{1}$$

The demand for module m, possibly null, is $\sum_{s=1}^{s=S} x_{sm}$. It is then useful to create *auxiliary variable* $y_m = 1$ if AM m is chosen. This binary variable is related to the decision variables x_{sm} by constraint (2) in which constant Ω is a big value (for example $\Omega = \sum_{s=1}^{s=S} d_s$). Constraint (2) is sufficient because the cost function to be minimized integrates variable y_m, weighted by fixed cost g_m.

$$\sum_{s=1}^{s=S} x_{sm} \leq \Omega \cdot y_m, \forall m = 1..M \tag{2}$$

Let $u_{mc_k}^k$ be a *decision variable* that corresponds to the demand for AC c_k from SAC k used to produce the AM m. This variable is only utilized if AC c_k can be assembled in module m $(\rightarrow b_{mc_k}^k = 1)$. The total demand for AC c_k from SAC k, possibly null, is noted $\sum_{m=1}^{m=M} u_{mc_k}^k$. The relation (3) enforces that module m is composed of one AC from each SAC and that demand for each AC from AM m is equal to the total demand for m.

$$\sum_{c_k=1}^{c_k=C_k} u_{mc_k}^k = \sum_{s=1}^{s=S} x_{sm}, \forall m = 1..M, \forall k = 1..K \qquad (3)$$

One must create *auxiliary variable* $v_{mc_k}^k = 1$ if AC c_k from SAC k is chosen for module m. This binary variable is related to the decision variables $u_{mc_k}^k$ by constraint (4). The constraint [5] enforces that the AM m uses only one AC from each SAC.

$$u_{mc_k}^k \leq \Omega \cdot v_{mc_k}^k, \forall m = 1..M, \forall k = 1..K, \forall c_k = 1..C_k \qquad (4)$$

$$\sum_{c_k=1}^{c_k=C_k} v_{mc_k}^k = y_m, \forall m = 1..M, \forall k = 1..K \qquad (5)$$

One must introduce a second *auxiliary variable* $s_{c_k}^k = 1$ if AC c_k from SAC k is chosen for one or several modules. This binary variable is related to the decision variables $u_{mc_k}^k$ by constraint (6). This constraint is sufficient because the cost function to be minimized integrates variable $s_{c_k}^k$, weighted by fixed cost $w_{c_k}^k$.

$$\sum_{m=1}^{m=M} u_{mc_k}^k \leq \Omega \cdot s_{c_k}^k, \forall k = 1..K, \forall c_k = 1..C_k \qquad (6)$$

The above formulation rests on the implicit assumption that there is no constraint on possible combinations of ACs assembled in a module. It is, however, possible that ACs c_{k_1} and c_{k_2} belonging to SACs k_1 and k_2 cannot be assembled in the same module, in particular for reasons of interfacing. In this case, the Boolean parameter $\lambda_{c_{k_1} c_{k_2}}^{k_1 \wedge k_2} = 1$ is used to represent this coupling restriction; alternatively it will be = 0. This leads to creation of the Boolean matrix $\Lambda^{k_1 \wedge k_2}$ for each couple of SACs whose ACs can be interfaced. This restriction results in the introduction of constraint (7) to deal with cases of incompatibility.

$$u_{mc_{k_1}}^{k_1} + u_{mc_{k_2}}^{k_2} \leq \sum_{s=1}^{s=S} x_{sm}$$
$$\forall m = 1..M, \forall k_1 = 1..K, \forall k_2 = 1..K/k_2 \neq k_1 \wedge \lambda_{c_{k_1} c_{k_2}}^{k_1 \wedge k_2} = 1, \forall c_{k_1} = 1..C_{k_1}, \forall c_{k_2} = 1..C_{k_2}$$
$$(7)$$

In some cases, impossibility of coupling ACs c_{k_1} and c_{k_2} belonging to SACs k_1 and k_2 may be lifted through a junction component whose impact in the target function is fixed cost $\theta_{c_{k_1} c_{k_2}}^{k_1 \wedge k_2}$ and direct variable production cost $\eta_{c_{k_1} c_{k_2}}^{k_1 \wedge k_2}$. This situation is expressed by the Boolean parameter $\gamma_{c_{k_1} c_{k_2}}^{k_1 \wedge k_2} = 1$, or 0 in the absence of a junction component coupling ACs c_{k_1} and c_{k_2}. This leads to the use of Boolean matrices $\Gamma^{k_1 \wedge k_2}$ in addition to matrices $\Lambda^{k_1 \wedge k_2}$. These matrices are such as $\gamma_{c_{k_1} c_{k_2}}^{k_1 \wedge k_2} \leq \lambda_{c_{k_1} c_{k_2}}^{k_1 \wedge k_2}$, the junction components lifting the coupling prohibition. One then introduces *decision variable* $\pi^{k_1 \wedge k_2}_{mc_{k_1} c_{k_2}}$ standing for the demand for junction component to lift the coupling prohibition of ACs c_{k_1} and c_{k_2} belonging to SACs k_1 and k_2 for the purposes of module m. This variable is used only where $\gamma^{k_1 \wedge k_2}_{c_{k_1} c_{k_2}} = 1$. In order to force $\pi^{k_1 \wedge k_2}_{mc_{k_1} c_{k_2}}$ to be equal to the demand for module m if ACs c_{k_1} and c_{k_2} are selected, we introduce constraint (8), dedicated to coupling incompatibilities. The total demand of this junction component is noted $\sum_{m=1}^{m=M} \pi^{k_1 \wedge k_2}_{mc_{k_1} c_{k_2}}$. And constraints (7) is to be replaced by constraint (9).

$$u^{k_1}_{mc_{k_1}} + u^{k_2}_{mc_{k_2}} \leq \sum_{s=1}^{s=S} x_{sm} + \pi^{k_1 \wedge k_2}_{mc_{k_1} c_{k_2}}$$

$$\forall m = 1..M, \forall k_1 = 1..K, \forall k_2 = 1..K, \forall c_{k_1} = 1..C_{k_1}, \forall c_{k_2} = 1..C_{k_2}/k_2 \neq k_1 \wedge \gamma^{k_1 \wedge k_2}_{c_{k_1} c_{k_2}} = 1$$

$$(8)$$

$$u^{k_1}_{mc_{k_1}} + u^{k_2}_{mc_{k_2}} \leq \sum_{s=1}^{s=S} x_{sm}$$

$$\forall m = 1..M, \forall k_1 = 1..K, \forall k_2 = 1..K, \forall c_{k_1} = 1..C_{k_1}, \forall c_{k_2} = 1..C_{k_2}/k_2 \neq k_1 \wedge \lambda^{k_1 \wedge k_2}_{c_{k_1} c_{k_2}} + \gamma^{k_1 \wedge k_2}_{c_{k_1} c_{k_2}} = 1$$

$$(9)$$

One must introduce a second *auxiliary variable* $\rho^{k_1 \wedge k_2}_{c_{k_1} c_{k_2}} = 1$ if the solution needs a junction components for coupling ACs c_{k_1} and c_{k_2} from SACs belonging to SACs k_1 and k_2 used for one or several modules. This binary variable is related to the decision variables $\pi^{k_1 \wedge k_2}_{mc_{k_1} c_{k_2}}$ by constraint (10). This constraint is sufficient because the cost function to be minimized integrates the variable $\rho^{k_1 \wedge k_2}_{c_{k_1} c_{k_2}}$, weighted by fixed cost $\theta^{k_1 \wedge k_2}_{c_{k_1} c_{k_2}}$.

$$\sum_{m=1}^{m=M} \pi^{k_1 \wedge k_2}_{mc_{k_1} c_{k_2}} \leq \Omega \cdot \rho^{k_1 \wedge k_2}_{c_{k_1} c_{k_2}}$$

$$\forall k_1 = 1..K, \forall k_2 = 1..K, \forall c_{k_1} = 1..C_{k_1}, \forall c_{k_2} = 1..C_{k_2}/k_2 \neq k_1 \wedge \gamma^{k_1 \wedge k_2}_{c_{k_1} c_{k_2}} = 1$$

$$(10)$$

The *objective function* to be minimized is the weighted sum of binary variables corresponding to the sum of fixed costs and variable costs, proportional to the quantities to be produced. The three fixed costs are those induced by the selected AMs, $\sum_{m=1}^{m=M} f_m \cdot y_m$, the selected ACs, $\sum_{k=1}^{k=K} \sum_{c_k=1}^{c_k=C_k} w^k_{c_k} \cdot s^k_{c_k}$ and by the junction components $\sum_{k_1=1}^{k_1=K_1} \sum_{k_2=1, k_1 \neq k_2}^{k_2=K_2} \sum_{c_{k_1}=1}^{c_{k_1}=C_{k_1}} \sum_{c_{k_2}=1}^{c_{k_2}=C_{k_2}} \theta^{k_1 \wedge k_2}_{c_{k_1} c_{k_2}} \cdot \rho^{k_1 \wedge k_2}_{c_{k_1} c_{k_2}}$. Three variable costs, proportional to the quantities to be produced, have to be distinguished.

- Total demand for AM m, $\sum_{s=1}^{s=S} x_{sm}$, is to be weighted by its direct variable cost g_m, inducing partial cost $\sum_{m=1}^{m=M} g_m \cdot \sum_{s=1}^{s=S} x_{sm}$.
- Total demand for AC c_k from SAC k, $\sum_{m=1}^{m=M} u^k_{mc_k}$, is to be weighted by its direct variable cost $v^k_{c_k}$, inducing partial cost $\sum_{k=1}^{k=K} \sum_{c_k=1}^{c_k=C_k} v^k_{c_k} \cdot \sum_{m=1}^{m=M} u^k_{mc_k}$.

- Finally, total demand for the junction component linking ACs c_{k_1} and c_{k_2} belonging to SACs k_1 and k_2, $\sum_{m=1}^{m=M} \pi_{mc_{k_1} c_{k_2}}^{k_1 \wedge k_2}$, is to be weighted by its direct variable cost $\eta_{c_{k_1} c_{k_2}}^{k_1 \wedge k_2}$, inducing partial cost $\sum_{k_1=1}^{k_1=K_1} \sum_{k_2=1, k_1 \neq k_2}^{k_2=K_2} \sum_{c_{k_1}=1}^{c_{k_1}=C_{k_1}} \sum_{c_{k_2}=1}^{c_{k_2}=C_{k_2}} \eta_{c_{k_1} c_{k_2}}^{k_1 \wedge k_2} \cdot \sum_{m=1}^{m=M} \pi_{mc_{k_1} c_{k_2}}^{k_1 \wedge k_2}$.

This cost function is an affine function that combines, for every selected item (AC or AM), an expenditure that depends on production volume equal to demand to be met, plus a fixed cost independent of volume. It is possible, as in Giard (1999, 2001), to formulate the problem in a more complex cost function, being "monotonically non-decreasing and piecewise linear" and to integrate the cost synergy (positive or negative) resulting from simultaneous production of several ACs at the same plant. This transformation of the problem, easy to operate but not selected here, substantially increases the number of variables.

3.2.2 Temporal and Spatial Dimensions Included in the Objective Function

Though seemingly static, this model is flexible enough to efficiently integrate change in demand, which only impacts direct variable costs. It can also easily be customized to take new AC launch dates into account.

AS demand induces AM demand and, consequently, AC demand. Taking into account the change of demand over time involves replacing d_s by d_{st}, and thus $u_{mc_k}^k$ by $u_{mc_k t}^k$, for periods t belonging to a common economic horizon, and to discount production costs using an appropriate periodic discount rate α. In the absence of change in direct variable costs, assuming their real value is constant, the discounted partial cost of AC c_k, chosen for illustration, is $v_{c_k}^k \cdot \sum_{t=1}^{t=T} \sum_{m=1}^{m=M} u_{mc_k t}^k \cdot (1 + \alpha)^{-t}$. Function $u_{mc_k}^k = \sum_{t=1}^{t=T} u_{mc_k t}^k \cdot (1 + \alpha)^{-t}$ restores the initial formulation which is to apply instantly to all the direct variable costs of the target function. Three additional remarks may be made.

- By factoring in demand change over time through discounted demand one can address demand beyond the first year simply by changing the lower limit of summation. This device is valuable where new services are coming up or where certain services are slated to replace current services.
- Where some ACs (or AMs) are in the pre-development study phase, the fixed costs associated with the selection of such products is a discounted value of their development cost and, if necessary, investment. Certain constraints must then be included in the formulation of the problem since an AC which is in the study phase cannot be mounted on an AM selected to satisfy immediate demand for one or more ASs. This can result in dividing certain services into two: demand for existing products being defined prior to launch of new ACs while demand for forthcoming products will be defined subsequently. The related data consistency issue is to be dealt with upstream of optimization process.
- Defining the relevant economic horizon (H) presents methodological difficulties common to all economic analyses in connection with product launches; it will therefore not be addressed here.

Coefficients for the target function implicitly include a *spatial dimension*: the location of AC and AM production plants determines manufacturing costs. If one supposes the location of final assembly lines to be predetermined along with their assigned production, the shipping costs to final delivery are hardly impacted by any decisions. The choice of AM produced in a given plant only impacts assembly cost, which is integrated in direct variable cost. If an AM is produced at multiple plants, this reasoning is valid only if the economic impact is similar. The choice of location of a production plant for new ACs impacts direct variable cost, which includes manufacturing costs as well as delivery costs of the ACs to the AM plants. The choice is relatively straightforward in the absence of impact from decisions concerning other ACs which ought to be manufactured at the same site to achieve synergies. To take such synergies into account, one should adjust the formulation of the problem by integrating supply chain design considerations. This aspect is left aside here.

4 Numerical Example

We have implemented this model on a real case of an automotive company. We take as an example the engine cooling system of cars. Our example that rests on functional definition for linking parts to services, takes into account 178 AMs that need 3 SACs: radiator (RAD), charged air cooler (CAC) and fan. Those three SACs have respectively 71, 40 and 61 ACs. Some CAs from two different SACs cannot be combined freely. The AMs aim at meeting a list of 390 ASs. Matrices a_{sm} and $b^k_{mc_k}$ are around 96 % null. With this set of data the number of variables created is 11989 and the number of constraints is 10499. Xpress-IVE solved it with an optimal solution in 3.5 s as it is linear. For more information (table of notations, data and results) see Example (http://www.lamsade.dauphine.fr/~giard/Detailed_Exemple.zip).

The solution permits to reduce drastically the diversity of the two BOM levels. The number of AMs goes from 178 to 82, the number of RAD goes from 71 to 24, the number of CAC goes from 40 to 15 and the number of FAN goes from 61 to 23. The optimal solution found uses junction components for 8 (RAD, FAN) 2 (RAD, CAC) and 12 (CAC,FAN).

5 Conclusion

The multi-level standardization approach we propose delivers several advantages compared to previous approaches. It relies on a multi-functional standpoint readily implemented by business players and engineers to define the needs (ASs), the AMs and the ACs. It supports simultaneous standardization of AMs and of all the SACs they comprise while taking into account any interfacing incompatibilities and allowing for introduction of junction components. The BOM then stems from this optimization process. The sets may integrate existing components (or modules) as well as others that are still in the design stage. The definition of ASs can be made at a sufficient level of aggregation, which is that used by many configurators, such that demand forecasts are relevant. Finally, the economic model factors the temporal and spatial dimensions both of which are crucial for business.

References

Agard, B., Bassetto, S.: Modular design of product families for quality and cost. Int. J. Prod. Res. **51**(6), 1648–1667 (2013)

Agard, B., Penz, B.: A simulated annealing method based on a clustering approach to determine bills of materials for a large product family. Int. J. Prod. Econ. **117**(2), 389–401 (2009)

Agard, B.,Tollenaere, M.: Conception D'assemblages Pour La Customisation de Masse. Mécanique Ind. **3**(2), 113–119 (2002)

Baldwin, C.Y., Clark, K.B.: Managing in an age of modularity. Harvard Bus. Rev. **75**, 84–93 (1997)

Baud-Lavigne, B., Agard, B., Penz, B.: Mutual impacts of product standardization and supply chain design. Int. J. Prod. Econ. **135**(1), 50–60 (2012)

Chatras, C., Giard, V.: Economic variety control and modularity. In: ILS'5 Conference in Breda, Netherlands (2014)

Dahmus, J.B., Gonzalez-Zugasti, J.P., Otto, K.N.: Modular product architecture. Des. Stud. **22**(5), 409–424 (2001)

Dupont, L., Cormier, G.: Standardisation d'une famille ordonnée de composants dont le coût d'obtention est concave. In: MOSIM 2001, pp. 509–513 (2001)

Fisher, M., Ramdas, K., Ulrich, K.: Component sharing in the management of product variety: a study of automotive braking systems. Manage. Sci. **45**(3), 297–315 (1999)

Fonte,W.G.: A de-proliferation methodology for the automotive industry. Massachusetts Institute of Technology (1994). http://dspace.mit.edu/handle/1721.1/12064

Giard, V.: Analyse Économique de La Standardisation Des Produits" Cahier GREGOR (1999)

Giard, V.: Economical analysis of product standardization (Binder edn.). In: IFAC/IFIP/IEEE 2000. Elsevier (2001)

Lamothe, J., Hadj-Hamou, K., Aldanondo, M.: An optimization model for selecting a product family and designing its supply chain. Eur. J. Oper. Res. **169**(3), 1030–1047 (2006)

Martin, M.V., Ishii, K.: Design for management and control of production and logistic variety: developing standardized and modularized product platform architectures. Res. Eng. Des. **13**(4), 213–235 (2002)

Perera, H.S.C., Nagarur, N., Tabucanon, M.T.: Component part standardization: a way to reduce the life-cycle costs of products. Int. J. Prod. Econ. **60–61**, 109–116 (1999)

Renard, C.: The standards ISO 3-1973, ISO 17-1973, SO 497-1973 and ANSI Z17.1-1973

Rai, R., Allada, V.: Modular product family design: agent-based pareto-optimization and quality loss function-based post-optimal analysis. Int. J. Prod. Res. **41**(17), 4075–4098 (2003)

Rutenberg, D.P.: Design commonality to reduce multi-item inventory: optimal depth of a product line. Oper. Res. **19**(2), 491–509 (1971)

Sanchez, R., Mahoney, J.T.: Modularity, flexibility, and knowledge management in product and organization design. Strateg. Manag. J. **17**(S2), 63–76 (1996)

Sered, Y., Reich, Y.: Standardization and modularization driven by minimizing overall process effort. Comput. Aided Des. **38**(5), 405–416 (2006)

Swaminathan,J.M., Tayur, S.R.: Managing broader product lines through delayed differentiation using vanilla boxes. Manage. Sci. **44**(12-part-2), S161–S172 (1998)

Ulrich, K.T.: The role of product architecture in the manufacturing firm. Res. Policy **24**(3), 419–440 (1995)

Knowledge Sharing Using Product Life Cycle Management

Pham Cong Cuong[1], Alexandre Durupt[1], Nada Matta[2(✉)],
Benoit Eynard[1], and Guillaume Ducellier[2]

[1] University of Technology of Compiegne,
Compiegne, France
{phamcong,alexandre.durupt}@utc.fr
[2] University of Technology of Troyes,
Troyes, France
{nada.matta,guillaume.ducellier}@utt.fr

Abstract. Information Systems, used to share information, lead to the growth of heterogeneous data and then the dependencies between them. Thus, the links and dependencies among heterogeneous and distributed data are more and more complex during daily activities of users (engineers, etc.). Ontology is currently used to enhance the knowledge sharing and the data integration in many information systems. Our contribution is to propose a methodology to facilitate the exploitation (interrogation and sharing) of data in an organization.

Keywords: Knowledge sharing · PLM · Ontology

1 Introduction

Information Systems, used to share information, lead to the growth of heterogeneous data and then the dependencies between them. Thus, the links and dependencies among heterogeneous and distributed data are more and more complex during quotidian activities of users (engineers, etc.). The data exploitation (interrogation and sharing) has to be adapted to the context of large data and complex dependencies. To overcome this current inconvenience, more and more research works have investigated and studied the Semantic Web (SW) concepts and techniques, as well as their applications to improve the capabilities of PLM solutions in order to efficiently manage lifecycle data. Ontology is a key component of SW in which concepts and the relationships between concepts can be expressed in natural language and understandable by both of human and machine. Ontology is therefore used to enhance the knowledge sharing and the data integration in many actual information systems. Our contribution is to propose a methodology to facilitate the exploitation (interrogation and sharing) of data in an organization. Thus, the PLM domain is considered for industrial companies where the users are engineers. A global approach to construct an ontological model facilitating data exploitation is therefore illustrated from PLM context.

© IFIP International Federation for Information Processing 2015
S. Umeda et al. (Eds.): APMS 2015, Part I, IFIP AICT 459, pp. 376–382, 2015.
DOI: 10.1007/978-3-319-22756-6_46

2   Knowledge Sharing

Knowledge play an indispensable role in the long-term sustainability and success of organization. The need for processes that facilitate the creation, sharing and leveraging of individual and collective knowledge has emerged recently for this reason.

Knowledge sharing (KS) has been introduced as one of the major activities of knowledge management and some definitions of knowledge sharing can be found in the literature [4]. KS can be defined as activities of transferring or disseminating knowledge from one person, group or organization to another. The individuals initially create knowledge but it can be produced and held collectively. At the most basic level; knowledge sharing involves the process through which knowledge is transferred between a source and a recipient by using knowledge sharing techniques.

Information technology (IT) provides techniques to capture knowledge, categorize, search, extract content information and present it in more meaningful formats across multiple contexts of use. Some authors [5, 7, 8] have invested their efforts to construct platforms that enable knowledge sharing by using ITs. Sato et al. [5] used XML Linking Language (XLink) as a method of knowledge representation describing and proposed architecture for sharing that knowledge among users.

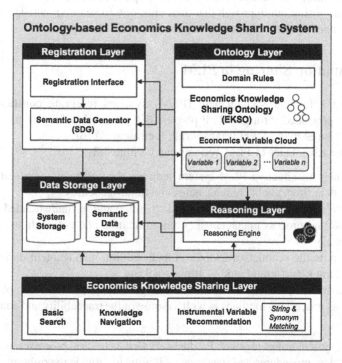

Fig. 1. Ontology-based economics knowledge sharing system architecture [7]. In this architecture, different levels are defined, related to the difference between data and knowledge. Ontology is enriched from data by generating semantic data related to ontology concepts. Reasoning engine is used when a data is searched. It allows to infer data using logic links between concepts.

He used the peer-to-peer technology to help users to better understand how to reuse existing knowledge on computer networks. Zhang et al. [8] tried to re-define knowledge resources in the network by object-oriented thinking and proposed three-layer knowledge sharing model. By using technologies on Web 2.0, a knowledge-sharing system is built on the Internet, allows the knowledge acquisition, sharing, extension and retrieving. Several knowledge-sharing systems use ontologies, which are defined as an explicit formal specification of a shared conceptualization [2]. For instance, Yoo et al. [7] proposed a system based on ontology expressing economics knowledge and Semantic Web technologies. Figure 1 presents the architecture of this system that consists of five layers: registration, ontology, data storage, reasoning and economic knowledge sharing. Users can register economics knowledge pertaining to a certain economics paper. They define then the metadata and the relationships between notions discussed in the paper. According ontology model, the system transforms this knowledge into semantic data in a machine-understandable format. Two functions: basic search and knowledge navigation were implemented.

OntoShare [1] is another ontology-based knowledge sharing system, in which, as users contribute information to the community, a knowledge resource annotated with metadata is created by using ontologies that have been defined using Resources Description Framework Schema (RDFS) and populated using RDF.

Before proposing our approach that uses ontology to share knowledge in PLM, let us describe main problem of sharing information in PLM.

3   Information Sharing in PLM

The Product Lifecycle Management (PLM) systems integrate constantly all the information produced throughout all phases of a product's lifecycle to everyone in an organization at every level (managerial, technical…) [6].

Some key advantages of PLM systems can be noted [3]:

- Establishing an effective PLM system reduces the enormous data resources to a coherent data flow, avoids redundancies and heterogeneities.
- PLM enables the collaboration through distributed and virtual/extended enterprises (workflow and process management, communication and notifications, secure data exchange…)
- PLM permits the product structure and its evolution management during different steps and track-performed modifications tracking.
- PLM is a mature solution to tackle the heterogeneity, growth and complexity of the data and its processing methods as well as some of the traceability and confidentiality issues.

So, PLM system brings together: Products, service, activities, processes, people, skills, data, knowledge, procedures and standards…. It aims to provide the right information for the right people at the right time. It provides an efficient solution to handle the complex and heterogeneous data resources and a mature method to track the evolution and modification of these data.

However, along with these advantages, it also exists some issues:

- Lack of strong stakeholders, ICT tools as well as a common standard between PLM systems causes data integrity problems and limits the access to and sharing of product information and knowledge distributed,
- Another issue of PLM community is the increasing of need for product lifecycle knowledge capitalization and reuse in order to reduce time and cost.
- Database exploitation requires a good understanding of database structure as well as data model especially in the context where the data is heterogeneous and the links and dependencies among data are complex.

To answer these problems, we aim to use ontology to enhance knowledge sharing in PLM. The difficulties in data exploitation and technical information in PLM systems come from the low-level of data model representation, the increasing of the complexity of links and dependencies among heterogeneous data. To exploit data from database, it requires a deep understanding of data model and the dependencies between these data. Ontology promises an efficient solution to enable the sharing this understanding. The data model and the complex relationships could be also presented obviously, visually and easily to perceive by using ontology.

4   Our Approach to Share Knowledge in PLM

The main problem in information management is to manage the evolution of data and links between information. Each user introduces his own view when he/she adds a new data. So, information search based on database becomes complex. Otherwise, knowledge engineering techniques as shown before provide techniques, which help from one side to respect the logic of a user and from another side to share knowledge. We propose to use knowledge sharing techniques based on ontology and inference engine in order to help in data management in PLM (Fig. 2). In fact, ontologies must be

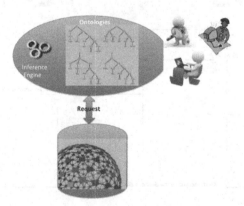

Fig. 2. Architecture of knowledge sharing in PLM. Inference engine can be used when a user ask for data from PLM. It follow ontologies in order to generate several links between data. The system can then transform these links in a data request which is used for database.

defined to represent user views. Ontologies' low-level concepts have to be linked to data in database, or unless respect the variable name of these data. An inference engine can help to build a data request and generate links using the propagation of relations between concepts. We present in the following an example of this work for researcher working in bio-imaging (GIN) lab.

4.1 Building Ontology in GIN Lab

To ensure a concrete view, we started our work by interviewing some scientists in a research institute where the complexity, variety, heterogeneity and growth of data resources have been handled by using PLM solutions. The goal of this interview is to identify the real needs of researchers, the difficulties in manipulating with information system during daily activities. In fact, most of scientists have difficulties in data querying and they almost cannot accomplish this task without helps of database technicians. For this reason, a visual, dynamic query interface that contains contents non-technician and user-proper, is required and acts an important role in system. Furthermore, as showed in the Fig. 3, the knowledge sharing process in bio-imaging GIN Laboratory initiates by data querying from PLM database through this query interface. Providing an efficient interface therefore becomes crucial and essential.

We define an ontology corresponding of the use logic of information in database. Information belongs to three major categories: **Tools**, **Data**, and **Process** (Fig. 4). Several relations exist between these concepts like **Use, Follow** and **Provide** (Fig. 5).

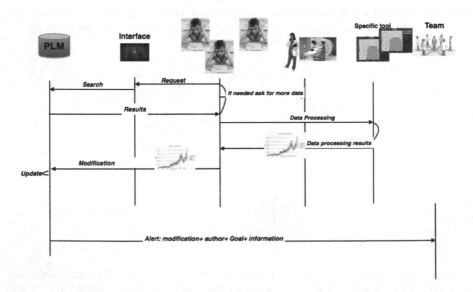

Fig. 3. Knowledge sharing in Bio-Imaging GIN Lab.

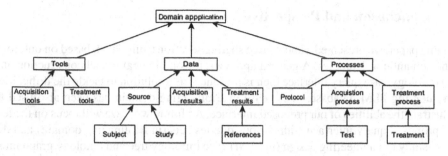

Fig. 4. Conceptual tree of ontology. Three main concepts are used "Tools", "Data" and "Process". These concepts are manipulated in different ways: in acquisition, treatment, or results.

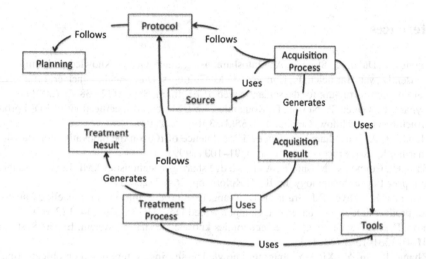

Fig. 5. Conceptual graph of ontology. Data acquisition follows different protocol in order to acquire information from several sources. Acquisition results are then manipulated in treatments, respecting protocols in order to provide results.

4.2   Ontology Based Querying Interface

By using ontology tree and ontology graph, ontology-based graph query interface helps users to make a query more easily. By using the ontology tree and ontology graph, users can understand the relationships among concepts and directly choose query parameters. Users also can choose a query in query history to re-execute, modify or complete it. When a user completes his query, our system does as following

1. Identifying nodes links, following relations in ontologies.
2. Generating an output query in a format understandable and executable by Query Processor, XQuery Engine for example.
3. Executing the output query on PLM data file (.xml or .json format).
4. Results are then visualized as a graph and data in the Interface query.

5   Conclusion and Perspective

In this paper, we presented a knowledge sharing solution using PLM, based on ontology and semantic web studies. A general approach for ontological model construction and an ontology-base query interface then is presented as a solution to tackle the difficulties in querying PLM database. A use case in BioImaging domain has been also used to illustrate the abilities of our proposed interface. As future work we will focus on the test of proposed query interface with various queries sets (in BioImaging domain) and the case study of engineering design (in PLM). The ontology tree and ontology graph must be also developed to cover all concepts in BioImaging domain. Ontology will be implemented in semantic web language (RDF, SPARQL) in order to use inference engine for information search. We plan to test different inference engine for this aim.

References

1. Davies, J., Duke, A., Stonkus, A.: Ontoshare: using ontologies for knowledge sharing
2. Fensel, D., van Harmelen, F., Horrocks, I., McGuinness, D.L., Patel-Schneider, P.F.: OIL: an ontology infrastructure for the semantic web. IEEE Intell. Syst. **16**(2), 38–45 (2001)
3. Eynard, B., Gallet, T., Nowak, P., Roucoules, L.: UML based specifications of PDM product structure and workflow. Comput. Ind. **55**(3), 301–316 (2004)
4. Hendriks, P.: Why share knowledge? The influence of ICT on the motivation for knowledge sharing. Knowl. Process Manage. **6**(2), 91–100 (1999)
5. Sato, H., Otomo, K., Masuo, T.. A knowledge sharing system using XML Linking Language and peer-to-peer technology. In: IEEE Xplore, pp. 26–27 (2002)
6. Sudarsan, R., Fenves, S.J., Sriram, R.D., Wang, F.: A product information modeling framework for product lifecycle management. Comput. Aided Des. **37**(13), 1399–1411 (2005)
7. Yoo, D., No, S.: Ontology-based economics knowledge sharing system. Expert Syst. Appl. **41**(4), 1331–1341 (2014)
8. Zhang, J., Liu, Y., Xiao, Y.: Internet knowledge-sharing system based on object-oriented. IEEE Xplore **1**, 239–243 (2008)

Organizational Capability in Production Scheduling

Emrah Arica[✉], Sven Vegard Buer, and Jan Ola Strandhagen

Department of Production and Quality Engineering, Norwegian University of Science
and Technology, Trondheim, Norway
{emrah.arica,ola.strandhagen}@ntnu.no,
svenvegb@stud.ntnu.no

Abstract. The performance of the production scheduling activities is highly
influenced by the organizational factors in a particular manufacturing environment. Based on the analysis of the relevant literature, this paper proposes a capability maturity model for organizational capability in production scheduling. The
paper contributes to theory by building upon the results of the field-based studies
on human and organizational factors in scheduling, and developing a framework
for assessing the organizational maturity in production scheduling. The model
can be utilized by the practitioners to map and evaluate the organizational capability in their scheduling practice.

Keywords: Production scheduling · Organizational factors · Capability maturity
model

1 Introduction

The production scheduling activities take place in the context of production planning
and control (PPC) which aims for aligning demand and capacity, while providing high
quality products with maximum time and cost efficiency. The scheduling activities deals
with allocating the production orders to limited resources over given time periods, and
can be divided roughly into two parts: (1) initial generation of the schedules (2) updating
the schedules (i.e. rescheduling) in the face of unscheduled events.

The need to adopt the schedules to unscheduled events is a matter of practical reality.
The real life planners spend most of their efforts to monitor and react on problems [1].
These events can change the status of resources, such as material shortage and machine
breakdowns, as well as the status of orders, such as rush order, quality problems, and
due date changes. They in turn may result in deviations to schedules and plans, and
eventually affect the performance [2].

The insights of the field-based scheduling studies indicate that the advanced
computer technology can generate the initial schedules; however, the rescheduling
process involve additional human logic, information gathering, and organizational
efforts to reach at informed effective decisions [2–4]. The rescheduling process often
take place with intense time pressure and an unclear overview of the situation [5]. In
order to clarify the situation, efforts take place to acquire information from a number of
sources that can be humans or different information systems in the organization.

© IFIP International Federation for Information Processing 2015
S. Umeda et al. (Eds.): APMS 2015, Part I, IFIP AICT 459, pp. 383–390, 2015.
DOI: 10.1007/978-3-319-22756-6_47

On one hand, these field-based reports generated very valuable and rich insights on human, technological, and organizational factors of scheduling practice from different real life cases. On the other hand, many of the field-based studies have been too broad and unstructured, and have attempted to cover a large human and organizational factors in planning and scheduling domain [6]. The lack of building on each other's findings leads to the lack of frameworks upon which to shape any generalizations. Without generalizable findings, theory and knowledge cannot influence the planning and scheduling practice [6].

In this paper, we have analyzed the field-based reports in literature and listed a set of organizational factors that influence the production scheduling performance. These factors are further adopted to generate a capability maturity model (CMM) for organizational capability and maturity. The model can be utilized to assess the organizational maturity of manufacturing companies in their production scheduling activities.

2 Literature Findings

2.1 Organizational Factors in Production Scheduling

Organizational Structure. The organizational structure of the PPC roles and departments has an influence on scheduler's performance, by for example influencing the possibilities of executing the schedule in its original form [7]. The organizational structure should reflect the requirements of both initial scheduling and rescheduling activities [5]. The rescheduling process necessitates extensive communication and feedback efforts within the organization to clarify and evaluate the situation and take effective rescheduling decisions, as clearly illustrated by the in-depth case study of de Snoo et al. [2]. As such, the structure should reflect the interdependencies and facilitate effective handling of different situations triggered by different types of unscheduled events.

In this respect, the physical location of the scheduler matters due to the vertical, i.e. between planning and control levels, and horizontal, i.e. between the schedules of the shop floor units, interdependencies and communication efforts. Especially, the proximity between the schedulers and the shop floor enables schedulers to more easily obtain information from production and other employees, and, therefore, to effectively handle unscheduled events [4]. A central physical location contributes to the scheduler's role as an information node and problem solver.

Schedulers' Interconnections. As the essence of communication and feedback efforts, relevant and timely information is essential for the scheduler in order to make effective decisions [6]. Gathering the relevant information in a timely manner for effective scheduling/re-scheduling decisions is highly dependent on schedulers' contact points in the organization. A basic example of a scheduler's contact point is that schedulers need situational information about the production from the operators to maintain feasible schedules, while operators need information about production schedules and schedule changes [8]. Depending on the situation and required information, other interconnections for schedulers can be people from purchasing, sales, quality, finance, human resources, and other support groups [7].

In this respect, it is important for the scheduler to be integrated with his/her contacts. A good relation have positive effects on social commitment, cooperation, consensus, and work satisfaction, besides the improved scheduling performance [8]. If they are in an isolated situation without knowledge of the production status and outputs, the expected production outputs will also be uncertain [7]. The scheduler will have some challenges in understanding the requirements of the different departments, trying to strike a compromise, and to convince everyone that the recommended solution is the best one. It is therefore important that the scheduler is well acquainted with his colleagues and will know how and when to utilize these people in the best manner in order to solve problems [9].

Facilitation of the Communication and Coordination Efforts. Communication and information sharing efforts among the parties located in different departments of the organization should be facilitated to improve the timeliness of the information gathered. This can be done by using procedures to guide the communication efforts in different situations as well as suitable information technologies that can facilitate it [10]. Combined with the knowledge of the interconnections, the communication facilitation can ensure an efficient information flow, and thereby result in a positive influence on the production scheduling performance.

A good example of such procedure is provided by de Snoo et al. [2] in order to guide the event handling and rescheduling process with respect to the type of events. Nevertheless such procedures should be supported by providing the relevant information to relevant people in the relevant situation. To achieve this, the fit between the organizational role and the employed information systems plays an important role; which means the consistency between the information systems and the responsibility, authority, and skills of the associated roles [11].

Prior to adjusting the information systems in accordance with the organizational roles, the decision making authorities of different organizational roles in the scheduling activities should also be specified. This issue is especially important to identify the decision making autonomy of the shop floor personnel when reacting on unscheduled events and taking rescheduling decisions. The shop floor personnel play a vital role in rescheduling process, because of being closer to the production processes and problem area [1, 2, 12]. Especially if the shop floor operates outside the working hours of the planners and schedulers, it is basically unavoidable to have the shop floor operators making scheduling decisions [12]. The concept of autonomy relates to how much a unit can decide for themselves, and how strict the commands from their managers are [7]. The more detailed and constrained these instructions and guidelines form the higher authority is, the less autonomy exists [7].

The lack of such clarification of decisional roles may lead to excess coordination and communication efforts which can diminish the timeliness of the rescheduling, as well as inappropriateness of the decisions taken under incomplete information. Accordingly, when fitting the decision support systems for scheduling tasks and roles, it is crucial to define what decisions should be taken by the schedulers and what decisions by the shop floor personnel [12].

Synchronization of the Performance Goals Across the Organization. The theoretical scheduling models are usually driven by one or several pre-defined performance measures that aim for optimizing the shop floor efficiency such as minimization of makespan and/or throughput times of the jobs [13]. More advanced scheduling/rescheduling measures consider the stability, robustness, and instability (nervousness) of the schedules [14].

However, the industrial practice is far from considering such advanced measures. In the scheduling practice optimization might not be a relevant issue, especially in the continuous rescheduling decisions. Most practitioners make re-scheduling decisions based on compromises, balancing the interests of different organizational parties [15]. The scheduling decisions often take place in the middle of conflicting goals and performance criteria from different departments [4, 16, 17]. As such, the most appropriate performance criteria may not be obvious in different situations [17]. Typically one organizational role is far from satisfied with the efforts of the other one [18]. For instance, operators could be dissatisfied with the schedulers' understanding of the actual reality on the shop floor. On the other hand, schedulers could be frustrated by operators not following the schedules or that they are slow to communicate plan disturbances.

Therefore, the organization should focus on common understanding and synchronization of the performance goals of different groups in the organization. The chosen performance measurements should reflect the business' overall goals, and they should work together to achieve an overall improvement.

Training and Continuous Improvement. Lean thinking and continuous improvement are also relevant ideas to enhance the production scheduling performance. There are different means of continuously improving the scheduling performance such as training of the scheduler, and identification and elimination of non-value adding activities in the scheduling tasks.

It is evident that the scheduler should have the essential training or education in the work he/she is going to carry out. This is needed to develop/adopt scheduling methods/mechanisms customized to the production context in which the schedules should be developed and carried out successfully. A step forward in training activities is to ensure that the scheduler has a thorough understanding of the processes, resources, and products they are being asked to schedule [4]. The scheduler should gain the ability to recognize hidden relationships, be aware of possible problems that can occur, and identify possible alternative resource assignments [6].

In this respect, experience and knowledge exchange between the schedulers and the shop floor personnel is of high importance. The operators have plenty of valuable information about the production situation that will benefit the schedulers in their work. Previous shop floor work experience can also be a major benefit for the scheduler in his/her tasks [4]. A well-trained scheduler can anticipate the potential events that can disturb the schedules and produce robust schedules that take the uncertainties of the manufacturing environment into account [6, 10]. Furthermore, he/she can have a better understanding of the communication efforts and actions that needs to be carried out in the rescheduling process.

Another means of continuously improving the scheduling performance is directly linked to the lean thinking, which is basically eliminating the non-value adding activities in the scheduling practice. This can for example be done by identifying and eliminating the compensation tasks that take place within the scheduling activities, but not necessarily adding value to the scheduling task outputs. Jackson et al. [19] defines the compensations tasks as activities that are necessary to compensate for some kind of problem, limitation, or failure in the overall system. Within scheduling and control, this could for instance be; data management because of a poorly designed information systems, use of compensatory systems because the formal system is inadequate, and duplication of effort because of bad coordination [10]. Compensation tasks are non-value adding in the long term and should be identified and eliminated or reduced [17].

Such continuous improvement activities contribute to enhance the organizational factors discussed in the earlier sections, and result in enhanced scheduling and control performance. For instance, identification of the inadequacy of the formal systems to obtain the necessary information for scheduling can trigger improvement activities for a better fit between the roles and information systems. All in all, the organization should establish clear procedures or mechanisms for continuous improvement activities to help the schedulers with analyzing their work, identify the compensation tasks, and eliminate them.

2.2 Capability Maturity Models

A capability maturity model gives a company the opportunity to assess and compare the maturity of its operations relative to an industry best practice [20]. A maturity model consists of a sequence of maturity levels for a class of objects that last from a bottom stage, which represents initial states e.g. characterized by an organization having little capabilities, up to the highest stage of total maturity [21].

Maturity models can be used to assess the competence of IT systems support in specific processes, such as proposed by Powell et al. [22] for ERP support in Lean production. They can also be used to evaluate the maturity of business processes such as proposed by Grimson and Pyke [23] for the assessment of the sales and operations planning process.

These models have been developed on the basis of different suggestions on maturity levels, depending on the topic of interest. In this study, we have adopted the ISO/IEC 15504 standard that defines a reference model for assessing and determining the organizational maturity in a set of organizational processes [24]. Each maturity level encompasses all of the elements of the lower levels. The maturity levels are defined as follows.

- Level 0. Incomplete: The process is not implemented or fails to achieve its process outcomes
- Level 1. Performed: Achieves the fundamental process outcomes.
- Level 2. Managed: The process is executed in managed fashion (planned, tracked, verified, and adjusted).
- Level 3. Established: The process is managed with clearly defined principles and procedures.

- Level 4. Predictable: The established process is consistently performed within defined limits to achieve its outcomes.
- Level 5. Optimizing: The predictable process dynamically changes and adopts to effectively meet relevant current and projected goals.

3   CMM for Organizational Capability in Production Scheduling

The performance of the production scheduling process can be influenced by many different factors (e.g. the characteristics of the manufacturing environment, implemented technologies). However, the scope of this study and proposed CMM contains the essential organizational elements for effective production scheduling and rescheduling activities. On the basis of the analysis of literature findings on organizational factors, the model in Fig. 1 is proposed with maturity levels and corresponding organizational elements.

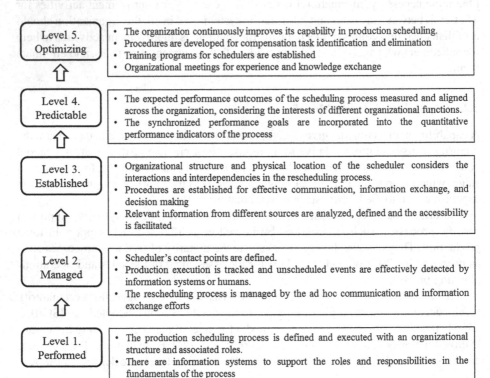

Fig. 1. CMM for organizational capability in production scheduling

4   Conclusion

This study investigated the organizational factors that influence the performance of the production scheduling activities. A capability maturity model (CMM) with a five level scale for the organizational maturity in the production scheduling activities were developed, on the basis of the organizational elements identified through the literature findings. The developed model can act as a catalyst to assess the organizational capability and maturity of a manufacturing company in its production scheduling activities as well as can provide guidelines for improvements in this respect. Further work should apply and test the CMM in multiple case studies of varying industrial settings, in order to test its validity and generalizability.

References

1. McKay, K.N., Wiers, V.C.S.: The human factor in planning and scheduling. In: Herrmann, J.W. (ed.) Handbook of Production Scheduling, pp. 23–57. Springer Science + Business Media, Inc, New York (2006)
2. de Snoo, C., van Wezel, W., Wortmann, J., Gaalman, G.J.C.: Coordination activities of human planners during rescheduling: case analysis and event handling procedure. Int. J. Prod. Res. **49**, 2101–2122 (2011)
3. Cegarra, J.: A cognitive typology of scheduling situations: a contribution to laboratory and field studies. Theor. Issues Ergon. Sci. **9**, 201–222 (2008)
4. Berglund, M., Karltun, J.: Human, technological and organizational aspects influencing the production scheduling process. Int. J. Prod. Econ. **110**, 160–174 (2007)
5. de Snoo, C., van Wezel, W.: Coordination and task interdependence during schedule adaptation. Hum. Factors Ergon. Manuf. Serv. Ind. **24**, 139–151 (2014)
6. Crawford, S., Wiers, V.C.: From anecdotes to theory: a review of existing knowledge on human factors of planning and scheduling. In: MacCarthy, B.L., Wilson, J.R. (eds.) Human Performance in Planning and Scheduling, pp. 15–43. Taylor & Francis, London (2001)
7. McKay, K.N., Wiers, V.C.: The organizational interconnectivity of planning and scheduling. In: Planning in Intelligent Systems: Aspects, Motivations, and Methods, pp. 175–201 (2006)
8. de Snoo, C., van Wezel, W., Wortmann, J.: Does location matter for a scheduling department?: a longitudinal case study on the effects of relocating the schedulers. Int. J. Oper. Prod. Manag. **31**, 1332–1358 (2011)
9. Karltun, J., Berglund, M.: Contextual conditions influencing the scheduler's work at a sawmill. Prod. Plann. Control **21**, 359–374 (2010)
10. MacCarthy, B., Wilson, J.: Influencing industrial practice in planning, scheduling and control. In: MacCarthy, B.L., Wilson, J.R. (eds.) Human Performance in Planning and Scheduling, pp. 451–461. Taylor & Francis, London (2001)
11. Strong, D.M., Volkoff, O.: Understanding organization-enterprise system fit: a path to theorizing the information technology artifact. MIS Q. **34**, 731–756 (2010)
12. Wiers, V.C.: The relationship between shop floor autonomy and APS implementation success: evidence from two cases. Prod. Plann. Control **20**, 576–585 (2009)
13. Pinedo, M.: Scheduling: theory, algorithms, and systems, 4th edn. Springer, New York (2012)
14. Sabuncuoglu, I., Goren, S.: Hedging production schedules against uncertainty in manufacturing environment with a review of robustness and stability research. Int. J. Comput. Integr. Manuf. **22**, 138–157 (2009)
15. Hozak, K., Hill, J.A.: Issues and opportunities regarding replanning and rescheduling frequencies. Int. J. Prod. Res. **47**, 4955–4970 (2009)
16. MacCarthy, B.L., Wilson, J.R., Crawford, S.: Human performance in industrial scheduling: a framework for understanding. Hum. Factors Ergon. Manuf. Serv. Ind. **11**, 299–320 (2001)

17. MacCarthy, B.: Organizational, systems and human issues in production planning, scheduling and control. In: Herrmann, J.W. (ed.) Handbook of Production Scheduling, pp. 59–90. Springer, Berlin (2006)
18. De Snoo, C., van Wezel, W.: The interconnectivity of planning and shop floor: case description and relocation analysis. In: Fransoo, J.C., Waefler, T., Wilson, J.R. (eds.) Behavioral Operations in Planning and Scheduling, pp. 31–43. Springer, Berlin (2011)
19. Jackson, S., Wilson, J.R., MacCarthy, B.L.: A new model of scheduling in manufacturing: tasks, roles, and monitoring. Hum. Factors J. Hum. Factors Ergon. Soc. **46**, 533–550 (2004)
20. Netland, T.H., Alfnes, E.: Proposing a quick best practice maturity test for supply chain operations. Measuring Bus. Excellence **15**, 66–76 (2011)
21. Becker, J., Knackstedt, R., Pöppelbuß, J.: Developing maturity models for IT management. Bus. Inf. Syst. Eng. **1**, 213–222 (2009)
22. Powell, D., Riezebos, J., Strandhagen, J.O.: Lean production and ERP systems in small-and medium-sized enterprises: ERP support for pull production. Int. J. Prod. Res. **51**, 395–409 (2013)
23. Grimson, J.A., Pyke, D.F.: Sales & operations planning: an exploratory study and framework. Int. J. Logistics Manag. **18**, 322–346 (2007)
24. Rout, T.: SPICE and the CMM: is the CMM compatible with ISO/IEC 15504. In: AquIS 1998 (1998)

Linking Information Exchange to Planning and Control: An Overview

Kasper Kiil[1]([⊠]), Heidi C. Dreyer[1], and Hans-Henrik Hvolby[1,2]

[1] Department of Production and Quality Engineering,
Norwegian University of Science and Technology,
S.P. Andersens veg 5, 7491 Trondheim, Norway
{kasper.kiil,heidi.c.dreyer}@ntnu.no, hhh@celog.dk
[2] Department of Production, Aalborg University,
Fibigerstraede 16, 9220 Aalborg, Demark

Abstract. This paper creates an overview of previous research which has been conducted related to how information exchange can improve planning and control decisions in order to establish directions for future research. By synthetizing literature reviews, more than 130 unique papers are considered in the analysis. It is identified that most research only examines a dyad relation, and there exist a strong focus on how to improve the order replenishment by using demand and inventory level information. Case studies, simulation models, and inclusion of more complex network structures is suggested for future research.

Keywords: Information exchange · Planning and control · Future research

1 Introduction

The constant search for cost reductions and efficiency gains without compromising other performances measures creates an enormous pressure on planning along the supply chain. Exchanging information, e.g. inventory levels, customer demand, forecast, among supply chain partners for improving planning and control decisions has been emphasized as an effective mean to improve performance [4, 14, 15]. Some of the cited benefits includes e.g. reduction of bull-whip effect, better and faster response to customer, greater visibility, reduced inventories, and increased service level [2, 11, 13]. Exchanging information has even been recognized as the core of collaborative supply chain management [13, 16]. However, there exist no overview of the many small conclusions which have been made [7, 16, 17] and this lacking overview complicates the process of trying to understand how information exchange influences planning and control decisions [12].

This study starts the journey of linking information exchange to planning and control by establishing the necessary overview through examining and synthesizing previous literature reviews. The objective of the study is to answer what research there previously has been conducting related to information exchange and planning and control in order to establish areas of future research.

© IFIP International Federation for Information Processing 2015
S. Umeda et al. (Eds.): APMS 2015, Part I, IFIP AICT 459, pp. 391–398, 2015.
DOI: 10.1007/978-3-319-22756-6_48

2 Background

Information Exchange. Information sharing and information exchange appear to be used interchangeably and they both refer to the extent to which operational, tactical or strategic information is available between supply chain members [16, 19]. Information exchange has been studied for decades and its impact on supply chain performance can be traced back to the work of Forrester [6] where the bull-whip effect was first conceived. Causes and recommendations to counteract it has been widely discussed and joint solutions as collaborative planning, replenishment and forecasting (CPRF) has been proposed as well (see e.g. [14, 5]). Today, it is well established that increased information exchange can lead to higher supply chain performance [15, 20]. Even though, it is well-understood that it can lead to higher performance, the road of how to get there is still blurred: "Despite the progress, the research underscored the fact that many SC managers do not fully understand the nature and role of an information-sharing capability. Thus, a proven, well-traveled path with well-defined signposts to the development of this important SC capability has not yet been established" [3, p. 241].

Design of Planning and Control. Assuming information is exchanged with supply chain partners a vast amount of literature investigates how it may be utilized [7, 8]. The application is usually through improved planning and control decisions, i.e. how much to order, when to order, routing decisions, inventory allocations, safety stock etc. [9]. References [10, 18] have explained how planning and control, and its underlying decisions, should be designed in accordance with (1) market requirements, (2) product characteristics and (3) process type. However, information exchange is not included as a basis for how planning decisions should be designed. Even though, numerous studies explicitly focus at how those two are connected and how planning and control decisions can be designed (and improved) if specific information is available. Other authors have previously emphasized this concern: "no studies have addressed aspects related to information sharing as a determinant of planning approach." [12, p. 148]. Essentially, there exist no encapsulating framework, or well-traveled path [3], to understand how information exchange influences planning and control decisions, nevertheless the field has still received many valuable but separate contributions [19].

Linking Information Exchange to Planning and Control. Previously, the type of information exchanged has been grouped into 20 categories ranging from demand information to what type of forecasting model or time fence settings the different supply chain partners apply [8]. Planning and control decisions has been divided into eight categories with facility location as the most strategic and order replenishment and shipment decision as the most operational [8]. The purpose of this paper is to connect these two dimensions, and the underlying categories, by generating an overview of which type of information (exchanged between supply chain partners) there previously has been examined to improve planning and control decisions. Secondly, it should be considered *how* this research has been conducted. The applied method (analytical, simulation, etc.) and the supply chain structure (dyad, divergent, etc.) condenses the most important parts of how the research has been conducted, and has also been used in previous review papers [7, 17].

3   Research Design

To grasp the tremendous amount of available literature on information exchange and planning and control literature reviews can provide valuable information. The initial literature search for this study discovered several literature reviews, but none of them directly linked information exchange to planning and control decisions. Therefore, this study assembles previous review papers to create this link and overview. The research process can be divided into two main steps:

Step 1: Locating Studies. First, only published academic articles and proceedings was chosen to be included. Second, to not only rely on a single database four databases (Scopus, ScienceDirect, Google Scholar, and Emerald) were selected. Third, keywords like information exchange, information sharing and collaboration was combined with supply chain at all four databases. Fourth, to reduce the number of articles and ensure a relative novel result a 15-year time period spanning from (including) 2000 to 2014 was selected. 32 papers was identified in this at this stage, this is predominantly because only review papers, and potential review papers, were selected for further evaluation.

Step 2: Selection and Evaluation. A comprehensive review [8] presents a conceptual framework of seven dimensions in order to categorize this type of literature. This framework was later applied in a simplified version with four dimensions [17]. Those four dimensions correspond to what has been discussed in the beginning of this paper and are conveyed in this paper. The first two considers *what* type of information and *which* planning and control decisions. The last two is concerned with *how* the research was conducted, giving these four dimensions:

1. Type of information exchanged
2. Type of planning decision
3. Applied method
4. Supply chain structure

The 32 review papers from the step 1 were read more in detail and only review papers which had specified those four dimensions (for the papers they reviewed) was selected for further analysis. As an example, the review by Giard and Sali [7] was excluded as they did only specify the planning decision as being either operational, tactical, or strategic which were considered too coarse. Six review papers from the period between 2000 and 2014 was identified to fulfill the selection criteria [1, 8, 13, 17, 19, 21]. Within the six review papers, a total of 176 papers and 131 unique papers had been reviewed.

As the previous review papers provide the main data for the subsequent analysis, their selection process specifies what papers there ultimately are included. The most common keywords used within the six selected review papers includes, supply chain information sharing, flow coordination, supply chain dynamics and collaboration. Some of them have applied a rather broad search approach in operation management related journals [8, 19] other focus explicitly on modeling papers [1], and some solely on two stage supply chain structures [17]. It should be noted that the chosen method, of only using review papers as the main data source, do not guarantee that all relevant (unique) papers are identified and included, however the method is still highly suitable to indicate previous trends.

4 Analysis and Discussion

Haung et al. [8] present 20 different categories of which type of information to exchange, and eight categories of different planning and control decisions. The 131 unique papers has been classified according to those categories and are presented in Table 1.

Table 1. Number of papers examine the relation between information exchange and planning and control decisions [1, 8, 13, 17, 19, 21].

		PLANNING AND CONTROL DECISION								
		Facility Location	Outsourcing	Production & distribution	Capacity Allocation	Inventory Allocation	Safety Stock	Order Replenishment	Shipment	Not specified	Sum
INFORMATION EXCHANGED	Demand forecast	0	0	3	1	3	1	7	1	2	18
	Production schedule	0	0	4	0	0	0	3	1	0	8
	Forecasting model	0	0	0	0	1	0	0	0	0	1
	Time fence	0	0	1	0	0	0	0	0	0	1
	Inventory level	0	0	1	1	6	3	21	5	3	40
	Backlog cost	0	0	0	0	0	0	1	0	0	1
	Holding cost	0	0	0	0	0	0	3	0	0	3
	Service level	0	0	0	0	1	0	0	0	1	2
	Capacity	2	4	3	0	0	0	6	1	1	17
	Manufacturing leadtime	0	0	0	0	1	0	3	0	1	5
	Cost of process	2	3	3	0	0	0	1	0	0	9
	Quality	0	0	0	0	0	0	1	0	1	2
	Delivery	0	0	1	0	0	0	3	3	1	8
	Delivery lead time	0	0	0	0	0	0	2	0	0	2
	Variation of lead time	0	0	1	0	0	0	1	1	3	6
	Demand (e.g. POS)	0	1	4	2	2	0	41	3	11	64
	Demand variability	0	0	0	1	0	0	6	0	3	10
	Batch size	0	0	2	0	0	0	5	1	0	8
	Demand correlation	0	0	0	0	0	0	3	0	0	3
	Delivery due date	0	0	1	0	0	0	1	1	0	3
	Not specified	0	0	1	0	2	0	6	0	8	17
	Sum	4	8	25	5	16	4	114	17	35	228

Table 1 specifies that e.g. seven unique papers has investigated the exchange of demand forecast in order to make better decisions related to order replenishment. If a paper has investigated how exchange of demand forecast could be used to improve both inventory allocation and order replenishment a full point has been assigned to both inventory allocation and order replenishment.

Clearly, the first comment from Table 1 is that sharing demand information (i.e. sharing downstream demand, especially by the end customer, with upstream facilities), in order to improve order replenishment (i.e. how a business entity places an order) is the single most investigated relation between information exchange and planning and control decisions. Out of the 131 unique papers almost one-third had this particular relation included. The exchange of inventory levels and demand forecast, to improve decisions related to order replenishment, has also received a great amount of attention.

Planning and Control Decision. Of the eight different planning decisions, order replenishment has been considered in almost all papers; remarkably 114 papers includes this decision. Production and distribution planning is considered in 25 papers while 17 papers investigates shipments (i.e. shipment within the same tier or emergency shipments where one tier is exclude [8]). Surprisingly, decisions related to inventory allocation, safety stock, or capacity allocation has only received very little attention from previous literature. It is surprising as it would be expected that sharing customers forecast or point-of-sales data could improve the focal company's own forecast and hereby obtain lower safety stock levels. Also, if a complete chain is examined, the total inventory level could might be reduced if it is allocated according to where the demand is expected.

Exchange of Information. Of the 20 different kinds of information possible to exchange demand, inventory level, and demand forecast are the top three followed by capacity and demand variability as forth and fifth. With demand, demand forecast, and demand variability included in top five a tendency of how downstream information, compared to upstream information, can be utilized is indeed present [1]. It could be expected that sharing upstream inventory levels and variability in delivery time may provide confidence further down the supply chain and could help decrease inventory levels. Also, even though the shelf life, or age of inventory, is not included in Table 1 it has been showed how it can improve performance [4].

Supply Chain Structure. To fully understand the research, which previously has been conducted related to information exchange and planning and control, Table 2 presents how it has been conducted by comparing the applied method and the supply chain structure from the 131 unique papers. From the table it can be concluded that nearly half of the papers studies a dyadic structure. Dyadic being the most common supply chain structure followed by serial and divergent which have been in examine in respectively 24 and 23 papers. On the other hand, less than 7 % of the papers adopts the more comprehensive network perspective. Reference [8] explains that dyadic structure is too simple to be compared with real supply chains and some of the implications should only be applied on a conceptual level. However, only involving two entities keeps the complexity down and makes it possible to apply an analytical (i.e. calculus

Table 2. Applied method and supply chain structures in the reviewed papers from Table 1 [1, 8, 13, 17, 19, 21].

		SUPPLY CHAIN STRUCTURE						
		Dyadic	Divergent	Convergent	Serial	Network	Not speci-fied	Sum
APPLIED METHOD	Analytical	34	12	4	7	0	2	59
	Systems dynamic	4	0	0	13	0	0	17
	Discrete event Simulation	2	4	3	1	0	0	10
	Mixed integer pro-gramming	2	0	0	0	6	0	8
	Game Theory	1	1	2	0	1	0	5
	Agent based mod-eling	13	5	2	3	2	1	26
	Not specified	1	1	0	0	0	10	12
	Sum	57	23	11	24	9	13	137

and probability) method [19], which may also explain the high occurrence of the analytical method combined with the dyadic structure.

Applied Method. With the high concentration of analytical method and dyadic structure the analytical method is the most common applied method overall. Simulation methods like discrete event simulation and agent based simulation are used across most supply chain structures, while systems dynamic mostly have been applied in serial supply chain structures. Interestingly, no case studies have been included which, besides simulation, appear as a suitable method if a complete supply chain network should be examined. Using the case study approach may also provide new ideas for what type of information to share, and offer examples of what are most common and beneficial to share.

5   Conclusion and Future Research

This paper contributes to the current body of knowledge on information exchange by explicitly showing and clarifying what previous research that have been conducted and how it has been conducted. First, the exchange of demand information and inventory levels, in order to improve order replenishment decisions, has received the highest amount of attention. Second, a tendency within information exchange is to investigate how downstream information can be exploited upstream [1]. Third, a common approach is to simplify the problem to a dyad supply chain structure and solve it analytically [8, 19]. Fourth, the use of both simulation and empirical studies are argued to be effective but not fully exploited methods. They also holds the power of analyzing the more complex network structure. Fifth, rudimentary issues, as which type of information to exchange and with whom is still unclear, and no well-traveled path exist [3, 13, 16]. Those five points summaries the outcome of the six review papers. However, to further develop the link from information exchange to planning and control and better understand the how it influences three directions for future research are deduced:

Research Design. It was highlighted that especially the network structure has previously been overlooked. Only studying dyad and simple supply chain structures may not provide the complete necessary knowledge [19]. It is expected, that this could be accommodated by using simulations models or using in-depth case studies where before and after situations are evaluated through essential performance measurements.

Level of Information Exchange. Information exchange can occur at different levels [19] and from the six reviews at least four dimensions defines the level of information exchange a supply chain applies. First, frequency and timeliness; this addresses the issue of how often and how far in advance the information should be exchanged to provide the highest benefit. Second, the information content specifies what type of information to exchange. Third, information detail concerns if information should be exchanged at e.g. SKU level or product family level and if it should be in e.g. monthly, weekly or daily time buckets. Fourth, neighborhood relates to the number of supply chain partners, which should receive and send the information. For future research it could be examined how to actually measure this level of information exchange and provide a generic framework, but also to examine the relationship to different planning and control levels.

Challenges and Benefits. Future research should be concerned with the impact on the supply chain performance and the challenges of implementing it. Some of the challenges of sharing data between individual companies is that it requires a great amount of trust, or willingness, as well as secure technical solutions for smooth connectivity [3]. How can a company safely share detailed forecasts with a supplier, if the supplier also supplies the company's biggest competitors? On the other hand, future research should also give some attention to how the benefit should be measured and distributed between various partners.

This paper present the academic perspectives on information exchange and planning and control. It will be continued with a case study of a network supply chain to examine what type of information there currently is exchanged, if the type of information identified through the six review papers include all types of information relevant to consider, and how the information is linked to the planning and control decisions in the case companies.

Acknowledgements. This paper is part of the Norwegian research project Retail Supply Chain 2020 funded by the Research Council of Norway and participating industrial companies. The four year project was initiated in 2014 and this paper especially contributes on one of the four key research areas of designing new advanced planning and control models through information exchange.

References

1. Choi, H.P.: Information sharing in supply chain management: a literature review on analytical research. Calif. J. Oper. Manag. **8**(1), 110–116 (2010)
2. Dev, N.K., Caprihan, R., Swami, S.: Strategic positioning of inventory review policies in alternative supply chain networks: an information-sharing paradigm perspective. Int. J. Logistics Res. Appl. Lead. J. Supply Chain Manag. **16**(1), 14–33 (2013)
3. Fawcett, S.E., Wallin, C., Allred, C., Magnan, G.: Supply chain information-sharing: benchmarking a proven path. Benchmarking Int. J. **16**(2), 222–246 (2009)
4. Ferguson, M., Ketzenberg, M.: Information sharing to improve retail product freshness of perishables. Prod. Oper. Manag. **15**(1), 57–73 (2006)
5. Fliedner, G.: CPFR: an emerging supply chain tool. Ind. Manag. Data Syst. **103**(1), 14–21 (2003)
6. Forrester, J.: Industrial dynamics: a major breakthrough for decision makers. Harvard Bus. Rev. **36**(4), 37–66 (1958)
7. Giard, V., Sali, M.: The bullwhip effect in supply chains: a study of contingent and incomplete literature. Int. J. Prod. Res. **51**(13), 3880–3893 (2013)
8. Huang, G.Q., Lau, J.S., Mak, K.L.: The impacts of sharing production information on supply chain dynamics: a review of the literature. Int. J. Prod. Res. **41**(7), 1483–1517 (2003)
9. Jacobs, F.R., Berry, W.L., Whybark, D.C., Vollmann, T.E.: Manufacturing Planning and Control for Supply Chain Management, 6th edn. McGraw-Hill, New York (2011)
10. Jonsson, P., Mattsson, S.A.: The implications of fit between planning environments and manufacturing planning and control methods. Int. J. Oper. Prod. Manag. **23**(8), 872–900 (2003)
11. Jonsson, P., Mattson, S.A.: The value of sharing planning information in supply chains. J. Phys. Distrib. Logistics Manag. **43**(4), 282–299 (2013)
12. Kaipia, R.: Coordinating material and information flows with supply chain planning. Int. J. Logistics Manag. **20**(1), 144–162 (2009)
13. Kumar, R.S., Pugazhendhi, S.: Information sharing in supply chains: an overview. Procedia Eng. **38**, 2147–2154 (2012)
14. Lee, H.L., Padmanabhan, V., Whang, S.: The bullwhip effect in supply chains. Sloan Manag. Rev. **38**(3), 93–102 (1997)
15. Li, G., Hong, Y., Wang, S., Xia, Y.: Comparative analysis on value of information sharing in supply chains. Supply Chain Manag. **10**(1), 34–46 (2005)
16. Moberg, C.R., Cutler, B.D., Gross, A., Speh, T.W.: Identifying antecedents of information exchange within supply chains. Int. J. Phys. Distrib. Logistics Manag. **32**(9), 755–770 (2002)
17. Montoya-Torres, J.R., Ortiz-Vargas, D.A.: Collaboration and information sharing in dyadic supply chains: a literature review over the period 2000–2012. Estud. Gerenciales **30**(133), 343–354 (2014)
18. Olhager, J., Rudberg, M.: Linking manufacturing strategy decisions on process choice with manufacturing planning and control systems. Int. J. Prod. Res. **40**(10), 2335–2351 (2002)
19. Sahin, F., Robinson, E.P.: Flow coordination and information sharing in supply chains: review, implications, and directions for future research. Decis. Sci. **33**(4), 505–536 (2002)
20. Thatte, A.A., Rao, S.S., Ragu-Nathan, T.S.: Impact of SCM practices of a firm on supply chain responsiveness and competitive advantage of a firm. J. Appl. Bus. Res. **29**(2), 499–530 (2013)
21. Yang, Z., Zhang, L.: Information sharing in supply chain: a review. J. Digit. Inf. Manag. **11**(2), 125–130 (2013)

More Than What Was Asked for: Company Specific Competence Programs as Innovation Hothouses

Hanne O. Finnestrand, Kristoffer Magerøy[✉], and Johan E. Ravn

Industrial Management, SINTEF Technology and Society, Trondheim, Norway
{hanne.o.finnestrand,kristoffer.mageroy,johan.e.ravn}@sintef.no

Abstract. The development of a company towards high-quality products and services demands higher skills among employees. Furthermore, companies providing extensive training are more likely to be productive and innovative. The question explored in this paper is how the demand for flexibility and high innovation rates in high-tech companies affects the choice of "making or buying" necessary skills. In order to study this, we have made use of organizational theory supported by empirical findings in two Norwegian companies experiencing the need for being flexible and facing challenges regarding increasing innovation pressure. Through our industry insights and specifically the case studies presented, we are led to conclude that in-house training programs contribute to build important prerequisites for flexible organizations with capability to innovate and change.

Keywords: In-house training · Company specific competence programs · Employee skills · Vocational workers · Flexible and innovative companies · Case study

1 Introduction

Research indicates that most Western countries with a skilled and educated but high-cost work force are moving towards high-tech manufacturing industries [1]. Consumers demand a broader range of high quality products and services and there are continuing developments in ICT that can enable more flexible manufacturing systems. Danford et al. [2] and White et al. [3] hold that the interest for highly qualified and flexible workers can be understood as a response to changes in the market and technological conditions. For instance, when studying the automobile industry, MacDuffie [4] found that companies that want to adapt a more flexible form of automobile assembly require more highly skilled workers. These are workers with the knowledge and ability to undertake the problem solving implied by this mode of production.

In addition to vocational training at school or as apprenticeship, most workers acquire their job skills at the work place as in-house training or in training offered by externals [5]. However, the factors that are related to such workplace rewards as employment stability, income, and occupational status also predict access to training opportunities. This means that highly educated workers participate more often than less educated workers such as vocational workers in workplace training, and workers in higher status

© IFIP International Federation for Information Processing 2015
S. Umeda et al. (Eds.): APMS 2015, Part I, IFIP AICT 459, pp. 399–405, 2015.
DOI: 10.1007/978-3-319-22756-6_49

occupations are more likely to receive training than workers in more marginal positions [6, 7]. Also when it comes to workplace training, vocational workers are not prioritised. Bills and Hudson [5] observed enormous differences in training rates across occupations. Upper level workers, like managers and professionals, participate in training at far higher rates than less well-positioned workers do.

Furthermore, people who work with customers and products often know more about the way the organization operates than people in staff and senior management positions. Shop floor workers may therefore be in a better position to make suggestions and develop innovations than others. Knowing that companies in advanced manufacturing are dependent on a production system that adapts and changes fast according to the demands in the market, such companies should therefore see the need for a highly qualified work force that is involved in and informed about the company's value creating activities – and with the necessary skills to both produce and adapt when necessary. Altogether, the need for highly skilled vocational workers is high and even increasing as advanced manufacturing develops further into flexible customer-centric organizations. When making an effort in acquiring those workers, companies can either choose to "buy" a skilled workforce by careful and selective hiring, or "make" a skilled workforce by the provision of training [8]. The question explored in this paper is how the demand for flexibility and high innovation rates in high-tech companies affects the choice of "make or buy". In order to study this, we have made use of organizational theory supported by empirical findings in two Norwegian companies experiencing the need of being flexible and facing challenges regarding increasing innovation pressure. One of the companies is a manufacturing company developing and producing specialized products, while the other is a yard delivering steel constructions to the off-shore oil and gas industry.

Development of Skills

Organizational researchers have claimed that skills inside a company are key to success. In a world where access to information is fast and widespread, those organizations who can create and use their own knowledge are likely to be able to build and sustain competitive advantage [9, p. 6]. From the "make or buy" perspective, there is evidence that employers gain from providing or supporting training, just as employees gain from participating in it. Companies that provide extensive training are more likely to be productive, innovative, and competitive [5]. Also, research on situated learning has demonstrated the benefit of utilizing authentic contexts [10], where the operators can simulate a scenario and learn based on both realistic and relevant situations on the job to increase their understanding of the interplay between tools, techniques and environment.

A manufacturing company that starts developing high-quality products and services must increase its response and innovation rate. To do so, it has to abandon the tight control-oriented approach and rely on workforce agility and responsibility. This requires higher skills and other kinds of skills among the employees. Boxall and Purcell [11] argue that there are major differences in what is invested in employees between high-tech manufacturing companies, on the one hand, and labour-intensive, low-tech manufacturing industry on the other. Companies can profit from teaching operators to solve technical problems as they occur, instead of calling in specialist technicians for problem solving and delaying the production [12]. Because companies rely on skilled workers in high-tech manufacturing, workplace practices centred on employee participation are assumed to pay off. This does not directly mean that in-house training programs can facilitate and contribute to a more flexible and innovative organization. However, Bessant [9] found that high involvement workplace practices encourage innovation, change and problem-solving activities on the shop floor, it involves more people in the process and by this create more opportunity for innovations to be developed. As in-house training creates new meeting arenas and often put focus at internal processes and procedures, as well as facilitates professional discussion, it is assumable that it leads to higher involvement workplace practices. And, hence, cause innovation opportunities.

2   Methodology

An instrumental case study approach is adopted. We have carried out case studies in two different companies as evidence from multiple cases is generally considered more compelling than a single case study [13]. An instrumental case study provides insight into a particular issue, redraw generalizations, or build theory [14]. As with most instrumental case studies, the research team wanted to create a new theory by building on and testing existing theory. Findings from the empirical investigation are compared with literature to bring further detail and structure to current issues. Data is collected through workshops, semi-structured interviews and meetings with representatives of the case companies.

3   Case Studies

The presentation of each case study starts with a short introduction to the company, followed by a summary of the most relevant findings. In order to anonymize the companies, we have named them company A and company B.

Company A

Company A develops and produces power distribution systems for oil and gas installations and is given a lead development role within the global corporate. The centre counts 200 permanent employees, educationally dispersed between unskilled workers, vocational workers, engineers, masters and PhDs. In addition to this comes around 40 consultants and temporary employees. Reduced appreciation of the profession and recruitment problems are considered some of the company's biggest future threats. The company has gone from traditional batch production to more unique and complex one-of-a-kind products designed in collaboration with customers. This change implied other kinds of skills on the shop floor as well as in engineering. A typical project may consist of approximately 4,000 assembly hours and 2,500 engineering hours [15]. Introduction of more advanced manufacturing, with customized products, flexible automation and computer aided manufacturing imply that the work systems become more technologically complex. This increasing complexity puts increased demands on workers' skills and knowledge. Supplementing manual skills and tacit knowledge, workers also are required to perform tasks like machine set-up and programming, which used to be reserved for technicians and engineers [16].

There is also a qualitative change in the necessary repertoire of skills. Besides professional or technical skills, there is an increased need of communication and social skills. Because the products are developed in collaboration with the customers in order to fit the customers' exact needs, the products end up as unique with their unique work plan. This means that the engineers seldom were able to submit fixed work plans to the shop floor that were ready to be used. The skilled workers on the shop floor often saw that they had to make adjustments to the work plans in order to make them practical. The practical skills of the shop floor workers ended up as very important in this kind of production and the division between blue-collar work tasks and engineering tasks was in other words blurred [15]. Thus, distinct technical competences and skills must be accompanied by broader competencies and skills, like learn to learn, critical problem solving, cultural awareness, collaboration and communication.

To avoid lay-offs but remain flexible, company A has chosen to utilize a certain amount of temporary workers. However, this increases the demand for internal teaching, and if the percentage of temporary workers passes somewhere between 10–20 %, then they experience a drop in productivity. Still with lower percentages of temporary workers, the training of them takes valuable focus from apprentices and their learning process. The trend of increased turnover has the same effect, as it demands more training of newly-hired employees. Altogether, the wear and tear at senior vocational workers who continuously remain in a teaching situation can exceed the rational boundaries. This can potentially result in lack of motivation, absent of time to self-development and limited possibility to contribute to continuous improvement efforts. Avoiding such a trend is important, as a strong professional culture is considered key to maintain a powerful innovative environment.

Combining the recruitment challenge, usage of temporary workers, higher turnover, increased complexity, growing demand of workers' skills and knowledge, as well as the enhanced need of communicational and social skills, this has led the company to realize that they need to develop an overall strategy for in-house training. They acknowledge the need to prioritize more time and resources to educational purposes and the strategy will treat training of senior vocational workers as well as apprentices and temporary employees. They realize that as the company has evolved from batch production to complex one-of-kind products, the possibility to hire sufficient-skilled vocational workers has been reduced and they have to develop required skills themselves. As the personnel safety representative puts is: *"Mass production is out of the question, so we can't buy our way to competence."*

Company B
Company B delivers large steel constructions for use on oil and gas offshore platforms and onshore process plants. The deliverables are described as projects and take years to complete. Usually, the company employs about 500–600 employees but the exact number of employees varies due to the market situation, which can change quite drastically over just two to three years. This means that company B has for several years been through many periods characterized by temporary redundancies, lay-offs, very short duration of the contracts, and a constant threat of close downs just to be followed by very high activity and even too much work in periods. In 1999/2000 there was a huge

crisis in the Norwegian offshore industry which left company B in an unusually difficult situation. For more than a year the company had no deliveries which meant that the company had to lay-off the entire work force – some of them temporary, and as much as 400 employees permanently. The management and the union worried that the company would lose important competencies when laying off that many employees and decided to carry out an outstanding effort in skill development among the employees. They aimed on new contracts and the skill development program was done in order to qualify the company for new contracts.

The management emphasized in particular three arguments for carrying out a skill development program. Firstly, the difficult situation demanded other kind of competencies than the company used to offer. In order to utilize new markets, the employees also needed to turn their skills in new directions. Secondly, the management claimed that the employees needed not only new skills, but also more skills. Thirdly, in order to be more flexible and take on different projects, operators were encouraged to take more than one certificate of apprenticeship.

The union supported the management's project on saving the company through development of skills. They argued that knowledge within one work task such as welding was very helpful, for example when scaffolding. A welder doesn't only build in accordance to what he or she has learned, but actually how he or she would have liked it to be if they were to do the welder job. In other words, they argued for getting ready for a greater understanding of the entire work process.

The shop stewards also argue that workers with several certificates of apprenticeship or formal skills are in a better position to keep their jobs in difficult periods. Although there is no job in their own local company, there may be temporary jobs within the company group. And in these situations, a broader spectrum of skills increases the possibilities for a temporary job other places. One of the shop stewards pointed out, *"If people are interested in traveling – there is always work."*

To develop certain workers' skills turns out to be a shop union strategy in getting ready for workforce reductions after the union format:

> *"We have said that in relation to workforce reduction, the seniority principle is still the most important argument. However, we see that skills are increasingly more important and there is more and more focus on the right skills when we have to cut the workforce. That's the reason why we want to participate and interfere in the discussion about who is to be offered education and courses. Otherwise, some managers may say that, "I want you here for a long time – I will offer you this and that in order for you to stay here longer." I don't know whether we have been good at it, but we have at least tried to offer this"* (shop steward, company B).

The company chose to focus on five areas when up-skilling the employees: multidisciplinarity, use of ICT, and particular expertise in logistics, management development, and team development. The skill development program lasted for almost two years and most of it was financed through public funding. When the program ended, the employees had all together carried out more than 50 000 day's work on skill development. Almost all training had been in-house training in collaboration with local colleges.

In retrospect the HR-manager claims that the difficult situation the company experienced in 2000 have left them with very useful experiences of the importance of a skill development program that not only make ready for necessary competence, but also enables employees to understand what kind of competence they need and how to acquire this competence. The HR-manager now reports that employees have started to demand more training, employees are taking responsibility for their own skill development, and vocational workers require training on areas they would never require earlier, like courses within engineering, coaching, logistics, and administration.

4   Discussion and Conclusion

From a human resource perspective, training and education are often funded in two aspects; the need for offering attractive work places and keeping employees motivated; and second, the need for continuously maintaining and developing the company's knowledge base. Neither the findings from company A nor company B are contradictory to this; however, they contain some elements that draw a wider picture of the motivation behind and the impact caused by on-the-job training.

As presented in the introduction, the development of a company towards high-quality products and services demands higher skills among employees. Furthermore, companies providing more training are more likely to be productive and innovative. However, why should companies facing high demands of flexibility and innovativeness put more effort into establishing company specific competence programs? What make them differ from high-tech mass production companies and why can't they buy external training programs or hire high-skilled workers? Research on situated learning has demonstrated that in-house learning increases the understanding of the interplay between tools, techniques and environment, but this does not cover the different needs companies that rely on flexibility are facing, compared with more stable companies. However, through our industry insights and specifically the case studies presented, we believe that an in-house training program contributes to build some important prerequisites for flexible organizations with capabilities to innovate and change.

Firstly, a company specific competence program provides a structure and a system capable of effectuating changes faster. It is also likely, that persons dedicated to the competence program are better skilled to develop new procedures and the following sharing of new practice. The increased understanding of entire work processes after the extensive training in company B support this as a possible enabler.

Secondly, a more highly skilled and innovative workforce are found key to flexible organizations. Company A has experienced that the evolution to batch and one-of-a-kind production has put pressure on internal training programs. They also pinpoint that innovativeness is determinant on a strong professional focus, which is likely to be increased by structured training. But also the increasing challenges of hiring highly skilled workers support the need for in-house training.

Thirdly and finally, a more applicable workforce increases flexibility. As seen in company B, a broader set of skills can increase the possibility to take temporary jobs at other locations within the corporate or within neighbouring companies in industrial clusters. For organizations exposed of large fluctuations, such opportunities can be key to maintain competence in the area through periods of lay-offs.

Altogether this result in the following proposition: Company specific competence programs contribute at building dynamic and flexible organizations and increase their capability to face change in technology and marked. Future research should investigate this further, including each of the prerequisites proposed and their cause-effect relations.

This work has been conducted with support from the project *Verdikjede fagarbeider* supported by The Regional Research Counsil of Mid-Norway and the research project *HPWS.no* supported by The Research Council of Norway.

References

1. Ashton, D.N., Sung, J.: Supporting workplace learning for high performance working. International Labour Organization (2002)
2. Danford, A., Richardson, M., Stewart, P., Tailby, S., Upchurch, M.: Partnership, high performance work systems and quality of working life. New Technol. Work Employ. **23**(3), 151–166 (2008)
3. White, M., Hill, S., Mills, C., Smeaton, D.: Managing to Change? British Workplaces and the Future of Work. Palgrave Macmillan, Basingstoke (2004)
4. MacDuffie, J.P.: Human resource bundles and manufacturing performance: organizational logic and flexible production systems in the world auto industry. Ind. Labor Relat. Rev. **48**, 197–221 (1995)
5. Bills, D.B., Hodson, R.: Worker training: a review, critique, and extension. Res. Soc. Stratification Mobility **25**(4), 258–272 (2007)
6. Frazis, H., Gittleman, M., Joyce, M.: Correlates of training: an analysis using both employer and employee characteristics. Ind. Labor Relat. Rev. **53**(3), 443–462 (2000)
7. Arulampalam, W., Booth, A.L., Bryan, M.L.: Training in Europe, IZA Discussion paper series, NO. 933 (2003)
8. Knoke, D., Janowiec-Kurle, L.: Make or buy? The externalization of company job training. Res. Sociol. Organ. **16**, 85–106 (1999)
9. Bessant, J.: High-involvement innovation: building and sustaining competitive advantage through continuous change. Wiley, Chichester (2003)
10. Lave, J., Wenger, E.: Situated Learning: Legitimate Peripheral Participation. Cambridge University Press, Cambridge (1991)
11. Boxall, P., Purcell, J.: An HRM perspective on employee participation. In: Wilkinson, A., Gollan, P.J., Marchington, M., Lewin, D. (eds.) The Oxford handbook of participation in organizations, p. XV. Oxford University Press, Oxford (2010). (624 p)
12. Wall, T.D., Corbett, J.M., Clegg, C.W., Jackson, P.R., Martin, R.: Advanced manufacturing technology and work design: towards a theoretical framework. J. Organ. Behav. **11**(3), 201–219 (1990)
13. Yin, R.K.: Case Study Research: Design and Methods. Sage publications, Thousand Oaks (2009)
14. Stake, R.E.: Multiple Case Study Analysis. The Guilford Press, New York (2006)
15. Finnestrand, H.O., Ravn, J.E.: Prosjektindustri - partssamarbeid og nye organisasjonsformer. In: Brøgger, B. (ed.) Å tjene på samarbeid: medvirkning, partssamarbeid, bedriftsutvikling. Gyldendal akademisk, Oslo, p 173 s (2007)
16. Knutstad, G., Ravn, J.E.: Technology utilization as competitive advantage-a sociotechnical approach to high performance work systems. In: Advanced Materials Research, pp 555–561. Trans Tech Publ (2014)

Prediction of Process Time for Early Production Planning Purposes

Mads Bejlegaard[✉], Thomas Ditlev Brunoe, and Kjeld Nielsen

Department of Mechanical and Manufacturing Engineering, Aalborg University,
Aalborg, Denmark
bejlegaard@m-tech.aau.dk

Abstract. The production ramp-up process is critical to stay competitive and to capture market share but there are some common problems encountered during ramp-up. Among others one problem is related to the maturity of the production processes, including unforeseen bottlenecks. This paper contributes to the production planning part of the ramp-up process by showing how to predict the process time for new parts that is to be introduced in an existing manufacturing environment. A statistical model based on historical product-data is applied and the potential advantages of the model are outlined.

Keywords: Regression · Ramp-up · Production planning · Reconfigurable manufacturing systems

1   Introduction

In the context of changing market conditions due to globalization, companies experience fluctuations in product demand besides the need of introducing new innovative products more often [6]. Hence, the ramp-up process is critical to stay competitive and to increase market share. The production ramp-up is introduced in the new product development (NPD) but little literature studies in detail the ramp-up issue [11]. One common characteristic of the ramp-up phase is the lack of planning reliability [8]. In a comprehensive study on production ramp-up, common problems encountered during ramp-up are classified and includes problems which are related to the maturity of the production processes [11]. This includes slow set-ups, unforeseen bottlenecks, and manufacturability of the products (i.e. product design-process fit) [11]. The ability to accurately predict the process time for new parts that are to be introduced in an existing or new manufacturing environment can prevent or reduce the above mentioned problems by increasing the accuracy of the production planning (i.e. design of the manufacturing system).

The Reconfigurable Manufacturing System (RMS) is a new manufacturing system paradigm which is partly designed to meet these ramp-up issues. Thus RMS works towards the ability to rapidly adapt to new market conditions (i.e. change to the exact capacity and functionality needed when needed) [7]. However, new parts or a new product family introduced in existing manufacturing environments will often be

© IFIP International Federation for Information Processing 2015
S. Umeda et al. (Eds.): APMS 2015, Part I, IFIP AICT 459, pp. 406–413, 2015.
DOI: 10.1007/978-3-319-22756-6_50

incorporated in a balanced flow, which is why accurate prediction of process times to predict future requirements to the manufacturing system in an early stage is relevant. Ideally the RMS provides the ability to change functionality of existing systems and machines to suit new production requirements and scale the capacity by adding, removing or rearranging manufacturing resources and system components [7]. However, a prediction of the process time will still provide beneficial knowledge of the capacity needed when reconfiguring the system.

Some manufacturing equipment can provide the information of the expected process time, e.g. a robot programmed for a certain cycle. However, this information will only be available after the programing, and thus prediction of the process time on an earlier stage is valuable in the context of rapid configuration on a system level (see Fig. 2), e.g. balancing a line. Furthermore, it is difficult to predict the process time on manual processes. However, it is easier to adjust the capacity on manual manufacturing processes due to the human flexibility; early information of the process time still has influence on the ramp-up in relation to the production planning.

This paper addresses the issue of late knowledge of the actual time it takes to produce new parts that are to be introduced in a new or existing manufacturing environment. Similar work has not been identified whereas many methods have been developed for cost estimation [2, 3, 10], and [12]. One of these determines a method for using historical data for cost estimation for quotation purposes using statistics [1]. Likewise, this paper presents a case study of applying a statistical model. In this case for time estimation sufficiently accurate for a more precise estimation of process times for the purpose of more accurate production planning during ramp-up. Thus, it is shown that it is possible to predict process times.

2   Method

An extract of historical, registered process time was made from the database of an ERP system in a large Danish manufacturer of industrial equipment, while the rest of the data used was manually gathered from a CAD system. The historical process time is the mean of registered process time related to a part from the last five quarters. The research is based on a part family and the related processes in a welding department as visualized in [14]. First of all, parts undergoing the same processes running through the welding department were divided into families. Second, a family was selected and the routing deduced, all in order to demarcate the analysis (Fig. 1).

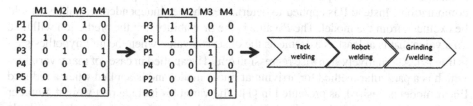

Fig. 1. Part family clustering for routing formation in order to demarcate the analysis, where M's are machines (i.e. cell level in Fig. 2) and P's are parts.

The data consists of the parts in this particular part family, how many times they were produced, and the process time for each time they were produced in the sample period. The rest of the data (referred to as product-data) includes part weight, number of subcomponents, part dimensions (i.e. area and volume).

A linear regression analysis is applied to analyze the relations between the independent variables (i.e. product-data) and the dependent variables (i.e. historical, registered process time related to the product parts undergoing the processes in the chosen routing). As illustrated in Fig. 2, the regressions are made on various levels of the manufacturing system as described by [14] first on the segment level and successively traversing to lower levels until an acceptable level of accuracy is obtained. The analysis takes it starting point at the segment level as a relation between process time and product data is expected to show when the overall process technology gets common to all included parts, e.g. welding, machining etc. As a function of effect size (i.e. relation between variables) and the level of significance a sample size between 12 and 30 is required [5]. Hereby, you can argue that the validity of the analysis gets unreliable if the sample size gets under 12, when it is divided in underlying levels, even with a strong relation between variables.

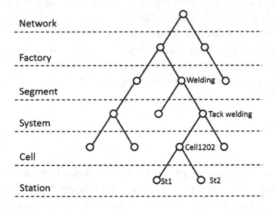

Fig. 2. Breakdown structure of the manufacturing system, inspired by [13, 14]

Some of the independent variables can appear insignificant or appear as noise to the result. One method to find the most precise combination of variables is to test all alternative combinations of the independent variables that can be considered. Although, only a maximum of seven independent variables are used it will imply testing 13,699 linear combinations. Instead P is applied to determine whether independent variables should be excluded from the model. The P-value is the probability that the prediction will take on a value that is at least as extreme as the observed value when the null hypothesis H_0 is true [9]. Alternatively stepwise regression could be applied in cases of many variables which is a particular method for arriving at linear model and is applied when a reduced linear model is desired, as presented in [1]. The variables include part weight, number of subcomponents, part dimensions (i.e. area and volume), which was the available product information. The mandatory data is the time used on each part in each process.

Depending on the sequence in which the regressions are made the process time from the first process in the routing of the part family (i.e. the dependent variable) can be applied as an independent variable for the next regression etc.

In order to determine the system level (see Fig. 2) on which, an acceptable prediction accuracy is obtained an evaluation criteria must be set. It is often seen that residual sum of squares (R^2 or modified R^2), i.e. how well the observed data fits the model, is used. However as it is argued in [1], it may be difficult to translate this measure into a business term, why Mean Absolute Percentage Error (MAPE) can be used instead as an evaluation criteria to compare the predicted values the observed values.

3   Results

Figures 3, 4, and 5 show the results for the analysis performed to determine the level accuracy in predicting the process time. Since the regression analysis was carried out on the manual tack welding cell as the first of the three cells in the particular routing, this only included four independent variables. Thus one variable can be added to the pool of independent variables for each step (i.e. move from one system area to the next based on the routing). However, the results on system level (including tack welding, robot welding and grinding/welding) did not obtain the desired level of accuracy.

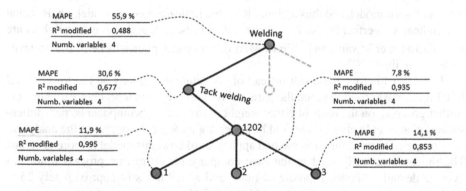

Fig. 3. Results related to tack welding and the identification of prediction accuracy at each of the included manufacturing system levels

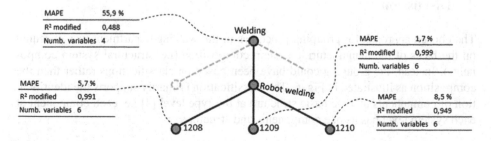

Fig. 4. Results related to robot welding and the identification of prediction accuracy at each of the included manufacturing system levels

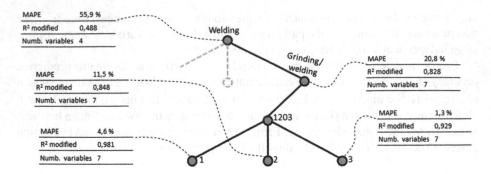

Fig. 5. Results related to grinding/welding and the identification of prediction accuracy at each of the included manufacturing system levels

For this reason these were broken down into cells or stations (if only one cell was represented) to obtain more accurate predictions.

MAPE is the measure of how much the predicted time values in average deviate from the observed time values using the regression model. R^2 represents how well the regression model describes the variation in the observed data. The R^2 indicates how well the data fits the model, and thus a higher R^2 value indicates a better model, i.e. R^2 equal to 1 indicates a perfect fit. As it is illustrated in Figs. 3, 4, and 5, fewer variables are related to a lower R^2 value and a higher MAPE. This can explain why cell 1203 achieves better result than 1202.

To further improve the result instead of dividing into stations on the lowest level (see Fig. 2) it was tried to group the parts on the basis of the independent variables, i.e. further grouping on the basis of either weight, number of subcomponents, part dimensions (i.e. area and volume). This did however not improve the output of the analysis.

Compared to the estimation method applied until now, this model is more accurate. The methods currently used in the case company for estimating process times has average deviations between predicted times and actual times of approximately 25 % while the results presented gives an MAPE of 7.5 %.

4   Discussion

The chosen approach for grouping processes in the welding department was executed on the basis of the manufacturing system composition (i.e. structural system components). Instead, the grouping could have been based on classifications rather than the composition as illustrated in Fig. 6. The classification primarily supports the identification of components and the basic structure at the type level [4] i.e. each component at each system level has its one components and structure.

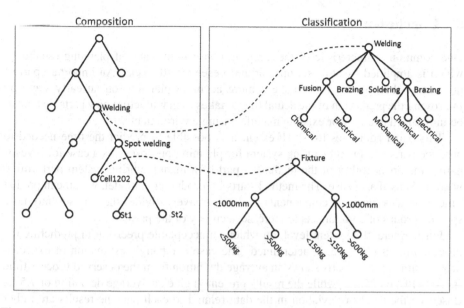

Fig. 6. Both composition and classification can be applied as two different approaches for structuring a process breakdown for the purpose of identifying commonalities in processes. Inspired by [4]

It is not unusual that one observation deviates 25 % from the average of the observed time values in the sample period, even when potential outliers is sorted from the rest. The operators' time consumption at the included stations tends to have a higher degree of fluctuation for manual processes compared to semi-automated processes. This may be due to semi-automated processes' fixed procedures but in general the fluctuation may be caused by a lack of responsibility to the customer process and an insufficiently implemented process execution procedure. This can explain better prediction accuracy for the semi-automated process using the regression model. For this reason the accuracy of the result may be improved if the sequence of regression analyses switched to start on the basis of data from processes with fixed procedures and then use the dependent variable from this analysis as an independent variable in the next etc., instead of following the sequence of the routing.

Since the model uses historical data it is worth considering how to keep the data on which the predictions are made, updated. Most of manufacturing processes are underlying continues improvements and new parts are constantly introduced, and thus new data emerges. Furthermore, it would be reasonable to expect increasing learning curves following process changes, thus increased efficiency of employees could be expected. The updating frequency of the data then becomes an important issue. This issue is currently not addressed, but it will be crucial to update the data when changes occur to the process. Knowledge of the frequency of which updated procedures or process changes occurs could be used to infer an appropriate updating frequency.

5   Conclusion

One common characteristic of the ramp-up phase is the lack of planning reliability, which is amplified by slow set-ups and unforeseen bottlenecks. An important part of preventing these issues is to make a more accurate planning on an early stage by improving the prediction of the actual time it takes to manufacture new parts that are to be introduced in a new or existing manufacturing environment.

This paper addresses to which extent it is possible to predict the time needed to produce parts in a manufacturing system for planning purposes. As a case for investigating the applicability of the method, a part of a manufacturing system performing welding is used as a case. The method starts by producing a model, which can predict time for a wide range of components, and successively divides the data set into more specific groups of components to increase accuracy of the predictions.

Furthermore, the system level, on which an acceptable precision in predicting the process time is obtained, is determined. The case company's estimation of expected process time for new parts shows an average deviation from the observed process time (i.e. MAPE) on 25.2 % while the results presented give an average deviation of 7.5 %. Based on the level of deviation in the data related to each part the results are rather promising. The results further indicated a relation between the prediction accuracy and the level of automation, since the prediction of the process time on a semi-automated process had greater accuracy. It is likely that information of competence level could be included to increase the prediction accuracy on manual processes, e.g. include information on operators capabilities or if the work is performed by an apprentice. However, this would conflict with the broad use of the model unless operators with certain levels of competencies are permanently dedicated specific processes.

The model can be applied in many contexts, e.g. introducing a new part or new products in an existing or new manufacturing environment if the necessary historical data to predict the process time is available. This can potentially reduce the costs related to inaccurate production planning (i.e. reduce the cost of slow set-ups and unforeseen bottlenecks). In cases of high MAPE, the model can be used as an indicator that the process is not properly designed or that tools are not appropriate for the job, i.e. indirectly, the model can indicate that one process is not performing as well as the majority of the processes.

Using the model in relation to the composition structure gives a generic approach while using the classification approach is more likely to be individual. The composition structure follows the hierarchical structure that is easy to apply but classification structures could provide a higher prediction accuracy of process time.

The greatest challenge in utilizing the model is the issue of updating when process changes occur. Nevertheless, knowledge of the frequency of which updated procedures or process changes occurs could be used to infer an appropriate updating frequency.

References

1. Brunoe, T.D., Nielsen, P.: A case of cost estimation in an engineer–to–order company moving towards mass customisation. Int. J. Mass Customisation **4**, 239–254 (2012)

2. García-Crespo, Á., Ruiz-Mezcua, B., López-Cuadrado, J. L. et al.: A review of conventional and knowledge based systems for machining price quotation. J. Intell. Manuf. 1–19
3. H'mida, F., Martin, P., Vernadat, F.: Cost estimation in mechanical production: the cost entity approach applied to integrated product engineering. Int. J. Prod. Econ. **103**, 17–35 (2006)
4. Jørgensen, K.A.: Information Modelling of Product Families. Unpublished (2011)
5. Karlsson, C.: Researching Operations Management. Routledge, London (2009)
6. Koren, Y.: The Global Manufacturing Revolution: Product-Process-Business Integration and Reconfigurable Systems. Wiley, Hoboken (2010)
7. Koren, Y., Shpitalni, M.: Design of reconfigurable manufacturing systems. J. Manuf. Syst. **29**, 130–141 (2010)
8. Meier, H., Homuth, M.: Holistic ramp-up management in SME-networks, pp. 123–128 (2006)
9. Montgomery, D.C.: Introduction to Statistical Quality Control, 5th edn. Wiley, Hoboken (2005)
10. Shtub, A., Versano, R.: Estimating the cost of steel pipe bending, a comparison between neural networks and regression analysis. Int. J. Prod. Econ. **62**, 201–207 (1999)
11. Surbier, L., Alpan, G., Blanco, E.: A comparative study on production ramp-up: state-of-the-art and new challenges. Prod. Plann. Control **25**, 1264–1286 (2014)
12. Verlinden, B., Duflou, J., Collin, P., et al.: Cost estimation for sheet metal parts using multiple regression and artificial neural networks: a case study. Int. J. Prod. Econ. **111**, 484–492 (2008)
13. Westkämper, E., Westkaemper, E.: Research for Adaptive Assembly, pp. 15–17 (2006)
14. Wiendahl, H., ElMaraghy, H.A., Nyhuis, P., et al.: Changeable manufacturing-classification, design and operation. CIRP Ann. Manuf. Technol. **56**, 783–809 (2007)

Information Logistics Means to Support a Flexible Production?

Susanne Altendorfer-Kaiser[✉]

Industrial Logistics, Montanuniversitaet Leoben, Leoben, Austria
susanne.altendorfer@unileoben.ac.at

Abstract. The information economy is characterized by an excessive supply of data and information, which makes it difficult to establish an optimal information management. Therefore, this paper deals with the challenge of how an efficient information logistics can be established. An approach using the lean philosophy for identification and categorization of information is presented. The paper concludes with the importance of Information logistics and how lean information flows support a flexible production.

Keywords: Information flow · Information systems · Muda · Production

1 Background

Under the theme Industry 4.0 the manufacturing industry, especially in Germany and Austria, works on the creation of increasingly intelligent, autonomous and decentralized subsystems that should lead to more competitive production and logistics processes. Therefore the effective and economical integration of information and decision-making bodies is relevant. If this integration is efficiently performed on all system and corporate levels this can be the key success factor.

Despite the increased use of currently available technologies such as RFID or semi-autonomous control of production and logistics facilities the immediate intra- and inter-company transfer of information along the supply chains is often very limited. However in times of growing competitiveness and shorter times-to-market an efficient and cost-optimized material flow can arise only through the sophisticated integration of production and information processes. Thus, the collection and use of information is of increasingly importance.

Due to recent developments and trends such as Industry 4.0, Big Data, Data Analytics data and/or information is omnipresent. This apparent advantage can be quickly turned into a drawback: there is an oversupply of data that are not beneficial information to their environment and this also includes more disadvantages than potential for a company. This flood of data means that the truly relevant information may not be located at the time needed.

Just by the strong interconnectedness, availability and information overload, it is essential for companies to have the right information at the right time in the right form at the right place for the right person [2, 18].

© IFIP International Federation for Information Processing 2015
S. Umeda et al. (Eds.): APMS 2015, Part I, IFIP AICT 459, pp. 414–421, 2015.
DOI: 10.1007/978-3-319-22756-6_51

This aspect, however, is still often underestimated as the subject of information is still very strong anchoring purely in the IT department. Here, the data management is the main focus during the transformation of the physical data. It would be just a strategic necessity for companies to bring the information flows with the material flows in harmony. Information and communication technologies (ICT) are here a key technology in order to targetly embed the information flows with the production processes. Reference [17] However, the importance of ICT is not yet completely defined precisely in the area of information logistics and still in science there are different views.

Therefore this paper deals with the importance of Information logistics and how lean information flows support a flexible production.

2 Terms and Definitions

The competitiveness of companies in the future is strongly influenced by the way they do business. Here, knowledge becomes an integral production factor. And knowledge is based on information. Nowadays information is omnipresent – it is the time of the so-called information society. Not only in our private lives we are confronted with information also the daily business is formed by an information overload.

Especially for companies the right information at the right time is nowadays a crucial asset. Barney defines information as one resource (among others) that enables "the firm to conceive of and implement strategies that improve its efficiency and effectiveness" [3]. Nevertheless it is not the quantity that is important. It is the quality of information that comes into value.

Here Floridi defined the general definition of information (GDI) as a tripartite way: σ is an instance of information, as semantic context, if:

- (GDI.1) σ consists of one or more data;
- (GDI.2) the data in σ are well-formed;
- (GDI.3) the well-formed data in σ are meaningful [5].

In order to talk about the quality of information in general and for logistics in particular, it is important at this point to define the terms data, information and knowledge, to connect information and logistics in a more appropriate way (Fig. 1).

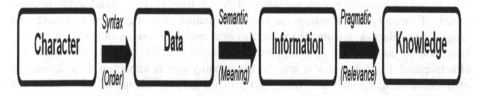

Fig. 1. Interconnection between data, information and knowledge 1

- *Data*: The noun data is defined as facts and statistics collected together for reference or analysis. The term itself comes from the Latin plural of "datum".

- *Information*: For this paper the relevant definition of information is defined as something that is conveyed or represented by a particular arrangement or sequence. The term information origins in the Latin verb "*informare*" (in English "to inform"), which means 'to give from' or 'to form an idea of'. Furthermore the Latin noun "*informatio*" had already had the meaning of concept and idea".
- *Knowledge*: Knowledge comes from the verb "to know", which is of Germanic origin. Knowledge means facts, information, and skills acquired through experience or education and can refer to theoretical and practical understanding of a subject. Furthermore it can be divided between implicit and explicit knowledge.

Especially data, its generation, storage and use in form of information is essential for the material flow (illustrated in Fig. 2).

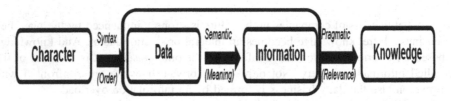

Fig. 2. Important areas of the information logistics for the material flow [1, 6]

Nevertheless, the importance of information and related information and communication technologies must be recognized for logistics and their benefit aspects of logistics must be placed in the foreground. Current developments in the field of auto-ID technologies and cyber-physical systems provide high potential for the logistics area, but can only be used up completely when both the logistics and the information relevant factors are considered. Only through an appropriate symbiosis of information and material flows can be directing support the logistics, according to the principle "IT enables business" [12]. Therefore, it is desirable to consider the information logistics as a design element and give it an appropriate role in logistics.

3   Information Flow Management for Information Logistics

Nowadays information is omnipresent – it is the time of the so-called information society. Especially for companies the right information at the right time is nowadays a crucial asset. Barney defines information as one resource (among others) that enables "the firm to conceive of and implement strategies that improve its efficiency and effectiveness" [3]. Nevertheless it is not the quantity that is important. It is the quality of information that comes into value. But it is not only the quality of information that matters. What's even as important is that the information is at the right time at the right place. Here the six R's of logistics matter for the proper information flow management.

The following Table 1 shows the six R's of logistics applied on information [2].

Table 1. 6 R's of logistics applied on Information [2]

R's	Information context
Right information	Necessary for the user
Right time	Decision-supportive
Right quantity	As much as necessary
Right place	Accessible for the user
Right quality	Detailed enough and usable
Right costs	Reasonable price

To support the realisation of an adequate information flow management within the company, the concept of IT as enabler of process change is still on the forefront although dates already back to [4, 7]. A change in information systems is possible as the technological progress over the years has opened new possibilities to support the organizational reengineering. However, information system aspects have often been left out of consideration in reengineering projects. Information systems often have had and still have the status of being a matter of course and therefore their integration is often not thoroughly considered [8]. Thus companies are far too often behind in their information technologies. Software systems are often out-dated and poorly structured. The need for agile software architecture to support IFM becomes evident when the need for more flexibility and reduced costs in the daily business urges companies to restructure.

Martin defines a company as an open, socio-technical system with an organisation that has the goal to supply its customers in a satisfactorily way and by doing so making profit [9]. As open system it has a lot of interfaces to the outside world, as shown in Fig. 3.

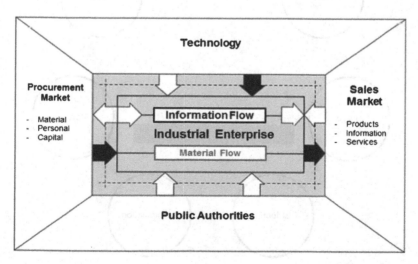

Fig. 3. Interfaces of a company [translated to English based on [10]]

Highlighted in this figure is the information flow, which runs in parallel to the material flow. This already shows the importance of a defined information flow and a well established information flow management. And an IFM is not only necessary for intra-company flows but also for the whole supply chain. Vogt puts a lot of weight on the importance of information along the supply chain: "Information regarding the demand for, quality of the products, and other factors such as financing, and guarantees, will flow up and down the supply chain to keep every member informed of the current state of affairs pertaining to their products. This information must be timely and accurate as the manufacturing of the products must be adjusted to the demand as quickly as possible" [13].

4   Identification of Relevant Information – Impossible?

Information logistics has many parallels to the production logistics. Thus, the logistical principle of "6R" can be applied to the information and the information life cycle can certainly see similarities with the product life cycle.

With the life-cycle model for information it is possible to identify which phases information pass through (Fig. 4).

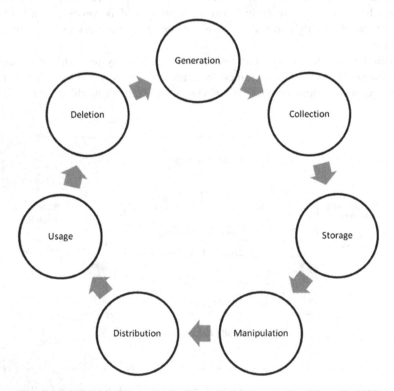

Fig. 4. Information life cycle (developed after the product life cycle [19])

In a further step, corresponding tasks can be defined and assigned to appropriate technologies for the realization of the individual phases. (This aspect however is not addressed in this paper).

What is, however, treated in the literature very little, are the ways to stem the flood of information by controlling the information life cycle and make a categorization of value-added and non-value-added information. Therefore, in this section an opportunity is presented in the context of production management to identify relevant information.

The car manufacturer Toyota achieved to stabilize the organization through a targeted focus on the prevention of waste in the production process, resulting in high quality products resulted. The resulting strategies and methods to eliminate internal waste (Muda) helped Toyota in the 1970s and 1980s [7]. Considering the current process structure of modern enterprises certain parallels between production and information processes in terms of avoiding waste can be drawn. Modern hardware and software solutions promise greater transparency and increased efficiency through the collection and analysis of numerous data. However, due to the high density of information it is often difficult to assess them according to their percentage of completion. The apparent security to hoard all the relevant data proves in many cases than risk losing sight of what is essential. Omnipresent media such as the Internet allow an enterprise-wide manipulation, which on one hand is a significant advantage of modern technology, but on the other hand also enhances the potential for information-related waste. For this reason, it requires a strict editing and plausibility check of information, which can be created by the definition of cross-company practices. As a basis for the establishment of such standards, the detection and localisation of wastes might be used. Therefore, an attempt is made based on Chapados [20] to transfer the types of waste as defined by Taiichi Ohno [21] within production to waste types of information (Table 2).

Table 2. Muda of information compared to muda of production [21]

Muda of production	Muda of information
Over production	Production of wrong information
Idle times	Delay in the information retrieval
Transport	To many interfaces
Production	No clear definition what kind of information is needed
Movements	High effort of transformation
Stock	Inefficient storage
Maintenance	Missing or wrong information

The resulting "Muda of information" should identify the main causes of a possible "Over informatisation" so as to identify targets for efficient data management. It was also discussed explicitly in addition to usually quickly identifiable wastes to those shapes that result from previous errors. One example for this is the inefficient allocation of access rights. But also the involvement of too many interfaces contributes negatively to the overall efficiency of the information process and thus to inefficiency of the overall process. The success of this, at first trivial-sounding approach is, however, boycotted by several sites as compared to the outdated structures or non-acceptance of the user. Therefore, the industrial desensibilisation to information processes and media must be pursued. The creation of common structures and standards represents a proven form to reduce and prevent information-related wastes.

5 Conclusion and Outlook

Information Logistics has a great potential to support the processes of a company and the whole production area. Especially initiatives like cyber-physical systems, Internet of Things and Industry 4.0 are strongly heading in the direction of smart factory and horizontal and vertical integration along the supply chain. At this point information logistics will be an essential cornerstone. With the ongoing research we will strongly investigate on the information flow management and the necessary methods and techniques for information logistics.

This paper highlights information as becoming increasingly important and targeted identification and categorization of the information would be necessary. Therefore, it is essential to consider information logistics as an independent and significant part of the company. A deficit in the field of information logistics is partly due to the fact that there are no uniform standards or no industry-wide reference models, such as the information logistics should best be integrated into the company and can be achieved as an ideal link between information logistics and production. Only in this way, depending on the flow of information, production can be optimized.

References

1. Auer, T.: Wissensmanagement: Reizwort oder zeitgemäße Notwendigkeit, Publikation im Controller-Leitfaden 12/2008, WEKA Verlag (2008)
2. Augustin, S.: Informationswirtschaft und Informationslogistik im Industrieunternehmen. Montanuniversität Leoben, München (1990)
3. Barney, J.: Firm resources and sustained competitive advantage. J. Manage. **17**, 99–120 (1991)
4. Davenport, T.: Process Innovation: Reengineering Work Through Information Technology. Harvard Business School Press, Boston (1993)
5. Floridi, L.: Information: A Very Short Introduction, pp. 3–59. Oxford University Press, Oxford (2010)
6. Hacker, W.: Informationsflussgestaltung als Arbeits- und Organisationsoptimerung. Jenseits des Wissensmanagements. vdf Hochschulverlag AG an der ETH Zürich (2007)
7. Hammer, M., Champy, J.: Reengineering the Corporation: A Manifesto for Business Revolution. HarperCollins Publishers, New York (2003)
8. Kawalek, J.: Rethinking Information Systems in Organizatons. Integrating Organisational Problem Solving. Routledge, New York (2008)

9. Martin, H.: Transport-und Lagerlogistik.Planung, Struktur, Steuerung und Kosten von Systemen der Intralogistik. Springer Vieweg, München (2011)

10. Osterloh, M., Frost, J.: Prozessmanagement als Kernkompetenz: Wie Sie Business Reengineering strategisch nutzen können (Processmanagement as Core Competence: How to strategically use Business Reengineering). Gabler Verlag, Wiesbaden (2006)

11. Semar, W.: Weiss + Appetito Holding AG - Software für den ganzen Konzern. In: Wölfle, R., Schubert, P. (eds.) Dauerhafter Erfolg mit Business Software – 10 Jahre Fallstudien nach der eXperience Methodik, pp. 51–64. Carl Hanser, München (2009)

12. Sundblad, S., Sundblad, P.: Business improvement through better architected software. Microsoft Archit. J. (2007)

13. Vogt, J.J., Pienaar, W., de Wit, P.W.C.: Business Logisitics Management: Theory and Practice, 2nd edn. Oxford University Press, South Africa (2005)

14. Gudehus, T.: Logistik. Grundlagen-Strategien-Anwendungen, 4th edn. Auflage, München (2010)

15. Winter, R., Dinter, B.: Integrierte Informationslogistik (2008)

16. Eversheim, W., Luczak, H.: Industrielle Logistik, 8th edn. Auflage, Mainz (2004)

17. Straube, F.: e-Logistik. Ganzheitliches Logistikmanagement (2004)

18. Zsifkovits, H.: Schwerpunkte der Industrielogistik. In: WINGbusiness 4, S. 12–13 (2014)

19. Schuh, G., Schmidt, C.: Produktionsmanagement: Handbuch Produktion und Management, 2. Auflage (2014)

20. Chiarini, A.: Lean Organization: from the Tools of the Toyota Production System to Lean Office (2013)

21. Chapados, C: Eight wastes of information. http://toyotaproductionsystemus.wordpress.com/2013/05/04/eight-wastes-muda-of-information/. Abrufdatum 10 Jan 2014

22. Dahlgaard, J., Dahlgaard-Park, S.: Lean production, six sigma quality, TQM and company culture. TQM Mag. **18**, 263–281 (2006)

Why Do Plant Managers Struggle to Synchronize Production Capacity and Costs with Demand in Face of Volatility and Uncertainty?

Obstacles Within Strategizing Volume-Oriented Changeability in Practice

Manuel Rippel[✉], Johannes Schmiester, and Paul Schönsleben

D-MTEC, BWI Center for Industrial Management, ETH Zurich, Zurich, Switzerland
mrippel@ethz.ch

Abstract. Production plants are currently facing an increase in volatility and uncertainty of demand volumes. This environmental condition comes with highly fixed costs and capacity structures, which are mostly planned on the basis of forecasts and demand projections. Thereby, changing demand causes variances in manufacturing unit costs, endangering production plants' profitability, competitiveness and liquidity. Hence, synchronizing capacities and costs with demand volumes becomes an essential target for plant managers in the face of demand volatility and uncertainty. Approaching this target in practice entails various obstacles due to dynamic and interdependent target conflicts as well as a lack of a dedicated and applicable strategizing approach. In this paper, these obstacles are disclosed and evaluated based on action research cases.

Keywords: Uncertainty · Volatility · Resilience · Changeability · Strategizing

1 Introduction

Production plants are currently facing an increasingly volatile and uncertain environment. Demand volatility materializes in fluctuations with shorter cycles and higher amplitudes. Spillovers from a company's market environment (e.g. financial markets, political conflicts, trade embargos) enhance the dynamics behind demand volume fluctuations. Disruptions as a distinct form of volatility due to extreme events are likely to happen more frequently and severely affect companies [1]. These extreme events are highly distinctive in their characteristics making each a one-of-a-kind event [1]. A variety of scientific approaches and concepts have been developed regarding the responsiveness towards changing business environments of organizations and organizational units in the manufacturing sector [2]. There is still no uniform understanding and terminology in academia, neither in one discipline nor cross different disciplines. Instead, several terms (e.g., flexibility, changeability, agility, resilience) are used with partly different, partly overlapping focuses [3–5]. In addition, technical issues are given priority, and an integration of disciplinary perspectives is mostly left unregarded [2].

© IFIP International Federation for Information Processing 2015
S. Umeda et al. (Eds.): APMS 2015, Part I, IFIP AICT 459, pp. 422–430, 2015.
DOI: 10.1007/978-3-319-22756-6_52

Recently conducted action research cases (in eight production plants in six countries over two years) addressed in depth strategizing and implementing abilities in production plants to handle demand volatility and uncertainty. These cases mainly provide the data for this paper and constitute the basis of the presented findings.

The objective of this paper is to identify and evaluate the obstacles for economically and competitively handling demand volatility and uncertainty in production plants. The purpose is to provide the explicitly revealed problem context for further research on an academically sound and practically relevant approach for strategizing the required abilities of production plants. Therefore, the following reflection questions will be answered by presenting and evaluating the observed and experienced problem context and circumstances in managerial practice:

(a) Which implications have demand volatility and uncertainty on production plants?
(b) Which obstacles arise and hamper managers when dealing with the implications?

2 Implications of Demand Volatility and Uncertainty

The first step examines the fundamental issues that arise from the external environmental factors demand volatility and uncertainty and the effect they have on the "production plant." Based on this, a dedicated target is derived and defined.

Volatility is exacerbated by a high degree of uncertainty, making it almost impossible for manufacturing companies to predict future demands and interfering fluctuations and disruptions. In addition, progressing globalization sets requirements for manufacturing companies (e.g. in regard to competitiveness, sourcing and supply chain management) [6]. Production plants face increasing pressure by corporate entities regarding their competitiveness to external peers (e.g. within Make-or-Buy decisions, performance benchmarks). Furthermore, production plants are also exposed to increasing competition in their own manufacturing networks (e.g. within relocation decisions from high-wage to low-wage countries). Demand forecasts and scenarios are often the main basis for planning and decision-making in industrial practice. These forecasts are based either on mathematical extrapolation of historical data or on individual experiences of experts. As the frequency and extent of extreme events increases and are hardly possible to forecast in an uncertain world, their assumptions and recommendations often turn out to be wrong, and plans and decisions regarding capacity structure of production plants fail to materialize.

The above mentioned environmental factors affect capacity structures of manufacturing plants, which are typically characterized by a high level of fixed costs. These structures refer to the main production factors, people, assets and resulting cost positions. Due to their rigid and specific nature, investments into fixed assets can often be regarded as sunk costs, and the related depreciation and financing costs make up a significant share of manufacturing plants' fixed costs [7]. When volatile and uncertain demand markets clash with high levels of rigid fixed costs at the manufacturing plant, high variances of unit costs evolve, which significantly impact the plant's operational performance, i.e. its profitability. Variances of unit costs occur when the antecedent projected unit costs cannot be realized since deviations emerge between forecasted and factual production volume. In particular, the fixed cost cannot be absorbed as intended in the forecast. It is not about managing volatility and uncertainty because their occurrence cannot be influenced as external factors. What can be managed is the ability of the system to handle these economic and competitive factors.

Taking these problems into account, a synchronization of capacities and costs with demand volumes becomes an essential target for the production plant management (see Fig. 1). As an idealized target state: Manufacturing costs always emerge simultaneously with the production output as well as with the demanded and appropriately provided capacity. In growth phases, delivery reliability can be ensured while manufacturing costs increase less than production output in order to reduce unit costs and enhance profit margin. In decline phases, manufacturing costs can be adapted downwards according to the descending production output. This kind of synchronization is defined as volume-oriented changeability (VoC), which should ensure robust and sustainable profitability and competitiveness of a production plant [7]. VoC was introduced as concept in order to specifically focus on and address the challenges, obstacles, requirements and solutions of handling the implications of volume fluctuations in industrial practice [7, 8]. VoC can be regarded as a specific subset of the broad concept of changeability [3] and should contribute to a company's demand-responsive supply chain [9].

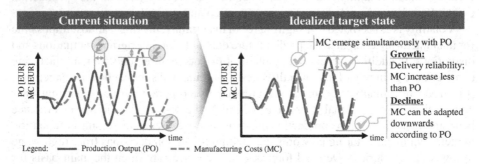

Fig. 1. Volume-oriented changeability – Synchronizing capacity and costs with demand.

3   Obstacles When Dealing with Implications

Dealing with the above mentioned implications involves preventively changing and influencing the system's configuration and characteristics as well as to taking measures when necessary. Plant managers should take action and prepare the plant by strategizing and implementing VoC with the goal of synchronizing capacities and costs with demand fluctuations. Arising obstacles are identified and evaluated in the following.

3.1   Business Cycle-Continuous Profitability (O1)

The intended synchronization of costs and capacities with demand volume is mostly guiding plant managers towards reducing fixed costs and increasing the share of variable costs. Thereby, conflicts evolve in a multi-period perspective (see Fig. 2).

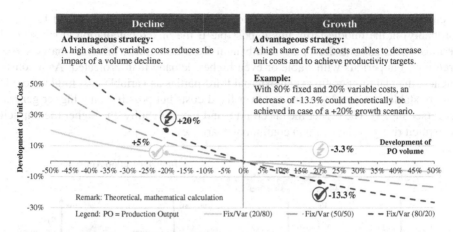

Fig. 2. Development of unit cost dependent on production output and share of fixed costs.

While during decline phases (recession and crisis) variable costs contribute to stabilizing the unit cost level, fixed costs degression effects cannot be realized during growth phases (recovery and expansion). Nevertheless, these effects are requested as an inbuilt contribution to achieve productivity targets. Accordingly, plant managers face the dilemma of choosing diametric-advantageous alternatives for configuring their system: On the one hand, the preventively built-in adjustment abilities would be very advantageous for potential declines since negative impact on the product margin can be mitigated. This strategic orientation requires configuring the production plant with a high percentage of variable costs. On the other hand, the (almost) effortless contribution to productivity targets (and possibly associated personal incentives related to high productivity achievements) is appreciated for potential growth. This approach involves a configuration of the plant's structure with a high percentage of fixed costs.

3.2 Multi-period Competitiveness (O2)

Several approaches for handling volatility and uncertainty propose a transfer of the inevitable entrepreneurial risks to third parties (e.g. via outsourcing to suppliers, via buy-order-transfer models to service providers or via temporal work to employees). Eventually, this transfer of risks mostly is not for free.

In a socio-technical dimension, transferring the entrepreneurial risk to those third parties might adversely affect among others the innovativeness of the company (e.g. if own know-how gets lost after outsourcing to suppliers), the satisfaction and state of health of employees, or the attractiveness of the production plant as employer. Frequently, these risk premiums cannot be explicitly revealed. The effect is very indirect and elusive since the implications will appear in the long term. Therefore, the extent is often not transparent to the management at the time the decision must be made. In a financial dimension, this external third party might charge this "risk premium" in comparison to proprietary, in-house production. Apparently, it keeps the unit costs (i.e. price as allocated costs) constant despite lower quantity of purchased units in comparison to captive production (in particular in the case of cost centers). In the short-term and (probably) in the middle-term, this is possible if the mixed calculation along several periods works and the third party can benefit from an implicit price surcharge ("risk premium") in periods with stable or even higher demand than projected. As a consequence, the plant integrating such external third parties as variable cost might provide a more stable unit cost level due to lower fixed costs but possibly on a higher general level (see Fig. 3). The higher the uncertainty and incalculability, the higher the implicit or explicit risk premium, which continuously arise every period.

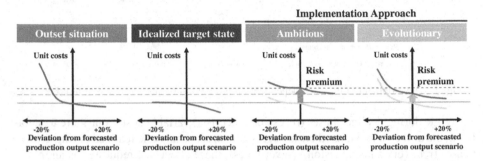

Fig. 3. Unit costs dependent on demand fluctuation and implementation approach (schematic).

Besides, one-time costs within the implementation increase the costs for the ability to synchronize capacity and costs with demand. These (financial and social) costs will depend on the approach to build up the ability. In order to achieve the target sooner than later and to a higher extent ("ambitious" approach), more offensive and proactive measures and significant initial structural adaptations will be required (e.g. to preventively replace employees by temporary workers). In contrast, to achieve the target step-by-step and to a lesser extent ("evolutionary" approach), a combination of proactive and reactive measures are preferred. Initial structural adaptations are restrictively conducted, but every upcoming opportunity to build up VoC is utilized (e.g. if an employee retires, his position is refilled by a temporary worker). The faster and more comprehensive the target is achieved, the more expensive the approach will be.

The financial risk premium can also be non-transparent at times and might be priced unknowingly. Thus, the reverse case can be considered as well. The revealing of implicit price surcharges as well as actively and explicitly discussing risk sharing could be utilized to reduce the price. Nevertheless, the accruing additional costs for the risk premiums for VoC give rise to the core issue and an inevitable debate on principles between plant and corporate management. How valuable is the adjustment potentials for our company? How much do we want and can we afford to invest in these potentials? The main downside is, when thinking and acting with a focus on isolated single periods, these costs endanger the competiveness of the company (in comparison to competitors) or of the plant (in comparison to external suppliers or other plants, which are less prepared for these scenarios). The benefits might emerge if the accumulated costs over a multitude of periods are compared between both options. Using demand scenarios could even so cause biases due to the inevitable uncertainty.

3.3 Multi-dimensional Performance (O3)

The synchronization of costs and capacities with demand volumes implies a variety of target conflicts when applied by practitioners in strategic management of manufacturing plants. At first, the synchronization has implications for other target dimensions and can stand in conflict to these. Other target dimensions affected by the synchronization are technical targets (e.g. capacity and capability targets such as speed, productivity, quality or innovativeness, etc.), financial targets (e.g. cash-flow and profit targets, such as manufacturing costs and liquidity, etc.) and social targets (e.g. employee satisfaction and employer attractiveness consisting of employee motivation, market power on the labor market, etc.) [7, 10]. In these target dimensions, the synchronization can have impacts that can be beneficial or contradicting with existing strategies. For example, buy-order-transfer models can lower the cash outflow but also decrease the ability of the plant to be innovative since the asset is owned and operated by an external party. In addition, these multi-dimensional target conflicts become dynamic since the weighting of the target dimensions varies with the individual above mentioned phases of the business cycles. While during growth delivery reliability might be prioritized, liquidity becomes the main focus during declines. Accordingly, strong dependencies of multi-dimensional performance with the business cycle-continuous profitability (O1) and multi-period competitiveness (O2) exist since the target prioritization is subject to temporal aspects. These dynamics of the target conflicts are to be considered when building up structures, during planning processes, and have to be included in performance measurement and assessment tools.

3.4 Vigorous Effectiveness (O4)

The obstacle of vigorous effectiveness explicitly describes the degree to which the idealized target state of synchronizing (see chapter 2) can be achieved.

The factor "extent" details how far capacities and respective costs can be adjusted to demand fluctuations and accordingly the extent to which the targeted underlying issue can be solved. The achievable extent strongly depends on the potential to influence the costs by means of appropriate and available levers. The management of fixed costs is an essential element in order to adapt costs to demand fluctuations. Cost remanence as a characteristic of the plant is a main issue which needs to be addressed [11]. The extent of fixed costs is often underestimated since the effective influenceability and particularly the reducibility of the plant's cost structure is over-optimistically estimated. Besides, production plants struggle to adapt their costs in supportive and administrative functions. However, these cost positions should not be neglected since 50 % are bound in support processes, and their cost structure mainly consists of fixed costs [12]. The factor speed characterizes how fast capacities can be adjusted to demand fluctuations. Many companies take action if the market demand and associated production volumes will not evidently recover. Only then do they evaluate, select, and implement measures to adapt capacity. Capacity costs continuously accumulate in doing so, and this cannot be compensated for later on. Interdependencies to O1, O2 and O3 are apparent.

3.5 Practice-Oriented Applicability (O5)

Practitioners have difficulties implementing existing approaches and tools since important requirements might not be given (e.g. data availability, data consistency, data quality) or too laborious to apply so that effort and benefits (e.g. gained knowledge by an analysis) bear no proportion. In addition, some tools are too complex to allow explanation to occasional users or the results to senior management. If many assumptions are necessary and a lot of time and effort required to explain the underlying hypotheses and background fundamentals, various decision makers tend to insufficiently understand and trust the results and consequently reject it as basis for their decision making. However, the opposite trend can also be observed: increasingly gathering and analyzing huge amounts of data, building more complex mathematical models and simulations for decision making. These might help to understand the implications of external factors on the considered system. However, it should be questioned whether quantifying and projecting future risks and their probability of occurrence based on data of the past will lead to reliable results for practitioners in face of uncertainty. In particular, extreme events like black or grey swans [13] can hardly be quantified. Gigerenzer argues that incorrectly assuming to know risks in an uncertain world and using complex calculations and mathematical models for future predictions might result in an illusion of accuracy and certainty within decision making and erroneous beliefs [14].

4   Conclusion and Outlook

Based on observations and experiences within action research cases in industrial practice, the implications of demand volatility and uncertainty on production plants are analyzed. Variances of unit costs occur when the antecedent projected unit costs cannot be realized since deviations emerge between forecasted and factual production volume. They significantly impact the plant's operational performance, i.e. its profitability. Therefore, volume-oriented changeability (VoC) sets the target to synchronize production capacity and costs with demand fluctuations. Arising obstacles are identified and evaluated when developing strategies to build up structures in order to synchronize costs and capacity with demand volumes in practice. The obstacles can be distinguished in approach-immanent and target-immanent and are summarized in Fig. 4. Based on these obstacles, requirements can be derived for further research on an academically sound and practically relevant approach for strategizing volume-oriented changeability (VoC) as the ability to economically and competitively handle demand volatility and uncertainty in production plants.

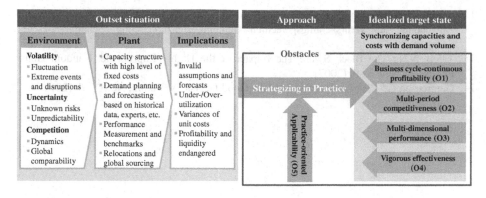

Fig. 4. Problem context causing obstacles within achieving VoC-related target.

References

1. Tainton, J., Nakano, M.: The behavioural effects of extreme events in global supply chains. In: Grabot, B., Vallespir, B., Gomes, S., Bouras, A., Kiritsis, D. (eds.) Advances in Production Management Systems, Part II. IFIP AICT, vol. 439, pp. 62–70. Springer, Heidelberg (2014)
2. Kampker, A., Burggräf, P., Gartzen, T., Maue, A., Czarlay, D.: Analysis of socio-technical structures in order to increase the changeability of producing companies. Adv. Mater. Res. **907**, 181–196 (2014)
3. Wiendahl, H.-P., ElMaraghy, H.A., Nyhuis, P., Zäh, M.F., Wiendahl, H.-H., Duffie, N., Brieke, M.: Changeable manufacturing – classification, design and operation. CIRP Annals Manufact. Technol. **56**(2), 783–809 (2007)
4. Nyhuis, P., Reinhart, G., Abele, E. (eds.): Wandlungsfähige Produktionssysteme Heute die Industrie von morgen gestalten. PZH Verlag, Garbsen (2008)
5. Petit, T.J., Fiksel, J., Croxton, K.L.: Ensuring supply chain resilience: development of a conceptual framework. J. Bus. Logistics **31**(1), 1–21 (2010)
6. Koch, S.N.: Methodik zur Steigerung der Wandlungsfähigkeit von Fabriken im Maschinen- und Anlagenbau. Dissertation (2012)
7. Rippel, M., Schmiester, J., Wandfluh, M., Schönsleben, P.: Building blocks for volume-oriented changeability of assets in production plants. IN: 48th CIRP Conference on Manufacturing Systems - CIRP CMS (2015) [in press]
8. Rippel, M., Lübkemann, J., Nyhuis, P., Schönsleben, P.: Profiling as a means of implementing volume-oriented changeability in the context of strategic production management. CIRP Annals Manufact. Technol. **63**(1), 445–448 (2014)
9. Sheffi, Y.: The Resilient Enterprise: Overcoming Vulnerability for Competitive Advantage. MIT Press, Cambridge (2005)
10. Rippel, M., Budde, J.-W., Friemann, F., Schönsleben, P.: Building blocks for volume-oriented changeability in personnel cost structure of manufacturing companies. In: Grabot, B., Vallespir, B., Gomes, S., Bouras, A., Kiritsis, D. (eds.) Advances in Production Management Systems, Part III. IFIP AICT, vol. 440, pp. 463–470. Springer, Heidelberg (2014)
11. Zell, M.: Kosten- und Performance Management – Grundlagen – Instrumente – Fallstudien. Gabler, Wiesbaden (2008)

12. Remer, D.: Einführen der Prozesskostenrechnung: Grundlagen, Methodik, Einführung und Anwendung der verursachungsgerechten Gemeinkostenzurechnung. Schäffer-Poeschel, Stuttgart (2005)
13. Taleb, N.N.: The Black Swan: The Impact of the Highly Improbable. Random House Publishers, New York (2007)
14. Gigerenzer, G.: Risk Savvy: How to Make Good Decisions. Viking, New York (2014)

How to Support Plant Managers in Strategizing Volume-Oriented Changeability in Volatile and Uncertain Times – Deriving Requirements for a Practice-Oriented Approach

Manuel Rippel[✉], Johannes Schmiester, and Paul Schönsleben

D-MTEC, BWI Center for Industrial Management, ETH Zurich, Zurich, Switzerland
mrippel@ethz.ch

Abstract. Volume-oriented Changeability (VoC) contributes to a production plant's profitability and competitiveness in the face of increasing demand volatility and uncertainty, which is characterized by more frequent and severely affecting extreme events. Strategizing VoC in practice entails overcoming obstacles due to dynamic and interdependent target conflicts. Currently, a dedicated and applicable approach is lacking. Based on identified obstacles, requirements are derived for providing plant's general managers conceptual and methodical support within strategizing VoC. The requirements constitute the result of this paper and should be taken into account by subsequent research on academically sound and practical relevant approaches for the defined purpose.

Keywords: Uncertainty · Volatility · Resilience · Volume-oriented changeability · Strategizing · Demand-responsive supply chain

1 Introduction

The environment of production plants is characterized by increasing demand volatility and uncertainty, which also comprises major disruptions due to extreme events, like grey or black swans [1, 2]. As the frequency and extent of those fluctuations and extreme events as well as the number of unknown risks in an uncertain world is increasing, it is hardly possible to use common forecasting methods anymore. Assumptions and derived decisions regarding configuring production resources of plants often turn out to be wrong. A multitude of scientific approaches and concepts have been developed, and these often focus on technical-related topics [3]. The concept of volume-oriented changeability (VoC) was introduced [4, 5] with the target of synchronizing capacities and costs with demand fluctuations. VoC can be regarded as a specific subset of the broad concept of changeability [4]. It should provide added value for plant managers or managers in charge as project managers to strategize and/or implement procedures to economically and competitively handle implications of demand volatility and uncertainty. The plant level including the interface towards corporate management is still being widely neglected in the research on responsiveness of organizations and organizational units towards volatility and uncertainty. Existing scientific

© IFIP International Federation for Information Processing 2015
S. Umeda et al. (Eds.): APMS 2015, Part I, IFIP AICT 459, pp. 431–438, 2015.
DOI: 10.1007/978-3-319-22756-6_53

approaches are either designed for the company level [6], supply chain level [7], manufacturing network level [8], or on the factory level, which mainly focuses on topics with high relevance for operations and logistics closely related to the shop floor [3, 9, 10]. There is a lack of attention in literature to providing practically relevant and applicable approaches and tools that address important fields and occurring obstacles within strategizing VoC of production plants. These obstacles (summarized in Chap. 2) were identified in recently conducted action research cases (in eight production plants in six countries over two years) regarding strategizing abilities of production plants in the face of demand volatility and uncertainty. They were evaluated by Rippel et al. [11]. Based on this findings and the same action research cases, this paper derives requirements for an approach for strategizing the ability of production plants to economically and competitively handle volatility and uncertainty. The purpose is to provide the key parameters for subsequent research on an academically sound and practice-oriented approach.

2 Revealing Obstacles Within Strategizing VoC

Obstacles, classified as target-immanent or approach-immanent, were identified and evaluated by Rippel et al. [11] and summarized in the following:

Business cycle-continuous profitability (O1) considers the arising trade-off between stability of unit costs (advantageous: high share of variable costs) in decline phases and exploitation of fixed costs degression effects (advantageous: high share of fixed costs) in growth phases. **Multi-period competitiveness (O2)** addresses that risks are transferred to third parties in order to handle volatility and uncertainty, which comes at a price. The "risk premiums" might exist in a non-transparent form due to their indirect and long-term nature (e.g., innovativeness or attractiveness of the company as employer). **Multi-dimensional performance (O3)** reveals that the synchronization of costs and capacities with demand volumes has implications for other target dimensions of technical, social and financial natures. These implications can be supportive or obstructive to existing strategies and implied target dimensions. **Vigorous effectiveness (O4)** refers to the extent and speed as essential factors within VoC. Accordingly, the scope should not be limited to production functions but include support and administrative functions of the plant. Furthermore, plants lose time to actually interpret the changes of the business environment but then might decide and act too rigorously due to time pressure and accumulating manufacturing costs. **Practice-oriented applicability (O5)** indicates that many approaches lack applicability in practice due to their partly single-disciplinary nature, unfeasible requirements in terms of required data and effort due to the frequently enormous complexity. Besides, many assumptions and forecasts are required but might include fragile and erroneous input in face of uncertainty with unknown risks.

3 Deriving Requirements for Strategizing VoC in Practice

Based on the identified obstacles, requirements for a practically relevant and effective approach for strategizing VoC are derived and incipient hypotheses of possible solutions are given in the following.

3.1 Purpose-Oriented Requirements

The category "purpose-oriented" comprises three requirements which details the purpose of the underlying target of VoC, which is synchronizing capacity and costs with demand fluctuation.

Solution Concreteness. Approaches should explicitly address challenges, obstacles and solutions for handling volume fluctuations in production plants and contributing to a demand-responsive supply chain. Instead of generally covering various change drivers and dimensions, solutions specifically for volume fluctuations have to be defined. Thereby, plant managers should be guided by what necessarily and concretely needs to be considered in order to preventively implement measures and adapt structures, behavior and activities. For doing so, an approach should suggest relevant and important fields of action to be considered and possible enablers and levers. Solution concreteness mainly contributes to tackling the obstacles O4 and O5.

Financial Explicitness. This requirement incorporates the relevance of financial considerations within managerial decision making. Beyond providing the technical possibilities to scale capacity in case of demand in-/decrease, approaches have to stress financial impacts both regarding additional costs for VoC potentials but also the target effectiveness, namely the degree of synchronization between capacities and production costs and resulting stability of unit costs and profit margins. Besides costs and capacity, the cash-flow of a production plant is endangered in the considered market environment. As fixed costs often comprise fixed cash outflows and investments into fixed structures imply amounts of bound capital, fluctuating cash inflows driven by demand volatility put severe pressure on the plant's liquidity. An approach should clearly differentiate between and make transparent the above named types and significance of financial impacts (i.e., cash-flow effective and/or profit-&-loss effective), since the effect might vary [12]. An approach should reflect and define a project-specific understanding, priorities and expectations (of involved stakeholders) as well as ambition level regarding profitability and competiveness related to cash-flow and/or profit-&-loss impacts. This should set clear guidance for the solution search within the strategizing project and finally assess the target achievement. In particular, financial explicitness addresses the obstacles O4 and O2.

Uncertainty-Adequate. The approach to be developed should sufficiently incorporate the characteristics and constraints of uncertainty, which are considered in this paper as "the insufficiency or imperfection of knowledge or information critical to decision-making, concerning the past, present or future events, or conditions within and surrounding an organizational system" [13, p. 401]. Within this paper and the VoC concept, we assume that neither objective nor subjective probabilities are present, which makes rational decision-making nearly impossible [14]. This requirement sets the most challenging criteria since it is questioning common approaches to model and to evaluate benefits of changeability. Significant limitations exist in modeling the system, and these reduce the practical relevance in the end. The ensuing results might incorporate an illusion of accuracy and certainty [15]. According to Gigerenzer, "When we face a complex problem, we look for a complex solution. And when it doesn't work, we seek an even more complex one. In an uncertain world, that's a big error. Complex problems do not always require complex solutions." [15, pp. 14] Therefore, a robust approach should incorporate simple and heuristic elements where possible and reasonable. The requirement "uncertainty-adequate" would address obstacles O5, O2 and O1.

3.2   System Boundary-Dependent Requirements

Within the system boundary-dependent requirements, the focus is to define which system elements, interfaces and interdependencies have to be investigated and where design possibility exists within the considered system "production plant" [14].

Strategic Plant Level. Taking account the underlying problem mentioned above, strategic management at the production plant is likely to be the hierarchical level in charge of responding effectively to volatile and uncertain demand volumes. This level is relevant since manufacturing costs are highly sensitive due to fixed cost components and main fixed costs are bound on this system level [16]. Main fixed costs of a production plant consist of assets and personnel costs, in particular in indirect plant functions. It is at the strategic plant level where structures, (i.e., people and assets) are determined and planned upon. Measures to synchronize costs and capacity with demand can be implemented by taking a holistic perspective and has probably the highest leverage potential since plant management is not limited to managing production functions but also several supportive functions. Therefore, an approach should holistically address the strategic plant level and define the system boundaries accordingly. The manufacturing network, supply chain and company level are considered as supersystem, whereas the factory level (in the narrower, production-related sense) and further downward levels are defined as subsystem. The specific needs and obstacles of a plant's general managers to handle demand volatility and uncertainty should be addressed. In particular, their permitted and authorized scope for action should be appropriately taken into consideration since this scope might set significant limitations and restrictions to modifying and intervening in the plant and further cross-organizational processes, structures and patterns. Thus, this requirement mainly addresses obstacle O4 and additionally O3 and O5.

Interdisciplinary Solution Space. Basically, a multitude of approaches, measures and solutions for different partial problem aspects and occurring tasks within the broad concept of changeability exist [3, 10]. Since VoC-relevant measures were developed from a multitude of different disciplines (e.g., finance and sourcing, engineering and factory planning, supply chain management, human resource), an integrated toolkit is barely available for holistic, strategic management level. The intentions and priorities of the various disciplinary streams differ and are sometimes contradictive to each other [5]. For example, technical approaches to increase the changeability of production systems, which could be advantageous from an engineering perspective, might stand in contrast to measures proposed by asset management approaches. Therefore, a portfolio of solution options and alternatives from different disciplines should be comprehensively revealed and an overview of specific measures provided for practitioners in order to be able to compare dis-/advantages of measures and resulting target conflicts, to select plant-specific appropriate measures and to combine their impacts. Interdisciplinary solution space is beneficial in taking obstacles O3 and O4 into account.

3.3 Organization Concept-Oriented Requirements

Based on the above mentioned system level, the organizational concept of the plant has to be considered according to management aspects and dimensions since system-dependent contradictions and restrictions originate here [4]. Partly, they can be influenced by the plant management in the short-, middle- or long-term.

Socio-Technical Management Aspects. A socio-technical system is a hybrid form of a social system and a technical system and consists of interrelated elements of both system types [17]. Therefore, a production plant can be considered a socio-technical system since it consists of human beings and technical devices interacting with each other [18]. Socio-technical analysis of VoC means to consider not merely comprising human and technical system elements and their interactions but to extend the view beyond that and integrate in particular behavioral and activity-oriented aspects. In order to include this understanding, the system aspects "structure," "behavior" and "activities" should be addressed in an integrated manner [19]. In regard to synchronizing capacities and costs with demand volumes, the following topics of these aspects can be considered as relevant: Structure consists of resources mainly in the form of personnel and assets as well as organizational structure and processes [20]. This structure is the object that is managed in relation to volatile and uncertain demand volumes. Here, preventive measures are to be applied in order to make the structure compliant with its environment. Behavior refers to the decision-making, underlying rationales and cognitive biases of management (as function) and managers (as individuals) in a production plant. Here, attitude towards risk, time preferences, degree of commitment and cohesiveness play an important role [4]. When it comes to the described environment, decision-making regarding uncertainty in practice as well as established incentive, steering and performance measurement systems influencing the social practices are to be investigated. Activities on the strategic level comprise the strategy development and formulation process, here referred to as strategizing, in order to adjust structures and behavior, to implement measures and to conduct detailed studies and projects afterwards. Including the management aspects significantly influences the speed of action and the culture of decision making and addresses obstacles O1, O2 and O3.

Management Dimensions. As defined above, the strategic plant management is the relevant system level to be considered. According to Bleicher [19], the focus of strategic considerations are strategic programs as well as the design of fundamental structures, systems of management and of the problem solving behavior of the relevant individuals. However, this management dimension should not be considered independently since manifold interdependencies take place [19]. Bleicher also argues that the task of strategic management is to influence the alignment of activities, which are established by the normative management and which focus on general targets, principles, norms and guidelines. The operational management focuses on the implementation of conceptual specifications of the normative and strategic level by means of operations according to capabilities and resources [19]. However, unexpected events can occur as obstacles within operations, which require changing future expectations (visions of the normative level) and strategies (programs of the strategic level) [19]. Accordingly, the normative and the operational plant management level has to be considered in an integrative manner within strategizing VoC. However, the potential to influence might be limited since important aspects are largely given by corporate directives (e.g., role and functions of the plant within the manufacturing network and supply chain) and can just be "translated or completed" by local plant management. Furthermore, behavior aspects of the normative level (e.g., plant-specific characteristics of corporate culture) can be indirectly influenced in the long-term. The implementation on the operational level might require adaptations to local (cultural and legal) conditions (e.g., social practices, concerns and reservations due to events in the past, formal and informal leadership, statutory participation of employees) [20]. These could incorporate plant-specific restrictions if plant management cannot directly and fully influence them. Therefore, an approach should integrate management dimensions beyond the strategic level as a generic framework in order to enable adaptation to plant-specific conditions and restrictions within strategizing. Thereby, it focuses on obstacles O3, O4 and O5.

3.4 Contextual Requirements

The contextual requirements address areas beyond the plant- or project-specific system boundaries, which should be investigated due to their relevance as input for strategizing VoC or due to the impact of VoC on them. They incorporate relevant relations to the hierarchical superior (supersystem) and subordinate systems (subsystem), which affect setting management priorities. Hence, the contextual prerequisites, the organizational and strategic embeddedness of the plant into the manufacturing network and the company as a whole and inter-organizational implications are to be regarded [21].

Consistent Strategic Alignment. The above summarized obstacles [4] highlight the complexity of the underlying problem. The obstacles O1 and O2 reveal existing and dynamic changing target conflicts for managers. The obstacles O3 and O4 worsen and cause further target conflicts due to various existing interfaces and interdependencies between different target dimensions, management aspects and interests of stakeholders across several organizational and hierarchical company levels [4]. These kind of target conflicts often exist in management aspects of networked systems [19] and involve cross-hierarchical practices [5]. An approach should make these target conflicts transparent to decision makers, probe the causes of them and provide options to balance them. Consistent strategic alignment should address the obstacles O3, O2 and O1.

Coherent Strategic Alignment. This requirement takes into account the subordinate production-related system level as well as the interfaces towards corporate management and network management. The subordinate levels include crucial elements in regard to cost structure (e.g., labor, material and machinery) and comprise technical and/or technological potentials or limitations. The superior levels set the rules and assignments for the plant management. Lastly, it is within each plant management's target scope to identify and sustain its strategic value within the company's manufacturing network (e.g., within performance measurement, which might focus on benchmarks of the plant in relation to internal and external competitors). Thus, it is necessary to closely look at the temporal preferences of the organization and individuals (i.e., incentive systems) regarding realizing benefits. The requirement focuses on obstacles O1, O2 and O3.

3.5 Approach-Oriented Requirements

Many theoretically founded management approaches are too complex or too generic to be directly applied in practice. Besides, various approaches are lacking clear guidance on how to be applied in practice. Kerr et al. point out seven key principles for developing industrially relevant strategic technology management toolkits [22]: Since strategic problem solving is a social process, it should be developed under participation and social interaction of individuals, i.e. **human-centric**. The mode of this interaction and participation shall be **workshop-based** since it offers the opportunity to merge individual knowledge into collective knowledge which is crucial in face of the complexity of strategic problems. The process shall be **neutrally-facilitated** by an individual external to the system. The process shall remain **lightly processed**, i.e. flexible. It includes alternating steps of divergence and convergence as well as plenary and small group sessions. Different tools shall be integrated. Results shall be in a **modular** form. The tools should be **scalable** and applicable at different levels within the organization. It should be **visualized** both in the application and in the output. These should also serve as guiding principles for an applicable approach for strategizing VoC. In order to get solid results within a limited timeframe, existing approaches might need to be adapted.

4 Conclusion and Outlook

The target of volume-oriented changeability (VoC), synchronizing of capacities and costs with demand fluctuation, should ensure the plant's profitability and competitiveness. However, obstacles arise within the strategizing. Practitioners' on the plant level require methodical and conceptual support to realign their strategy regarding structure, activities and behavior in a socio-technical perspective. Within this paper requirements are presented in order to provide scientific researchers a guideline for developing an academically sound and practice-oriented approach that support plant managers in strategizing VoC. The requirements also function as criteria to evaluate existing scholarly approaches regarding their appropriateness for the given problem context.

References

1. Akkermans, H.A., Van Wassenhove, L.N.: Searching for the grey swans: the next 50 years of production research. Int. J. Prod. Res. **51**, 6746–6755 (2013)
2. Taleb, N.N.: The Black Swan: The Impact of the Highly Improbable. Random House Publishers, New York (2007)

3. Kampker, A., Burggräf, P., Gartzen, T., Maue, A., Czarlay, D.: Analysis of socio-technical structures in order to increase the changeability of producing companies. Adv. Mater. Res. **907**, 181–196 (2014)
4. Rippel, M., Lübkemann, J., Nyhuis, P., Schönsleben, P.: Profiling as a means of implementing volume-oriented changeability in the context of strategic production management. CIRP Annals Manufact. Technol. **63**(1), 445–448 (2014)
5. Rippel, M., Schmiester, J., Wandfluh, M., Schönsleben, P.: Building blocks for volume-oriented changeability of assets in production plants. In: 48th CIRP Conference on Manufacturing Systems - CIRP CMS (2015) [Submitted]
6. Friedli, T.: Technologiemanagement – Modelle zur Sicherung der Wettbewerbsfähigkeit. Springer, Berlin (2006)
7. Petit, T.J., Fiksel, J., Croxton, K.L.: Ensuring supply chain resilience: development of a conceptual framework. J. Bus. Logistics **31**(1), 1–21 (2010)
8. Lanza, G., Moser, R.: Strategic planning of global changeable production networks. In: 45th CIRP Conference on Manufacturing Systems (2012)
9. Wiendahl, H.-P., ElMaraghy, H.A., Nyhuis, P., Zäh, M.F., Wiendahl, H.-H., Duffie, N., Brieke, M.: Changeable manufacturing – classification, design and operation. CIRP Annals Manufact. Technol. **56**(2), 783–809 (2007)
10. Nyhuis, P., Deuse, J., Rehwald, J.: Wandlungsfähige Produktion. Heute für morgen gestalten. PZH Verlag, Garbsen (2013)
11. Rippel, M., Schmiester, J., Schönsleben, P.: Why do plant managers struggle to synchronize production capacity and costs with demand in face of volatility and uncertainty? – Obstacles within strategizing volume-oriented changeability in practice. In: Umeda, S. et al. (eds.): APMS 2015, IFIP AICT 440 (2015)
12. Taschner, A.: Business Cases - Ein anwendungsorientierter Leitfaden, 2nd edn. Springer Gabler, Berlin (2013)
13. Ilevbare, I.M., Probert, D., Phaal, R.: Towards risk-aware roadmapping: influencing factors and practical measures. Technovation **34**, 399–409 (2014)
14. Haberfellner, R., de Weck, O., Fricke, E., Vössner S.: Systems Engineering. Grundlagen und Anwendung, 12th edn. Orell Füssli Verlag, AG Zürich (2012)
15. Gigerenzer, G.: Risk Savvy: How to Make Good Decisions. Allen Lane/Penguin Group, London (2014)
16. Wildemann, H.: Fixkostenmanagement – Leitfaden zur Anpassung von Kostenstrukturen an volatile Märkte. TCW, München (2009)
17. Zink, K.J.: Soziotechnische Ansätze. In: Luczak, H.V. (ed.) Handbuch Arbeitswissenschaft. Schäffer-Poeschel Verlag, Stuttgart (1997)
18. Schönsleben, P.: Integral Logistics Management. Operations and Supply Chain Management Within and Across Companies, 3rd edn. CRC Press, Boca Raton (2012)
19. Bleicher, K.: Das Konzept Integriertes Management, 8th edn. Campus Verlag, Frankfurt am Main (2011)
20. Gagsch, B.: Wandlungsfähigkeit von Unternehmen Konzept für ein kontextgerechtes Management des Wandels. In: Bea, F.-X., Kötzle, A., Zahn, E.: zahlr. Abb. Schriften zur Unternehmensplanung 64 (2002)
21. Schnetzler, M.: Kohärente Strategien im Supply Chain Management—eine Methodik zur Entwicklung und Implementierung von Supply Chain-Strategien. Dissertation, ETH Zurich (2005)
22. Kerr, C., Farrukh, C., Phaal, R., Probert, D.: Key principles for developing industrially relevant strategic technology management toolkits. Technol. Forecast. Soc. Chang. **80**, 1050–1070 (2013)

Job Shop Scheduling with Alternative Machines Using a Genetic Algorithm Incorporating Heuristic Rules -Effectiveness of Due-Date Related Information-

Parinya Kaweegitbundit and Toru Eguchi[✉]

Graduate School of Engineering, Hiroshima University, Higashihiroshima, Japan
eguchi@hiroshima-u.ac.jp

Abstract. This paper deals with an efficient scheduling method for job shop scheduling with alternative machines with the objective to minimize mean tardiness. The method uses a genetic algorithm incorporating heuristic rules for job sequencing and machine selection. Effective heuristic rules for this method have been proposed so far. However due-date related information has not been included in the heuristic rule for machine selection even though the objective is to minimize mean tardiness. This paper examines the effectiveness of due-date related information for machine selection in this method through numerical experiments.

Keywords: Job shop scheduling · Alternative machines · Tardiness · Heuristic rule · Genetic algorithm

1 Introduction

This paper deals with an efficient scheduling method for job shop scheduling with alternative machines. Some research papers related to this problem have been proposed in the literature [1, 2]. In this problem, the machine for processing each operation is not fixed only one; there can be alternative machines. Not only the sequence of jobs on machine, but also the machine which process each operation must be selected for this scheduling. We have already proposed a scheduling method using a genetic algorithm incorporating heuristic rules [3, 4]. In this method, heuristic rules for job sequencing and machine selection are embedded in the search of genetic algorithm. The performance of scheduling is improved using the knowledge of the rules. The rules for job sequencing are used when a machine became idle and there are multiple waiting jobs to be processed on the machine. The rules give priority values for the waiting jobs and the job with the highest priority value is selected as the next job to be processed on the machine. The rules for machines selection are used when a machine finishes processing an operation of a job. The rule gives values for candidate machines to process the next operation of the job. We have examined various heuristic rules for incorporation when the objective of scheduling is to minimize mean tardiness. As a result, (SL/RPN) + SPT rule [5] performed best for job sequencing. (WINQ + RPT + PT) × PT rule [6] performed best for machine selection. Although the objective of scheduling is to

S. Umeda et al. (Eds.): APMS 2015, Part I, IFIP AICT 459, pp. 439–446, 2015.
DOI: 10.1007/978-3-319-22756-6_54

minimize mean tardiness, the machine selection rule does not include due-date related information. In this paper, we examine the effectiveness of considering due-date related information for machine selection rules. Numerical experiments are carried out to show the effectiveness of including the information.

2   Job Shop Scheduling with Alternative Machines

The scheduling problem considered in this paper is described as follows: Consider the job shop that consists of R work centers. Each work center $W_r(r \in \{1, 2, \ldots, R\})$ has M_r machines. The operation to be processed in a work center is performed on one of the machines in the work center. Each Job $J_i(i = 1, 2, \ldots, I)$ has n_i operations $\{o_{ij}(j = 1, 2, \ldots, n_i)\}$ that are processed by the increasing order of the operation number j. The operation o_{ij} is processed on a work center $Wz_{ij}(z_{ij} \in \{1, 2, \ldots, R\})$ and the routings of the operations through work centers are diverse. We assume that $Wz_{ij} \neq Wz_{i,j+1}$ for $j = 1, \ldots, n_i - 1$. The processing time of the operation o_{ij} on machine k ($k = 1, 2, \ldots, Mz_{ij}$) is p_{ijk}. Operations cannot be interrupted (non-preemption). Each machine can process only one job at a time; each job can be processed only on one machine at a time. The objective of scheduling is to minimize the mean tardiness defined as follows:

$$T = \sum_{i=1}^{I} \max(0, C_i - d_i)/I \tag{1}$$

where C_i and d_i are the completion time and the due-date of job J_i, respectively.

3   Scheduling Optimization Using a Genetic Algorithm

In this chapter, the genetic algorithm used in this paper is described. In the genetic algorithm, each operation has a gene for job selection and genes for machine selection. The number of genes for machine selection is the same as the number of candidate machines which can process the operation. Each gene for machine selection is prepared for each candidate machine. Each gene for job selection and machine selection is coded as a real value between 0 and 1. The set of genes for all the operations of jobs corresponds to a chromosome.

Decoding is carried out using a feed-forward scheduling simulation in which the genes are considered as priority values for job selection and machine selection. When machine finishes processing an operation of a job, the job goes to the input buffer of one of the candidate machine which can process the next operation of the job. The machine which has the largest value of gene is selected as the next machine to process the next operation. When a machine became idle and there are multiple waiting jobs to be processed in the input buffer of the machine, one of the waiting job is selected and is started to be processed on the machine. The job with the highest value of gene is selected as the next job. By this method, when all the operations of jobs are completed, a schedule is obtained. The mean tardiness of jobs in the schedule is used for calculating the fitness. The individual which has the smaller mean tardiness is defined to have the higher fitness in this method.

An elite strategy is adopted in this paper. The best 20 % of individuals are copied to the next generation. The other 80 % individuals are generated using crossover by randomly selecting two individuals from the current generation. In crossover, 30 % genes are randomly selected from one individual and the other 70 % genes are randomly selected from another individual. The rate of mutation is 1 %. For the detail construction of this genetic algorithm, refer to the literature [5, 7].

4 Genetic Algorithm Incorporating Heuristic Rules

4.1 Incorporation of Heuristic Rules

Although the genetic algorithm alone described in Chap. 3 can search the optimal schedule, the performance is not good. The performance of scheduling can be improved by incorporating problem specific knowledge. Eguchi et al. have proposed the job shop scheduling method using a genetic algorithm incorporating a priority rule for job selection [7]. In this method, when decoding, a job is selected using not only the value of gene for job selection but also the value calculated by applying a priority rule. Specifically, the job with the highest value of the multiplication of the gene and the priority value calculated by the rule is selected as the next job to be processed. By this method, the knowledge of priority rule can be embedded in the search of genetic algorithm. As the same way, machine selection rules can be incorporated for machine selection. Specifically, the machine which has the highest value of the multiplication or division of the gene for machine selection and the value calculated using a machine selection rule is selected as the machine to process the next operation [3, 4].

4.2 Job Selection Rules

From our previous research [3], the best priority rule for job selection is (SL/RPN) + SPT rule [5] as follows:

$$pri_{ij} = \frac{1}{p_{ijk}} \left(\max\left[\frac{d_i - t - rpt_i}{rpn_i}, 0 \right] + 1 \right)^{-1}. \tag{2}$$

The value of rpt_i represents the total processing time of remaining operations. If an operation has alternative machines, the mean processing time is used. The value of rpn_i represents the number of remaining operations. When a machine became idle and there are multiple waiting jobs to be processed at time t, the job with the highest value of pri_{ij} is selected as the next job. This paper used this rule for job selection.

4.3   Machine Selection Rules

Also from the previous research [3], the best machine selection rule is (WINQ + RPT + PT) × PT rule [6]. This rule is the combination of WINQ, RPT and PT. These rules select the next machine as follows:

- PT: The rule selects the machine which has the shortest processing time to process the next operation of the job.
- NINQ: The rule selects the machine which has the smallest number of waiting jobs.
- WINQ: The rule selects the machine which has the smallest summation of the processing times of waiting jobs.
- WINQ + RPT + PT: The rule selects the machine which has the smallest summation of (1) the processing times of waiting jobs, (2) the remaining processing time currently being processed on the machine and (3) the processing time of the next operation when the operation is processed on the machine.
- (WINQ + RPT + PT) × PT: The rule selects the machine which has the smallest value of {((1) + (2) + (3)) × (3)}.

The rules described above are not using due-date related information. Because the objective of scheduling is related to due-dates, machine selection using due-date related information seems to be effective. In this paper we examine new machine selection rules using due-date related information as follows.

- MAX MIN SLACK: The rule calculates slack value (= due-date − current time − sum of remaining processing time) for each waiting job in the input buffer of machine. Then the minimum slack value is selected for each machine. Finally, the machine which has the largest value of the minimum slack value is selected as the machine to process the next operation. The objective of this rule is to select the machine which has larger slack in terms of minimum value.
- MAX TOTAL SLACK: The rule calculates the sum of slack values for all the waiting jobs in the input buffer of machine. Then the machine which has the largest value of the sum of slack values is selected as the machine to process the next operation. The objective of this rule is to select the machine which has larger slack in terms of total value.
- MIN MAX (SL/RPN) + SPT: The rule calculates the value of Eq. (2) for each waiting job in the input buffer of machine. Then the maximum value of it is selected for each machine. Finally, the machine which has the smallest value of the maximum value is selected as the machine to process the next operation. The smaller value of Eq. (2) corresponds to larger slack value. Therefore, the machine with smaller value of the maximum value of Eq. (2) is selected.
- MIN TOTAL (SL/RPN) + SPT: This rule calculates the sum of the values of Eq. (2) for all the waiting job in the input buffer of machine. Then the machine which has the smallest value of the sum of the values is selected as the machine to process the next operation.
- MIN MAX CR + SPT: This rule uses CR + SPT rule [8] instead of (SL/RPN) + SPT in MIN MAX (SL/RPN) + SPT.

- MIN TOTAL CR + SPT: This rule uses CR + SPT rule [8] instead of (SL/RPN) + SPT in MIN TOTAL (SL/RPN) + SPT.
- MIN MAX ATC: This rule uses ATC rule [9] instead of (SL/RPN) + SPT in MIN MAX (SL/RPN) + SPT.
- MIN TOTAL ATC: This rule uses ATC rule [9] instead of (SL/RPN) + SPT in MIN TOTAL (SL/RPN) + SPT.
- MAX MIN EDD: This rule selects the earliest due-date in the input buffer of machine. Then the machine with the maximum value of it is selected as the next machine to process the next operation.
- MAX TOTAL EDD: This rule calculates the sum of the due-date for all the waiting job in the input buffer of machine. Then the machine which has the largest value of it is selected as the machine to process the next operation.

5 Numerical Experiments

5.1 Numerical Conditions

Numerical experiments are carried out to examine the effectiveness of the method in this paper. The number of job is 100. There are eight work centers ($R = 8$) in the shop floor. Each work center has two machines ($M_r = 2$). Any operation assigned to work center can be processed on both machines in the work center. The number of operations n_i for each job is randomly determined between 4 and 8. The order of work centers to process each operation of a job is determined randomly. It is assumed that one of the machines in a work center can process the operations faster than the other machine. The processing time of an operation on the most efficient machine is determined by the uniform distribution between 5 and 100. The processing time on the other machine in the same work center is determined by multiplying a speed factor by the processing time on the most efficient machine. The speed factor is randomly determined by the uniform distribution between 1 and 2. The due-dates of jobs are determined based on TWK method [10]. The problems with two different levels of due-date tightness are generated. When the due-dates of jobs are loose, the number of tardy jobs is set to about 10 %–15 % by tuning the due-date factor in TWK method. When the due-dates of jobs are tight, the number of tardy jobs is set to about 25 %–30 %. The thirty problems are randomly generated. The scheduling performance is evaluated by the mean value of Eq. (1) for the thirty problems and the standard deviation from the best rules. For all the conditions, (SL/RPN) + SPT rule is used for the job selection rule.

5.2 Experimental Results

Tables 1 and 2 show the experimental results when using heuristic rules alone. These are the results obtained not using the genetic algorithm. For both due-date tightness levels, (WINQ + RPT + PT) × PT rule for machine selection performed best. The best rule using due-date related information was MAX MIN SLACK.

Table 1. Mean tardiness using heuristic rules alone in the loose due-date condition

Machine selection rules	Mean tardiness	S.D. from the best
PT	755.8	102.5
NINQ	56.9	16.5
WINQ	59.7	18.4
WINQ + RPT + PT	34.9	11.8
(WINQ + RPT + PT) × PT	24.0	0.0
MAX MIN SLACK	60.3	19.9
MAX TOTAL SLACK	70.6	23.2
MIN MAX (SL/RPN) + SPT	68.1	21.9
MIN TOTAL (SL/RPN) + SPT	66.0	20.2
MIN MAX CR + SPT	85.8	27.8
MIN TOTAL CR + SPT	72.7	21.9
MIN MAX ATC	73.2	24.2
MIN TOTAL ATC	66.1	19.8
MAX MIN EDD	61.7	18.6
MAX TOTAL EDD	82.0	29.6

Table 2. Mean tardiness using heuristic rules alone in the tight due-date condition

Machine selection rules	Mean tardiness	S.D. from the best
PT	837.6	92.2
NINQ	97.9	17.1
WINQ	99.6	17.6
WINQ + RPT + PT	65.5	9.1
(WINQ + RPT + PT) × PT	45.2	0.0
MAX MIN SLACK	96.4	19.4
MAX TOTAL SLACK	103.2	18.6
MIN MAX (SL/RPN) + SPT	107.8	25.1
MIN TOTAL (SL/RPN) + SPT	101.2	21.5
MIN MAX CR + SPT	126.1	23.4
MIN TOTAL CR + SPT	110.2	22.1
MIN MAX ATC	114.3	25.3
MIN TOTAL ATC	108.5	22.5
MAX MIN EDD	99.4	19.4
MAX TOTAL EDD	123.2	28.5

Tables 3 and 4 show the experimental results when using the genetic algorithm incorporating heuristic rules. MAX MIN SLACK rule is used as a machine selection rule which includes due-date related information. When incorporating MAX MIN SLACK rule, the minimum slack value can be negative. Therefore, when the value of minimum slack is s, the value $s^+ = \exp(s)$ is calculated and the maximum value of the multiplication of s^+ and the value of gene is used for machine selection in the genetic

Table 3. Mean tardiness using the genetic algorithm incorporating heuristic rules in the loose due-date condition

Machine selection rules	Mean tardiness	S.D. from the best
GA + PT	22.4	8.5
GA + NINQ	16.9	5.3
GA + WINQ	17.4	5.4
GA + WINQ + RPT + PT	12.0	2.4
GA + (WINQ + RPT + PT) × PT	9.9	0.0
GA + MAX MIN SLACK	20.4	8.0

Table 4. Mean tardiness using the genetic algorithm incorporating heuristic rules in the tight due-date condition

Machine selection rules	Mean tardiness	S.D. from the best
GA + PT	46.4	10.2
GA + NINQ	38.6	5.4
GA + WINQ	39.0	5.2
GA + WINQ + RPT + PT	31.1	3.0
GA + (WINQ + RPT + PT) × PT	26.7	0.0
GA + MAX MIN SLACK	45.5	9.8

algorithm. The results in Tables 3 and 4 indicate that (WINQ + RPT + PT) × PT rule performed best for incorporation for both due-date tightness levels.

6 Conclusion

In this paper, a genetic algorithm incorporating heuristic rules is applied for job shop scheduling with alternative machines. There are two decision situations in this scheduling: job sequencing and machine selection. (SL/RPN) + SPT rule is used for job sequencing. Various machine selection rules are examined. Some rules such as WINQ, NINQ, (WINQ + RPT + PT) × PT are the ones which do not include due-date related information. Because the objective function for scheduling in this paper is mean tardiness, due-date related information seems to be important also for machine selection rules. However, the experimental results show that the best machine selection rule is (WINQ + RPT + PT) × PT rule both when using heuristic rules alone and when applying the genetic algorithm incorporating the heuristic rules. (WINQ + RPT + PT) × PT rule works for load balancing. Numerical results suggest that it is not necessary to include due-date related information in machine selection if the due-date related information is considered in job selection and load balancing is considered in machine selection appropriately.

References

1. Nasr, N., Elsayed, E.A.: Job shop scheduling with alternative machines. Int. J. Prod. Res. **28** (9), 1595–1609 (1990)
2. Moon, I., Lee, S., Bae, H.: Genetic algorithm for job shop scheduling problems with alternative routing. Int. J. Prod. Res. **46**(10), 2695–2705 (2008)
3. Kaweegitbundit, P., Eguchi, T.: Job shop scheduling with alternative machines using genetic algorithm incorporating heuristic rules. In: Mechanical Engineering Congress, 2014 Japan [MECJ-14], No. 14-1, S1420140. The Japan Society of Mechanical Engineers, Tokyo (2014)
4. Eguchi, T., Kaweegitbundit, P., Hoshino, N., Daido, T., Murayama, T.: Job shop scheduling with alternative machines–experimental evaluation of the scheduling method using a genetic algorithm incorporating heuristic rules–. In: Manufacturing Systems Division Conference 2015, No. 15-8, pp. 95–96. The Japan Society of Mechanical Engineers, Tokyo (2015)
5. Yoda, M., Eguchi, T., Murayama, T.: Job shop scheduling for meeting due dates and minimizing overtime using genetic algorithm incorporating new priority rules. J. Adv. Mech. Des. Syst. Manufact. **8**(5), paper no. 14–00076 (2014)
6. Eguchi, T., Oba, F., Toyooka, S., Sato, Y.: A machine selection rule for dynamic job shop having alternative machines with different processing times. J. Jpn. Soc. Precis. Eng. **72**(4), 459–464 (2006)
7. Eguchi, T., Oba, F., Kozaki, S.: Dynamic scheduling using the mixture of a genetic algorithm and a priority rule. Trans. Jpn. Soc. Mech. Eng. Ser. C **71**(703), 1047–1053 (2005). (in Japanese)
8. Anderson, E.J., Nyirenda, J.C.: Two new rules to minimize tardiness in a job shop. Int. J. Prod. Res. **28**(12), 2277–2292 (1990)
9. Vepsalainen, A.P.J., Morton, T.E.: Priority rules for job shop with weighted tardiness costs. Manage. Sci. **33**(8), 1035–1047 (1987)
10. Conway, R.W.: Priority dispatching and job lateness in a job shop. J. Ind. Eng. **16**(4), 228–237 (1965)

Big Data Technology for Resilient Failure Management in Production Systems

Volker Stich, Felix Jordan[✉], Martin Birkmeier, Kerem Oflazgil, Jan Reschke, and Anna Diews

Institute for Industrial Management, RWTH Aachen University (FIR), Aachen, Germany
{volker.stich,felix.jordan,martin.birkmeier,kerem.oflazgil,
jan.reschke,anna.diews}@fir.rwth-aachen.de

Abstract. Due to a growing complexity within value chains the susceptibility to failures in production processes increases. The research project BigPro explores the applicability of Big Data to realize a pro-active failure management in production systems. The BigPro-platform complements structured production data and unstructured human data to improve failure management. In a novel approach, the aggregated data is analyzed for reoccurring patterns that indicate possible failures of the production system, known from historic failure events. These patterns are linked to failures and respective countermeasures and documented in a catalog. The project results are validated in three industrial use cases.

Keywords: Failure management · Big data · Complex event processing · Production control · Pattern management

1 Introduction

The amount of data generated in production companies is continuingly growing. One reason for this development is the advancing integration of system control and measurement utilities within the production, due to new cost-efficient, high-performance information technologies. These allow for an intelligent connection of different production systems units and in general an increased interconnectedness of the production systems in total. The idea of interconnected machines and the overall production integration is labelled as *"Industry 4.0"* in Germany. Industry 4.0 aims at the systematic network integration of machines to make efficient use of the company's available information resources [1]. As part of this development, the value of production data and the hereby generated information has obtained increasing value for a company. The following approach illustrates a new strategy on how big amounts of data can be systematically used for a failure management system in production.

In a world with complex production procedures and globally operating corporate groups, an efficient failure management system can be a significant advantage in competition. With downtime costs on average as high as 22.000$ per minute, failures should be avoided or at least detected as soon as possible [2].

S. Umeda et al. (Eds.): APMS 2015, Part I, IFIP AICT 459, pp. 447–454, 2015.
DOI: 10.1007/978-3-319-22756-6_55

The research project BigPro addresses this issue by creating a Big Data driven, pro-active failure management system, capable of processing various data from the production environment. Within the platform, the generated production data will be analyzed for data patterns that indicate possible failures in the production system.

2 Literature Review

2.1 Big Data

In 2001 the Meta Group (Gartner) proposed a report about future data management, proposing the three dimensions: Variety, Velocity and Volume [3]. The term Big Data was not yet invented, but the data classification into the three V's prevailed and has been supplemented in 2013 by the dimension Veracity in an IBM study [4].

The dimension *Volume* is still the most common perception of Big Data and describes the amount of data that is generated and processed, at times comprising of petabytes of data. *Velocity* describes the speed at which the data is generated and processed, with special emphasis on the increasing significance of real-time data transmission. The fact that the majority of data is unstructured or semi-structured is regarded by the dimension *Variety*. The newly introduced dimension *Veracity* covers the aspect of the uncertain quality of data and the outcome of data analyses, taking into account that data is partially imprecise, nuanced, and may be redundant or incomplete [5].

Big Data introduces new capabilities of data storage, processing, and analysis. With increasing data sources in companies the available data in companies exceeds their processing capabilities. This not only holds true for the data volume, but also for its variety. With roughly 80 % of the data being unstructured or semi-structured, the ability to consider all kinds of data for analytical tasks, infused by Big Data technology, is of great importance for a company's success. The processing data in real-time is another important aspect that makes Big Data technology capable for failure management systems, since a short reaction time to identify failures is of crucial economic importance for production companies [6].

2.2 Complex Online Optimization and Complex Event Processing

The term *complex online optimization* summarizes hard to solve optimization problems with high response time requirements while including different decision makers and project phases [7]. These challenges exist especially when a failure occurs or is suspected and the production system needs to be stabilized. In most classic failure management approaches, production managers try to cushion failures by including buffers within the production plan. However, there are new approaches which introduce a dynamic component to adapt production plans to occurring failures, e.g. simulation-based rescheduling. Most of these approaches concentrate on a particular machine, ignoring the succeeding production steps and the changes that come with the adjustment of the production plan for the following machines. The BigPro approach includes different kinds of data from several decision-making levels to create a comprehensive failure management in production. This approach includes not only the already mentioned rescheduling concept, but also approaches of event-based failure identification and prevention activities, which are part of an automated data analysis.

Complex event processing (CEP) describes the direct tracking, processing and analyzing of data streams in near real-time. The aim of complex event processing is to gain insight in data patterns and identify meaningful business events within a complex data context [8, 9]. The advantage of complex event processing is that these event streams can be processed directly on the data stream. This technology shows great potential for the use in an intelligent and agile production, where great amounts of data from different sources such as sensor-data streams, service data and external data need to be analyzed on-the-fly. In BigPro this technology will be used to analyze failure patterns to initialize preventive actions. Here, not only current but also past event patterns are considered to create a larger information basis and make the forecasting system more reliable and resilient.

2.3 FMEA Incident Management

The failure mode and effects analysis is an established systematic technique, used to identify and analyze failures and failure types. The FMEA analysis enables the detection of failure possibilities and weak points within a process and identifies proactive measures to prevent these failures [10]. Furthermore, FMEA optimizes existing processes and can even be used to bundle all information regarding past detected failures and their connection for further use. The FMEA method therefore is a suitable tool to define failure groups as part of the reactive failure management in BigPro.

2.4 Mood Tracking and Sentiment Analysis

Monitoring human related data such as emotions and physical activities have gained increasing awareness in many different research areas [11]. However, stress management in production context is a rather new research area. Due to newly deve-loped biosensors it is possible to measure different parameters such as heart rate variability, heart beat or skin conductance which are reliable indicators for stress. This information can be merged in a production environment to identify stressful situations and prevent failure or production downtime by taking measures accordingly.

Sentiment Analysis refers to the analysis of written human interaction to identify the emotional state of the author, at the time the message was written. A message can contain not only an informative, but also an emotional message [12]. The analysis of human data will be included in BigPro as another potential failure indicator to gain better insight into the production system, and improve failure management.

2.5 Identified Research Gap

The integration of Big Data technology into a failure management system has not yet been put to the test. This enables the merge of structured and unstructured data in a production context and to create a more precise virtual image of the production system. It also requires more sophisticated CEP algorithms to better process and merge structured and unstructured data in a failure management context. To ensure portability of the solution, another challenge is to cover three different use cases with very distinct information systems and business cases.

After the data is processed and a potential failure is recognized, a user-oriented visualization is necessary to suggest or initiate countermeasures. Depending on the failure's seriousness and impact on production, countermeasures need to be taken by persons from different hierarchies with different authorization levels in the company. Hence, a user-oriented visualization (management decides on aggregated information, while production workers require actual information on machine status) of failures needs to be developed. Furthermore, the integration of human data as an indicator for failures requires new data privacy concepts.

3   Big Data for Production Failure Management

3.1   Failure Recognition with Big Data to Increase Production Resilience

To detect possible failures all production data (e.g. sensor data, order data from the ERP system and other information systems, production environment data, …) will be gathered and analyzed. As part of the BigPro approach the influence of the persons within the production - the heart of a production- will be considered as well. In fact, the worker's input and his working experience is of great importance to gain better insights in the production system's condition. Unusual observations such as growing noise emission or oil leakage stay mostly unnoticed, but can be detected by experienced workers. As part of this project, different sources of human input are tested regarding their failure management suitability: text analyses of intranet department news, maintenance comments as well as voice recognition within the production itself are potential data sources.

Human data, as well as data from production assets will be automatically analyzed and handled by complex event processing methods. In addition, not only current but also past information from failure situations are processed to detect reoccurring patterns and improve the platform's failure forecasting capabilities. After patterns are detected, the probability of an occurring failure is determined to define the data's quality and to decide whether correcting actions will be taken.

Applying Big Data – technology to the production data allows for the consideration of all data (structured or unstructured) relevant for the production process, making the digital representation of the production more comprehensive. Thus, the more data and information is available in real-time, the better the planning, controlling and managing of production systems can be performed, while responsiveness to unforeseeable events increases. All these aspects pave the way to a more resilient production system suffering of fewer unplanned production downtimes.

3.2   Big Data for Failure Prevention and Reaction Management

After patterns have been detected, adequate countermeasures need to be defined for the pro-active character of the failure management system in BigPro. As a supporting tool for the creation and evaluation of specific reactive actions the FMEA analysis will be used. For known patterns a reactive action will be defined in the failure management platform and documented in a countermeasure catalog. For an identified pattern with a high probability rate the previously defined countermeasure might be initiated automatically by the system. Patterns with a lower probability of occurrence can be forwarded to the person in charge as a failure warning with a reaction proposal. Thus, the risk of the production from going into downtime is reduced. The catalog will be extended in an ongoing validation process. To eventually use this technology for different production branches cross-sector solutions need to be generated.

3.3 Failure Visualization

As a subordinate theme this research aims to visualize information about possible failures, their urgency, and possible reasons with proposed countermeasures.

Information should be visualized differently for different groups of employees. While the production manager needs failure notifications about urgent failures, the machine operator needs all types of information about the machines that are in his area of responsibility. He also needs a different degree of information and is used to more technically detailed information. His information may include information about resource shortage or signs of increasing wear as well as a drop in oil pressure. This personalized way of failure visualization creates a more transparent and user-oriented workflow while increasing efficiency of the failure management system.

4 BigPro for a Resilient Failure Management in Production

The project BigPro unites new data processing approaches with an emphasis on failure management strategies. The aim of the project is the creation of new usable concepts and tools in regards to the failure detection, failure handling and failure visualization. The project takes place in close collaboration with three project partners to test created solutions in action within their production systems.

The project partners are of varying size with a range of different production systems to study and ensure the manifold application possibilities of the BigPro platform.

4.1 The Overall Approach

Information plays an important role in this project. To realize an effective and efficient failure management system, it is important to consider the right pieces of information in the right context. The project's Big Data approach allows for the consideration of all kinds of data and information, without the need to specify relevant information beforehand. Thus, all available data can be gathered, analyzed, and used in the BigPro platform for a data-based failure management.

BigPro will extend the data processed for analysis from the production environment (production machine data, environmental data, and order data) with unstructured, human data. Thus, a more complete digital image of the production is gained. Impressions, such as unusual machine noises or flawed machine operations are difficult to track with ordinary sensors. BigPro will be capable to capture and understand human input, and will use this additional information for the failure management.

The overall goal of BigPro is to enable a pro-active failure management for producing companies. This goal is carried out by developing algorithms for data pattern analysis. These algorithms examine existing data pools for patterns during production failures. Detected data patterns will be correlated with the related failure and included in the catalog of countermeasures. BigPro platform will use this data base to compare current data stream from the production environment with the known patterns. In case of a match, the system will warn, that a specific failure might occur. If a known and established countermeasure is recognized, it will be suggested to the responsible user.

Next, to initialize and conduct pro-active or re-active countermeasures, it is important to identify the appropriate management/decision level to address the failure. Here, it is important to provide the required information visualized user-oriented and in the right aggregation level.

The project comprises of the following tasks to implement a Big Data platform for failure management in production systems:

- Creating an information landscape for each use case, and developing a concept to determine data and information reliability for the failure management system,
- Evolving algorithms for CEP data pattern management as basis for a pro-active failure management,
- Creating an expandable catalog of countermeasures, correlated with identified data patterns, and
- Developing new, user-oriented visualization concepts for different decision levels.

4.2 Use Cases Descriptions

The first use case is part of a research environment to test the interaction between practice and research. Based on a real production environment, electrically powered pedal carts are being assembled in a small-batch production. The factory is equipped with modern machinery and assisted by voice-based systems such as Pick-by Voice commissioning. Due to research activities, the data environment is extended on a regular basis. This leads to a dynamic data generation environment and a high variety and veracity of data. As part of research it is possible to study employees as indicators of disturbance in more detail than in actual companies.

The second partner has started to digitalize its hand moulding shop by installing RFID technology linked to the ERP system to increase process transparency. These data are extended by data pulled from the involved production machines. This use case represents the data availability of a typical SME. The company does not yet have a total failure management system but with up to six weeks of throughput time for each product, it is of the utmost importance, that failures and resulting production disturbances can be avoided.

The production process of the third partner requires the interaction of a high number of production machines, each creating a significant volume of data points that need to be merged to extend the already existing failure management system. The integration of human created content promises further insights into the production process and its stability.

4.3 Challenges in BigPro

The three use cases and their diverse production and business backgrounds mean a significant challenge to BigPro. Each partner demands for a specific problem solution in a specific context. To ensure transferability of the solution, three measures need to be taken: First, the partner specific problems need to be generalized to examine transferability options. Second, a set of standard BigPro elements to address the generic problems will be defined. These sets comprise of involved information objects, as well as required information sources (e.g. sensors). Third, the catalog's logic to gather countermeasures needs to receptive for all three partner's requirements.

Further challenges arise from the integration of structured and unstructured data. Especially the aspired inclusion of human-generated content poses a challenge for the BigPro platform. On the one hand, it is necessary to generate data without interfering with the workers' working routines. Thus, analyses were run to identify already existing human interfaces within the treated use cases. On the other hand, there is still the complexity of digitalizing input and processing the retrieved data into context-related content. Therefore, the system will be taught in terms and context by reading in documents and manuals of the respective process.

5   Conclusion and Outlook

An efficient failure management plays an important role for production companies. Scrap and downtime are cost drivers that need to be avoided. Since data and information play an increasingly important role in companies and for decision makers, it seems natural to use data for a failure management system. BigPro introduces comprehensive approach by using Big Data methods for more precise failure detection. A Big Data platform will be developed capable of processing structured and unstructured data, generated in the production environment.

Unlike other approaches, BigPro not only uses data from production machines and environment sensors, but stresses the worker's capabilities to indicate disturbances and failures. By digitalizing the human input, and merging it with machine data on the BigPro platform, the digital image of the production is more complete, and serves a better decision basis. On this basis, data pattern analyses are run to detect looming failures in production. This goal drives another challenge: the combination of historic and real-time data, as well as the correlation with data patterns and related failures.

Finally, a concept for a user-oriented visualization to better support decision makers is required. This concept ensures that only information relevant for a person is shown (management decides on aggregated information, while production workers require actual information on machine status).

In the first project phase the technical and business-driven use case requirements have been gathered, discussed and documented. Next, the BigPro platform will be initiated based on the documented requirements. In parallel, the information landscape is drawn, to identify relevant information objects. Based on the information objects, the data pattern analysis will start.

Acknowledgements. The BigPro project is promoted by the German Federal Ministry of Education and Research (Project number 01IS14011A-I), in the context of the operational program *ICT 2020 –Research for Innovation.* The project will end in August 2017.

Special thanks go to: Asseco AG, C. Grossmann Stahlguss GmbH, Cognesys GmbH, i2solutions GmbH, Robert Bosch GmbH, Software AG, FZI Forschungszentrum Informatik, Werkzeugmaschinenlabor der RWTH Aachen.

References

1. McKinsey Digital. Industry 4.0- How to navigate digitization of the manufacturing sector. Industry report, McKinsey & Company (2015)
2. Industry News. Downtime Costs Auto Industry $22 k/Minute. http://news.thomasnet.com/companystory/downtime-costs-auto-industry-22k-minute-survey-481017 (2006)
3. Laney, D.: 3-D Data Management: Controlling Data Volume, Velocity and Variety. META Group Original Research Note (2001)
4. Schroeck, M., et al.: Analytics: the real-world use of big data. IBM Institute for Business Value - executive report, IBM Institute for Business Value (2012)
5. Bloehdorn, S., Fromm, H.: Big Data—Technologies and Potential. Enterprise-Integration (2014)
6. Zikopoulos, P., Eaton, C.: Understanding Big Data: Analytics for Enterprise Class Hadoop and Streaming Data. McGraw-Hill Osborne Media, New York (2011)
7. Grötschel, M., Krumke, S.O., Rambau, J.: Online Optimization of Complex Transportation Systems. Springer, Berlin (2001)
8. Cugola, G., Margara, A.: Processing flows of information: from data stream to complex event processing. ACM Comput. Surv. (CSUR) **44**(3), 15 (2012)
9. Grauer, M., et al.: An approach for real-time control of enterprise processes in manufacturing using a rule-based system. In: Multikonferenz Wirtschaftsinformatik (2010)
10. Goebbels, S., Jakob, R.: Geschäftsprozess-FMEA: Fehlermöglichkeits-und Einfluss-Analyse für IT-gestützte Geschäftsprozesse. Symposion Publishing GmbH (2004)
11. Mishne, G., De Rijke, M.: MoodViews: tools for blog mood analysis. In: AAAI Spring Symposium: Computational Approaches to Analyzing Weblogs (2006)
12. Pang, B., Lee, L.: Opinion mining and sentiment analysis. Found. Trends Inf. Retrieval **2**(1–2), 1–135 (2008)

Selection of Molding Method for CFRP Automotive Body Parts - Resin Injection vs. Compression

Yuji Kageyama[1(✉)], Kenju Akai[2], Nariaki Nishino[2], and Kazuro Kageyama[2]

[1] Kanazawa Institute of Technology, Nonoichi, Japan
y_kageyama@neptune.kanazawa-it.ac.jp
[2] The University of Tokyo, Bunkyō, Japan
akaikenju@gmail.com, Nishino@tmi.t.u-tokyo.ac.jp,
kageyama@giso.t.u-tokyo.ac.jp

Abstract. The carbon fiber reinforced plastic (CFRP) is now drawing attention in the automotive industry and has also recently been adopted for manufacturing bodies of mass produced electric vehicles. The CFRP molding method for automobile body can be largely categorized into the injection and compression methods. The essential difference between the two lies in whether or not the process involves an intermediary material and it became evident that this had a significant impact on quality and productivity. An evaluation was performed to determine which of these methods the valid method for basic molding, is by comparing the nature of such intermediary material with main components of automobile body, which led to the discovery of fundamental issues. A review on how technical developments thus far were considered with regards to such issues, it became evident that while significant progress was being made there was still a divergence from the expected target.

Keywords: Carbon fiber reinforced plastic(CFRP) · Automobile industry · Molding method

1 Trends in Automobile Body Components and Expectations for CFRP [1]

A consideration of the transition of the materials used for automobiles indicates that the use of steel is on a gradual decline, while the use of lightweight materials, such as aluminum and resin, is starting to increase. The same is true for structural materials, with the use of pillars made from high-tension steel and aluminum for outer panels on the increase. CFRP, on the other hand, continues to be popular in the field of motor sports, such as F1 racing, since its use has been attributed to the sharp drop in the number of accident-related deaths of drivers. There has been an increase in the number of instances of its use for the structural components of supercars. It has been difficult to adopt this material for mass-produced automobiles, however, due to reasons such as its high cost. CFRP has, however, recently been seen in environmentally friendly vehicles,

© IFIP International Federation for Information Processing 2015
S. Umeda et al. (Eds.): APMS 2015, Part I, IFIP AICT 459, pp. 455–463, 2015.
DOI: 10.1007/978-3-319-22756-6_56

such as in the body of the BMW i3 and the stack frame of the Toyota Mirai. The material not only improves performance such as driving stability through weight reduction, but it is also expected to provide a means of reducing negative legacies, such as environmental problems.

2   CFRP Molding Methods Currently Applied to Automobile Bodies

Although there are great expectations for CFRP as a material for automobiles, its status has not yet been firmly established due to issues with cost and productivity. There has, however, been an overall reduction in cost. Carbon fiber manufacturers, furthermore, have set their sights on the development of carbon fiber with a higher number of filaments in the strands, not only for aerospace but also for automotive applications. Researchers have developed innovative varieties of carbon fiber specifically for automobiles, without the constraints of conventional carbon fiber manufacturing techniques, and further development is expected. In terms of productivity, on the other hand, a salient issue has been the time-consuming detachment of the product from the autoclave mold. This is the final step after the cutting, pasting, and layering of dozens of resin-soaked carbon fiber sheets in the mold, which are then sintered in an autoclave. Resin transfer molding (RTM), which is a resin injection method and carbon fiber sheet molding compound (C-SMC), which is a press method, have been adopted as innovative construction methods for the Lexus LFA sports car [1]. High-pressure RTM (HP-RTM) molding has furthermore been implemented as an improvement over RTM and adopted for the engine hood and roof of the Lexus RCF. The construction method that used to be called structural reaction injection molding (S-RIM) formed the basis for the development of HP-RTM. Molding that can be completed within 3 min is now a reality, due to the improvement of equipment and the development of rapid curing resins. The fact that the body of the i3 model from BMW, which is a mass-produced electric vehicle, uses this construction method is truly ground-breaking. This will certainly be a trend to follow in the future. The current situation is such that a variety of other CFRP molding methods for automobiles are being researched, developed, and proposed. Research into CFRP using thermoplastic resins has recently been attracting considerable attention, with particular emphasis on special molding methods such as the thermoplastic CFRP sheet compression method.

3   Analysis of CFRP Molding Methods for Automobile Bodies

While it is obviously good that the industry is proposing a variety of CFRP molding methods for automobiles, not all molding manufacturers can quickly set up their equipment to start their research and begin mass production. All of these molding methods require special molding facilities which are not readily available and are, of course, quite expensive. In addition, material manufacturers often comment that, while they are interested in researching CFRP as a material for the future, they are at loss regards determining the molding method on which they should concentrate. Even if they were to concentrate on one particular molding method, they still would not know which components should be targeted, to whom they should offer their materials, or with whom they could consult in their efforts.

3.1 Two Molding Methods

We considered the two CFRP molding methods that are currently gaining the greatest attention for application to automobile bodies. Our findings are listed in Table 1. In many cases, the molding methods could be largely categorized into two types, namely, the injection type and the compression type. The injection type is often used to create relatively large components such as body frames or outer panels and includes methods such as RTM molding. This type of molding method has been applied to mass-produced vehicles such as the i3 from BMW, through the adoption of the HP-RTM molding method. This is a wet method that involves impregnating the carbon fiber base material (that has been formed into the shape of the intended product) with liquid resin. This is then composited and reactively cured with heat or the like. The compression method, on the other hand, is a dry method. The carbon fiber base materials are impregnated with resin in advance. The intermediary material, which has been half-cured or solidified, is made to flow under high pressure. It is in this aspect that the method differs from the injection method. These methods have actually been adopted for secondary frame components or outer panels made of C-SMC or trunk lids made by prepreg compression molding (PCM), as was adopted for the Nissan GT-R. The stack frame of the Toyota Mirai, which is a fuel cell vehicle, is molded using a

Table 1. CFRP molding method for automobile body

	RTM	VaRTM	HP-RTM	SMC	PCM	TP Prepreg
Molding Method	Static Mixing Resin Transfer	Vacuum-assisted Resin Transfer	Impingement mixing Reaction Injection	Long fiber random sheet press	Prepreg sheet press	Thermoplastic Prepreg sheet press
Actual implementations	• Sports cars Body frame Engine hood, roof (MacLaren SLR, Lexus LFA, etc.)	• Sports cars Roof (Lexus LFA, etc.)	• Eco cars Body, roof (BMW i3) • Sports cars Roof, engine hood (Lexus RCF etc.)	• Sports cars Secondary frame (Lexus LFA, Lamborghini, etc.) Engine hood inner (Lexus RCF, etc.)	• Sports cars Trunk lid (Nissan GTR)	• Eco cars Stack frame (Toyota Mirai)
Features * Material • Design • Production	Resin, Carbon fiber Large scale integrated structure (in excess of external panel dimensions) Low pressure molding, Medium molding time Onsite composite process			Intermediary material (Resin + Carbon fiber) Small to medium scale molded parts (up to external panel dimensions) High pressure molding Short molding time Composite process performed by material manufacturer		
Type	Injection			Compression		
Method	Wet			Dry		
	Carbon fiber base material is impregnated with liquid resin, then reactive cured or solidified.			Semi-cured or solidified intermediary material is made to flow under high pressure then reactive cured or solidified		
Difference in molding methods	Whether or not to use an __intermediary material__					

compression method, using a thermoplastic resin CFRP intermediary material, which has drawn considerable attention in recent years. The fundamental difference between these two methods is in whether they use an intermediary material, which has been prepared by compositing the resins and fibers in advance. These methods can be broadly categorized into the compression method that uses an intermediary material and the injection method that does not use any such material, with materials being composited within a mold, instead.

3.2 Differences Between Two Molding Methods

The fundamental difference between these two methods is whether an intermediary material is used for preparing the composite material. Next, we will consider how this difference affects the level of quality or productivity (Fig. 1).

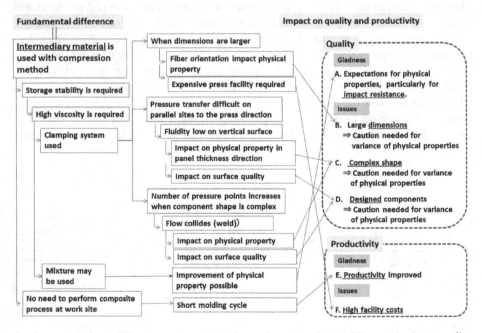

Fig. 1. Impact from difference between injection and compression molding methods on quality and productivity

An advantage of using an intermediary material is that the number of compositing processes at the manufacturing site is reduced by one. This leads to the shortening of the molding cycle, which better enables mass production. Conversely, the stability of the intermediary material during storage presents an issue, since it incorporates unreacted resin. There are, of course, a number of aspects with regards to stability, but the most important of all relates to the prevention of resin outflow from an intermediary material in the storage environment. A raised level of viscosity is therefore required of the resin. Increasing the viscosity has a significant impact on quality and productivity. First of all, to mold a material into the shape of the product by using a mold, it is necessary to apply pressure to the intermediary material. This is provided by a press-based clamping system. When the projected area of the product becomes large in such a case, even higher pressures becomes necessary to make the intermediary material flow. Depending on the product dimensions, very expensive press facilities may be necessary. Furthermore, fiber can easily be oriented in the flow direction and the variance in the physical properties can become significant, potentially having an impact on the surface quality of the product. The nature of this method is such that the pressure is less likely to be applied to the product sections in the direction of the mold clamping, which tends to adversely affect the fluidity of the intermediary material. The deterioration in the fluidity of the material has an impact on the physical properties and surface quality. When the shapes of the components are complex, the physical properties and surface quality of the product can vary. Furthermore, when the component shape is complex, the number of pressurizing points must increase, which leads to an increased number of locations where the flows caused by pressurization run into each other. This is more of an issue when the viscosity is high, such that the flows are unable to mix, which can have a significant impact on the physical properties and surface quality. Resin, however, is quite good at mixing, and thus can be used as a filler for shock absorption and for filling other functional materials. Taking advantage of this aspect, it would be possible to predict that, while the intermediary material is less likely to flow, the physical properties can be improved. This would be particularly advantageous for parts that need to be collision resistant.

There are advantages related to mass productivity and the respective physical properties attainable with the compression method which features the use of an intermediary material. However, caution is required in such aspects as the dimensions of the product, the complexity of the shape, or the design properties. The injection method offers the opposite properties.

3.3   Main Components of Automobile Body and Two Molding Methods

The properties of the two molding methods described above and the required characteristics of the main components of an automobile body were compared to evaluate their compatibility. The results are listed in Table 2. The components were categorized into the body frame, lids that are opened and closed, reinforcements, as well as interior and exterior components. Parts were selected from these categories. In terms of productivity, furthermore, the assumption was that the components were mass produced for automobiles that are built at a rate of 10,000 units per month, in order to accommodate the need for future conversion to CFRP.

We first considered the floor pan, a body panel of significant dimensions. Since this panel is characterized by complex concaves and protrusions in the tunnel sections, an evaluation based on the results described above pointed to the injection method as being more suitable than the compression method. On the other hand, sub-frames and side sills, which are frame elements, have medium-scale dimensions and are relatively simple in shape. For these reasons, evaluation pointed to the compression method being

Table 2. Fundamental molding method and main issues from aspects of "respective automobile components"

Category	Component						Molding method	Issues
Body frame	Floor panel	Large	Complex	None	Medium	Large	Injection	Productivity (molding cycle)
	Sub-frame	Medium	Simple	None	Large	Large	Compression	Facility cost (press pressure)
	Side sill	Medium	Simple	None	Large	Large	Compression	Facility cost (press pressure)
Lids	Engine hood –Outer	Medium	Simple Complex	Available	Small	Large	Compression Injection	Facility cost (press pressure) Productivity (molding cycle)
	– Inner	Medium	Simple	None	Medium	Large	Compression	Facility cost (press pressure)
	Back door –Outer	Medium	Simple Complex	Available	Medium	Large	Compression Injection	Facility cost (press pressure) Productivity (molding cycle)
	– Inner	Medium	Simple	None	Large	Large	Compression	Facility cost (press pressure)
Enforcements	Engine mount, etc.	Small	Simple	None	Medium	Large	Compression	Facility cost (press pressure)
Interior and Exterior	Rear spoiler	Small	Simple	Available	Small	Large	Compression	—
	Rocker panel, etc.	Small	Simple	Available	Small	Large	Compression	—

more suitable. However, the injection method would have to be developed for mass production, while a press facility with a capacity of at least 1000 tons would be needed for the compression method. There are still issues with mass production, however, which will be a requirement in the future. Lids such as engine hoods and tailgates were considered in terms of their being bonded structures with inner and outer panels. Such components have medium-scale dimensions but attention to design is particularly important for the outer panel. Demands for shapes range from quite simple ones to complex ones such as bulges on engine hoods or spoiler-integrated types for tailgates. It would appear that the molding method must be decided according to the complexity of such shapes. Even in the case of lids, for instance, they are not all the same and the required physical properties vary from one to another. Tailgates, for instance, require a certain degree of impact resistance to be able to withstand rear-end collisions, while the impact resistance of engine hoods cannot be increased due to the necessity to provide pedestrian protection. Another aspect that should be noted with regards to the design is the sense of unity for the entire vehicle. If the outer panels were to be produced using different molding methods, then a difference in the surface quality would arise. As a result, the likes of the paint coating that is performed as a post-process would also need to be changed. Thus, the manufacturing issue shifts from the molding method to the paint finishing. Therefore, the method used to mold lids must be selected at the stage where the product is being commercialized. In any event, there is no doubt that issues related to the molding method, which are similar to those for the body frame, will also arise in such instances.

Reinforcement components such as engine mounts, or interior and exterior components such as rear spoilers and rocker panels, tend to be well suited to the application of the compression method due to their required characteristics and, as such, fundamental problems should not arise.

It is possible to evaluate whether the injection or compression method is compatible with the main components of an automobile body, although there are some for which it was difficult to make a selection, such as the lids described above. Both molding methods incur significant issues that must be resolved to accommodate the need for mass production in the future.

4 Discussions Relating to CFRP Molding Methods for Automobile Bodies

In the future, it will be vital to identify the direction in which improvements will have to be made, by addressing trends in the technologies that have already been developed, in relation to the problems related to the two molding methods described above. Figure 2, below plots the fundamental problems with the injection method on the horizontal axis, while the pressure applied by the press, which is the main issue with the compression method, is plotted on the vertical axis. On this graph, we have plotted representative examples that have been developed to date.

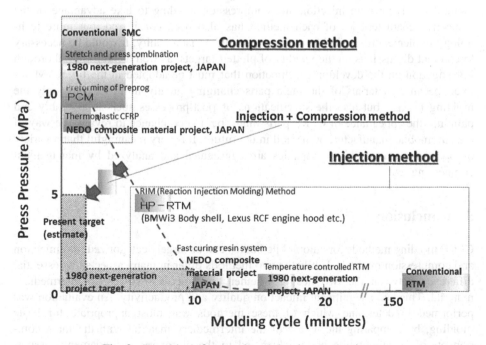

Fig. 2. Transition of research and development on issues

More than 30 years ago, in 1980, the "Research and Development for Next Generation Composite Materials" project was started as a national effort, which brought up similar discussions. RTM, which is an injection method, was referred to as "temperature-regulated RTM" and attempts were made to develop a technology to significantly reduce the molding cycle. On the other hand, research was conducted to develop technology for reducing the pressure exerted by the press, which came to be known as the "stretch and press combined method" for SMC, which is a compression method. The relevant targets are also indicated in the diagram and while a considerable number of successes were obtained, significant failures were also confirmed [2]. Since then, the New Energy and Industrial Technology Development Organization (NEDO) has been established and rapid-curing resins have been developed for the while thermoplastic-resin CFRP has been researched for application to the compression method. This study is ongoing, with the ultimate goal of developing a thermoplastic-resin CFRP. The figure shows that the targets set in 1980 have been partially achieved. The targets, however, have changed as the expectations for CFRP grew, with molding cycles in the order of 1 min now expected, which is significantly less than what was initially expected. Conversely, the trend is toward less demanding press capacities. A general purpose press will often have a capacity in the order of 500 MPa, as plotted in the figure. Further margins for improvement have emerged in this area, however.

HP-RTM has been adopted as the injection method for the body of the BMW i3 as well as the engine hood and roof of the Lexus RCF, as described above, while PCM was adopted as the compression method for the trunk lid of the Nissan GT-R. In every one of these cases, however, the plotted targets have not been satisfied. A multiple method involving both injection and compression molding to take advantage of the respective characteristics of each method has also been considered, but more technology implementations will be necessary to make that a reality. It would be necessary to conduct discussions on the validity of plotted targets, as well as perform a thorough investigation on the development direction that must be adopted in the future. Moreover, because materials of the main parts changing greatly influences not only the molding process but also the specifications of post-processes such as assembly and painting, the appearance of CFRP parts might be a good chance to review the way of the automobile manufacturing method in the future. It is very meaningful that a variety of opinion of automobile companies are aggregated and analyzed by management engineering, etc.

5 Conclusion

CFRP molding methods for automobile bodies can be largely categorized into injection and compression methods. While the two methods differ in many aspects, the essential difference between the two lies in whether the process involves an intermediary material. This had a significant impact on quality and productivity. An evaluation was performed to determine which of these methods was most appropriate for basic molding, by comparing the nature of the intermediary material with the main components of an automobile body, which led to the discovery of fundamental issues.

A review of technical developments attained up to this point, considering these fundamental issues, was undertaken. As a result, we found that, while significant progress had been made, there was still a divergence from the expected target. It became clear that further development and control of the resin employed for the CFRP was important to establishing a direction to take to attain improvements. In the future, our aim is to gain an understanding of the validity of the established targets, perform quantification of the fluidity targets for the resin by simulation, and achieve further improvements in the technical aspects through enhanced collaboration with resin manufacturers. We also intend to make plans for implementing analyses and discussions not only relating to the technical aspects but also to business management.

References

1. Kageyama, Y.: Today's and future's CFRP technologies for automobile (special issue on increasing enhancements and applications of carbon fiber plastics in automobiles). J. Soc. Automot. Eng. Jpn. **68**(11), 75–81 (2014). http://ci.nii.ac.jp/naid/40020256901
2. Japanese Standards Association: Next Generation Composite Material Technology Handbook, 1990

Paraconsistent Artificial Neural Network Applied in Breast Cancer Diagnosis Support

Fábio Vieira do Amaral[1(✉)], Jair Minoro Abe[1],
Alexandre Jacob Sandor Cadim[2], Caique Zaneti Kirilo[2],
Carlos Arruda Baltazar[2], Fábio Luís Pereira[1], Hélio Côrrea de
Araújo[1], Henry Costa Ungaro[2], Lauro Henrique de Castro Tomiatti[2],
Luiz Carlos Machi Lozano[2], Renan dos Santos Tampellini[2],
Renato Hildebrando Parreira[1], Uanderson Celestino[1],
Rafael Espirito Santo[1], and Cristina Côrrea Oliveira[1]

[1] Graduate Program in Production Engineering, Paulista University-UNIP,
Dr. Bacelar 1212, CEP 04026-002 São Paulo - SP, Brazil
{favamaral, f.luis01}@gmail.com,
jairabe@uol.com.br, hhca@globo.com

[2] Ungraduate Computer Science, Paulista University-UNIP,
St. Vergueiro 1211, CEP 01504-000 São Paulo - SP, Brazil
{carlosarrudabaltazar, cardimajs}@gmail.com,
{caiquez.kirilo, henry_tnt_07, tomiattil,
renan.tampellini}@hotmail.com, luizlozano@icloud.com

Abstract. In this work, a Paraconsistent Classifier for the diagnosis of breast cancer based on the attributes of mamographic images was developed. The system uses a neural network with decision making from the final results of processing each set of attributes was created. In order to mitigate the effects of false positives diagnoses and true positives. In order to analyze the performance of the Paraconsistent Classifier, the results will be compared with the results of the following classifiers: Multi-Layer Perceptron (MLP), a dual stage classifier (ART2LDA) based on Adaptive Resonance Theory (ART) and a classifier implemented with nonlinear optimization techniques and combinatorics, associated with the classification capabilities of Radial basis Functions - (RBF-Simulated Annealing).To perform the simulations, two different databases were used. The first one, to classify calcifications, is composed of 143 samples divided into 64 benign cases and 79 malignant cases represented by form. The performances of the classifiers in discriminating benign and malignant cases are compared in terms of area under the Receiver Operating Characteristic Curve (Az). The higher the value of Az, the better the performance of the classifier.The experiments with calcifications show: Paraconsistent Classifier (Az = 0.986), MLP classifier (Az = 0.70), ART2LDA Classifier (Az = 0.696) and RBF Classifier - Simulated Annealing (Az = 0.94). For experiments with mammographic masses and tumors show: Set 1, Paraconsistent Classifier (Az = 0.939), MLP classifier (Az = 0.994), ART2LDA Classifier (Az = 0.901) and RBF Classifier - Simulated Annealing (Az = 0.912). Set 2, Paraconsistent Classifier (Az = 0.935), MLP classifier (Az = 0.994), ART2LDA Classifier (Az = 0.890) and RBF Classifier - Simulated Annealing (Az = 0.924). Set 3, Paraconsistent Classifier (Az = 0.875), MLP classifier (Az = 0.970), ART2LDA Classifier (Az = 0.850)

© IFIP International Federation for Information Processing 2015
S. Umeda et al. (Eds.): APMS 2015, Part I, IFIP AICT 459, pp. 464–472, 2015.
DOI: 10.1007/978-3-319-22756-6_57

and RBF Classifier - Simulated Annealing (Az = 0.996). Set 4, Paraconsistent Classifier (Az = 0.500), MLP classifier (Az = 0.887), ART2LDA Classifier (Az = 0.767) and RBF Classifier - Simulated Annealing (Az = 0.907). Set 5, Paraconsistent Classifier (Az = 0.929), MLP classifier (Az = 0.987), ART2LDA Classifier (Az = 0.884) and RBF Classifier - Simulated Annealing (Az = 0.998). Set 6, Paraconsistent Classifier (Az = 0.939), MLP classifier (Az = 0.982), ART2LDA Classifier (Az = 0.885) and RBF Classifier - Simulated Annealing (Az = 0.999). In the case of the Paraconsistent Classifier, the eighth experiment was composed of the total image attributes relating to mammographic masses and tumors (Az = 0.939). In the particular case of the RBF-Sort Simulated Annealing experiment with all the image attributes, it was proved its unfeasibility, due to the complexity of their algorithm, where the processing time tends to infinity for a larger number of elements. For the experiments, the Paraconsistent classifier used 20 % of the samples for the neural network training, against the total number of samples available minus one for the other classifiers.

Keywords: Attributes of images classifier · Breast cancer · Computer-Aided diagnosis · Paraconsistent annotated evidential logic Et · Paraconsitent artificial neural network mammography

1 Introduction

Breast cancer fills second place in cancer occurrences in the world, with 22 % of all the new cases each year. If diagnosis point and treatment occurs in start, healing prognosis is favorable. [3].

In world population, the average after life reach five years after diagnosis in 61 % of the cases.

Brazil epidemiological illness profile subdued special attention in politic decisions of federal government. Breast cancer brings high mortality rate, because is only diagnosed in final stages. The Plan for Strengthening Prevention Actions and Quali-fication of the Diagnosis and Treatment of Cervical and Breast Cancers, released on March 2012, is an example of this premise. The incentive of X-ray exam realization in breast of caring population also belongs in this prevention politics [1, 2].

Breast X-ray (mammography) is the most indicated for detect early the presence of nodes inside breasts. Clinical exam and others image and lab exams could also support the diagnosis.

The exam shows a variety of adipose tissue, parenchyma and normal and abnormal tissues. The radiologist should analyze abnormally, using attributes, dimension, form and texture. After analysis is possible to identify illness presence. Then analyze if the node is actually a bad one, besides the fact that most of them are not [1, 2].

The risk of a wrong diagnosis, false positive or false negative, is high. Clinical exams shows that some Brazilian cities has 50 % of mammography tests with difficult in reading and diagnosis. The process realized during the exam is highly important for exams quality [1, 2].

For reach acceptable trust level, is necessary to raise the prediction of positive values. The percentage of breast cancer cases identified in mammography and confirmed by biopsy that can reach 30 %. Considering the traumatic aspect and costs for biopsy realization, it is relevant an alternate computational capable of raise distinguish between good and bad items found. This method could work well as decision-making tool. The radiologist would use this tool as part of the analysis protocol of mammography. With this, the wrong diagnosis would been minimized and the exam recommendations of biopsy reduced [1, 2].

This work treat to propose a tool capable of analyze and classify good and bad mammography attributes and a change in the process.

Attribute image classification will be supported by paraconsistent artificial neural network. This tool does not manipulate mammography. In this part of the work will be treated only aspects related to calcification. To practice this simulations will be used a database, obtained from segmentations treated in mammography acquired with Department of Radiological Sciences and Diagnosis Imaging Foothills Hospital, located in Calgary, Alberta, Canada, this database is built from 69 good cases and 79 bad ones, identified manually from a radiologist specialized in mammography. From this point, the identifications determine the factors in Momentum (m), Compaction factor (c) and Fourier description (f) [1, 2].

2   Digital Images Attributes

The computed detection of good masses, bad tumors and calcification in mammography are not simply filled with Neural Networks specialized in ordinary recognition. In existing ordinary recognition (as mammography) built by neural networks, identify forms from borders and patterns (image segmentation), so, localizing frontiers between background and pattern. In this recognizing, the better image definition of frontier in patterns the better results of border detection. In mammography, most of the good masses, just like good calcifications, has well-defined aspects and frontier (borders) with high contrasted degree. Forms of good calcifications can be circular and oval shaped. Contour of the benign masses beyond the circular and oval form, could also present the macro lobular form, shown in Fig. 2 [9]. The border transition is clear from inside the dense tissue from outside, less dense. Malignant calcifications, although, seems to have cloudy contrast and frontier not so clear. Malignant calcification outlines shows lobular shape, and malignant tumors shows microlobulated shape. In this case, the transition of interne tissue (denser), from extern is not very clear or defined. However, some benign masses such as fiber adenoma could present erased borders in mammography.

About the convexity and concavity of masses shape, we could see that the most benign masses presents convex shapes. Some of them are concaved or speculated. However, malignant tumors could present both convex and concaved, and even predominant tentacles shape. And if compared, benign masses and malignant tumors, are both homogeneous in terms of density and distribution (Figs. 1 and 2) [9, 10].

Given these facts, if a neural network was trained for pattern recognizing of masses and benign and malign calcification, it would be, depending on network implementation, an efficient benign masses recognizer, but not so efficient detecting malign tumors, sometimes not recognizing fiber adenomas. Therefore, neural networks trained to recognize only patterns are not well suited and recommended to support cancer diagnosis, because it lacks where radiologists need it the most, identify cancer.

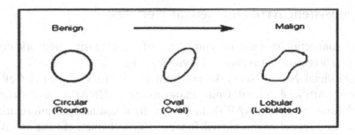

Fig. 1. Morphology of calcification visualized in Mammography [10].

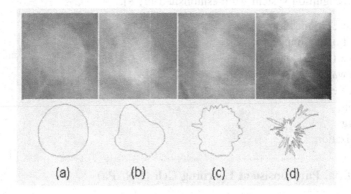

Fig. 2. Shape examples, benign (a) and (b), malign (c) and (d) [9].

The fact that the simply pattern recognizing has few or no application in mammography, shape factors, distinctness detection of masses outline and measures of texture are the answer CAD (Computer-Aided Diagnosis) for diagnosing attributes extraction in mammography.

Parameters that describe calcifications identified in mammography:

- Momentum (m)
- Fourier (f)
- Compaction factor (C)
- Radial (r)
- Distance (d)
- Standard detour of the radial distance
- Tumor Border Roughness Index(R)
- Spiculated shape index (SI):
- Entropy: , wherein
- Second momentum:
- Momentum difference:
- The inverse momentum difference:
- Correlation : linear brightness dependence Measure:
- Ac (acutance)

3   Paraconsistent Artificial Neural Network

Features of connectionist structure composed of an extensive network components supported by paraconsistent Annotated Evidential Et. [7, 8].

These Artificial Neural Networks are built from Artificial Neural Cells forming Paraconsistent Artificial Neural Units Paraconsistent (UNAP's) and Arificial Paraconsistent Neural Systems (SNAP's) that direct, treat and analyze information signals obtaining a close model of the mental functions that characterize the behavior of the human brain [7, 8].

Based on these criteria and foundations that enable the implementation of CNAP's necessary recognition system were established [7, 8].

- Analytical Connection
- Simple Logic Connecton
- Selective Logic Connection
- Passageway
- Complementation
- Decision
- Learning
- Memorization

3.1   Artificial Paraconsistent Learning Cell (CNAPa)

As part of this memory unit or as standards in primary sensor layers, in other words, all information learned or stored, must pass for such cell (Fig. 3).

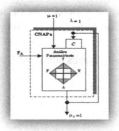

Fig. 3. Representation of CNAPa [7, 8]

3.2   Artificial Paraconsistent Decision Cell (CNAPd)

This cell act as a node of decision in RNAP's. In your entry, applying two signals from another network area, resulting in only one exit that matches one conclusive analysis of these entries (Fig. 4) [8].

The possible output values are:

- Output equals to 1 represents the pattern "True".
- Output equals to 0 represents the pattern "Falsity".
- Output equals to 0.5 represents the pattern "Uncertainty".

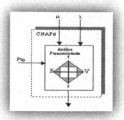

Fig. 4. Representation of CNAPd [7, 8]

3.3   Simple Logic Artificial Neural Paraconsistent Cell (CNAPCls)

Establishes the logical connective OR (maximization) between degrees of belief applied to the input of the cell, telling you which of the two signals applied to the input of the cell has the highest value, setting the signal at the output.

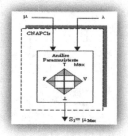

Fig. 5. Representação de uma CNAPCls [7, 8]

4   Paraconsistent Analyzer

Considering traumatic aspects and the cost for realization of biopsy, and is relevant an alternative computational way capable of raise distinguish between benign and malign calcification. This method works like a decision support tool. The radiologist would use this tool as a protocol stage, helping mammography analysis. With this, wrong diagnosis would been lowered and biopsy exam recommendation.

This software will implement a RNAP for each image attribute (m, c and f), and in the process ending it will show the diagnosis.

In the image below, the process of paraconsistent classification. This process will be similar to calcification classifications [11].

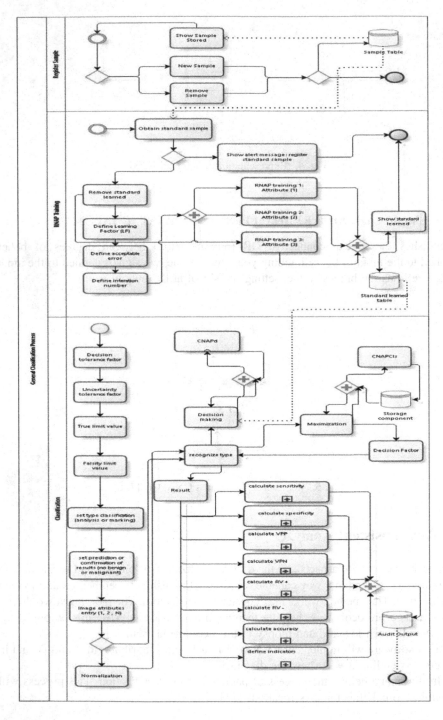

4.1 Network Composition

Main part of the network is built by a group of CNAPa that learn and spread for others parts of the network.

The second layer is composed by CNAPd, aiming establish the evidence degree between standard stored in CNAPa.

The third layer is built by CNAPCl, created for maximization, forming a competitive network, in which only one value is understood as winner [11].

4.2 Database Register Used for RNAP Training

For network training it is not necessary a high number of values.

4.3 RNAP Training

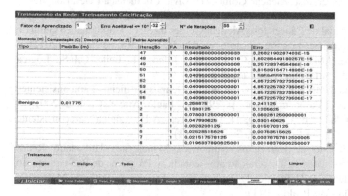

4.4 RNAP Classification

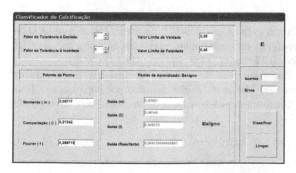

This module function can obtain a value resulting of network process, capable of determinate if a newer sample is benign or malign, and shows quality and reliability of classification through calculations of sensibility, specificity, predicted positive value, predicted negative value, likelihood positive reason, likelihood negative reason and accuracy. And how much true positive, false positive, true negative and false negative it has.

5   Final Conclusions

The paraconsistent analyzer in its first version could reach 94 % hits for calcification.

Considering the diagnosis errors could reach 50 % in extreme cases, there was a significant reduction of diagnosis with false positives or false negatives.

RNAP characteristics also need to be quoted.

- Low number of samples needing.
- In this tool case, there was no detraining in network, so required less time training.
- The algorithm complexity implemented also presents easy mastery.

References

1. Espírito-Santo, R.: Discriminação de Classes Fundamentada em Técnicas de Otimização Não Linear e Combinatória Associadas a Funções de Base Radiais: Um estudo de Caso em Mamografia. Tese apresentada à Escola Politécnica da Universidade de São Paulo para o obtenção do título de Doutor em Engenharia. Área de Concentração: Sistemas Eletrônicos. São Paulo (2004)
2. Espírito, S.R., Lopes, R.D., Rangayyan, R.M.: Classification of breast masses in mammograms using radial basis functions and simulated annealing. Int. J. Cogn. Inf. Nat. Intell. 3(3), 27–38 (2009). www.igi-global.com
3. Instituto Nacional de Câncer José Alencar Gomes da Silva. Coordenação Geral de Ações Estratégicas. Coordenação de Prevenção e Vigilância. Estimativa 2012 : incidência de câncer no Brasil / Instituto Nacional de Câncer José Alencar Gomes da Silva, Coordenação Geral de Ações Estratégicas, Coordenação de Prevenção e Vigilância. Inca, Rio de Janeiro (2011)
4. Da Costa, N.C.A., Abe, J.M., Murolo, A.C., Da Silva Filho, J.I., Leite, C.F.S.: Lógica Paraconsistente Aplicada. Atlas, São Paulo (1999)
5. Da Silva Filho, J.I., Abe, J.M.: Fundamentos das Redes Neurais Artificiais Paraconsistentes destacando aplicações em Neurocomputação, p. 298. São Paulo, Arte & Ciência (2001)
6. Abe, J.M., Da Silva Filho, J.I., Celestino, U., de Corrêa, A.H.: Lógica Paraconsistente Anotada Evidencial Et. Editora Comunicar, Santos (2011)
7. Pereira, F.: Reconhecimento de Caracteres Numéricos Manuscritos Utilizando Redes Neurais Artificiais Paraconsistentes. Dissertação apresentada ao Programa de Pós-Graduação em Engenharia de Produção da Universidade Paulista para obtenção do título de Mestre em Engenharia de Produção. São Paulo (2011)
8. Silva, F.J.I., Abe, J.M.: Fundamentos das Redes Neurais Artificiais Paraconsistentes. Arte & Ciência, São Paulo (1999)
9. Hillary, A., Rangayyan R.M., Desautels, J.E.L.: An indexed atlas of digital mammograms. In: Peitgen, H.-O. (ed.) Digital Mammography, pp. 309-311. Springer, Heidelberg (2003)
10. Bruce. L.M., Adhami, R.R.: Classifying mommographic mass shapes using the wavelet transform modulus-maxima method. IEEE Trans. Med. Imaging, 18(12) (1999)
11. do Amaral, F.V.: Classificador Paraconsistente de atributos de imagens mamograficas aplicado no processo de diagnostico do câncer de mama assistido por computador. Tese apresentada ao Programa de Pós Graduação em Engenharia de Produção na Universidade Paulista – UNIP, São Paulo (2013)

Project Management, Engineering Management, and Quality Management

Start of Production in Low-Volume Manufacturing Industries: Disturbances and Solutions

Siavash Javadi[✉] and Jessica Bruch

Design, Innovation and Engineering Department, Mälardalen University,
Eskilstuna, Sweden
{siavash.javadi,jessica.bruch}@mdh.se

Abstract. Reducing disturbances during start of production of new products is of high importance to assure that products reach the market on-time with the intended quality and volume. Therefore, identification and elimination of sources of such disturbances is necessary. Since the literature about such disturbances in low-volume manufacturing industries are limited, this paper is aimed to identify the common sources of such disturbances and the possible solutions to mitigate them in low-volume manufacturing industries. A multiple-case study has been conducted to achieve this aim. The results show that main sources of disturbances are lack of opportunities to test and refine products, considering the production system "as is" and putting extensive focus on product functionality rather than its manufacturability. Moreover, using the knowledge and experiences from production of previous similar products is identified as a source of learning and compensation for lack of opportunities for test and refinement.

Keywords: Product introduction · Low-volume · Industrialization · Production start-up

1 Introduction

Manufacturing companies are forced to launch new products to the markets in shorter intervals due to factors such as globalization, rapidly emerging technologies and shorter product life cycles (Bellgran and Säfsten 2010, Chryssolouris 2006). Achieving shorter time to market protects the companies from crucial consequences such as losing markets and revenue and early outdating of the products (Hendricks and Singhal 2008, Adler 1995). However, the start of production is mainly characterized by high level of disturbances (Almgren 2000, Nyhuis and Winkler 2004) which usually lead to longer production cycle times (Apilo 2003, Terwiesch and Bohn 2001), lower production output (Juerging and Milling 2005, Terwiesch et al. 2001) and lower quality of products (Almgren 1999b, Nyhuis and Winkler 2004, Terwiesch et al. 2001).

Most of such disturbances during the start of production can be prevented or mediated by preparatory activities before the start of production which are mostly carried out during the product introduction process (Säfsten and Aresu 2002, Almgren 1999c, Fjällström et al. 2009). The product introduction process is defined as the transition from product design to production and incorporate the activities which make the product

© IFIP International Federation for Information Processing 2015
S. Umeda et al. (Eds.): APMS 2015, Part I, IFIP AICT 459, pp. 475–483, 2015.
DOI: 10.1007/978-3-319-22756-6_58

manufacturable and prepare it for production (Bellgran and Säfsten 2010, Johansen and Björkman 2002). Therefore, identification of sources of such disturbances at the start of production and eliminating or mitigating them by improving the product introduction process is necessary.

Improvement of the product introduction process in low-volume manufacturing industries requires solutions which are tailored to the requirements of such industries (Maffin and Braiden 2001, Surbier et al. 2013). The literature about the sources of disturbances during the start of production of new products in low-volume manufacturing industries is very limited (Surbier et al. 2013). Therefore, the aim of this paper is to identify the sources of disturbances during the start of production of new products in low-volume manufacturing industries and to suggest general solutions for mitigating them.

The study focuses on disturbances related to product and production system not cover issues related to the external variables such as suppliers or customers. The research is based on a multiple-case study in a low-volume manufacturing company.

2 Disturbances During Start of Production

Sources of disturbances during the start of production have been studied mostly in form of case studies and in context of high-volume manufacturing industries (Surbier et al. 2013). Different researchers have studied and categorized the sources of disturbances in different ways such as Almgren (2000), Nyhuis and Winkler (2004) and Surbier et al. (2013). However, all of the named studies mention product and production system among main sources of disturbances. The product-related disturbances are summarizes by Surbier et al. (2013) as insufficient product specifications and lack of product maturity. The production system-related disturbances are described as lack of production process maturity, manufacturability of the product and product-production system fit (Surbier et al. 2013).

Most of these disturbances can be prevented by the activities carried out during the product introduction process. The product introduction process, also known as the industrialization process (Bellgran and Säfsten 2010, Berg 2007) is the closing and one of the key process of product development projects (Bellgran and Säfsten 2010, Johansen and Björkman 2002, Ruffles 2000). During the product introduction process, product and production system are developed, tested, refined and adapted together (Fjällström et al. 2009, Ruffles 2000).

The main phases of the product introduction process in high-volume manufacturing industries are conceptual study, development of engineering prototypes, pilot production, pre-series production and production ramp-up (Bellgran and Säfsten 2010, Johansen and Björkman 2002). Product and production system are designed during the conceptual study. The product is developed, tested and refined by development of engineering prototypes. During pilot and pre-series productions the production system and product are tested, refined and adapted together. Finally during the production ramp-up remaining bugs are removed and expected production goals such as production volume, time and quality are reached (Johansen 2005, Ulrich and Eppinger 2012). Adler (1995) summarises the mechanisms for coordination of product introduction process into four categories based on the level of interaction between product design and production: standards, plans and schedules, mutual adjustment and teams. The level of novelty of the product and production systems defines the complexity the product introduction process (Adler 1995, Tidd and Bodley 2002, Almgren 1999a).

3 Low-Volume Manufacturing Industries

Low-volume manufacturing industries are usually characterized by yearly production volumes between 20–500 products, high variety, complexity and customizability of products and full make-to-order production policy (Jina et al. 1997). In addition, new products are usually designed to be produced in the existing production systems to avoid high investment cost (Qudrat-Ullah et al. 2012). Therefore, the production systems in such industries are usually designed to offer high flexibility to be able to produce various products. Such flexibility is usually provided by using universal production equipment, highly-skilled workers, low level of automation and shared production resources among different products (Hill 2000, Qudrat-Ullah et al. 2012). Such characteristics lead to lack of opportunities to test and refine product and production system and adapting them together due to few number of prototypes, limitations of pre-series productions and infeasibility of conventional production ramp-up (Javadi et al. 2013). In other word, opportunities to remove or mitigate disturbances at the start of production in low-volume manufacturing industries are limited in these industries. Therefore, identification of sources of disturbances and developing alternative solutions instead of applying the common approach of test and refinement during later phases of product introduction process is necessary in low-volume manufacturing industries.

4 Method

Since the empirical studies about the disturbances during the start of production in low-volume manufacturing industries are limited, case study was selected as the research method. The first hand study of the subject of the research is expected to lead to increased understanding about it (Eisenhardt 1989, Voss et al. 2002). Therefore, a multiple-case study design was selected to achieve the aim of this research.

Four product development projects were selected as the case studies. Two of the cases were studied in real-time which are hereafter called Project A and B. Project A was a small product modification project whereas Project B was a large product development project, i.e. a general modification of a product. Project A was followed for 11 months from October 2012 to September 2013. Project B was followed up for 14 months from October 2012 to January 2014. The two other cases were finished product development projects which were studied retrospectively which are hereafter called Project C and D. Project C was again a small project whereas project D was a large project. The studied events of Project C and D had happened during respectively 11-month and 20-month periods.

Multiple sources were utilized for data gathering including semi-structured interviews and document studies. Informal conversations were also carried out mostly to complete the data about the background of the company and projects and other required data. Among the documents, a database which was used for registering and following up the disturbances related to the products during the production of new products was one of the main sources of data. In addition, people who were involved in the projects were interviewed to complete and verify the gathered data. In total, 29 semi-structured face to face interviews were conducted with people who were involved in different phases of the projects as well as the production engineers, production flow leaders and operators. Time of the interviews varied between 30–80 min. In Case A and B observation of the events of the projects were also used as a sources of data.

The intention with the multiple-case study design was to compare the disturbances at the start of the production of new products in different projects with different scopes. It also helped to study the effect of the changes in the coordination methods of product introduction process on the disturbances during the start of production in the real-time cases in comparison with the retrospective ones.

Deducted conclusions in all four case studies were validated through triangulating the collected data from different sources (Yin 2013). Collected data from the cases was continuously recorded, summarized and transferred to a case study record and iteratively analyzed. The suggested process by Eisenhardt (1989) was utilized for analyzing the data by conducting within and then cross-case analyses and a comparison with the literature.

5   Empirical Findings

5.1   The Company

The company was a Swedish designer and manufacturer of underground construction and mining equipment. The company produced products with yearly production volume lower than 100 units in 4 main families. Each product has several variants with high level of customizability with many different options to fulfill the requirements of different customers and markets.

5.2   Product Development Projects

The goals of Project A and Project C were modifying a module of the products with minimum possible changes of other modules whereas Project B and Project D were started with the aim of general upgrade and modification of the products.

The general arrangements for the projects were similar. Each project was managed by a multidisciplinary team which consisted of a project manager, designers, production engineers, a product introduction project leader, and representatives from marketing and service departments. Due to high number of ongoing product development projects, all the project team members had to divide their time between different projects. Production engineers were also responsible for ongoing production activities.

All of the four products were planned to be assembled in the existing assembly lines and no new production system development were planned. As a results, minimizing the changes in the existing assembly lines were one of the goals in all of the projects.

Besides the above-mentioned similarities, the main difference between small and large projects regarding the product introduction process was that no prototype were planned for the small projects. The production of the upgraded products were started directly as normal commercial production. In contrary, the project plan of large products included production of one prototype and one product as pre-series production. In Case B the number of pre-series productions could be increased to four products depending on customer demands for the product.

In addition, some new coordination methods were introduced and used more formally in Case A and Case B in comparison with the retrospective cases, Case C and Case D. Design reviews were used to inform the production engineers and flow managers about the new features of the products and include their perspective in the product design. The production requirements were also gathered at the beginning of the new projects and were categorized and prioritized by the product introduction project leaders. These requirements were transferred in form of a list to the designers to be considered in the product design.

5.3 Disturbances Related to the Product

A considerable part of the studied disturbances in the problem reporting database were related to the lack of information or wrong information about *connecting parts*. Some example of connecting parts are nuts and bolts, cable sets and hydraulic hoses. In several instances, the information on the bill of material or drawings did not match the real product. Suggesting wrong sizes of screws and hoses, or wrong cable connections on the documents are some examples of these problems. In some cases, no information was given to the production about these parts and the operators had to find the parts by try and error or based on their experiences. This type of disturbances was categorized under *missing/wrong information about connecting parts.*

Another major share of disturbances was related to problems with assembling parts and components. In many occasions, the parts could not be assembled on the products due to non-conformity of parts interfaces, difficulty of accessing the place of the part on the product or the possibility of damaging other parts during the assembly work. This category of disturbances was named *design for assembly* disturbances.

Other types of disturbances ranged from non-functioning parts and components to the wrong or late delivery of them which were categorized as *other*. Figure 1 shows the share of each type of disturbances in the studied projects.

As Fig. 1 shows, around half of the disturbances in all of the projects were caused by missing or wrong information about connecting parts. This share was reduced in the real-time cases (A and B) comparing to the retrospective ones (C and D). The disturbances caused by design for assembly problems had also considerable share varying from 20 to 33 % of disturbances. However, these share was less in the large projects (B and D).

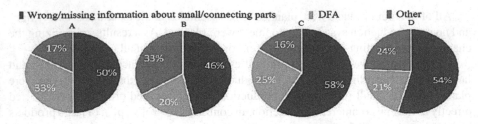

Fig. 1. Shares of each type of disturbances in each case

5.4 Disturbances Related to the Production System

Disturbances related to the production system were mostly caused by late consideration of the required changes in the production system which were necessary to produce new products. Late delivery of the required tools and fixtures, overlooking the limitations of lifting and moving equipment and overestimating the available production capacity of the production system were some of the observed examples of these disturbances. In general, lack of considering the production requirements were repeatedly occurred in different sources data.

6   Sources of Disturbances and Possible Solutions

As the results suggest, lack of considering manufacturability of the products by neglecting design details and design for assembly criteria consist 70–80 % of the product-related disturbances in all cases. Due to prioritizing functionality of the products over its manufacturability in the product development process, usually details of the product design were not considered sufficiently before handing over the product to the production. The limited shared resources among different product development projects are not sufficient to cover all the design priorities. Therefore, the problem of under-prioritizing manufacturability of the product was intensified. However, the newly implemented tools and methods for coordination of the product introduction process such as design reviews have reduced this kind of disturbances in both Case A and Case B compared to Case C and Case D by 8 %. In addition, lack of opportunities to test and refine the products does not allow to remove such disturbances before handing over the product to production. Interestingly, the share of design for assembly disturbances were less in the large projects which had higher number of prototypes and consequently more opportunities were available to test and refine the products.

Another source of disturbance was late consideration of the required changes in the production system. Whereas under-prioritizing manufacturing requirements is also a usual problem in high volume production industries, it is intensified in low-volume manufacturing industries. Since no new production system is developed for new products in low-volume manufacturing industries and products are designed to be produced in the existing production system, the production system is usually considered "as is". Therefore, the required adjustments and changes in the production system is left to the very late stage of product introduction process if they are not totally ignored.

All in all, the characteristics of low-volume manufacturing industries intensifies the disturbances related to product and production system during the start of production mentioned by Surbier et al. (2013). Examples of such disturbances are lack of deign details, lack of considering manufacturability of products and late consideration of required changes in the production systems.

The results justify that utilizing more interactive product introduction coordination mechanisms such as design reviews suggested by Adler (1995) and Tidd and Bodley (2002) can reduce the disturbances during the start of production. However, the similarity of the types of disturbances and even their share in the disturbances in the real-time and retrospective cases suggests that the production of earlier similar products can be used as a very valuable source for learning and improvement in low-volume manufacturing industries. The similarity of the products and use of almost unchanged production systems increase the similarity of the product development projects to a high extent. Therefore, learning from similar problems in similar projects can be used as a compensation for lack of opportunities for test and refinement in the product introduction process in low-volume manufacturing industries. However, the knowledge about disturbances in production should be constantly gathered and shared with the product development teams. This knowledge should also be used efficiently by product development teams and especially by the product designers.

7   Conclusions

Regarding its aim, the paper provides an insight about the sources of disturbances during the start of production in low-volume manufacturing industries which are lack of opportunities for test and refinements, late consideration or ignoring required changes in production system and extensive focus on product functionality rather than its manufacturability. Furthermore, learning from production of similar previous products is identified as a valuable source for compensating lack of opportunities for test and refinement and mitigating other sources of disturbances. In this regard, the paper provides the practitioners in low-volume manufacturing industries with an insight to how to reduce disturbances during the start of production of new products by considering required activities in earlier phases of the product introduction process.

The main limitation of this research is excluding external variables of the product introduction process which could be investigated in future. In addition, a more detailed study of the solutions and facilitators could be another topic for further research.

References

Adler, P.S.: Interdepartmental interdependence and coordination: the case of the design/manufacturing interface. Organ. Sci. **6**, 147–167 (1995)

Almgren, H.: Pilot Production and Manufacturing Start-up in the Automotive Industry. Principles for Improved Performance. Chalmers University of Technology, Gothenburg (1999a)

Almgren, H.: Start-up of advanced manufacturing systems–a case study. Integr. Manuf. Syst. **10**, 126–136 (1999b)

Almgren, H.: Towards a framework for analyzing efficiency during start-up: an empirical investigation of a Swedish auto manufacturer. Int. J. Prod. Econ. **60**, 79–86 (1999c)

Almgren, H.: Pilot production and manufacturing start-up: the case of Volvo S80. Int. J. Prod. Res. **38**, 4577–4588 (2000)

Apilo, T.: New product introduction in the electronics industry. In: 17th International Conference on Production Research, Blacksburg, USA (2003)

Bellgran, M., Säfsten, K.: Production Development: Design and Operation of Production Systems. Springer, London (2010)

Berg, M.: Factors Affecting Production Ramp-Up Performance. Jönköping University, Jönköping (2007)

Chryssolouris, G.: Manufacturing Systems: Theory and Practice. Springer Science + Business Media, Incorporated, Berlin (2006)

Eisenhardt, K.M.: Building theories from case study research. Acad. Manag. Rev. **14**, 532–550 (1989)

Fjällström, S., Säfsten, K., Harlin, U., Stahre, J.: Information enabling production ramp-up. J. Manuf. Technol. Manag. **20**, 178–196 (2009)

Hendricks, K.B., Singhal, V.R.: The effect of product introduction delays on operating performance. Manag. Sci. **54**, 878–892 (2008)

Hill, T.: Manufacturing Strategy: Text and Cases. Irwin/McGraw-Hill, New York (2000)

Javadi, S., Bruch, J., Bellgran, M., Hallemark, P.:. Challenges in the industrialization process of low-volume production systems. In: International Conference on Manufacturing Research 2013. Cranfield university press, Cranfield (2013)

Jina, J., Bhattacharya, A.K., Walton, A.D.: Applying lean principles for high product variety and low volumes: some issues and propositions. Logistics Inf. Manag. **10**, 5–13 (1997)

Johansen, K.: Collaborative product introduction within extended enterprises. Institutionen för konstruktions- och produktionsteknik (2005)

Johansen, K., Björkman, M.: Product introduction within extended enterprises. In: Proceedings of ISCE 2002 International Symposium on Consumer Electronics, Ilmenau, Germany (2002)

Juerging, J., Milling, P.M.: Interdependencies of product development decisions and the production ramp-up. In: The 23rd International Conference of the System Dynamics Society, Boston, MA, USA (2005)

Maffin, D., Braiden, P.: Manufacturing and supplier roles in product development. Int. J. Prod. Econ. **69**, 205–213 (2001)

Nyhuis, P., Winkler, H.: Development of a controlling system for the ramp-up of production systems. In: Proceedings of the International Conference on Competitive Manufacturing, pp. 4–6 (2004)

Qudrat-Ullah, H., Seong, B.S., Mills, B.L.: Improving high variable-low volume operations: an exploration into the lean product development. Int. J. Technol. Manag. **57**, 49–70 (2012)

Ruffles, P.C.: Improving the new product introduction process in manufacturing companies. Int. J. Manuf. Technol. Manag. **1**, 1–19 (2000)

Surbier, L., Alpan, G., Blanco, E.: A comparative study on production ramp-up: state-of-the-art and new challenges. Prod. Plan. Control, 1–23 (2013)

Säfsten, K., Aresu, E.: Assembly system design and evaluation of 15 manufacturing companies in Sweden. Manuf. Syst. **31** (2002)

Terwiesch, C., Bohn, R.: Learning and process improvement during production ramp-up. Int. J. Prod. Econ. **70**, 1–19 (2001)

Terwiesch, C., Bohn, R., Chea, K.: International product transfer and production ramp-up: a case study from the data storage industry. R&D Manag. **31**, 435–451 (2001)

Tidd, J., Bodley, K.: The influence of project novelty on the new product development process. R&D Manag. **32**, 127–138 (2002)

Ulrich, K.T., Eppinger, S.D.: Product Design and Development. McGraw-Hill, New York (2012)

Voss, C., Tsikriktsis, N., Frohlich, M.: Case research in operations management. Int. J. Oper. Prod. Manag. **22**, 195–219 (2002)

Yin, R.K.: Case Study Research: Design and Methods. SAGE Publications, Los Angeles (2013)

Improving Service Quality in Public Transportation in Brazil: How Bus Companies are Simplifying Quality Management Systems and Strategic Planning to Increase Service Level?

Helcio Raymundo[✉], João Gilberto Mendes dos Reis, Pedro L.O. Costa Neto, Oduvaldo Vendrametto, Emerson Rodolfo Abraham, Marcos O. Morais, Carla C. Parizi, Sivanilza Teixeira Machado, Helton R.O. Silva, and Antônio S. Brejão

Paulista University - Postgraduate Studies Program in Production Engineering, Dr. Bacelar 1212, São Paulo, São Paulo 04026002, Brazil
{helcioru,politeleia,oduvaldov,prof.sergiobrejao}@uol.com.br,
{betomendesreis,kaa_ell}@hotmail.com,
{emerson_abraham,sivateixeira}@yahoo.com.br,
marcostecnologia@ig.com.br,
ccapraraparizi@gmail.com

Abstract. Improving the service quality in public transportation is essential for convinced users to abandon the use of private cars. However, to improve service quality, companies need to adopt a quality management system and strategic planning which is not an easy task. This paper presents a way of simplifying a Quality Management System (QMS) and developing a Simple Strategic Planning (SSP) to be adopted for bus transportation companies. A methodology is developed and showed in this paper, together with a case study that illustrate the system. A Brazilian Bus Company applied the methodology and reached an improvement of their service levels with low costs.

Keywords: Bus companies · Public transportation · Strategic planning · Quality management systems

1 Introduction

Improving service quality is a key-factor to persuade drivers to change the private car for the public transportation systems [1]. Reducing private transport use and increasing public transportation is not an easy task, because it is necessary to change the behavior of potential users [2]. Moreover, the advantages of car use consist in allowing a door-to-door transportation without travel on foot and sharing space with others passengers. Therefore, the biggest challenge for public transportation companies is providing high service quality to attract passengers, while trying to cut their costs [3].

© IFIP International Federation for Information Processing 2015
S. Umeda et al. (Eds.): APMS 2015, Part I, IFIP AICT 459, pp. 484–491, 2015.
DOI: 10.1007/978-3-319-22756-6_59

A way of starting to change this situation involves the understanding of these companies in adopting a management model with parameters to improve service level. Thus, these management models need to answer some questions: (i) How the information of importance is collected and interpreted? (ii) How the strategic guidelines of the company become Action Plans? (iii) How the Action Plans are applied in practice? and (iv) How the effectiveness of the Action Plans is measured in relation to the strategic guidelines?

In Brazil, public transportation is a pool that involves public and private companies. Generally, rail services operate for public companies and bus services for private companies. The bus companies often struggle to produce enough knowledge generated by selecting and reviewing the information, which ultimately reduces confidence in strategic planning [4]. This situation occurs because they do not know how clearly the information is interconnected, and what the highest priority in each process is? This causes a loss of time, because it generates an analysis of information that is sometimes disconnected from the strategic actions.

Furthermore, bus companies believed that Quality Management Systems - QMS are costly, and increase internal bureaucracy. At the same time, strategic planning is seen as too expensive and a complex process, usually requiring external consultants [4]. In addition, they believe that strategic planning produces guidelines that are oftentimes not connected with the reality of enterprises [4].

In an environment of crisis and with the threat of unsatisfactory profitability, it is recommendable that the bus companies have a solid and efficient decision-making process. However, for the majority of the time, it is difficult for them to recover losses as a result of ill-conceived action strategies or action plans badly implemented or partially implemented.

The service level of bus companies increases considerably when they begin to understand, accept and apply concepts of QMS and strategic planning [4,5]. The first element is the foundation, because, among other things, it focuses on customers; and the second element is the driver for the future, as it streamlines the companies' actions. However, in both cases, the base is always the source, the collection, the organization and the processing of the information to feed the relevant indicators that adequately measure the quality and efficiency of the processes that produce the actions of the enterprises.

Previous researches focused on analyzing service quality of public transportation studying user behavior, government regulations and polices [1–3,6,7]. Unfortunately, none of these studies are concentrated in understanding that the problem of service quality is linked with inefficiency of model management of transportation companies.

The purpose of this paper is to study how a Simple Strategic Planning (SSP) and a simplifying QMS can contribute for increased service level and quality in bus companies operating in Brazil.

2   Methodology

This article presents a methodology to simplify a QMS and develop SSP to apply in management of bus companies. The purpose of this methodology is to allow that companies reach better service levels improving their management systems. To show the utility of this methodology, our study was divided based on the following steps:

- **The first step:** a study on the importance of information to increase service levels and transportation systems is conducted. Its purpose is understand the scenario in which companies need to improve the service quality;
- **The second one:** The simplifying QMS and SSP are developing considering the studies of [4, 5, 8–13].
- **Finally:** one case study is performed to illustrate the methodology and its results.

3   Information

3.1   Demand

The demand information, generally, is not freely available, because the decision-makers of companies, normally the owners themselves, usually establish specific ways to deal with this kind of information. Nevertheless, the information of demand is a fundamental element to establish priorities, particularly related to the market [5].

Some indicators of demand that can be used in some levels of the organization to increase service level and bring satisfactory results. The most common indicators are IPK - Index of Passengers per Kilometer and PDV - Total Passengers per Day and per Vehicle. It should also be noted that the simple analysis of these two indicators may generate decisions that influence the profitability of bus companies. For example, if a bus line shows PDV lower than another one, the first one may be more profitable [14].

3.2   Customer Satisfaction

Customer satisfaction is an indicator that has been used by some bus companies in Brazil. However, this occurs only due to the worsening of the illegal transportation phenomenon. This phenomenon consists of transportation services, mainly by one vehicle, a van or a minibus, driven by its own owner. This kind of transportation operates without proper agency permits or certificates.

Illegal operators often do not have proper insurance; they do not conduct background checks for employees, also illegal, or perform regular safety inspections on their vehicles. However, they were very popular, especially in the 1990s and 2000s, because they were faster and more comfortable than regular buses in many Brazilian cities [9]. This reality obligates bus companies to improve their operations, buying new buses and training bus drivers.

3.3   Operational

Operational information can be considered the most complex and less trustworthy in bus companies. This kind of information is generated in various sectors, from several sources and is usually shown masked to avoid exposing the shortcomings or weaknesses of the sector responsible for its gathering [10].

This kind of information is based on key performance indicators - KPI. To develop a strategic planning three of them need to be considered [8]:

- **Compliance Factor (in relation to what was planned)**: It measures how effectively the planning was fulfilled, because the strict use of a set of resources (no more, no less) was planned and therefore its use should be exactly as planned. Otherwise, there is evidence of the occurrence of wastage;
- **Mean Kilometer Between Failure MKBF**: It measures the efficiency of preventive maintenance of the buses and how much the potential failures can jeopardize the Compliance Factor, thus generating customer dissatisfaction, and damaging the image of the company; and
- **Complaint Index (by kilometer)**: It shows the extent to which the operation of the service is meeting customer expectations. This indicator should be analyzed by subgroups, such as crew, offer, comfort etc., enabling better understanding of each of the registered complaints.

3.4   Market

Market information is usually difficult to be generated and managed as it represents competitive information. Therefore, it is considered highly confidential. The reason to have good market information is justified to understand the company's position in respect to your competitors [15]. Many companies cannot always determine who their real competitors are, making it difficult to establish properly what their weaknesses and threats are.

4   Simplifying a Quality Management System

A management system is the interconnection of components to achieve a specific objective more effectively in an organization. These components include the organization itself, resources and processes. Therefore, people, equipment and knowledge, in a certain cultural environment, are part of the system as well as the documented policies and practices [11].

Quality Management System, according to the ISO 9000 standard [11], with a focus on customer satisfaction, is described as how to introduce and use quality management in an organization. The ISO standard is based on a number of quality management principles, including a strong customer focus, the motivation and implication of Top Management, the process approach and continual improvement.

Hence, under these conditions, it is crucial for the organizations to understand the customers requirements and to use them to develop business processes that deliver an acceptable level of services.

Therefore, these customer satisfaction processes must be monitored and measured to ensure they will deliver the results the customers demand. This is called a process control.

In order to simplify the QMS it is recommendable that organizations adopt and pay attention to the results of three key elements [13]:

- **Customer Satisfaction:** It means understanding what customer satisfaction is and making sure that every employee understands how to deliver it;
- **Corrective Action:** It means identification of the sectors in the company that are not satisfying the customer's needs and taking corrective action to make sure that this never happens again; and
- **Preventive Action:** It means identifying sectors within the company that are at risk of not satisfying the customer's needs, understanding the marketplace trends, capabilities and threats to satisfying the customer, and then taking preventive action to make sure that this never happens in the first place.

5   Developing a Synthetic Model for Strategic Planning

The changes of paradigms and values have influenced the management of organizations, and have forced the bus companies to promote substantial changes to meet the demands of the market. Hence, it was essential for these companies to adopt a strategic planning and to take into account the needs of the market, technological innovations, new customer segmentation and application of up-to-date administration techniques, simplified and effective.

There is no one perfect strategic planning model. Each organization ends up developing its own nature and model of strategic planning, often by selecting a model and modifying it as they go along in developing their own planning process [13].

In our study we develop a Simple Strategic Planning to be used for bus companies. The SSP is divided in some steps:

- **The first step:** is to establish comparative parameters with the competititors;
- **Second:** is to analyze the current situation of the bus company;
- **Third:** is to determine where the company wants to be and where it wants to go;
- **Fourth:** is to define or to realign the companys mission;
- **Fifth:** consists in establishing the main goal of the company taking into consideration: the weaknesses and threats and the needs of the stakeholders. The main goal must be deployed in action plans for each sector of the company and sectorial goals must be established for each sector and each process;
- **Sixth:** is to develop parameters and indicators to monitor effectively the main goal and sectorial goals. The scheme can be seen in Fig. 1.
- **Seventh:** is to ensure that the information related to the main goal and sectorial goals is trustworthy; and finally
- **Eigth:** it is necessary to apply continually the PDCA cycle (Plan, Do, Check, Action), as represented in Fig. 2.

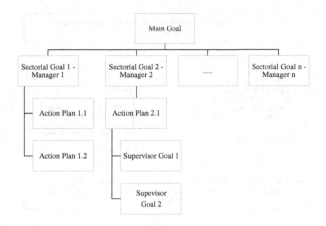

Fig. 1. Deployment of Main Goal in Sectorial Goals

6   Case Study

The Bus Company adopted in this case study was partly professionalized according to its size and fairly well-organized. This company was trying to implement a QMS, when they started experiencing some issues. The implementation of the QMS did not take off because, according to the Board of Directors, there would be no effective senior management commitment. Moreover, according to the senior manager, the quality could represent unbearable additional costs.

The Diagnosis [4] showed that both were part of the reason, but it went further. It was proved that the strategic planning was almost inexpressive. The Suggested Solution [4] was simplifying QMS and convinced the Board of Directors to obtain an ISO 9001:2008 certification. Thus, a SSP was adopted to help bus company to manage its service level.

It should be said that an ISO 9001: 2008 certification in a bus company has one main conceptual difficulty in interpreting the requirements of the standards, originally designed to be applied to manufacturers and not to services. In practice, and in fact, the main difficulty is to transform the existing informal procedures into formal procedures and implement them.

Once the SSP was adopted, it clearly demonstrated the strategic importance of the achievement of the ISO 9001:2008 certification, not the opposite, as was being disclosed in the company previously. The results were that the certification activities were quickly completed in just nine months. The company prepared 100 % of its procedures, set most of the informal procedures, prepared and applied internal audit, pre-audit and certification audit.

The estimated impact on the costs of hiring an accredited certification authority and a consultant, training and the time consumed by the managers and other employees involved, will be about 1 % of total annual revenue, spent in 12 months. The costs are being offset by productivity improvement, a new structure and a competitive company image.

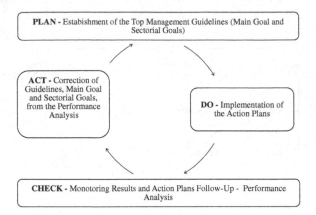

Fig. 2. PDCA Cycle

Completing the process of improving management, the Bus Company has simplified its QMS and has achieved growing results of profitability, superior customer service level and image enhancement.

7   Conclusions and Outlook

The paper allows the conclusion that the adoption of a simplified QMS linked with a Simple Strategic Planning and supported by the information may define or redirect the bus companies strategies. A case study of a Brazilian bus company showed that it increased service levels and consumer satisfaction adopting a SSP and a simplifying QMS, using the ISO 9001:2008. The costs represented 1 % of annual company revenue.

The improvement in service levels and quality in public transportation is very important to increase the numbers of passengers in the system and reduce the use of private cars that generates intensive traffic in peak and non-peak hours. The solution for emission reduction of CO_2 in the atmosphere, the efficiency of land use and the reduction of travel time is public transportation. Hence, this study contributed to recommend ways to improve quality of services and to increase the use of public transportation in the cities for bus companies and governments.

References

1. Liou, J.J., Hsu, C.C., Chen, Y.S.: Improving transportation service quality based on information fusion. Transp. Res. Part A: Policy Pract. **67**, 225–239 (2014)
2. Lai, W.T., Chen, C.F.: Behavioral intentions of public transit passengers: the roles of service quality, perceived value, satisfaction and involvement. Transp. Policy **18**(2), 318–325 (2011)

3. Maha, A., Bobalca, C., Tugulea, O.: Strategies for the improvements in the quality and efficiency of public transportation. Procedia Econ. Finance **15**, 877–885 (2014)
4. Raymundo, H., Vendrametto, O., dos Reis, J.G.M.: Knowledge management in public transportation: experiences in brazilian bus companies. In: Grabot, B., Vallespir, B., Gomes, S., Bouras, A., Kiritsis, D. (eds.) Advances in Production Management Systems, Part II. IFIP AICT, vol. 439, pp. 603–610. Springer, Heidelberg (2014)
5. US Department of Commerce: Information Security. Technical report, US Department of Commerce (2011). http://www.nist.gov
6. Barros Pestana, C., Peypoch, N.: Productivity changes in Portuguese bus companies. Transp. Policy **17**(5), 295–302 (2010)
7. Yeh, C.H., Deng, H., Chang, Y.H.: Fuzzy multicriteria analysis for performance evaluation of bus companies. Eur. J. Oper. Res. **126**(3), 459–473 (2000)
8. Austin, R.D.: Measuring and Managing Performance in Organizations. Addison-Wesley, Boston, MA (2013)
9. Cervero, R.: Informal Transport in the Developing World. UN-HABITAT, Nairobi (2000)
10. Dunlop, D., Stewart, W.: Central Area Bus Operational Review. Technical report. http://www.gw.govt.nz
11. ISO: Management system standards (2015). http://www.nist.gov
12. U.S. Small Business Administration: Planning and Goal Setting for Small Business. Technical report, U.S. Small Business Administration, USA (2015). https://www.sba.gov
13. Westcott, R.: Simplified Project Management for the Quality Professional: Managing Small And Medium-size Projects. Amer. Society for Quality, Milwaukee (2004)
14. ANTP: Sistema de Informaes da Mobilidade Urbana (2015). http://www.antp.org.br
15. Tirole, J.: Market Power and Regulation (2014). http://www.nobelprize.org

A Study on the Effect of Dirt on an Inspection Surface on Defect Detection in Visual Inspection Utilizing Peripheral Vision

Ryosuke Nakajima[✉], Yuta Asano, Takuya Hida,
and Toshiyuki Matsumoto

Aoyama Gakuin University, Kanagawa, Japan
{d5613005,a5711002}@aoyama.jp,
{hida,matsumoto}@ise.aoyama.ac.jp

Abstract. This study focuses on adhered dirt to a product in production process, and also considers the relationship between dirt of inspection surface and defect detection in visual inspection utilizing peripheral vision. Specifically, images of inspection surface in an actual factory are analyzed using image analysis to do modeling. Moreover, dirt of inspection model, location and characteristics of defect are designed as experimental factors, and their effect on defect detection rate are evaluated. As a result, it is clarified that the defect detection rate becomes suddenly lower getting to the inspection surface dirtier. Consequently, defect that can be detected easily becomes harder to detect according as the inspection surface is dirtier.

Keywords: Visual inspection · Dirt · Peripheral vision · Defect detection

1 Introduction

In order to supply high-quality products to the market, manufacturing industries have given product inspection as much attention as processing and assembling. There are two types of inspections: functional inspection and appearance inspection. In functional inspection, the effectiveness of a product is inspected. In appearance inspection, small visual defects such as scratches, surface dents and unevenness of the coating color are inspected. The automation of functional inspection has advanced because it is easy to determine whether a product works or not [1]. However, it is not as simple to establish the standards to determine whether the appearance of a product is defective. First, there are many different types of defects. Second, the categorization of a product as non-defective or defective is affected by the size and depth of the defect. Third, some products have recently become smaller and more detailed. Finally, production has shifted to high-mix, low-volume production. It is thus difficult to develop technologies that can discover small defects and to create algorithms that identify multiple types of defects with high precision. Therefore, appearance inspection still depends on visual inspection using human senses [2].

Recently, a visual inspection method utilizing peripheral vision was proposed [3–7], and the effectiveness of the method has been tested in manufacturing factories [8].

© IFIP International Federation for Information Processing 2015
S. Umeda et al. (Eds.): APMS 2015, Part I, IFIP AICT 459, pp. 492–499, 2015.
DOI: 10.1007/978-3-319-22756-6_60

Human vision is divided into two ranges. Central vision is the 1–2° range of vision on either side of the center of the retina. The remaining range of vision is called peripheral vision. The spatial resolution of human vision decreases significantly with increasing angle from the center of the retina [9]. The visual inspection method utilizing peripheral vision involves two process: first, a wide range is searched by peripheral vision; then, the defect is decided by the high spatial resolution of the central vision. Thus, low-level processes such as sampling and characteristics clustering are processed by peripheral vision, next high-level processes such as discrimination is processes by central vision to reduce the amount of information to be processed. From this, an efficient visual information processing is realized [10], the visual inspection method utilizing peripheral vision which can be realized high accurate inspection in a short time has been expected.

In order to prevent dust in the air and on clothing from adhering to the product, it is generally recommended that visual inspection for a high-quality product be performed in a clean room. However, in situations where the production process becomes more complex and more outsourcing in recent years, it is often not conducted in a clean room. Also, there are many cases where visual inspection process is not a clean room because of constraints of existing equipment and economic problems. This is the present situation that must be inspected the dirty inspection surface in visual inspection. That is, in a situation where both the dirt that can be removed and the defect that cannot be removed are mixed, inspectors are required to detect only the defect. This causes reduced defect detection accuracy.

In order to consider the relationship between the amount of dirt on the inspection surface and accuracy of defect detection, this study analyzes images of inspection surfaces in an actual factory and creates a model for dirt density based on the pixel values of the images. Then, experiments are conducted using dirt density, defect location and defect characteristics as experimental factors. The effects of these factors on defect detection accuracy are examined.

2 Analysis and Modeling of Dirt

2.1 Analysis of Dirt in Actual Factory

In order to analyze conditions of dirt on an inspection surface, a field survey at Company X, which performs visual inspections, was implemented. The company produces transparent parts for automobiles. Neither the production process nor the visual inspection process is conducted in a clean room. Therefore, the visual inspection is performed in location where the inspection surface is dirty.

In the field survey, images of the inspection surface used for the visual inspection process are taken by a camera; these images are then sorted in order of dirtiness. In order to evaluate the distribution of pixel values, histograms of these images are analyzed as shown in Fig. 1. As the results, it was obtained that both the dispersion of pixel values in the image and the shape of the histograms are changed according to the amount of dirt on the inspection surface.

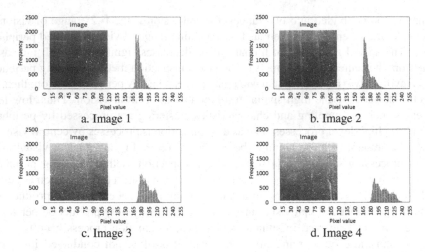

Fig. 1. Frequency of pixel value for each photographed image

2.2   Modeling of Dirt

2.2.1   Quantification of Dirt

The analysis method explained in Sect. 2.1 is applied to the inspection surface in the factory in order to quantify the dirt. A known amount of dirt is intentionally scattered on the inspection surface intentionally, and the relationship between the applied and the distribution of pixel values in the photographed image is considered.

As for an inspection surface of a product, the product with a height of 100 mm and a width of 100 mm in the company is used. As for dirt, the powders with a diameter of 0.18–0.25 mm are used. The powders are scattered during the production processes to prevent the products from coming into contact with each other, and those are one of the typical dirt in the visual inspection process.

The amount of scattered powder varied from 0.0 g to 1.0 g, in 0.1 g increments, and the histogram for each level of powder is examined. The results for the 0.0 g, 0.3 g, 0.6 g and 0.9 g levels are shown in the bar graph in Fig. 2. It was obtained that the dispersion of pixel values in the image is varied according to the amount of scattered powder.

2.2.2   Formulation of Dirt

Using the pixel values derived in Sect. 2.2.1, to formulation of the dirt is considered. Specifically, to determine the dispersion of pixel values for each amount of scattered powder, kernel density estimation is applied. The commonly used Gaussian kernel function k(x) (Reference) is employed in this study. It is calculated using Eq. (1), where x is the frequencies of the pixel value. Bandwidth h is calculated in Eq. (2) using the standard deviation, σ, of the frequencies of the pixel values. Then, the kernel dispersion f̂k(x) is calculated in Eq. (3) using the kernel function k(x) and the bandwidth h. The results for the 0.0 g, 0.3 g, 0.6 g and 0.9 g levels are shown in the line graph in Fig. 2. It was found that it is possible to estimate the probability density function of the distribution of pixel values with high accuracy.

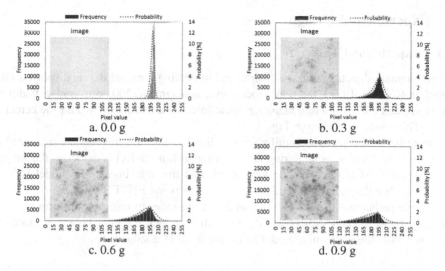

Fig. 2. Frequency and probability of pixel value for each scattered amount of dirt

$$K(x) = \frac{1}{\sqrt{2\pi}} e^{-\frac{1}{2}x^2} \tag{1}$$

$$h = \frac{0.9\sigma}{256^{\frac{1}{5}}} \tag{2}$$

$$\hat{f}k(x) = \frac{1}{256h} \sum_{i=0}^{255} k\left(\frac{x - xi}{h}\right) \tag{3}$$

2.2.3 Imaging of Dirt

Using the probability density function shown in Sect. 2.2.2, the ability to create images of specific amounts of dirt is considered. First, the pixel values are assigned to create image according to the probability density function. Then the pixels are colored according to the pixel values. The results for the 0.0 g, 0.3 g, 0.6 g and 0.9 g levels are shown in image of Fig. 3. It was found that it is possible to create the images corresponding to desired amounts of scattered powder.

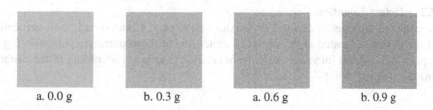

Fig. 3. Created images for each application amount of dirt

3 Experimental Design

3.1 Experimental Task

Experimental subjects are tasked with visual inspecting a model that is displayed on a monitor (CG276, EIZO Inc.). A model with a height of 300 mm, and a width of 300 mm, and a black 10 mm diameter circle (used as a fixation point) on the center is used. This model is shown in Fig. 4.

In order to lead inspection utilizing peripheral vision, the subjects are requested to fix only at the fixation point during the experiment. If no defect is detected, the subject presses the SPACE KEY on the key board, and the next inspection model will be displayed. If a defect is detected, the subject presses the ENTER KEY.

The experimental layout is shown in Fig. 5. In order to ensure a uniform viewing distance between each subject and the inspection model, the chin holder is placed at 400 mm from the inspection model to fix the head of a subject.

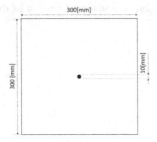

Fig. 4. Inspection model

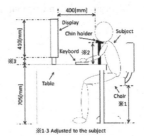

Fig. 5. Experimental layout

3.2 Experimental Factors

3.2.1 Dirt Density of the Inspection Model

The dirt density with each inspection model is realized by using a background image that is created as described in Sect. 2.2.3. Four images (0.0 g, 0.3 g, 0.6 g and 0.9 g) shown in Fig. 3 are employed in the experiment. The image of 0.9 g of dirt was chosen as the upper limit, after factory of Company X confirmed that the inspection surface is never dirtier than the image representing 0.9 g of dirt. Hereafter, the four types of the inspection model are called Non dirty (0.0 g), Slightly dirty (0.3 g), Somewhat dirty (0.6 g) and Very dirty (0.9 g) respectively.

3.2.2 Defect Location

The inspection model is divided into sixteen parts (4 × 4 horizontally and vertically), and the defect is located at the center of either one of these parts. As shown in Fig. 6, the parts are divided into four areas, from area (1) to area (4) according to the distance from the fixation point.

3.2.3 Defect Characteristics

The characteristics of the defects are defined by the luminance contrast between the inspection model and the defect, and the size. The shape of all defects is circular. The luminance contrast of each defect is one of three different levels: 0.10, 0.15 and 0.20. There are also two types of defects in the factory: those that are darker than the inspection surface, such as scratches, and those that are brighter than defects than the inspection surface, such as adhered inks. Therefore, the luminance contrast of each defect is also specified as either dark or bright.

The size of the defect is specified by a diameters of 1.0 mm, 1.5 mm and 2.0 mm. These defects are determined by assuming the standard of the appearance inspection.

All defects employed in the experiment are shown in Fig. 7. The experiment is conducted for the four different location areas (sixteen parts) of defect, three different luminance contrast levels, two different types of defect, and three different sizes of defect. This gives a total of 288 (location parts (16) × luminance contrast (3) × dark and bright (2) × size (3)) defective inspection models for each level of dirt on the inspection models.

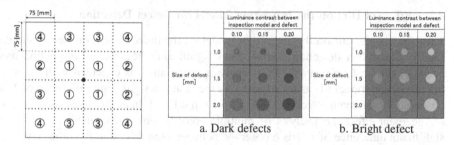

Fig. 6. Defect location

Fig. 7. Defects employed in experiment

3.3 Experimental Procedure

Twelve subjects, between aged of 21 and 26 years, are employed in this experiment. Only subjects with a corrected eyesight score greater than 1.0 are employed. In order to familiarize the subjects with the experiment, an overview and the procedure of the experiment are explained, and the preliminary experiment are tasked. In the experiment, to inspect 578 (288 non-defective and 288 defective) inspection models is tasked for each dirt of the inspection model.

The experimental room temperature is set between 18 and 24 °C, and the humidity is set between 40 and 60 %. Since the luminance of the inspection model and the defect are affected by external and internal light (such as fluorescent lighting), the experiment is conducted in a dark room. The purpose and contents of the experiment are explained to the subjects in writing, and the informed consent of all subjects is obtained.

Using the results of the experiment that are obtained by the above procedures, the defect detection rate is calculated, which is the number of detected defects divided by the number of total defect. It is expressed in Eq. (4) and used as the evaluation index.

$$Defect\ detection\ rate[\%] = \frac{Number\ of\ detected\ defects}{Number\ of\ total\ defects} \qquad (4)$$

4 Experimental Results and Discussion

4.1 Individual Characteristics of Subjects

Using the defect detection rate, the effect of the dirt of the inspection model is examined. Owing to the possibility that the individuality of the subject might have affected the result, the uniformity of the results for all subjects is verified.

The defect detection rate of the subjects for each level of dirt on the inspection model is shown in Fig. 8. As the result of the Smirnov-Grubbs test (significance level 1 %) shows, there are no outlier values in the defect detection rates of any of the subjects. Therefore, the data from all twelve subjects are used.

4.2 Effect of Dirt on the Inspection Model on Defect Detection

The effect of the dirt on the inspection model on the defect detection rate is shown in Fig. 9. The defect detection rate becomes significantly less as the inspection model becomes dirtier. One-way ANOVA (analysis of variance) is executed with the dirt on the inspection model (4) as for a factor. As the result, a significant difference of 1 % is observed for the main effect [$F(3, 44) = 45.17$, $p < 0.01$]. In addition, as sub-effect tests of the main effect, an analysis of multiple comparisons is executed. As a result, a significant difference of 1 % is 6 observed between Non dirty and the other levels, and between Slightly dirty and Very dirty, whereas a significant difference of 5 % is observed between Slightly dirty and Somewhat dirty.

Based on the above results, in order to realize high defect detection accuracy with visual inspection utilizing peripheral vision, such inspection should be performed only when there is no dirt on the inspection surface. To accomplish this, it is necessary to take measures such as washing the inspection surface prior to the visual inspection process or making a clean room for the visual inspection process.

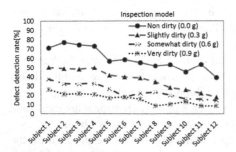

Fig. 8. Defect detection rate for each subjects

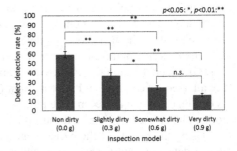

Fig. 9. Defect detection rate for each inspection model

5   Conclusion

In order to consider the relationship between the dirt on the inspection surface and defect detection in visual inspection utilizing peripheral vision, images of an inspection surface in an actual factory were analyzed, and the dirt was modeled. Then, the dirt density of an inspection model, defect location and defect characteristics were designed as experimental factors, and the experiment was conducted with twelve subjects. As the result, it is clarified that the defect detection rate becomes significantly less as the inspection surface becomes dirtier. Consequently, it is shown that the importance of a clean inspection surface for a highly accurate visual inspection process.

In future studies, we will consider in more detail the relationship between the dirt on the inspection surface and defect detection for each location area and for each characteristics of the defect.

Acknowledgement. This study was supported by Grant-in-Aid for JSPS Fellows (14J09642).

References

1. Aoki, K.: Review on in-process inspection. Jpn. J. Non-Destr. Inspection **60**(8), 433–435 (2013)
2. Nickles, G.M., Melloy, B.J., Gramopadhye, A.K.: A comparison of three levels of training designed to promote systematic search behavior in visual inspection. Int. J. Ind. Ergon. **32**, 331–339 (2003)
3. Sasaki, A.: Syuhenshi Mokushikensahou. Jpn. Inst. Ind. Eng. Rev. **46**(4), 65–75 (2005)
4. Sasaki, A.: Syuhenshi Mokushikensahou. Jpn. Inst. Ind. Eng. Rev. **46**(5), 61–68 (2005)
5. Sasaki, A.: Syuhenshi Mokushikensahou. Jpn. Inst. Ind. Eng. Rev. **47**(1), 55–60 (2006)
6. Sasaki, A.: Syuhenshi Mokushikensahou. Jpn. Inst. Ind. Eng. Rev. **47**(2), 53–58 (2006)
7. Sasaki, A.: Syuhenshi Mokushikensahou. Jpn. Inst. Ind. Eng. Rev. **47**(3), 67–72 (2006)
8. Sugawara, T., Shinoda, S., Uchida, M., Sasaki, A., Matsumoto, T., Niwa, A., Kawase, T.: Proposal of a new inspection method using peripheral visual acuity focusing on visibility and inspection angle of defective items during product inspection. J. Jpn. Ind. Manage. Assoc. **62**(4), 153–163 (2011)
9. Ikeda, M.: Meha Naniwo Miteiruka. Heibonsha 1–289 (2004)
10. Yoshida, C., Toyoda, M., Sato, Y.: Vision system model with differentiated visual fields. Inf. Process. Soc. Jpn. **33**(8), 1032–1040 (1992)

The Main Problems in the Design and Management of MOOCs

Luis Naito Mendes Bezerra[⊠] and Márcia Terra da Silva

Graduate Program in Production Engineering, Paulista University-UNIP,
Dr. Bacelar St. 1212, São Paulo, Brazil
luisnaito@yahoo.com.br, marcia.terra@uol.com.br

Abstract. Despite the global scale, the wide range of courses and the high number of enrollments, some challenges have been emerging for the universe of the MOOCs (Massive Open Online Courses), especially those related to project and management aspects. This article aims to identify the main problems faced by the managers of the MOOCs. Hence, an exploratory study was carried out through the analysis of existing publications in academic databases. The results show that after the survey it was possible to identify and analyze six problems, the main one of which was the very low completion rate of this type of course.

Keywords: MOOCS · Problems of MOOCS · Challenges of MOOCS

1 Introduction

Recently there emerged a new modality of distance education, known as MOOC (Massive Open Online Course). The MOOCs are open courses, with fully online format, without preconditions, without initial billing rates and with the potential to distribute education on a global scale, including to enable students from developing countries have access to institutions and courses of quality at low cost [1–3].

In 2011, about 3 years after the first MOOC[1] had been offered, Sebastian Thrun created the Artificial Intelligence course at Stanford University that attracted more than 160,000 students from 190 countries. As from 2011, the growth of this distance education modality has been breathtaking, with the initial emergence of three big hubs – Coursera, Udacity and EdX – for the provision of MOOCS [4–6].

The research shows that the main reasons for the interest of students in MOOCs can be summarized in four relevant aspects: interest in learning about certain subjects; knowledge increase; updating on some previously seen subject or learning something specific that should contribute to the professional development [7, 8].

However, despite the global scale having been reached, the large number of students served and the considerable growth in the number of courses, some challenges have been

---

[1] The first MOOC was created in September 2008 in Canada.

© IFIP International Federation for Information Processing 2015
S. Umeda et al. (Eds.): APMS 2015, Part I, IFIP AICT 459, pp. 500–506, 2015.
DOI: 10.1007/978-3-319-22756-6_61

appeared in the universe of the MOOCs. Several authors have researched problematic aspects in the design and management of these courses, such as, for example, the pedagogical model [9, 10] and the quality of MOOCs [11].

Through this paper, based on a bibliographical study, the main problems in the design and management of MOOCs can therefore be objectively identified and analyzed beyond pointing out the most significant problem and clarifying how the issues relate to each other.

In addition to this introduction, this paper is divided into six parts. In the initial section, the methodology used to achieve the objective of this research is presented, then a study on the main problems in the design and management of MOOCs. Afterwards, the results and analysis are shown, followed by conclusions and, eventually, the bibliographical references.

2 Methodology

From an exploratory, non-systematic study, conducted through the analysis of existing publications in academic databases, such as Springer, Science Direct, ERIC database, ACM Digital Library and Google Scholar, the main problems in the design and management of MOOCs were identified.

The bibliographic survey covers the period between the offer of the first MOOC in 2008 [12] and the year in which the research has been conducted (2015). After reading and analyzing titles and abstracts, 20 articles that constitute this analysis were selected.

3 Main Problems in the Design and Management of MOOCs

The MOOCs, as already said, have a huge potential to provide free education on a global scale, with the opportunity of democratizing access to higher education of good quality [2]. No doubt his growth has been quite expressive. Only in Europe, according to the website of [13], which gathers data about the MOOCs in European countries, 510 courses were offered in April 2014. In the same year, in September, there were 770 courses, a growth of 50.98 % [13].

Despite the apparent expansion, the MOOCs model is the target of a lot of criticism and concerns because, besides being a still recent teaching mode, it is often compared, erroneously, to traditional distance education courses and also seen as competitor of face-to-face teaching. Such concerns, however, can be considered unfounded since they are modalities with differentiated goals and functions.

The MOOCs, due to their open character and short duration, do not allow for the issue of undergraduate or graduate certificates and furthermore carry out a complementary role to distance education and face-to-face teaching, providing students the opportunity to expand their knowledge and/or have a professional update. Another important point that distinguishes them from distance education and private face-to-face teaching is the fact that the services offered by MOOCs are free of fees because their business model is different from traditional education institutions [3] as will be discussed below.

The following is an attempt to interrelate the main problems encountered in literature regarding the design and management of these courses.

– **Business Model** – some authors cite the MOOCs as a new business model for higher education institutions. Even though the courses are exempt from fees for registration and access to content, institutions may charge fees for issuing certificates. According to the author [12], the business model of the MOOCs is related to the one adopted by technology companies, such as Google and RedHat Linux, which provide a basic service to customers, then offer add-ons to be paid for. In the case of MOOCs, the charge for the certificate would be the complementary service. Considering the large number of students, such an initiative could generate a sustainable business model [1, 12]. However, at this point, such a model is accessible only for a small portion of educational institutions, such as Harvard, Stanford and MIT, which are using their long tradition and excellent academic reputation to receive sufficient funds to pay for the costs of creating platforms for content production and distribution on a large scale, resulting in the creation of for-profit companies and inspired by the model of Silicon Valley startups such as Coursera (Stanford University) and Edx (MIT and Harvard) [6]. The MOOCs can also serve as a marketing element to the major institutions of higher education, mainly for institutions of great reputation and prestige like the previously already mentioned ones. According to the author [6], about 65 % of all students who enrolled on the Coursera platform reside outside of the United States, a fact that could help to attract more foreign students who would pay substantial registration fees for attending face-to-face undergraduate and graduate courses.
– **Very Low Completion Rate of the Courses** – a concern often raised in the surveys conducted on the MOOCs relates to the fact that thousands of students enroll but only a small part of them have completed the courses. Abandonment in this teaching modality is generally quite high, currently around 90 % [6, 14–18]. According to the author [19], the completion rate is related to the number of people who receive the certificate or are approved to the course. According to the author [20], the completion rate of MOOCs cannot be compared to that of face-to-face courses or even traditional distance education because MOOCs students do not pay tuition and also do not receive university credits; hence the motivation for its completion is largely inherent in the model of the course itself.
– **Certification** – the majority of MOOCs are adaptations of subjects offered in the degrees of higher education institutions around the world. Thus, they do not configure a full degree course and their certification could generate some questions, such as if being free of cost, they would have the same value as a paid face-to-face course. Moreover, it would be important to analyze how potential employers assess such certificates [1, 2].
– **Pedagogical Model** – the most accepted classification for the approach or pedagogical model is the one that divides the MOOCs into two categories: cMOOCs and xMOOCs, according to authors like [6, 9, 21–23]. In this context, the cMOOCs constitute the first generation – beginning in 2008 – with a focus on creating and generating knowledge through interaction among the participants. In this model, the participants are encouraged to use a variety of technologies and to reflect on their learning, following the principles of connectivism which considers the

intense interaction between the participants as fundamental for the construction of knowledge. The xMOOCs are the second generation – beginning in 2012 – with pedagogical approach based on behaviorism and more traditional format. Counting on content and assessments based on previously provided teaching materials. In this model, monitoring and mentoring actions are less systematic, with discussion forum and automated assessment. This is the model that prevails today, being adopted by the major platforms Coursera and edX [24–26].

– **Quality** – According to the author [27], the concern with quality in the MOOCs is related to the problem of high drop-out rates in this type of course. Still according to the same authors, how can MOOCs managers declare quality learning in their courses, if students are failing to complete the same? Again according to the author [27], the MOOCs should follow the same quality principles applied in traditional courses because, to a great extent, they derive from undergraduate disciplines, being produced by the same faculty, with the same material, however, adapted to the new environment. Therefore, it is important to be concerned with the issues involving the guarantee (quality assurance) and improvement (quality enhancement) of the quality of MOOCs. The quality assurance process is mentioned in the works of [11], dealing with a quality program called UNED MOOC and also by [27], dealing with the model named OpenupEd Quality Label.

– **Validation and Plagiarism** – according to the author [2], a fundamental aspect and a great challenge for the MOOCs is to ensure that the works are original and valid. To do so, a system to prevent and detect plagiarism of the activities generated by the students is necessary. Still according to the same authors, the platform Coursera studies to deploy a software for detecting plagiarism, just as Udacity and Edx which formed a partnership with Pearson VUE, a test center provider, to validate the tests in supervised form. However, it is important to highlight that this practice entails generating cost to students.

Table 1 summarizes the six problems and the author(s) that were used as a reference.

Table 1. summary of problems and authors

#	Problem	Author(s)
1	Business model	1; 12; 6
2	Very low completion rate of the courses	14; 15; 6; 16; 17; 18; 19; 20
3	Certification	1; 2
4	Pedagogical model	6; 21; 22; 23; 9; 24; 25; 26
5	Quality	27; 11
6	Validation and plagiarism	2

4   Results and Discussion

This section is dedicated to the presentation of the relations between the previously presented differing concepts.

The business model currently adopted by the big hubs in the offer of MOOCs, as Coursera, Udacity and Edx, considers that such courses aim to reach a large number of students, attracted by the opportunity to participate in courses offered by major institutions of higher education like Harvard, MIT and Stanford [18].

Although there are no registration fees or tuition, educational institutions may have a new source of financial resources through charging for issuing certificates. For example, the University of Washington, which is part of the Coursera platform, is testing a hybrid model, which introduces more rigor in granting academic credits and also considers charging a fee for the issuance of the certificate [12]. However, the sustainability of such a model can be compromised if the courses have a high drop-out rate, around 90 % [19]. Hence, increasing the retention of students would be a measure of paramount importance to ensure the sustainability of the currently practiced business model.

The work of [20] suggests some measures to increase the retention rate such as attending the students according to the pace and profile of each individual, teachers who motivate the student to complete the course, with the use of techniques such as the recognition of the results achieved by the students, beyond increasing the participation and interaction between students and teachers in the discussion forums for each course. Additionally, thinking of increasing retention, the MOOC managers should also be concerned with issues involving quality guarantee (quality assurance) and improvement of quality (quality enhancement) of the MOOCs.

The issuance, validity, form and the market acceptance of the certificates issued by institutions that offer MOOCs is another aspect that has caused concern and discussion among those involved in the MOOC segment. To the extent that such certificates are accepted by employers and educational institutions, it is likely that this fact affects the way the MOOCs are seen in relation to traditional teaching. Further discussion can be found in the works of authors [28–30].

Of all the problems pointed out in the survey, the main challenge and key problem for the MOOC managers is related to the very low completion rate of this type of course. Such a problem is caused by the quality of the courses and also by the adopted pedagogical model. It is necessary to also consider that the higher the completion rate of a particular course is, the more students could potentially pay for the certificates of completion issuance, contributing to the business model being sustainable.

5   Conclusions

The research aimed at identifying and analyzing the main problems in the design and management of MOOCs, based on a bibliographical study. After the research it was possible to identify six relevant issues, such as the very low completion rate, the certification of the courses, the pedagogical model, the process involving the assurance and improvement of the MOOC quality, the acceptance of the certificates, in addition to the concern with validation and plagiarism in this type of course.

The analysis showed that the main challenge for MOOC managers is to increase the retention rate of their courses. From the management point of view, the reduction of the drop-out rate, nowadays around 90 %, would make it possible that the business model becomes more feasible once it would allow that more students could complete the courses and, therefore, consider the payment of fees for the certificate issuance. Furthermore is important that employers know the MOOCs better and increasingly accept such certificates in the same way that face-to-face course certificates are accepted.

The concern with quality is another aspect to be considered by the managers because the adoption of quality assurance and improvement programs would be timely to meet the expectations of students and increase the retention rates of the courses.

In a general analysis, for consolidating the business model of the MOOCs, the issues involving the pedagogical model, the increase of the completion rate and the acceptance of the certificates need to be thoroughly questioned and analyzed in order to achieve a level of maturity which is sufficient to ensure sustainability and continuity of this education modality.

The main contribution of this research was to interrelate the main problems in the design and management of MOOCs as to then identify the most significant problem, in this case the very low completion rate, beyond examining how the issues interrelate.

In terms of future work, a deeper study about the main reasons for the high drop-out rates in MOOCs is suggested.

References

1. Hyman, P.: In the year of disruptive education. Commun. ACM **55**, 20–22 (2012)
2. Cooper, S., Sahami, M.: Reflections on Stanford's MOOCS. Commun. ACM **56**, 28–30 (2013)
3. Ong, B.S., Grigoryan, A.: MOOCs and universities: competitors or partners? Int. J. Inf. Educ. Technol. **5**, 373–376 (2014)
4. Little, G.: Massively open? J. Acad. Librarianship **3**, 308–309 (2013)
5. Mallon, M.: MOOCs. Public Serv. Q. **9**, 46–53 (2013)
6. Sandeen, C.: Integrating MOOCS into traditional higher education: the emerging "MOOC 3.0" era. Change Mag. High. Learn. **45**, 34–39 (2013)
7. Fini, A.: The technological dimension of a massive open online course: the case of the CCK08 course tools. Int. Rev. Res. Open Distrib. Learn. **10** (2009)
8. Belanger, Y., Thornton, J.: Bioelectricity: A quantitative approach Duke University's first MOOC (2013)
9. Vardi, M.Y.: Will MOOCs destroy academia? Commun. ACM **55**, 5 (2012)
10. Fournier, H., Kop, R., Durand, G.: Challenges to research in MOOCs. J. Online Learn. Teach. **10**, 1–15 (2014)
11. Read, T., Rodrigo, C.: Toward a quality model for UNED MOOCs. ELearning Pap (2014). http://www.openeducationeuropa.eu/en/article/Toward-a-Quality-Model-for-UNED-MOOCs
12. Dellarocas, C., Van Alstyne, M.: Money models for MOOCs. Commun. ACM **56**, 25–28 (2013)

13. Open Education Europa (2014). http://openeducationeuropa.eu/en/european_scoreboard_moocs
14. Daniel, J.: Making sense of MOOCs: musings in a maze of myth, paradox and possibility. J. Interact. Media Educ. **2012**, 1–20 (2012)
15. Morris, L.V.: MOOCs, emerging technologies, and quality. Innov. High. Educ. **38**, 251–252 (2013)
16. Hew, K.F., Cheung, W.S.: Students' and instructors' use of massive open online courses (MOOCs): motivations and challenges. Educ. Res. Rev. **12**, 45–58 (2014)
17. Wilkowski, J., Deutsch, A., Russell, D.M.: Student skill and goal achievement in the mapping with Google MOOC. In: Proceedings of the first ACM conference on Learning @ scale conference, pp. 3–10. ACM (2014)
18. Alraimi, K.M., Zo, H., Ciganek, A.P.: Understanding the MOOCs continuance: the role of openness and reputation. Comput. Educ. **80**, 28–38 (2015)
19. Jordan, K.: Initial trends in enrolment and completion of massive open online courses. Int. Rev. Res. Open Distrib. Learn. **15** (2014)
20. Khalil, H., Ebner, M.: MOOCs completion rates and possible methods to improve retention-a literature review. In: World Conference on Educational Multimedia, Hypermedia and Telecommunications, pp. 1305–1313 (2014)
21. Welsh, D.H., Dragusin, M.: The new generation of massive open online course (MOOCS) and entrepreneurship education. Small Bus. Inst®. J. **9**, 51–65 (2013)
22. Zutshi, S., O'Hare, S., Rodafinos, A.: Experiences in MOOCs: the perspective of students. Am. J. Distance Educ. **27**, 218–227 (2013)
23. Saadatmand, M., Kumpulainen, K.: Participants' perceptions of learning and networking in connectivist MOOCs. MERLOT J. Online Learn. Teach. **10**, 16–30 (2014)
24. Blanco, Á.F., García-Peñalvo, F.J., Sein-Echaluce, M.: A methodology proposal for developing adaptive cMOOC. In: Proceedings of the First International Conference on Technological Ecosystem for Enhancing Multiculturality, pp. 553–558. ACM (2013)
25. Clow, D.: MOOCs and the funnel of participation. In: Proceedings of the Third International Conference on Learning Analytics and Knowledge, pp. 185–189. ACM (2013)
26. Kennedy, J.: Characteristics of massive open online courses (MOOCs): a research review, 2009–2012. J. Interact. Online Learn. **13**, 1–16 (2014)
27. Rosewell, J., Jansen, D.: The OpenupEd quality label: benchmarks for MOOCs. INNOQUAL Int. J. Innov. Qual. Learn. **2**, 88–100 (2014)
28. Li, X., Chang, K., Yuan, Y.: Massive open online proctor: protecting the credibility of MOOCs certificates. In: Proceedings of the CSCW – Collaboration in the Open Classroom, pp. 1129–1137. ACM (2015)
29. Schroeder, R.: Emerging open online distance education environment. Continuing High. Educ. Rev. **76**, 90–99 (2012)
30. Venkatesh, N.: Analysis on massive open online courses (MOOC): opportunities and challenges towards 21st century online education. Int. J. Appl. Innov. Eng. Manage. (IJAIEM) **3**, 203–220 (2014)

Assessing the Relationship
Between Commodity Chains:
Ethanol, Corn and Chicken Meat

Eder Ferragi and Irenilza Nääs[✉]

Graduate Program in Production Engineering,
Paulista University-UNIP, Dr. Bacelar St. 1212, São Paulo, Brazil
irenilza@gmail.com

Abstract. Energy and food are two issues of fundamental importance in the scenario of global production and consumption. This study seeks to describe, measure and analyze the interrelationship between the results of global commodity chains of corn, ethanol and broiler. We considered the interconnectivity through the chains inputs and outputs within the production of both food and biofuel. Based on the production of the three commodities in the United States and Brazil, the Social Network Analysis (SNA) metrics was used to calculate quantitative indicators of centrality (outdegree and indegree) of the products in relation to each other. The study allowed the identification of degree indices for each product at three different times over a period of twelve years. Results indicated the importance and evolution of the relationship between the outputs of each commodity chain throughout the studied period.

Keywords: Agribusiness · Social network analysis · Interrelated global chains

1 Introduction

According to the conceptual approach of the global commodity chain – GCC [1], the first dimension of the chain is an input – output structure, which describes the transformation process of raw materials and other inputs in the final products. In this approach, the ethanol, the corn and the broiler chains are interconnected. From a global point of view the final product of the corn chain can be an input of the ethanol chain, and both corn and ethanol chains outputs provide inputs for the broiler chain. A great part of the studies found in current literature define the border of the chain or network analysis based on one single product or commodity [2–4], and therefore, fail to consider important aspects that refer to the inter-relationship between one chain and another. Defined as a network of labor and production processes the supply chain concept surpasses the issues of the transformation processes and goes on to consider the ways in which people, places, and processes are related to each other in the global economy [4]. The second dimension of the chain includes a configuration of geographical outline [1] considering transportation and communication, as well as institutional structures from each region, grounded in the world system theory [5]. According to this concept, it is understood that the productive processes is developed following a relationship based on

© IFIP International Federation for Information Processing 2015
S. Umeda et al. (Eds.): APMS 2015, Part I, IFIP AICT 459, pp. 507–514, 2015.
DOI: 10.1007/978-3-319-22756-6_62

some logic/concern between countries in the southern hemisphere and the northern hemisphere. The commodity chain approach becomes global and changes the focus of production in a specific country to a specific commodity. Consequently the focus is how the agents in the several countries cooperate or diverge from the rules to govern the chains and take ownership of the profits generated [6].

Given the relevance of agribusiness in the national and global scenario, the present study relates the total production of ethanol, corn and broiler chains in Brazil, and in the United States, the world's largest producers of these commodities [7]. The Social Network Analysis – SNA and the Graph theory [8] were applied in the quantitative analysis. A chain is composed of nodes and links, which connect the nodes. In the SNA the nodes (people or companies) are connected to each other through links, and patterns can be analyzed and calculated at two different levels: analysis of the nodes and analysis of the entire chain. In the first case, it is possible to assess the involvement and importance of a particular node about the complete chain [9, 10]. It is possible to calculate centrality rates that measure the degree (the link's volume of direct relation with the other nodes), the closeness (the indirect linking capability with the other nodes in the chain), and the betweenness (which considers the possibility of relationship between different groups of nodes that compose the chain) [9].

Regarding the chain in its' completeness the SNA metrics allow the calculation of density, centralization and complexity rates, which enables the possibility to observe the organization of the whole chain from the point of view of the set of links of which it is composed of [11].

The present study aimed to identify a quantitative instrument that allow to indicate the importance degree of a commodity chain output in relation to others chain's outputs. We seek for contributing to the analysis of the global commodity chains and their inter-relations, both in particular moments as well as in their evolution through time.

2   Methodology

To analyze the relationship between the mentioned chains, the outputs were considered as the total production of each commodity (ethanol, corn, and broiler). It was assumed that the total of the annual production represents the result of a complex business that involves previous decisions based on price [12, 13], climate [14], availability of natural resources [15], labor [16], and economic and governmental politics [17], as well as an interaction with other areas of knowledge such as biology, agronomy, mechanics, chemistry, physics and sustainability [18, 19].

The values were obtained from the data published by the organizations USDA – United States Department of Agriculture, RFA – Renewable Fuels Association, National Chicken Council, CONAB – Companhia Nacional de Abastecimento (National Supply Company), ÚNICA – União da Indústria da Cana-de-Açúcar (Brazilian Sugarcane Industry Association), e UBABEF – União Brasileira de Avicultura (Brazilian Poultry Union). Although the measurements are expressed in different units by the countries, all of the values were transformed in metric tons (1,000 kg) for comparison purposes. The studied period covers the years 2000, 2006 and 2012 (Fig. 1).

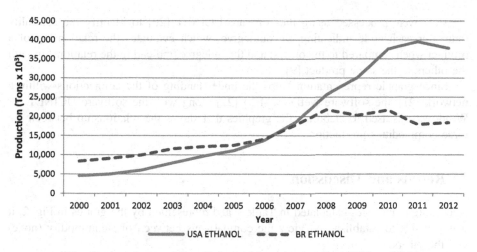

Fig. 1. American and Brazilian ethanol production from 2000 to 2012

To establish a comparison between the outputs of the chains, the proportions were calculated for each commodity production over the production of the other two. Values expressing the rate of the importance of each one over the two others were obtained, in terms of quantity produced in Brazil and in the United States, in the selected periods (Table 1). Ethanol, corn, and broiler were considered as nodes within a simplified network. The links between the nodes were quantified using the values expressed in Table 1.

Table 1. Compared production of ethanol, corn, and broiler in the USA and Brazil

		Brazil			United States		
		2000	2006	2012	2000	2006	2012
Product		Production[a]			Production[a]		
Ethanol		8367.35	14096.81	18348.79	4635.72	13807.62	37825.20
Corn		42289.70	51369.90	81007.20	251854.00	267503.00	273819.52
Broiler		5980.00	9340.00	12650.00	13702.80	15930.31	16621.08
Relation							
a	b	Ratio[b]			Ratio[b]		
Corn	Ethanol	5.05	3.64	4.41	54.33	19.37	7.24
Corn	Broiler	7.07	5.50	6.40	18.38	16.79	16.47
Ethanol	Corn	0.20	0.27	0.23	0.02	0.05	0.14
Ethanol	Broiler	1.40	1.51	1.45	0.34	0.87	2.28
Broiler	Corn	0.41	0.18	0.16	0.05	0.06	0.06
Broiler	Ethanol	0.71	0.66	0.69	2.96	1.15	0.44

[a]Production = 10^3 tons
[b]Ratio = a/b

Data were processed using the software UCINET [20] to identify the centrality index for each node indicating the outdegree, which evaluates the relationship of a product when compared to the others; and the indegree, indicating the relationship with the others to the same product [9].

Since graphic representation helps the understanding of the connections within a network [21], the software NetDraw 4.14 [22] along with the software UCINET for Windows was used to elaborate the graphics that shows the relationship between the three commodities production.

3   Results and Discussion

According to the rates calculated in Table 1 and represented by the graphs in Fig. 2, it was possible to establish and view the comparisons between one commodity (node) and the others.

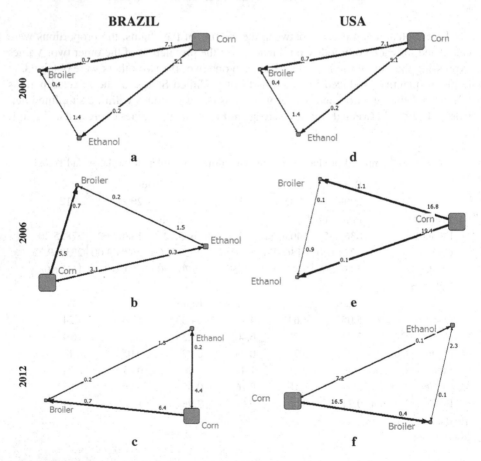

Fig. 2. Graphic representation of the relationship between ethanol, corn and broiler production in Brazil and in the U.S.A, from 2000 to 2012.

The size of the nodes is proportional to the volume of the specific production. The lines that connect the nodes indicate the relationship between the volume of production of each good, and the numbers next to the nodes indicate the ratio between the production of a good *versus* the other one it is related to. It was possible to observe the relationship and the evolution of ethanol, corn, and broiler productions through time: in 2000, 2006 and 2012 in Brazil (Fig. 2a–c), and in the United States (Fig. 2d–f).

The aim of the paper was the development of an indicator that enable to assess the ratio of an element (node) not only with one another, but with all the other elements (nodes) that are part of the network. The values of the networks structural properties were compared: density (the ratio of all ties that are actually present to the number of possible ties), degree centrality (which refers to the amount of immediate ties the actor has within the network, %), closeness centrality (which relates the distance of an actor to all others in the networks by focusing in the distance from each actor to all others, %), betweenness centrality (which views an actor as being in a favoured position to the extent that the actor falls on the geodesic paths between other peers in the network, %), clustering coefficient (which refers to the average of the densities of the neighbour-hoods of all actors), clique (which is a sub-set of a network in which the actors are more closely and intensely tied to one another than they are to other members of the net-work), N-clique (which is used to define an actor as a member of a clique if they are connected to every other member of the group at a distance greater than 1, with N being the length of the path allowed to make a connection to all other members), node (which is the same as element or actor), edge (which is the same as relationship), and geodesic distance (which is the length of the shortest path between the actors). However, we focused on the indegree and outdegree of the networks studied.

Using the software UCINET, was possible to calculate the outdegree (which measures the degree of importance of each product over all the others), as well as the indegree (that measures the importance of all the others over it) [9, 24].

Table 2 shows the indegree and outdegree of each product in Brazil and the United States during the period studied. Thus, a single indicator is introduced to assess the relation of production between a specific commodity with all the others considered in the chain or network.

Table 2. Outdegree and indegree values of the ethanol, corn and broiler chains output

	Brazil			United States			Total		
	2000	2006	2012	2000	2006	2012	2000	2006	2012
Outdegree									
Ethanol	160	178	168	036	092	242	070	119	208
Corn	1212	914	1081	7271	3616	2371	3756	2405	1844
Broiler	085	084	085	301	121	050	158	099	060
Indegree									
Ethanol	576	430	510	5729	2052	768	2413	1234	684
Corn	034	045	039	007	011	020	011	017	024
Broiler	847	701	785	1872	1766	1875	1560	1372	1404

The results obtained in Brazilian data indicate a relatively smooth trajectory for the three commodities considered. In the case of the ethanol derived from cane sugar, the outdegree slightly increased, ranging from 1.60 in 2000 to 1.68 in 2012. The corn showed a slight decline of its outdegree, ranging from 12.12 to 10.81. No change in the broiler's importance degree compared to the other two commodities was observed at the same period. These indicators reinforce the lack in Brazilian policy to encourages biofuel production [25], neither to favor the production of grain, feed and poultry, whose advances occur despite the financial constraints, lack of supportive transport logistics and distribution infrastructure [26, 27].

On the other hand, in the United States, the evolution of the degree of importance of ethanol when compared to the decrease of the importance of corn and chicken, confirm both the policy of encouraging the production of renewable energy as an alternative to fossil fuels derived from oil [28–30], as well as the productivity leap achieved by ethanol chain, whose outdegree jumped from 0.36 in 2000 to 2.42 in 2012. The evolution of the importance of ethanol in the last twelve years occurs despite the outdegree declined of the corn, its main raw material, from 72.71 to 23.71; and also the chicken outdegree decreased from 3.01 to 0.50 which used the same corn as a feedstock.

Considering the production total amount of the three commodities in both the United States and Brazil, it was detected a large increase in importance in the biofuel chain over the food chains (corn and broiler). The evolution of the ethanol outdegree from 0.70 in 2000 to 2.08 in 2012, compared with the food chains such as corn and broiler which outdegree decreased from 37.56 to 18.44 and from 1.58 to 0.60 respectively in the same period, have contributed with quantitative evidences to the food *versus* fuel discussion.

4 Conclusions

The values of outdegree and indegree were obtained for the three simplified studied commodity chains, using the SNA concept. The calculation of these values and the visualization of the network allow assessing the output behavior of a chain, about one another over time. Further studies are recommended to include the full extent of the commodity chain to have a more precise view of the interrelations of the agribusiness chains.

References

1. Gereffi, G.: The organization of buyer-driven global commodity chains: how U.S. retailers shape overseas production networks. In: Gereffi, G., Korzeniewicz, M. (eds.) Commodity Chains and Global Capitalism, pp. 95–122. Praeger, Westport (1994)
2. Thompson, G.F.: Between Hierarchies and Markets: The Logic and Limits of Network Forms of Organization. Oxford University Press, New York (2003)
3. Talbot, J.M.: The comparative advantages of tropical commodity chain analysis. In: Bair, J. (ed.) Frontiers of Commodity Chain Research, pp. 93–109. Stanford University Press, California (2009)

4. Bair, J.: Global commodity chains – genealogy and review. In: Bair, J. (ed.) Frontiers of Commodity Chain Research, pp. 1–34. Stanford University Press, California (2009)
5. Wallerstein, I.: The rise and future demise of the world capitalism system: concepts for comparative analysis. Comp. Stud. Soc. Hist. 16(4), 387–415 (1974)
6. Talbot, J.M.: Tropical commodity chains, forward integration strategies, and international inequality: coffee, cocoa and tea. Rev. Int. Polit. Econ. 9(4), 701–734 (2002)
7. Ferragi, E.M., Nääs, I.A.: Ethanol, corn and broiler: the interdependence between the global chains. Braz. J. Biosyst. Eng. 9(1), 01–10 (2015)
8. Borgatti, S.P., Mehra, A., Brass, D.J., Labianca, G.: Network analysis in the social sciences. Science 323, 892–895 (2009)
9. Freeman, L.C.: Centrality in social networks: conceptual clarification. Soc. Netw. 1, 215–239 (1978)
10. Wasserman, S., Faust, K.: Social Network Analysis: Methods and Applications. Cambridge University Press, Cambridge (1994)
11. Kim, Y., Choi, T.Y., Yan, T., Dooley, K.: Structural investigation of supply networks: A social network analysis approach. J. Oper. Manage. 29, 194–211 (2011)
12. Mitchell, D.: A note on rising food prices. World Bank Policy Research Working Paper 4682. The World Bank Development Prospects Group (2008). http://econ.worldbank.org
13. Ajanovic, A.: Biofuels versus food production: does biofuels production increase food prices? Energy 36(4), 2070–2076 (2011)
14. Lobell, D.B., Schlenker, W., Costa-Roberts, J.: Climate trends and global crop production since 1980. Science 333, 616–620 (2011)
15. Nusser, S.M., Goebel, J.J.: The national resources inventory: a long-term multi-resource monitoring programme. Environ. Ecol. Stat. 4(3), 181–204 (1997)
16. Radhakrishna, R.: Agricultural growth, employment, and poverty: a policy perspective. Econ. Polit. Wkly. 37(3), 243–245, 247–250 (2002)
17. Krueger, A.O., Schiff, M., Valdés, A.: Agricultural incentives in developing countries: measuring the effect of sectoral and economywide policies. World Bank Econ. Rev. 2(3), 255–271 (1988)
18. Demirbas, A.: Political, economic and environmental impacts of biofuels: A review. Appl. Energy 86(Supplement 1), S108–S117 (2009)
19. US EPA – U.S. Environmental Protection Agency. National Agriculture Center. http://www.epa.gov/agriculture/ag101/printcrop.html
20. Borgatti, S.P., Everett, M.G., Freeman, L.C.: UCINET ® 6.0. Analytic Technologies, Natick (2002)
21. Hanneman, R.A., Riddle, M.: Introduction to Social Network Methods. University of California, Riverside (2005). http://faculty.ucr.edu/~hanneman/
22. Borgatti, S.P.: NetDraw Software for Network Visualization. Analytic Technologies, Lexington (2002)
23. Studder, D.: Data visualization and discovery for better business decisions. TDWI best practices report. TDWI research (2013). http://tdwi.org
24. Opsahl, T., Agneessens, F., Skvoretz, J.: Node centrality in weighted networks: generalizing degree and shortest paths. Soc. Netw. 32(3), 245–251 (2010)
25. Farina, E., Rodrigues, L., Souza, E.L.: A política de petróleo e a indústria de etanol no Brasil. Interesse Nacional 64–75 (2013)
26. Valdes, C., Lopes, I.V., Lopes, M.R.: Changing food demand challenges Brazil's farm sector. Braz. Agric. 27–33 (2009)
27. EMBRAPA, Empresa Brasileira de Pesquisa Agropecuária. Embrapa Milho e Sorgo (2012). https://www.embrapa.br/milho-e-sorgo

28. Figueira, S.R., Burnquist, H.L.: Programas para álcool combustível nos Estados Unidos e possibilidades de Exportação do Brasil. Agric. São Paulo. **53**, 5–18 (2006)
29. Sorda, G., Banse, M., Kemfert, C.: An overview of biofuel policies across the world. Energy Policy **38**, 6977–6988 (2010)
30. Banerjee, A.: Food, feed, fuel: transforming the competition for grains. Dev. Change **42**, 529–557 (2011)

Information Quality in PLM:
A Product Design Perspective

Stefan Wellsandt[1,3](✉), Thorsten Wuest[2], Karl Hribernik[1],
and Klaus-Dieter Thoben[1,3]

[1] BIBA - Bremer Institut Für Produktion Und Logistik GmbH,
Bremen, Germany
{wel,hri,tho}@biba.uni-bremen.de
[2] Industrial and Management Systems Engineering,
Benjamin M. Statler College of Engineering and Mineral Resources,
West Virginia University, Morgantown, USA
thwuest@mail.wvu.edu
[3] Faculty of Production Engineering, University of Bremen, Bremen, Germany

Abstract. Recent approaches for Product Lifecycle Management (PLM) aim
for the efficient utilization of the available product information. A reason for this
is that the amount of information is growing, due to the increasing complexity of
products, and concurrent, collaborative processes along the lifecycle. Additional
information flows are continuously explored by industry and academia – a
recent example is the backflow of information from the usage phase. The large
amount of information that has to be handled by companies nowadays and even
more in the future, makes it important to separate "fitting" from "unfitting"
information. A way to distinguish both is to explore the characteristics of the
information, in order to find those information that are "fit for purpose"
(information quality). Since the amount of information is so large and the
processes along the lifecycle are diverse in terms of their expectations about the
information, the problem is similar to finding a needle in a hay stack.
This paper is one of two papers aiming to address this problem by giving
examples why information quality matters in PLM. It focuses on one particular
lifecycle process, in this case product design. An existing approach, describing
information quality by 15 dimensions, is applied to the selected design process.

Keywords: Product lifecycle management · Quality management · Usage
data · Product design · Data quality · Usage information

1 Introduction and Problem Description

Closing the information loops along the product lifecycle is a recent effort undertaken
by research projects [1, 2]. One of the reasons why closing information loops is so
important is the expectation that designers and manufacturers will be able to create
products (and services) of higher quality. This expected increase in product quality is
largely based on the assumption that information about the products' in-use behavior
('usage information') will lead to better decisions in processes like product design.

© IFIP International Federation for Information Processing 2015
S. Umeda et al. (Eds.): APMS 2015, Part I, IFIP AICT 459, pp. 515–523, 2015.
DOI: 10.1007/978-3-319-22756-6_63

Usage information can substantiate decisions and thus increase their transparency within collaborative working environments. Recent research on information about product usage typically focuses on the capabilities and general appropriateness of different approaches, methodologies or solutions that make usage information available to certain decision-makers (e.g. [3, 16]). Important for the actual integration of the information is the technical capability and a use/business case, as well as the adequacy of the information for the given case. Due to the heterogeneity of usage information, it is difficult to decide what information is actually relevant for a certain decision process – currently, the quality dimensions for usage information are largely unknown.

This paper will discuss the importance of information quality in PLM. For reasons of complexity the scope of the paper has to be significantly limited. This is done by focusing on one exemplary information loop (i.e. from usage to design). Furthermore, only one decision-process is selected for the following discussion.

2 Related Work

2.1 Information Flows in PLM

Handling product data and information along the complete product lifecycle is stated as PLM [4]. A product's lifecycle can be structured into three subsequent phases stated as 'beginning of life' (BOL), 'middle of life' (MOL) and 'end of life' (EOL). The concept of PLM was further extended during the EU-funded large-scale research project PROMISE – it demonstrated the possibilities of closing information loops among different processes of the lifecycle [5]. The recent concept of PLM is illustrated in Fig. 1. Internal information flows within the phases are not covered in the illustration.

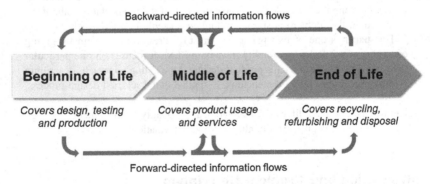

Fig. 1. A product lifecycle model and its major information flows [6]

Among the three lifecycle phases, two types of information flows can be established. The forward-directed flows are the ones that are typically mandatory to design, produce, service and dismiss the product. Backwards-directed flows are typically optional and allow optimization and control of processes. One recent example for optimization is the improvement of product design through the integration of usage information from the MOL phase – this approach is sometimes called 'fact-based design' [7].

Following the working-definition argued by Wellsandt et al., usage information is "[...] *any product-related information that is created after the product is sold to the end customer and before the product is no longer useful for a user*" [6]. Usage information can originate from sources like product embedded sensors, maintenance reports, shopping websites, social networks, product reviews and discussion forums [8]. Information from these heterogeneous sources feature very different characteristics concerning their format (e.g. structured vs. unstructured data), scope (e.g. plain data vs. multi-media) and the lifecycle activities covered in the content (e.g. use, maintenance and repair).

2.2   Information Quality (IQ)

The topic of IQ has been intensely discussed for at least two decades; several sophisticated definitions for 'information quality' exist. Since the purpose of this paper is not to discuss these fundamental concepts, a thoroughly discussed definition is selected for this paper. From a general perspective, the quality of information can be defined as the degree that the characteristics of specific information meet the requirements of the information user (derived from ISO 9000:2005 [9]). Based on this understanding, Rohweder et al. propose a framework for information quality that is an extension of the work conducted by Wang and Strong [10] – it contains 15 information quality dimensions that are assigned to four categories as summarized in Table 1.

Table 1. Dimensions of information quality [11]

Quality category	Scope	Quality dimensions
Inherent	Content	Reputation; free of error; objectivity; believability
Representation	Appearance	Understandability; interpretability; concise representation; consistent representation
Purpose-dependent	Use	Timeliness; value-added; completeness; appropriate amount of data; relevancy
System support	System	Accessibility; Ease of manipulation

The selected definition of information quality is split into four categories, i.e. inherent, representation, purpose-dependent and system support. Each category has dimensions that characterize information by two to five dimensions. A description of some definitions of these quality dimensions is provided in Table 2.

Table 2. Selection of quality dimensions and their description (based on [11])

Quality dimension	Description
Reputation	Credibility of information from the information user's perspective
Free of error	Not erroneous; consistent with reality
Objectivity	Based on fact; without judgement
Believability	Follows quality standards; significant effort for collection and processing
Understandability	Meaning can be derived easily by information user
Interpretability	No ambiguity concerning the actual meaning; wording and terminology
Concise representation	Clear representation; only relevant information; suitable format
Consistent representation	Same way of representing different information items
Accessibility	Simple tools and methods to reach information
Ease of manipulation	Easy to modify; reusable in other contexts

In order to receive a specific statement about the actual quality of an information item, the as-is characteristics of the item must be compared with the required characteristics. The better the matching is, the higher the information quality is considered.

3 Methodology and Scope

In order to substantiate the framework proposed by Rohweder et al., the requirements of the information users (decision-makers) must be identified and compared with the proposed IQ dimensions (see Table 1). For this purpose, the information flow from MOL to BOL is targeted in this paper – the main subject is usage information. The targeted decision-making process is 'requirements elicitation', an information-intensive decision-making processes conducted early in product design.

Process Description. Requirements elicitation (REL) is a systematic, and oftentimes iterative, process aiming to retrieve information from users (and other stakeholders) – the main result of this process is a list of explicit user requirements [12]. Techniques for information retrieval include surveys, questionnaires and observation. Recent approaches, like fact-based-design, aim for the retrieval of actual product usage information, in order to improve, for instance, the requirements list (see Sect. 2.1).

Required Characteristics. In literature, quality dimensions for the results of the elicitation activity, i.e. documented requirements, are readily available (e.g. IEEE 830 standard and [13]). A non-comprehensive list of requirements quality (RQ) dimensions is provided in Table 3. It is valid both for individual requirements and whole lists of requirements. RQ dimensions and IQ dimensions have overlapping in some areas.

Additional, but more general, information requirements result from decision-making in business environments, e.g. cost-efficiency of collection and use of information.

Table 3. Quality dimensions for requirements according to IEEE 830 and [13]

Criterion	Description
Valuable	Has a specific economic value or benefit for the business
Correct	Free from errors and in accordance with facts
Clear	Only one way to understand the requirements; no ambiguity
Understandable	Target audience can perceive the intended meaning
Complete	All relevant requirements are captured
Consistent	Not containing any logical contradictions
Assessable	Importance or relevance can be estimated
Verifiable	Fulfillment is testable in limited time
Modifiable	Variable components and the influences in case of changes are clearly identifiable
Traceable	Identifiable; connected to other requirements and documents
Relevancy	Fulfills a specific stakeholder need or goal (e.g. needed for realization)
Realizable	Can be realized in practice; resource efforts are estimated

4 Discussion

The quality dimensions in Table 3 describe desired characteristics of documented requirements, i.e. an output of the REL activity. In a PLM scenario, like fact-based-design, the requirements can be derived from usage information effectively serving as an input of the REL activity. Deriving requirements from usage information requires some kind of analysis and interpretation of the information, in order to get valuable design knowledge. Since usage information and requirements are involved in the elicitation activity, their quality characteristics might be related to each other. The relation between the two sets of quality dimensions will be substantiated in the following. For reasons of complexity, each IQ dimension will be put into the context of one RQ dimension at most. Therefore, the given examples for relations among RQ dimensions and IQ dimensions are not meant to be comprehensive – there are, most likely, other influences that are not covered in this paper. Since this paper lacks a specific use case for REL, the 'use'-scope of IQ dimensions is not further covered in this paper. The discussion is structured according to the four categories summarized in Table 1.

4.1 Content Scope

Reputation (rep). Quality dimensions, like the ones in Table 1, can be difficult to instantiate for a company, for instance when expertise or resources are lacking. In these cases, previous positive experience with usage information sources can outweigh the lack of precise estimations for the IQ. The reputation is relevant for decision-making in general, thus also relevant for REL.

Free of Error (foe). An error is something produced by mistake [14]. Concerning usage information, errors can occur in at least two areas, i.e. measurements and human-authored contents. In case of measurements, errors can be caused by, for instance inappropriate calibration of sensors, poorly placed sensors and measuring wrong events. In case of human-authored information, errors can be a result of, e.g. unskilled authors (e.g. typos and wording) and limited knowledge of authors (e.g. wrong statements and conclusions). When deriving requirements from erroneous usage information, the resulting requirements might be corrupted (e.g. reflecting a non-existent user need) – therefore, the correctness of requirements benefits from correct usage information.

Objectivity (obj). A characteristic of human-authored feedback information is its subjectivity – also stated as response-bias [15]. When dealing with user responses (e.g. in online discussions) information users generally need to take response-bias into account. Measurements, on the other hand, are more 'objective', since they do not have a response-bias [16]. Due to influences like the response-bias, REL decision-makers may not be able to derive requirements that fulfill the 'complete'-dimension – the available usage information (e.g. from weblogs or forums) is limited/scoped by the perceptions of its author.

Believability (bel). Information that is used to elicit requirements can be extracted from product reviews. These reviews may be authored by renowned professionals that are familiar with a product and terminology to describe it (higher bel) or by common users with unknown identity, knowledge and skills (lower bel). In addition, the reviews can be based on a structured, transparent testing process (higher bel) or an unstructured/unknown process (lower bel). The dimension might influence the "correct"-dimension of the REL process, since a higher believability of usage information might be associated with less errors effectively reducing potential corruption of requirements. Further the dimension is related to the "objectivity"-dimension.

4.2 Appearance Scope

Understandability (und). Human authored usage information, e.g. user feedback in discussion forums, is created by users with different backgrounds (e.g. writing skills, language and expertise on topic). The language, for instance, is an important factor in REL as it limits the understandability of usage information. In a similar way, raw measurement data from sensors (e.g. without graph plotting) are barely understandable by decision-makers. Not being able to take these kinds of usage information into account for REL may lead to an incomplete requirements list (e.g. missing key requirements).

Interpretability (int). Extracting the meaning of usage information can be difficult in case that important context information is lost or originally not provided. Missing context may cause ambiguity of usage information. Measurement protocols, for instance, require context information about the sensor that was used to collect the data. In case this context is not provided, tolerances of measurement remain unclear. This IQ-dimension affects the RQ-dimension for "correctness", as ambiguous usage information may lead to erroneous assumptions and finally to flawed requirements.

Concise Representation (ccr). Usage information that is based on human-authored contents is not necessarily uniform. Product reviews may contain a mixture of media, like text, pictures and videos, or different languages. When dealing with these information in the REL process, an in concise representation makes analysis more time consuming.

Consistent Representation (csr). Contents generated in the Internet (e.g. weblogs, discussion forums) do not follow standardized procedures. Text can be created freely following limited formal structures, such as templates in 'WordPress' and form fields of forum posts. Content can further contain media formats like pictures and videos. Multimedia formats of usage information require more elaborate tools and in general more effort for analysis. Therefore, consistent representation benefits cost-efficient collection and use of information during the REL process.

4.3   Use Scope

The five IQ dimensions of the 'use' scope are not covered further in this paper, since at this stage, no specific use case has been chosen. Without a use case, the range of possible requirements from REL is too large to provide value to this paper.

4.4   System Scope

Accessibility (acc). Getting access to usage information (in a technical sense) is challenging for several reasons. Usage information is, for instance:

- distributed across different sources (e.g. weblogs and databases);
- heterogeneous concerning its format, i.e. representation;
- potentially copyrighted or otherwise restricted (e.g. forum with registration).

Furthermore, the collection of usage information may require special skills and/or knowledge (e.g. data or text mining). Barriers for easy accessibility affect the 'complete'-dimension of requirements, since restricted or too costly access to information might result in missing requirements (that could be derived from the information).

Ease of Manipulation (eas). Usage information, like product reviews and posts in discussion forums, may contain pictures and videos. These contents are provided in formats that can be difficult to manipulate (e.g. video stream). The 'eas'-dimension is also ambiguous in relation to REL, since manipulation might not be desired by decision makers. The requirements should be framed in a way that they reflect the user's expectations and needs. Ease of manipulation might affect the 'correctness'-dimension of requirements when manipulation of usage information leads to wrong conclusions. An example concerns losing context information during a copy and paste procedure – in consequence, decision-makers might take wrong assumptions about product or user behavior.

5 Conclusion and Outlook

While the availability of new information sources, such as usage information in design, provides new opportunities to improve products (see [3, 7]), newly created information flows and new kinds of information can introduce problems along the lifecycle. Feeding usage information into the BOL phase, for instance, can cause issues in related decision-making processes. These issues can affect product quality in a negative way, e.g. when incorrect or incomplete requirements are elicited based on flawed usage information. The impact of flawed information may further affect later stages of the lifecycle such as maintenance, disassembly and disposal of products. Therefore, the example provide in this paper helps to justify why IQ has to be considered more thoroughly in PLM. In future research, the following aspects should be considered, in order to extend the understanding of IQ in PLM:

- Collection of additional cases from all lifecycle phases (e.g. production, sales, maintenance and EOL scenarios).
- The adequacy of IQ dimensions for each case has to be argued. This requires an analysis of decision-making processes.
- Interdependencies of IQ dimensions need to be detailed. This should be substantiated by practical examples from use cases.

Acknowledgement. This project has received funding from the European Union's Horizon 2020 research and innovation programme under grant agreement no. 636951 (Manutelligence) and grant agreement no. 636868 (Falcon).

References

1. Falcon Project: Feedback mechanisms across the lifecycle for customer-driven optimization of iNnovative product-services. http://www.falcon-h2020.eu. Accessed 16 July 2015.
2. Manutelligence Project: Product service design and manufacturing intelligence engineering platform. http://www.manutelligence.eu/. Accessed 21 Apr 2015
3. Abramovici, M., Lindner, A.: Knowledge-based decision support for the improvement of standard products. CIRP Ann. Manuf. Technol. **62**(1), 159–162 (2013)
4. Kiritsis, D.: Closed-loop PLM for intelligent products in the era of the internet of things. Comput. Aided Des. **43**(5), 479–501 (2011)
5. Promise Project: promise-innovation.com. http://promise-innovation.com/components. Accessed 26 Mar 2015
6. Wellsandt, S., Hribernik, K., Thoben, K.-D.: Sources and characteristics of information about product use. In: Procedia CIRP, 25th CIRP Design Conference, Haifa (2015)
7. Røstad, C.C., Henriksen, B.: ECO-boat MOL capturing data from real use of the product. In: Rivest, L., Bouras, A., Louhichi, B. (eds.) PLM 2012. IFIP AICT, vol. 388, pp. 99–110. Springer, Heidelberg (2012)
8. Wellsandt, S., Hribernik, K., Thoben, K.-D.: Content analysis of product usage information from embedded sensors and web 2.0 sources. In: ICE Conference 2015, Belfast (in press)

9. International Organization for Standardization, ISO 9000:2005: Quality Management Systems – Fundamentals and Vocabulary. International Organization for Standardization, Geneva (2005)
10. Wang, R.Y., Strong, D.M.: Beyond accuracy: what data quality means to data consumers. J. Manage. Inf. Syst. **12**(4), 5–33 (1996)
11. Rohweder, J., Kasten, G., Malzahn, D., Piro, A., Schmid, J.: Informationsqualität – Definitionen, Dimensionen und Begriffe. In: Hildebrand, K., Gebauer, M., Hinrichs, H., Mielke, M. (eds.) Daten und Informationsqualität, pp. 25–45. Springer, Heidelberg (2008)
12. Jiao, J.R., Chen, C.-H.: Customer requirement management in product development: a review of research issues. Concurr. Eng. **14**(3), 173–185 (2006)
13. Ebert, C.: Systematisches Requirements Engineering, 4th edn. dpunkt.verlag (2012)
14. Merriam Webster Dictionary. http://www.merriam-webster.com/dictionary/error. Accessed 12 June 2015
15. Sampson, S.E.: Ramifications of monitoring service quality through passively solicited customer feedback. Decis. Sci. **27**, 601–622 (1996)
16. Dornhöfer, M., Fathi, M., Holland, A.: Applying rules for representing and reasoning of objective product use information exemplarily for injection molding machines. Inform. Eng. Inf. Sci. **252**, 616–623 (2011)

Managing Evolving Global Operations Networks

Alona Mykhaylenko[✉], Brian Vejrum Wæhrens, and John Johansen

Centre for Industrial Production, Aalborg University, Aalborg, Denmark
amy@business.aau.dk

Abstract. For many globally dispersed organisations, the home base (HB) is a historic locus of integrative and coordinating efforts that safeguard overall performance. However, the dynamism of global operations networks is increasingly pulling the centre of gravity away from the HB and dispersing it across the network, challenging the HB's ability to sustain its centrality over time. To counteract this tendency, this paper addresses the gap in the literature regarding the development of the network management capability of the HB within the context of its network. Data was collected through a retrospective longitudinal case study of an intra-organisational operations network of one OEM and its three foreign subsidiaries. The findings suggest a row of strategic roles and corresponding managerial capabilities, which the HB needs to develop depending on the changing subsidiaries' competencies and HB-subsidiary relationships.

Keywords: Network management · Capabilities · Global operations

1 Introduction

It is well recognised that the basis for the sustainable performance of the global operations networks is found in the integration and coordination mechanisms that are available to the organisation [1]. For many companies, the home base (HB) is historically the locus of such managerial "centrality". It takes the lead with regard to setting and maintaining standards, as it embeds historical knowledge and capabilities, which are the basis of operations excellence. However, concerns have been raised about the increasing dispersion and dynamism of global operations networks pulling the centre of gravity away from the HB, thereby calling into question the HB's capability to sustain such centrality over time [2, 3]. Such tendencies can potentially endanger both the performance of the HB and the sustainable competitiveness of global organisations as a whole, especially those which maintain rooted operations. This makes it particularly important to address the issue of how an HB can continuously sustain and develop its network management capabilities. The existing research has overlooked the fact that global operations networks are dynamic entities of which the HB is a part; thus, its managerial capability may be influenced by the network and the changes that occur within it, and should be studied in its context. Therefore, this paper aims to understand how the network management capability of the HB firm is impacted by the process of its network evolution. To do so, we choose to focus on the internal

© IFIP International Federation for Information Processing 2015
S. Umeda et al. (Eds.): APMS 2015, Part I, IFIP AICT 459, pp. 524–531, 2015.
DOI: 10.1007/978-3-319-22756-6_64

operations network of a global company; the lead entity is located at the HB, which performs both local operations and global corporate functions, while the wholly owned foreign subsidiaries are regarded as network members.

2   Theoretical Background

Managing a global network is challenging due to the high costs and capability demands of coordinating dispersed activities over distances [4], changing roles of the network members [5], increasing tendencies to offshore high-value functions, changing boundary decisions [6]. Such changeability draws attention away from how organisations should structure and manage operations networks and towards how they can continuously sustain the existing managerial capabilities and develop new ones.

Recognizing the importance of the network management capability researchers disagree about its content. Some describe it as the traditional coordinating and controlling, others refer to more indirect forms of influence [7], while third ones [8] suggest that it will depend on the type of network and the HB properties. In line with such thinking, some authors tried to classify network types and suggest the activities for their management. Of particular interest is the work by Harland et al. [9], offering a taxonomy of supply networks, based on the network dynamism and the focal firm influence. They also suggest managerial activities required for each network type.

Therefore scholars strived to define network management capabilities precisely, omitting the fact that, first, many organisations are not born but rather develop into networks, and their managerial capabilities evolve accordingly [10]. Second, as the HB is a part of its network - its managerial capability may be influenced by changes in the network. Therefore the managerial capability of the HB needs to be understood in the context of its network's evolution. Regarding the latter, the evolving roles of the network members have been addressed before. One of the well-known works describes strategic roles of subsidiaries [5], whose development process can be summarized in 3 stages: (1) value-addition (subsidiary exploits and depends on parent's knowledge, striving to add value with efficient and effective production); (2) competence center (subsidiary gains more autonomy and complex tasks, introduces minor process and product improvements); (3) center of excellence (subsidiary gains global responsibility, becomes knowledge source for other network members). However the question of how network members impact each other in the process of their co-evolution has largely been understudied [11]. As an exception Mugurusi and Boer [12] outline general tendency in the evolution of the HB-subsidiary relationships: they tend to get tighter due to learning and mutual adjustment. And to our knowledge, the impact of the network evolution on the managerial capabilities of the HB has not been addressed. To cover this gap we approach network management as a multiplicity of activities aimed at influencing the network members to achieve a common goal [7]. HB capacity to produce such activities is referred to as a managerial capability, which generally implies a set of resources and knowledge of their usage [19]. To capture such activities in the process of network evolution, the latter is defined as temporal sequence of events that create and alter the global network configuration [13] over time.

3 Methodology

An in-depth retrospective case study strategy was chosen for this work because it allows us to study the longitudinal change process and focus on understanding the dynamics present within single settings [14]. The case studies are often criticised for providing little basis for scientific generalization, as they are situation specific. Others consider this to be strength because, as the findings are unstable over time, the context gains particular importance, making a case study particularly beneficial [15].

The main selection criteria were company's long offshoring history and active altering of global operations. The case company originated in 1976 in Denmark and became one of the leading industrial goods companies. It has production facilities in Denmark, the United States (US), Slovakia and China; it employs 1,600 people worldwide; 80 % of its products are customised solutions. The study tracked the company's offshoring history between 1999 and 2014. The data were collected through semi-structured interviews, archival documents and on-site observations to enable the triangulation of the findings. In total, 28 interviews lasting 1.5 h each were conducted with managerial and operational staff at the Danish HB and affiliates in China and Slovakia. To capture important network configuration changes in retrospect, an event-sampling approach was employed. Subsequent data analysis was focused on the state of the network configuration during key events, corresponding roles played by the HB and the enabling and challenging factors. Initially, the process "story" was written up based on the interviews at the HB and was then presented to the key informants to verify the overall accuracy. It was then enriched after the investigation at the subsidiaries, followed by a workshop with the management.

4 Case Description

The first offshore facility was established in 1999 in the US. In 2005, a new facility was opened in China and in 2007 in Slovakia - each serving its own market. Driven by customer requests for better prices, larger volumes and faster delivery, a low range of standard products was "replicated" from the HB to the subsidiaries by the HB staff with product-specific production expertise. They were temporary relocated to the sites, addressing the HB production with any arising issues. Achievement of quality targets was closely overseen by Danish expatriates.

Around 2009 the appearance of global customers and the lack of production capacity at the HB made the HB team up with the subsidiaries and coordinate such joint projects. Moreover, due to the increase in sites' product modification capabilities and localization of supplier bases, consultation requests towards the HB became more complex. The HB became less capable of suggesting quick solutions and started involving other sites. With no connections existing among the latter the HB was mediating such communication. Rapid growth of production volumes in 2011 significantly increased the load on the HB operations staff. Having their own local operations to attend to, they became slower and less effective in responding and making decisions - a bottleneck in global operations. To relieve the load and promote alignment, the HB staff started disseminating a variety of corporate procedures, thereby reducing their own involvement in certain activities. They also started facilitating direct communication among the sites by establishing regular official global meetings and introducing global communication rules. Also HB management started promoting a "global thinking" culture and introduced better communication systems and the partial automation of certain procedures. HB also started standardization of main production processes.

Around 2013 the HB picked up an active tendency of delegating global responsibility for some products to the subsidiaries due to the lack of production capacity at the HB, as well as to encourage development of their competencies and utilize chea-per R&D resources. The HB was supposed to maintain involvement in "higher-level" decisions. Previously formalised communication and coordination were supposed to enable the subsidiaries to operate in accordance with corporate demands, without the HB interventions. However, frequent deviations from standards in subsidiaries' operations currently pose concerns about the sustainability of alignment in the organisation. Moreover, some delegated responsibilities are performed less effectively by the subsidiaries than by the HB staff. And the HB management currently has little leverage to improve the situation. Previously, when any problems occurred, the HB domestic operations were there to intervene with support and control. However, currently they have limited capability, resources and motivation to help due to the reduction in the number of common operations with the subsidiaries. Moreover the sites started facing resistance from the HB in the approval and support of their improvement suggestions.

5 Discussion

Change in the HB Influence in the Network. A highlight of the transition process in the early stages was the HB prominent in promoting and directing performance of its subsidiaries. However, later the situation changed as the sites became more capable and autonomous. Comparing the case company situation to the network taxonomy offered by Harland et al. [9], finding itself in the "dynamic" part of the classification the HB also has gradually moved from the high- to the low-influence quadrant. Harland et al. explain such influence by the volumes produced at the HB relative to other players in the network and perceived indirect network value of the HB (HB's image in the network relating to its innovation drive). These correspond to the situation experienced by the case company. However, perceived network value of the HB was also determined by the contribution, which the HB was able or willing to make into the value-creating activities of the sites. As Lavie [16] explains it, a party with lower capability level may experience a need for learning from the more capable partner, thus being in a more dependent position. Therefore competence levels of the subsidiaries can be added to the taxonomy as an important determinant of the HB influence.

The character of managerial activities of the HB in different quadrants also supported predictions of Harland's et al. [9] framework: when the HB had high influence over the network these activities were related to direct network managing, while shifting to the "coping with the network" mode, when the influence decreased. However, the framework does not explain why and how the focal firm can move towards the influence reduction, and the possible existence of intermediate states, which would require yet another set of capabilities from the HB. Moreover, it overlooks the importance and potential influence of relationships in the network on the HB capabilities. To approach this gap we will consider the evolution of the subsidiaries' competencies and subsidiary-HB relationships. We will approach the former using the subsidiary strategic roles framework by Ferdows [5], and the latter – using the model by Snehota and Hakansson [17], distinguishing between three core dimensions of business relationships: resource ties, activity links and actor bonds.

Evolution of the Network and HB Managerial Capabilities.

Stage 1. Value Addition. The subsidiaries started at the lowest competence levels and worked towards improving their internal performance [5]. In such situation they engaged in no knowledge creation of their own and had to rely heavily on knowledge inflows, resources and guidance from the parent [18]. Therefore the main competencies required from the HB here were functional expertise, ability to transfer it to the subsidiary, and careful quality control [19, 20]. At this stage relationships emerged between the subsidiary and the HB as a result of emergence of resource ties (material as flow of components and immaterial as inflow of knowledge) and actor bonds between the HB operations and a new offshore production operation, which emerged as a result of cross-business sharing and transfer of resources and homogeneity of operations [12]. Therefore the role of the HB here may be described as an "implementer".

Stage 2. Competence Center. Due to the development of subsidiaries' competencies (and under certain environmental pressure) their focus changed towards creating synergy in the operations network, and learning. Hence the subsidiaries needed the HB help in providing connections with other network actors, making them "fit in" the global network and facilitate joint knowledge development [5], [12]. To accomplish this, the HB used its reputation and connections within the network and initially more global outset – the so-called positional and relational capabilities [21]. Coordination capabilities were also required to align globally dispersed activities [22]. As for the HB-subsidiary relationships, they developed through activity links resulting from the need to coordinate tasks across the network [12], and the need for joint knowledge development. Therefore existing resource and actor bonds were expanded by activity links, while the HB role here may be described as a "networking agent". Here the HB also enjoyed the highest influence level as it provides the network actors with the mutual access [9]. However, the greater the interdependence is, the more intensive the activity links become, which complicates working across distances [23], requiring more managerial intervention [22]. This caused scarcity and inefficiency of the HB human resources, required to maintain activity links. To relief the load the HB started encouraging actor bonds among the subsidiaries, creating trust and partnership necessary for real-time interaction and joint knowledge creation (partnering capability) [12, 19]. Creation of shared systems and processes, supported by IT capabilities, indicates the strengthening of the resource and actor bonds, facilitating the activity links. Therefore, while creating direct links among the subsidiaries, the HB reduced those with itself that also reduced the HB influence in the network.

Stage 3. Center of Excellence. As the subsidiaries assumed global responsibility for some products, the HB preserved high-level decision rights and occasional interventions – a function close to an "orchestrating" role described by Möller et al. [19]. Having no leverage of actual involvement into operations it instead requires strong communication and persuasive skills, thorough understanding of subsidiaries' operations and their business networks [24]. Also as the subsidiaries became capable of generating knowledge [18], the HB had to facilitate knowledge outflows from these sites [25], as well as to mobilize them for a common action when needed [19]. However the case company lacks such capabilities at the moment. Previously they were ensured by involvement of the HB domestic operations into the sites' operations through activity, resource and actor bonds. However, as the products under the subsidiaries' global responsibility are not produced at the HB, the HB-subsidiary activity links vanished. This caused gradual fading of all other links, challenging the HB know-ledgeability about the network and effectiveness of its strategic role.

The empirical results, supported by the literature, allowed us distilling the strategic roles of the HB (corresponding to the evolution of the subsidiaries' strategic roles) and managerial capabilities necessary to fulfill these roles (Table 1).

Table 1. Co-evolution of the subsidiaries and managerial capabilities of the HB

Subsidiaries' strategic roles	HB strategic role	Managerial capabilities of the HB
Stage 1. Value-addition	**Implementer**	Product-specific production expertise; ability to transfer production expertise to the sites; quality control
Stage 2. Competence center	**Networking agent**	Positional, relational and coordination capabilities; facilitation of joint knowledge development
		IT capability; partnering capability
Stage 3. Center of excellence	**Orchestrator**	Communication and persuasive skills; knowledgeability about operations and networks of the subsidiaries; motivating and mobilizing network members; facilitation of knowledge sharing

Evolution of the HB-Subsidiary Relationships. According to the literature, the HB-subsidiary relationships are important for the subsidiaries' performance and tend to get tighter with time [12]. However, we observed a process of gradual "distancing" of the HB from the subsidiaries as a result of activity links becoming a burden for the HB. This indicates that the important aspect in maintaining the managerial capability at the HB lies in having a certain "critical mass", in terms of both the number of people and their capabilities, rather than the general notion of the organisation's size, as well as the challenge of the domestic resources utilization to balance the local and global needs. Previous research showed that globalisation is less challenging for larger companies than for their smaller counterparts, lacking resources for operational and corporate support of their global operations. However, as the findings showed, the companies that are considered large may face similar problems. Moreover, we can suggest that the intensity of the activity links and resource scarcity at the HB may be another mediator of the HB-subsidiary relationship (apart from earlier suggested congruence between the "system properties" of the nodes and the environmental dynamism [12]), promoting their dissolution, rather than tightening.

Network Types and HB Managerial Activities. As Harland et al. [9] predicted, HB managerial activities will depend on its influence in the network. However, as our case showed, such activities are also dictated by the HB-subsidiary relationships: for example, weakening of the latter reviled the need for activities meant to keep the HB knowledgeable about the subsidiaries' operations. Therefore we suggest expanding the networks taxonomy by including a dimension of the HB-subsidiary relationships.

6 Conclusion

This work addresses a gap in the literature on the change of the network management capability of the HB within the context of its network. In particular, we investigated how the evolution of subsidiaries' competencies and HB-subsidiary relationships impact the ability of the HB to manage its global network. We distilled the strategic roles and managerial capabilities, which the HB needs to adopt with the change in relationships and roles of its subsidiaries. These can be of a particular importance for practitioners, who strive to develop their subsidiaries, while preserving the HB as an influential actor. We also shed a light on the factors promoting the disintegration of the HB-subsidiary relationships (rather than their tightening, as the extant literature emphasises). Based on the latter we also made suggestions to improve the existing supply networks classification. The results also indicated the importance of the HB size and domestic operations for its ability to perform its managerial roles effectively. The main limitations of the study include the use of only one company, rendering highly suggestive results. They are expected to be generalisable to most industrial goods companies, but will benefit from the replication across various industries.

References

1. Kotabe, M., Mudambi, R.: Global sourcing and value creation: opportunities and challenges. J. Int. Manag. **15**(2), 121–125 (2009)
2. Ciabuschi, F., Dellestrand, H., Holm, U.: The role of headquarters in the contemporary MNC. J. Int. Manag. **18**(3), 213–223 (2012)
3. Feldmann, A., Olhager, J., Fleet, D., Shi, Y.: Linking networks and plant roles: the impact of changing a plant role. Int. J. Prod. Res. **51**(19), 5696–5710 (2013)
4. Contractor, F.J., Kumar, V., Kundu, S.K., Pedersen, T.: Reconceptualizing the firm in a world of outsourcing and offshoring: the organizational and geographical relocation of high-value company functions. J. Manag. Stud. **47**(8), 1417–1433 (2010)
5. Ferdows, K.: Made in the world: the global spread of production. Prod. Oper. Manag. **6**(2), 102–109 (1997)
6. Slepniov, D., Waehrens, B.V., Jørgensen, C.: Global operations networks in motion: managing configurations and capabilities. Oper. Manag. Res. **3**(3–4), 107–116 (2010)

7. Knight, L., Harland, C.: Managing supply networks: organizational roles in network management. Eur. Manag. J. **23**(3), 281–292 (2005)
8. Järvensivu, T., Möller, K.: Metatheory of network management: a contingency perspective. Ind. Mark. Manag. **38**(6), 654–661 (2009)
9. Harland, C.M., Lamming, R.C., Zheng, J., Johnsen, T.E.: A taxonomy of supply networks. J. Supply Chain Manag. **37**(3), 21–27 (2001)
10. Ferdows, K.: Managing evolving global production networks. In: Galvan, R. (ed.) Strategy Innovation and Change: Challenges for Management, pp. 149–162. Oxford University Press, Oxford (2008)
11. Cheng, Y., Farooq, S., Johansen, J.: International manufacturing network: past, present, and future. Int. J. Oper. Prod. Manag. **35**(3), 392–429 (2015)
12. Mugurusi, G., de Boer, L.: What follows after the decision to offshore production? A systematic review of the literature. Strateg. Outsourcing Int. J. **6**(3), 213–257 (2013)
13. Srai, J.S., Gregory, M.: A supply network configuration perspective on international supply chain development. Int. J. Oper. Prod. Manag. **28**(5), 386–411 (2008)
14. Eisenhardt, K.M.: Building theories from case study research. Acad. Manag. Rev. **14**(4), 532–550 (1989)
15. Dubois, A., Gadde, L.E.: Systematic combining: an abductive approach to case research. J. Bus. Res. **55**(7), 553–560 (2002)
16. Lavie, D.: The competitive advantage of interconnected firms: an extension of the resource-based view. Acad. Manag. Rev. **31**(3), 638–658 (2006)
17. Snehota, I., Hakansson, H. (eds.): Developing Relationships in Business Networks. Routledge, Londres (1995)
18. Gupta, A.K., Govindarajan, V.: Knowledge flows and the structure of control within multinational corporations. Acad. Manag. Rev. **16**(4), 768–792 (1991)
19. Möller, K., Svahn, S., Rajala, A., Tuominen, M.: Network management as a set of dynamic capabilities. Helsinki School of Economics, Helsinki (2002)
20. Youngdahl, W.E., Ramaswamy, K., Dash, K.C.: Service offshoring: the evolution of offshore operations. Int. J. Oper. Prod. Manag. **30**(8), 798–820 (2010)
21. Hall, R.: A framework linking intangible resources and capabiliites to sustainable competitive advantage. Strateg. Manag. J. **14**(8), 607–618 (1993)
22. Anderson, E.G., Davis-Blake, A., Erzurumlu, S., Joglekar, N., Parker, G.: The effects of outsourcing, offshoring, and distributed product development organization on coordinating the NPD process. In: Loch, C., Kavadias, S. (eds.) Handbook on New Product Development Management. Elsevier, Amsterdam (2007)
23. Kumar, K., van Fenema, P.C., Von Glinow, M.A.: Offshoring and the global distribution of work: implications for task interdependence theory and practice. J. Int. Bus. Stud. **40**(4), 642–667 (2009)
24. Vahlne, J.E., Schweizer, R., Johanson, J.: Overcoming the liability of outsidership—the challenge of HQ of the global firm. J. Int. Manag. **18**(3), 224–232 (2012)
25. Ambos, T.C., Ambos, B., Schlegelmilch, B.B.: Learning from foreign subsidiaries: an empirical investigation of headquarters' benefits from reverse knowledge transfers. Int. Bus. Rev. **15**(3), 294–312 (2006)

Production Cost Analysis and Production Planning for Plant Factories Considering Markets

Nobuhiro Sugimura[✉], Koji Iwamura, Nguyen Quang Thinh,
Kousuke Nakai, Seisuke Fukumoto, and Yoshitaka Tanimizu

Graduate School, Osala Prefectuture University, Sakai, Japan
sugimura@me.osakafu-u.ac.jp

Abstract. Much emphasis is now given to development of fully closed and controlled plant factories, aimed at supplying various vegetables safely and constantly. However, one of the most important issues of the plant factories is the high production costs due to the investment and equipment in the factories and the daily operations. Systematic methods are considered here increase the delivery prices of the vegetables and to reduce the running costs in the plant factories.

Keywords: Plant factories · Production planning · Cost analysis

1 Introduction

Much emphasis is now given to development and application of fully closed and controlled plant factories, aimed at supplying various vegetables safely and constantly. Many plant factories have been equipped and operated in suburban areas and downtowns for supplying the safe and high quality vegetables directory to the markets [1, 2]. However, one of the most important problems of the plant factories to be solved is the production costs due to the investment and equipment in the factories and the daily operations. A mathematical model is proposed in the research to estimate the production costs of the vegetables due to the investment, equipment and operations, based on the production conditions of the vegetables and their production volumes in the plants. The proposed model are verified by comparing the estimated production costs by the proposed model with ones of the real plant equipped in Osaka Prefecture University [3].

A production planning method is proposed to select a suitable production plans of the vegetables to be cultivated in the daily operations of the plant factories referring to the forecasting model developed to estimate the market prices of the vegetables. The market prices are forecasted by applying a GP (Genetic Programming) model representing the relationships between the market prices and the weather data.

An electric power supply market is also discussed to get the electric power for the plant factories, aimed at reducing the electricity costs, since the plant factory requires large amount of electric power for the lighting sources and the air conditioning equipment.

© IFIP International Federation for Information Processing 2015
S. Umeda et al. (Eds.): APMS 2015, Part I, IFIP AICT 459, pp. 532–540, 2015.
DOI: 10.1007/978-3-319-22756-6_65

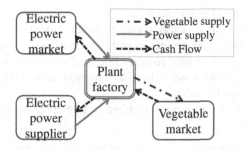

Fig. 1. Vegetable market and electric power market

2 Plant Factories and Their Markets

Plant factories are production systems which constantly produces safe and high quality vegetables rapidly and constantly. However, the production costs in the plant factories are higher than the ones of the conventional farms, due to initial investment costs including plant constructions, air conditioning equipment, lighting devices and production equipment and also running costs for electric power supply. Therefore, two markets are considered in the research to reduce the operation costs and to increase the selling prices of the produced vegetables.

Figure 1 shows the vegetable markets and the electric suppliers related with the plant factories. The vegetable markets are the markets dealing with the vegetables produced by both the conventional farms and the plant factories, and the market prices are determined based on the supplies and the demands in the markets. The market prices of the leaf lettuces dynamically change day by day due to various environmental conditions, and the selling prices are increased if the delivery timing is fit to the date with high prices of the lettuces. Therefore, a suitable production plans are required to deliver the lettuces to the high price markets.

As regards the electric power supply, two types of supply systems are considered. They are, conventional electric power suppliers and electric power markets. The plant factories get most of the required electric powers from the conventional suppliers and a part of the electric powers from the markets to decrease the procurement costs.

The following three issues will be discussed in the paper to manage the plant factories based on the vegetable markets and the electric power markets.

(1) Production cost analysis of plant factories,
(2) Production planning of plant factories based on vegetable market prices, and
(3) Purchasing electric powers from electric power markets

3 Production Cost Analysis of Plant Factories

The production costs of the vegetables produced in the plant factories are classified in to following items.

(1) Construction costs of plant factories,
(2) Machinery costs of plant factories, such as pallets to seed vegetables, conveyers to transport the pallets, and devices to pick up the grown-up vegetables,
(3) Lighting source costs to give required photon flux density of the vegetables,
(4) Air-conditioning device costs to keep the environments in the plant factories, such as temperature and humidity,
(5) Running costs for the electricity required to operate the plant factories, and
(6) Other running costs.

The individual cost items are investigated based on the documents and data in the web-sites to estimate the production costs of one piece of the vegetables. The cost items considered here include such items as the construction costs of the plant factory buildings for an unit area, the conveyer costs for an unit length, the lighting device costs for the fluorescent lights and/or LED lights required to cultivate the vegetables, the air-conditioning costs to remove an unit kWh heat, and the power purchasing costs for an unit kWh.

The cost items are analyzed and a set of formulas are developed to estimate the production costs for the individual pieces of the vegetables. By applying the formulas, the production costs for the leaf lettuces are estimated for the cases of the fluorescent lights and the LED lights. For an example, Eq. (1) gives the photon flux requirement of the lighting sources to produce the vegetables, which is one of the most important formulas for designing the plant factories.

$$PF = PFD \times S_p \times V_{all} \times \eta_L \tag{1}$$

where,
PF [μmol s^{-1}]:   Total photon flux required in the plant factories.
PFD [μmol m^{-2} s^{-1}]:   Photon flux density required to the lighting sources to cultivate the vegetables.
S_p [m^2]:   Areas which the individual vegetables occupy.
V_{all}:   Total number of vegetables in the plant factories.
η_L: Efficiency of the lighting sources.

The numbers of the lighting sources are estimated by applying Eq. (1), and the capacity and the electric powers of both the lighting sources and the air-conditioning systems are estimated based on the numbers and the electric powers of the lighting sources.

The basic specification of the plant factories considered here is summarized in Table 1, based on the experimental plant factory in Osaka Prefecture University. Table 2 shows the specification of the leaf lettuces produced in the experimental plant factories. Whole plans of the plant factories for both fluorescent lights and the LED lights have been designed based on the specifications, and the production costs are estimated for individual pieces of the lettuces.

The estimated costs are summarized in Table 3 for the plant factories equipped with the fluorescent lights and ones with LEDs. The estimated costs are roughly same with the production costs of the existing plant factories. The differences of the cost items

Table 1. Specification of a plant factory

Daily production	5,000 [pieces]
Capacity	25,000 [pieces]
Lighting sources	Fluorescent lights or LED
Efficiency of light	80 [%]

Table 2. Specification of a leaf lettuce

Cultivation period	25 [days]
Photon flux density	150 [μmol m^2 s^{-1}]

Table 3. Summary of production costs for plant factories (Yen/Piece)

	Plant factories equipped with fluorescent lights	Plant factories equipped with LED
Lighting source	9.88	58.9
Air conditioning	14.2	2.19
Construction	11.0	11.0
Equipment	2.78	2.78
Seeds, water, etc.	6.10	6.10
Electric power	88.4	28.4
Total cost	132	109

between two light sources are also roughly same as the existing plant factories. In the case of ones equipped with LED lights, the lightning device cost is high, but the air-conditioning cost and the electricity costs are low, due to high efficiency and low energy consumption of the LED lights against the fluorescent lights.

4   Production Planning and Purchasing of Electric Power

4.1   Estimation of Wholesale Market Prices

A suitable production plans for the Plant factories are required to produce and to supply the vegetables in suitable timing to the markets. A production planning method is discussed in the section based on the market price estimation of the lettuces.

The market prices of lettuces are changing day by day due to surrounding conditions such as seasons, weather, and climate [4]. Many research works have been carried out to forecast the vegetable market prices by applying the ARIMA model of the time series analysis and the Neural Network model [5, 6]. However, it is required to establish long-term forecasting methods for the production planning, due to the long lead time in the plant factories. Therefore, the correlations between the wholesale market prices in Tokyo and the various parameters of the weather such as temperature, humidity, and so on, were firstly analyzed, and it was found that the lowest temperature

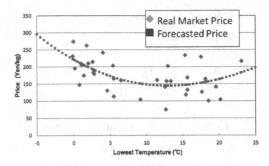

Fig. 2. Relationships between real market prices and forecasted prices

has highest correlations with the lettuce prices. A genetic programming (GP) based system has been developed to forecast the market prices of the lettuces based on the time series data of both the market prices and the lowest temperature. The formulas to forecast the market process are generated by applying the GP method based on the training data of the prices in the real markets and the lowest temperature in every month for 8 years. Equation (2) shows the obtained formula represented by the polynomial for forecasting the prices.

$$EP = \sum_{k=0}^{n} k_n LT^n \qquad (2)$$

where,
EP: Market prices of leaf lettuces
LT: Lowest temperature
k_n: Constants

The formulas are applied to the forecast of the market prices for 3 years other than the training data for 8 years. Figure 2 shows the evaluation results, which give the relationships between the real wholesale market prices and the forecasted prices. Equation (2) obtained here is applied to the production planning of the plant factories to deliver the vegetables to the markets at suitable timing.

4.2   Production Planning Based on Market Prices

A production planning method is proposed based on the forecasting system of the wholesale market prices. This method selects a suitable vegetable to be cultivated in daily operations.

Two types of plant factories are considered in the present research. They are,

(1)   Factory A produces only leaf lettuces, and
(2)   Factory B has the capability of producing both leaf lettuces and another vegetable called β.

The following items are assumed for the ease of production planning.

(a) The factory B has the equipment to produce two vegetables and the production costs are higher than ones of the factory A,
(b) Both the leaf lettuces and the vegetable β have same cultivation period of 25 days,
(c) The vegetable β can be sold by the price same as the production costs, and
(d) The retail vegetable market prices are higher than the wholesale market prices in either 3, 3.5 or 4 times.

The following procedure is proposed to carry out production planning.

STEP 1: Forecasting of lowest temperature and wholesale market prices
        The lowest temperature of 25 days after are firstly forecasted based on the weather forecast and the wholesale market prices of the lettuces are also estimated by applying Eq. (2). The cultivation period in the plant factories is set to be 25 days, and the production planning requires the forecast of the market prices of 25 days after, in order to select the cultivation operations in the next day.

STEP 2: Selection of vegetables to be cultivated in the nest day

    (1) Plant factory A
        The production planning system for the plant factory A selects the one of the following tow operations for the next day.
        (a) Cultivating lettuces, if the forecasted price is higher than the production costs, or
        (b) No cultivation, if the forecasted price is lower than the production costs.

    (2) Plant factory B
        The production planning system of factory B selects one the following two operations for the next day.
        (a) Cultivating lettuces, if the forecasted price is higher than the production costs, or
        (b) Cultivating vegetable β, if the forecasted price is lower than the production costs.

In the plant factory B, the vegetable β is cultivated to avoid the loss of the running cost, for the cases that the forecasted lettuce price is lower than the production costs. However, the production cost of the plant factory B is higher than one of the plant factory A, due to the additional production equipment for two types of vegetables.

4.3 Purchasing of Electric Power from Market

As regards the electric power supply, two suppliers are considered in the research. One is the conventional electric power suppliers, which provide the electricity by the fixed prices based on the long term contracts. Another is electric power markets, in which the amount of power supply and the prices are determined based on the daily supplies and

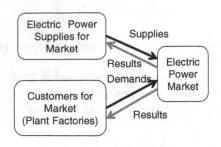

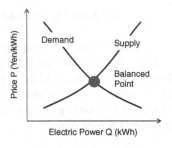

Fig. 3. Electric power market   **Fig. 4.** Market mechanisms

demands, such as Nord Pool in EU and JEPX (Japan Electric Power eXchange) in Japan [7]. Figures 3 and 4 show a structure of the electric power markets and the relationships between the balanced prices and the amount of the electric power supplied to the markets, respectively.

When the vegetables to be cultivated in the next day are fixed, the total electric power requirement is estimated and the demands to the electric power market are determined. The demand of the plant factory is sent to the market, and the market determines the amount of electric power and its price in the next day.

5 Simulation Results

One year simulations of both the factories A and B have been carried out by applying the forecasted prices and the real prices of the lettuces from January to December, 2010. As regards the electric power market, a statistical simulation model is proposed, which include 10 suppliers and 20 customers including the plant factory. The daily supplies and demands of the individual suppliers and customers are selected randomly in the simulations.

Figure 5 shows the simulation results about the profits of the plant factories A and B. The profits of both the factories depend on the market price of the lettuce. When the market price is low, the combined production of the factory B reduces the loss by producing the vegetable β. The simple production of the factory A gets the higher profit

Fig. 5. Profit of plant factory

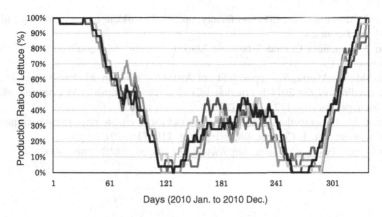

Fig. 6. Production volumes of lettuce in plant factory B

in the case of high market price. The combined production in factory B is not so efficient, if the market price is high and stable. The production volumes in factory B is summarized in Fig. 6. The percentage of the lettuce is high in the winter seasons, since the market price is high due to low temperature, as shown in Fig. 3. The simulations have been carried out for five times due to the statistical characters of the market price forecasting. The individual lines in Fig. 6 show the different simulation results, but all the tendency are almost same.

6 Conclusions

A plant factories and its production planning system are discussed in the paper. The followings are concluded.

(1) The production cost items are considered to plan and to estimate the production costs of individual piece of leaf lettuces, based on the investigations of the experimental plant factories in Osaka Prefecture University and related documents.

(2) A genetic programming (GP) based method is proposed to forecast the future prices of the lettuces, since the long lead time of 25 days are required for cultivating the lettuces.

(3) A production planning system for the plant factories is proposed to select a suitable vegetable to be cultivated in every day operations, aimed at increasing the profits and decreasing the operation costs.

References

1. Takatsuji, M.: Fully Controlled and Closed Plant Factory, pp. 63–65. Ohmsha Ltd, Tokyo (2007). (in Japanese)
2. Outline of Facilities (R&D Center for the Plant Factory). http://www.plant-factory.21c. osakafu-u.ac.jp/english/index.html

3. Takatsuji, M., Mori, Y.: LED Plant factory, pp. 10–27. Nikkan Kogyo Shimbun Ltd., Tokyo (2011). (in Japanese)
4. Tokyo Metropolitan Central Wholesale Market. http://www.shijou.metro.tokyo.jp/torihiki/. (in Japanese)
5. Shukla, M., Jharkharia, S.: Applicability of ARIMA models in wholesale vegetable market. In: Proceedings of the 2011 International Conference on Industrial Engineering and Operations Management, pp. 1125–1130 (2011)
6. Nasira, G.M., Hemageetha, A.: Forecasting model for vegetable price using back propagation neural network. Int. J. Comput. Intell. Inf. **2**(2), 110–115 (2012)
7. Japan Electric Power eXchange. http://www.jepx.org/english/aboutus/index.html

Enhancing an Integrative Course in Industrial Engineering and Management via Realistic Socio-technical Problems and Serious Game Development

Nick Szirbik[1]([⊠]), Christine Pelletier[2], and Vincent Velthuizen[3]

[1] IEM/Operations/University of Groningen, Groningen, The Netherlands
n.b.szirbik@rug.nl
[2] IBS/Hanze University of Applied Sciences, Groningen, The Netherlands
c.m.pelletier@pl.hanze.nl
[3] Trias Informatica, Groningen, The Netherlands
vincent.velthuizen@triasinformatica.nl

Abstract. This is a position paper. It discusses specific educational issues encountered during the Systems Engineering Design course at the Industrial Engineering and Management master program at the University of Groningen. It explains first the concept of an integrative course, an innovation that was applied first in this master program. It explains the causes and effects of two observed educational shortcomings of this course, and it links these to the extant literature. Finally, the paper proposes two ideas to address these shortcomings.

1 Introduction and Background

According to the current standards on engineering education [1], the courses in an engineering study program can be classified either as lecture-centric (LC), problem-based (PB or inquiry- based), project-assisted (PA), or project-centric (PC sometimes, these courses are named capstone courses). In the Industrial Engineering and Management (IEM) study program at the University of Groningen (RUG, in the Netherlands), an innovative learning paradigm has been developed and applied in the last decade: the integrative course. This kind of course is one that is placed at the end of the curriculum schedule, and requires the application of knowledge and skills learnt from the majority of the previous courses. The integrative courses are meant to apply both paradigms of problem-based learning and project-centric learning. This concept may sound similar to the capstone course [10].

Currently, at IEM, there is an accumulated experience of teaching integrative courses over the past 8 years, and there has been confirmation that the outcomes of these courses are the desired ones. The first source of confirmation has been the short-term and long-term feedback given by the graduates and alumni from the last decade. The second source was the industry, and the third source was

© IFIP International Federation for Information Processing 2015
S. Umeda et al. (Eds.): APMS 2015, Part I, IFIP AICT 459, pp. 541–548, 2015.
DOI: 10.1007/978-3-319-22756-6_66

the formal accreditation reports of the IEM program, revealing an increase in the quality of the master theses produced in the last years.

Despite the apparent success of the integrative courses revealed by these sources, the teachers who are involved in their development are aware of two major shortcomings that reduce the effectiveness of teaching in the integrative manner. The extant literature [6] and exchange of experience (via personal channels) on the subject show that these shortcomings are not unique at RUG. The first shortcoming is the lack of realism and veracity of the "problem" that is to be solved by the designs developed during the integrative study. The second shortcoming is the lack of cognitive engagement between the teams and individual students who are doing the designs for the coursework, leading to a fragmented project development, and also a lack of communication and alignment in the integrative process. Later in this paper, the authors propose two ways to mitigate these shortcomings.

In the Netherlands, the higher education in engineering is provided by some of the existing public universities. In addition to these, there are a few dozen universities of applied sciences (UAS) and offering bachelor and more recently master level programs in various engineering disciplines.

During the 1990s, two change tendencies emerged in Dutch universities. The first change was driven by the industry, which asked more vocally for engineering students with skills like team work, context and problem complexity understanding, the ability to diagnose complex problems, communicate the findings, and the preparedness to coordinate solution efforts. At its core, this request challenged the old style of "chalk and talk" (i.e. LC) teaching. The universities responded in various ways, one being by applying PB learning, and another by inviting more and more professionals as guest lecturers. It was quickly learned later that PB learning is not the single or even the best solution for engineering.

The second change was to respond to the demand of the industry for a more multi-disciplinary kind of graduate. The response was a new type of engineering study program, namely the IEM. These master degrees are supported in each of these universities by a similar bachelor study program in IEM. Students who earn a bachelor degree in Industrial Engineering from an UAS can follow a special adaptation coursework for half a year and then start one of these master studies in IEM.

These IEM programs appeared exactly when PC and PB learning started to be applied in various engineering programs universities in the world. The disciplines that can be taught in PB style are those where knowledge is rather encyclopedic and less hierarchical (that is, the order in which the concepts are learned is not so important). The emphasis in these courses is to investigate a "situation/problem", and find its causes (diagnostic). This is similar to the initial application of problem-based learning in medicine [11], and students learn and put together the pieces of knowledge along the way in finding the causes of the investigated "problem" (i.e. finding a diagnostic for it).

For those disciplines where knowledge is strictly hierarchical, the style of teaching is either PA or PC. The emphasis in PA courses is on analysis. The "problem/opportunity" that triggers the design is given by the teacher, and its causes and diagnosis are clearly established beforehand. The students have to analyse and specify requirements for a future design.

The disciplines taught in PC style, like for example software project management and control systems design (for robotics), have a strong emphasis on the design itself - the problem, stakeholders, and the requirements are mostly given beforehand by the teacher. Typically, project teams are smaller, of 3–5 students, each having a small portion of the design to tackle. Design of different teams are sometimes integrated into bigger designs, spurning collaboration between teams. Periodic presentations of the teams help that knowledge and acquired skills (and again, mistakes) are shared and discussed.

2   The Integrative Course and Its Shortcomings

At RUG, the master IEM program is ending with courses that apply an integrative approach. The emphasis is on technical integration, but both courses (the course in Systems Engineering Design and the course in Sustainable Engineering) have still a strong managerial/economic-related part.

In the integrative courses, all the learning styles (LC, PB, PA, and PC) are applied. There are plenary lectures, which present mostly examples of problems, stakeholders, requirements and design solutions. The "problem" has to be found/defined/invented by the students - with teacher's assistance. Then, students have to analyze specify the requirements of a complex and multidisciplinary system, and finally develop a conceptual design that meets the requirements and can stand a formal design assessment - an evaluation phase that is also performed by the students. Finally, the teachers role is that of the "buyers" of the design, who are involved in the design in iterative stages of its development, revealing its shortcomings, gaps, and inconsistencies.

The course Systems Engineering Design is the "oldest" integrative course in the IEM master program at RUG. Students are organized in teams of 3–4 students, and teams are organized in "triads" (three teams) of 10–13 students each. Each triad has a separate student who plays the role of system integrator. The tasks of the project are to define first - separately for each triad - a specific multi-disciplinary problem (which has to be more or less realistic), and explore the "stakeholders' " wishes. Next, the teams have to analyse and specify the requirements of a system that addresses the effects of the problem - each team in the triad specializes in a specific set of requirements. Finally, the system has to be designed in terms of a context-placed operational architecture, comprising a functional architecture described in IDEF0 and a generic physical architecture with alternatives for components and interfaces. The final deliverable is a dossier that is supposed to participate in a Request for Proposals (RfP) for such a system. The project is quite equivalent (albeit much shorter in time and smaller in scope) to the pre-inception phase [2] in a system development process.

The operational architecture has to be built by using a systems engineering CAD system (CORE^{tm}9 from the Vitech Corp.), which incorporates also requirements engineering tools. This CAD system allows for collaborative design and the integration of separate structures/interactions of functions and components that were designed by different teams. A recent example of system designed was a bio-gas producing and storage infrastructure, which was supposed to replace/upgrade an existing infrastructure for fossil gas in a clearly delimited region. Because this course runs in parallel with the Sustainable Systems course, many problems are related to environmental issues, alternative fuels, and novel energy systems.

The students are encouraged to view this course as a "serious game", where they compete to "sell" their design to the issuers of the RfP (see presentation [12]), and there is a constant competition for the best team and best triad. Moreover, the teachers (as a separate team) are developing each year a system in parallel with the students, sometimes as part of a triad with two other student teams. If a student team delivers a better project than the teachers, who get always a mark 9 (on a scale from 5 to 10), that student team gets the maximum mark. Each year, one or even two student teams manage to "beat" the teachers' team.

This course is popular with other students than the IEM master program, for whom the course is compulsory. Each year, 15–20 % of students are taking this course as elective, and they are coming from master programs like Computing Science, Energy and Environmental Science, Chemical Engineering, Economet-rics, and even Law. They bring even more disciplinary knowledge and skills into the triads, and also ways of thinking that are new for the IEM students and even the teachers. The course is highly sought by exchange students also, who are studying at RUG only for a semester. However, there are also shortcomings.

Problem-based learning assumes that the problem is real, existing in a real context. In PB courses in medicine for example, the students are given a real patient case, which they have to investigate and diagnose. In PB courses in engineering, the students go into the field (typically a company) and are given or identifying a real problem. However, due to time and resource limitations, courses that have a design project at their core, hardly can cope with overloading the coursework with a diagnostic phase. Another typical issue is that teachers that are teaching in PC style, have limited experience with the PB approach. The net result is that in PC course that starts with a "problem" that is made up, typically by the teachers, who try to communicate its details as well as they can to the students. However, the problem "exists" only in the mind of the teachers, and many times, students do not grasp or have a really good understanding what the problem really is. The single way to figure out, is to continually "interview" the teachers about the problem, but many times this can lead to even more confusion. The net effect is that students are losing interest in the problem and in the project, going out from the "immersion", "make-believe", and "flow" state that make them feel like in an engaging game.

A simple solution (applied currently in the course Systems Engineering Design) is to let the students define the problem/opportunity themselves (with some teacher feedback). They have to describe it in a scenario-like narrative, and expand the details as they go with the design. However, this approach leads to other undesired effects. The problem becomes part of the design itself, and in order to have an ele-gant and technologically interesting design, the problem is changed in ways that bend reality. Especially the quantitative aspect of the problems are suffering, and this can lead to problems that do not have a holding in physical reality, because the assumptions made lead to the violation of the laws of physics. The net effect is that students realize the lack realism of their problem at some moment, and again, they lose interest in the project overall. If they remain immersed and that happens many times, this creates an even more dangerous learning effect, because the students may remain convinced that this kind of unrealistic problems and designs exist in reality. If the students are "brought back to reality" during the final presentation or the previous feedback sessions with the teachers, this will create a sense of failure, and again, they lose interest and are not engaged anymore. These effects have been observed by other researchers who attempted to use elements of PB learning in PC settings [3, 8].

The second shortcoming is related to the design phase; after the problem, stakeholders, and requirements have been clearly established. Students working in design teams tend to divide the work in chunks that are doable by single students (using the given CAD system) and integrate this separately made work later. Except for the feedback sessions, the work does not need to be integrated, and students tend to work in isolation. This leads to fragmentation lack of focus and understanding of the system as whole - and less cognitive engagement between team members and the teams in the triad. In this phase, the students put most of the effort in mastering the CAD environment and produce the functional and physical designs. Unfortunately, this leads to less communication, low team performance, no collaboration-induced creativity, friction between team members (because they do not understand properly what the others are doing), frustration, and in the end boredom or anxiety. The "flow" mental state sought by using the serious game in the design competition is not achieved any more by some teams. There is no motivation to finish with an exciting result, and there is no intrinsic curiosity left to explore and find alternatives and new ideas for the design. Because the used CAD system is a folder and menu based system that has a graphical interface for IDEF0, the whole work seems to become 99 % mouse clicks and menu navigation, at odds with a creative process, and distracting the students from team communication and reciprocal creative thinking. This kind of effects have been observed for many years in real design projects that use CAD systems [5, 7], and it is not surprising to find these in PC courses that use CAD systems and teamwork.

An interesting finding came out last year, when members of a triad of students played a digital multi-player serious game, which was developed by the gas industry with RUG collaboration. This triad was the one that developed the bio-gas system, and it had the opportunity to visualize the system they were designing in the form of a business game, which mimicked the development of the bio-gas infrastructure, with implications to the gas markets and investments. At the end of the game, these students were interviewed to find out if the game playing helped them in the process to design their bio-gas system. The most interesting finding of these interviews was that the game actually improved communication within the triad in the "boring" design phase (the game-playing took place in the second half of the course), and helped them to keep an eye on the whole of the system, and remain engaged in achieving an satisfying result. This was in line with findings in the literature [4]. The identification and validation of these two shortcomings have been done via qualitative research: observation of how students work during tutorial classes, end-of-course survey via open-question forms, and "post-mortem" workshops with students who volunteered to participate, where various aspects of the course were discussed openly, and the findings formalized.

3   Proposed Solutions

For the first shortcoming (problem's lack or realism), the proposed solution is to have a real problem owner, and a real problem. The IEM students who are doing their master thesis in the study year that follows the Systems Engineering Design course are following a three phase curriculum: first a LC course on Research Methodology (with an emphasis on Design Science Research aspects), second a Research Project, and third a Design Project. The last two phases, or at least the last phase, take place in the context of a company, which is the problem owner for the design of the student.

When the Systems Engineering Design course starts (in April), the senior master students who are doing their master thesis project are well advanced in their track, that is, in the middle of the Design Project phase. At that moment, the problem they have to address by their design is very clear, and they started to implement the improvement, or a novel process, or a novel product, or a system that addresses this problem. There are in total 40–50 students whose thesis and design project is in this status. The idea is to recruit a number of students as teaching assistants (TAs) for the Systems Engineering course which is smaller than equal than the number of triads in course. The selection would be based on their previous performance in the course, and the nature of their design (if its scope is a complex, multi-disciplinary system, the better). These students will play the role of problem owners and main stakeholders in the design of a similar system by a triad. There is no need to have an exactly similar scope and nature of the system, but it is expected the problem owner will keep the assumptions made more realistic.

This approach is expected to be advantageous not only for the triad, which will be helped to keep the problem and the design realistic, and drive the design from the problem and not vice-versa. The problem owner student can use the triad as an exploratory design team, and apply their ideas in its own thesis work.

For the second shortcoming (fragmentation of focus during the design phase), the idea is to develop a simple board game that mimics the development of the proposed system. This idea was actually proposed by the students who played the serious game for bio-gas infrastructure. They complained that the digital game was too restrictive and impossible to adapt to their own ideas about the proposed bio-gas system. Because the game had a previous non-digital version, a board-game where game pieces mimicking the components of the system where place on a map, they argued that it would have been more interesting and useful to have a board game that was easy to change according to the changes they made in their own design. The board can be hand drawn each time the game is played, and new pieces (representing new components) can be improvised easily from old board game pieces, or even 3D printed. The rules of the game should reflect the behavior of the system and its development. The main issue with such a game is its final purpose, which is important for its developers [9]. The current view is that such a game is to be developed to allow stakeholders to play to understand better the system design, and also its potential development. The players who will play the roles initially will be students themselves, but they will design the game having in mind that the real players will be stakeholders. If a problem owner student is attached to a triad that designs a game, this student can participate as a real stakeholder, and also bring the game within the company where the real design project takes place, and engage the potential stakeholders to play the game, communicating the proposed design in a user-friendly manner.

However, the main educational purpose of the game is to prevent fragmentation and bring together the triad members in the phase when they tend to work too much in isolation. To enforce that the game is played regularly, the triad coordinator student should be tasked to organize gaming session twice per week, and have sometimes teacher participation if that is possible. For example, the last feedback session of the course should involve the teachers as players in the newly developed games.

4   Discussion and Future Work

When applying these ideas, some problems can be envisaged. For example, if there are 8–9 triads in a course, that will necessitate an early planning and strict coordination. The 8–9 appropriate problem owners within the group of senior master students have to be found before the course starts. Also, these problem owners should have design tasks, or at least contexts, that qualify as "complex system designs". The intention is that for the first year of idea's application, only a few triads (2, maximum 3) will be matched with a problem owner. At the time of writing, 2 master students who are finishing their master thesis, and a PhD student are already allocated to the role of problem owner. When the course will be taught this year, 3 triads will face a real problem from a company, and their assumptions will be "guarded" by a student tasked for this role.

For the design of the board game, expertise in game design is needed - and it is currently sought after. Initially, there will be only one triad that will attempt a board game design, and only those students who have experience and interest with games will be asked to volunteer for this triad. The intended system design for this experiment will be an electric energy storage infrastructure, modelled on the previous bio-gas infrastructure and its related board game. The teachers and the study program will invest supplementary effort and resources in this triad, and the experience will be carefully documented.

An important follow up to applying these ideas is to assess the impact of these improvements, short term and long term, and communicate the results and eventually interact with programs that have similar approaches. A related research theme is to investigate if there is an advantage in designing a serious board (+digital) game for the stakeholders in the pre-inception and inception phases of the design of real systems.

5 Conclusions

The use of serious games seems to be promising for improving the effectiveness of PC learning and integrative learning in engineering education, especially in IEM programs. For the moment, there is little experience in applying them, and quick and efficient ways to develop board games that mimic a system's development are yet to be discovered and evaluated.

References

1. ABET: Criteria for Accrediting Engineering Programs (2012). http://www.abet. org/uploadedFiles/Accreditation/Accreditation_Step_by_Step/Accreditation_ Documents/Current/2013_-_2014/eac-criteria-2013-2014.pdf
2. Buede, D.M.: The Engineering Design of Systems: Models and Methods. Wiley, New York (2009)
3. Fink, F.K.: Integration of engineering practice into curriculum 25 years of experience with problem based learning. In: ASEE/IEEE Frontiers in Education Conference, Session 11a2, 7–12 (1999). http://fie.engrng.pitt.edu/fie99
4. Honey, M.A., Hilton, M. (eds.): Learning Science Through Computer Games and Simulations. National Academies Press, Washington (2011)
5. Kosmadoudi, Z., Lim, T., Ritchie, J., Louchart, S., Liu, Y., Sung, R.: Engineering design using game-enhanced CAD: the potential to augment the user experience with game elements. J. Comput. Aided Des. **45**, 777–795 (2013). Elsevier
6. Lattuca, L.R., Terenzini, P.T., Volkwein, J.F.: Engineering change: a study of the impact of EC 2000, executive summary. ABET, Baltimore, MD (2006)
7. Luczak, H., Beitz, W., Springer, J., Langner, T.: Frictions and frustrations in creative-informatory work with CAD systems. In: Bullinger, H.-J. (ed.) Human Aspects in Computing: Design and Use of Interactive Systems and Work with Terminals. Elsevier (1991)
8. Mills, J.E., Treagust, D.F.: Is problem-based or project-based learning the answer. Eng. Educ. (4) (2003). http://www.aaee.com.au/journal/2003/mills_treagust03. pdf
9. Pasin, F., Giroux, H.: The impact of a simulation game on operations management education. Comput. Educ. **57**, 1240–1254 (2011)
10. Paulik, M.J., Krishnan, M.: BA competition-motivated capstone design course: the result of a fifteen-year evolution. IEEE Trans. Educ. **44**(1), 67–75 (2001)
11. Smith, K.A.: Inquiry and cooperative learning in the laboratory. In: Proceedings of the ABET/Sloan Conference on Distance Learn. Practice Oriented Professions (2002)
12. Szirbik, N.: Experiencing the systems engineering process as a serious game. Presentation at the CORE-users Conference, Washington, DC (2013). Available as video at https://www.youtube.com/watch?v=0C-mMIrxqyA

Performing Supply Chain Design in Three-Dimensional Concurrent Engineering: Requirements and Challenges

Ottar Bakås[✉], Kristoffer Magerøy, Børge Sjøbakk,
and Maria Kollberg Thomassen

Industrial Management, SINTEF Technology and Society, Trondheim, Norway
{ottar.bakas,kristoffer.mageroy,borge.sjobakk,
maria.kollberg.thomassen}@sintef.no

Abstract. Designing the supply chain at the same time as developing new innovative products and efficient production processes holds the potential of being a source of competitiveness for a pressured manufacturing industry. This paper studies actors that influence the practices of three dimensional concurrent engineering (3DCE). Developing product, process and supply chain in parallel requires considerable cross-functional coordination and strong supplier involvement. A single case study of a large manufacturer of security products and systems was applied to explore current practices in an ongoing new product development (NPD) project. Five key challenges were found as barriers to performing supply chain design within this complex collaborative effort. Also, five requirements are suggested as enablers to organizations that aim for reaping the benefits of integrating supply chain design in their development process. By understanding the retirements and challenges of this process, the potential of 3DCE can be released and create value for practitioners in industry.

Keywords: Three dimensional concurrent engineering · 3DCE · New product development · Supplier involvement · Supply chain design · Case study

1 Introduction

Norwegian manufacturing firms experience intensified global competition from companies located in low-cost countries. Instead of competing only on price, many companies focus on developing advanced product and services that provide a premium value to their customers and users. In order to stay on top of the innovation cycle, managing new product development (NPD) processes becomes critical [1, 2]. Concurrent engineering of both product and process have been one response in order to make sure that product is meeting the customer needs and at the same time enable design for manufacturing. Shorter product life cycles, together with increased demand heterogeneity and the creation of several niche markets, are forcing many companies to respond faster, provide higher degree of customization and reduce their time-to-market [3]. Achieving this requires stronger collaboration with suppliers and partners in the supply chain. These developments imply the need to go beyond the scope of concurrent engineering which include product and process design. Fine [4] named this expansion

© IFIP International Federation for Information Processing 2015
S. Umeda et al. (Eds.): APMS 2015, Part I, IFIP AICT 459, pp. 549–557, 2015.
DOI: 10.1007/978-3-319-22756-6_67

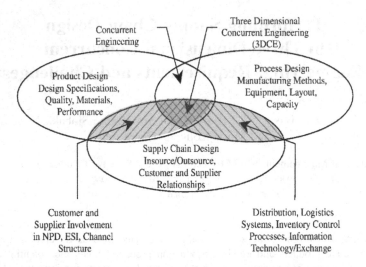

Fig. 1. Scope of paper within 3DCE. Source: Ellram et al. [5], modified from Fine, 1998, p. 146 [4].

three-dimensional concurrent engineering (3DCE) and defined it as *"...the simultaneous development of product, process and supply chain"* (Fig. 1).

Despite a significantly growing interest in 3DCE, there is limited empirical evidence on current practices and experiences. While conceptual benefits and opportunities are well described [4–6], few researchers have addressed issues with such approaches, especially from a supply chain practices perspective. Ellram et al. [5] argue that while the answers to these procedural issues are fairly straightforward and common sense, it is their execution that creates a challenge. Similarly, van Hoek and Chapman [7] call for research that study the early efforts to leverage supply chain capability as part of the product development team in practice. Hence, the purpose of this paper is to present empirical findings from an on-going NPD project utilizing the ideas of 3DCE. The objective is to understand requirements and challenges related to performing 3DCE in practice. The study starts with an assessment of existing literature on the topic, and then uses empirical data from an on-going case to verify, modify and expand these factors in a summarizing framework.

2   Requirements and Challenges Addressed in Literature

Concurrent engineering calls for significant cross-functional coordination. Adding the dimension of supply chain design in a 3DCE approach strengthens the need for external collaboration through supplier involvement. In the following section, requirements and challenges of 3DC will be presented, focusing on the intersections between product-supply and process-supply areas.

Early consideration of the supply chain perspective in the product development process is critical [6, 8]. van Hoek and Chapman [8] argue that the need for NPD and supply chain to align is only increasing, and that supply chain management should be included from the beginning with the same level of authority as product and process development. Supply chain management should no longer need to clean up after NPD. Ellram et al. [5] argue that top management support and involvement of functional leadership would likely be necessary in order to orchestrate such coordination. Issues that need to be addressed in parallel are: efficient flow of new products, ramp-up of supply chain activities such as sourcing, manufacturing and distribution, as well as other related activities supporting the commercialization of the product [6]. van Hoek and Chapman [7] have developed a model showing this evolution from a situation where alignment is limited to the final stages of NPD, to a situation where new products are seen as a joint mission for supply chain and product development (Fig. 2). Consequently the focus shifts from product availability, further through increased coordination and efficiency, and finally a focus at leveraging the supply chain capabilities to help drive revenue and market impact.

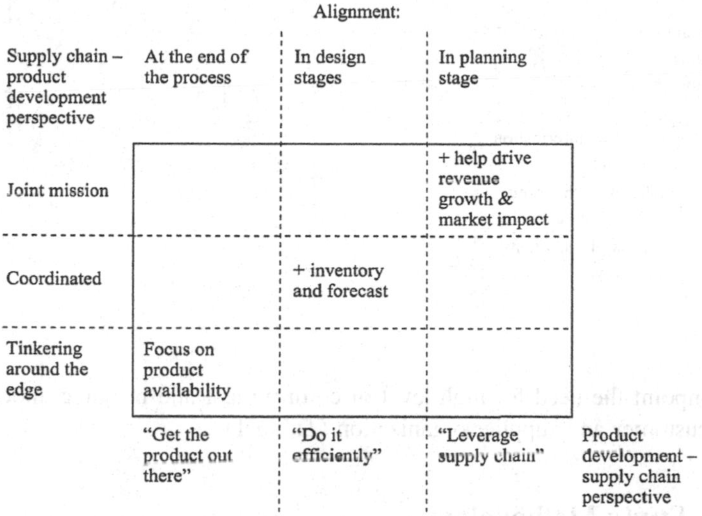

Alignment:

Supply chain – product development perspective	At the end of the process	In design stages	In planning stage
Joint mission			+ help drive revenue growth & market impact
Coordinated		+ inventory and forecast	
Tinkering around the edge	Focus on product availability		
	"Get the product out there"	"Do it efficiently"	"Leverage supply chain"

Product development – supply chain perspective

Fig. 2. Aligning product development and supply chain [7].

Achieving early supplier involvement (ESI) can provide benefits of improved product quality, increased manufacturability, reduced time-to-market and development costs and decreased product cost [9]. Further, it also provide strategic benefits at the organizational level such as learning effects, access to new capabilities and insights into future directions for supplier product range [9]. On the other side, disadvantages and challenges are found to be risk of leaking important information and knowledge [10], risk of being stuck with wrong partner or technology [11], loss of bargaining power [9], and uncertainty related to suppliers competence and motivation [11]. To really leverage the opportunities created by supplier involvement, Christopher [12] highlights three important prerequisites: (1) a rationalized supplier base, (2) a high level of shared information and (3) the need for multiple, collaborative working relationships across the organizations at all levels. A view that is supported by McIvor and Humphreys [13]

Table 1. Summary of factors affecting the integration of supply chain design in 3DCE

Prerequisites for coordination and execution of 3DCE	Challenges with performing 3DCE	Ellram et al. [5]	Cousins et al. [9]	Gadde and Snehota [10]	von Corswant and Tunälv [11]	Christopher [12]	McIvor and Humphreys [13]
Involvement of top management and functional leadership		x					
Rationalized supplier base						x	
Wide information sharing						x	
Resource allocation and collaboration on multiple levels						x	x
	Risk of information leaks		x				
	Stuck with wrong partner/technology				x		
	Loss of bargaining power		x				

as they pinpoint the need for high level of commitment and resource allocation from both the customer and supplier organization (Table 1).

3 Case Study Methodology

A case study approach is adopted to investigate challenges experienced in a company that is about to adopt a 3DCE process to improve their new product development practices. When the research is of an exploratory nature and the researchers investigate contemporary events, Yin [14] proposes a case study research method. The research was designed as a single case study in order to be able to understand the complex nature of the three-dimensional concurrent engineering in a NPD-project with a planned time line of about 24 months.

An instrumental case study provides insight into a particular issue, redraw generalizations, or build theory [15]. The purpose here is to provide insight into practical experiences with operating NPD project based on the principles of 3DCE.

As with most instrumental case studies, the research team wanted to provide insight into the issue of requirement and challenges of 3DCE by building on existing theory and comparing this with experiences from the field. Findings from the empirical investigation are compared with literature to bring further detail and structure to current issues.

Data is collected through workshops, interviews, and meetings with representatives of the case company. The data material currently contains transcripts from 9 interviews with managers from all involved departments in their development process and participation in 9 monthly meetings in a cross-functional development team. Document studied includes strategy documents, plans, organizational descriptions, policies and procedures and KPI data.

The case company is a large-sized manufacturer of safety and surveillance solutions with almost 400 employees globally and headquarters in Norway. They produce equipment and systems for securing assets and personnel used within multiple industries, such as construction, maritime, and oil and gas. They have a wide range of products within their portfolio. The case study on 3DCE is related to development of a new generation of one of their core high-volume products.

4 Results and Discussion

4.1 Challenges with Integrating Supply Chain Design in 3DCE

The issue of *supplier involvement* created much debate in the case company. There were much discussions about whether to involve a supplier of the core material of the product directly into the development project team. And if so, which supplier should be selected? The company had a long standing relationship with supplier A, and had only recently started to purchase some parts from supplier B. Supplier A was initially suggested due their long common history. The purchasing department had recently identified that supplier B had more advanced production technology. Supplier B were perceived to be more flexible and willing to adapt, and was finally chosen in the team.

Even though supplier B had provided important knowledge on product materials and insights on manufacturability, there has been one identified challenge in this close supplier involvement. There is a tendency that the supplier is answering 'yes' to most questions on whether a specific feature or process will be possible for the new product. This inherent optimism might be explained by a fear of losing the long-term production contract in the next phase of the project. It might also be explained by the fact that the supplier's sales department has been the main contact point, and little collaboration has included other functions.

For the second core component in the product, a supplier was not invited to join the development project. The team feared a situation of "supplier lock-in", and wanted to have the opportunity to perform a price competition on the developed component between multiple potential suppliers, without having too strong ties with one single producer.

Within issues of *cross-functional coordination*, the decision making process was found to be challenging by the case company. Three-dimensional concurrent engineering inherently expands the numbers of objectives for the project: marked requirements on features, design for manufacturing and logistical requirements all impose a set of requirements for the end product. In many cases, these objectives are conflicting. In this case, the market wanted to have numerous product variants in order to manage pricing mechanisms across multiple industries, whereas the supply chain perspective calls for having fewer set of variants to keep in stock in many storage locations across the globe. Further, single decision variables were found to influences the solution space significantly on other product components. It is found challenging to design organizational routines and procedures that secure sufficient involvement of multiple stakeholders into these complex discussions.

Further, the project mandate was found to be an important factor for the coordination processes. The case data suggest that differentiated understanding of mandate and roles in the development process is a challenging factor. The case data also suggest that the role of top management is central and underutilized in the development process. Last, the lack of a specific supply chain role in the organization can lead to issues of souring, production and distribution is not as clearly represented in the discussions on central decisions for the product design. The project is organized under the technology/R&D unit of the organization, and operations departments are under-represented in the team.

4.2   Requirements for Integrating Supply Chain Design in 3DCE

The following factors were found in the case data to represent important prerequisites for integrating supply chain topics in the development process:

- Clarified key decision points in the process. The case company is applying a product road map following the stage-gate models, with 5 main decision points with their separate review boards. Production and supplier processes are described in the road map.
- Core suppliers must be involved from early on. Their motivation might depend on their contractual situation with the core company, whether they are paid for their work in the development process, or they are secured a minimum volume of production in the operational phase.
- A clear mandate that is communicated to all parties.
- Involvement of top management and all relevant functional units, with fixed meeting intervals. The company are using cross-functional teams to coordinate across functions, units and locations.

4.3   Framework

The findings of the case have made us able to propose a framework for requirements and challenges of integrating supply chain design in three-dimensional concurrent engineering (Table 2).

Table 2. Framework for performing supply chain design in 3DCE

Influencing factors:	Requirements (R)	Challenges (C)	Found in literature	Supported in case
1. Involvement of top management and functional leadership	R		x	x
2. Rationalized supplier base	R		x	Inconclusive
3. Wide information sharing	R		x	
4. Resource allocation and collaboration on multiple levels	R		x	x
5. Clear mandate communicated to all	R			x
1. Risk of information leaks		C	x	
2. Fear of being stuck with wrong partner/technology		C	x	x
3. Loss of bargaining power		C	x	x
4. Unclear and complex decisions making process		C		x
5. Lack of supply chain role: voice of logistics in team		C		x

5   Conclusion

The framework in Table 2 emphasizes five key requirements and challenges of achieving true integration of supply chain design in three-dimensional concurrent engineering. These five factors can serve as an important guideline with DOs and DON'Ts for managers and project managers in concurrent engineering projects.

For the case company, three specific advantages have been identified from applying the principles of 3DCE:

1. Selection of more proper components. Experiences from previous NPD projects within the case company show that components have been included in the product design, where the timeline for 'last-buy' from supplier had passed, making the availability of product components challenging and more costly.

2. Increased focus on product variants and customer-order decoupling point. A maturity level of understanding of the consequences of high number of product variants for supply chain control can be observed.
3. Selection of right suppliers as partners. Increased collaboration on supplier selection has given the company access to new capabilities and competence that it did not have available previously.

We call for further research on validation of the framework with more empirical data in a multiple case study in different industry sectors. Another interesting line of research will be to investigate how principles of three-dimensional concurrent engineering can be applied in small and medium-sized enterprises, where access to resources is lower.

Designing the supply chain at the same time as developing new products and efficient production processes holds the potential of being a source of competitiveness for a pressured manufacturing industry by contributing to reduced cost and time-to-market. The effect of working concurrently with products, process and supply chain needs to be examined further with additional empirical studies.

References

1. Carrillo, J.E., Franza, R.M.: Investing in product development and production capabilities: the crucial linkage between time-to-market and ramp-up time. Eur. J. Oper. Res. **171**(2), 536–556 (2006)
2. Fine, C.H.: Clockspeed-based strategies for supply chain design. Prod. Oper. Manage. **9**(3), 213–221 (2000)
3. Fixson, S.K.: Product architecture assessment: a tool to link product, process, and supply chain design decisions. J. Oper. Manage. **23**(3–4), 345–369 (2005)
4. Fine, C.H.: Clockspeed: Winning Industry Control in the Age of Temporary Advantage. Basic Books, New York (1998)
5. Ellram, L.M., Tate, W.L., Carter, C.R.: Product-process-supply chain: an integrative approach to three-dimensional concurrent engineering. Int. J. Phys. Distrib. Logistics Manage. **37**(4), 305–330 (2007)
6. Hilletofth, P., Eriksson, D.: Coordinating new product development with supply chain management. Ind. Manage. Data Syst. **111**(2), 264–281 (2011)
7. van Hoek, R., Chapman, P.: From tinkering around the edge to enhancing revenue growth: supply chain-new product development. Supply Chain Manage. Int. J. **11**(5), 385–389 (2006)
8. van Hoek, R., Chapman, P.: How to move supply chain beyond cleaning up after new product development. Supply Chain Manage. Int. J. **12**(4), 239–244 (2007)
9. Cousins, P., et al.: Strategic Supply Management: Principles Theories and Practice. Person Education, Harlow (2008)
10. Gadde, L.-E., Snehota, I.: Making the most of supplier relationships. Ind. Mark. Manage. **29**(4), 305–316 (2000)
11. von Corswant, F., Tunälv, C.: Coordinating customers and proactive suppliers: a case study of supplier collaboration in product development. J. Eng. Tech. Manage. **19**(3–4), 249–261 (2002)

12. Christopher, M.: The agile supply chain: competing in volatile markets. Ind. Mark. Manage. **29**(1), 37–44 (2000)
13. McIvor, R., Humphreys, P.: Early supplier involvement in the design process: lessons from the electronics industry. Omega **32**(3), 179–199 (2004)
14. Yin, R.K.: Case Study Research: Design and Methods. Sage Publications, Inc., Thousand Oaks (2009)
15. Stake, R.E.: Multiple Case Study Analysis. The Guilford Press, New York (2006)

Learning Evaluation Using Non-classical Logics

Genivaldo Carlos Silva$^{(\boxtimes)}$ and Jair Minoro Abe

Graduate Program in Production Engineering, Paulista University,
Rua Dr. Bacelar 1212, 04026-002 São Paulo, SP, Brazil
gcsilva@ig.com.br, jairabe@uol.com.br

Abstract. Among the various existing methods used in teachers' evaluation, one of the most used is the survey of the students themselves. This method may have incomplete (paracompleteness), conflicting or inaccurate results as they often deal often with subjective and contradictory opinions. This work presents a case study using a non-classical logic, to analyze these conflicting views. The Paraconsistent Annotated Evidential Eτ Logic proves to be helpful in the analysis of these data types in order to see more clearly the items that should be improved.

Keywords: Paraconsistency · Non-classic logics · Teacher evaluation

1 Introduction

Several countries have intensely discussed more efficient ways to analyze the performance of teachers in an institution so they can provide the best possible learning to their students.

According to Derrington [1] the function of the director of the institution remains a key component in the evaluation of teachers, but a more comprehensive evaluation model incorporating a greater body of evidence will produce a more accurate view of teachers' skills. There are many other methods, including the self-reflection of teachers, student performance data and feedback from students. Concerning on feedback from students, one of the methods is the survey of the opinions themselves.

This research is a case study that uses a mathematical approach by evidential Eτ paraconsistent logic, applied to the analysis of the results of research conducted with students in teachers' evaluation. It is expected, in this research, that the results obtained can give a clearer view of the relevance of the analyzed items, as well as its importance in the general context of assessment, showing those items that need to be improved.

2 Background

Abrami [2] shows that this model should not only include the evaluation of all teacher assignments, but also incorporate the socioeconomic and cultural context in which the professional works.

© IFIP International Federation for Information Processing 2015
S. Umeda et al. (Eds.): APMS 2015, Part I, IFIP AICT 459, pp. 558–564, 2015.
DOI: 10.1007/978-3-319-22756-6_68

Fenwick [3] discusses the process, often difficult to assess the effectiveness of teaching in terms of student learning outcomes and suggests approaches to micro and macro level evaluation of teachers using student outcomes.

According to LaFee [4], students are very close to their teachers and are in a good position to assess their activities in room and know what works or not in their learning. According to Ferguson [5] even in developed countries like the USA, the school system is developed in some respects and underdeveloped in others. The main reasons for this underdevelopment are structural gaps and systemic inefficiencies in the education system to prepare young people for employment.

Rosenshine and Furst [6] identified some factors that influence learning, such as clarity, teacher orientation tasks, student involvement, among others.

The project "The Measure of Effective Teaching [7] - founded by the Bill & Melinda Gates - studying methods that provide a more effective learning and among the elements used in the project is a survey of a dozen thousands of students who answer questions about their experiences on education. The results of the survey were used as one of the evaluation tools and feedback to teachers. However, this method may have incomplete, conflicting and inaccurate data, and risk evaluate metrics that have little to do with the really important behaviors of teachers face to educational goals due to because it is subjective opinions. DE MELO [8].

Abe [9] presents some aspects of paraconsistent systems and its applications in various fields.

2.1 Paraconsistent, Paracomplete and Non-alethic Logics

In what follows, we sketch the non-classical logics discussed in the paper, establishing some conventions and definitions. Let T be a theory whose underlying logic is L. T is called inconsistent when it contains theorems of the form A and $\neg A$ (the negation of A). If T is not inconsistent, it is called *consistent*. T is said to be *trivial* if all formulas of the language of T are also theorems of T. Otherwise, T is called *non-trivial*.

When L is classical logic (or one of several others, such as intuitionistic logic), T is inconsistent if T is trivial. So, in trivial theories the extensions of the concepts of formula and theorem coincide. A *paraconsistent logic* is a logic that can be used as the basis for inconsistent but non-trivial theories.

A *theory* is called *paraconsistent* if its underlying logic is a paraconsistent logic. Many logicians have appreciated issues such as those described above. In 1910, the Russian logician Nikolaj A. Vasil'év (1880–1940) and the Polish logician Jan Lukasiewicz (1878–1956) independently glimpsed the possibility of developing such logics. Nevertheless, Stanislaw Jaskowski (1996–1965) was in 1948 effectively the first logician to develop a paraconsistent system, at the propositional level.

His system is known as 'discussive' (or discursive) propositional calculus. Independently, some years later, the Brazilian logician Newton C.A. da Costa (1929-) constructed for the first time hierarchies of paraconsistent propositional calculi C_i, $1 \leq i \leq \omega$

of paraconsistent first-order predicate calculi (with and without equality), of paraconsistent description calculi, and paraconsistent higher-order logics (systems $NF_i, 1 \leq i \leq \omega$).
Another important class of non-classical logics are the paracomplete logics.

A logical system is called *paracomplete* if it can function as the underlying logic of
theories in which there are formulas such that these formulas and their negations are
simultaneously false. Intuitionistic logic and several systems of many-valued logics are
paracomplete in this sense (and the dual of intuitionistic logic, Brouwerian logic, is
therefore paraconsistent).

Consequently, paraconsistent theories do not satisfy the principle of non-
contradiction, which can be stated as follows: of two contradictory propositions, i.e.
one of which is the negation of the other, one must be false. In addition, paracomplete
theories do not satisfy the principle of the excluded middle, formulated in the following
form: of two contradictory propositions, one must be true. Finally, logics that are
simultaneously paraconsistent and paracomplete are called *non-alethic logics*.

3 Methodology

According to Rosenshine and Furst [6] and the report Student Perception Surveys
and Their Implementation [7], a set of factors (Sn) was extracted, which constituted
the research with students. The factors chosen were Attention, Control, Plainness,
Knowledge, Magnetism, Checking and Reinforcement. Each factor has five statements,
which shall be assigned grades from 0 to 10 for both possibilities, "Acceptance" and

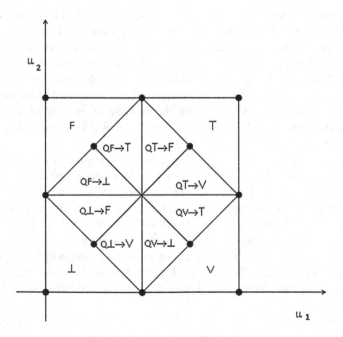

Fig. 1. Paraconsistent logic states

"Rejection", representing respectively the Belief and Disbelief levels for each statement. The results were analyzed according to Paraconsistent Logic Annotated Evidential Eτ and presented in graphs using the paraanalizer algorithm according Da Silva Filho [10] and compared according to Fig. 1.

Where:

Falsity	F
Truth	V
Inconsistency	T
Paracompleteness	⊥
Quasi-falsity tending to paracompleteness	QF → ⊥
Quasi-falsity tending to inconsistency	QF → T
Quasi-paracompleteness tending to falsity	Q⊥ → F
Quasi-paracompleteness tendendo truth	Q⊥ → V
Quasi-inconsistency tending to truth	QT → V
Quasi-inconsistency tending to falsity	QT → F
Quasi-truth tending to paracompleteness	QV → ⊥
Quasi-truth tending to inconsistency	QV → T

Figure 2 shows the table with the data for the operational research group, with the same methodology used for B and C groups.

3.1 Data Analysis

In Fig. 3, we have the result of the paraanalyzer algorithm analysis that shows that factors S1, S3 and S6 Attention - Plainness - Checking respectively, are considered viable, which means that they have been evaluated and do not require improvements.

On the other hand, we see that the factors S2, S4, S5 and S7 were considered inconclusive, it means, the information is not enough to lead to a decision on the items evaluated and eventually would require some improvement to achieve better evaluation levels.

4 Outcomes of Logic Eτ

Figure 4 shows the result of global analysis, located on the near Quasi-truth tending to inconsistency area in the Square Unit of the Cartesian plan (SUCP), which indicates that some factors need to be improved in order to have a better assessment of the teacher.

PERFORMANCE EVALUATION SURVEY						
Group:		GROUP A				
Experts:		1		2		3
Statements		Acept	Rejc.	Acept	Rejc.	Acept	Rejc.
Attention							
S1	My teacher treats me with attention when I need help.	9	1	7	5	9	1
	My teacher is nice when I ask questions.	7	1	7	6	1	0
	My teacher makes me feel that he really cares about me.	8	1	7	5	9	1
	My teacher encourages me to do my best.	9	0	7	5	9	0
	My teacher gives us time to explain our ideas.	7	0	5	5	6	2
Control							
S2	My colleagues behave the way my teacher wants.	6	2	3	8	5	7
	Our class stays busy and does not waste time with useless.	6	1	4	7	4	8
	The behavior of students in the class affects our learning.	7	0	8	2	6	10
	Behavior of students in class are the teacher annoyed.	6	2	5	6	5	6
	Students of class treat the teacher with respect.	6	6	9	9	10	2
Plainness							
S3	In class, we learn to correct our mistakes.	7	1	6	3	8	1
	My teacher explains things clearly.	8	0	3	6	9	2
	I understand that I will be learning in this class.	6	2	6	4	7	1
	My teacher knows when the class understand or not a subject.	7	1	6	4	9	0
	If do not understand something, my teacher explain otherwise.	7	1	5	4	8	1
Knowledge							
S4	My teacher encourages us the read.	10	0	5	6	10	0
	My teacher encourages the class to study.	8	1	8	6	8	1
	My teacher encourages research.	8	1	7	6	10	0
	My teacher asks students to better explain they give.	2	2	7	0	7	4
	I think the lesson we learn more every day.	2	10	6	0	8	1
Magnetism							
S5	My teacher takes work to home.	7	1	6	5	7	1
	Homework help me learn.	7	1	6	5	8	0
	This class does not keep my attention and I get bored.	9	0	6	5	9	0
	My teacher makes learning enjoyable.	4	8	7	7	5	6
	My teacher makes the lessons are interesting.	6	6	9	0	8	1
Checking							
S6	My teacher, while teaching, asks us if we inderstand.	8	1	7	6	9	0
	My teacher asks questions to make sure we are following.	7	0	6	5	8	0
	My teacher tell us what we are learning and why.	7	1	6	4	9	0
	My teacher encourages us to share our knowledge.	7	1	5	5	9	0
	Students speak and share their ideas on the work of the class.	8	1	7	4	10	0
Reinforcement							
S7	My teacher takes the time to summarize what we learn every day.	6	1	4	8	6	2
	When my teacher takes a job, he explains it to help me understand.	7	1	4	8	7	1
	We received comments on activities to see where mistakes.	0	9	10	0	6	1
	The comments I receive help me understand how to improve.	0	9	10	0	7	3

Fig. 2. Operational research data - Group A

Number of factors chosen >					7	
	A AND B AND C		Level requirement		0,550	
			Conclusions			
Factor	Band	μ_{1R}	μ_{2R}	Bel Deg	Disb Deg	Decision
S01	F1	0,90	0,20	0,70	0,10	VIABLE
S02	F1	0,60	0,60	0,00	0,20	NOT CONCLUSIV
S03	F1	0,80	0,20	0,60	0,00	VIABLE
S04	F1	0,90	0,60	0,30	0,50	NOT CONCLUSIV
S05	F1	0,70	0,20	0,50	-0,10	NOT CONCLUSIV
S06	F1	0,90	0,20	0,70	0,10	VIABLE
S07	F1	0,70	0,30	0,40	0,00	NOT CONCLUSIV
global analysis		0,79	0,33	0,46	0,11	NOT CONCLUSIV
	Global Point					

Fig. 3. Features analysis table

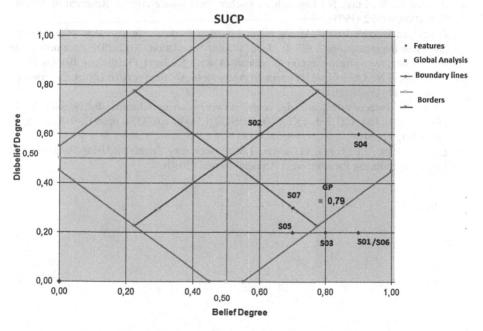

Fig. 4. Features analysis with logic states graphic

5   Conclusion

The study achieved its goal in order to provide a tool to assess a group opinion. They may be contradictory, considering the weight of each opinion from the many experts, which in this case study are students of an institution. With this tool it is possible to identify features that can and should be improved.

This analysis can also be applied in all types of educational institutions and companies in which they have conflicting information for decision-making.

References

1. Derrington, M.L.: Changes in teacher evaluation: implications for the principal's work. Delta Kappa Gamma Bulletin. **77**, 51–54 (2011)
2. Abrami, P.C.: How should we use student ratings to evaluate teaching? Res. High. Educ. **30**, 221–227 (1989)
3. Fenwick, T.J.: Using student outcomes to evaluate teaching: a cautious exploration. N. Dir. Teach. Learn. **2001**, 63–74 (2001)
4. LaFee, S.: Students Evaluating Teachers. Education Digest. **80**, 4–10 (2014)
5. Ferguson, R.F., Danielson, C.: How framework for teaching and tripod 7Cs evidence distinguish key components of effective teaching. In: Designing Teacher Evaluation Systems: New Guidance from the Measures of Effective Teaching Project (2014)
6. Rosenshine, B., Furst, N.: Research on teacher performance criteria. Research in Teacher Education, 37–72 (1971)
7. Policy and Practice Brief: "Asking about Teaching Students, Student Perception Surveys and Their Implementation", Bill & Melinda Gates Foundation, 2012; PDF document at the address http://www.metproject.org/downloads/Asking_Students_Practitioner_Brief.pdf
8. De Mello, G.N.: Observação da interação professor-aluno: uma revisão crítica. Cadernos de Pesquisa. **12**, 19–28 (2013)
9. Abe, J.M.: Paraconsistent artificial neural networks: an introduction. In: Negoita, M.G., Howlett, R.J., Jain, L.C. (eds.) KES 2004. LNCS (LNAI), vol. 3214, pp. 942–948. Springer, Heidelberg (2004)
10. Da Silva Filho, J.I., Torres, G.L., Abe, J.M.: Uncertainty Treatment Using Paraconsistent Logic - Introducing Paraconsistent Artificial Neural (2010)

Scrum as Method for Agile Project Management Outside of the Product Development Area

Ronny Weinreich[1](✉), Norbert Neumann[1], Ralph Riedel[2], and Egon Müller[2]

[1] Robert Bosch GmbH, Central Purchasing Automotive 5 (CP/AB5),
Im Birkenwald 32-46, 70435 Stuttgart, Germany
{ronny.weinreich, norbert.neumann}@de.bosch.com
[2] Department of Factory Planning and Factory Management,
Technische Universität Chemnitz, Erfenschlager Straße 73,
09125 Chemnitz, Germany
{ralph.riedel, egon.mueller}@mb.tu-chemnitz.de

Abstract. In recent years Agile Project Management (APM) and especially the Scrum framework have grown in popularity in order to deal with "vuca" business environments. Scrum has become more and more common practice in software development and has already been tested in a few hardware domains. But is it also applicable outside the development area? The paper aims to show potentials and limitations in the use of Scrum in a purchasing environment and describes implemented customizations.

Keywords: Agile project management · Scrum · Case-study · Non-development · Purchasing

1 Introduction

Present business environment became "vuca", which means companies have to face an increasing volatility, uncertainty, complexity and ambiguity [1]. To deal effectively with these challenges they need to develop certain capabilities. In recent literature agility is frequently mentioned, while the concept itself is defined very heterogeneously and comprises many sub-disciplines [2]. Agile Project Management (APM) as one of them seems to provide successful approaches [3].

Relevant experience issues mainly from software development and rarely from hardware development [3]. Outside the product development there are only scattered papers which address the potential of agile approaches, e.g. in the field of factory planning [4] or sales [5]. For this reason the paper tries to figure out potentials and limitations for APM outside of the product development area based on a case-study in a purchasing environment.

Therefore the article presents some theoretical basics on Agile Project Management and Scrum followed by a comparison of differences between the fields of product development and non-development. Thereafter the research methodology is described

© IFIP International Federation for Information Processing 2015
S. Umeda et al. (Eds.): APMS 2015, Part I, IFIP AICT 459, pp. 565–572, 2015.
DOI: 10.1007/978-3-319-22756-6_69

as well as the analyzed case. Finally the paper concludes with the evaluation and discussion of the results and an outlook on future research intentions.

2   Theoretical Background and Research Methodology

2.1   Agile Project Management

The need for APM as well as its ideas, concepts and methods originated from the field of software development [3]. Its success story began after the articulation of the agile manifesto [6], which brought high attention to the field [7]. APM is based on the principles of agile manufacturing and lean management.

The most common method in APM is Scrum (see Sect. 2.2), followed by Kanban and several methods, which are mainly focused on software development. A broad field of hybrid or customized solutions exists besides these stand-alone methods. The field where APM is most common is software development. Other domains where APM has already been adopted are (hardware) product development and process optimization [8, 9].

2.2   Scrum

In the field of project management the term "Scrum", which is originally a formation in rugby sports, was at first mentioned in 1986 in an article of Takeuchi and Nonaka. They describe self-organized and "multilearning" project teams which work cross-functional and subtly controlled in overlapping development phases [10]. Sutherland and Schwaber took these findings and the term "Scrum" and developed in the early 1990s the today known framework, which was first presented in 1995 [11].

Scrum is defined as "a framework within which people can address complex adaptive problems, while productively and creatively delivering products of the highest possible value" [12, p. 3]. The underlying principles are transparency, inspection and adaption, which are be followed by using a special iterative process (see Fig. 1), a special role model (see Table 1) and a number of artifacts [12]. Most of these artifacts are not defined by the framework itself but are good practices in the field of APM.

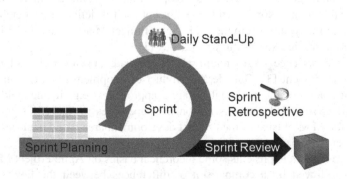

Fig. 1. Events during a sprint within the Scrum framework

Table 1. Roles and their responsibilities within the Scrum framework

Role within Scrum	Responsibilities
Scrum master	Facilitator of team and product owner; maintains motivation and self-organization of the team; moderator of the daily stand-up and the sprint retrospective
Product owner	Interface to all customers and stakeholders; prioritizes the back log items in order to maximize the value of team results; moderator of sprint planning and sprint review
Development team	Self-organization and continuous improvement of productivity; works on back log items to deliver value to the customer; responsible to fulfill product owner's requirements

Examples are the use of (kanban-) taskboards, pair working or the use of estimation techniques like planning poker [13, p. 24].

Moreover, Scrum requires an agile culture, which focuses on collaboration and creation while hierarchy and competition step back. The structural elements of Scrum support this. It could be noticed that these values are partially contrary to those of hierarchical organizations. As a consequence the implementation of Scrum requires many changes in the field of management [11].

2.3 Development of Social Systems

In order to show commonalities and differences between possible areas for the application of APM it seems to be worthwhile to analyze the systems they work with. Therefore Table 2 shows a number of attributes, adopted from systems theory [14].

As purchasing builds up the interface to other companies (suppliers) the authors interpret it as an area for social systems development.

Table 2. Comparison of development areas

Attributes	Software development	Hardware development	Social Systems development
Elements	Data	Data; physical objects	People
Relations	Technical interplay	Technical interplay	Communication
Dynamics	Non-emergent	Non-emergent	Emergent
Behavior	Complicated; deterministic or stochastic;	Complicated; deterministic or stochastic;	Complex; contingently
Testing and results	Directly testable; direct result	Simulated or prototyped; direct result	Simulated or direct; delayed results
Memory	Amnesic or resettable	Resettable or replaceable	Reminding; existing path dependence

Especially the differences in terms of system behavior and testing possibilities lead to the question, how these special circumstances affect the application of Scrum and which necessities for customizations can be derived from that.

2.4 Research Methodology

Due to the explorative and primarily qualitative character of the research question a case study approach was first chosen as suitable research methodology. A case study can be described as the "detailed examination of a single example of a class of phenomena" [15, p. 34]. In the current stage of research this approach is useful to first provide hypotheses, which can be tested systematically later on with a broader empirical basis [16].

A case study research design has the following components shown in Table 3 [17, 18] with its equivalents in our particular case.

Table 3. Research design

Component	Equivalents
The study's questions	Is it possible to apply SCRUM successfully in non-development domains and in living systems as organizations? What phenomena result from the particular domain of application?
The study's propositions	SCRUM as an agile project management method is applicable in non-development domains and it leads to better, faster, more goal-oriented, more focused, more flexible and more creative problem solving processes The non-development domain leads to some particularities
The study's units of analysis	One concrete case in the purchasing department of a big automotive supplier with several events (on-site-training, CSM-workshop, daily stand-ups, sprint plannings and review, retrospectives) and project team members, the team coach, the product owner. Information was gathered from interviews, document analysis and participatory observation
The logic of linking the data to the propositions	Conclusions build on a qualitative analysis of documents, interviews and observations, including a classification scheme and qualitative variables
The criteria for interpreting findings	History of events; time effects, accumulations of particular conditions; correlations with specific roles, environmental impacts etc.; outcomes of the project; opinions, emotions, satisfaction of the participants

The case study itself can be seen as embedded in a superordinated cycle of action research because the research itself is participative, i.e. the researcher is more or less part of the team, as well as problem-identification, planning, action and evaluation are interlinked [19]. The knowledge created in the research process is to be fed back in the system to improve the system's resp. the agile project's processes and outcomes [20].

3   Case Study Analysis

3.1   Case Description

The analyzed case was a single project in a loss-making business division of a global automotive supplier. The project goal was to secure break even by reduction of expenses. Because the biggest expenditure item was material cost the focus was mainly on purchasing but also on logistics and production. Therefore the participants of the project came from different departments and different countries in order to build up a cross-functional (or functional dissolved) and multinational team. Each team member was more or less specialist of his domain which is required by the high specificity of the automotive branch.

The project environment contained many stakeholders and a high management attention, which implied many internal politics and a high dynamic. So a "vuca" environment was given. For that reasons the chosen operating system was Scrum, in order to be able to cope with the named circumstances:

- iterative process to adapt on changes due to the existing dynamics
- cross-functional and self-organized team, scraped together at one location and supported by a Scrum Master to create required creativity
- Product Owner to handle needs of stakeholder and management

The team has been grown during the project from twelve to 15 members (inclusive Scrum Master and Product Owner). Five people were transposed during the observed project time due to several reasons, e.g. job change or limited secondment.

Nobody in the team had experience with APM. Therefore the Product Owner and Scrum Master got a CSM-certification first while the whole team got a 2-day-training to introduce in Scrum. Besides this the first four sprints (8 weeks) were supported by a consultancy.

Less than 50 % of the team staff had practical experience within the problem field.

The team was co-located for only three days per week (Tuesday to Thursday) because the employees came from all over Europe. The used task-board was not digitalized in order to have all participants most of the time at the same location to secure direct communication and full participation. Other used artifacts were an impediment log, an overall roadmap to show the strategy (comparable to a release plan), an availability plan of all team members and a central server in order to have full access to all documents and information.

The chosen sprint length was two weeks, while every sprint contained the planning meeting, four stand-ups (twice a week), the sprint review and the sprint retrospective.

The vision was formulated as the amount of cost the team had to reduce. The backlog items to reach this vision consisted of ideas from the whole team but were prioritized by the Product Owner.

The observer (first author), which is CSM as well, had the function of a scientific attendant. Mostly he participated in the Scrum events, e.g. planning, review and retrospective, to gather data and to act like a promoter, consultant or questioner.

4 Evaluation Results and Discussion

Due to the limited extent of this article the evaluation focuses mainly on insights which are linked to the special environment of social systems development and the automotive business. Already known issues like team development, cultural change or the influence of disturbances from different sources could be also recognized but are not addressed in this paper.

The most difficult challenge while implementing Scrum in the non-development area is the fact that there is only a limited possibility to test ideas and solutions (see Table 2). Trying e.g. a new negotiation concept like it is usual in purchasing all tests would be real-time within the living system. This means to use a trial-and-error-approach is only possible at a high risk. As a consequence the team decided to implement quality gates due to the criticality of a task fail. Low criticality allowed that team members could decide for themselves or by four-eye-principle; high criticality needed the involvement of the Product Owner or sometimes the stakeholders. A problem which the authors observed is that these offered a possibility for micro-management by the Product Owner or the stakeholders. Thereby, self-organization of the team and an autonomous idea creation, concept development and testing were more or less blocked. Another issue regarding the involvement of different parties is about speed. The more people are involved, the more time for decision making was needed (see e.g. [21]). To overcome endless discussions in some places it was chosen to introduce the sociocratic consent moderation approach [22, p. 9], which promises faster decisions with a higher quality by minimizing rejection and veto instead of maximizing agreement.

Critical is also the granularity of items. If they are too restricted, often the solution is intended by the formulation of the task. So the team could not determine the way of solving the problem and as a consequence creativity is limited.

Micromanagement and a restricted granularity of the tasks showed a negative impact on team motivation and the trust in the method Scrum, especially because the team members, who are all experts in their field, expected from an agile approach a more open way to work.

Another issue resulted from the social systems scope and from the specificity of different domains in automotive business. The one Product Owner did not have the competence for all domains and sometimes the translation from the stakeholders into the team failed. So it was inevitable that even team members had to talk directly to stakeholders, which is originally not intended within the Scrum framework. Later it was chosen to install a Chief Product Owner and three Product Owners each for specific areas in order to deal with the high complexity. Scrum Planning was split in two parts – one hour for the whole team moderated by the Chief Product Owner, one hour for planning within the specialized area. Thereby, the team was divided in smaller sub-teams (3–7 people) even though they constantly tried to act and optimize as a whole.

After three month of work a strategic change could be recognized. While at the beginning the overall project roadmap was structured by qualitatively described problem fields (purchasing material fields) without any relation to saving potentials, later on it changed to a prioritized action plan oriented at the relation between saving potential, estimated lead time and inherent risk. This implies that especially in case that the problem field is very complicated and the team is not familiar with it a set up time is needed. So in early sprints analysis and idea creation outweigh while later execution is more focused. This means not that there is a cut between a kind of planning sprints and executing sprints. Planning and execution are always done in parallel in order to adjust over the whole project time.

5 Conclusion and Future Research

It can be concluded that most of the elements of Scrum can be used also within a project in the purchasing area while some of them need some customization. In addition, there are other critical aspects, e.g. the difficulty to manage the variety of specialists in order to create a common team or to find the right granularity of tasks and targets.

Therefore especially in environments like automotive with a less agile culture as well as in social systems development further qualitative research is required. On a long-term perspective broader quantitative research should aim at clarifying the most effective tools and principles of APM and how those contribute to project success.

Also the used sociocratic consent moderation approach needs much more scientific investigation as it is relatively new, less used and differing from traditionally known decision methods like the autocratic decision by a powerful superior or the decision by election as it is used in a democracy.

References

1. Bennett, N., Lemoine, J.G.: What a difference a word makes: understanding threats to performance in a VUCA world. Bus. Horiz. **57**, 311–317 (2014)
2. Jentsch, D.: Wandlungsfähigkeit im Management produzierender Unternehmen. Chemnitz, IBF (2015)
3. Riedel, R.: Systemische Fabrikbetriebsplanung auf Basis eines kybernetisch-soziotechnischen Modells. Chemnitz, IBF (2012)
4. Reinema, C., et al.: Agiles Projektmanagement – Einsatzpotentiale und Handlungsbedarfe im Rahmen von Fabrikplanungsprojekten. ZWF **108**, 113–117 (2013)
5. van Solingen, Rini., et al.: Scrum in sales. How to improve account management and sales processes. In: AGILE 2011, pp. 284–288. IEEE Computer Society, Salt Lake City (2011)
6. Beck, K., et al.: Manifesto for Agile Software Development (2001). www.agilemanifesto.org
7. Dingsøyr, T.: A decade of agile methodologies: towards explaining agile software development. J. Syst. Softw. **85**, 1213–1221 (2012)
8. Komus, A.: Status Quo Agile 2014. In: 2nd International Study on Application of Agile Methods, Koblenz, (2014). www.status-quo-agile.com

9. Conforto, E.C., et al.: Project Management Agility Global Survey. CEPE, Cambridge (2014)
10. Takeuchi, H., Nonaka, I.: The new new product development game. Harvard Bus. Rev. **64**, 137–146 (1986)
11. Maximini, D.: The Scrum Culture. Introducing Agile Methods in Organizations. Springer, Berlin (2015)
12. Schwaber, K. Sutherland, J.: The scrum guide. The defenitive guide to scrum: the rules of the game (2013). http://www.scrumguides.org/docs/scrumguide/v1/scrum-guide-us.pdf
13. Conforto, E.C., et al.: Can agile project management be adopted by industries other than software development? Proj. Manage. J. **45**(3), 21–34 (2014)
14. Ropohl, G.: Allgemeine Systemtheorie. Einführung in Transdisziplinäres Denken. Berlin, Edition Sigma (2012)
15. Abercrombie, N., Hill, S., Turner, B.S.: Dictionary of Sociology. Penguin, Harmondsworth (1984)
16. Flyvbjerg, B.: Five misunderstandings about case-study research. Qual. Inq. **12**(2), 219–245 (2006)
17. Rowley, J.: Using case studies in research. Manage. Res. News **25**(1), 16–27 (2002)
18. Yin, R.K.: Case Study Research; Design and Methods. Sage, Thousand Oaks (2003)
19. Waterman, H., Tillen, D., Dickson, R., de Koning, K.: Action research: a systematic review and assessment for guidance. Health Technol. Assess. **5**(23), 1–157 (2001)
20. Susman, G.I.: Action Research: A Sociotechnical Systems Perspective. In: Morgan, G. (ed.) Beyond Method: Strategies for Social Science Research. Sage Publications, London (1983)
21. Godwin, W.F., Restle, F.: The road to agreement: Subgroup pressures in small group consensus processes. J. Pers. Soc. Psychol. **30**, 500–509 (1974)
22. Buck, J.A., Endenburg, G.: The creative forces of self-organization. sociocratic Center Rotterdam (2012)

A Behaviour Model for Risk Assessment of Complex Systems Based on HAZOP and Coloured Petri Nets

Damiano Nunzio Arena[1(✉)], Dimitris Kiritsis[1], and Natalia Trapani[2]

[1] École Politechnique Fédérale de Lausanne,
STI-IGM-LICP ME, Station 9, CH-1015 Lausanne, Switzerland
{damiano.arena,dimitris.kiritsis}@epfl.ch
[2] Dipartimento di Ingegneria Industriale (D.I.I.), University of Catania,
Viale Andrea Doria 6, 95125 Catania, Italy
ntrapani@dii.unict.it

Abstract. To support the knowledge of specialists during a HAZOP brainstorming session, a support system, which is able to automatically generate a preliminary HAZOP report was developed. The support system, which is based on Coloured Petri Nets (CPNs), simulates the behaviour of the system when different abnormal scenarios occur. The research demonstrates that integration of CPNs and HAZOP is very effective to obtain a smart tool for risk assessment of complex systems, improving the HAZOP analysis procedures.

Keywords: Major hazard identification · HAZOP · Coloured petri nets

1 Introduction

Today more than ever, safety in process industries represents an extremely important issue, which requires development and adoption of procedures helpful for carrying out a formal identification of hazard and risk assessment generated by the system complexity both in design phase and during operations. HAZOP (Hazard and Operability) analysis is a structured technique used to execute a systematic examination of process risks in major hazard plants. Although it is really time-consuming and requires significant human and economic resources, it is still most dependent tool for risk identification in chemical and petrochemical plants.

A brief literature review of these studies is discussed in order to set the state-of-the-art of a potential HAZOP automation.

2 Literature Review

A method, called HAZID, was the forerunner for the computer aided hazard identification [1]. McCoy set out to develop a tool for hazard identification based on fault propagation, but did not aim that this tool would necessary emulate HAZOP. McCoy obtained a more efficient tool by the creation of a computer program for hazard identification, which is a HAZOP emulator. The general approach appears similar to

© IFIP International Federation for Information Processing 2015
S. Umeda et al. (Eds.): APMS 2015, Part I, IFIP AICT 459, pp. 573–581, 2015.
DOI: 10.1007/978-3-319-22756-6_70

HAZOPExpert [2], a system based on a strong graphical interface which allows the user to easily specify piping and instrument diagrams but it is not meant to replace the HAZOP team. Its objective is to automate the routine aspects of the analysis as much as possible, thereby allowing the team to focus on more complex aspects of the analysis that cannot be automated. An evolution of HAZOPExpert for Batch processes (BHE) was first developed by Srinivasan and Venkatasubramanian, and later improved by other researchers [3]. Thereafter, the same authors developed an auto-mated HAZOP analysis tool for chemical processes called PHASUITE and based on Petri Nets [4].

In the past few years, researchers have concentrated on combining HAZOP with dynamic simulation [5], with Signed Directed Graph [6] or with techniques able to catch the structural aspects of process plants, such as Digraphs [7], D-higraphs [8], Case-Based Reasoning, [9], and Cause-Implication Diagrams [10, 11]. Most recent studies, on HAZOP methodology and its automation, was done by Lotero-Herranz and Galàn [12]. The use of Petri Nets, as a modelling language for batch or continuous processes, has proven to be efficient and powerful, but there is a lack in literature about the use of CPNs [13] for hazard.

3 HAZOP Methodology

Hazard and Operability (HAZOP) study is a well-known methodology for hazard identification, useful in design phase as well as in operational phase, for analysing chemical process hazards. In order to identify causes and consequences of deviations in complex systems, a multidisciplinary team of experts applies a set of guidewords to the process sections, during structured brainstorming sessions. The analysis of problems within a HAZOP study is qualitative, but integration with quantitative risk assessment methodology is well documented [14].

Although this method is very liable for hazard identification in complex systems and to support risk drive engineering in manufacturing [15], also useful for, however, the limitations of HAZOP study have been widely discussed [14], motivating academic and industrial researchers in seeking technological solutions for obtaining a more efficient application of this methodology.

Hence, the aim of this paper is to propose an HAZOP study carried out by ana-lysing the propagation of several faults through different connected models that are based on Coloured Petri Nets (CPNs), taking advantage of the enhanced characteristics that will be discussed in the following section.

4 Coloured Petri Net Language and CPN-Based Model

Coloured Petri Nets (CPNs) is a discrete-event graphical modelling language for constructing models of concurrent systems and analysing their properties. CPNs combine the modelling advantages of Petri Nets and compactness of the high level functional programming language Standard ML. The CPN modelling language is a general-purpose modelling language, i.e., it is not aimed at modelling a specific class of systems, but is aimed towards a very broad class of systems that can be characterized as concurrent systems.

A CPN model of a system is both state and action oriented. It describes the states of the system and the events (transitions) that can cause the system to change state. By performing simulations of the CPN model, it is possible to investigate different scenarios and explore the behaviour of the system, using customizable tokens, places, transitions and functions. The formal definition of CPNs a coloured Petri net model is a nine-tuple:

$$CPN \{\Sigma, P, T, A, N, C, G, E, IN\}$$

where Σ is a finite set of non-empty types, called colour sets, P is a finite set of places, T is a finite set of transitions, A is a finite set of arcs, N is a node function, C is a colour function, G is a guard function, E is an arc function, IN is an initialization function. Further details on CPN can be found in [12].

The potential integration between HAZOP and CPN is studied in order to extract a behavioural model of e.g. process plant the related HAZOP analysis. The paper presents an on-going research, which shows the potential of CPN and HAZOP integration to obtain a support system for HAZOP studies. In fact, a library of component and behaviour model of typical chemical plant equipment is being developed, each component will be able to be connected with others in order to easily reproduce the P&ID (Piping and Instrumentation Diagram) of the plant, like so the system processes and information flow.

The first step for system modelling is the drawing up of a list of relevant process parameters concerning each equipment type: i.e. Flow In and Out, Level (for vessels and tanks, Pressure, Temperature, Reaction (only for reactors).Then, the mental process, through which logical connection between causes of a failure and its consequences, typical of HAZOP study, needs not only a complete knowledge of all the components failure modes but a full understanding of the so-called propagation of a failure inside and outside the component. Failure is intended as a deviation from the "normal behaviour", e.g. high level within the vessel, low flow and so on. The concept of "normal behaviour" is related to the functioning of the system, and then it is not a static condition because it evolves together with the system.

Therefore, two further steps must be performed:

- The collection of all the typical causes of failure concerning each one of the modelled components;
- The creation of CPN-based mechanism, which emulate the propagation of failures.

The first of these steps can be tackled by leveraging CPN colour sets. Data related to typical accidents together with their impact on the involved process variables will be collected and represented through their proper colour sets. Then, the second one is the most challenging. The automation of the so-called "failures propagation" is crucial in order to detect causes and consequences related to all the possible failures that can occur in the system. Causes and Consequences of the process variable deviations, which are related to analysed node/section/plant, constitute the main elements of a HAZOP analysis. Therefore, in this context, we define:

- Internal Cause: An occurring fault within the component that causes a deviation on the component parameter (e.g., accidental event).
- External Cause: The propagation of a deviation from an upstream component might be the cause of a failure within the analysed one.
- Internal Consequence: Deviating process variable within a component might produce one or more internal faults.
- External Consequence: An internal deviation might propagate through downstream components. It might potentially be the external cause of a downstream deviation.

Finally, HAZOP methodology uses a set of guidewords and parameters from which it is possible to define the above-mentioned deviations by their combination (e.g. No/Less/More Flow, Less/More Pressure, Less/More Temperature, etc.). Hence, successive issues in terms of creating models that emulate the propagation of failures through an industrial plant as well as reproducing the information flow in detail is summarized in Fig. 1.

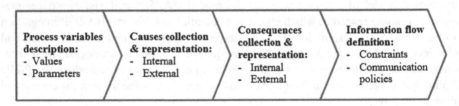

Fig. 1. Sequence of issues in modelling process

4.1   Declarations

'CPN Tools' [16] constitute the modelling framework, which has been adopted in order to create behavioural models of industrial components such as a tank, a pump, a valve, etc. 'CPN Tools' is used for editing, simulating, state space and performance analysis of CPN models. Moreover, it supports untimed and timed hierarchical CPN models.

Figure 1 shows the types of data that are consumed within the model. In this context, coloured tokens and their properties seem particularly suitable to represent either Process variables or Causes, Consequences and Information Flow policies.

Thus, according to both the given definition of a Coloured Petri Net (Sect. 3) and editing framework rules, a CPN model of a component requires:

- A colour set for each kind of:
  - Process variable (VAL: Z | VL | L | N | H | VH);
  - Internal and external cause or consequence (STRING);
- A set of places that may store/contain all those information modelled by colour sets.
- A set of transitions, arcs and functions, which run and control the correct information flow.

"VAL" colour set represents all the "qualitative" values that can be reached by a process variable in the CPN model. It has been defined to represent the qualitative value that can be reached from any process variable, for instance, "Z" = Zero, "VL" = Very Low, L = Low, N = Normal, H = High, VH = Very High.

4.2   Components

The entire analysed section of the plant comprises of 4 elements such as, 2 valves, 1 vessel, and 1 pump. Each of the CPN models is made up of these primitive elements:

- **Places**, depicted as circles and necessary for storing information about the process variables;
- **Transitions**, used for running the above mentioned information;
- **Arcs**, connect places and transitions by driving the information flow.

Those components are consuming the above-mentioned data such as, process variable values modelled by tokens, flow policies defined by SML functions etc.

Thus, starting from previous definitions together with many available information concerning the analysed node, further issues in terms of specificity of the modelling component have been tackled during its translation into CPN model.

Figure 2 shows a snippet of the vessel model, which is made up of 5 places and 10 transitions. These are able to consume information concerning the vessel's process variables such as, temperature, pressure, level, flow-in, and flow-out, and satisfy its working policies through guards, arc and other functions.

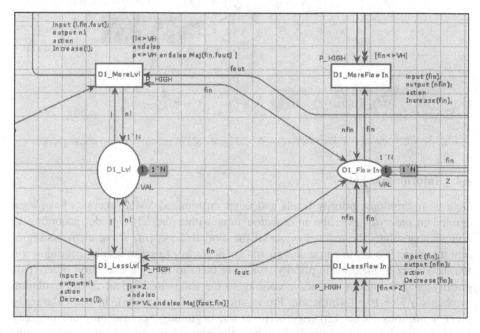

Fig. 2. CPN model – vessel (D1)

4.3   Causes and Consequences

Each grey place (see Fig. 2), which models a specific process variables, may be connected with green depicted places and transitions, which are used in order to use data related to internal and external causes (see Fig. 3). Each of those causes acts on one or more specific process variables, thus, it acts on the qualitative information modelled by a token that is stored within the relative place. During a simulation of the CPN model, the occurrence (or firing) of a green transition triggers a ripple effect, which may change the state of the involved components, according to predefined communication policies. Much of the same applies to the consequences (purple places and transitions, Fig. 4).

A purple transition is enabled when specific conditions are reached by the system, which leads a component to fail in a specific way. As previously mentioned, a ripple effect is triggered when the system state changes, hence, the new state that is reached from each involved component may represent the disruption cause of a linked component. More details are given in the next section.

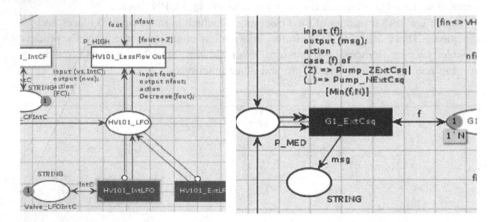

Fig. 3. CPN model – valve causes   **Fig. 4.** CPN model – pump consequences

4.4   Information Flow

Guards, inscriptions, priority levels and other customized SML functions have been defined in order to drive the information flow within the CPN model according to policies that reflect the real behaviour of the modelled system. These elements represent the model's core, in particular, guards are necessary to set bounding conditions on transitions firing, meanwhile priority levels are there to rule the execution order. This priority level definition is made according to the following typical failure evolution mechanism I $\rightarrow$ P$\rightarrow$T (Initiation, Propagation, and Termination). In particular, only green transitions (Sect. 4.3) may occur at the beginning because they are the only enabled ones (Initiation of the fault). Then, the propagation of a fault is due to component's features and communication policies. This stops when a final state has been reached.

Therefore, it is possible to obtain a "behaviour forecast report" from the CPN-based system by randomly firing initiating causes and tracking the system behaviour.

5 From CPN Model to HAZOP

Once the CPN model has been developed, it is possible to extract data that will guide the HAZOP study executed by experts. Simulation of propagation of failures through the modelled system reveals interesting data about its response to those typical component failures. The term "controlled" means, it is always possible to get meaningful outputs from each firing (stop criteria have been set out not to reach meaningless states).

Therefore, CPN Tools simulation produces a ".txt" file, which exactly reports a list of all the binding elements involved during the so-called token game.

Report data should be collected even by monitoring functions or mined by external tools such as ProM [16] or CPNaaS (on-going project). However, data collected from simulation have been translated into a HAZOP like form through an Excel VBA macro ad hoc designed to manage those data. The HAZOP report is still in a raw format (Fig. 5), which includes only guidewords, causes and consequences, but further developments may include important information such as automatic control systems and safeguards.

PARAMETER	GUIDEWORD	CAUSE	CONSEQUENCE
Flow	More	HV101 IntC = "Locked-Open Valve"	HV101 MoreFlowOut
			G1 MoreFlowIn
			G1 MorePressIn
		FCV105 IntC = "Locked-Open Valve"	FCV105 MoreFlowOut
			Butene flow increase into downstream units.
		FCV105 ExtC = "ManuallyOpenValve"	FCV105 MoreFlowOut
			Butene flow increase into downstream units
		D1 ExtC = "Uncontrolled Inlet Flow Increasing"	D1 MoreFlowIn
			D1 MoreLvl
			D1 MorePress
			G1 LessFlowOut

Fig. 5. HAZOP report – "more flow" deviation

6 Discussion and Conclusions

The markings of a CPN represent the states of the modelled system. Once the analysed system has been modelled, the most linear procedure seems to be exploring all the possible states that system may be achieved (by performing a reachability analysis) and then analysing each path. However, this is a complex process in terms of time and computational effort. This could be at odds with proposed goals concerning time saving and process simplification for a HAZOP study.

Therefore, simulating a CPN model and by reading values from the generated report, it is possible to extract all the information needed to perform a HAZOP analysis of the modelled system. For the time being the simulation has been run on a small model just to analyse both feasibility and effectiveness of the results. The under development "CPN component library" may help in expanding the model easily and quickly. Lastly, the solution obtained by translating CPN Tools report data through Excel does not represent a final product but just the quickest way to get a readable one as above mentioned. However, comparing it with an "old style" HAZOP report, the "automated" HAZOP report shows almost all the risk cases together with representing an environmentally friendly and time saving way of working. This is why the use of CPNs, in order to model the behaviour of the plant through which we can obtain a HAZOP analysis, represent a possible integration between those two methodologies, moreover, it provides a very useful and smart tool both for hazard identification process and to assess operational matters which affect production dependability and resilience.

References

1. McCoy, S.A.: HAZID, a computer aid for hazard identification 1. Trans. IChemE Part B Process Saf. Environ. Prot. **77**(B6), 317–327 (1999)
2. Vaidhyanathan, R., Venkatasubramanian, V.: HAZOPExpert: an expert system for automating HAZOP analysis. Reliab. Eng. Syst. Saf. **53**(2), 185–203 (1996)
3. Venkatasubramanian, V., Zhao, J., Viswanathan, S.: Intelligent systems for HAZOP analysis of complex process plants. Comput. Chem. Eng. **24**(9–10), 2291–2302 (2000)
4. Zhao, C., Bhushan, M., Venkatasubramanian, V.: PHASUITE an automated HAZOP analysis tool for chemical processes, part I: knowledge engineering framework. Process Saf. Environ. Prot. **83**(6), 533–548 (2005)
5. Wu, J., Zhang, L., Liang, W., Hu, J.: A novel failure model for gathering system based on multilevel flow modelling and HAZOP. Process Saf. Environ. Prot. **91**(1–2), 54–60 (2013)
6. Isshiki, K., Munesawa, Y., Nakai, A., Suzuki, K.: HAZOP analysis system compliant with equipment models based on SDG. In: Ali, Moonis, Bosse, T., Hindriks, K.V., Hoogendoorn, M., Jonker, C.M., Treur, J. (eds.) IEA/AIE 2013. LNCS, vol. 7906, pp. 460–469. Springer, Heidelberg (2013)
7. Boonthum, N., Mulalee, U., Srinophakun, T.: A systematic formulation for HAZOP analysis based on structural model. Reliab. Eng. Syst. Saf. **121**, 152–163 (2014)
8. Rodriguez, M., De la Mata, J.S.: Automating HAZOP studies using D-higraphs. Comput. Chem. Eng. **45**, 102–113 (2012)
9. Cui, L., Shu, Y., Wang, Z., Zhao, J., Qiu, T., Sun, W., Wei, Z.: HASILT: an intelligent software platform for HAZOP, LOPA, SRS and SIL verification. Reliab. Eng. Syst. Saf. **108**, 56–64 (2012)
10. Nemeth, E., Cameron, I.T.: Cause-implication diagrams for process systems. their generation, utility and importance. Chem. Eng. Trans. **31**, 193–198 (2013)
11. Toth, A., Hangos, K.M., Werner-Stark, A.: A structural decomposition-based diagnosis method for dynamic process systems using HAZID information. J. Loss Prev. Process Ind. **31**, 97–104 (2014)
12. Lotero-Herranz, I., Galàn, S.: Automated HAZOP using hybrid discrete/continuous process models. Comput. Aided Chem. Eng. **32**, 991–996 (2013)
13. Jensen, K., Kristensen, L.M., Wells, L.: Coloured petri nets and CPN tools for modelling and validation of concurrent systems. Int. J. Softw. Tools Technol. Transf. **9**(3–4), 213–254 (2007)

14. Rausand, M.: Risk Assessment: Theory, Methods, and Applications. Wiley, New York (2013)
15. Trapani, N., Macchi, M., Fumagalli, L.: Risk driven engineering of prognostics and health management systems in manufacturing. In: 15th IFAC, Ottawa, 11–13 May 2015
16. CPN Tools Homepage. http://cpntools.org

Importance of Bidimensional Data Matrix Code Against Medicine Counterfeiting

André Gomes de Lira Muniz[(⊠)], Marcelo Nogueira, and Jair Minoro Abe

Graduate Program in Production Engineering in Software Engineering Research Group at UNIP,
University Paulista, São Paulo, Brazil
a.gdelira@gmail.com marcelo@noginfo.com.br jairabe@uol.com.br

Abstract. In the recent years the world has faced significant problems related to public health and the counterfeiting of medicines, which has become a critical factor for the world population. It was verified that studies on this scope are few and the concern is due to the fact that It represents many losses, reaching the value of 8 millions reais with counterfeit medicines in 2013 and lack of traceability. This study aims to present a national and global screen view of tracing systems using the bidimensional code Data Matrix by showing its importance and use in hospitals. It is an applied research with qualitative and descriptive approach, relying on bibliometric study on databases such as ScienceDirect, Portal Capes and Ebsco on the period comprehended between 2004 and 2014 and using the keywords traceability, drugs, health care and Data Matrix. The results show that the theme is not well explored on the scientific community, achieving ten papers on the previously mentioned databases. It is considered an important subject concerning to financial health on a company.

Keywords: Traceability · Medicine · Data matrix

1 Introduction

The pharmaceutical industry was held responsible for problems arising from the use of medicines in the use chain [1]. However, the current situation and advances in tracking, reverse logistics, interchangeability of specific drugs and regulations have provided a meaningful way to address this issue. Currently beyond the financial aspect, consumer safety became mandatory from the perspective of responsibility and business ethics.

Prioritize the safety and quality of products and services contributes decisively to customer loyalty, and strengthening the relation-ship between patient and health institutions. This situation is critical and patient safety in hospitals is a matter to be analyzed in depth in society [1]. Every year, thousands of people suffering from medical errors caused by flaws in the administration of medication and hospital procedures. A set of "best practices" has been developed and implemented by organizations that demonstrate an awareness in management processes, activities and relationship with patients. The challenge of improving its internal processes, based on continuous improvement with the technological support and new working methods. Traceability shall then be a way for industry and health organizations to implement

© IFIP International Federation for Information Processing 2015
S. Umeda et al. (Eds.): APMS 2015, Part I, IFIP AICT 459, pp. 582–588, 2015.
DOI: 10.1007/978-3-319-22756-6_71

management systems, providing efficiency in its operations, customer value and to remain competitive in the market.

Before the proposed objective, opposite the importance of the topic and its application, analyze the traceability of pharmaceutical drugs operating in Brazil, conducting applied research, given that it is not pure science; quantitative because they are used figures on counterfeit drugs in Brazil; and descriptive, for he knows the main object of study. Supported by pillars of traceability, which is the ability to track bidirectional forward with application or location of the same [2], evaluation of historical medications, with their resilience through recorded identifications, allowing the tracking of what is considered as sources of consultations.

2   A Bias of the Problem

In recent years the world is faced with significant problems related to public health and counterfeit drugs has become a critical factor for the world's population. The drug falsification of its holistic approach can vary according to country [3]. May classify drug counterfeiting the form of manufacturing the pharmaceutical product by someone not authorized to do so by copying or imitating the original without permission and with the purpose of deception or fraud by selling the product as if it were the original.

Aiming to solve the problem of definition of counterfeit medicines, the World Health Organization - WHO established a definition: "Counterfeit medicine is one which is deliberately and fraudulently subject to a change of identity and/or source. In conclusion that the product can be or generic brand and may include products with the correct or incorrect composition without active components, with insufficient active components or with a packaging false" [4]. In Brazil, according to Law No. 8,072/90, counterfeiting is a heinous crime, prompting the offender to be penalized without the traditional mercies as bail, pardon and others, that despite the rigidity of the sentence, in an attempt to inhibit such crimes, not extinguish the problem. The society, government and industry must find solutions that restrain counterfeiting with effective mechanisms for control of production and distribution of medicines.

Faced with this challenge, the private sector, society and government leaders around the world have sought effective ways to combat counterfeiting. We know that, to a greater or lesser degree of difficulty, the current mechanisms in the package can still be played and lead the consumer to a misunderstanding that can be fatal.

2.1   Global Trends

The creation of the World Health Organization, a specialized agency for health in 1948 developed of norms, standards and processes in search of a suitable level of health for all people. WHO aims the quality of drugs at the international level and that makes recommendations to combat and prevent counterfeit drugs requiring not only cooperation between institutions but also at international level.

With the rise of international trade in drugs and ease in Internet sales was the rapid expansion of the counterfeit goods trade. With that in 2006 WHO held an international task force to combat Counterfeit pharmaceuticals (IMPACT), composed by Interpol Intellectual Property Organization, and the agencies and associations of countries that seeks to share knowledge to identify problems, seek solutions and coordinate activities.

In Brazil, the creation of ANVISA in 1999 began regulating the supervisory process in the country, it is one set up a body with special authority to direct and independent public administration.

The first fake ID case in Brazil was registered in 1877. In 1991, was identified nine brands of tetracycline antibiotics were forged eleven that existed in the market.

The drug counterfeiting practices worsened between 1997 and 1998 being registered 172 cases of forgery by the Ministry of Health. Appeared counterfeit medicines for the treatment of prostate cancer, for example Androcur Schering of Brazil, led to worsening of the disease and died at least five patients who used the fake medicines.

Competition in the Brazilian drug market is being fought not only by national and foreign companies, there's a new competitor that is in pursuit of revenue from this market in 2013 had revenues of 3 trillion [5]. According appointment of the National Anti-Piracy Forum - FNCP, suppliers of smuggled, counterfeit and pirated products have a turnover of 30 billion dollars in the last year (2013). Counterfeiting and smuggling of products generate damage amounting to eight billion dollars a year representing 20 % of the total market and about five billion dollars of tax evasion and in Brazil,it is considered a heinous crime, this number doubles the world average of 10 %, as shown by WHO studies [5].

The IRS conducted the seizure of more than 40 million dollars in smuggled medicines since 2010, and at first the door of counterfeit products in Brazil is Paraguay which accounts for 20 billion two-thirds of ticket dollars per year in illegal products. Traceability of medicines in the production chain aims at prevention and drug misuse weakening and reducing counterfeit products, enabling the identification of lots with quality problems or of dubious origin and quickly re-moving market.

3 Tracing – Using the Automating Tool for Medicine Safety

With technological advances and influences imposed by contemporary society has required adoption of increasingly bold solutions requiring restructuring of the productive sectors based on efficiency, so having an effective production ceased to be a differential and became a synonym for survival in the corporate panorama. The veracity in the economy and consumer market demand establish crucial factors in the survival of an enterprise, synonyms such as price, quality, innovation, term commitment to the safety of people and the environment are not evident guarantees attesting product quality [6]. The ability to enter detailed information about the origin and characteristics of the products distributed, according to batches or individually, at various stages of the production chain, has become an important instrument of commercial advantage. In addition to representing a key condition to meet the demands of consumers.

Law 11,903, of January 14, 2009, deals with the traceability of production and consumption of drugs [7]. Ratifies the law 12 097 of 24 November 2009, where debate the concept and application of traceability in the supply chain of bovine meat and buffalo. Finally, the law 12.305, of August 2, 2010, establishing the national solid waste policy [6]. This set of law refers traceability in Brazil to a new level, transferring to businesses, industries, businesses, insurance companies, hospitals and others the responsibility of collecting products put on the market. On international standards ISO 9000 is the following definition, traceability is defined as the ability to trace the history, applications or the location of products from its origin to the consumer [8]. The hospital side, traceability is the hospital's ability to control the receipt, distribution, dispensing and administration of batch and validity of drug processes [6]. To set, traceability in this study was used to Occam's razor, so traceability is defined as the origin of the product identification from the raw materials used, production process, market distribution to consumption [9]. As a result of tampering and counterfeit drugs is notorious the need to establish a process to control the product distribution chain to the end consumer, the process control should identify the lot and the validity and be registered so that they can monitor the stages of the entire cycle in jail where he is. In hospital approach, lack of process control directly affects the hospital control and that the hospitals studied alternatives to address this lack of information and to control properly the information concerning the product, new technologies for identification and product traceability comes in market, including the two-dimensional code.

3.1 The Risks of Palliative Solutions and Innovation

The work of relabeling is a stopgap solution and can bring some risks to update data because the control process has a heavy reliance on human interaction and a methodology that guarantees some checkpoints and data validation during the information chain. And for this control to be effective it is necessary to invest in labor-work which increases the cost of operation. There is also the entrance possibility in the stock of medicine with error in the hospital and, therefore, is essential to control of lots and the internal redistribution of products by updating controls and information systems.

One possible risk is duplication of information and the potential damage and to corrupt the traceability of medicines during the time he is active in the system. Therefore, validate the quality of labels, printing program, as well as keeping the maintenance of printers, and have adequate quality control process promotes sustainable solution.

According to a study from the Institute of Medicine (2001) shows that even in first world countries, such as in the United States at a rate of 24 % utilization in reading bar codes in hospitals to make the conference of the product before being effective dispensing and to control inventory 29.9 % using this technology. Therefore proper identification in the pharmaceutical industry is relevant [10]. The creation of the two-dimensional code that has a variable format may promote the information that hospitals need and thus meet the need of retagging and yet increase the quality assurance in medicine. While reading the new code, automatic batch data import and validity restrict the occurrence of error for the inclusion of data in the system and thus expand the inventory management assurance company. Based on studies conducted on the status of the hospital pharmacy by the American Society of Health-System Pharmacists (ASHP) highlights the cost reduction and expansion of security, mobilizing the fitness industry and the supply of drugs in individual doses and identified with bar codes, as identified in the study group of GS1 Brazil. This requires adapting the packaging and the code for single doses. This will be possible because, you can register up to 55 characters in a print only 2–3 mm^2. Importantly, the GS1 Data Matrix code is being used in various medicines and ease of reduced printing and of great importance to the unit or small doses consumption.

3.2 Application in the Medical Field

In January 2009 it was published the Law 11,903, which creates the National System of Drug Control, which must be done through identification system, with the use of the capture, storage and electronic data transmission technologies. Companies will have a gradual period of three years for the implementation of the Data Matrix system. This law will bring numerous benefits to the industry, such as better control and security in the fight against counterfeiting, smuggling and theft; traceability of products by auto-mated records systems.

Data Matrix is a worldwide used model that allows the identification of various features and product information through encryption that guarantees the traceability of the products from the beginning of the production process to end use. The data matrix was chosen for use in medicine because it has the ability to in-stall in smaller sized packages, such as medical and surgical equipment. Some companies are already deploying the system. Pharmaceutical industries as Eurofarma concluded its implemen-tation in 2009; Baxter, who in March 2009 put its entire line with new print system; some hospitals in São Paulo as the German Hospital Oswaldo Cruz and the Hospital Israelita Albert Einstein also already part of users of the Data Matrix code.

3.3 Benefits of Using the Data Matrix in the Hospital Area

As well as the industries of medicines, which are currently required to use the Data Matrix code is believed that this logo will also be an obligation to suppliers of hospital products in this way, companies in this sector, are already anticipating and so making use this code in marketing your products has the following benefits.

Alignment with the industry, given the mandatory implementation; Ease of tracea-bility of products and medicines; Process improvement; Precise handling of inventories reflecting an improvement in purchasing management; Cost savings because there is no more need to use labels and ribbons; Of waste volume reduction is also a gain, because there is no longer a need to issue labels that future would be discarded.

All work in health aims to patient safety. An efficient traceability system is an-other component for ensuring the safety through the safe use of medicines and hospital medical supplies.

Noted that CT - Surgical Technique Trade Hospital Materials LTDA, importer of hospital supplies in 2011 invested in this technology and thus provided its customers yet another benefit [11]. Finally the author connotes that some of the customers already using Data Matrix in the use of medications such as German Hospital Oswaldo Cruz and the Hospital Israelita Albert Einstein mentioned above.

4 Materials and Methods

The present work, with quantitative essence, has descriptive and bibliographical character. To proceed the investigation, a bibliometric study was performed. According to [12], a bibliometric research consists on applying statistical techniques and mathematical patterns to descript aspects from literature and other means of communication. Initially, scientific papers were selected for data collecting related to tracing using Data Matrix on medicines of health services. Choosing the papers was due to their representativeness on scientific research on academic scope. A time gap is 10 years was considered, between 2004 and 2014. The papers were collected from a research containing the following keywords: traceability, datamatrix, health care and drugs. The sampling resulted in ten papers from the following sources: Science Direct, Portal Capes and Ebsco. After selection, a database was created to perform the bibliometric analysis with origin, author, title and correlated keywords for each paper, as follows (Fig. 1).

Origem	Autor	Título	Drugs	Traceability	DataMartrix	HealthCare
Science Direct	R. Ducommuna, S. Gloora, P. Bonnabry	Risk of errors related to deficiencies in the identification of drug unit doses	x	x		x
	F.J. Lagrange and F. Jacq	Developing an innovative oral unit dose robot dispenser: Patient care performance and industrial perspectives	x			x
	Luca Mainetti and Luigi Patrono and Maria Laura Stefanizzi and Roberto Vergallo	An innovative and low-cost gapless traceability system of fresh vegetable products using RF technologies and EPCglobal standard				
	Ahmed Musa and Angappa Gunasekaran and Yahaya Yusuf	Supply chain product visibility: Methods, systems and impacts		x		
	J. Plimmer	Trends in Packaging of Food, Beverages and Other Fast-Moving Consumer Goods (FMCG)		x		
	E. Raingeard, J.-C. Fréville, G. Grimandi, A. Truchaud	Intérêt de l'automatisation de la distribution du médicament – méthode de comparaison des technologies disponibles sur le marché français		x		x
	George Roussos	Computing with RFID: Drivers, Technology and Implications		x		
Ebsco	Dennison, Avery	France is first to to set the code.	x	x	x	
	Stobie, Craig	On the right track.				
	Plain-Jones, Charlie	When Simple isn't Good Enough.	x	x	x	x

Fig. 1. Bibliometric study of keywords (source, authors).

It is noteworthy that not part of the object of this study, the other processes involved, nor other specific variables for mining of the above mentioned data, i.e. presenting a structure chain of medical supplies, as this would be an extension of this outbreak, which I would refer to other types of studies that were not in the midst of the objectives.

5 Final Considerations

Performing this study enabled a better understanding about the work and importance of Data Matrix Bidimensional code. It was noticed that scientific literature does not explore this subject as it should, as management mistakes may cause high organizational impacts, leading the company to financial, ethical and moral losses. A significant rise on companies from diverse sectors that have adopted Data Matrix for identification of their products, particularly the pharmaceutical industry, as its use is mandatory due to law 11.903 that creates National System of Medicine Control.

For several times the responsible for hospital pharmacies have found obstacles which restrain the development of tracing projects and it is not uncommon that the reason is lack of support or financial resources. However, it is worth noting that there are solutions that adapt to a wide variety of budgets, as it has been exposed.

It is also worth noting that, facing the costs generated by error and time spent with workforce do not add value and offer more risks. They are factors that may show the quick feedback of the investment.

In addition, the focal point is the attention to regulations. With this study, it is expected the health assistance reaches a higher quality level, when it comes to authentic products and legal origin, as well as expect that a regulation for primary packages based on GS1 Data Matrix is created.

Acknowledgements. This work has been supported by FCT – Fundação para a Ciência e Tecnologia in the scope of the project: PEst-OE/EEI/UI0319/2014 by Portugal and University Paulista - Software Engineering Research Group by Brazil.

References

1. Camargo, F.: Rastreabilidade: sinônimo de eficiência e segurança, s.l.: s.n. (2006)
2. Mello, C.H.P., da Silva, C.E.S., Turrioni, J.B., de Souza, L.G.M.: ISO 9001: 2000: Sistema de Gestão da Qualidade para Operações de Produção e Serviços. s.l.: Atlas (2002)
3. Virella, D.: Falsificação de medicamentos. Uma realidade à qual é preciso dar atenção. Acta Pediátrica Portuguesa, **39**(1), 46–50 (2008)
4. Who, W.H.O., others.: General information on counterfeit medicines, s.l.: s.n. (2007)
5. CFF, C.F.d.F.: O mercado negro de medicamentos, s.l.: s.n. (2014)
6. Rocha, R.U.G.D.: Fluxo da informação no sistema de rastreabilidade em uma empresa do segmento eletrônico, Curitiba: s.n. (2012)
7. Nogueira, E., Neto, G.V.: Counterfeit drugs and law N. 11.903/09: legal aspects and impacts. Revista de Direito Sanitário **12**(2), 112–139 (2011)
8. Santos, A.R.D.: Rastreabilidade "do laboratório à mesa:": um estudo da cadeia produtiva da indústria de carne suína na empresa Doux, Caxias do Sul: s.n. (2014)
9. Malta, N.G.: Farmácia Hospitalar Rastreabilidade de medicamentos na farmácia hospitalar, s.l.: s.n. (2014)
10. Kreysa, U., Denecker, J.: Enabling safer patient care automatic identification standards for pharmaceutical and medical devices, pp. 32–35. International Hospital Federation Reference Book (2007/2008)
11. Souza, D.L.D., Souza, G.D., Bregenski, L.A., Fraiz, S.: Data Matrix, Curitiba: s.n. (2010)
12. Araújo, C.A.: Bibliometria: Evolução história e questões atuais. Em questão **12**(1), 11–32 (2006). Porto Alegre

"The Fast and the Fantastic" Time-Cost Trade-Offs in New Product Development vs. Construction Projects

Youcef J-T. Zidane[1][✉], Asbjørn Rolstadås[1], Agnar Johansen[2], Anandasivakumar Ekambaram[2], and Pavan Kumar Sriram[1]

[1] NTNU, Trondheim, Norway
{youcef.zidane,asbjorn.rolstadas,pavan.sriram}@ntnu.no
[2] SINTEF, Trondheim, Norway
{agnar.johansen,siva}@sintef.no

Abstract. Today, in new product development projects, "NPDs", time is the cutting edge. The time to market in new product development projects is a key factor in the competition between innovative companies. Research has shown that time can be managed, and speed too. Our concern in this paper is to study the time factor in the case of new product development projects based on a time-cost trade-off curve, which is important for the project success by delivering the product as fast as possible. We will explain the motivation behind delivering fast in NPD projects. In construction projects, a customer initially contracts for a project from a contractor based on specifications, budget and delay. Time to market is a key success factor in new product development projects. Does time to delivery have high importance in construction projects? We conclude by showing the significance of NPD projects' speed with respect to management in construction projects.

Keywords: New product development projects · Construction projects · Time-cost trade-offs · Time to market · Time to delivery

1 Introduction

For more than two decades, the time to market in new product development projects has gradually become the cutting edge. In fact, as a strategic weapon, time is the equivalent of money, productivity, quality, even innovation. In production, in new product development, and in sales and distribution, time represents the most powerful source of competitive advantage (Stalk and Hout 1990, 2003) – particularly in markets where the first mover has a strong advantage (Stalk and Hout 1990, 2003; Brown and Eisenhardt 1998; Cordero 1991; Mahmound-Jouini et al. 2004). There are several companies in place that have employed time-based strategies, such as the mobile telephony industry, the automotive industry, and many other types of industries where production starts by developing new products. Delivering faster new product development projects in these markets reduces costs, increases profits and creates values (Schmelzer 1992; Mahmound-Jouini et al. 2004).

© IFIP International Federation for Information Processing 2015
S. Umeda et al. (Eds.): APMS 2015, Part I, IFIP AICT 459, pp. 589–597, 2015.
DOI: 10.1007/978-3-319-22756-6_72

This paper is particularly concerned with the time-cost trade-offs in construction projects. The time-cost trade-off curve is explained in general, followed by a qualitative analysis of the same curve and its transformation in new product development projects and of how the changes happened in less than three decades to achieve the high efficiency and effectiveness that we now know within this type of projects. The curve will be used in reflecting on the actual situation within the construction industry. Four successful construction projects from other countries are presented to show that the construction industry can learn from the industry's notable innovative projects.

The research results presented are derived from the "SpeedUp" research project in Norway, which focuses on large complex construction projects. The main objective of SpeedUp is to develop and test the knowledge base that can contribute to the reduction of the total implementation time of complex projects.

2 Time-Cost Trade-Offs in a Project

There is a strong relationship between a project's time to delivery and its total costs. For some types of costs, the relationship is in direct proportion; for other types, there is a direct trade-off. For the sum of these two types of costs, somewhere in the red curve in Fig. 1, there is an optimum project duration for minimum total costs. By understanding the time-cost relationship, one is better able to predict the impact of a schedule change on project cost. The costs associated with the project can be categorized as direct costs or indirect costs (Kerzner 2009).

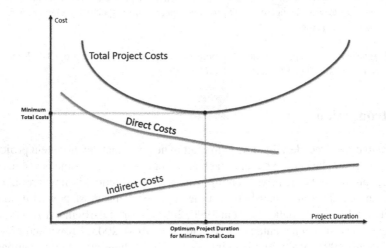

Fig. 1. Time-cost trade-offs (Source: Kerzner 2009, p. 520)

Direct costs are those directly associated with project activities, for instance salaries, travel expenses, subcontracting and project materials and equipment that have been purchased directly. If the speed of the project is increased in order to decrease project duration, which is called crashing project's activities, the direct cost increases; consequently more resources must be allocated to speed up the project delivery (Kerzner 2009;

Pmbok 2013). Indirect costs are those not directly associated with explicit project activities; for example taxes, cost related to administration and its staff, and office renting. Such costs tend to some extent to be relatively steady per unit of time over the project life cycle. This is not always the case, including large-scale projects where their cycles end after several years; here, the net present value should be taken into consideration. Per se, the total indirect costs decrease as project duration decreases. One basic assumption that needs to be made when estimating project costs is whether the estimates will be limited to direct project costs only or whether the estimates will also include indirect costs. So, indirect costs are those costs that cannot be directly traced to a specific project and that therefore will be accumulated and allocated equitably over multiple projects by some approved and documented accounting procedure (Pmbok 2013). Furthermore, the project cost is the total sum of direct and indirect costs.

The purpose behind balancing time and cost is to avoid wasting resources. If the direct and indirect costs can be accurately obtained, then a region of feasible budgets can be found, bounded by the early-start and late-start activities. Time–cost trade-off relationships are made by searching for the lowest possible total costs (i.e., direct and indirect) that likewise satisfy the region of feasible budgets. These methods, like the Critical Path Method (CPM), contain the concept of slack time and the maximum amount of time that a job may be delayed beyond its early start without delaying the project completion time. The optimum project duration is determined by the critical path, and this will determine the minimum total costs of the project (Kerzner 2009). One of the most important problems in projects is the time-cost trade-offs. Crashing the project's schedule would lead to increment in the project cost (Marco 2011; Mohmoud Belal et al. 2013).

3   Methodology

In order to attain the research objective, a literature review has been done on the concept of time-cost trade-offs in new product development projects and construction projects. Although many authors have written about the time-cost trade-offs based on quantitative methods, nothing, to the best of our knowledge, has been said about the explanation of the time-cost trade-off curve and its interpretation by relating it to the efficiency and effectiveness of the project. During the course of this paper, we have mainly used the results of the work conducted by some researchers on NPD projects and construction projects and not limited to Hutchinson (Hutchinson 2007), Demartini and Mella (2011), Schmelzer (1992), Mahmound-Jouini et al. (2004) and Karlsson et al. (2008). Construction project cases studied by the School of Civil Engineering at the University of Leeds were used to look at their time and cost overrun to try to allocate them on the time-cost trade-off curve in construction projects. The same is done for the four cases used from Karlsson et al. (2008) to come up with a new assumption about the time-cost trade-off curve. For NPD projects, the time-cost trade-off curve is a qualitative conceptual interpretation coming from the changes taking place in industries that are based on innovative projects from a few decades ago until the present. This is based on the interpretation of Stalk and Hout (1990, 2003), Schmelzer (1992) and Hutchinson (2007).

4 Time-Cost Trade-Offs in NPD Projects

The evolution of time-based competition follows a continually evolving global manu-facturing environment, where the order winners quickly become order qualifiers (Hutch-inson 2007). The manufacturing industries, which are based on innovation and NPD, have struggled to keep up with the global competition in the new millennium, as the basis of competition has shifted from cost to quality, to variety, and now to speed; where time to market has been becoming more important than the amount of invested money and accounting (Hayes et al. 2005; Hutchinson 2007).

Most innovative companies in this new era of globalization are more concerned with time reduction as their first/major priority, than cost reduction (Ansoff 1965; Porter 2008; Rich and Hines 1997; Demartini and Mella 2011). Hutchinson (2007) and based on an adaptation from Blackburn (1991), as illustrated in Fig. 2, concerning the long-term trends in manufacturing. Graphs for the 1950s, 60s, 70s, 80s, 90s, 2000s and beyond on the x-axis are made, and plotting lines indicate roughly how industry norms have changed from decade to decade. Changes in the periods present a revealing picture of the evolution towards time-based competition that is almost universal across all industries.

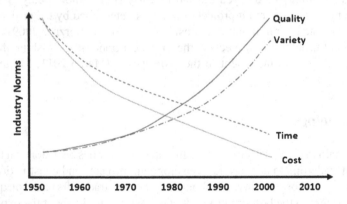

Fig. 2. The trend of manufacturing: towards time-based competition (Source: Hutchinson 2007, p. 34)

Our aim here is to understand the NPD projects and to reflect and learn how the same behavior can be relevant to construction projects. By going through the literature about NPD projects, we tried to interpret the information in a conceptual, qualitative way to develop the time-cost trade-offs curve, as illustrated in Fig. 3. We can see that NPD projects went through two paths crossing three major states ("0", "1" and "2"). State "0" depicts many companies that are cost-reduction oriented; this is because the markets are closed and less newcomers enter the local market. One example that illustrates this: Less Japanese cars were sold in Europe a few decades ago than what is the case nowadays. When globalization appeared, the survivors were the companies that changed direction from cost-reduction orientation to time-reduction orientation. The value of time (time-to-market) increased, and this increment led companies to crush their NPD projects to be first in the market, thus ensuring their survival (Moving gradually from state "0.1", "0.2", etc., as the competition increases, till state "1"). Based on some case studies, Schmelzer (1992) explains that when comparing an increase in the total project costs of 50 % (crashing the project, state "0.1" and up) versus trying to fit the optimum path duration (state "0"); the latter will be more harmful.

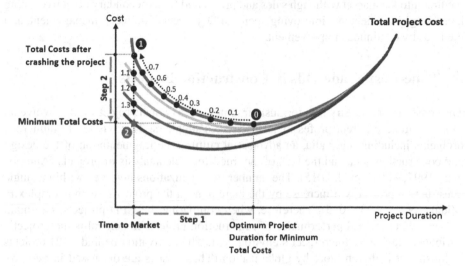

Fig. 3. Time-cost trade-offs in NPD projects

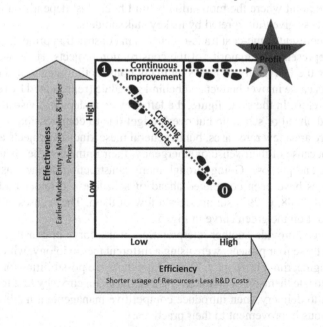

Fig. 4. The steps based on efficiency vs. effectiveness matrix of time-based management

Being maximum effective will ensure the company's competitive advantage in the market. On the other hand, companies want maximum profits from their NPD projects, and they increase efficiency to its maximum while they have the maximum effectiveness. Figure 4 is based on Schmelzer (1992) after combining it with Fig. 3. The leading companies are those ended in the state "2", where they are (1) highly effective by being the first into the market with high sales and prices and (2) as secondary objective, being increasingly efficient by improving their NPD projects' delivery management and methods by continuous improvement.

5   Time-Cost Trade-Offs in Construction Projects

The construction industry is notoriously fragmented; a typical project would involve up to six or more different professional disciplines/suppliers. This has led to numerous problems including, inter alia, an adversarial culture, the fragmentation of the design and construction data, and the lack of the true life-cycle analysis of projects (Anumba et al. 1997; Zidane et al. 2015). The number of organizations involved within a single construction project will increase by the increment in the project size and complexity (Zidane et al. 2013, 2015). Therefore, when comparing the NPD projects, one main reason behind the bad performance of construction projects in general is the project's attributes - including the project's environment. The motivation behind NPD projects to finish fast is driven more by globalization (These issues are discussed in Sect. 6). However, construction projects cannot be generalized in that way; each project is singular to the point where the motivation behind being fast depends on the definition of project success given/interpreted by its key stakeholders.

Figure 5 represents time-cost trade-off curves in construction projects. The red zone to the right represents the majority of the construction projects. Here, we refer to the study done by the University of Leeds on many construction megaprojects in Europe; all the projects came in over budget and behind schedule (represented by red dots in the red zone in Fig. 5). In the same figure, the left grey zone depicts construction projects that are ended ahead of schedule but over budget due to compression or crashing the projects. There are a few rare cases, but in general these kinds of projects are motivated to speed up because of their sense of emergency, their immediate needs to materialize their outcome and purpose. Going through many construction project cases, we found that some cases have been completed ahead of schedule and under budget. Table 1 (Karlsson et al. 2008, p. 297) summarizes a few of them. These cases are represented by the green dot on the green curve in Fig. 5.

The cases can provide another interpretation of the curve in construction projects, knowing that these four projects were using a different methodology, which is based on concurrent engineering philosophy. That means there are possibilities for construction projects to allocate themselves on the left side of the green curve by first looking for the value of time to delivery, then introduce competitive management methods, and keep using continuous improvement to their practices.

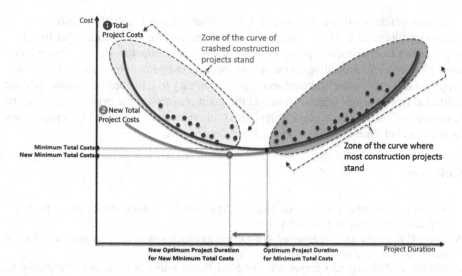

Fig. 5. Time-cost trade-offs in construction projects

Table 1. Four cases of medium-size construction projects ended ahead of schedule and under budget (Source: Karlsson et al. 2008, p. 297)

Project type	Country	Planned duration	Estimated cost (US$ million)	Ahead of schedule	Cost saving US$
Mixed-use office building	Finland	3 years	25	29 working days	17300
School	Sweden	10 months	7.5	4 calendar months	81000
Commer-cial retail store	UK	1 year	25	20 working days	19000
Educational training center	USA	10 months	5.2	46 working days	27000

6 Conclusion

Time to market in NPD projects has not the same emphasis and value compared to time to delivery in construction projects. Due to the different attributes, stimuli, environments of each type of projects, we cannot apply all the learnings from NPD projects directly into construction projects. Nevertheless, knowing that NPD projects exhibited the same behaviors before globalization, and that they transformed gradually to effective and efficient projects after the emergence of globalization, one can assume that the same may happen to construction projects. A contractor or contractors deliver construction projects in general, depending on the size of the project by involving subcontractors and suppliers and many other stakeholders. This is contrary to NPD projects, since they are delivered from a single organization and the main players are the organization and the consumers. This difference plays a significant role in each key stakeholder's perception on the effect of time-to-delivery in construction projects.

References

Ansoff, H.I.: Corporate Strategy: An Analytic Approach to Business Policy for Growth and Expansion. McGraw-Hill, Boston (1965)

Anumba, C.J., Baron, G., Evbuomwan, N.F.O.: Communications issues in concurrent lifecycle design and construction. BT Technol. J. **15**(1), 209–216 (1997)

Blackburn, J.: Time-Based Competition: the Next Battleground in American Manufacturing. Business One Irwin, Homewood (1991)

Brown, S.L., Eisenhardt, K.M.: Competing on the Edge. HBS, Cambridge (1998)

Cordero, R.: Managing for speed to avoid product obsolescence. J. Prod. Innov. Manag. **8**, 283–94 (1991)

Demartini, C., Mella, P.: Time competition. The new strategic frontier. IBusiness **3**, 136–145 (2011)

Hayes, R., Pisano, G., Upton, D., Wheelwright, S.: Pursuing the Competitive Edge. Wiley, New York (2005)

Karlsson, M., Lakka, A., Sulankivi, K., Hanna, A., Thompson, B.: Best practices for integrating the concurrent engineering environment into multipartner project management. J. Constr. Eng. Manag. **134**(4), 289–299 (2008)

Kerzner, H.: Project Management: a Systems Approach to Planning, Scheduling and Controlling, 10th edn, pp. 516–531. Wiley, New York (2009)

Mahmound-Jouini, S.B., Midler, C., Garel, G.: Time-to-market vs. time-to-delivery managing speed in engineering, procurement, and construction projects. IJPM **22**, 359–367 (2004)

Marco, A.: Project Management for Facility Constructions- a Guide for Engineers and Architects, vol. VIII. Springer, Berlin (2011) (189 p, 90 illus)

Mohmoud Belal, A., Nusair, I.A., Badra, N.M.K., Hasan, M.K.: A procedure for using bounded objective function method to solve time-cost trade-off problems. IJLRST **2**(2): 21–25 (2013). ISSN (Online):2278-5299

Porter, M.E.: On Competition, Updated and Expanded Edition. Harvard Business School Press, Boston (2008)

Project Management Institute PMI. A Guide to the Project Management Body of Knowledge (pmbok Guide), 5th edn. Newtown Square (2013)

Rich, N., Hines, P.: Supply-chain management and time-based competition: the role of the supplier association. IJPDLM **27**(3–4), 210–225 (1997)

Hutchinson, R.: The Impact of Time-Based Accounting on Manufacturing Performance. PhD thesis, University of Toledo (2007)

Schmelzer, H.S.: Organisation und Controlling von Produktentwicklungen: Praxis des wettbewerbsorientierten Entwicklungsmanagements. S-P Verlag, Stuttgart (1992)

Stalk, G. Jr., Hout, T.M.: Competing Against Time: How Time-based Competition Is Reshaping Global Markets. Free Press, New York (1990, 2003)

University of Leeds. Megaproject. http://www.mega-project.eu/ (2015)

Zidane, Y.J.-T., Johansen, A., Ekambaram, A.: Megaprojects-challenges and lessons learned. Procedia Soc. Behav. Sci. **74**, 349–357 (2013)

Zidane, Y.J.-T., Stordal, K.B., Johansen, A., Raalte, S.V.: Barriers and challenges in employing of concurrent engineering within the Norwegian construction projects. Procedia Econ. Finance **21**, 494–501 (2015)

Introducing Engineering Concepts to Secondary Education Through the Application of Pedagogical Scenarios in "Manuskills" Project

Maria Margoudi[✉] and Dimitris Kiritsis

École Polytechnique Fédérale de Lausanne (EPFL), Lausanne, Switzerland
{maria.margoudi,dimitris.kiritsis}@epfl.ch

Abstract. The current paper identifies the lack of engineering concepts taught in secondary education and to this end proposes a new approach to be followed. The contents of the aforementioned approach are subject to the EU project Manuskills and the research conducted in its concept. The utilization of pedagogical scenarios is proposed as a tool for secondary school teachers towards the incorporation of engineering concepts into their teaching practice. The nature and the characteristics of pedagogical scenarios that constitute them appropriate for this purpose will be reported and analyzed.

Keywords: Engineering education · STEM · Manuskills · Pedagogical scenario

1 Introduction

The outcomes of this paper are subject to relevant research carried out in the concept of the EU project Manuskills. Manuskills' main aim is to raise awareness for specific manufacturing concepts, both in the secondary and higher education level. As a result of this attempt, a new need has emerged about introducing a new approach for the incorporation of engineering education to the current secondary education's program. In order to realize the objective of the project, a new approach was structured, leveraging the pre-existing concept of "pedagogical scenarios" and adapting it to the needs of engineering education. In the following chapters, the significance and the necessity of the pedagogical scenarios for the integration of engineering in secondary education will be argued.

2 Theoretical Framework

Following the advances in engineering education, it becomes evident that the first real reference to engineering related concepts for students doesn't occur until tertiary education. According to relevant researches, a large number of secondary school students fail in reaching math and science proficiency [1]. In order to support the broadening of engineering within each one of the rest of the school subjects, the STEM (Science, Technology, Engineering and Mathematics) concept has been introduced. As mentioned

© IFIP International Federation for Information Processing 2015
S. Umeda et al. (Eds.): APMS 2015, Part I, IFIP AICT 459, pp. 598–605, 2015.
DOI: 10.1007/978-3-319-22756-6_73

by Gonzalez and Kuenzi [2], STEM education refers to teaching and learning in the fields of science, technology, engineering, and mathematics. It typically includes educational activities across all grade levels. The importance of STEM education increases proportionately to the dependence of our society to technology. Consequently, it is vital that when students graduate from high school are comfortable with the STEM principles.

At this point, a special reference should be made to engineering education and the benefits it can provide for secondary education. First of all, engineering motivates students' learning of math and science concepts, which make technology possible. The engineering approach to learning, also enables the acquisition of knowledge irrelevant to STEM disciplines, like reading, writing, communication and design. The interdisciplinary nature of engineering, described above, occurs as a result of the kind of problems it addresses. Some of the learning gains of students, when engaging with engineering problems, are listed by Portsmore and Rogers [3]. In more detail, students learn to: (1) identify and formulate a problem, (2) design a solution, (3) create and test a solution, (4) optimize and re-design and (5) communicate and disseminate the solution.

The review of the relevant literature presents an ambiguous picture. On the one hand, the fact of engineering education concepts providing an effective tool for students is generally accepted and recognized. On the other hand, engineering concepts are rarely addressed before university level education.

3 Purpose and Vision

The gap described in the theoretical framework, concerning the non-application of engineering concepts in secondary education, has several causes. Firstly, schools do not incorporate into their curricula a special subject for engineering. Even more importantly, very few teachers have knowledge of engineering concepts and therefore do not feel confident of including them in their teaching. Finally, a main cause for the low effectiveness and motivation regarding STEM education is the use of consolidated methods, techniques and tools by teachers.

In the current paper we suggest the use of pedagogical scenarios, as a means that will enable the incorporation and application of several different concepts of engineering education into secondary education.

The approach that will be described in the following chapters is developed under the EU funded project (FP7 609147) Manuskills.

4 Manuskills Project

Manuskills is a EU funded project (FP7 609147) which is oriented towards engineering education and specifically manufacturing. In more detail, Manuskills' main aim is to raise manufacturing awareness and even to develop the learner's understanding for specific manufacturing concepts, both in the secondary and higher education level [4].

The main target groups that the project is aiming at are teenagers and young adults, since, in general, they represent the most important beneficiaries of STEM and manufacturing education.

In order to achieve its goals, the project encompasses a series of experiments (available on Manuskills' Platform, http://demo.manuskills.org/). Each one of these experiments include the application of a delivery mechanism, which stands for cutting-edge ICT educational tools and the corresponding methods, so that the delivery of a course or even a concept, regarding STEM and/or manufacturing education, can be succeeded in a proper and contemporary frame. After following a searching and testing process, of both traditional and innovative tools, that are somehow linked to manufacturing education, the final bank consists of the following delivery mechanisms: Serious games, Simulations, Educational videos, Teaching Factory and Virtual Reality applications (Fig. 1).

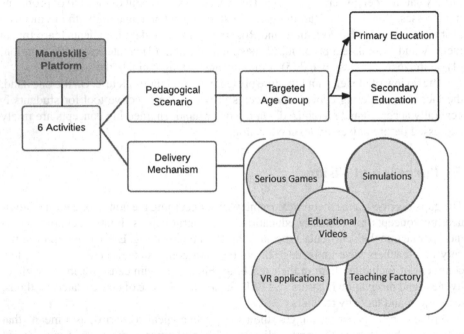

Fig. 1. Manuskills' approach

While preparing the application approach to secondary education, a new need arose. Since there is no specific school subject addressing engineering in general or especially manufacturing, a new way of incorporating our experiments to the existing secondary school's subjects was required. Moreover, another important aspect of the required solution was the fact that most secondary school teachers are not familiar with engineering concepts, and therefore feel intimidated about incorporating them into their teaching practice.

Manuskills' answer to the aforementioned problem is the incorporation of pedagogical scenarios, to each one of the experiments, in order to introduce the aforementioned delivery mechanisms, to both secondary and tertiary education.

5   Pedagogical Scenarios

A pedagogical scenario –also referred to in literature as Educational Scenario or just Scenario- is a technology supported learning plan meant to be used by a teacher or any individual who is interested in incorporating technological features into a teaching procedure. As mentioned by Yiannoutsou and Kynigo [5] the pedagogical scenarios are tools for teachers and describe the main elements of a plan of pedagogical activity, which employs the use of technology. Moreover, referring to the structure of their contents, they address aspects of the activity such as the epistemology of the domain, the social orchestration, the duration, the role and use of the tool. Despite all the aforementioned characteristics, the fact that makes a pedagogical scenario unique and that radically differentiates it from a simple learning plan, is the special reference made to the added educational value of the planned activities, in other words clarifying the nature of the innovation and the factors that determine its necessity [6].

For the needs of Manuskills project and towards the aim of a unified structure, the same template was used for all the pedagogical scenarios. The mentioned template consists of four interdependent modules, each of which contains several sections. The modules describe in detail the identity of the scenario, its application framework, the teaching-learning process to be followed and finally the implementation activities [7].

In the following paragraphs, we aim at giving a more detailed insight and a clearer view to the reader for each one of the described modules of the scenarios, as implemented and used for the purposes of the project (Fig. 2).

The first module provides a detailed view of the scenario's identity by clarifying several structure-related issues. Analytically, the reader receives details on the appropriate age group of students, as well as on the suggested school subjects to which the scenario could find application. Following these basic information, the cognitive domain that forms the scenario's background is briefly along with the scenario's learning objectives in terms of skills-to-be acquired by students. This module ends with a brief presentation of the topic and the rational of the scenario and also the added value of the activities that it encompasses.

The second module focuses on the application framework of the scenario and encompasses vital information for a teacher concerning the practical aspects of integrating the activity into a school's classroom. A special reference is made to the level and the pre-existing knowledge that the students are expected to possess, in order to engage with the scenario's activities. Also, the role that both the teacher and the students are expected to play, in terms of class orchestration, is described. All the aforementioned information of this module are topped with details concerning the time allocation of the activities and their duration, as well as details on the software applications and educational materials needed for the attainment of the planned activities.

The next module of the pedagogical scenario is referring to the teaching and learning process that is expected to take place. It is the most theoretical of all the modules and it basically constitutes necessary theoretical background of the scenario. It includes details on the cognitive terms used and the pedagogical framework that it encompasses in its activities. Finally, the teaching methodology and accompanying strategies are listed and briefly explained.

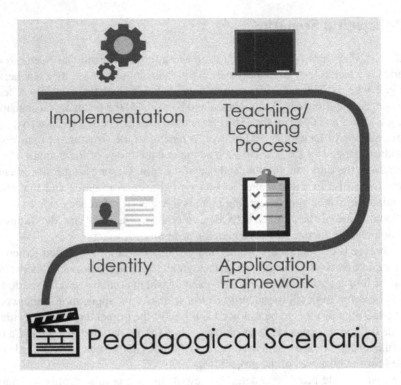

Fig. 2. Pedagogical scenario's structure

The fourth and final module is also considered to be the most important one. The subject of this module are the actual activities that constitute the pedagogical scenario. All the activities are listed and described in a chronologically structures way. For this purpose, the whole procedure is divided into phases and for each phase practical information are provided, like its duration, teacher's and students' role etc.

In order to enable the reader form a more clear view on the scenario's structure, which was employed for the needs of Manuskills [7], all the modules and their contents are analytically listed below:

1. Scenario Identity
   (a) Creators
   (b) Subject Matter
   (c) Topic of Scenario
   (d) Rational of Scenario
   (e) Added Value
2. Scenario Application Framework
   (a) Level & Pre-existing Knowledge of the Students
   (b) Class Orchestration
   (c) Social Orchestrator
   (d) Time Allocation & Duration
   (e) Software Application & Materials

3. Teaching-Learning Process
   (a) Theoretical Framework
   (b) Pedagogical Framework-Model
   (c) Methodological Framework-Model
   (d) Goals-Expected Results
4. Scenario Implementation
   (a) Learning Activities
   (b) Worksheets
   (c) Enrichment of Scenario.

6 Added Value for Engineering Education

The first module of the pedagogical scenario's structure concerns the "Scenario Identity" and it contains information about the target group of the scenario, such as the age of students and their learning level. For engineering education this translates into engineering content adapted appropriately to the needs of each age and learning level. Another section of the same module is dedicated to the corresponding school subject or learning domain, in general. This section aims at incorporating various engineering concepts into already existing school subjects (such as Math, Science etc.). Also, particular emphasis is placed on the correspondence to each country's official curriculum. Finally, an important section refers to the added value of each particular scenario, explaining the profits gained from the use of technology for the optimal presentation and explanation of engineering concepts.

The second module of the pedagogical scenario is revolving around its "Application Framework". The sections of this module covers a wide range of information, including the level of pre-existing knowledge, the suggested classroom organization, time allocation and duration of the activities and details about the leveraged software or any other appropriate materials. All the aforementioned information constitute a useful and necessary tool in the hands of a teacher, in order to organize his/her teaching practice.

Another important module is the "Teaching – Learning Process", which consists of the necessary frameworks that eventually structure the theoretical, pedagogical and methodological background of the learning activities. Firstly, the section about the theoretical framework elaborates on basic engineering concepts related to the subject or the problem in question, providing all the necessary scientific references for the teacher to explore. The pedagogical and methodological frameworks refer to the organization of the teaching and learning, by providing state of the art didactic models and the latest teaching approaches to be followed. In support of the adopted theories, scientific references are available for the teacher.

The final module of a pedagogical scenario concerns its "Implementation". This module includes the most "practical" sections of a scenario. In more detail, sections referring to learning activities and worksheets can be found in this module, providing information and guidance, not only for the students involved, but also for the teachers.

7 Conclusions

At the beginning of this paper a knowledge gap was identified in the existing literature, concerning engineering education. In more detail, it is evident that even within STEM education, concepts that revolve around engineering do not find easily application into secondary education. The causes of the aforementioned situation cab be divided into three general categories, accordingly, there are school-related, teacher-related and tools-related causes.

School-related causes are linked to the fact that there is no particular school subject on engineering below the university education level. This situation makes it difficult for the teachers to identify a school subject that could be relevant for a particular engineering concept. The detailed description of a pedagogical scenario, of the previous chapter, makes clear its contribution to this particular issue by clarifying, each time, the appropriate school subject and learning domain for the taught engineering concept ("Scenario Identity" module).

The second cause relates to teachers themselves, as it is a fact that most of them are not familiar with engineering concepts and therefore do not feel confident in incorporating them into their teaching practice. In order to tackle this issue, the pedagogical scenario incorporates into its structure a variety of information about the basic concepts of the engineering subject in question each time ("Theoretical Framework" section). Moreover, many information about the teaching procedure in general are available ("Scenario Application Framework" module).

Finally, the third cause of the low inclusion of engineering related concepts in STEM education is closely linked to the use of consolidated tools by the teachers. A pedagogical scenario's structure is oriented towards providing appropriate methods, techniques and even technological tools' suggestions for teachers, towards incorporating engineering in their teaching practice ("Pedagogical Framework" and "Methodological Framework" sections).

Concluding, we argue that the pedagogical scenario approach is capable of incorporating all the necessary components to tackle the main causes that result to the low representation of engineering in STEM education and therefore enable the introduction of engineering concepts to even younger ages of students.

Acknowledgements. The research conducted in the frame of "Manuskills", leading to these results has received funding from the European Community's Seventh Framework Programme (FP7/2007-2013) under grant agreement no. 609147.

References

1. Kuenzi, J.J.: Science, technology, engineering, and mathematics (STEM) Education: background, federal policy, and legislative action (2008). Congressional Research Service Reports. Paper 35. http://digitalcommons.unl.edu/crsdocs/35
2. Gonzalez, H.B., Kuenzi, J.J.: Science, technology, engineering, and mathematics (STEM) education: a primer. Congressional Research Service, Library of Congress, Aug 2012

3. Portsmore, M.D., Rogers, C.: Bringing engineering to elementary school. J. STEM Educ. 5(3–4) July–December 2004
4. Perini, S., Oliveira, M., Costa, J., Kiritsis, D., Kyvsgaard Hansen, P.H., Rentzos, L., Skevi, A., Szigeti, H., Taisch, M.: Attracting young talents to manufacturing: a holistic approach. In: Grabot, B., Vallespir, B., Gomes, S., Bouras, A., Kiritsis, D. (eds.) APMS 2014, Part II. IFIP AICT, vol. 439, pp. 626–633. Springer, Heidelberg (2014)
5. Yiannoutsou, N., Kynigo, C.: Boundary objects in educational design research: designing an intervention for learning how to learn in collectives with technologies that support collaboration and exploratory learning. In: Plomp, T., Nieveen, N. (eds.) Educational Design Research – Part B: Illustrative cases, pp. 357–379. SLO, Enschede, the Netherlands (2013)
6. Kynigos, C., Kalogeria, E.: Boundary crossing through in-service online mathematics teacher education: the case of scenarios and half-baked microworlds. ZDM Math. Educ. 44(6), 733–745 (2012)
7. Fragkaki, M., (2008). Structure of learning scenarios. edutubeplus – a european curriculum related video library and hybrid e-services for the pedagogical exploitation of video in class. In: Deliverable WP6 Pedagogical Framework-Pilot Implementation/T61 Pedagogical Framework. http://www.academia.edu/5170480/Pedagogical_Scenario_Structure

Sustainability and Production Management

Energy Value-Stream Mapping
a Method to Visualize Waste
of Time and Energy

Rainer Schillig[1], Timo Stock[1,2(✉)], and Egon Müller[2]

[1] University of Applied Sciences Aalen,
Beethovenstraße 1, 73430 Aalen, Germany
{rainer.schillig,timo.stock}@hs-aalen.de
[2] University of Technology Chemnitz,
Erfenschlager Str. 73, 09126 Chemnitz, Germany
egon.mueller@mb.tu-chmnitz.de

Abstract. In the industry, the Value-Stream Mapping (VSM) method has been successfully used for years to reduce inventory and lead times. With this method, process steps in a value-stream can easily be divided into value-adding and non value-adding ones. However, the VSM does not provide any information about the energy consumption and, as a consequence; it does not give any hint at how much of the energy used actually serves value-adding purposes. This paper describes how the VSM can be extended to an Energy Value-Stream Mapping method (EVSM) which allows dividing the energy input of the production process in value-adding and non value-adding.

Keywords: Energy Value-Stream Mapping · Energy efficient production and logistics · Lean and green production · Toyota production system

1 Introduction

While the manufacturing industry is one of the main energy consumers, it is at the same time also the key factor for our prosperity. Considering the continuously rising energy costs and an increasing public awareness of the need for a sustainable economic activities, many branches of industry have declared energy efficiency their strategic business objective [1].

In Germany for instance, during the second half of the last century, labour productivity has increased almost fourfold, while energy productivity has not even doubled during the same period of time [2]. In the past, the industry's rationalizing efforts have been focused on increasing automation while simultaneously cutting down the cycle times.

When in the nineties of the last century the methods of the Toyota Production System (TPS), with its focus on systematical waste reduction came to be known in the Western World, numerous companies tried to adopt them for their own use. Since that time the TPS is considered as a benchmark for creating highly efficient value-streams and often it is also described as a lean production system [3].

© IFIP International Federation for Information Processing 2015
S. Umeda et al. (Eds.): APMS 2015, Part I, IFIP AICT 459, pp. 609–616, 2015.
DOI: 10.1007/978-3-319-22756-6_74

2 The Toyota Production System

Taiichi Ohno, who is one of the TPS's architects, described its essence as follows: ‚All we are doing is looking at the time line from the moment the customer gives us an order to the moment when we collect the cash. And we are reducing that time line by removing the non value-added wastes' [4], Fig. 1.

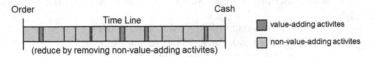

Fig. 1. Essence of the TPS according to [4]

Thereby he makes it quite clear; the point is to reduce non value-adding activities and not regarding details of the value-adding. To identify non value-adding processes for the first, Ohno divided activities into waste and work, Fig. 2. To identify waste systematically, he named 7 types of waste. Any work usually consists of a combination of value-adding and non value-adding activities.

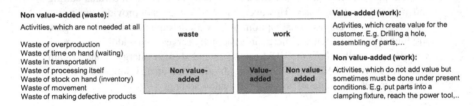

Fig. 2. Value-adding and non value-adding activities according to [4]

3 Value-Stream Mapping and Energy Value-Stream Mapping

Rother and Shook [5] presented in 1999 a method called Value-Stream Mapping which was apt for practical use. This method made it possible to look at the cycle times of work separately from the non value-adding lead time (waste). In their approach, the focus was on minimizing the lead time extending inventory (waste).

This approach may convey the impression that the process sequences within the cycle times (work) is, as a matter of principle, completely free from waste. However, this is not true. When taking a closer look, one can see almost always that the cycle time, of the manufacturing process itself, is composed of value-adding (t_{va} = time value-adding) and non value-adding (t_{nva} = time non value-adding) time sequences [6].

In literature there are several proposals in order to extend the VSM to an Energy Value-Stream Mapping (EVSM) [7–13]. Most of these approaches use a stepped 'energy line' to visualize the energy consumption alongside the process chain. The Environmental Protection Agency (EPA) [7] introduced EVSM by presenting the energy usage for each production step. Erlach and Westkämper [8] added two figures: The 'Energy Intensity' to describe the process-related energy consumption and the 'Degree of Efficiency' to evaluate the process efficiency in comparison with a benchmark process. Reinhart et al. [9] demonstrated in their approach how different forms of energy like electrical, gas or compressed air could be visualized. [8, 9] formulated guidelines to improve the energy efficiency of the value-stream called Energy Value-Stream Design. Shahrbabaki and Jackson [10] described in principal that energy in an EVSM should be divided into value-adding and non value-adding portions. They lack to explain how this could be done. Plehn et al. [11] extended the representation of the EVSM by an input/output model using the criteria energy, materials, water, waste and emissions. Posselt et al. [12] added the process related energy consumption of peripheral systems. Keskin and Kayakutlu [13] showed the link between Lean and energy efficiency and the effect of non value-adding time in terms of energy waste.

However none of these proposals is built on an exclusively dual assessment of the time and energy input only referring to the criteria value-adding or not. If the VSM should be extended to an EVSM regarding the energy consumption of the production processes the cycle times must not be regarded as completely value-adding automatically.

Aalen University of Applied Sciences, in cooperation with Chemnitz University of Technology, have developed a method, called 'Dual Energy Signatures' which allows to divide the process-related energy consumption by using the criteria 'value-adding' and 'non value-adding'. With this dualised approach the proven VSM method can be extended to an EVSM, in accordance with the principles of the TPS. The classification of energy into E_{va} (Energy value-adding) and E_{nva} (Energy non value-adding) opens up the possibility to divide the cycle times doubtless into t_{va} and t_{nva}, too.

4   How to Create a Dual Energy Signatures by Example of a Milling Process

In the Aalen University's milling laboratory experiments were taken on a 3-axis vertical machining centre, Hermle Type C 30 V. The machining process consisted in successively milling three grooves of different widths into a component made from heat-treated steel. Milling was done in full cut, with an infeed of 7.5 mm over a distance of 60 mm and using three HSS end mill cutters with diameters 8, 12, and 16 mm. In parallel, a power measurement was taken [14].

To identify the energy, required for the actual chip removal, the authors suggest: Comparing the energy consumption while processing (the workpiece) to a material with a very low density (air). Therefore the test set-up had a distinctive feature in so far as the first pass took place using an 'air cut', in other words processing without a workpiece, Fig. 3 - top. Thereby the production parameters should be maintained.

This made it possible to see what the energy signature of the process looked like without any workpiece contact. The second pass took place with workpiece contact, Fig. 3 - center. When both signatures are overlaid one gets the dual energy signature Fig. 3 - bottom. In this signature the value-adding elements of the process are clearly distinguishable, with regard to the input of energy as well as with regard to their duration, and can be differentiated unmistakably from the non value-adding elements of the process.

Details of these measurements are shown in Fig. 4. The light grey signature shows the electrical power consumption during air cut, while the dark grey signature shows the additional power consumption during chip removal. It is important to note, that

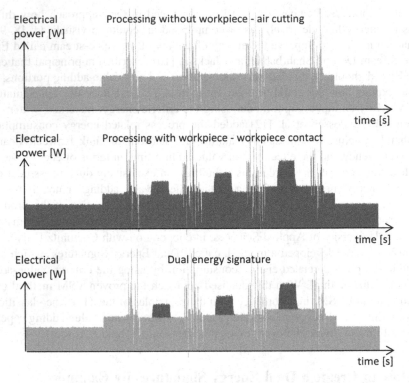

Fig. 3. Milling - air cutting vs. workpiece contact [according to 6]

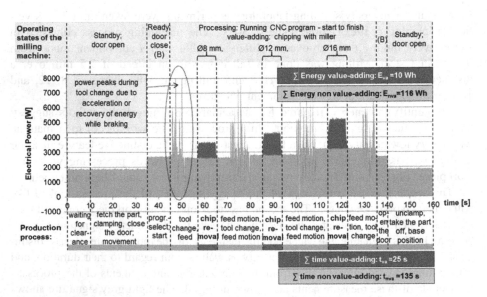

Fig. 4. Dual energy and time signature of a chip removal process [according to 6, 14]

only the actual chip removal process is value-adding. The value-adding times are marked by dark grey bars at the bottom.

The amount of energy which is required for chip removal only is about 10 Wh, the value-adding time which is needed therefore is 25 s in total. The non value-adding input of energy is 116 Wh, while the non value-adding input of time is 135 s. If it isn't possible to do an air cut, due to technical limitations, the energy required for the chip removal itself can also be calculated. Appropriate approaches are [15, 16]. Thereby a dual energy signature can be drawn as well.

5 Dual Resolution of Cycle Time and Energy Input

The value-adding efficiency of the process in terms of energy, as well as in terms of time, can now be defined as η_{Eva} and η_{tva}, Eqs. 1, 2. Therefore the value adding energy/time is divided by the total energy/time consumption of the process [1, 6, 14].

$$\eta_{Eva} = \frac{E_{va}}{(E_{va} + E_{nva})} \quad \eta_{Eva} = \frac{10 \text{ Wh}}{(10 \text{ Wh} + 116 \text{ Wh})} = 8\% \quad (1)$$

$$\eta_{tva} = \frac{t_{va}}{(t_{va} + t_{nva})} \quad \eta_{tva} = \frac{25 \text{ s}}{(25 \text{ s} + 135 \text{ s})} = 16\% \quad (2)$$

The use of dual signatures allows evaluating the production process in respect to the input of time and energy. The cycle time itself as well as the energy used within this cycle time is thereby consequently subdivided into value-adding and non value-adding parts. In the data box of the milling process the results are shown nominally, in form of figures, as well as proportionally in form of the bars beneath, Fig. 5.

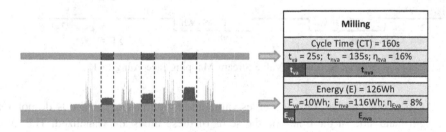

Fig. 5. Dual signature and data box according to [6, 14]

The low efficiencies show that the dual approach can help to reveal substantial improvement potentials within the production process itself. To increase the process efficiency, there are two approaches possible: One is to decrease the power level and thereby reducing the non value-adding energy (E_{nva}). This affects just the energy productivity. The other one is the reduction of non value-adding time (t_{nva}). That will lead to an increase in productivity and in addition to energy savings. When time is wasted and during this time energy is consumed, this amount of energy necessarily also has to be regarded as waste, too. Up to now the authors have analysed several different production processes like milling, casting, welding, injection moulding, handling, robotic and laser applications [1, 6, 17, 18]. For all of them a dualistic approach can be made. Further production processes are actually under research.

6 Energy Value-Stream Mapping

The analysis of the manufacturing process by means of dual energy signatures allows it to extend the VSM to an EVSM while maintaining the inner logic of the VSM [1]. The results of the investigated milling process are embedded into the EVSM, Fig. 6. A drilling process and the time and energy used for the transport between the production processes are added (assumed figures). Transport requires almost always energy, has a lead time extending effect and is not value-adding. Consequently the time (t_T = time Transport) and energy (E_T = Energy Transport) used for transport are considered as non value-adding. This is schematically shown by the rectangular function, Fig. 6.

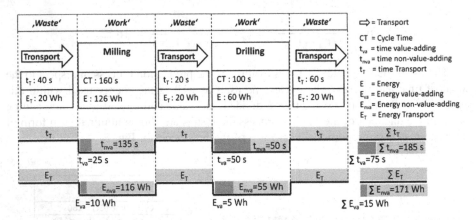

Fig. 6. Energy Value-Stream Mapping [according to 1]

As mentioned earlier, only t_{va} serves value-adding purposes, t_{nva} and t_T do not. On the right hand side of the time line the sums of these times are visualized. The same logic can be applied to the use of energy in EVSM. When optimizing energy value-streams it is important to look at the value-stream as a whole, this helps to avoid suboptimisations.

If there are processes which consume lots of resources (time, energy) or entail low value-adding efficiencies they should be seriously questioned in total. Only if it is impossible to find a more efficient manufacturing technology and a more suitable process, then as a second step the time and energy input which does not contribute to adding value can be reduced systematically.

7 Process Improvement by Dual Energy Signatures and Detailed Process Analysis

Electric energy is the product of power and time. As mentioned to increase the process efficiency, basically two approaches are possible: Reducing the process time or decreasing the power level [17]. However this requires detailed process knowledge and an analysis of all major components to allocate waste of energy.

Figure 7 shows the principal approach to improve the process efficiency by dual energy signatures and detailed process analysis. Like in Fig. 4, the value-adding time and energy, required for chip removal, are marked. From the point of view of energy only shares of the spindle and axle drive serves value-adding purposes. They drive the chip removal. As shown in Fig. 7 all the other components do not serve value-adding purposes. Especially the energy consumption outside the value-adding time should be questioned. Therefore stop and go systems for the different components should be installed, e.g. for lightning, control cabinet cooling, etc. If complete elimination of the energy consumption in non-value adding periods of time is not possible it should be at least reduced to a minimum.

This mythological approach provides a systematic to identify and question any kind of wasted time and energy.

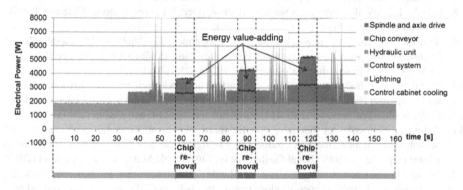

Fig. 7. Detailed process analysis

8 Summary

The analysis of value-streams that include time and energy data are becoming more and more important in the manufacturing industry. With the help of dual energy signatures the value-adding and the non value-adding inputs of time and energy within a production process can be determined, as desired by Ohno. This is shown by using the example of a milling process, in which the energy requirement during air cutting is contrasted with the energy requirement for a milling process with workpiece contact.

This distinction makes it possible to extend a VSM to an EVSM. Including transport in the EVSM offers the opportunity of visualizing not only its non value-adding energy requirement but also its lead time-extending effect. This methodical procedure provides a practical tool to process designers for a comprehensive analysis and improvement of value-streams.

References

1. Müller, E., Stock, T., Schillig, R.: Energy value-stream mapping – a method to optimize value-streams in respect of time and energy consumption. In: Zaeh, M.F. (eds.) Enabling Manufacturing Competiveness and Economic Sustainability. 5th International Conference CARV, pp. 285–290. Munich (2013)
2. Bundesministerium für Umwelt, Naturschutz und Reaktorsicherheit: Umweltwirtschaftsbericht 2011, Umweltbundesamt, p. 80. Dessau-Roßlau (2011)
3. Womack, J.P., Jones, D.T., Ross, D.: The Machine That Changed The World, p. 11. Free Press, New York (1990)
4. Ohno, T.: Toyota Production System. Beyond Large-Scale Production. OR: Productivity Press, Portland (1988)
5. Rother, M., Shook, J.: Learning to See. Value-Stream Mapping to Create Value and Eliminate Muda. Lean Enterprise Institute, Cambridge (2009)
6. Schillig, R., Stock, T., Müller, E.: Energiewertstromanalyse. Eine Methode zur Optimierung von Wertströmen in Bezug auf den Zeit- und Energieeinsatz. ZWF Jahrg. 107(1–2), 20–26 (2013)
7. U.S. Environment Protection Agency (EPA). The Lean and Environment Toolkit, pp. 21–34. http://www.epa.gov/lean (2007). Accessed 31 Mai 2015
8. Erlach, K., Westkämper, E.: Energiewertstrom. Der Weg zur Energie Effizienz Fabrik. Fraunhofer Verlag (2009)
9. Reinhart, G., Karl, F., Krebs, P., Maier, T., Niehues, K., Niehues, M., Reinhardt, S.: Energiewertstromdesign. Ein wichtiger Bestandteil zum Erhöhen der Energieproduktivität. wt Werkstattstechnik online, Jahrgang 101(4), 254–255 (2011)
10. Shahrbabaki, S.A.D., Jackson, M.: Green and lean production visualization tools; a case study exploring EVSM. In: Kersten, W. (ed.) International Supply Chain Management and Collaboration Practices, pp. 399–412. Josef Eul Verlag, Lohmar – Köln (2011)
11. Plehn, J., Sproedt, A., Gontarz, A., Reinhard, J.: From strategic goals to focused eco-efficiency improvement in production – bridging the gap using environmental value stream mapping. In: 10th Global Conference on Sustainable Manufacturing, Istanbul (2012)
12. Posselt, G., Fischer, J., Heinemann, T., Thiede, S., Alvandi, S., Weinert, N., Kara, S., Herrmann, C.: Extending energy value stream models by the TBS dimension – Applied on a multi product process chain in the railway industry. Procedia CIRP 15(2014), 80–85 (2014)
13. Keskin, C., Kayakutlu, G.: Value stream maps for industrial energy efficiency. In: PICMENT 2012: Technology Management for Emerging Technologies, pp. 2824–2831 (2012)
14. Müller, E., Stock, T., Schillig, R.: Dual energy signatures enable energy value-stream mapping. In: 23rd International Conference on Flexible Automation and Intelligent Manufacturing (FAIM), Porto (2013)
15. Denkena, B., Tönshoff, H.K.: Spanen - Grundlagen. Springer, Heidelberg (2011)
16. Schulz, H., Schiefer, E.: Prozeßführung und Energiebedarf bei spanenden Fertigungsverfahren. ZWF 93(6), 266–271 (1998)
17. Müller, E., Schillig, R., Stock, T., Schmeiler, M.: Improvement of injection moulding processes by using dual energy signatures. In: 47th CIRP Conference on Manufacturing Systems (CMS 2014), Windsor (2014)
18. Müller, E., Stock, T., Schillig, R.: A method to generate energy value-streams in productions and logistics in respect of time- and energy-consumption. Prod. Eng. Res. Dev. 8(1–2), 243–251. Springerlink.com (2014). Accessed 05 Dec 2013

Job-Shop like Manufacturing System
with Time Dependent Energy Threshold
and Operations with Peak Consumption

Sylverin Kemmoé-Tchomté[1], Damien Lamy[2],
and Nikolay Tchernev[2(✉)]

[1] CRCGM (EA 3849), Auvergne University, Clermont-Ferrand, France
Sylverin.KEMMOE_TCHOMTE@udamail.fr
[2] LIMOS (UMR CNRS 6158), Auvergne University, Aubière, France
lamy@isima.fr, Nikolay.Tchernev@udamail.fr

Abstract. In this study the Job-shop scheduling problem with energy considerations is considered. At each moment of the schedule an energy threshold must not be exceeded. This energy threshold is not fixed all along the schedule and can vary. The variation of energy is handled by inclusion of dummy operations. Furthermore, the operations that must be scheduled have a power profile presenting a high energy consumption (peak) at the beginning and a lower consumption after the peak's end. A mathematical formulation of the problem is proposed. This model is experimented on a short example with the CPLEX 12.4 solver. The schedules obtained show the relevance of the model. This study shows that new approaches for scheduling are no longer avoidable and that it is possible for enterprises to schedule efficiently their tasks according to energy constraints.

Keywords: Job-shop · Energy consumption · Energy threshold · Linear programing

1 Introduction

A linear model is proposed in this paper which goal is to extend a previous work [1] concerning the scheduling in a job-shop like manufacturing environment with an energy threshold which must not be exceeded. Operations presenting two distinct energy consumptions are considered as follows: a peak consumption at the beginning of the process and a nominal consumption after the peak's end. The previously proposed linear model [1] is extended in order to manage variations in the allowed energy threshold. Thus, the objective is to find the best feasible schedule of the problem where operations need electricity in order to be realized and where the instantly usable energy is constrained and varies with time. The model of the problem could have many applications especially in scheduling operations efficiently according to price variations during given periods, or avoid exceeding predefined consumption peaks that have been negotiated with the electricity supplier.

The rest of the paper is as follows. In the next section a literature review of articles including energy constraints is proposed. In the third section, the assumptions made in

© IFIP International Federation for Information Processing 2015
S. Umeda et al. (Eds.): APMS 2015, Part I, IFIP AICT 459, pp. 617–624, 2015.
DOI: 10.1007/978-3-319-22756-6_75

this study are presented. The fourth and fifth sections introduce a linear program modelling the problem and experiment results. Finally we conclude and give some directions for future research.

2 Related Work

In the literature, industrial problems such as minimizing the total completion time (makespan), the cost, and other objective functions have been widely studied. Although the energy efficiency in manufacturing is well-addressed in the literature (see for survey [2] only a few works addressed the energy consumption as an important constraint in scheduling [3]. However, several papers have spread on this subject concerning the "Green Manufacturing" these past years and a non-exhaustive review is proposed in this section.

Reference [4] proposed several methods and operational tools to minimize the energy consumption of factories. They present a mathematical formulation aiming at minimizing the total completion time of a set of operations while minimizing the total energy consumption. Their model handles the different states a machine can be in: idle, running, switch ON or OFF. Reference [5] showed that a more energy efficient system is more robust and thus less sensitive to breakdowns. They worked on the correlation between makespan, energy and robustness. By inclusion of variable speeds in the operation processes, a machine which is processing a task quickly will consume more energy but the treatment time will be reduced. Thus if a breakdown occur, the lost time could be caught up by increasing processing speed. The model of [6] consists in minimizing the carbon footprint, the makespan and the consumption peaks in a Flow-shop. In their work [7] authors proposed a solution which consists in avoiding consumption peaks on a production system, modelled as a Flexible Flow Shop. They use an Energy Aware Scheduling (EAS) on the existing schedule obtained with an APS (Advanced Planning and Scheduling). They finally note the fact that their model could be better, integrating variability of costs and energy need of machines which is constant in their study. Reference [8] took into account the variable prices of electricity during a day, including Time-of-Use (TOU) rates in a Flexible Flow-shop. It is observed that a few work have been done concerning the Job-shop with energy constraints and thus they proposed a Job-shop where both the total energy consumption and the total tardiness are minimized.

In a previous work [1], a linear model for the Job-shop with Energy Consumption Threshold (JS-ECT) is proposed where each operation has two different energy consumption: a high energy consumption at the beginning of the operation, called a peak consumption, and a lower energy consumption for the rest of the operation. In this mathematical formulation, the energy threshold is constant during the schedule. Thus, an improved linear program where this energy threshold could change over time is proposed. In the next section the assumptions used in this paper concerning the Job-shop with a Variable Energy Consumption Threshold (JS-VECT) where the operations to be scheduled present an electricity consumption peak at their start are presented.

3 Assumptions Used

3.1 Physical Assumptions

This study is based on the Job-shop theoretical model which is known to be a NP-Hard problem (see for review [9]). The Job-shop problem consists in scheduling a set of n jobs that have to be sequenced on m machines. Each job involves a set of operations, which must be processed in a pre-determined order. Each operation has to be processed on a given machine during a processing time and no pre-emption is allowed. A commonly used objective in Job-shop problem is the minimization of completion time of all jobs (makespan) by managing machine disjunctions.

3.2 Energy Assumptions

While doing the literature review concerning energy optimization on production systems, two things appeared. First, the operations are generally represented with constant energy consumption as shown in [7] where operations have a unitary consumption. However, it can be seen in the literature that machine operations have complex energy behavior where most of the time operations present an energy consumption peak at the start of processing as shown in the work of [10] concerning lasers. An example of real world energy profile for machines tool is given in Fig. 1. In this figure is also plotted the energy representation commonly observed in the literature and the representation chosen in this study. In the proposed representation the first part of the diagram represents the consumption peak and the second one corresponds to the processing energy consumption. Secondly, studies concerning scheduling under consumption peaks constraints often consider a constant available energy over time, however this available energy could vary over time because of a negotiated contract with the energy supplier, or in order to model the cost of instantly useable electricity.

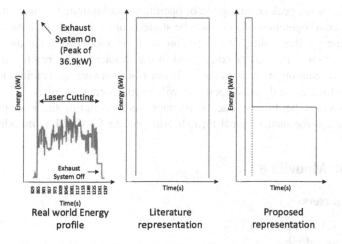

Fig. 1. Power profile of a machine and its representations [1]

In the Fig. 1, it can be easily understood that considering a constant energy consumption for the operations imply a possible loss of time while scheduling since some operations cannot be planed earlier because of an operation consuming more energy than really needed. Considering this assumption, it has been chosen to divide the operations into two sub-operations: one concerning the high energy consumption peak, and the other concerning the operating energy consumption. Finally, a variable energy threshold that must never be exceeded is introduced (*i.e.*: from 0 to 50 time units, 70 kW are allowed; from 50 to 80, 50 kW are allowed; etc. ...). An example of a schedule including a varying energy threshold and operations considering peak consumption is given in Fig. 2.

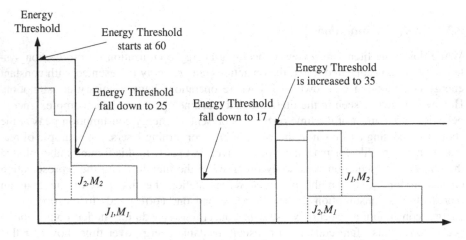

Fig. 2. A Gantt chart of a schedule involving energy threshold variations

In Fig. 2, two jobs must be processed: Job J_1, which routing pass through Machine M_1 and M_2, and job J_2 passing through M_2 and M_1. Vertical dotted lines represent the separation between peak consumption of operations and nominal consumptions. In this example, second operation of J_2 cannot be started earlier because of a reduction in the available energy threshold. This variation will be modelled with use of dummy operations which starting dates correspond to the moment of energy threshold change and energy consumption equal to the variation (*i.e.*: between threshold valued 60 and threshold valued 25, a dummy operation will need 35 energy units).

In this section the different energy assumptions used in this study are presented. In the next section the mathematical formalization of the JS-VECT is introduced.

4   Linear Modelling

4.1   Parameters

M : set of machines;
J : set of jobs;

V	: set of all the sub-operations ($|V| = 2 \cdot |M| \cdot |J|$);
T	: set of events corresponding to energy threshold change;
V^+	: set V adjoined with dummy vertices ($|V^+|=|V| + |T|$);
i, j, k, l	: indexes representing the different operations;
O_i	: global operation of the sub-operation i, $i \in V$;
J_i	: job of the operation i;
p_i	: duration of operation i;
T_k	: time of energy threshold change (i.e.: $k = 0$ corresponds to first threshold);
μ_i	: machine required to process sub-operation i, $\mu_i \in M$;
H	: a large positive number;
E_i	: energy required for processing the operation i;
E_{max}	: maximum energy that must never be;

4.2 Variables

C_{max}	: completion date of all operations also referred as the makespan of the schedule;
s_i	: starting time of sub-operation i;
$x_{i,j}$	: binary variable equal to 1 if sub-operation i is realized before sub-operation j and equal to 0 otherwise;
$y_{i,j}$	: binary variable equal to 1 if there is a non-null energy flow from sub-operation i to the sub-operation j and equal to 0 otherwise;
$\varphi_{i,j}$	: denotes the number of energy units transferred between entities of the system (could be real or dummy operations);

4.3 Linear Formulation

$$Min \; C_{\max} \tag{1}$$

$$s_i + p_i \le C_{max}, \; \forall i \in V \tag{2}$$

$$x_{j,k} + x_{l,i} = 1, \; \forall i,j,k,l \in V/i<j, \; k<l, \; O_i = O_j, \; O_k = O_l, \; i \ne k, \; \mu_i = \mu_k \tag{3}$$

$$s_j - s_i \ge p_i, \; \forall (i,j) \in V/i<j, \; J_i = J_j \tag{4}$$

$$s_j - s_i = p_i, \; \forall (i,j) \in V/i<j, \; O_i = O_j \tag{5}$$

$$s_j - s_i - Hx_{i,j} \ge p_i - H, \; \forall i,j \in V/O_i \ne O_j, \; \mu_i = \mu_j, \\ mod(i,2) = 0, \; mod(j,2) = 1 \tag{6}$$

$$\sum\nolimits_{j \in V^+} \varphi_{0,j} \le E_{max} \tag{7}$$

$$\sum_{j \in V^+} \varphi_{0,j} = E_j, \ \forall j \in V^+ / i \neq j \tag{8}$$

$$\sum_{j \in V^+} \varphi_{0,j} \leq E_i, \ \forall i \in V^+ / i \neq j \tag{9}$$

$$\varphi_{i,j} = min(E_i, E_j), \ \forall (i,j) \in V / i < j, \ O_i = O_j \tag{10}$$

$$s_k = T_{k-|V|}, \ \forall k \in V^+ \backslash V \tag{11}$$

$$\varphi_{i,j} \leq H.y_{i,j}, \ \forall i,j \in V^+ / i \neq j \tag{12}$$

$$y_{i,j} \leq \varphi_{i,j}, \ \forall i \in V^+ / i \neq j \tag{13}$$

$$s_j - s_i - Hy_{i,j} \geq p_i - H, \ \forall (i,j) \in V^+ / J_i \neq J_j \tag{14}$$

$$\varphi_{j,i} = 0, \ \forall (i,j) \in V / i < j, \ J_i = J_j \tag{15}$$

The first line (1) refers to the objective of the problem: minimizing the completion time of all operations (makespan). Constraints (2) give the expression of the makespan. Constraints (3) represent the precedencies for sub-operations occurring on the same machines (i.e.: whether the first sub-operation of a global operation is scheduled before a second sub-operation on another global operation, or vice versa). Constraints (4) define the starting dates of operations according to job's sequence. Constraints (5) ensure that, if i and j are two sub-operations referring to the same global operations, then j is processed directly after the end of the sub-operation i. Constraints (6) adjust the starting dates of operations that belong to different jobs but need the same machine. Constraint (7) avoids to exceed the maximal energy threshold when processing the operations. Constraints (8) ensure that the sum of energy flowing from dummy operations, sub-operations and energy threshold is equal to the energy needed for the sub-operation j. Constraints (9) ensure that the sum of energy flowing from dummy operations or the sub-operation i to the other ones never exceeds the energy that was used for its processing. Constraints (10) is a cut corresponding to a flow of energy between first and second sub-operation of the same global operation. Constraints (11) fix the starting dates of the dummy operations that represent the variation of the energy threshold over time. Constraints (12) ensure that if there is an energy flow from i to j then $y_{i,j} = 1$. If $y_{i,j} = 0$ then no flow is possible from i to j. Constraints (13) stipulate that if there is no need of a flow from i to j ($\varphi_{i,j} = 0$), then necessarily $y_{i,j} = 0$, however if $y_{i,j} = 1$ then necessarily $\varphi_{i,j} > 0$. Constraints (14) adjust the starting dates of sub-operations which need to wait before the end of previous operations in order to not exceed the energy threshold available at the moment. Constraints (15) stipulate that no flow is possible between two sub-operations i and j, if i and j belong to the same job and if i is processed before j.

5 Results

The validity of the above linear program has been tested on a set of small examples (including the one presented in Fig. 2) randomly generated. The linear model is solved using CPLEX 12.4 solver. In Fig. 3 is presented the Gantt diagram of a problem without any energy consideration and the Gantt diagram of the same problem extended with energy consumptions and an energy threshold varying over time. In this figure, it is also plotted the energy consumed by each operation to show the impact of the threshold on the schedule.

On Fig. 3 it can be stressed that third operation of J_3 is the most consuming one and can only be scheduled during a given time-window, thus all its predecessors on the job must be scheduled before. The other operations start only if enough energy is available. Finally, it can be clearly seen that two things can affect the schedule while considering a variable energy threshold: the moment energy threshold change and the value of allowed energy after a change. According to chosen values it is possible that no schedule will fit the energy threshold profile.

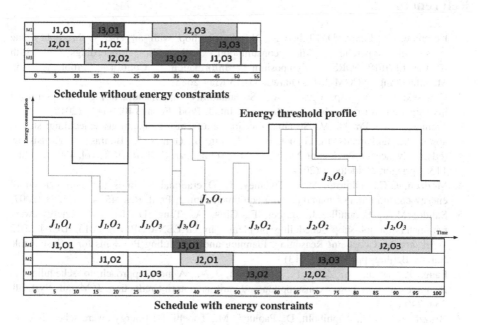

Fig. 3. Impact of the energy threshold on schedules

6 Conclusion and Future Work

In this study the problem of the Job-shop with a Variable Energy Threshold Constraint (JS-VECT) is addressed. The linear model considers operations that have two types of energy consumption: a huge energy consumption, and a nominal energy. Furthermore, the available energy at each moment of the schedule could change over time. This is modelled by inclusion of dummy operations which have a predefined energy consumption and whom starting dates are fixed. The linear model provides exact solutions for small scale instances, but is quickly overtaken with the increasing of jobs and machines. In the future larger scale instances for the problem will be treated with the use of a metaheuristic. Several perspectives appear as future works. Indeed, the energy threshold is considered as a parameter in this study, and it could be really interesting to consider it a variable to be calculated thus leading to a bi-criteria problem where the objective is to display a Pareto graphic of the possible solutions. Another perspective is to consider due dates since starting dates of operations are modified in order to respect the energy threshold, and with them the ending dates of operations or jobs. Finally, it could be interesting to add other objectives such as minimizing the cost of the production by inclusion of time-of-use considerations, or minimizing the total energy needed in the planning.

Acknowledgments. This work was financially supported by the French Public Investment Bank (BPI) and granted by the ECOTHER project.

References

1. Kemmoe, S., Lamy, D., Tchernev, N.: A job-shop with an energy threshold issue considering operations with consumption peaks. In: Proceedings of 15th IFAC/IEEE/IFIP/IFORS Symposium Information Control Problems in Manufacturing INCOM 2015, Ottawa, 11–13 May 2015
2. Gunasekaran, A., Spalanzani, A.: Sustainability of manufacturing and services: investigations for research and applications. Int. J. Prod. Econ. **140**, 35–47 (2012)
3. Trentesaux, D., Prabhu, V.: Sustainability in manufacturing operations scheduling: stakes, approaches and trends. In: Grabot, B., Vallespir, B., Gomes, S., Bouras, A., Kiritsis, D. (eds.) Advances in Production Management Systems, Part II. IFIP AICT, vol. 439, pp. 106–113. Springer, Heidelberg (2014)
4. Mouzon, G.C., Yildirim, M.B., Twomey, J.: Operational methods for minimization of energy consumption of manufacturing equipment. Int. J. Prod. Res. **45**, 4247–4271 (2007)
5. Salido, M.A., Escamilla, J., Barber, F., Giret, A., Tang, D., Dai, M.: Energy-aware parameters in job-shop scheduling problems. In GREEN-COPLAS 2013: IJCAI 2013 Workshop on Constraint Reasoning, Planning and Scheduling Problems for a Sustainable Future, Beijing, pp. 44–53 (2013)
6. Fang, K., Uhan, N., Zaho, F., Sutherland, J.W.: A new approach to scheduling in manufacturing for power consumption and carbon footprint reduction. J. Manuf. Syst. **30**, 234–240 (2011)
7. Bruzzone, A.A.G., Anghinolfi, D., Paolucci, M., Tonelli, F.: Energy-aware scheduling for improving manufacturing process sustainability: a mathematical model for flexible flow shops. CIRP Ann. Manuf. Technol. **61**, 459–462 (2012)
8. Luo, H., Du, B., Huang, G.Q., Chen, H., Li, X.: Hybrid flow shop scheduling considering machine electricity consumption cost. Int. J. Prod. Econ. **146**, 423–439 (2013)
9. Jain, A.S., Meeran, S.: Deterministic job-shop scheduling: past, present and future. Eur. J. Oper. Res. **113**(2), 390–434 (1999)
10. Kellens, K., Costa-Rodrigues, G., Dewulf, W., Duflou, J.R.: Energy and resource efficiency of laser cutting processes. In: Proceedings of the 8th International Conference on Photonic Technologies, Physics Procedia, vol. 56, pp. 854–864 (2014)

Environmental Management Practices
for the Textile Sector

Barbara Resta[⊠], Stefano Dotti, Albachiara Boffelli,
and Paolo Gaiardelli

Department of Management, Information and Production Engineering,
CELS - Research Group on Industrial Engineering, Logistics and Service
Operations, Viale Marconi 5, 24044 Dalmine, BG, Italy
{barbara.resta,stefano.dotti,albachiara.boffelli,
paolo.gaiardelli}@unibg.it

Abstract. Environmental sustainability is gaining more and more relevance for textile companies. However, there are often problems with application, even in the most committed companies. In this paper, an empirical typology of Italian textile firms that discern the patterns of practices used in response to environmental issues and concerns that affect such industry is proposed. The resulting typology is composed by three types: Best practice, Good practice and Bad practice. Each type is then characterised in terms of firm's characteristics and perceived environmental competitiveness benefits. The discussion of some open issues deriving from the empirical analysis precedes the final conclusion.

Keywords: Environmental sustainability · Environmental management practices · Environmental competitiveness · Textile sector

1 Introduction

Over the past decades, many companies have started to included environmental considerations into their business activities in order to decrease or eliminate the impact of these activities on the natural environment [1]. The concept of corporate environmental management [2] was introduced at the beginning of the '90s to help managers handle this new situation, translating the concept of environmental sustainability into a managerial tool for company managers. Although previous studies have made significant contributions to the literature on environmental issues, much still remains to be learnt about how companies include this challenge and opportunity into new strategic and operational options [3]. Moreover, most of the existing studies are too general and theoretical, and the assumption that all the business are facing a similar environmental problem is rarely appropriate [4]. The specific industrial context tends to shape the strategies and management systems that exist at the firm-level due to its unique regulations and the influence of its stakeholders [5]. In particular, the textile sector is one of the industries mostly affected by environmental issues and concerns: it is one of the world's largest industries, while also one of the most polluting [6]. Thus, sustainability principles, strategies and tools have then become essential for textile companies to stay competitive in the market [7].

© IFIP International Federation for Information Processing 2015
S. Umeda et al. (Eds.): APMS 2015, Part I, IFIP AICT 459, pp. 625–631, 2015.
DOI: 10.1007/978-3-319-22756-6_76

In such a context, this article aims at developing an empirical typology of the Italian textile companies by statistically identifying consistent and recurring patterns (types) of environmental management practices.

The paper is organised as follows. The next section outlines the theoretical background of the study. In Sect. 3, the research methodology will be described by presenting the research model and the empirical study carried out in the Italian textile sector. In Sect. 4, the research findings are discussed and implications of the findings are presented. Finally, the last section (Sect. 5) closes the paper with the most relevant conclusions and future research directions.

2   Theoretical Background

Environmental Management Practices (EMPs) refer to all the measures and activities aimed at reducing the environmental impact caused by a company's business. Despite many management practices are often lumped together as simply "environmental", it is important that practices are effectively distinguished from one another. Sroufe et al. [8], classified the practices on the basis of their scope, that might be operational, tactical or strategic, thus pertaining to different foci, representing different resource commitments and targeting a wide range of goals and objectives. The authors continued underlying that for a firm to be committed to environmental management, it must be aware of holistic environmental concerns, coordinating and integrating activities across operational, tactical and strategic levels. Another standpoint, relying on the resource-based view, was embraced by Lucas [9], where the EMPs were categorised along two dimensions: the different capital investment types and the stages at which they affect the production process, while Colicchia et al. [10] distinguished between intra-organisational and inter-organisational environmental practices. The former refers to practices related to company "in-house" processes, while the latter to initiatives that imply collaboration and trust among multiple supply chain members. In general, it can be affirmed that researchers have surveyed firms' adoption of EMPs, identifying their adoption either within a specific sector, or across industries, considering specific firm size, or adopting a longitudinal perspective. EMPs have also been studied in relation to environmental and economic performance and influencing factors. However, due to the lack of an exhaustive framework for EMPs, each paper relies on a different set of practices drawn by the authors from the literature on environmental issues. To fill this gap, Resta et al. [11] proposed a comprehensive classification framework for environmental sustainability practices by combining a systematic literature review with a web content analysis of ten European sustainability leaders, selected according to the Dow Jones Sustainability Europe Index. The resulting theoretical framework, containing 57 practices divided into 6 areas, represents a reference framework for EMP and is potentially applicable to every sector. In particular, it was used to survey the Italian Textile, Clothing and Leather (TCL) industry by content-analysing the corporate websites. As one of first research devoted to understanding the practices for environmental sustainability in the Italian TCL supply chain, although it is exploratory in nature, some interesting findings were hypothesised from this study. However, the direct collection of empirical data is necessary to validate the current research findings and to further describe the distribution of the environmental sustainability phenomenon in the considered population and to analyse how such phenomenon contribute to corporate competitiveness. In particular, two main research question arise: "Are there consistent and recurring patterns of environmental practices which can be viewed as an empirical typology?"; "What are the competitiveness benefits related to each type?". Therefore this study attempts to: (i) discern empirically the patterns (or types) of practices used by Italian textile companies in response to environmental issues and concerns that affect such industry, (ii) analyse which are the main firm characteristics (in terms of size, production segment, vertical integration, and environmental strategy) of each individuated type, and (iii) identify the environmental competitiveness benefits that are related to each type.

3   Research Methodology

A descriptive survey research has been conducted to shed light on the above-mentioned research questions.

3.1   The Conceptual Model

Measures for environmental management practices were drawn from [11] and were finalized during a pilot study. Several associations, both at national and European level, were also consulted. In total, 33 measures were considered, categorised into 13 categories (Product, Raw materials, Packaging, Supply chain, Transportation, Environmental Management System (EMS), Energy management, Water management, Waste management, Air emission management, Materials, Culture, Governance). For each practice, managers were asked to indicate its use (dummy variable: 0 = "not used"; 1 = "used") in the company. For each category, the intensity of EMPs was computed with an index constructed as a single scale of continual variation $[0,..,1]$ (where 0 = worst EMP profile; 1 = best EMP profile), which allowed the practice aggregation process at category level.

Measurement of competitiveness is complex because no commonly accepted definition of this concept exists and, consequently, it should include as many business performance dimensions as possible to provide a holistic view of environmental management's effects on firms' competitiveness [12]. Therefore, a firm's self-assessment approach based on a number of items has been employed. Environmental competitiveness self-assessment was thus measured by asking managers to select the perceived competitive benefits from a list. Then, the items were aggregated into 3 categories (Revenue growth, Cost savings and Compliance and risk), computed with an index constructed as a single scale of continual variation $[0,..,1]$ (where 0 = no environmental competitiveness; 1 = high environmental competitiveness).

3.2   Data Collection and Analysis

The primary data for this study was collected through a web survey in June–July 2014. The questionnaire was administered to the total population of Italian textile companies included in the AIDA database (NACE code: 13) having an email contact publically available, totalling 1509. In total, 303 usable responses returned to the authors, corresponding to a response rate of 20 %. In order to identify consistent and recurring patterns of environmental practices, agglomerative hierarchical cluster analysis was employed to group the textile companies into homogeneous categories. The software used to perform the cluster analysis statistical calculation was the IBM® SPSS® Statistics Version 20.

4   Results and Discussion

4.1   Cluster Analysis Results

Initially, the number of clusters had to be chosen. The hierarchical agglomerative clustering method to form groups was employed. During the course of agglomeration, squared Euclidean distance was used to calculate the distance between each pair of companies. As a result, three types (clusters) were formed. The profile of the variables for the solution with three clusters is presented in Table 1.

Discriminant analysis confirmed results of the cluster analysis in verifying that all the companies were properly classified in their groups.

Table 1. Cluster analysis of environmental practice implementation

Cluster / Practices	1	2	3	Total average
Product	0.40	0.36	0.24	0.29
Raw materials	0.60	0.39	0.35	0.40
Packaging	0.52	0.36	0.31	0.35
Supply chain	0.48	0.37	0.26	0.32
Transportation	0.50	0.44	0.30	0.37
Environmental Management System (EMS)	0.33	1.00	0.00	0.34
Energy management	0.61	0.43	0.28	0.37
Water management	0.71	0.29	0.15	0.27
Waste management	0.63	0.55	0.44	0.50
Air emission management	0.71	0.24	0.11	0.23
Materials	0.74	0.47	0.31	0.42
Culture	0.52	0.34	0.17	0.27
Governance	0.33	0.23	0.04	0.14

Cluster 1. Best Practice. This group represents 42 companies (14 % of the sample), and is characterised by a high receptivity to environmental issues, that are expressed in the highest level of practice implementation in all the categories but EMS. The group has the largest average turnover and the highest vertical integration: 33 % of the companies covers up to 4 production segments. The cluster is characterised by the highest level of environmental strategic proactivity (2,33/3,00) and a medium level of cost savings (0,39) and competitiveness (0,30) perceived benefits.

Cluster 2. Good Practice. This group contains 88 firms (29 % of the sample), that show a medium level of practice implementation. In average, companies included in this group have smaller dimension and a lower vertical integration compared to Group 1: 21 % of the companies covers up to 3 production segments. The cluster is characterised by a high level of environmental strategic proactivity (2,23/3,00) and a medium level of cost savings (0,34) and competitiveness (0,30) perceived benefits.

Cluster 3. Bad Practice. This group represents 57 % of the surveyed companies. These 173 firms expressed the lowest implementation of environmental management practices in all the categories. In average, companies included in this group have the lowest environmental proactivity (1,89/3,00), the smallest dimension (in terms of turnover) and the lowest vertical integration: 16 % of the companies covers up to 2 production segments. The companies perceive a low level of cost savings (0,23) and competitiveness (0,22) benefits.

4.2   Environmental Practice Analysis and Discussion

Considering the average for all the companies, practices showing the highest level of implementation are: (i) waste management, in particular waste reduction (48 % of the sample) and separate waste collection (89 %); (ii) use of process materials, in particular the use of certified materials (60 %); and (iii) use of raw materials, that are sustainable (64 %) and certified (51 %). Practices presenting the worst implementation level are: (i) Culture; (ii) Air emission management; and (iii) Governance.

Moving from Best to Bad practice, the implementation level decreases in all the categories but EMS. This last aspect represents a warning point for companies belonging to Cluster 1: despite such firms declare to implement a high number of environmental practices in all the areas, apparently they do not have a systematic management system in place.

Overall, it can be stated that only a part of the Italian textile companies are fully concerned and committed about environmental issues and recognise the importance and necessity of incorporating environmental approaches into their management practices (Cluster 1). However, their similarities with Cluster 2 firms in terms of environmental strategic proactivity and perceived benefits poses a doubt about their leadership position: it is hard to imagine how a sustainability agenda with this many focus areas can break through and get the necessary buy-in to be successful. While there are several areas that companies need to comply with, it might be better to concentrate on a few themes and strategic priorities. To develop a clear set of priorities, it is important to start by analysing what matters most along the entire value chain, through internal analysis and consultations with stakeholders, including customers, regulators, and nongovernmental organizations. This process should enable companies to identify the sustainability issues with the greatest long-term potential and thus to create a systematic agenda. Once the priorities are identified, the next step is to develop a fact base from which to define the practices that need to be implemented. Companies have several management tools available, such as Environmental Performance Management Systems, supported by proper Environmental Management Information Systems and controlled through flexible governance structures. All these tools find a strong basis into a pervasive culture for environmental sustainability.

5 Conclusion

Environmental sustainability is gaining more and more relevance for textile companies since it can positively contribute to the firm's value creation process. Several companies are starting to pave the way towards sustainability through different management systems and approaches. The objective of this study was to identify and characterise groups of Italian textile companies that are statistically similar to each other considering the environmental management practices they adopt. This was carried out using a cluster analysis. Three types were identified: Best, Good and Bad practice. Moving from Best to Bad practice, average turnover and vertical integration decrease, as well as the implementation level of environmental management practices in all the categories (but EMS). The analysis showed that, although sustainability is somewhere on the corporate agenda, there are often problems with execution, even in the most committed companies, and the necessity to focus on a limited set of strategic priorities was highlighted. Finally, some directions for future research can be pointed out to expand this work: (i) include in the sample textile companies from other countries; (ii) enlarge the conceptual model to social sustainability aspects; and (iii) test the relationship between the implementation of environmental management practices and companies' financial results.

References

1. Bonini, S., Bové, A.: Sustainability's Strategic Worth: McKinsey Global Survey results. McKinsey & Company, New York (2014)
2. Greeno, J.L.: Rethinking corporate environmental management. Columbia J. World Bus. 27 (3–4), 222–232 (1992)
3. Madsen, H., Ulhi, J.: Have trends in corporate environmental management influenced companies competitiveness? Greener Manage. Int. 44, 74–88 (2003)
4. Hubbard, G.: Strategic Management: Thinking, Analysis and Action. Prentice-Hall, Sydney (2000)
5. Chang, D., Kuo, L., Chen, Y.: Industrial changes in corporate sustainability performance–an empirical overview using data envelopment analysis. J. Clean. Prod. 56, 147–155 (2013)
6. European Commission: Sustainability of textiles. Retail Forum for Sustainability, no. 11 (2013). http://ec.europa.eu/environment/industry/retail/pdf/issue_paper_textiles.pdf

7. Smith, N.: Corporate social responsibility: whether or how? Calif. Manage. Rev. **45**, 1–25 (2003)
8. Sroufe, R., Montabon, F., Narasimhan, R., Wang, X.: Environmental management practices. Greener Manage. Int. **40**, 23–40 (2002)
9. Lucas, M.T.: Understanding environmental management practices: integrating views from strategic management and ecological economics. Bus. Strateg. Environ. **19**(8), 543–556 (2010)
10. Colicchia, C., Marchet, G., Melacini, M., Perotti, S.: Building environmental sustainability: empirical evidence from logistics service providers. J. Clean. Prod. **59**, 197–209 (2013)
11. Resta, B., Dotti, S., Pinto, R., Bandinelli, R., Rinaldi, R., Ciarapica, F.E.: Practices for environmental sustainability in the textile, clothing and leather sectors: the Italian case. Int. J. Oper. Quant. Manage. **20**(3), 193–225 (2014)
12. Wagner, M., Schaltegger, S.: The effect of corporate environmental strategy choice and environmental performance on competitiveness and economic performance: an empirical study of EU manufacturing. Eur. Manage. J. **22**(5), 557–572 (2004)

Life Cycle Assessment Electricity Generation from Landfill in São Paulo City

Marise Barros Miranda de Gomes[1,2(✉)], José Benedito Sacomano[1],
Fabio Papalardo[1], and Alexandre Erdmann da Silva[2]

[1] Post Graduate Program in Production Engineering,
Universidade Paulista (UNIP), Dr. Bacelar St. 1212, Sao Paulo, SP, Brazil
marise.gomes@superig.com.br
[2] Centro Universitário Das Faculdades Metropolitanas Unidas – FMU,
São Paulo, Brazil

Abstract. A municipal solid waste landfills are complex systems, because your waste in a landfill body has a large heterogeneous mixture, high levels of different organic and inorganic matter. Environmental problems are results about intense urbanization, but different solutions offered for alternatives mitigating the environmental impacts. These solutions are the best practices in the recovery of such wastes when disposed of in landfills. But recent concepts in modern landfill management, in the São Paulo City, incorporate strategies in their life cycle, so since the beginning of the landfill, different techniques have been tested to stabilize the amount of methane gas emissions and energy recovery. This work finds the perspective, sustainability electricity generation, these uses of landfill gas are divided into electricity generation and direct use. The scenery, study sustainability indicators are Bandeirantes Landfill, with application of fuzzy logic to estimate production methane for energy generation.

Keywords: Landfill · Fuzzy logic · Sustainability · Recovers energy · Renewable energy

1 Introduction

Recent concepts in modern landfill management, incorporate sustainability indicators in their life cycle, when the beginning of the landfill, many techniques are tested to stabilize the amount of methane gas emissions, included estimations using linear and no-linear models [1]. Energy recovery is one of the indicators of sustainability for landfills, but these systems necessitates estimation of gas released and its energy potential [2].

Sustainability, it's a term created by the Helmholtz Institute [3], an important center of research and technology from Germany, highlights the use of energy and natural resources in an efficient, safe and sustainable way. Therefore, it defines the minimum requirements that are universally valid for the global sustainable development, unconventionally. It assigns the deficit of sustainability indicator to the forecasts of global energy shortage, to power supply or generation, to the extraction of raw materials and waste disposal without its energy recovery.

© IFIP International Federation for Information Processing 2015
S. Umeda et al. (Eds.): APMS 2015, Part I, IFIP AICT 459, pp. 632–639, 2015.
DOI: 10.1007/978-3-319-22756-6_77

This methodological approach is based on the integrative sustainability concept developed by the Helmholtz Association. Its large idea is that the abstract notion of sustainability has to be adapted to a specific local situation, in this case, Bandeirantes Landfill, in order to make its meaning clear. Therefore, it defines the minimum requirements that are universally valid for the global sustainable development, unconventionally. It assigns the deficit of sustainability indicator to the forecasts of global energy shortage, to power supply or generation, to the extraction of raw materials and waste disposal without its energy recovery.

Landfills operating and maintenance costs are expensive for Brazilian municipalities, resolution 404 of the National Environmental Council and the law 11.107/2005, complementary to each other, assist in retrenchment strategies by the landfill sharing between municipalities in the same region [4, 5]. The first one establishes a set of guidelines to obtain environmental licensing for small landfills, and the second one sets norms for the management in intermunicipal consortium [6].

It is estimated that Brazil has 1,723 landfills [7]. The soil is prepared so that garbage does not affect the environment, does not cause bad odors, and does not contribute to visual pollution or to the proliferation of animals. When the waste decomposes it generates leachate: a pollutant liquid, methane gas, and other pollutants. Methane causes pollution and it is about 20 times worse for the Earth's climate than carbon dioxide emissions.

The motivation of this study reinforces that the technical parameters adopted to determine the energy potential of this type of enterprise have been developed to landfills in other countries. Therefore, design features, its operation, waste types and climatic conditions are different in the national landfills, endangering the sustainability of the landfill as an alternative energy source.

1.1   A Review the Life Cycle Bandeirantes and Parameters Reference

From 2008, the Bandeirantes landfill began to operate as an independent producer and supplier of electricity. The expectation of this last phase is estimated to expire in 2030. The highest peak of sustainable production and methane generation was recorded in 2004, when it was still operating as a landfill.

Estimate the total amount of methane gas produced in landfills, variables such as time and phases of waste decomposition should be considered. Besides these influencing factors, the degradation process influences the potential to generate methane gas, which can reach about 400 m^3/ton of dry residue [8].

Indeed, was presented the results of a study conducted in 20 landfills in northern Germany [9]. The variations in the generation of methane depend on landfill soil compaction, on rainfall, and on the concentration of each type of material in different points. The climatic conditions of each region analyzed, as well as the operation of landfills, are also factors that influence the quality and quantity of production of methane gas. Finally, the research by this author also considered the amount of oxygen penetrating into the soil, the t soil type and its granularity and distribution of the amount of water in various parts of the landfill. Soil type and its granularity and distribution of the amount of water in various parts of the landfill.

Many procedures and methodologies evaluated two methods for the estimation landfill gas sustainability [10]. One of them is called design method of IPCC [11] and the method of first-order decay known as the equation of USEPA [12]. These authors recommend further research on different methods, but concluded that the design method estimates lower rates of methane generation, since it brings into account the average of dispose of different cases of waste, leading to inaccurate results.

2 Methodology

2.1 Study Theoretical About Emission Factor and Collection Factor

The first equations of calculation methods for estimating methane generation did not consider the emissions, part of which migrated to the atmosphere and others were absorbed and degraded in the surface layers of the territorial plan of the landfill, among many other parameters. According to the IPCC [11], different methods and mathematical models were used to estimate the emissions in landfills. This variability did not allow the application in regions or even in countries, due to the heterogeneity of climate, soil, rainfall, among other factors.

It was conducted in a study on the application of the mathematical model in different CDM projects in developing countries, comparing with the measured results [13]. The countries involved in the study were Brazil, China, Argentina and Chile. The author's conclusion was that the models refer to different optimal precisions of the actual measurements and cannot adequately explain the composition of the wastes and the site conditions which are different from the landfills in developed countries.

Research also emphasizes that the initial model evolved in order to improve accuracy because of the variables that affect the chemical reactions [14]. They indicate constraints on the models such as the complexity of gas generation, depending on several variables, according to the particular conditions of each landfill, such as soil, moisture, and climate.

Thus, in order to calculate the methane generation in this study, we used Eq. 1, as follows.

$$Q_{CH4} = L_0 * R * (e_{-kc} - e_{-kt}) \tag{1}$$

Where:

Q_{CH4} = Methane generated in year t (m^3/year);
L_0 = Potential of methane generation (m^3/ton);
R = Annual average of garbage input at the dump, (ton/year);
K = Methane generation rate = 0.04 (half life from 4 to 2 years);
c = year since the closure;
t = year since the beginning of the activity (year).

It is noteworthy that, in the Eq. 1, the variables c and t are equivalent to the variables t and y respectively presented in Eq. 1. In Eq. 1, there is the representation of the sum (Σ) of all years for the decay variable. There is also a technical motivation for adopting another tool instead of the one proposed by USEPA [12].

The first-order equation, Eq. 1 has the period of 1 year as time, and not the time in its lower part, for example, the production of gas in each second of time. Making projections of gas production at all time points would be limited, even if finitely. Only supercomputers could perform some processing on this level of accuracy, adding the projections of the landfill gas lifecycle of 20, 30, 40 or more years ahead.

The potential methane generation capacity, or L_0, describe the total amount of methane gas potentially produced by a metric ton of waste as it decays. EPA determined that the appropriate values for L0 range from 56.6 to 198.2 m^3 per metric ton or megagram (m^3/Mg) of waste, in practice. Except in dry climates where lack of moisture can limit methane generation, the value for the L_0 depends almost entirely on the type of waste present in the landfill. The higher the organic content of the waste, the higher the value of L_0, this is a sustainability factor. Note that the dry organic content of the waste determines the L0 value, and not the wet weight measured and recorded at landfill scale houses, as water does not generate LFG. Some tools have a refers sets L_0 to a default value of 170 m^3/Mg to represent a conventional landfill.

Abrelpe [15] highlights the difficulty of finding the database in order to estimate accurately the values of L0 and k. It recommends the adoption of the rating factor of the waste disposal site, Table 1. This factor is associated with L0 variable and it influences the potential of methane gas generation.

Table 1. Emission factor - EF

Site	Emission Factor (EF)
Landfill	1.0
Controlled landfill	0.8
Trash dump	0.4

This emission factor associated with the site of residue destination interferes with the estimated portion of generation of methane gas. Landfills have factor 1 of 100 %. It is estimated that these sites have adequate control regarding the handling and compaction of waste [16].

The Table 2 presents the simulation results of the matrix that combines the emission factor and the collection factor with three types of disposal sites, according to the Eq. 2.

$$LO' = [EF] * [CEF] \qquad (2)$$

Table 2. Simulation result for L_0'(m^3/ton)

Site category	EF = 0.6	CEF = 0.85
1	0.6	0.85
2	0.48	0.68
3	0.24	0.51

In the simulation shown in Table 2, the three categories were divided into 1 for landfill, 2 for controlling landfill and 3 to trash dump. The last one had the lowest result regarding the L_0' variable. The blue column was coded for the results of 60 % collection percentage and the red column to 85 % performed collection.

The results emphasize that the collection factor affects the emission factor, the lower the collection factor the lower the potential for methane gas production. When the collection factor tends to increase, the potential for methane generation tends positively too. Although the collection factor is the same for landfills and controlled landfills, the numbers remained different in the two cases (EF and CEF).

2.2 Application of Fuzzy Logic Model for Estimating the Production of Methane Gas in Landfill

Fuzzy logic is widely used in a machine control, for example. The term fuzzy refers to the logic involved can deal with concepts that cannot be expressed as the "true" or "false" but rather as "partially true".

This paper presents fundamental ways an existing model for the numerical assessment of sustainability called sustainability assessment by fuzzy evaluation.

About the uncertainties of solid waste characteristics, as well as the complex physical, chemical, and biological processes taking place within the Bandeirantes landfill, motivated advanced modeling techniques to be applied; mathematical modeling and fuzzy logic systems [17].

3 Results and Discussion

3.1 Simulation Potential Emissions from Energy Recover

In this modeling of the sustainable production of electricity, the Bandeirantes landfill is named as Thermal Power Plant. The tests represent three scenarios.

In the simulation shown in chart following, the three categories were divided into 1 for landfill, 2 for controlling landfill and 3 to trash dump. The last one had the lowest result regarding the Potential of methane generation variable, Fig. 1.

Figure 1 Simulink Fuzzy was coded for the results of 60 % collection percentage for trash dump and the to 85 % performed collection decrease for controlling landfill. The potential of methane generation had the following results in the simulation compiled.

See Fig. 1, the first fuzzy logic when landfill, it is not possible. The simulation of this scenario shows, in Fig. 1, that there was an improvement in the performance of methane gas generated in all sites of waste disposal, even more at the trash dump. The simulation of this scenario shows, in Fig. 1, that there was an improvement in the performance of methane gas generated in all sites of waste disposal, even more at the dump. The two locations of inappropriate disposal had their emissions increased.

The simulation was repeated, by changing the vector order of the matrix elements. The result was exactly the same, proving that the result of the first simulation was

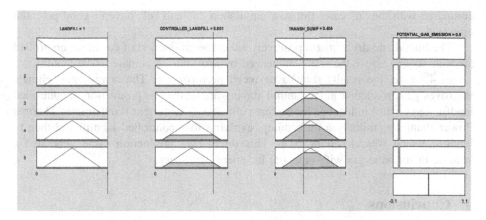

Fig. 1. Simulation result for L_0 (m³/ton) with simulink fuzzy

correct, thus confirming the increase in methane generation in plants considered inadequate, but with the amount of gas production that is not used.

The performance in humid and dry climates improves gas production and affects it in semi-humid climate, according to the result of Fig. 2. Although it has adopted the worst values for methane production, the performance to landfill is better in the "b" case when

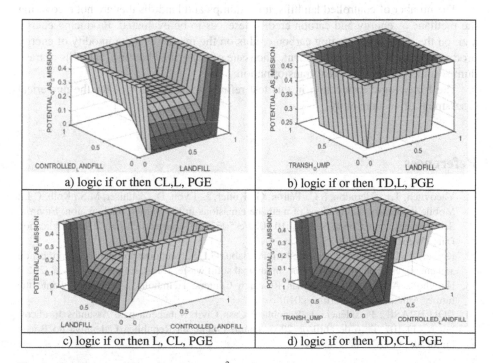

a) logic if or then CL,L, PGE

b) logic if or then TD,L, PGE

c) logic if or then L, CL, PGE

d) logic if or then TD,CL, PGE

Fig. 2. Simulation surface result for L_0 (m³/ton) – L (landfill); TD (trash dump); CL (controlled landfill); PGE (Potential gas emission)

compared with the "d" case. But case simulation "a" and "c", haven't good potential emissions.

The humid and dry climates positively affect the production of gas in the controlled landfill, staying above the result influenced by semi-humid climate in the landfill.

In 4th case, the results show a balanced performance. The semi-humid climate improves gas production in the landfill staying above the gas production in controlled landfill and landfill influenced by the three climates. The current Bandeirantes Thermal Power Plant was initially a trash dump, evolving to a controlled landfill and then to landfill, which was closed in 2006. This three-stage production cycle generated a volume of methane gas with potential for energy recovery.

4   Conclusions

They work with fuzzy logic in the future when the project goes into operation as a plant, and they do not consider the methane potential in the production cycle, discarding energy production since the establishment of the plant. In this scenario, the plant did not value 50 %; this corresponds to the production of 2,356,207 MWh. It would be possible to fuel the plant and still have 2,244,175 MWh.

This simulation doesn't show that by 2030, the plant will produce $1,424,148,778$ m^3 of GHG (**greenhouse gas**). The potential emission for recovering energy it's a good performance when increase disposal trash.

The number of controlled landfills, trash dumps and landfills that are not recovering the methane as energy and carbon credits deserves to be evaluated. Producing energy and, on the other hand, trading carbon credits on the market as a commodity of energy production can be a good investment. The issue of controlled landfills, landfills or trash dumps undergo a recent great transformation.

The fuzzy logic application in this test refines and extends tool for the numerical assessment of sustainability.

References

1. Yacovitch, T.L., Herndon, S.C., Pétron, G., Kofler, J., Lyon, D., Zahniser, M.S., Kolb, C.E.: Mobile laboratory observations of methane emissions in the Barnett Shale region. Environ. Sci. Technol. Am. Chem. Soc. doi:10.1021/es506352j. Accepted 23 Feb 2015. Publication Date (Web): 9 March 2015
2. Kumar, A., Dand, R., Lakshmikanthan, P., Babu, G.L.S.: Methane production quantification and energy estimation for Bangalore municipal solid waste. J. Inst. Eng. **95**(1), 19–27 (2014)
3. Helmholtz Association of German Research Centers: Helmholtz – with energy into the future. Annual report, Berlim (2010)
4. DOU BRASIL: Presidência da República. Casa Civil. Subchefia para Assuntos Jurídicos. Lei n°. 11.107, de 6 de abril de 2005. Diário Oficial da República Federativa do Brasil. Publicada no DOU de 7.4.2005

5. CONAMA: Conselho Nacional do Meio Ambiente. Resolução Conama n° 404, de 11 de novembro de 2008. Estabelece critérios e diretrizes para o licenciamento ambiental de aterro sanitário de pequeno porte de resíduos sólidos urbanos. (Publicação – Diário Oficial da União – 12/11/2008)

6. MMA: Ministério do Meio Ambiente. Agenda 21 brasileira: resultado da consulta nacional/Comissão de Políticas de Desenvolvimento Sustentável e da Agenda 21 Nacional, 2nd edn., vol. 158, p. 93. Ministério do Meio Ambiente, Brasília (2004)

7. MMA. Ministério do Meio Ambiente. Gestão do Lixo. Aterros Sanitários (2010). http://www.brasil.gov.br/sobre/meio-ambiente/gestao-do-lixo/aterros-sanitarios. Acesso em 31 May 2013

8. ALVES, I. R. F. S.: Análise experimental do potencial de geração de biogás em resíduos sólidos urbanos, 118 phase, pp. 33–34. Dissertação de Mestrado - Universidade Federal de Pernambuco. Programa de Pós-Graduação em Engenharia Civil (2008)

9. ALVES, I. R. F. S.: Análise experimental do potencial de geração de biogás em resíduos sólidos urbanos, 118 folhas, pp. 33–34. Dissertação de Mestrado - Universidade Federal de Pernambuco. Programa de Pós-Graduação em Engenharia Civil (2008)

10. Mendes, L.G.G., Magalhães, S.P.: Estimate methods of biogas generation in a sanitary landfill. Universidade Estadual Paulista – UNESP. Faculdade de Engenharia, Campus Guaratinguetá – FEG. Departamento de Energia – DEN. Rev. ciênc. exatas, Taubaté **11**(2), 71–76 (2005)

11. IPCC - Intergovernmental Panel on Climate Change" Guidelines for National Greenhouse Gas Inventories (1997). http://www.ipcc-nggip.iges.or.jp/public/gl/invs6.html. Acessado em 29 May 2012

12. USEPA – Environmental Protection Agency: United States International Best Practices Guide for Landfill Gas energy Projects. Landfill Gas Modeling. Global Methane Initiative. Capítulo 6, 14 pp 63–67 (2012)

13. Stege, G.A.: Methane Emission Reductions Achieved by Landfill Gas Projects in Developing Countries, p. 6. SCS Engineers, Phoenix (2009)

14. Worrell, W.A., e Vesilind, P.A.: Solid Waste Engineering, 2nd edn., 401 pp. 118–119. Cengage Learning, Boston (2011)

15. ABRELPE. Atlas Brasileiro de emissões de GEE e Potencial Energético na Destinação de Resíduos Sólidos. Abrelpe – Associação Brasileira de Empresas de Limpeza Pública e Resíduos Especiais. Diretor Executivo: Carlos R.V. Silva Filho, 172p (2012)

16. ONU – United Nations: Sustainable development challenges. World economic and social survey, 181 pp. 68. Department of Economic and Social Affairs, UN, New York (2013)

17. Abdallah, M., Warith, M., Narbaitz, R., Petriu, E., Kennedy, K.: Combining fuzzy logic and neural networks in modeling landfill gas production. World Acad. Sci. Eng. and Technol. **5** (2011) (International Scholarly and Scientific Research & Innovation)

Improving Factory Resource and Energy Efficiency: The FREE Toolkit

Mélanie Despeisse(✉) and Steve Evans

Institute for Manufacturing, University of Cambridge, Cambridge, UK
{md621, se321}@cam.ac.uk

Abstract. Eco-efficiency is defined as the concept of doing more with less; in other words, creating goods and services while preserving natural resources and reducing waste and pollution during manufacturing. This paper presents a toolkit for eco-efficiency at factory level: the Factory Resource and Energy Efficiency (FREE) toolkit. It contains five key elements; (1) see waste, (2) find solutions, (3) set targets, (4) assess yourself, and (5) create good habits. The FREE toolkit contains a range of games, tools and methods mapped against these five elements to integrate sustainability into factory activities. This paper presents the toolkit structure and an example of the journey for eco-efficiency.

Keywords: Eco-efficiency · Energy efficiency · Environmental performance · Resource efficiency · Sustainability · Sustainable manufacturing · Toolkit

1 Introduction

While factories are a source of economic and social value, they are also viewed as a cause of environmental problems. The emergence of concepts such as eco-efficiency, cleaner production, and industrial ecology [1–3] challenges this negative view of manufacturing. These concepts promote a radical change in perception of the role of industry from causing environmental degradation to becoming a driver for sustainability. They bring together men, money, machines and materials into more efficient configurations to support the transformation of our society towards sustainability [4]. This paper focuses on eco-efficiency. It aims to reduce material and energy intensity, increase service intensity of goods and services, reduce dispersion of toxic materials, improve recyclability, use renewable resources, and extend product life [3].

Factories are a key determining factor of the efficiency with which resources are converted into products and services. However, environmental performance variation of up to 400 % has been observed between factories producing similar products with similar technology [5]. This occurs at different levels, from variation across industry sectors to variation across the processes within a single factory (Fig. 1).

This research adopts a positive view of the role of industry in moving towards sustainability. The Factory Resource and Energy Efficiency (FREE) toolkit presented here seeks to promote eco-efficiency practices in factories. Eco-efficiency is defined as "doing more with less" as applied at factory level; in other words, creating goods and services while preserving natural resources and reducing waste and pollution during

© IFIP International Federation for Information Processing 2015
S. Umeda et al. (Eds.): APMS 2015, Part I, IFIP AICT 459, pp. 640–646, 2015.
DOI: 10.1007/978-3-319-22756-6_78

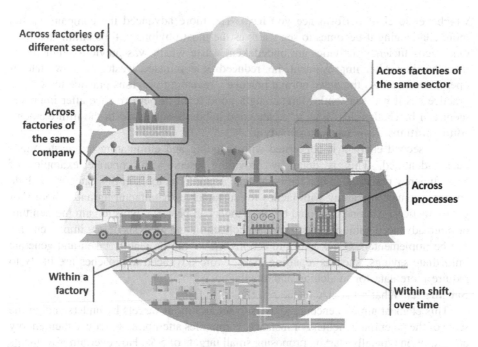

Fig. 1. Environmental performance variation at different levels *(Illustration by Aanand Davé)*

manufacturing. The following sections describe the toolkit structure and an example of its use with a generic sequence for getting started with eco-efficiency.

2 The Toolkit Structure

This paper presents the interim results of the Eco-Efficiency Grand Challenge – Environmental Performance Variation (EPV project) conducted by the EPSRC Centre for Innovative Manufacturing in Industrial Sustainability [6]. The EPV project aims to improve the overall sustainability of manufacturing by reducing environmental performance variation between factories and help elevate (future) factory sustainability performance. To address performance variation, a series of tools for factory eco-efficiency, ranging from games to advanced modelling techniques, were collected. This collection of tools forms the FREE toolkit presented in this paper. It aims to support the integration of eco-efficiency into daily activities. The toolkit is structured around five key elements. Each element is described below with a guiding question and associated activities for eco-efficiency.

See waste. What is your waste worth?

In this first part of the toolkit, users learn to identify and value waste. This stage may seem trivial but companies often overlook their waste as they are part of "normal practice"; because the manufacturing operations are up and running, it is typically assumed that there is no need to improve the operations. However, proactive companies argue that there are always improvements to be made if we look for them, whichever level of performance you have. The more advanced the company is, the more challenging it becomes to see waste as the most obvious will be eliminated first. Once eco-efficiency activities are undertaken, waste which was previously ignored is made visible. After improvement, i.e. reduced or eliminated waste, the new state of operations becomes the new "normal practice", revealing previous practice to be "bad practice" as it was wasteful. Maintaining a good level of performance after improvement can be challenging; how to create good habits is addressed in the fifth element. **Find solutions.** How can you remedy it?

The second element is concerned with reducing and eliminating the waste previously identified. This is done by providing users with concrete examples of eco-efficiency practices so that they may take action. The tools in this category include an improvement hierarchy with tactics for sustainable manufacturing and a library of good practices. Actions promoted by these tools can be quick wins to gain momentum, or more advanced solutions requiring data collection and analysis before improvements can be implemented. Quick wins are actions which can be readily taken and generate immediate savings, such as repairing leaks. More advanced approaches are likely to require more data for modelling and simulation.

Set targets. What's the size of the prize?

This element aims to encourage users to set ambitious targets by understanding the scale of the potential benefits. For instance, companies attempting to reduce their energy consumption typically start by proposing small targets of 5 %. However, improvements made by other companies show that savings of 20–80 % are achievable [4]. It also shows that eco-efficiency activities are not about small, marginal improvements but can result in radical improvements if integrated into daily activities. Setting ambitious targets can encourage companies to view eco-efficiency as an approach for factory operations as opposed to an add-on on top of "normal practice".

Assess yourself. Where are you now?

The fourth element of the toolkit focuses on assessing current levels of performance through qualitative and quantitative methods. Quantitative assessment tools include key performance indicators (KPIs) and modelling tools. These quantitative methods provide a strong basis for target setting as suggested in the previous section. Assessment tools can also be qualitative and do not require any data collection. They can be used to aid understanding of eco-efficiency, identify strengths and weaknesses of the company in various dimensions of eco-efficiency, as well as identify areas with the best potential for improvements.

Create good habits. Where to from here?

The final element of the toolkit aims to systematise eco-efficiency improvement activities. Tools in this section include training programmes, modelling tools and systematic use of indicators to track and further improve performance. Training is required to integrate eco-efficiency into daily activities and empower employees to seek and make resource efficiency improvements. By making eco-efficiency a work habit, it can be fully integrated into the factory operations on a daily basis and scale up the impact. Eco-efficiency cannot be considered as a one-time activity as it may result in only temporary improvement with the performance going back to pre-improvement levels as good practices are not maintained. This section of the toolkit is key to turning eco-efficiency good practices into standard practice.

3 An Example of the Journey to Eco-Efficiency

This section presents a collection of tools and a recommended sequence (Fig. 2) to get started with eco-efficiency. The journey and tools are mapped against the five elements of the FREE toolkit to provide structure and clarity. The tools presented here can help understanding, assessing and improving environmental performance with a step-wise approach. The sequence proposed is not necessarily the most appropriate for all companies but it is a generic one which will generate results. The FREE toolkit can also be used to develop a customised approach to eco-efficiency with more advanced tools.

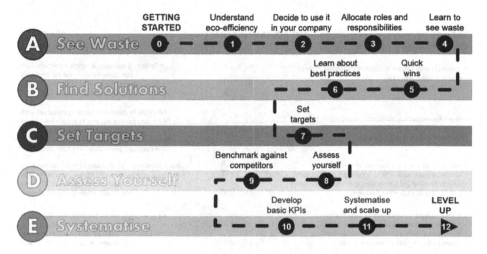

Fig. 2. Recommended sequence for getting started with eco-efficiency

Before implementing eco-efficiency, basic understanding of the concept and what it means in practice is required (step 1). This can be achieved with educational tools such as training and guide books [3, 7, 8]. These tools allow the company to see that becoming more eco-efficient is feasible and have significant benefits. This can lead to the company deciding to implement eco-efficiency in its operations (step 2). Responsibility then needs to be allocated so that designated people can lead the eco-efficiency activities (step 3).

Next, the company needs to learn to see waste (step 4) by looking at operations through a new lens to make waste visible. At this stage, low hanging-fruit and quick wins help gain momentum and engage more people in looking for improvements (step 5). One approach to identify immediate savings is to take a tour of the production facilities during non-operating hours and identify leaks or any equipment running which should be switched off. This exercise can be described as a "factory sensory experience" as it is guided by sound, smell, temperature, etc. The exercise can be enhanced through the use of technology (e.g. thermographic camera, electromagnetic and ultrasonic flow meter). Another exercise adopted by some companies is a collaborative treasure hunt. This exercise brings together experts from different factories to perform a walkthrough of the facilities and identify improvement opportunities [9]. Those experts may come from other companies and other industrial sectors. It allows knowledge and good practices to be transferred.

Further learning about good practices can be done through analysing documented cases [10] and databases [11] of best practices. Those information sources may be overwhelming as they contain a large number of examples and thus it is challenging to find specific, relevant information for a given company [12]. To simplify access to examples of sustainable manufacturing practices (step 6), a list of strategies and tactics [13] have been developed to support effective learning and ease access to specific solutions (Fig. 3).

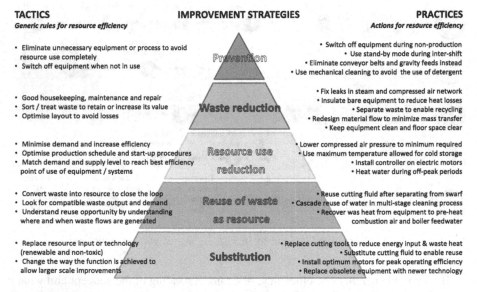

Fig. 3. Improvement strategies, tactics and examples of practices for sustainable manufacturing

The next step proposed is to start using resource saving targets (step 7). By understanding the size of the prize, companies can set ambitious targets and make eco-efficiency a competitive activity in the company. Non-financial rewards and recognition have been identified as drivers for employee motivation, creativity and empowerment [14]. Understanding the size of the prize will help scale up the impact of eco-efficiency activities across the factory.

At this stage, qualitative assessment tools (step 8) can help identify areas of strength and weakness with no data collection required. Tools such as the Capability Assessment Grid for Eco-efficiency (CAGE) framework and the RAMP tool [15, 16] provide a basis for such qualitative assessment of companies' maturity in various dimensions of eco-efficiency. These assessments rely on the user's existing knowledge about the company in terms of resource management and environmental management system in place. In addition, these tools can be used for internal and external benchmarking (step 9). When used internally in a company, benchmarking enables intra- and inter-factory learning by transferring knowledge and practices from high to low performing areas.

While a qualitative assessment can help understand current level of maturity for eco-efficiency, a more quantitative assessment is needed to identify areas with the greatest opportunities for improvement, i.e. where most resources are being consumed and waste generated. A quantitative analysis can be supported by converting factory data into KPIs (step 10). Typical KPIs include energy, water, waste, and air emissions [4]. Factory modelling can help further the quantitative analysis and support the identification of improvements in a more systematic manner (step 11). Various modelling techniques can be used depending on the granularity of data available and the intended purpose of the factory model [17, 18]. More advanced factory modelling techniques are particularly powerful to identify system-wide improvements [17, 19].

4 Conclusions

This paper introduced the FREE toolkit with examples of tools for eco-efficiency. The proposed journey to get started with eco-efficiency games and tools includes a selection of tools readily implementable. These tools are engaging, simple, and easy to use as they require little (if any) data. This helps overcome the first barriers to eco-efficiency (steps 1–3 in Fig. 2).

The examples provided are: collaborative treasure hunt and other factory games to identify areas of improvement, qualitative self-assessment tools to identify areas of strengths and weaknesses, good practices for sustainable manufacturing, and tools for making sense of factory data and developing performance indicators.

Most of the tools presented in this paper will play a role across multiple elements of the toolkit as they can address multiple aspects of eco-efficiency. For instance, a factory modelling tool can be used to quantify current performance as well as simulate the effect of scheduling or technological change on energy performance. Another example is using benchmarking tools to assess current performance and set targets.

The five elements of the FREE toolkit can also provide a framework for companies to develop their own approach to eco-efficiency. As companies make progress and better understand how eco-efficiency fits into their activities, they can customise their journey using the five elements of the FREE toolkit to match their specific needs.

Acknowledgements. The author wishes to acknowledge the Engineering and Physical Sciences Research Council (EPSRC) for funding this project, the EPV team (Aannd Davé, Lampros Litos and Simon Roberts) for their participation and valuable inputs to the project, and the EPSRC Centre for Innovative Manufacturing in Industrial Sustainability and industrial partners for their support.

References

1. Ehrlich, P.R., Holdren, J.P.: Impact of population growth. Science **171**(3977), 1212–1217 (1971)
2. Schmidheiny, S.: Changing Course: A Global Business Perspective on Development and the Environment. MIT Press, Cambridge (1992)
3. Lehni, M., Pepper, J., Eco-efficiency: creating more value with less impact (2006). World Business Council for Sustainable Development, North Yorkshire. http://www.wbcsd.org/web/publications/eco_efficiency_creating_more_value.pdf. Accessed 13 April 2015
4. Evans, S., Bergendahl, M.N., Gregory, M., Ryan, C.: Towards a Sustainable Industrial System, with Recommendations for Education, Research, Industry and Policy. University of Cambridge, Institute for Manufacturing, Cambridge (2009)
5. Bocken, N., Morgan, D., Evans, S.: Understanding environmental performance variation in manufacturing companies. J. Prod. Perform. Manag. **62**(8), 856–870 (2013)
6. EPSRC Centre for Innovative Manufacturing in Industrial Sustainability. http://www.industrialsustainability.org/. Accessed 10 April 2015
7. UNEP. Resource Efficient & Cleaner Production (RECP) Programme. http://www.unep.org/resourceefficiency/Business/CleanerSaferProduction/ResourceEfficientCleanerProduction/tabid/102615/Default.aspx. Accessed 10 April 2015
8. Carbon Trust. Tools, guides & reports. http://www.carbontrust.com/resources/guides
9. Next Manufacturing Revolution. New Resource Efficiency Tool: Collaborative Treasure Hunts. http://www.nextmanufacturingrevolution.org/new-resource-efficiency-tool-collaborative-treasure-hunts/
10. The Compressed Air Challenge. Library. https://www.compressedairchallenge.org/library/. Accessed 11 April 2015
11. Industrial Assessment Centers Database. http://iac.rutgers.edu/database/. Accessed 11 April 2015
12. Roberts, S.J.F., Ball, P.D.: Developing a library of sustainable manufacturing practices. Procedia CIRP Conf. Life Cycle Eng. **2014**, 159–164 (2014)
13. Despeisse, M., Oates, M.R., Ball, P.D.: Sustainable manufacturing tactics and cross-functional factory modelling. J. Clean. Prod. **42**, 31–41 (2013)
14. Amabile, T.M.: How to kill creativity'. Harvard Bus. Rev. **76**(5), 76–87 (1998)
15. Litos, L., Evans, S.: Maturity grid development for energy and resource efficiency management in factories and early findings from its application. J. Ind. Prod. Eng. **32**(1), 37–54 (2015)
16. Institute of Environmental Management & Assessment (IEMA). Resource Action Maturity Planner (RAMP). https://www.iema.net/rmramp. Accessed 10 April 2015
17. Despeisse, M., Ball, P.D., Evans, S., Levers, A.: Industrial ecology at factory level—a prototype methodology. Proc. Inst. Mech. Eng. Part B J. Eng. Manuf. **226**(10), 1648–1664 (2012)
18. Davé, A., Oates, M.R., Turner, C., Ball, P.D.: Factory modelling: the impact of data granularity and quality on production and building architecture system simulation outputs. Int. J. Energy Sect. Manage. Emerald (accepted) (2015)
19. Davé, A., Ball, P.B.: Factory modelling: data guidance for analysing production, utility and building architecture systems. In: Proceedings of the 11th International Conference on Manufacturing Research (2013)

Social Environmental Assessment in the Oil and Gas Industry Suppliers

Hamilton Aparecido Boa Vista[1], Fábio Ytoshi Shibao[1],
Geraldo Cardoso de Oliveira Neto[1], Lúcio T. Costabile[2(✉)],
Marcelo K. Shibuya[2], and Oduvaldo Vendrametto[2]

[1] Master Program in Environmental Management and Sustainability, Ninth July
University-UNINOVE, Francisco Matarazzo Avenue, 612, São Paulo, Brazil
geraldo.prod@ig.com.br
[2] Graduate Program in Production Engineering, Paulista University-UNIP,
Dr. Bacelar St. 1212, São Paulo, Brazil
luciotc@terra.com.br

Abstract. The aim of this study was to determine whether the adoption of
social environmental qualification affects the environmental performance
of companies operating or seeking careers in the oil and gas sector as suppliers
or potential suppliers, through a survey of companies based in the ABC region
in São Paulo, Brazil. The results showed strong agreement in relation to meeting
social and environmental requirements for oil and gas operators. Another finding
was that the certifications influence positively the environmental, economic and
social performance of companies.

Keywords: Supplier qualification · Social and environmental performance ·
Oil and gas

1 Introduction

The Brazilian equatorial margin is one of the most promising areas for exploration and
production of oil and gas as part of the so-called "Golden Triangle", composed with the
Gulf of Mexico, west coast of Africa and Brazilian coast. The discovery of oil
deposited in the open sea (offshore), exceeds this layer of salt on the ocean floor, called
"pre-salt", reaches depths of more than 7000 m below the sea level. Moreover, it can
lead Brazil to become a leading oil producer [1].

The exploration and production of oil and gas in the pre-salt area is an opportunity
for expansion and diversification of the Brazilian economy; therefore, in order to
improve technical and productive knowledge, it is essential to develop efficient and
competitive suppliers in the supply area of goods and services for this chain [2].

The Brazilian government adopted the Law number 12.351 in December 22nd
2010, creating the bidding system for the activities in the pre-salt area. This was the
starting point for the development of local suppliers policy for the oil and gas sector in
Brazil [3]. For Petrobras Oil Company, increasing local suppliers is a priority because it
aims to increase its business in the long term, create a sustainable perspective, create
new jobs and strengthen the national economy [4].

© IFIP International Federation for Information Processing 2015
S. Umeda et al. (Eds.): APMS 2015, Part I, IFIP AICT 459, pp. 647–654, 2015.
DOI: 10.1007/978-3-319-22756-6_79

The literature review identified several studies about environmental qualification of suppliers studying several variables such as: green supply chain management [5–7], social environmental responsibility [8–11], qualification of suppliers [4, 11–13], social practices [4, 14, 15], environmental practices [5, 7, 14], social environmental investments [16, 17], business performance [18], social performance [14, 19], environmental performance [7, 18, 20, 21], economic performance [7, 17, 22] and environmental proactivity [7, 16, 20, 23]. By analyzing the existing articles about environmental qualification of suppliers, it was found the need to study the relationship between these variables together, because some studies consider some of these variables; however, they did not find any study to present all variables simultaneously.

Thus, the aim of this paper is to verify that for the Brazilian oil and gas industry suppliers the social environmental qualification has provided a better performance for the both. The study was considered relevant because of the risk associated with the environmental impacts of exploration activities and the oil and gas production as well as the social-economic importance of the activity for the Brazilian society. Furthermore, it was considered the fact that this sector has been pioneer in the preparation of guidelines for corporate environmental management.

It has been also considered the relevance of oil activity and the social and environmental impacts of the exploration and production of offshore oil and gas fields of the "Tupi" and "Libra" that make up the Santos Basin, near the defined region for research. Therefore, it is important to the study the issues related to social and environmental performance of companies in the area of goods and services installed in the ABC Region, which is economically important for the State of São Paulo, Brazil.

In this context, this study is expected to make sure that the adoption of qualification practices established by major operators in the sector in Brazil, positively affect the social environmental performance of companies participating in or aspiring to participate in business opportunities in the oil and gas supply chain, considering the degree of risk of the activities and planned investments for the development of an oil and gas local industry, being able to meet the ongoing expansion in the sector.

2 Methodology

To achieve the proposed objectives, a methodological procedure conducted a descriptive research of the quantitative type, in which the objective is to evaluate the structural relationships of the proposed measurement model based on improved theoretical findings and validated by experts [24].

The operationalization of the variables was used as the unit of analysis for companies of goods and services that provide or intend to provide for oil and gas sector in which, are interested in obtaining their qualification criteria according to Petrobras Oil Company regulations in Brazil.

Were considered as subjects of the research the directors or managers to develop activities related to procurement, engineering, environment, social responsibility, safety, logistics, human resources and other related.

For the operation of the measurement model was designed a data collection instrument, based on the theoretical foundation [25], for the constructs: social practices, environmental practices, social environmental investments, social performance, environmental performance, economic performance and social environmental proactivity.

As a result of bibliographic research we developed a conceptual framework for the development of research, as shown in Fig. 1.

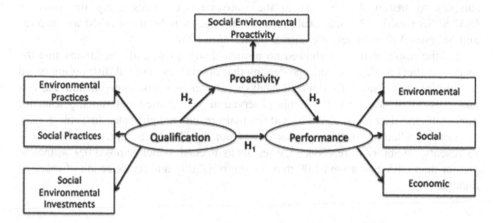

Fig. 1. Conceptual framework

The requirements of the market and its growing environmental expectations put pressure on suppliers to qualify for improving the performance of the contractor. Specifically, environmental practices, social practices and social environmental investment provided with products and/or services to the Brazilian oil and gas sector [26]. Based on the expected relationship between quality and environmental performance the first hypothesis arises.

H_1: The qualification process for oil and gas operators positively affects the social and environmental performance of companies in the ABC region.

Proactive companies typically implement environmental practices beyond the requirements of laws and regulations, while the reactive companies only seek regulatory compliance of these requirements [7, 27].

Therefore, in the conceptual framework the environmental proactivity is a second interdependent variable that can have a significant contribution or contingent effect on the relationship of the variable independent qualification and variable dependent performance; moreover, its influence has mediating effect and its role in relation depends on the initial hypothesis. Thus, the second hypothesis is:

H_2: The qualification process positively affects the social and environmental proactivity of companies in the ABC region.

After, the third case emerged:

H_3: The environmental proactivity positively affects the social and environmental performance of companies in the ABC Region.

In social surveys collecting data on people through observation is difficult; therefore, the researcher can use the questionnaires that have the advantage of being less expensive for its implementation, avoid biased judgments and allows respondents feel comfortable to respond due anonymity [29].

The research instrument was submitted for consideration by the respondents. Eighty questionnaires were collected; however, it was found the existence of 15 missing data; therefore, the data were considered not acceptable. Then, it was used 65 samples to treatment according to the statistical techniques using the software IBM SPSS version 22. Additionally, the test Komolgorov-Smirnov (K-S) was applied and Shapiro-Wilk to assess the normal distribution [30].

As the result of the test showed no normal distribution, and considering that the usual statistical methods for data processing that do not have normal distribution based on multiple regression, discriminant analysis, cluster analysis, experimental analysis and cross-tabulation [29]. From this observation was carried out running tests for nonparametric data Kruskal-Wallis and the main results are presented in Table 1 [25].

For the reliability of the data was carried out the Cronbach Alpha test, because it represents the ability to reproduce the results as needed, which showed 0.974, that is, greater than 0.05 and around 1.00 maximizing reliability and reproduction of research data [25].

3 Results and Discussion

It was observed that the majority of respondents were in the age group from 31 to 60 years (83 % of respondents) and there was greater participation of professionals aged between 31 and 40 years (33.8 % of respondents), and that most of the respondents have higher education and graduation (86.1 % of respondents) which may indicate a prerequisite for the position of this person in the company.

It was noted that the vast majority of respondents within the hierarchy of the companies is situated from the range of professionals with seniority (86.2 % of respondents). The corporate function in the company 38.5 % of respondent exercised executive position in the company, which provides conclusion that the subject matter the board of the organizations participated of the survey.

In addition, most respondents worked in the company three years or more (87.7 % of respondents). The largest shares were professional with over 10 years in the company (35.5 % of respondents). The company time leads us to infer that respondents have sufficient knowledge of the company's management processes.

It was subsequently performed testing normality K-S and Shapiro-Wilk, in both tests all had lower values assertions 0.001 indicating non-adherence normal curve [25] and Cronbach Alpha test to verify the reliability of data [25] that presented 0.974.

Then the test was performed for non-parametric data [25]. The main results are summarized in Table 1.

Regarding H_1, respondents showed strong agreement in relation to meeting social and environmental requirements for oil and gas operators. Noted that the greatest degree of agreement occurred in respondents that work time above 10 years in the company. The treatment to social and environmental requirements of the operators is directly related to the qualification construct [12, 13].

Table 1. Summary cross-tabulation

	Assertive	n[1]	A[2]	N[3]	D[4]	Chi-Sq[5]	Df[6]	Sig[7]
Age group (31–40 years)	Provides its customers with information on product safety	22	19	1	2	10,719	4	0.30
Worked in company (10 years more)	Performs audit environmental performance of suppliers	23	4	5	14	9,404	3	0.24
Worked in company (10 years more)	Meets social and environmental requirements of oil and gas operators	21	17	4	0	8,126	3	0.43

[1]Number of events (n)
[2]Number of respondents who agree with the assertive (Agree)
[3]Number of respondents who do not agree nor disagree with the assertive (Agree nor Disagree)
[4]Number of respondents who disagree with the assertive (Disagree)
[5]Chi-square
[6]Degree of freedom
[7]Significance (p)

It is emphasized that the age group 31–50 years old had the highest degree of agreement in relation to financial resources as important for the environmental performance of companies [16, 17]. Regarding the initiative to provide safety information of products and/or services to your customers can be considered an environmental proactive measure contributing positively to the businesses performance, supporting the findings of [16, 23].

On the other hand, there was a discordance of the respondents regarding the practice of environmental audits of suppliers regarding time spent in the company. Despite the practice of holding environmental audits of suppliers was positive for environmental performance [18, 20, 21], the data were inconclusive.

Referring H$_2$, it was observed that the Mann-Whitney test made the cross-tabulation of the responses to the variable "Your company already provides for the oil and gas sector", the results as the existence of the commitment to the fundamental rights worker safety by the company you work, promote respect for the fundamental rights of its employees and meet all the social and environmental requirements for oil and gas operators, the most respondents agreed (36 respondents), even those who work in companies that do not provide for the oil and gas sector (23 respondents), denoting that the sample respondents agree that for the environmental qualification is important the Social and Environmental Practices [14, 15]. Thus, the process for social environmental qualification of suppliers encourages the adoption of the practices for this purpose [15].

The cross-tabulation of the variable certifications in relation to the other assertions made possible show a high degree of agreement of respondents, and not related to the fact of the companies they own certification. Therefore, the variables related to social environmental practices and performance were confirmed positive [7, 14, 17–22].

Regarding H$_3$, it was identified about ISO 14001 certification, it was found dis-agreement regarding environmental performance audits of suppliers. It should be noted that most of the responding companies were not certified and certified companies have strong agreement. Showing that environmental certification influenced the degree of agreement of the sample. Therefore, the environmental certification should be encouraged to improve the environmental performance of companies located in the ABC region. The suggestion is that a more detailed research would be better in the future.

The certification for the finding affects the environmental proactivity of enterprises, confirms the assumption [22], as a "win-win" situation, in which, both the environ-mental and the organizational performances of companies would be favored with effective environmental management.

4   Conclusions

The process of qualification of operators does not affect the environmental performance of companies according to the sampling plan of the survey, that is, the central hypothesis was not confirmed (H$_1$), because the respondent companies consider that the qualification is associated only to the process of highlighting the safety information of the products and/or service and not the need to be certified. Thus, these companies do not achieve control practices through audits, due to the low quantity of certified companies, showing a weakness in relation to performance.

In relation to (H$_2$), it was found that companies understand that the use of social and environmental qualification process for suppliers drives the adoption of practices for this purpose. However, they do not consider that the most important is the fact they have certification, but if the supplier has environmental practices in routine work. Therefore, the certification has not been confirmed as proactive for environmental qualification of suppliers.

However, it was observed effect of the environmental proactivity of business (H$_3$), trusting that the environmental certification should be encouraged as a practice and not as necessary documentation. The most important is to verify that suppliers have environmental practices adopted proactively, improving performance.

An important aspect of this analysis is the lack of control through social envi-ronmental audits on suppliers. Due to this finding, suppliers located in the ABC region should consider the implementation of the practice of holding social environmental performance audits of its suppliers, because the literature review indicated positive results regarding the improvement of environmental performance and necessary for the insertion of the company in Green Supply Chain.

The conceptual framework that was tested can be used to provide managers and researchers with constructive support to managerial decision-making and for future academic research. A limitation of this study was unable to generalize the results by sample, which happened only with suppliers located in the ABC region. Moreover, it is suggested to further studies in order to obtain a larger sample, another point is to verify that the practice of social environmental audit in suppliers can improve social envi-ronmental performance.

References

1. ANP. Agência Nacional do Petróleo, Gás Natural e Biocombustíveis. Brasil esta ente as mais atraentes oportunidades exploratórias do Mundo (2014). http://www.anp.gov.br. Accessed 30 Jan 2015
2. Guimarães, E.A.: Política de conteúdo local na cadeia de petróleo e gás: uma visão sobre a evolução do instrumento e a percepção das empresas investidoras e produtoras de bens. Confederação Nacional da Indústria [CNI] (2012). Brasília. http://www.portaldaindustria. com.br/cni/iniciativas/eventos/2012/08/1,5241/seminario-internacional-conteudo-local-e-politicas-para-a-competitividade-na-cadeia-de-petroleo-e-gas-p-g.html. Accessed 20 March 2015
3. Brasil. Presidência da República. Lei Nº 12.351, de 22 de dezembro de 2010. Dispõe sobre a exploração e a produção de petróleo, de gás natural (2010). Brasília: Presidência da República. Accessed 9 Jan 2015
4. Petrobras. Petróleo Brasileiro SA. Incentivo ao Desenvolvimento (2014b). http://www. petrobras.com.br/pt/sociedade-e-meio-ambiente/sociedade/incentivo-ao-desenvolvimento/. Accessed 28 Jan 2015
5. Falatoonitoosi, E., Leman, Z., Sorooshian, S.: Modeling for green supply chain evaluation. Math. Probl. Eng. **2013**, 1–9 (2013)
6. Pires, S.R.I.: Gestão da cadeia de suprimentos (Supply Chain Management): conceitos, estratégias, práticas e casos. Atlas, São Paulo (2009)
7. Srivastava, S.K.: Green supply-chain management: a state-of-the-art literature review. Int. J. Manag. Rev. **9**(1), 53–80 (2007)
8. Barbieri, J.C., Cajazeira, J.E.R.: Métodos para integrar a responsabilidade social na gestão (2013). http://www3.ethos.org.br/cedoc/metodos-para-integrar-a-responsabilidade-social-na-gestao/#.U6SplPldVch. Accessed 20 Jan 2015
9. Bobsin, M.A., Lima, G.B.A.: Gestão de segurança, meio ambiente e saúde: proposta de estrutura de sistema e metodologia de avaliação de desempenho. Boletim Técnico Organização & Estratégia **2**(3), 357–377 (2005)
10. Elkington, J.: Canibais com garfo e faca. Makron Book, Finland (2001)
11. Petrobras. Petróleo Brasileiro SA. Relacionamento com Investidores (2014a). http://www. investidorpetrobras.com.br/pt/indice-de-sustentabilidade-da-dow-jones-djsi.htm. Accessed 18 Jan 2015
12. Rao, P., Holt, D.: Do green supply chains lead to competitiveness and economic performance? Int. J. Oper. Prod. Manag. **25**(9), 898–916 (2005)
13. Vanalle, R.M., Lucato, W.C., Santos, L.B.: Environmental requirements in the automotive supply chain–an evaluation of a first tier company in the Brazilian auto industry. Procedia Environ. Sci. **10**, 337–343 (2011)
14. Ministério do Meio Ambiente [MMA]. Cartilha A3P: Agenda ambiental na administração pública (5th edn.). Brasília, DF. (2009)
15. Pinto, L.F.G., Rodrigues, A., Macedo, D., Girardi, E.A.: Contributions of socio-environmental certification to the sustainability of the citrus industry in Brazil. Citrus Res. Technol. **34**(1), 9–16 (2013)
16. Nyaga, G.N., Whipple, J.M., Lynch, D.F.: Examining supply chain relationships: do buyer and supplier perspectives on collaborative relationships differ? J. Oper. Manag. **28**(2), 101–114 (2010)
17. Surroca, J., Tribó, J.A., Waddock, S.: Corporate responsibility and financial performance: the role of intangible resources. Strateg. Manag. J. **31**(5), 463–490 (2010)

18. Bowen, F.E., Cousins, P.D., Lamming, R.C., Faruk, A.C.: Horses for courses: explaining the gap between the theory and practice of green supply. Greener Manag. Int. **35**, 151–172 (2001)
19. Melo Neto, F.P., Froes, C.: Gestão de responsabilidade social corporativa: o caso brasileiro. Qualitymark Editora Ltda, Rio de Janeiro (2004)
20. Jabbour, A.B.L., Jabbour, C.J.: Are supplier selection criteria going green? Case studies of companies in Brazil. Ind. Manag. Data Syst. **109**(4), 477–495 (2009)
21. Kannan, D., Jabbour, A.B.L.D.S., Jabbour, C.J.C.: Selecting green suppliers based on GSCM practices: using fuzzy TOPSIS applied to a Brazilian electronics company. Eur. J. Oper. Res. **233**(2), 432–447 (2014)
22. Porter, M.E., Van der Linde, C.: Toward a new conception of the environment-competitiveness relationship. J. Econ. Perspect **9**, 97–118 (1995)
23. Jabbour, A.B.L.D.S., Jabbour, C.J.C., Latan, H., Teixeira, A.A., de Oliveira, J.H.C.: Quality management, environmental management maturity, green supply chain practices and green performance of Brazilian companies with ISO 14001 certification: direct and indirect effects. Transp. Res. E Logistics Transp. Rev. **67**, 39–51 (2014)
24. Diehl, A.A., Tatim, D.C.: Pesquisa em ciências sociais aplicadas: métodos e técnicas. Prentice Hall, São Paulo (2004)
25. Hair Jr., J.F., Blach, W.C., Badin, B.J., Anderson, R.E., Tatham, L.R.: Análise Multivariada de Dados; tradução Adonai Schlup Sant'Ana, 6th edn. Bookman, Porto Alegre (2009)
26. Zhu, Q., Sarkis, J., Lai, K.H.: Institutional-based antecedents and performance outcomes of internal and external green supply chain management practices. J. Purch. Supply Manag. **19**(2), 106–117 (2013)
27. Chandraker, R., Kumar, R.: Evaluation and measurement of performance of GSCM in Chhattisgarh Manufacturing Industries (INDIA). Int. J. Appl. Innov. Eng. Manag. (IJAIEM) **2**(6), 240–249 (2012)
28. Selltiz, C., Wrightsman, L.S., Cook, S.W.: Métodos de pesquisa nas relações sociais. Medidas na Pesquisa Social. EPU2, São Paulo (2005)
29. Silva, D., Garcia, M.N., Farah, O.E.: Métodos quantitativos na pesquisa de marketing. In: Pizzinatto, N.K., Farah, O.E. (eds.) Pesquisa pura e aplicada em marketing. Atlas, São Paulo (2012)
30. Conover, W.J., Iman, R.L.: Rank transformations as a bridge between parametric and nonparametric statistics. Am. Stat. **35**(3), 124–129 (1981)

Power Optimization in Photovoltaic Panels Through the Application of Paraconsistent Annotated Evidential Logic Eτ

Álvaro André Colombero Prado[1(✉)], Marcelo Nogueira[1,2],
Jair Minoro Abe[1], and Ricardo J. Machado[2]

[1] Software Engineering Research Group, Paulista University, UNIP,
Campus Tatuapé, São Paulo, Brazil
py2alv@gmail.com, marcelo@noginfo.com.br,
jairabe@uol.com.br
[2] ALGORITMI Centre, School of Engineering, University of Minho,
Campus of Azurém, Guimarães, Portugal
rmac@dsi.uminho.pt

Abstract. The contrast between large urban centers and other isolated locations where even the most basic resources are scarce, leads the development of self-sustainable solutions, a panorama in which the electrical power is an important demand to be supplied. Through Bibliographic and Experimental research, plus practical implementation and testing, it was possible to develop a solution which fits within the proposed needs. This paper presents a self-oriented solar panel based on Paraconsistent Annotated Evidential Logic Eτ, its construction and practical tests, where an average yield of 3.19 W was obtained against 2.44 W from a fixed panel, representing an increase of 31.56 % in the overall power.

Keywords: Solar energy · Photovoltaic · Power optimization · Energetic sustainability · Paraconsistent annotated evidential logic eτ

1 Introduction

In present times, where the development of new technologies and enhancements for various aspects of daily life is a constant activity, many cases of very scarce resources are not rare, particularly in locations far from urban centers. One of the most important of these resources is the electricity, often unavailable because of large distances between distribution networks and the locations itself, or even because the great importance of local ecosystems [1].

Most of the solutions adopted in these cases normally results in high environmental impact, by using generators and combustion engines, offering physical risks to those who handle them in addition to its high greenhouse gas emissions. Following this panorama, an important method for obtaining electricity without burning fossil fuels is through a photovoltaic solar panel [2]. Supply only implies in the cost of equipment itself, with no carbon liberated during operation.

© IFIP International Federation for Information Processing 2015
S. Umeda et al. (Eds.): APMS 2015, Part I, IFIP AICT 459, pp. 655–661, 2015.
DOI: 10.1007/978-3-319-22756-6_80

However, an important problem is related to the positioning of the solar panel, which is often fixed and does not have the ability to follow the natural movement of the sun throughout the day [3]. Many authors propose the use of simple timer-based systems or even "perturbation and observation" algorithms to circumvent this problem, but without the ability to handle situations of inconsistency or contradiction in the collected data [4, 5].

By using embedded software, a controller board and a sample from the voltage provided by the photovoltaic panel, it is possible to obtain a correct positioning with a stepper motor mechanically attached to it. This alternative combined with the use of Paraconsistent Annotated Evidential Logic Eτ on the decision-making process by the embedded software seeks to provide an optimal performance by handling situations where the signals from the panel are not conclusive or contradictory. The self-sustainable design now proposed is intended to power small devices of everyday use, by charging batteries with good performance, plus a reduced environmental impact.

2 Paraconsistent Logic

2.1 Historical Background

The Genesis of Paraconsistent Logic originated in 1910, by the work of logicians N.A. Vasil'év and J. Łukasiewicz. Although contemporaries, they developed their research independently. In 1948, Jaskowski, encouraged by his professor Łukasiewicz, discovered Discursive Logic. Vasil'év wrote that "similar to what happened with the axioms of Euclidean geometry, some principles of Aristotelian logic could be revisited, among them the principle of contradiction" [6].

Going beyond the work of Jaskowski, the Brazilian logician Newton C.A. Da Costa has extended its systems for the treatment of inconsistencies, having been recognized for it as the introducer of Paraconsistent Logic; Abe [6], also a Brazilian logician, set several other applications of Annotated Systems, specially Logic Eτ, establishing the basic study of Model Theory and the Theory of Annotated Sets.

2.2 Certainty and Uncertainty Degrees

Founded on the cardinal points, and using the properties of real numbers, it is possible to build a mathematical structure with the aim of materializing how to manipulate the mechanical concept of uncertainty, contradiction and paracompleteness among others, according to Fig. 1. Such mechanism will embark the true and false states treated within the scope of classical logic with all its consequences. To this end, several concepts are introduced which are considered "intuitive" for the purpose above:

Perfectly defined segment AB: $\mu + \lambda - 1 = 0; 0 \leq \mu, \lambda \leq 1$
Perfectly undefined segment DC: $\mu - \lambda = 0; 0 \leq \mu, \lambda \leq 1$

The constant annotation (μ, λ) that focus on the segment has completely undefined the relationship $\mu - \lambda = 0$, i.e. $\mu = \lambda$. Thus, the evidence is identical to the positive evidence to the contrary, which shows that the proposition $p_{(\mu,\,\lambda)}$ expresses a blurring. It varies continuously from the inconsistency (1, 1) until the paracompleteness (0, 0).

Since the constant annotation $(\mu,\,\lambda)$ that focus on the segment has clearly defined the relationship $\mu + \lambda - 1 = 0$, i.e. $\mu = 1 - \lambda$, or $\lambda = 1 - \mu$.

Therefore, in the first case, the favorable evidence is the Boolean complement of contrary evidence and, second, the contrary evidence is the Boolean complement of favorable evidence, which shows that the evidence, both favorable and contrary 'behave' as if classic. It varies continuously from the deceit (0, 1) to the truth (1, 0). The applications are introduced as follows:

G_{ic}:[0, 1] × [0, 1] → [0, 1], G_{pa}:[0, 1] × [0, 1] → [−1, 0], G_{ve}:[0, 1] × [0, 1] → [0, 1], G_{fa}:[0, 1] × [0, 1] → [−1, 0].

Defined by:

Inconsistency Degree: $G_{ic}(\mu,\,\lambda) = \mu + \lambda - 1$, since $\mu + \lambda - 1 \geq 0$
Paracompleteness Degree: $G_{pa}(\mu,\,\lambda) = \mu + \lambda - 1$, since $\mu + \lambda - 1 \leq 0$
Truth Degree: $G_{ve}(\mu,\,\lambda) = \mu - \lambda$, since $\mu - \lambda \geq 0$
Falsehood Degree: $G_{fa}(\mu,\,\lambda) = \mu - \lambda$, since $\mu - \lambda \leq 0$

It is seen that the Accuracy Degree "measures" how an annotation $(\mu,\,\lambda)$ "distances" from the segment perfectly defined and how to "approach" of the state, and the true degree of Falsehood "measures" how an annotation $(\mu,\,\lambda)$ "distances" from the segment perfectly defined, and how to "approach" the false state.

Similarly, the inconsistency degree "measures" how an annotation $(\mu,\,\lambda)$ "distances" from the segment undefined and how "close" it is from the inconsistent state,

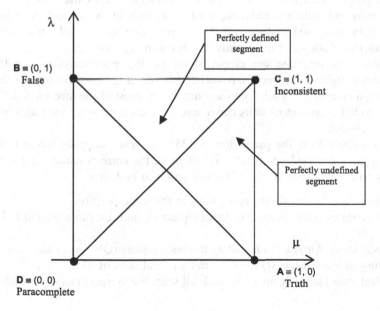

Fig. 1. τ reticulate [6]

and degree of Paracompleteness "measures" how an annotation (μ, λ) "distances" of the segment undefined, and how "close" it is from paracomplete. Is called G_{in} uncertainty degree (μ, λ) from an entry (μ, λ) to any of the degree of inconsistency or paracompleteness. For example, the maximum degree of uncertainty is in an inconsistent state, i.e. $G_{ic}(1, 1) = 1$. It is called the Certainty Degree $G_{ce}(\mu, \lambda)$ of an annotation (μ, λ) to any of the degrees of truth or falsity.

2.3   Decision States: Extreme and Not-Extreme

With the concepts shown above, it is possible to work with "truth-bands" rather than the "truth" as an inflexible concept. Perhaps more well said that truth is a range of certainty with respect to a certain proposition. The values serve as a guide when such a proposition is considered; for example, "true" in order to make a decision positively, and so on. The extreme states are represented by Truth (V), False (F), Inconsistent (T) and Paracomplete ($\perp$); and the not-extreme logical states by the intermediate areas between the states. The areas bounded by not-extreme values depend on each project.

2.4   Embedded Software

The embedded software was developed upon the spiral model, being followed by a risk analysis for all the following steps, since the adoption of software engineering and its assumptions are critical to project success [7].

Both evidence values are obtained with an interval of 500 ms between them, which allows a proper distinction and the capture of the logic states Paracomplete ($\perp$) – with low intensity and uniform λ and μ, representing a dimly lit room – and Inconsistent (T), with high-intensity and uniform μ and λ, representing an external environment with nuisances like shadows of trees, birds or other moving obstacles.

In order to optimize the output states of the para-analyzer algorithm, the non-extreme logic states were conveniently chosen (Fig. 2), according to the application requirements [8]. Taking into account that in most of the time the solar panel is exposed to light levels close to its maximum, the closest non-extreme states from truth (V) were elected.

Once switched on, the panel starts a 135° full scan, stopping where it finds the strongest favorable evidence (μ). From this point, the corresponding logic state found in this position will indicate the following action to be taken.

- Logical state Truth (V): the panel stays in the same position.
- Logical states Inconsistent and Paracomplete (T and $\perp$): run a second full scan of 135°.
- Logical states Almost-Truth tending to Paracomplete (QV $\to$ $\perp$) and Almost-Truth tending to Inconsistent (QV $\to$ T): run a partial scan of 81°.
- Logical state False (F): after a second full scan, the system enters in Standby mode.

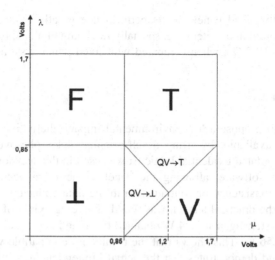

Fig. 2. Aspect of the lattice with corresponding voltage levels to the logic states.

3   Practical Implementation and Results

A single-axis traction system with a stepper motor was chosen, since it proved itself enough to provide a noticeable gain in performance combining simplicity, robustness and simplified maintenance [8]. In addition to the solar panel itself, the prototype has a set of batteries (for power and load circuits) with their respective charge controllers and a homemade Arduino based controller board.

In order to validate its operation, a series of daytime tests were done in a rooftop environment in November 2013, with good weather.

During three days the generated power was measured and compared with a fixed panel of the same type as the one used in the prototype. An increase of 31.56 % could be achieved in this particular days (Fig. 3) specially during the morning hours and late

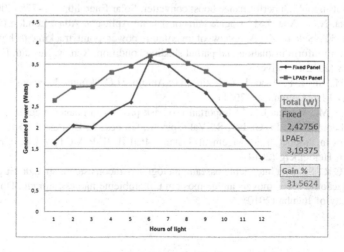

Fig. 3. Results obtained with the prototype.

afternoon, when the fixed panel has its performance greatly reduced. This result is similar to others found in the literature, specially in Huang et al. [9] (35.8 %) and Salas et al. [10] (2.8 %–18.5 %), when compared with fixed panel systems.

4 Conclusion

This paper aims to propose a low-environmental impact alternative for places where electricity is not available, by using a self-oriented solar photovoltaic panel. The Paraconsistent Annotated Evidential Logic Eτ was used in the decision-making process by the embedded software, allowing the panel to be more accurately positioned in situations of inconsistency or contradiction in the data collected.

According to the practical tests, it was found an average yield of 3.19 W provided by the proposed system against 2.44 W obtained from the fixed panel, which represents an increase of 31.56 %. This shows that the results are compatible with other similar systems [9, 10] and demonstrates that the actual implementation is perfectly feasible and capable of being implemented as a solution for manufactures of any type.

Acknowledgements. This work has been supported by FCT – Fundção para a Ciência e Tecnologia in the scope of the project: PEst-OE/EEI/UI0319/2014 by Portugal and University Paulista - Software Engineering Research Group by Brazil.

References

1. Bursztyn, M.A.: Difícil Sustentabilidade: Política Energética e Conflitos Ambeintais. Garamond, Paris (2001)
2. CRESESB, Centro de Referência para Energia Solar e Eólica Sérgio de Salvo Brito. Energia Solar: Princípios e Aplicações (2006)
3. Santos, J.L., Antunes, F., Chebab, A., Cruz, C.: A maximum power point tracker for PV systems using a high performance boost converter. Solar Ener. **80**, 772–778 (2005). Elseiver
4. Da Costa, N.C., Abe, J.M.: Lógica Paraconsistente Aplicada. Atlas, London (1999)
5. Ishaque, K., Salam, Z.: A review of maximum power point tracking techniques of PV system for uniform insolation and partial shading condition. Renew. Sustain. Ener. Rev. **19**, 475–488 (2012). Elseiver
6. Abe, J.M., Silva, F., João, I., Celestino, U., Araújo, H.C.: Lógica Paraconsistente Anotada Evidencial Eτ, Comunicar (2011)
7. Nogueira, M., Machado, R.J.: Importance of risk process in management software projects in small companies. In: Grabot, B., Vallespir, B., Gomes, S., Bouras, A., Kiritsis, D. (eds.) Advances in Production Management Systems, Part II. IFIP AICT, vol. 439, pp. 358–365. Springer, Heidelberg (2014)
8. Torres, C.R.: Sistema inteligente baseado na lógica paraconsistente anotada Eτ para controle e navegação de robôs móveis autônomos em um ambiente não estruturado. Doctoral thesis, University of Itajubá (2010)

9. Huang, B.J., Ding, W.L., Huang, Y.C.: Long-term field test of solar PV power generation using one-axis 3-position sun tracker. Solar Ener. **85**, 1935–1944 (2011). Elseiver
10. Salas, V., Olías, E., Lásaro, A., Barrado, A.: Evaluation of a new maximum power point tracker (MPPT) applied to the photovoltaic stand-alone systems. Solar Ener. Mater. Solar Cells **87**, 807–815 (2004). Elseiver

Flexible Ethanol Production:
Energy from Sugarcane Bagasse Might Help the Sustainability of Biofuels

Marcelo Kenji Shibuya[1(✉)], Irenilza de Alencar Näas[1],
and Mario Mollo Neto[2]

[1] Graduate Program in Production Engineering, Paulista University-UNIP,
Dr. Bacelar Street 1212, São Paulo, Brazil
{marcelo.shibuya,irenilza}@gmail.com
[2] UNESP - Campus Tupã, Domingos da Costa Lopes Street, Tupã, Brazil
mariomollo@gmail.com

Abstract. The ethanol industry in Brazil is going through a period of stagnation, resulting in the reduction of ethanol supply. The ethanol for automotive purposes may be anhydrous, which is used as an anti-detonating additive to gasoline; and hydrated ethanol, which can be used in the flex-fuel vehicles, which can use the biofuel, gasoline or a mixture of both in any proportion. This study is aimed to analyze the contribution that energy from the sugarcane bagasse could bring to the production of corn ethanol in plants adapted to operate with both sugarcane and the cereal. Therefore, it was considered, the surplus energy from sugarcane biomass and maize availability in the producing region. At the end of the article, the results are discussed by providing an analysis of the application of corn as alternative raw material for the production of ethanol in Brazil.

Keywords: Biofuel · Ethanol · Energy efficiency

1 Introduction

Anhydrous ethanol is the most important additive mixed with gasoline and hydrated ethanol can be used as an alternative fuel for flex-fuel vehicles that may either pure gasoline, hydrated ethanol or a mixture of both in any proportion [1, 2]. Since 2009, a reduction of hydrous ethanol demand in Brazil began, which rose from 16,471 million cubic meters in this year to the volume of 9,793 million cubic meters in 2013 [3]. Gasoline, on the other hand, was used in the volume of 25,409 million cubic meters in 2009, and trespassing the 39,678 million cubic meters in 2013.

The increase in fossil fuel consumption and the reduction of the biofuel demand is shown by [4] as a period of stagnation and expansion interruption about the sugarcane industry in Brazil. The same authors add that what contributed to this phase of stagnation was the government intervention in gasoline prices, which occurred from 2008 to 2012 to fight inflation rate. This interference has caused the price of commercial gasoline to fall to a price lower than the international oil barrel price, affecting the relative price of ethanol and the fossil fuel. Also, there was a decline in productivity in the sugar cane plantation, helping to intensify the crisis in the sector. Still, according to the

© IFIP International Federation for Information Processing 2015
S. Umeda et al. (Eds.): APMS 2015, Part I, IFIP AICT 459, pp. 662–669, 2015.
DOI: 10.1007/978-3-319-22756-6_81

authors, the reduction ethanol plants expansion and shifting of the biofuel supply, determined the increase in their prices to consumers and thus reduced their consumption.

Brazilian plants of ethanol production are self-sufficient in energy [5], which is one of the competitive advantages of the ethanol produced in the country. Under this approach, the combination of the availability of ethanol plants and surplus energy obtained from sugarcane bagasse and corn production in the same geographic region, corn ethanol would have conditions to be produced. Therefore, as defined by [6], there is a need to adapt these plants to operate with both raw materials. The author indicates that when the industrial plant originally built for processing sugar, starts to process corn it requires an investment of near US $ 8,5 million.

This article aims to analyze the additional ethanol that could be produced using corn as raw material, and the excess energy obtained from sugarcane bagasse in the plants located in the Midwest of Brazil. In this way, the additional ethanol produced from corn help make the Brazilian ethanol production sustainable. The present study was conducted in this geographic region because it has ethanol production from sugarcane and corn as raw material.

2 Literature Review

2.1 Sugarcane Ethanol and Corn Ethanol Production in the Midwest of Brazil

According to [7], the production of ethanol from sugarcane occurs simultaneously with the sugarcane harvest, that is, from March to December of each year. The author [3] define that the higher volumes of biofuels are produced in the intermediate harvest months, from July to September. This feature of production makes ethanol prices higher to consumers, in the offseason of sugarcane and start the production cycle, when the biofuel stocks tend to be at lower levels [3].

Brazilian production of ethanol from the sugarcane and the use of flex-fuel vehicles are world references in renewable energy [3]. The same author adds that ethanol production has promoted the rural development, diversification of energy sources, reduction of dependence on imported oil, and especially the reduction of air pollution and greenhouse gasses. The regional production of ethanol from sugarcane for the year 2013 is presented in Table 1.

Table 1. Brazilian regional production of ethanol (source: [3])

Region	Production 2013	Production Percentage
North	253.61	0.91%
Northeast	1,703.67	6.13%
Southeast	17,167.74	61.74%
South	1,475.83	5.31%
Midwest	7,207.75	25.92%
Brazil in Total	27,808.59	100%

Brazil is a pioneer in the production of sugarcane ethanol, has been successful in overcoming the initial challenges for developing this fuel, making efficient use of agricultural production technologies, modern management practices of crop, and the use of bagasse after grinding to generate heat and electricity for the production of ethanol [8]. Two crops of corn are harvested in Brazil per year [15]. The first crop has a cycle from October of one year to April of the following year; and the second crop (also known as a winter crop), occurs from January to July of the same year. The second crop of corn alternates the soil with soybeans. The potential of increasing production of corn to 72.239 million tons, in case of using all soybean planting area [9]. The same author adds that due to high costs of transporting the surplus production from the Midwest, the production of second maize crop of this region is economically attractive only in the periods of high international prices. These factors make the second maize is a viable alternative as raw material for ethanol production in this region.

Table 2 shows the production details in the Midwest region of Brazil. The states of Mato Grosso (MT), Mato Grosso do Sul (MS), and Goiás (GO) composes the region. Table 2 also indicates the respective amounts of ethanol plants installed, the average days of operation of the plants, and the quantities harvested in the second corn crop in 2013.

Table 2. Number of plants, average days of operation and the second corn crop (source: [3, 15, 16])

State	Quant. Plants	Average days of operation per year	Sugarcane ethanol produced in the crop of 2014 (10^6 m^3)	Second corn crop in 2012 (10^6 ton)
MS	23	222	2248.37	7,451.1
GO	36	183	3871.93	4,816.9
MT	9	173	1087.46	19,357.8

2.2 Corn Ethanol: The American Experience and Perspectives for Production in Brazil

In the United States, the ethanol produced from corn is currently the dominant biofuel, using 30 % of the total corn production in the country. According to [10], two processes are used to produce ethanol from corn: dry or wet milling. Milling ethanol by the wet method provides a greater amount of by-products such as corn oil, carbon dioxide gas, starch, and approximately 440 liters of anhydrous ethanol per ton of corn. Furthermore, ethanol production by the dry process has attracted major interest by producers, for providing a higher amount of biofuel production (460 L of anhydrous ethanol plus 380 kg DDGS-Distillers Dried Grains with Solubles) per ton of processed corn.

One of the disadvantages of the production of ethanol from corn is the impossibility of total utilization of biomass corn as a source of power generation, as occurs with the bagasse from sugarcane. According to [7, 11], the corn harvest generates straw, stem, leaves and cobs left n the field to preserve fertility and soil moisture. Thus, in the US, other energy sources are used, such as natural gas or shale gas. Regarding the characteristics of the raw materials used for ethanol production, sugarcane should be ground and processed within hours of harvest otherwise there is the loss of sucrose and, therefore, the reduction of the ethanol or sugar production [9]. On the other hand, corn does not undergo this problem and may be stored for long periods.

Data from December 2013 to April 2014 [12] from two plants in the state of Mato Grosso (MT) converted to operate simultaneously with sugarcane and corn, showed a production of 0.37 million cubic meters of ethanol from corn. The product used was the leftover of the winter crop in that state. It should be noted that the use of grain for ethanol production occurred precisely in the off-season of sugarcane, which occurs from December to April when the plants are interrupted for lack of sugarcane.

It was recently reported [12] the income earned by the plants installed in the state of Mato Grosso, with 0.352 m^3 of ethanol per ton of corn and 169.5 kg of DDGS per ton of corn. An important point to note, especially when analyzing the sustainability and competitiveness of ethanol production, is the consumption and how to obtain the energy used in industrial steps. In a published study [13] the authors state that the industrial processing of a ton of sugarcane, to obtain 85 L of ethanol consumes 1641.56 MJ, while processing a ton of corn produces 352 L of ethanol and consumes 3882.39 MJ of energy. These data become important when placed in the analysis of sugarcane bagasse that is the main source of supply of thermal and electric energy for ethanol production in the plants. According to [14], processing a ton of sugarcane generates 276 kg of bagasse with potential energy of 2503.71 MJ, and when the harvest is mechanized, it can obtain the amount of 165 kg per ton of cane straw harvested, which has the potential energy of 2143.64 MJ.

Considering the losses of 21 % in the conversion of the burning of sugarcane bagasse or straw, to obtain steam in the sugarcane plants [14], one can estimate that, to process a ton of sugarcane there is a brute availability of 2503.71 MJ of energy through bagasse, and consume of 525.78 MJ in the process of obtaining ethanol, with an extra amount of 336.37 MJ, which could be used to process corn for the production of ethanol.

3 Methodology

In this article, ethanol production potential in the Midwest region of Brazil was estimated through simulation, taking into account the use of sugarcane during their respective harvest and corn during the off season from sugarcane. The data used in the study was obtained from [3, 15, 16]. From these data, we estimated the potential contribution that corn ethanol could bring to the biofuel supply in the Midwest of Brazil. Calculations were performed in two different scenarios. In the first, the production of sugarcane ethanol was considered, in volumes achieved in 2013, and the excess energy from sugarcane bagasse being used for the production of corn ethanol. In this case, the limit of corn ethanol production could come from energy availability or availability of cereal in each analyzed state. The determinist simulation was adopted, and the production process variability was not considered (such as raw material quality).

In the second scenario use of energy from sugarcane bagasse and straw as energy source for obtaining the volume of ethanol was considered. In relation to the volume of corn used for ethanol production, it was necessary to consider between (1) the amount of corn processable due to the availability of energy; (2) the amount of grain from the harvest of the second crop; and (3) the amount of corn required for the production of 120 days of ethanol, having as a basis, the average volume obtained from the sugarcane.

The simulation of scenarios 1 and 2 are described by Eqs. 1, 2, 3 and 4.

$$D_{Ec} = \frac{V_e}{0,085} x2.503 \tag{1}$$

Where: D_{Ec} = energy available from the sugarcane bagasse (in MJ), V_e = volume of produced ethanol (m^3), 0,085 = volume of ethanol (m^3) produced per ton of sugarcane, 2.503 = Amount of energy obtained from the bagasse of 1 ton of sugarcane in MJ.

$$D_{Ep} = \frac{V_e}{0,085} x2.134 \tag{2}$$

Where: D_{Ep} = energy available from the sugarcane bagasse (in MJ), V_e = volume of produced ethanol (m^3), 0.085 = volume of ethanol (m^3) produced per ton of sugarcane, 2,503 = Amount of energy obtained from straw per ton of sugarcane in MJ.

$$E_{ex} = D_e x0.79 - E_c \tag{3}$$

Where: E_{ex} = Excess energy available to the industrial processing of corn (in MJ), D_e = Availability of energy from sugarcane bagasse (in MJ), E_c = energy used for the processing of sugarcane ethanol production (in MJ).

$$E_M = \frac{E_{ex}}{E_{pm}} x0,350 \tag{4}$$

Where: E_M = Volume of ethanol obtained from corn (in m^3), E_{ex} = Excess energy Available for the processing of corn ethanol (in MJ), E_{pm} = Energy necessary for the processing of 1 ton of corn (in MJ), 0,350 = Volume of ethanol obtained (in m^3) in the processing of 1 ton of corn.

4   Results and Discussion

Tables 3 and 4 show the results obtained from the simulations performed. On the first scenario, it was possible to estimate 2,537.9 cubic meters of ethanol from corn, an additional 35.21 % of the production of sugarcane ethanol. Note that in bold are the values of corn considered in the processing of ethanol.

In scenario 2, the use of available energy (from the former originator of sugarcane bagasse and straw), the volume of processable corn with the available energy, the daily amount of processable corn, and the corn harvested in 2013 crop were considered. In Table 2, in bold, there are defined the amount of corn that were considered for the

Table 3. Results of the simulation for scenario 1

State	Second corn crop - ref. 2013 (ton)	Processable corn due to excessive energy available (ton)	Excess Energy (10^6 MJ)	Sugarcane ethanol (m^3)	Corn ethanol (m^3)
MS	7,451,100	**2,291,755**	8,897	2,248,370	802,114
GO	4,816,900	**3,946,643**	15,322	3,871,930	1,355,176
MT	19,357,800	**1,108,444**	4,303	1,087,460	380,611
		Total		7,207,760	2,537,901

Table 4. Results of the simulation for scenario 2.

State	Second corn crop - ref. 2013 (ton)	Processable corn due to excessive energy available (ton)	Processable corn in 120 days of production. (ton)	Excess Energy (10^6 MJ)	Sugarcane ethanol (m^3)	Corn ethanol (m^3)
MS	7,451,100	13,829,704	**6,252,671**	53,692	2,248,370	2,188,435
GO	4,816,900	23,816,208	**3,175,978**	92,464	3,871,930	1,111,592
MT	19,357,800	6,688,957	**4,180,598**	25,969	1,087,460	1,463,209
		Total			7,207,760	4,763,237

production of ethanol, according to the conditions stated in methodology. Note that in this scenario, it was possible to obtain an additional 66.08 % compared to ethanol obtained from sugarcane.

The results of the study showed that ethanol produced from the cereal can give a large share of contribution to the increase of biofuel supply in Brazil. Thus, the deficit of biofuel announced by [4] would be minimized, giving conditions for the sector to re-grow with increasing demand for biofuel.

As defined by [6, 9], the present study considered the corn processed in off-season periods of sugarcane, that is, from January to April, when the ethanol processing plants are interrupted for lack of cane sugar. Thus, there is less inactivity in power plants, considering that the yield of sugarcane ethanol is produced from this raw material and other periods can use as a cereal raw material.

Another observation to be added is related to the sale price of corn ethanol by producing plants. As the production of corn ethanol is practiced in the offseason of sugarcane, as cited by [3], producers can benefit from it, and have more attractive prices in marketing their products.

Concerning the energy needed for producing ethanol from corn, the current study showed that the use of the excess sugarcane bagasse is possible to increase in 35.21 % the ethanol production; and the use of excess sugarcane bagasse and straw, can increase 66.08 %. Both studies considered the regional cereal availability, availability of energy and the maximum production by the State plants. These results show that the conversion of energy plants to operate with corn can help the energy efficiency of production facilities to increase production of biofuels with greater use of excess biomass. This energy efficiency is a competitive advantage of the plants prepared to operate with the two raw materials in relation to the typical American plants, as defined by [7, 11] which require external energy for processing corn.

Finally, we must add a note about the storage aspects of the two raw materials. As defined by [9], sugarcane must be processed hours after harvest, and corn can be stored for a longer period. The plants adapted to operate with both raw materials can benefit from this feature, because could be used to meet the agricultural productivity fluctuations of sugarcane, as reported by [4].

5   Conclusion

The study showed, for the Midwest region of Brazil, the additional volumes of ethanol that can be produced with the use of corn-producing plants previously adapted from only processing sugarcane ethanol. These results were obtained by simulation, considering the use of biomass from sugarcane. From the results obtained, it was possible to prove the energetic feasibility that the plants have to adapt to the operation with corn as raw material. Also to increasing the production, it is concluded in the present study that the use of corn can reduce inactivity of the ethanol plants in the off periods of sugarcane, using corn as raw material. Another benefit of the use of corn would be its use to minimize the effects of fluctuations in the production of sugarcane due to climatic factors. The results of the current study could be useful for both producers and policy makers. For producers, the study may predict the amount of ethanol that might be increased due to the addition of corn in the process. For policy makers, the study may subsidize information for the political decision-making process in biofuels in the country.

In future research, detailed studies could be carried out considering the monthly variation in the supply of sugarcane and the use of corn as an instrument to maintain the production in volumes of ethanol.

References

1. Coelho, S.T., Goldember, G.J., Lucon, O., Guardabassi, P.: Brazilian sugarcane ethanol: lessons learned. Energy Sustain. Dev. **X**(2), 26–39 (2006)
2. Freitas, L.C., Kaneko, S.: Ethanol demand under the flex fuel technology regime in Brazil. Energy Econ. **33**, 1146–1154 (2011)
3. ANP – Agência Nacional do Petróleo, Gás Natural e Biocombustiveis; Anuário Estatístico 2014. Brasília/DF. Disponível em http://www.anp.gov.br/?pg=60983#Se__o_2 consultado em 05 December 2014

4. Nogueira, L.A.H., Capaz, R.S.: Biofuels in Brazil: evolution, achievements and perspectives on food security. Glob. Food Secur. **2**, 117–125 (2013)
5. Dantas, G.A., Legey, L.F.L., Mazzone, A.: Energy from sugarcane bagasse in Brazil: an assessment of the productivity and cost of different technological routes. Renew. Sustain. Energy Rev. **21**, 356–364 (2013)
6. APROSOJA: I Forum Brasileiro de Etanol de Milho e Sorgo; Sorriso – MT (2013)
7. Hofsetz, K., Silva, M.A.: Brazilian sugarcane bagasse: energy and non-energy consumption. Biomass Energy **46**, 564–573 (2012)
8. Du, X., Carriquiry, M.A.: Flex fuel vehicle adoption and dynamics of ethanol prices: lessons from Brazil. Energy Policy **59**, 507–512 (2013)
9. BNDES. A Produção do Etanol pela Integração do Milho-Safrinha às Usinas de Cana de Açúcar: Avaliação Ambiental, Econômica e Sugestões de Política. Brasília (2014)
10. Hettinga, W.G., Junginger, H.M., Dekker, S.C., Hoogwijk, M., Mcaloon, A.J., Hicks, K.B.: Undestanding the reduction in US corn ethanol production costs: an experience curve approach. Energy Policy **37**, 190–203 (2009)
11. Crago, C.L., Khanna, M., Barton, J., Giuliani, E., Amaral, W.: Competitiveness of Brazilian sugarcane Ethanol compared to US corn ethanol. Energy Policy **38**, 7404–7415 (2010)
12. UNICA – União da Indústria da Cana de Açúcar, Relatório Final da Safra 2013–2014, disponível em http://www.unicadata.com.br/listagem.php?idMn=88. Access in 11 March 2015
13. Salla, D.A., Cabello, C.: Análise Energética na Produção de Etanol de Mandioca, Cana de Açúcar e Milho. Revista Energia na Agricultura, Botucatu, vol. 25(2), p. 32 a 53
14. Lamonica, H.M.: Produção de Vapor e Eletricidade – A Evolução do Setor Sucroalcooleiro, Workshop de Gestão de Energia e Resíduos na Agroindústria Sucroalcooleira (2007)
15. CONAB: Acompanhamento da Safra Brasileira – Grãos; V1 – Safra 2013/14, Brasília, Dez 2013
16. CONAB: Perfil do Setor do Açúcar e do Álcool no Brasil; vol. 5 – Safra 2011/2012, Brasília (2013)

Integrated Energy Value Analysis: A New Approach

L. Bettoni[(⊠)], L. Mazzoldi, I. Ferretti, L. Zavanella, and S. Zanoni

Department of Industrial Engineering, University of Brescia, Via Branze 38,
25123 Brescia, Italy
{l.bettoni,laura.mazzoldi,ivan.ferretti,
lucio.zavanella,simone.zanoni}@unibs.it

Abstract. The improvement of energy efficiency of 20 % is one of the three objectives of the EU Directive 20-20-20. To reach this goal, all production processes have to be analysed with reference to their energy consumption so as to identify actions aimed at removing or reducing energy wastes. From the Lean Production framework, the variation of the Value Stream Mapping (VSM), the Energy VSM (EVSM) is selected as a useful tool able to highlight the seven types of wastes identified by Ohno in Toyota Production System and energy wastes. This work aims at proposing a possible modification of the EVSM, which encompasses it within the Energy Audit and the Energy Balance Chart. The goal is to realize a deep energy analysis, highlighting energy wastes, in order to understand which corrective actions must be implemented or which corrections to energy reduction should be considered to reduce energy wastes.

Keywords: Energy flow · Energy analysis · Energy value stream · Energy audit · Lean and energy

1 Introduction

The study of energy consumption and costs in energy intensive sectors is of primary importance, because of the increase in energy price and its related environmental concerns. In literature, Energy issue is a wide topic, so it is faced from different point of view. Summarizing some of these, we want to highlight the magnitude of energy subject. Some studies have focused on the assessment models of energy consumptions of the system considered, which have the purpose to collect energy data allowing to highlight highest energy consumption process or equipment and quantitatively evaluate energy losses of an industry process [1–3]. Other studies deal with the measurement of the on-time energy consumptions, in order to straightaway solve different energy-decision problem, and on the solution of multi-objective energy problem related to energy policies, energy operations and management. As the survey in [4], which states that the Decision Analysis (DA) is largely applied to analyze Energy and Environmental (E&E) issues. Different researches are focalized on energy management system [5] or on technological solutions for reducing energy consumption and improving energy efficiency, in comparison with BATs (Best Available Techniques) standards, even if there is a poor knowledge of BATs [6, 7]. Energy intensive

© IFIP International Federation for Information Processing 2015
S. Umeda et al. (Eds.): APMS 2015, Part I, IFIP AICT 459, pp. 670–679, 2015.
DOI: 10.1007/978-3-319-22756-6_82

companies needs to identify all type of energy use in their processes, to divide which type of energy use is necessary for the production and which is removable (waste). All energy use, which is not strictly necessary for the production, is a cost that the customer is not willing to pay for. For this reason is necessary to provide to the energy intensive companies a useful tool which allows identifying this type of energy use. Even though there are lot contributions in literature, we observed a lack in the availability of an energy analysis able to bring out the different type of energy use. The objective of the Integrated Energy Analysis is to analyse energy use from a top down approach. This approach allows identifying at first macro-evidences of energy use and waste, and gradually highlighting how energy use and wastes are strictly related to production and logistical issues. This research is focused on tools able to identify and quantify energy consumption, waste, energy value and flow in an energy intensive production process. This study, highlighting energy wastes and anomalies and integrating tools derived from Energy and Lean analysis, proposes a new approach (named Integrated Energy Value Analysis) for the analysis of energy features of a production system. Related to other energy analysis, in this research the type of energy waste is pointed out. This information is important to identify the exact action to improve to reduce or remove it. The reduction of wastes is the main objective of Lean production, which aims at reducing costs, improving process flow and reducing lead times, to meet customer expectations and improve environmental quality and in order to achieve competitiveness. To apply the five tenets of Lean production, it is necessary to remove or at least reduce wastes "Whenever there is a product (or service) for a customer, there is a value stream. The challenge lies in seeing it" [9]. Therefore, to see the value stream of a product through the production process, a tool has been developed: the Value Stream Mapping (VSM). VSM is a suitable tool for waste identification and their subsequent elimination (or almost reduction), thanks to its graphical appeal. Some scientific works, as Erlach [10], face the issue of directly evaluating energy efficiency into Lean approach. Erlach introduces the energy contribution in the VSM including energy indicators such as Energy Intensity and Energy Density into the process box. Moreover, he defines eight design guidelines to derive measures for energy efficiency increase. Bogdanski [11] proposes an extended energy value stream approach, which introduces three innovative characteristics. The main novel feature is the introduction of the state of the machines, classified as ramp-up, processing and idle. For each state the measurement of power and time are collected, in order to consider dynamic energy profile. The second feature is the consideration of energy consumption of technical building service. The third distinction of the extended EVSM is the consideration of product related issues as technological characteristics and design. Another guideline about energy improvement through Energy Value Stream Analysis is the approach of the "Lean and Energy Toolkit", published by U.S. Environmental Protection Agency [12]. Efforts on Energy Value Stream Mapping are needed.

The remainder of the paper is organized as follows: in Sect. 2, the Integrated Energy Value Analysis methodology is introduced. In Sect. 2.1, the proposed Energy Audit approach is presented; the Energy Value Stream Mapping is explored in Sects. 2.2, 2.3 the Energy Balance Chart is studied in depth. The Future State is described in Sect. 3. The conclusions and further developments are summarized in Sect. 4.

2 The Methodology

The Integrated Energy Value Analysis (IEVA) is an integration of tools for the energy consumption assessment of an energy intensive process. The focus is on energy issues, so logistical performances are not encompassed by energy analysis and considerations.

Next to the seven wastes identified by Ohno [8], during the years researchers added some other wastes, considering different features of the system investigated and the need and criticism to the system itself, i.e. applying Lean and VSM to the service companies [13]. Power and energy are considered as additional wastes, but in the Integrated Energy Value Analysis, energy is the topic of the research. The IEVA analyses different kinds of energy consumptions (and wastes) related, e.g., to the state of the machines or the synchronization of the resources. The objective of the IEVA is to find the hidden energy wastes existing in the production process in order to remove, if possible, or reduce them by energy scheduling models.

Thanks to the analysis of the energy consumption of the machines, different states corresponding to different power levels are observed. In the *production* state, the machine produces and the power is consistent with the production effort. In the *holding* state, the machine doesn't produce, but the item newly worked out has not yet been released (i.e., the power is lower than in the production state, as the machine simply *holds* the item). In the *idle* state, the lowest power level, the machine is turned on but it is neither producing any items (i.e. no items are in process) nor holding them: nevertheless, some energy is still consumed due to auxiliary equipment of machines, which must be kept in function.

As for the VSM, the energy consumption can be Value-Added, (VA), Non Value-Added (NVA) and Necessary but NVA (NbNVA).

We identified different definitions of "energy waste". (a) When it is possible to consume less energy to produce the same output (i.e. quantity of produced products). (b) When energy is employed for NVA and NbNVA activities. And finally, (c) when energy is consumed supporting Lean thinking wastes, i.e. energy consumed for defective products, energy consumed for useless transportation, energy consumed for extra processing, defective production.

The IEVA focuses its attention on the first two definitions of energy wastes, i.e. (a) and (b), because the other ones are reduced or removed acting on Lean wastes. Thus, the energy wastes, which the IEVA focuses on, are:

- Energy consumption during Idle State (i.e. during the set-up),
- Energy consumption during Holding State,
- Energy Consumption for Overproduction,
- Energy lost for lack of Synchronization between energy-consuming resources and their associated auxiliary services.

The objective of the investigation is to create an "as is" analysis in order to verify energy consumptions, energy costs and energy wastes. The goal is to reduce both energy consumptions and costs, optimizing energy management, producing more products and consuming less energy, thus becoming "energy efficient". The IEVA allows the identification of energy wastes in order to find corrective actions able to remove or reduce them. The first step is to implement an Energy Audit, distinguishing processes and services resources and classifying resources as Value Added, Non Value Added and Necessary but Non Value Added. The second steps is to create the Energy Value Stream Mapping with related Energy Lines and study the wastes at each single resource (EVA-ENVA); study the synchronization between resources and related auxiliary services (vertical analysis – focus on the single machine). The last step is to create the Energy Balance Chart in order to compare takt time and energy consumption for those process resources, which are more energy consuming. At the end analyses the EBC in order to define an energy scheduling model suitable for the energy wastes reduction, considering the production time value (under/over takt time). In the following sections, the tools are analysed in detail.

2.1 Energy Audit

As first step of the IEVA methodology, the Energy Audit (EA) is performed. This technique uses the Lean organization approach in order to look for wastes in the energy use. The philosophy underlying this approach is based on the understanding of how energy is used in a particular process in order to discriminate what is strictly necessary (Value Added) and what can be improved (reduction or elimination of Non Value Added). The phases of the project can be summarized in (1) Energy Analysis, (2) Management analysis and finally (3) Root cause.

During the first phase the data of energy consumption (i.e., rated power, hours of operation per year, estimate of load and contemporary factors and efficiency) are collected and the consumptions at the resources are divided between electrical and thermal loads, with the aim of reconstructing the energy consumptions and costs, reporting a yearly energy balance. The energy balance allows the user to appreciate the annual energy consumption at each user (resource) and a Pareto analysis can be performed to identify the more expensive utilities in the energy perspective.

The Management analysis allows the management to identify system bottlenecks, by the analysis of production processes and the estimation of lead times, thus establishing the actual production rate of the system. The comparison between this value and the production capacity at each station within the process allows the identification of the non-utilized production capacity at the different stations as compared to the bottleneck. This assessment is very important because energy cost, as many other types of cost, can be divided into a fixed component and a variable component, and such components can be identified thanks to this specific activity. Moreover, the resources of the system are further classified as VA and NVA, by the analysis of the states of the machines (production state, holding state and idle state).

Finally, during the last phase of EA, technological improvements are identified and prioritized thanks to the Root cause analysis, which allows us to verify any possible improvement actions, understanding the motivations that underlie the costs currently incurred by the company.

2.2   Energy Value Stream Mapping

The EVSM is structured into three sections, as presented in Fig. 1: the Process of production flow (at the top), the Auxiliary service flows (in the middle) and the Energy lines (in the bottom). The EVSM is configured as a particular modification of the traditional VSM: changes are implemented in order to focus only on energy. In the process box of the EVSM, different values are specified: the energy consumption during production, the energy consumption during holding time and the uptime, i.e. the idle time of the process. All auxiliary services necessary for the production are shown in another process box, under the main process stream, and once again energy consumption and uptime are specified.

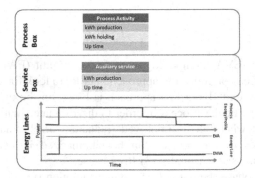

Fig. 1. EVSM configuration.

In the IEVA, instead of visualizing the time line, the Energy Lines is shown, distinguishing an energy value added line, EVA, (for the production state) and energy non value-added lines, ENVA (for the holding and idle states). Using this configuration, two analyses can be carried out, in order to obtain two kinds of outputs: (1) Identification of single resource's wastes: the inefficiencies of the single resource are analysed and (2) Identification of wastes related to the synchronization between process resource and related auxiliary service, which works together. Once the removable inefficiencies have been identified (so ENVA), this tool allows the user to define corrective action plans which enable to create the Future State. Figure 2 shows EVSM and Energy Line and Fig. 3 shows an example of the energy profile of a resource which changes its state over time.

In the EVSM, as well as the traditional VSM, the Future State shows the goals the company aims at in the future, i.e. the energy consumption has to be reduced during the holding and idle states, which are ENVA, with respect to the Current State. The most suitable method that can be applied to reduce holding and idle times has to be investigated using energy scheduling models, the development of which is not in the aim of this work.

The second analysis, allowed by the EVSM, includes both kinds of resources: process resource and auxiliary service resource. The aim is to verify whether the

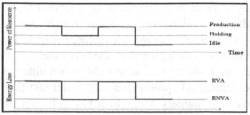

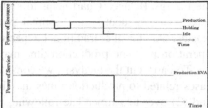

Fig. 2. EVSM and Energy Line

Fig. 3. Example of a waste for lack of Synchronism

auxiliary service resource is synchronized with its associated process resource or not. Often, in companies it is observed that the auxiliary service resource (for example, the fun) is in function even if it is not necessary for the associated process resource (for example the furnace), which is, e.g., in its holding state (or in its idle state). In this case the resources are not synchronized, Fig. 3, and an energy waste is present.

A possible Future State would be that the auxiliary service is turned off (or set to a minimum power level) when the process resource doesn't need it.

2.3 Energy Balance Chart

Another tool, derived from the VSM, is used during the Current State definition step, in order to identify other kinds of wastes and to determine the optimal configuration of the Future State: such a tool is the Balance Chart (BC). In the traditional BC, once defined the Takt Time, production times at all the resources (machines or operators or the production times to produce different products in a single machine) are pointed out, in order to identify the bottleneck of the system. Once located the bottleneck (which identifies a type of waste, as it breaks off the flow of the value at takt time), Lean thinking provides some solutions based on system's features, aiming at balancing the flow of the production mix. Thus, the BC allows the analysis of the Current State situation, highlighting the takt time, the resource production time, which has to be lower than the takt time, and the bottleneck of the system, for which the production time is higher than the takt time. In the energy perspective, there isn't an indicator suitable for quantifying how much energy is needed to define an energy efficient system and, at the same time, to maintain the logistic performances linked to the takt time. Therefore, the objective is to find the optimal (i.e. the minimum) energy consumption, in order to comply with both the takt time and the due date required by the customer. To build up an Energy Balance Chart it is necessary to analyze the energy consumption for the current cycle time, for that process resource that is more energy consuming. In order to find the cycle time that ensures the minimum energy consumption, the Total Energy function has to be minimized. The optimum found is the indicator that quantify how much energy is needed at the resource, maintaining the logistical performance. If it is possible to act on the production times of the machines, the Energy Balance Chart helps to highlight the energy behaviour of machines themselves and to identify the optimal production and holding times to reduce energy wastes. As for the traditional Operation Machine Production Balance Chart, the operation machine production time may be lower or higher than the takt time.

To carry out the analysis, we consider one resource or machine (M1): two different cases related to production times may be defined: (1) production time under takt time and (2) over takt time. The following machine, namely M2, which has to be replenished by M1, on the contrary, it runs at the takt time and there is no intermediate buffer between the two machines. So, in the first case (under takt time) the machine M1, once ended the production of the current item, stays in the holding state till the following machine becomes available to receive the item itself, i.e. till the takt time. In the second, M1 finishes the production later than the job completion by machine M2, which has to stay in idle state from the end of its production time (i.e. takt time) till M1 finishes to produce its item. The analysis is carried out in order to find the minimum energy consumption related to machine M1.

We assume that the production rate is variable, and that the energy consumption for production can be described as a convex function of the production time, while energy consumption for holding, on the other hand, decreases linearly when increasing the production time, i.e. it is proportional to the holding time.

Let us introduce the following notation in order to define the mathematical functions of energy consumption for production and holding states:

tt : takt time [time unit];
tp : production time of the resource [time unit];
th : holding time of the resource [time unit], defined as: tp, $th = tt - tp$
α, β, γ : coefficients of energy consumption for production function;
δ : coefficient of energy consumption for holding function;
Wp : power required for production [kW];
Wh : power required for holding [kW];

We also assume that the energy consumption for production, Ep, is a function of the production time, as in [14] by:

$$Ep(tp) = Wp \cdot (\alpha \cdot tp^2 - \beta \cdot tp + \gamma), \tag{1}$$

while the energy consumption for holding, Eh, is defined by:

$$Eh(th) = Wh \cdot \delta \cdot (tt - tp) \text{when } th > 0, 0 \text{ otherwise.} \tag{2}$$

The holding energy consumption is proportional to the holding time and decrease linearly increasing production time.

The Total Energy Consumption is the summation of energy consumption for production, Ep, and energy consumption for holding, Eh, and it is expressed by:

$$Etot(tp) = Wp \cdot (\alpha \cdot tp^2 - \beta \cdot tp + \gamma) + Wh \cdot \delta \cdot (tt - tp). \qquad (3)$$

The energy consumed when the resource runs at takt time is defined as:

$$Etakt = Etot(tp) \text{ when } tp < tt, Etakt = Ep(tt) \text{ otherwise.} \qquad (4)$$

The optimal combination of production time and holding time, which minimizes energy consumption, can be found by setting the first derivative of the total energy consumption function to zero, from which the optimal production time that minimizes energy consumption is derived as:

$$tp^* = \frac{Wp \cdot \beta + Wh \cdot \delta}{2 \cdot Wp \cdot \alpha}. \qquad (5)$$

The optimal production time tp^* is determined for the resources studied, i.e. the production time that minimizes the $Etot$, Fig. 4. Consequently, the optimal configuration of production time/holding time is defined, too. So the Energy Balance Chart (EBC), Fig. 5, can be drawn for different energy configurations, in order to compare the Current State of the resource studied and to determine the optimal configuration.

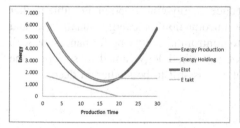

Fig. 4. Total energy consumption   **Fig. 5.** Energy Balance Chart

The EBC shows the distribution of energy consumptions for different production time values. Thanks to the EBC, it is possible to compare the current Total Energy Consumption with the minimum Total Energy Consumption, which represents the goal to be reached to become "energy efficient". It has to be noted that the EBC identifies the optimal energy trade-off between energy consumption for production and holding. In this study the logistic costs are not considered, so a trade-off between energy savings and logistic costs should be deeply investigated using additional analyses, i.e. energy scheduling models.

3 Future State

Once defined the energy consumption of the resources and the associated auxiliary services, through the Current State, it is possible to identify the areas of improvement, both management and technological. The type of corrective actions have to be investigated through different models, as the energy scheduling model. Once the results have been achieved from the Energy Value Stream Mapping and the Energy Balance Chart, thus determining the optimal solution, these tools can be revisited in order to edit and improve the Future State, as well as to highlight the energy goal of the system.

4 Conclusion

The proposed Integrated Energy Value Analysis (IEVA) is a method that allows the managers to investigate energy wastes at different levels of analysis. The Energy Audit, the Energy Value Stream and the Energy Balance Chart are the tools used to perform the IEVA. For the energy consuming resources, different states are classified (production, holding, idle) and each state is categorized as Energy Value Added or Energy Non Value Added. The evaluation of energy consumption is carried out for each single resource to analyze energy use during different states, and for the synchronisation of both resources and associated auxiliary services to highlight the hidden energy wasted because of the incorrect management of resources. The Energy Balance Chart, which allows to relate takt time and energy consumption, in order to understand the optimal energy scheduling model to apply so as to reduce energy consumption. Possible further developments of the present study are the introduction of energy quantitative and qualitative performance measures, in order to control the energy performances, as well as logistical ones. Finally, the definition of a methodology aimed at selecting the optimal energy scheduling model to be applied has still to be studied in deep.

References

1. Wei, Y.-M., Liao, H., Fan, Y.: An empirical analysis of energy efficiency in China's iron and steel sector. Energy **32**, 2262–2270 (2007)
2. Saidur, R., Rahim, N.A., Masjuki, H.H., Mekhilef, S., Ping, H.W., Jamaluddin, M.F.: End-use energy analysis in the Malaysian industrial sector. Energy **34**, 153–158 (2009)
3. Hong, G.-B., et al.: Energy flow analysis in pulp and paper industry. Energy **36**, 3063–3068 (2011)
4. Zhou, P., Ang, B.W., Poh, K.L.: Decision analysis in energy and environmental modeling: an update. Energy **31**, 2604–2622 (2006)
5. Ates, S.A., Durakbasa, N.M.: Evaluation of corporate energy management practice of energy intensive industries in Turkey. Energy **45**, 81–91 (2012)
6. European Commission - Integrated Pollution Prevention and Control (IPPC). Reference document on best available techniques for energy efficiency (2008)
7. Saygin, D., Worrell, E., Patel, M.K., Gielen, D.J.: Benchmarking the energy use of energy-intensive industries in industrialized and in developing countries. Energy **36**, 6661–6673 (2011)

8. Womack, J.P., Jones, D.T.: Lean Thinking: Banish Waste and Create Wealth in Your Corporation. Simon & Schuster, New York (1996)
9. Rother, M., Shook, J.: Learning to See: Value Stream Mapping to Add Value and Eliminate Muda. The Lean Enterprise Institute Inc, Brookline, MA (1999)
10. Erlach, K.: Energy efficiency in manufacturing using the energy value stream method for building an energy-efficient factory. In: Proceedings of APMS 2010 International Conference, Cernobbio, Como, Italy
11. Bogdanski, G., Schönemann, M., Thiede, S., Andrew, S., Herrmann, C.: An extended energy value stream approach applied on the electronics industry. In: Emmanouilidis, C., Taisch, M., Kiritsis, D. (eds.) Advances in Production Management Systems. IFIP AICT, vol. 397, pp. 65–72. Springer, Heidelberg (2013)
12. EPA. The Lean and Energy Toolkit. U.S. Environmental Protection Agency (2007) http://www.epa.gov/lean/toolkit/LeanEnergyToolkit.pdf
13. Pavnaskar, S.J., Gershenson, J.K., Jambekar, A.B.: Classification scheme for lean manufacturing tools. Int. J. Prod. Resour. 41(13), 3075–3090 (2003)
14. Tang, L., Che, P., Liu, J.: A stochastic production planning problem with nonlinear cost. Comput. Oper. Res. 39, 1977–19877 (2012)

An Integrated Production Planning Model with Obsolescence and Lifecycle Considerations in a Reverse Supply Chain

Swee S. Kuik[✉], Toshiya Kaihara, Nobutada Fujii,
and Daisuke Kokuryo

Graduate School of System Informatics,
Kobe University, 1-1 Rokkodai, Nada, Kobe, Hyogo 657-8501, Japan
kuik@kaede.cs.kobe-u.ac.jp, kaihara@kobe-u.ac.jp,
nfujii@phoenix.kobe-u.ac.jp,
kokuryo@port.kobe-u.ac.jp

Abstract. Environmentally conscious manufacturing and product recovery are considered as an important research in the current business scenario. This is due to the associated costs for virgin materials and waste disposal treatment that have been significantly increased in a yearly basis. Currently, there is a lack of modeling into the problems of remanufacturing production planning with component obsolescence and lifecycle constraints. In practice, the planning decisions may have direct impacts on the amount of wastage and disposal along a reverse supply chain. This article proposes an integrated production planning model with component obsolescence and lifecycle considerations, which helps minimise the total associated costs of production, costs of remanufactured products and components inventory holding, ordering costs, and disposal treatment costs. Numerical examples are also presented to demonstrate this production planning problem for remanufactured products using mixed integer programming optimisation. Finally, several contributions of this study and future works are discussed.

Keywords: Reverse supply chain · Remanufacturing · Obsolescence

1 Introduction

Manufacturers are now aware that product disposal to landfill may not be a viable solution to cope with the increased virgin material and disposal costs [1–3]. In supply chain perspectives, the depreciation due to its value loss for remanufactured products has a great influence on the profitability of manufacturers. Rapid improvement and development in science and technology has also resulted with shorter product lifecycle [4]. An appropriate production planning for shorter lifecycle products can help reduce the inventory holding costs and improve an overall supply chain performance. In addition, the remanufactured products could lose their perceived utility within end-of-life (EOL) stage [1–3]. To address these issues of obsolescence, manufacturers should consider to integrate this critical aspect in the time-period production planning horizon.

© IFIP International Federation for Information Processing 2015
S. Umeda et al. (Eds.): APMS 2015, Part I, IFIP AICT 459, pp. 680–688, 2015.
DOI: 10.1007/978-3-319-22756-6_83

In response to the significant changes in environmental rules and regulations, numerous manufacturers are also keen for implementing environmentally conscious manufacturing and product recovery with their supply chain partners for achieving significant amount of cost savings as a whole [2, 3]. Remanufacturing is currently known as one of the compromising alternatives to meet the stringent environmental challenges. By considering the alternative dispositions for handling EOL products, manufacturers can then minimise significant amount of waste disposal to landfill. There are organisations that are currently working on product recovery operations, such as Caterpillar, HP, Xerox, etc. [2]. For successful production planning, manufacturers need to consider the planning horizon with the obsolescence constraints that may directly impact on the depreciation value of remanufactured products.

At present, the development of production planning with obsolescence consideration for manufacturers is still at the budding stage [1, 3]. A major limitation is the complication of various types of remanufactured products and component obsolescence constraints, where it is subject to the depreciation value over a certain time-period planning horizon. If the obsolescence restriction is exceeded, any excessive inventory for obsolete products and components may need to be disposed entirely [1–3]. However, the total cost associated with the disposal treatment is considered as the financial burdens for manufacturers. The reduction of substantial amount of waste disposal by manufacturers is indeed a need for cost-effective improvement in a reverse supply chain.

In this article, an integrated remanufacturing production planning model is proposed with the considerations of component obsolescence restrictions. This developed model may help manufacturers to minimise overall supply chain costs. Section 2 presents the formulation of mathematical models in remanufacturing production planning problems. To demonstrate the usefulness of the proposed models, Sects. 3 and 4 present the numerical case examples with results analyses. Finally, the contributions of this study and future work are also discussed.

2 Mathematical Formulation

To address the obsolescence issues in production planning, the mixed integer programming (MIP) optimisation models are developed to analyse various scenarios of cost-effective production planning. In this study, there are two mathematical models with or without the incorporation of obsolescence issues that are presented for comparisons.

The first model is developed for an analysis to exclude the component obsolescence restrictions. Meanwhile, the second model is developed for an analysis to include component obsolescence restrictions. These optimisation models aim to minimise an overall associated cost of producing remanufactured products for the next planning horizon of T. The detailed mathematical formulations are discussed in the following sections. There are some key assumptions for the developed models that are considered in this study. The input parameters with continuous, integer and binary variables used for model formulation and evaluation are provided in Tables 1 and 2 respectively.

Table 1. Model Parameters

Symbol	Description
N	*Number of remanufactured product i, where $i = 1, 2, 3, \ldots N$*
J	*Number of component j, where $j = 1, 2, 3, \ldots J$*
T	*Planning horizon comprising of time period t, where $t = 1, 2, 3, \ldots T$*
f	*Time period f, upon receiving component j,*
R_i	*Unit cost of remanufactured product i*
C_j	*Unit cost of component j*
U_i	*Inventory holding unit cost for remanufactured product i*
H_j	*Inventory holding unit cost for component j*
A_i	*Fixed set-up cost for remanufactured product i*
G_j	*Fixed ordering cost for component j*
V_i	*Production capacity for remanufactured product i*
M_j	*Ordering capacity for component j*
α_j	*Disposal treatment unit cost for component j*
S_j	*Order lot size ordering for component j*
O_j	*Order lead-time for component j*

Table 2. Model variables

Symbol	Description
X_{it}	*Quantity of i produced in t period*
I_{it}	*Quantity of inventory i in t period*
y_{jt}	*Quantity of j ordered in t period*
L_{jt}	*Quantity of inventory j in t period*
L_{jtf}	*Quantity of inventory in t period upon receiving j at the end of f period*
β_j	*Quantity of disposal treatment j*
γ_{jrt}	*Quantity of usage in t period upon receiving j at the end of f period*
D_{it}	*Demand i in t period*
B_{ji}	*Bill of Material (BOM) with j of i*
e_j	*Obsolescence with j lifecycle*
a_{it}	*Fixed setup-up of i in t period (binary)*
P_{jt}	*Fixed (scheduled) ordering of j in t period (binary)*
p_{jt}	*Fixed ordering of j in t period (binary)*

- Types of the remanufactured products and components are known;
- Demands in the planning horizon are deterministic;
- Capacity in production and ordering are deterministic and constant;
- Quality aspect is excluded for either products or components;
- Considerations of obsolete components are deterministic and known;
- Transportation and distribution are beyond the scope of this study.

2.1 Model One Without Component Obsolescence and Lifecycle Constraints

This section presents the formulation of MIP model to evaluate production planning problem by excluding component obsolescence constraint. Using the above parameters and decision variables from Tables 1 and 2, the objective function of MIP model is formulated into eight terms as shown in Eq. (1).

$$MinZ = \sum_i \sum_t R_i X_{it} + \sum_j \sum_t C_j y_{jt} + \sum_j \sum_t C_j Y_{jt}$$
$$+ \sum_i \sum_t U_i I_{it} + \sum_i \sum_t A_i a_{it} + \sum_j \sum_t G_j P_{jt} \qquad (1)$$
$$+ \sum_j \sum_t G_j p_{jt} + \sum_j \sum_t H_j L_{jt}$$

Terms 1–3 are the cost associated with product-component in production and inventory aspects. Term 5 is calculated as the set-up associated costs in t period planning horizon. Terms 6 and 7 represent the cost associated with ordering components. Term 8 is the inventory cost associated with component in t period planning horizon. The model constraints are presented in Eqs. (2)–(8).

$$L_{jt} = L_{j,t-1} + S_j Y_{jt} - \sum_i B_{ji} X_{it} \qquad 1 < t \le o_j \quad \forall t,j \qquad (2)$$

$$L_{jt} = L_{j,t-1} + S_j y_{j,t-o_j} - \sum_i B_{ji} X_{it} \qquad t > o_j \quad \forall t,j \qquad (3)$$

$$I_{it} = I_{i,t-1} + X_{it} - D_{it} \qquad \forall t,j \qquad (4)$$

$$X_{it} \le V_i \qquad y_{jt} \le M_j \quad \forall t,j \qquad (5)$$

$$y_{jt} \le WP_{jt} \quad X_{it} \le Wa_{it} \quad Y_{jt} \le Wp_{jt} \quad \forall t,i \qquad (6)$$

$$X_{it}, y_{jt}, Y_{jt}, I_{it}, L_{jt} \ge 0 \qquad \forall t,i,j,f \qquad (7)$$

$$a_{it}, P_{jt}, p_{jt} \in (0,1) \qquad (8)$$

Equation (2) is the inventory balance associated with order and bill of materials (BOM). Equations (3) and (4) are the formulation of remanufactured products for the inventory balance to satisfy demand request. The constraints with related capacity, such as production and ordering are shown in Eq. (5). Meanwhile, Eq. (6) is formulated as the parameters used in binary form, if the values for y_{jt}, X_{it}, and Y_{jt}, and p_{jt} are more than zero, P_{jt}, a_{it}, and p_{jt} are also more than zero. These values of y_{jt}, P_{jt}, and p_{jt} can be expressed as one with W as a large positive number. In addition, Eqs. (7) and (8) represent the integer and binary decision variables used in the modelling.

2.2   Model Two with Component Obsolescence and Lifecycle Constraints

This section presents the formulation of MIP model to evaluate production planning with the restriction of component obsolescence. An objective function is formulated with nine terms as shown in Eq. (9), where Eqs. (10)–(25) are the constraints used for remanufacturing production modelling in this study.

$$
\begin{aligned}
MinZ = &\sum_i \sum_t R_i X_{it} + \sum_j \sum_t C_j y_{jt} + \sum_j \sum_t C_j Y_{jt} + \sum_i \sum_t U_i I_{it} \\
&+ \sum_i \sum_t A_i a_{it} + \sum_j \sum_t G_j P_{jt} \\
&+ \sum_j \sum_t G_j p_{jt} + \sum_j \sum_t \sum_f H_j L_{jtf} + \sum_j \alpha_j \beta_j
\end{aligned}
\tag{9}
$$

There are only two modified terms with this proposed model. Term 8 is modified to include the time-period upon receiving components and the end of obsolete time-period. The component disposal treatment cost is calculated as shown in the Term 9. The rest of the Terms 1–7 used are similar with the previous model in Eq. (1).

$$
I_{it} = I_{i,t-1} + X_{it} - D_{it} \qquad \forall t,j
\tag{10}
$$

$$
\sum_f^t L_{jtf} = L_{j0} + S_j Y_{jt} - \sum_i B_{ji} X_{it} \quad t=1 \quad \forall t,j,r
\tag{11}
$$

$$
\sum_f^t L_{jtf} = \sum_f^{t-1} L_{j,t-1f} + S_j Y_{jt} - \sum_i B_{ji} X_{it} \quad 1<t<e_j \quad t \geq e_j \quad \forall t,j
\tag{12}
$$

$$
\sum_{f=t+1-e_j}^t L_{jtf} = \sum_{f=t+1-e_j}^{t-1} L_{j,t-1f} + S_j Y_{jt} - \sum_i B_{ji} X_{it} \quad t \geq e_j \quad t \geq o_j \quad \forall t,j
\tag{13}
$$

$$
\sum_f^t L_{jtf} = \sum_f^{t-1} L_{j,t-1f} + S_j y_{jt} - \sum_i B_{ji} X_{it} \quad 1<t<e_j \quad t \geq o_j \quad \forall t,j
\tag{14}
$$

$$
\sum_{f=t+1-e_j}^t L_{jtf} = \sum_{f=t+1-e_j}^{t-1} L_{j,t-1f} + S_j y_{jt} - \sum_i B_{ji} X_{it} \quad t \geq e_j \quad t \geq o_j \quad \forall t,j
\tag{15}
$$

$$
\sum_i B_{ji} X_{it} = \sum_f \gamma_{jft} \quad 1 \leq t < e_j \quad \forall t,j,r
\tag{16}
$$

$$
\sum_i B_{ji} X_{it} = \sum_{f=t+1-e_j} \gamma_{jft} \quad e_j \leq t < T \quad \forall t,j,r
\tag{17}
$$

$$L_{jtf} = S_j Y_{jt} - \gamma_{jft} \quad f = t \quad t \leq o_j \quad \forall t, j, r \tag{18}$$

$$L_{jtf} = S_j y_{jt} - \gamma_{jft} \quad f = t \quad t \leq o_j \quad \forall t, j, r \tag{19}$$

$$L_{jtf} = L_{j,t-1,f} - \gamma_{jft} \quad f < t \quad t - f \leq o_j \quad \forall t, j, f \tag{20}$$

$$\beta_j = \sum_{t=o_j-1} \gamma_{j,t,t+1-o_j} \quad \forall t, j \tag{21}$$

$$X_{it} \leq V_i \quad y_{jt} \leq M_j \quad \forall t, j \tag{22}$$

$$y_{jt} \leq WP_{jt} \quad X_{it} \leq Wa_{it} \quad Y_{jt} \leq Wp_{jt} \quad \forall t, i \tag{23}$$

$$X_{it}, y_{jt}, Y_{jt}, I_{it}, L_{jtf}, \gamma_{jft}, \beta_j \geq 0 \quad \forall t, i, j, f \tag{24}$$

$$a_{it}, P_{jt}, p_{jt} \in (0, 1) \tag{25}$$

Equation (10) is the balance of inventory holding for product-component to satisfy demand request. Equations (11)–(15) are calculated as each time-period of orders is met with scheduled production planning. Equations (16) and (17) represent the production usage at each time-period with the obsolete components. Equations (18)–(20) are the expressions of inventory holding for product-component at each time-period. Equation (21) is derived to estimate excessive components to be discarded at the end of the obsolete time-period. In addition, the capacity constraints in relation to the production and ordering are established as shown in Eq. (22). Equation (23) represents the decision variable in binary form.

If the values of y_{jt}, X_{it}, Y_{jt}, and p_{jt} are more than zero, these variables of P_{jt}, a_{it}, and p_{jt} are also more than zero. As a result, these variables of y_{jt}, P_{jt}, and p_{jt} are one, where W is a large positive number.

Finally, Eqs. (24) and (25) represent the continuous and binary decision variables used in the modelling. In order to resolve the developed optimization models with obsolete component scenario in Eqs. (1) and (9), a CPLEX mixed integer optimization solver is used.

3   Numerical Example

This section discusses a numerical case example for production planning problem with the remanufactured products. In this example, a planning horizon is about 12 periods, which is used as a simulated case example. In this remanufacturing production planning example, there are three types (i.e. PT1, PT2 and PT3) of remanufactured product under examination. Each type of the remanufactured products has four separated components, which is named as CP1, CP2, CP3 and CP4. There are considered as the common components that are used by all types of the remanufactured products. Tables 3 and 4 show that the parameters used for both remanufactured products and components in the modelling. The obsolescence of time-period estimation for each

Table 3. Parameters used product i for modelling

	PT1	PT2	PT3
V_i	300	700	700
R_i	115	100	230
U_i	56	48	77
A_i	530	780	840

Table 4. Parameters used component j for modelling

	CP1	CP2	CP3	CP4
S_j	4500	4500	10000	10000
M_j	60	30	6	8
C_j	7500	22000	35000	23000
L_{jt}	4	5	5	3
α_j	6	8	9	6
G_j	420	540	680	460
O_j	30000	22000	5000	0

component is about 6 months for CP1, 3 months for CP2, 9 months for CP3, and 3 months for CP4 respectively.

Using Cplex optimisation solver, the results obtained without obsolescence issue showed that an overall minimum cost for the production planning was approximately $5,263,143 with the linear relaxation of approximately $4,829,131. The calculated value of optimality gap is about 0.0825. However, the results obtained with obsolescence issues revealed that an overall minimum cost for production planning was approximately $6,029,983 with the linear relaxation of approximately $5,528,876. The calculated value of optimality gap is about 0.0906. By comparing both models with or without obsolescence, the obtained results revealed that the total cost for production planning model with obsolescence as derived in Eq. (9) would be much higher than the total cost for production planning model without obsolescence as derived in Eq. (1). One of the primary reasons is that the product-component inventory holding and disposal are expressed as the cost associated terms of objective functions. In practice, the manufacturer should consider to maintain inventory stocks with quantities of the obsolete components as low as possible to avoid disposal costs after EOL constraints.

4   Results and Discussions

The obsolescence issues for remanufacturing production planning has been drawn significant attentions in recent years. To minimise the costs of producing the remanufactured products, there is a need to consider the obsolescence issues for product-component level in a production planning horizon. Figure 1 illustrates a

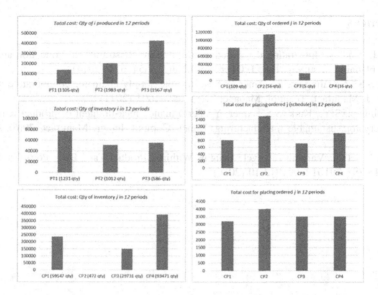

Fig. 1. A summary of total associated costs for producing 3 product types with 4 components

summary of product and component inventory variables with the total associated costs for this case example. This consideration may help resolve the oversimplified production planning problems. Two developed models have been compared with the remanufacturing production planning with and without obsolescence considerations. With three remanufactured product types ($N = 3$) and four separate components ($J = 4$), the proposed MIP model with obsolescence scenario consists of 1,107 variables with binary variables of 132, integer variable of 970 and continuous variable of 5. This model contains 2392 constraints used and non-zero coefficient of 1968.

5   Concluding Remarks

In this study, the proposed production planning model is developed by integrating the obsolescence issues for remanufactured products within a planning horizon. Comparisons of the obtained results from the developed models with and without obsolescence showed that the total associated costs with obsolescence are generally higher than the total associated costs without obsolescence. In addition, the contribution of this study is twofold. Firstly, the developed model addresses the obsolescence issue for remanufactured products in production planning problems. Secondly, the developed model aims to avoid the oversimplification of cost estimation in a reverse supply chain. For future works, different obsolete time-periods for the remanufactured product-component and variations of the inventory holding costs in production planning will be compared. Furthermore, the models can be extended by considering uncertainty of the consumer's demand requirements.

References

1. Pahl, J., Voß, S.: Integrating deterioration and lifetime constraints in production and supply chain planning: a survey. Eur. J. Oper. Res. **238**(3), 654–674 (2014)
2. Kuik, S.S., Nagalingam, S., Amer, Y.: Sustainable supply chain for collaborative manufacturing. J. Manufact. Technol. Manage. **22**(8), 984–1001 (2011)
3. Nagalingam, S.V., Kuik, S.S., Amer, Y.: Performance measurement of product returns with recovery for sustainable manufacturing. Robot. Comput.-Integr. Manufact. **29**(6), 473–483 (2013)
4. Zhao, Y., et al.: Varying Lifecycle Lengths Within a Product Take-Back Portfolio. J. Mech. Des. **132**(9), 091012–091012-10 (2010)

Cradle to Cradle Products, Modularity and Closed Loop Supply Chains

Kjeld Nielsen[✉] and Thomas Ditlev Brunoe

Department of Mechanical and Manufacturing Engineering, Aalborg University,
Fibigerstraede 16, 9220 Aalborg East, Denmark
kni@m-tech.aau.dk

Abstract. Cradle to Cradle (C2C) is a concept which is gaining acceptance as a way to design products which as a minimum are sustainable. This paper seeks to contribute to the C2C methodology by providing guidelines for determining product architecture in the product design process, which supports the C2C concept. The paper describes the linkages between product architecture and reusability in the technosphere (as opposed to the biosphere) which is an enabler for C2C. It is concluded that modular product architecture designing product families based on product platforms rather than designing individual products can enable C2C. Furthermore, reconfigurability also has potential to increase the reusability of parts of products.

Keywords: Sustainability · Eco-design · Cradle to cradle · Modular architecture

1 Introduction

This paper focuses on the specific challenges and opportunities in developing and manufacturing modular products when applying the "Cradle to Cradle" paradigm, and is an extension of the work published by Petersen et al. [10].

The concept "cradle to cradle" (C2C) was introduced by McDonough and Braungart [5, 6] as a way to "transform industry from a polluting and resource depleting system into a sustainable system of production". The concept has its origin in the work presented at EXPO 2000 as The Hannover Principles [7]. The main difference between C2C and traditional initiatives to reduce environmental impact are mainly focused on reducing the harmful impact of a product or process whereas C2C focuses not on reducing harmful impacts but seeks instead to remove them and replace them with non-harmful elements. One of the elementary ideas behind C2C is that industrial production should imitate the metabolism of nature where all waste from plants and animals is recycled to create new life by e.g. composting [5]. This is in contrast to the current prevailing industrial system, where products at the end of their useful life are disposed in landfills or incinerated which ultimately pollutes the environment. The materials used for this requires new harvesting of materials often starting in the supply chain as mining or quarrying. The mining and quarrying required for the new materials for manufacturing products is often resource

© IFIP International Federation for Information Processing 2015
S. Umeda et al. (Eds.): APMS 2015, Part I, IFIP AICT 459, pp. 689–696, 2015.
DOI: 10.1007/978-3-319-22756-6_84

consuming and polluting processes as well [8]. By introducing the C2C concept, McDonough and Braungart [5] seek to make a conceptual shift from the cradle to grave paradigm, where the aggregated environmental impact of a product in its single lifecycle is minimized, towards the C2C paradigm where the negative environmental impact is removed over several product lifecycles and materials are recycled infinitely. McDonough and Braungart [5] argue that industry should imitate nature by enabling materials used in industry to be recycled closed-loop, ideally without degrading material quality or disposing materials in landfills or incinerators. Materials used in products should either be (a) safely disposable in nature by using compostable materials and in this way contribute to renewing nutrients in the nature or farming or (b) recyclable in new products by extracting the materials, referred to as technical nutrients, and process them to become usable in a new product without degrading quality [2]. McDonough and Braungart refer to these two closed loops as the biosphere and the technosphere. In this paper, we shall focus mainly on products in which materials are recycled though the technosphere, i.e. non-organic products. The principles of C2C design and production are well in conformance with general principles of closed loop supply chains [4, 9], however in this context we will focus primarily on the principles specifically defined for C2C.

2   Cradle to Cradle Products and Production

Products, which are built from non-organic materials, should according to C2C be designed to support the material cycle of the technosphere, which is illustrated in Fig. 1. The cycle begins with a production process. The output of this process is a product, which for a period is used during its functional life. This part of the life cycle is identical to the traditional cradle to grave thinking, however in the following processes, the life cycle differs. Once the product becomes obsolete or fails, instead of discarding the product in a landfill or incinerating it as would traditionally be the case, the product is disassembled. The disassembly process outputs the components or materials used in the product, which is referred to as technical nutrients. The term "technical nutrient" emphasizes the analogy to the biological cycle, where degraded organic material provides nutrients for new plants or animals. The technical nutrients are then used for a new production process to output new products and thus a closed loop supply chain is achieved, where ideally no technical materials are wasted and no new materials need to be mined or extracted from natural resources.

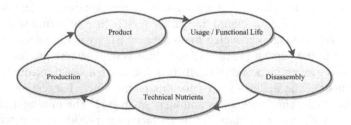

Fig. 1. The cycle of materials in the technosphere [5].

It is obvious that the design of a product will determine whether a product can be recycled in the C2C cycle or not. McDonough et al. [8] links the realization of the C2C vision to the 12 Principles of Green Engineering, which were first defined by Anastas and Zimmerman [1]. In the context of this paper, particularly three of these principles are of interests, which are:

- Principle 3: Separation and purification operations should be designed to minimize energy consumption and materials use [1].
- Principle 9: "Material diversity in multicomponent products should be minimized to promote disassembly and value retention" [1].
- Principle 11: "Products processes and systems should be designed for performance in a commercial afterlife" [1].

Following normally design procedures, product designs will determine how well these principles can be tracked. In order to follow principle 3, a product should be designed to that after a products useful life, it should be possible to separate it into recyclable materials. This includes that the product should be easy to disassemble into components, but also that the components should be recyclable with as little energy consumption as possible. This must be considered when designing the product by not choosing an architecture that is difficult to take apart as well as avoiding mixing materials in components, which will subsequently be difficult to separate. Principle 9 suggests minimizing material diversity in multiple components products, which is intended to support principle 3. By minimizing the number of different materials used in a product or component, fewer processes will be needed to separate and recycle the material at the end of its life and it will thus be more likely to be recycled. Principle 11 suggests that products, processes and systems should be designed for performance in a commercial afterlife; however, the content in this paper shall focus only on products in this context. This principle promotes re-use rather than re-cycling, since re-using a product most often consumes less energy and generally has a much lower environmental impact than recycling it.

Applying these principles naturally presents a number of challenges during product development, since some design considerations may suggest applying other principles than the 12 principles from Anastas and Zimmerman [1]. As will be shown in the following, choosing the right product architecture will enable the three principles presented above.

3   Product Modularity and Implications for Cradle to Cradle Products and Production

It is commonly acknowledged that the usage of modular product architecture is an efficient way of creating the product variety necessary in mass customization [3, 11, 12]. Furthermore, the usage of modular product design has proven to have a number of long-term positive effects on product development as well as manufacturing and logistics [11]. Numerous definitions of modular product architecture exist but in this context, the definition of modular product architecture defined by [13] is adopted. This definition states that products with modular architectures have the following properties: (1) One module, being a part of the product implements one or few functional elements and (2) The interactions and thereby interfaces between modules are well defined [13]. This applies to physical products and may to some extent apply to digital products. However, digital products variety can also be implemented without usage of a physical modular architecture, since products can be customized by non-physical means. Ulrich and Eppinger [13] define three different types of modularity: (1) Slot modular architecture, (2) Bus modular architecture, and (3) Sectional modular architecture. In the sectional-modular architecture however all interfaces between modules are identical, implying that modules can be combined randomly and no module is common to all products in a product family. This is in contrast to platform based product families, which are described below.

Modular product architecture broadly defined is often considered the opposite of integral product architecture, in which products are not logically divided in modules with clear interfaces [13]. This architecture is typically chosen for performance reasons, when size is an important optimization issue or if the product is produced in a volume, where the accumulated variable costs exceed the savings from choosing modular architecture.

3.1 Material Separation and Recycling

Considering principles 3 and 9, which suggest that separating materials should be as easy and less energy consuming as possible and that material diversity should be minimized, modular product architecture provides a number of possibilities compared to integral product architecture. The industry often tents to use modular product architecture as a way to reduce production complexity and will as a side effect have separated materials before final assembly. Disassembly of such modular products should/would be easier.

Using modular product architecture, components that are manufactured using certain materials can be incorporated into the same modules. This will be beneficial when disassembling the product for recycling, since each module can be regarded as a "product" itself, and following principle 9, this would minimize material diversity. In relation to disassembly and material separation, this is beneficial since each module after being disassembled would not need to be disassembled further to be recycled, assuming it is possible to design modules with only one material. If a module design must have multiple materials, pooling several components of the same material will be beneficial for logistics during disassembly, since each module will be disassembled to fewer material fractions. Using an integral product architecture will then opposite not be useful to fulfill principles 3 and 9. As an example a car wheel, which is modular, but the modules consist of two sub products the rim and the tire. The rim is recyclable, it consists of metal alloy (iron, steel, aluminum, titanium, etc.), but the tire consists of an integration of rubber mixture and metal material (steel) which as the alternative to landfills or incinerators could be re-used, but not re-used. Hence, the use of modular architecture makes it easier to follow the principles in design for C2C and contrary, the use of integrated architecture will likely make this more difficult.

Though ideally all materials used in a product should be recyclable to conform to the C2C principles, some companies may acknowledge a need for using materials, which cannot be recycled. However, even with some materials, which cannot be recycled, a company may wish to apply C2C partly by ensuring that the components that do not require the usage of non-recyclable materials can in fact be recycled in compliance with C2C. This can be achieved by defining the product architecture so that recyclable materials are included in certain modules, preferably minimizing material diversity c.f. above, and non-recyclable materials are included in other modules. By doing this, a partial recycling can be promoted as well as a safe disposal of non-recyclable materials.

3.2 Afterlife Reuse and Remanufacturing

In relation to principle 11, which states that products should be designed for an afterlife performance, modular product design also presents possibilities. However as described above this can primarily be achieved by considering each module as a product itself, so that modules rather than whole products are reused.

One example of this is extending products useful life by allowing end customers upgrade products by replacing a module. This can be achieved if the interfaces in a product are designed so that modules that provide functionality to the user become obsolete can be swapped with a new module providing updated functionality. One example of this is personal computers, where the modular architecture allows the end user to easily replace a hard drive or extension cards to add update functionality or performance. By doing this, the end customer will be able to use the product for a longer time since the product can be upgraded rather than discarded when obsolete.

An important prerequisite for this however is that a part of the product has a more stable functionality, i.e. the architecture should be designed so that "stable" functionality is separated from "unstable" functionality. "Stable" functionality is here defined as functionality that can be considered unchanged for a longer period. "Unstable" functionality is defined as functionality, which compared to the stable functionality needs to be changed more often. To enable product upgrades, and thereby extend the product's useful life, modules should contain either stable or unstable functionality rather than both. This is similar to product development strategies using product platforms in certain companies. When designing product families using a product platform, it is often chosen to include functionality, which is stable in a product platform differentiating the individual products by developing modules that are combined with the platform to form a product. However, the main goal of that effort is to reuse products and upgrade them to extend their life but rather to enable companies to reduce development cost, time and manufacturing costs as well. Although not presently used for supporting C2C principles, the experiences and methods from product platform development are expected to be possible to apply to C2C since the product architecture seems similar but with different optimization criteria.

In the description above, what determines whether functionality is stable or unstable is whether the functionality becomes obsolete. However, other criteria are also relevant in determining the stability of functionality. For some products, it can be expected that the user will change requirements for a certain type of product over time. In order to respect the C2C principles for such product, it would be necessary to determine which functionality the user would change requirements for most frequently and this functionality would become the unstable functionality.

Another approach, which can be relevant, is to define modules by their expected lifetime before failure. This is mainly relevant if the product contains components, which wear much faster than other leading to an entire product, which could become defect because of a single component or module. In this case, it would be possible to extend the useful life of the product by enabling replacement of the components, which wear fastest. To support this, the architecture could be designed so that fast wearing components are grouped in certain modules, while components that are more durable are grouped in other modules.

However, this approach can only be taken if it is possible to design the product so that the majority of end customers will be able to perform the replacement of modules themselves. If this were not possible, an option would be to allow the manufacturer to take back products once the customer does no longer want to use the product for any reason. Then the manufacturer would be able to process the product by replacing faulty or obsolete modules thereby producing a usable product again much the same way as described above for end customers. A different approach, which is relevant only for the manufacturer, would be to take back products from customers and disassemble the product into modules, which could then be used in a regular production of new products. This is different from the other approaches, since this approach would imply that reclaimed modules are transferred to stock after disassembly rather than whole products being "refurbished". Whatever approaches the manufacturer may choose if reclaiming old products for disassembly the requirements for designing a product architecture are much similar to the case where the customer replaces modules, i.e. grouping functionality by stability or expected time to failure.

4   Implications

4.1   Design Implications

As mentioned previously, what is described above can be considered the ideal way of designing product architecture for supporting C2C principles. However, in an industrial environment other considerations will be necessary. Product design decisions are often based on tradeoffs between different criteria. One challenge in designing for C2C is that optimizing for C2C may not conform to a company's other design criteria such as cost, performance etc. However at this point, no quantitative research has been conducted to analyze this and generalize the results, so tradeoff decisions would need to be based on case to case analyses.

Furthermore, it seems likely that the different design criteria within C2C could be contradicting when defining a product architecture. For example grouping similar materials in modules to promote recycling of materials could be contradicting the design criteria for grouping functionality in modules to promote module reuse. However, in this specific example, the requirement for reuse would usually be more important than grouping materials since reusing a product, or in this case module, would usually be less energy consuming and have a lower environmental impact than recycling the materials. Furthermore, the considerations regarding materials recycling and thereby grouping similar materials will be more important the shorter lifecycle the module has. i.e. this will be most important in modules with an unstable functionality or shorter expected time to failure.

In general, it is considered necessary to address product design as a design of product families rather than individual products. By thinking a product range as a whole product family, the reuse of modules can become more formalized helping companies to establish methods and procedures for designing products, which are robust to changes in functionality and usage of common modules, which will ultimately facilitate module reuse.

4.2   Practical Implications

There are a number of different issues, which could prove challenging when designing and manufacturing a product range applying modular architecture to conform to C2C. One issue is logistics. If a company is to reclaim products at the end of their useful lifecycle, logistics must be in place to handle the incoming products. Planning and scheduling of manufacturing using the disassembled modules could also prove challenging since it would be difficult to forecast the incoming reclaimed products. However, reverse logistics is already an established research area and solutions are being developed for this.

The length of life cycles for different product types varies vastly. For products, which have a long life cycle, companies may find it difficult to foresee which changes in functionality will be required within the product life cycle. Also for some product types, the product life cycle may even be longer than the company's existence, since an industrial environment is often highly dynamic with companies closing, being acquired or merged. It is obvious that company mergers will present challenges if reclaiming old product is part of the companies' product strategies.

Although this issue seems most important for products with long life cycles, the matter of determining the stability of functionality can also be in issue for products with shorter life cycles. For some product types companies compete by adding new functionality frequently, which would make it increasingly difficult for a company to determine which functionality will be obsolete in a short time. Hence, this issue can be relevant both to products with short and long life cycles.

5   Conclusions

Cradle to cradle is a concept, which is gaining broad attention as a solution to many of the environmental and natural resource challenges, which the world is faced with. Although some effort has been put into translating the principles to practical guidelines, it is still difficult to apply the principles in practice. Designing product ranges using modular product architectures however seems to present a number of possibilities to support C2C principles. The research conducted within modularity as well as companies' own practical experience with this could provide already established methods, which could easily be adapted to C2C design. However, this paper explores only the potential for applying modular design to C2C, and does not address specific issues practically and does thus not provide evidence that the approach is at all feasible, although it does seem likely.

We consider the issues presented in this paper as an area with a large research potential as well as an area, which could provide industry with guidelines for designing products, which have a lower environmental impact than currently. However, much more research and method development will need to be conducted, for example quantitative studies of product ranges to estimate the actual potential for different product types.

References

1. Anastas, P.T., Zimmerman, J.B.: Design through the 12 principles of green engineering. Environ. Sci. Technol. **37**, 94–101 (2003)
2. Bolton, S.: Design for a Cradle to Cradle (2010)
3. Brunø, T.D., Nielsen, K., Taps, S.B., Jørgensen, K.A.: Sustainability evaluation of mass customization. In: Prabhu, V., Taisch, M., Kiritsis, D. (eds.) APMS 2013, Part I. IFIP AICT, vol. 414, pp. 175–182. Springer, Heidelberg (2013)
4. Hatcher, G., Ijomah, W., Windmill, J.: Design for remanufacture: a literature review and future research needs. J. Clean. Prod. **19**, 2004–2014 (2011)
5. McDonough, W., Braungart, M.: Cradle to Cradle: Remaking the Way We Make Things. North Point Press, New York (2002)
6. McDonough, W., Braungart, M.: Design for the triple top line: new tools for sustainable commerce. Corp. Environ. Strategy **9**, 251–258 (2002)
7. McDonough, W., Braungart, M.: The Hanover Principles: Design for Sustainability. Papercraft, pp. 8–9 (1992)
8. McDonough, W., Braungart, M., Anastas, P.T., et al.: Applying the principles of green engineering to cradle-to-cradle design. Environ. Sci. Technol. **37**, 434–441 (2003)
9. Nielsen, K., Brunø, T.D.: Closed loop supply chains for sustainable mass customization. In: Prabhu, V., Taisch, M., Kiritsis, D. (eds.) APMS 2013, Part I. IFIP AICT, vol. 414, pp. 425–432. Springer, Heidelberg (2013)
10. Petersen, T.D., Nielsen, K., Joergensen, K.A.: Applying modular product architecture to cradle to cradle product. In: Proceedings of the 12th International MITIP Conference the Modern Information Technology in the Innovation Processes of the Industrial Enterprises, pp. 85–91 (2010)
11. Pine, B.J.: Mass Customization: The New Frontier in Business Competition. Harvard Business School Press, Boston (1993)
12. Tseng, M.M., Jiao, J.: Design for mass customization. Ann. CIRP **45**, 153–156 (1996)
13. Ulrich, K.T., Eppinger, S.D.: Product Design and Development. McGraw-Hill, New York (2008)

Factors for Effective Learning in Production Networks to Improve Environmental Performance

Alexander Schurig[1,3], Mélanie Despeisse[1(✉)], Eric Unterberger[2], Steve Evans[1], and Gunther Reinhart[3]

[1] Institute for Manufacturing, University of Cambridge, 17 Charles Babbage Road, Cambridge, CB3 0FS, UK
{mas254,md621}@cam.ac.uk
[2] Fraunhofer IWU Project Group Resource-Efficient Mechatronic Processing Machines, Beim Glaspalast 5, 86153 Augsburg, Germany
eric.unterberger@iwu.fraunhofer.de
[3] Institute for Machine Tools and Industrial Management, Technische Universität München, Boltzmannstrasse 15, 85748 Garching, Germany

Abstract. There is evidence that the environmental performances of factories operating under similar circumstances vary greatly, even within one company. This indicates that production sites are operated in different ways which suggests a potential for improvement. Previous research shows that collaboration within production networks can improve factory performance. Learning collaboratively across factories is a promising approach to reduce the environmental impact of production sites. Several companies recognised this opportunity. Processes and systems to support knowledge and know-how exchange within their production network are already in place. In this research a literature review and interviews were carried out to explore factors that influence learning between factories. Such factors are critical to develop an effective tool enabling learning across factories and thus environmental performance improvements.

Keywords: Interfactory learning · Environmental performance · Learning collaboratively

1 Introduction

Multinational production companies typically operate around the world. Factors—such as factory history, size, location, implemented production processes, or type of products manufactured—influence the measurable characteristics of each factory [1, 2].

On the one hand certain factors differ immensely across factories within a company and impact the factories' environmental performance, which is defined as the "measurable results of an organisation's management of its environmental aspects" [3]. For instance, older sites in a production network are built and equipped according to decade-old standards while more recently built sites follow contemporary standards and adopt newer, more efficient technologies. Some might be specialised in energy intensive manufacturing whereas others might focus on assembly. On the other hand several

© IFIP International Federation for Information Processing 2015
S. Umeda et al. (Eds.): APMS 2015, Part I, IFIP AICT 459, pp. 697–704, 2015.
DOI: 10.1007/978-3-319-22756-6_85

aspects, such as production processes, produced products or location, can be used to find clusters of factories operating under virtually equal circumstances [4], i.e. similar products, production technology and scale. However, the environmental performances of such factories vary even though they operate under comparable conditions. One reason for these variations can be an asymmetry of knowledge and know-how between factories. This asymmetry implies a potential for knowledge and know-how transfer as well as for learning. As a consequence the interaction of employees in and across factories to learn collaboratively can improve the environmental performance of the factories. Learning between factories, or interfactory learning, is a promising approach to reduce the environmental impact of factories. In this context, the research presented in this paper has three objectives:

- To find examples of systems, processes and tools already in place to support interfactory learning (knowledge and know-how exchange).
- To understand factors that hinder and amplify the learning as well as knowledge and know-how exchange between factories.
- To identify the requirements and specifications for a tool to effectively support interfactory learning for environmental performance improvement.

2   Methods

This research was conducted in two stages. First, the three objectives were addressed by undertaking a literature review in the field of learning and knowledge and know-how exchange Second, interviews conducted with three companies were analysed. Section three presents and discusses three core arguments for this study:

1. Environmental performance varies between factories operating in akin conditions.
2. A difference in performance is a potential for learning.
3. Learning collaboratively can improve factories' performance.

The interview partner's companies operate in the following sectors: pharmaceutical, automotive supply and aerospace industry. All companies employ more than 80.000 people and operate factories around the world. The interviewed expert of the aerospace company is the leader of a network of people responsible energy efficiency in manufacturing. In the pharmaceutical company two interviews were conducted. First an environment, safety and health (ESH) manager of a big plant with around 8.000 employees took part in the semi structured interview. Second a member of an internal committee that advises both the executive committee as well as the board of directors in ESH matters participated. Furthermore an ESH manager as well as an energy manager of an automotive supplier offered their answers. The interviewees are part of the personal network of the researchers. All the companies they work for are certified according to ISO 14001 which means that learning and knowledge exchange activities are ongoing. Furthermore it was important that the companies operate several factories around the world in order to examine interfactory learning. The chosen industries as well as the different positions of the interview partners allow comprehensive insights into how companies deal with learning as well as knowledge and know-how exchange across factories on different levels.

3 Performance Variation as Potential for Learning

Environmental performance variations can be perceived as an indicator pointing towards potential for learning within a company's network of factories. When factories operate under similar circumstances an asymmetry in knowledge regarding environmental performance improvements can lead to such differences. Researchers found that learning within a single factory and within a network of factories influences site performance positively. Thus, interfactory learning is a promising approach to improve the environmental performance of factories within a network.

Variation in Factories' Environmental Performance. Several groups of researchers have investigated environmental performance in various sectors (e.g. electronics, metal and dairy products) and have shown that there is a strong variation in performance between factories or farms. In the electronics industry, Nagel assessed 25 production facilities (13 in the USA, 7 in Europe, 4 in Asia, 1 in Canada) of printed board suppliers. Using data submitted by the suppliers the author calculated a normalized indicator. The results of the calculations and the submitted data showed that the environmental performances of the facilities vary. For example, to produce 1 kg of printed board the "best" supplier used 7.5 times less energy than the "worst" (taking into consideration only suppliers which submitted consistent mass balance data). The author explicitly states that the technology in each facility is comparable [5]. Therefore reasons for the variations can be diverse, including inefficient usage of the equipment or suppliers submitting unreliable data. In another study, Roberts & Gehrke presented similar results with five companies operating in New Zealand's metal working sector. Based on site visits and interviews with both the companies and local council staff the researchers found two types of correlations between business practice and environmental performance. First, practices that contribute to reducing waste and overhauling faulty equipment directly lead to less impact on the environment. Second, implementing management approaches, such as focusing on product and process quality, ongoing improvement and leadership as well as empowering employees lead to a better resource efficiency [6]. Finally, Van Passel et al. examined farm accountancy data of 41 dairy farms in Flanders, Northern Belgium. The researchers assessed the farms calculating an indicator consisting of economic and environmental aspects. They found two interesting conclusions. One is that well performing farms showed both good economic as well as a good environmental outcomes. The other one is that managers of underperforming farms tend to be older and show potential for additional education [7].

The three studies mentioned above focused on different companies producing similar products with similar production technology. Bocken et al. analysed companies with well-established environmental management systems and programs already implemented and running. The researchers found that, despite the environmental management systems in place, the environmental performances of factories within a single company can significantly vary. The reasons for these variations range from systemic to people-related [8]:

- Since every factory normally has a separate environmental management team the multi-site implementation of promising measures is difficult.
- Factories naturally operate in a rather isolated way which can even result in difficulties in circulating success stories in the production network.
- Unequal mind-sets and the varying levels of motivation of people responsible on-site also contribute to the environmental performance variations.

The above studies confirm that it is possible to assess and compare the environmental performance of factories operating under similar circumstances. Only one study deals with the environmental performance variation of factories within one company. However, the results of this study illustrate the potential for improving the environmental performance by exchanging knowledge and know-how as well as learning across factories of one company.

Performance Variation to Identify Potential for Learning. According to Senge et al. knowledge is the result of learning. In an organisational context the authors defined learning as "the continuous testing of experience, and the transformation of that experience into knowledge—accessible to the whole organization, and relevant to its core purpose" [9]. It can be concluded that others can use and understand this knowledge because it becomes available for the organisation.

Nonaka argues that organisational knowledge has its origin in individual knowledge, which can be explicit or tacit. Explicit knowledge is easy to share whereas sharing tacit knowledge can be challenging. The author offers insights into how to turn tacit into explicit knowledge [10]. Thus the transformation of experience into knowledge described in the definition above is addressed in this paper.

Learning and knowledge are related in a circular manner. Learning is the process which produces knowledge which again can be the starting point for further learning.

Su and Chen examined the relationship between two organisational learning mechanisms—conceptual learning and operational learning—and plant performance. Measuring an index based on cost, quality, flexibility and delivery the researchers found that both mechanisms influence the plant performance positively [1]. In other words, a higher quality of learning leads to both a broader knowledge base and a better plant performance. So, in order to improve the environmental performance of a plant one can consider improving the learning within the plant. Other plants that show a better environmental performance can play an important role in this improvement, because their better performance can be linked to a better ongoing learning and thus a broader knowledge base. Differences in the environmental performance of factories point to differences in knowledge and know-how. Thus the variations can be used as an indicator to identify learning potentials.

Learning Collaboratively to Improve Performance. Vereecke et al. examined eight manufacturing companies operating in different industries and each running four to 10 factories. Sites can, according to the authors, play four different roles in a network: isolated, receiver, hosting network player and active network player. Among other aspects the authors concluded that plants that transfer innovations to others also receive innovations from others in return. Although the mutual exchange of innovations seems to be beneficial for partnering factories, the performance regarding cost, quality or time measures was not connected to the role a factory plays in the network [2]. It is surprising that neither isolated factories struggle to reach expectations nor active network player factories outperform other network participants. That implies that plants do not benefit in participating in the knowledge exchange with other factories. Additionally declaring that factories interact in a network contradicts Bocken et al.'s finding that factories operate rather independently.

However, in a study 10 years later Vereecke and de Meyer reassessed the eight multinationals interviewing managers in headquarters. There are three interesting observations that the authors made:

- First, an expertise transfer from both other factories and headquarters to a factory with the clear objective of improving its performance took place [4]. This contradicts the conclusion of their earlier study that participating in exchanging innovations with other factories has no effect on a factory's performance.
- Second, over time the number of active network players increased. One reason is that companies progressively regard factories as a source of knowledge and know-how [4]. Hence better performing factories with a broader knowledge base can play an important role in improving the learning of weaker factories.
- Third, active network players can ensure their existence in the long term by creating and sharing knowledge even if it seems unfavourable in the short term [4]. Concluding this reinforces that factories benefit from exchanging knowledge in a network.

In the context of pollution prevention, pollution control and environmental management systems Gavronski et al. advise plant managers to take two aspects into consideration to improve environmental performance: to promote a trustful climate among the staff in the plant and to expand knowledge exchange beyond the borders of the factory itself. For the latter the researchers suggest two forms of engagement. In larger corporations other factories can be approached to exchange knowledge and know-how. Additionally managers can go beyond the borders of the cooperation to contact plants of other companies, e.g. customers or suppliers, but also academic institutions [12]. Vereecke and de Meyer emphasise the positive influence of knowledge exchange in a production network on the economic performance of plants. Gavronski et al. explicitly point out that exchanging knowledge and know-how improves the environmental performance of plants. Therefore both works underline the improvement potential inherent in learning and thought exchange in a production network.

4 Interview Results

The findings on how people learn and exchange knowledge in the environmental context within a company were grouped in clusters as shown in Table 1: individuals, the group they form and the way they interact.

Table 1. Clustered findings of analysis of interviews

The individuals	• Usually uncomfortable to directly contact known as well as unknown colleagues, third party facilitator needed • Strong influence of speaking a mutual language
The group	• Two to ten people • Common fields of knowledge and experience • Good personal relationships useful (several meetings, off-work gatherings)
The interaction	• Dramatically diverging role of competition between factories • Personal contact important but influenced by additional factors • No differences in technical tools used for communication • Inspiring role of shop floor visits • Regional and global conferences

The Individuals. All interviewed employees agreed that direct contact between colleagues in different factories needs to be facilitated or even enforced by a third party of the company. Providing contact details together with project descriptions does not comfort employees. Whereas not speaking the same language is a major hindrance, speaking the same language is a major amplifier for exchange and learning.

The Group. Best learning occurs in rather small groups of two to ten people. The three settings illustrated by the interviewees involved pre-selected individuals with matching interests, knowledge and know-how:

• Audit teams can either be composed of employees responsible for the field to be audited in other plants or of dedicated full-time auditors. Mixtures of these two line-ups are possible.
• Working groups are established for a limited time and deal with a specific issue that concerns different factories. People who are responsible for that topic in their factory participate in these groups.
• People responsible for the environmental performance of their factory meet up in regular personal meetings with colleagues from other factories throughout the year.

The exchange, collaboration and learning in these contexts is very lively. Good personal relationships influence the collaboration positively. However, to establish such beneficial relationships regular meetings and off-work gatherings are necessary. The longer colleagues know each other the easier it is for them to learn from each other.

The Interaction. Competition affected the companies interviewed in different ways. One company uses competition for making decisions on future investments in a production line for a new product. Thus competition is perceived as a hindering factor for interfactory learning in an environmental context. An interviewee of another company stated that a similar kind of competition might facilitate the cooperation between factories in future and that friendly competition ("Who saves more resources?") already occurs. In the third company at the end of each audit factories receive a school mark. Furthermore the performance of a factory is anonymously compared to other factories.

Face-to-face interactions between employees generally supports collaboration between factories. Nevertheless factors, such as varying openness of learning partners, trust, sympathy, etc. influence the exchange.

There are no decisive differences in the technological communication means the companies use to support collaboration and exchange. However, in general it is hard to access the right information in the correct situation, e.g. using a good practice database.

Shop floor visits play a major role in the interactions. The environment has a stimulating influence. In one case after visiting several own factories for learning purposes the next workshop will take place at a manufacturer operating in a different industry.

Furthermore all companies organise regional and global conferences as well as workshops to share knowledge and know-how as well as to establish personal networks. One company employs coordinators—hierarchically working between factories and the central functions—in USA, Mexico and China to organise such events.

In one company two major factories collaborate intensively. One reason for this unusually strong exchange is their regular mutual reporting to the top management.

5   Discussion and Conclusion

Differences in the environmental performance of factories operating under similar conditions lead to a potential for learning collaboratively. While new technologies can be an enabler for learning as they make more information available, finding the right information can be more time consuming. Therefore the direct interaction between colleagues in a suitable context promises to enable learning to happen.

The common testing of experiences and turning subsequent understandings into organisational knowledge supports improvements of factories' environmental impact. The interviews conducted in this study show that companies recognize interfactory learning as a means to improve factories' performance. Processes and systems originating from the field of knowledge management are already implemented and working. This paper discusses the conditions for a favourable learning environment.

The main findings of this study show that learning occurs when the people involved work on a concrete topic, such as an audit or a working group activity on a specific issue. According to the interview findings, effective learning currently takes place when employees with similar work backgrounds exchange experiences in small groups. This is due to the nature of the issues the participants are facing and thus the same good practices can be applied. In contrast conferences bring together people with different backgrounds. This may cause discomfort as employees need to directly contact unknown colleagues; it is therefore debatable whether this type of conferences is best to foster interfactory learning. However bringing together people with the same professional background can limit the impact of learning. When backgrounds and views only partly overlap, there is more potential for learning. One of the interviewed companies is using this approach to learn from other industrial sectors and spread the acquired knowledge across its manufacturing sites.

This research is part of a wider project on Environmental Performance Variation (EPV) conducted with the EPSRC Centre for Industrial Sustainability. This work contributes to the EPV project by uncovering factors for effective learning across factories. Based on these factors a tool will be developed to further support interfactory learning and convert it into a more effective means to improve the environmental performance of factories.

Acknowledgements. We would like to thank Dr. Peter Schnurrenberger, Andreas Peters, Peter Lunt, Marcus Dörr and Till Sieghart for their valuable contributions. We also wish to acknowledge the EPSRC Centre for Industrial Sustainability for their support.

References

1. Netland, T., Ferdows, K.: What to expect from a corporate lean program. Sloan Manage. Rev. **55**, 83–89 (2014)
2. Vereecke, A., van Dierdonck, R., de Meyer, A.: A typology of plants in global manufacturing networks. Manage. Sci. **52**(11), 1737–1750 (2006)
3. Perotto, E., Canziani, R., Marchesi, R., Butelli, P.: Environmental performance, indicators and measurement uncertainty in EMS context: a case study. J. Clean. Prod. **16**, 517–530 (2008)
4. Vereecke, A., de Meyer, A.: The dynamic management of manufacturing networks. Vlerick Leuven Gent Management School, Working Paper Series 2009/15 (2009)
5. Nagel, M.H.: Managing the environmental performance of production facilities in the electronics industry: more than application of the concept of cleaner production. J. Clean. Prod. **11**(1), 11–26 (2003)
6. Roberts, L., Gehrke, T.: Linkages between best practice in business and good environmental performance by companies. J. Clean. Prod. **4**(3–4), 189–202 (1996)
7. van Passel, S., Nevens, F., Mathijs, E., van Huylenbroeck, G.: Measuring farm sustainability and explaining differences in sustainable efficiency. Ecol. Econ. **62**(1), 149–161 (2007)
8. Bocken, N., Morgan, D., Evans, S.: Understanding environmental performance variation in manufacturing companies. Int. J. Prod. Perf. Manag. **62**(8), 856–870 (2013)
9. Senge, P.M., Kleiner, A., Roberts, C., Ross, R., Smith, B.: The Fifth Discipline Fieldbook: Strategies and Tools for Building a Learning Organization. Currency Doubleday, New York (1994)
10. Nonaka, I.: The knowledge-creating company. Harv. Bus. Rev. **69**(6), 96–104 (1991)
11. Su, H.C., Chen, Y.S.: Unpacking the relationships between learning mechanisms, culture types and plant performance. Int. J. Prod. Econ. **146**, 728–737 (2013)
12. Gavronski, I., Klassen, R.D., Vachon, S., Nascimento, L.F.: A learning and knowledge approach to sustainable operations. Int. J. Prod. Econ. **140**(2), 183–192 (2012)

Investments in Energy Efficiency with Variable Demand: SEC's Shifting or Flattening?

Beatrice Marchi[✉] and Simone Zanoni

Department of Mechanical and Industrial Engineering,
University of Brescia, via Branze, 38, 25123 Brescia, Italy
{b.marchi, simone.zanoni}@unibs.it

Abstract. In order to support energy efficiency improvement, it is essential to monitor the energy performance and to make benchmarking with similar process or related Best Available Techniques. Among different key performance indicators that compare similar processes, the most relevant for the industrial sector is the specific energy consumption (SEC). With regard to the energy demand in an industrial process, a variable and fixed portion can generally be distinguished: as a direct consequence the amount of energy used per unit of product (SEC) usually decreases while the production rate increases. It should be noted that often production processes face variable demand over their utilization. Aim of this work is to propose a novel decision model to support the identification of the more suitable investment in energy efficiency given the variable demand expected, explicitly considering that the effect of investments in energy efficiency can be categorized in two main categories: those shifting the SEC curve and those flattening the SEC curve.

Keywords: Energy efficiency · Investment · SEC · Uncertainty · NPV

1 Introduction

Energy efficiency is an essential part of a sustainable energy future as it helps reducing the energy consumption. In addition, energy efficiency leads to many other benefits, such as: it drives economic growth creating jobs and investment opportunities, it reduces greenhouse-gas emissions and air pollutants, it lowers fuel expenditures and it enhances energy security [1]. As it is shown in Fig. 1, the industrial sector is the greater energy consumer than any other end-use sectors, currently consuming about 50 % of the world's total delivered energy [2, 3]. Moreover, in Fig. 2 it is possible to observe that, over the next 20 years, the worldwide industrial energy consumption is expected to grow from 3,900 Mtoe in 2014 to 5,000 Mtoe in 2035 by an average of about 6 % per year [4].

Recently, energy efficiency in the industrial sector has emerged as one of the most significant manufacturing decision option and it is gaining an increasingly relevance [5, 6]. The key drivers for a gradual process of rethinking towards a more energy-efficient acting are: the energy turnaround in Europe including the "20-20-20" targets, the great impact of energy issue on the strategic objectives of industrial companies, which are costs, time and quality and, finally, the customers' increasing ecological awareness [7–9].

© IFIP International Federation for Information Processing 2015
S. Umeda et al. (Eds.): APMS 2015, Part I, IFIP AICT 459, pp. 705–714, 2015.
DOI: 10.1007/978-3-319-22756-6_86

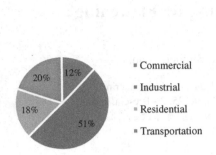

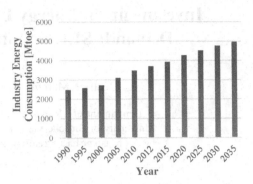

Fig. 1. World shares of total energy use by end-use sector, 2011 [2]

Fig. 2. Industrial sector energy consumption from 1990 to 2035 (Mtoe) [4]

However, industry often views energy as an operational cost instead of a competitive advantage: energy savings are perceived as incidental benefits of other actions rather than as a central value-generating proposition.

In order to reach higher levels of energy efficiency, it is important to monitor the progress of the energy performance of the company and to make comparisons with the performances of other firms (benchmarking). For that reason, key energy performance indicators (KPIs) have been introduced, such as the Specific Energy Consumption (SEC): i.e. the ratio between the total energy consumption and the physical/economic output value. Some of the advantages of this indicator are that it is not influenced by price fluctuations and can be directly related to process operations and technology choice. However, a comparison of energy use in different units and aggregate efficiency is effectively impossible without the conversion of the physical units' value into a common economic value [10].

Generally, the energy consumption profile of an industrial plant is given by two contributions: one is fixed, given the production plant, and the other is variable depending on the production rate. Thus, the amount of energy consumed per unit of product, and so the value of the specific energy consumption, decreases with the increase of the production rate, as the incidence of the fixed share decreases (Fig. 3). In many cases, industrial plants have to face variable, uncertain and discontinuous demands, e.g. days with high production and days with no production, working times alternate with idle times. For that reason, a wide range of production rate interests the production and the required flexibility results in reduced energy efficiency and increasing costs [11]. Even the specific energy consumption is subject to uncertainty, as it is a function of the production rate. Consequently, investments in energy efficiency can be divided in two subcategories: investments that reduce the specific energy consumption equally for all the production ("SEC vertical shifting") and investments that reduce the specific energy consumption differently for different production rate, i.e. flattening the curve of energy consumption ("SEC flattening"). See Fig. 3.

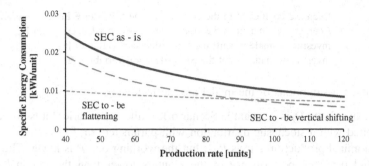

Fig. 3. Effects on the specific energy consumption of different energy efficient investment

The approach followed to evaluate the investments is the NPV (Net Present Value) method, in addition to the easier Payback period (PB), because, even if it is quite complex to apply, it gives better results and it allows comparing investments with different characteristics [8, 12]. This work analyses the most suitable investment in energy efficiency for a given industrial plant under constant and uncertain demand profile. The remainder of the paper is organized as follows: Sect. 2 introduces the notations and assumptions, Sect. 3 presents the mathematical models of the different scenarios considered, Sect. 4 provides numerical examples to illustrate the proposed models and, finally, Sect. 5 concludes the paper summarizing main findings and providing suggestions for future research.

2   Assumptions and Notations

This paper considers the problem of identifying the most suitable investment in energy efficiency for a given industrial plant and a given demand profile.

The notation of the model is:

D	Annual demand rate [unit]
P	Real production rate [unit/year]
P_{max}	Nominal production rate [unit/year]
n	Investment's lifespan [years]
a_0	Initial sensitivity coefficient on the constant of the SEC's curve
b_0	Initial sensitivity coefficient on the slope of the SEC's curve
a	Sensitivity coefficient on the constant of the SEC's curve
b	Sensitivity coefficient on the slope of the SEC's curve
a_{min}	Minimum value of the coefficient a
b_{max}	Maximum value of the coefficient b
$c_{0,en}$	Energy cost per unit of production before investment [€/unit]
c_{en}	Energy cost per unit of production after investment [€/unit]
p_e	Energy price per kWh [€/kWh]
SEC_0	Specific energy consumption before investment [kWh/unit]
SEC	Specific energy consumption after investment [kWh/unit]
S	Savings introduced with investments [€]
ρ	Discount rate
$\delta_{a,shift}$	Decrease coefficient in the constant of the SEC per € increase in I_{shift}

$\delta_{a,flat}$	Decrease coefficient in the constant of the SEC per € increase in I_{flat}
$\delta_{b,flat}$	Decrease coefficient in the slope of the SEC per € increase in I_{flat}
I_{shift}	Investment made to shift the SEC (decision variable) [€]
I_{flat}	Investment made to flat the SEC (decision variable) [€]

The main assumptions of the model are the following:

- The demand rate D_i is constant in Scenario 1, while in Scenario 2 it is uncertain and modelled with a stochastic distribution with parameters (α, β).
- The nominal production rate is P_{max} but the working one P is lower. Thus, due to the underuse, the performance of the plant is lower than the nominal one and inefficiencies are introduced.
- The effective production rate corresponds to the demand rate (L4L assumption).
- The SEC is usually represented by a power function of the production rate P. However, for simplicity, it has been considered an interval of production rate in which it is possible to approximate the SEC with a linear function (Fig. 4) of P, as following:

$$SEC = a - b \cdot P \tag{1}$$

- The energy price per kWh p_e [€/kWh] is assumed to be constant.
- The investment in vertical shifting, I_{shift}, has effect on the constant of the curve, a. While the investment in flattening, I_{flat}, has effect both on the constant, a, and on the slope, b, of the SEC's curve.
- Considering the diminishing marginal contribution of investments [13–15], a logarithmic investment function of the following form is used to describe the effect of the investments on the parameters of the specific energy consumption:

$$x = x_0 - \delta_x \cdot \ln(I_x) \tag{2}$$

where x identifies the SEC's parameter affected by the investment (i.e. a or b).

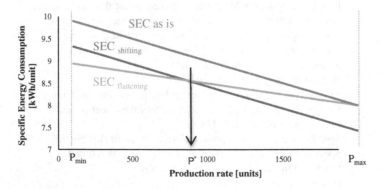

Fig. 4. Specific energy consumption function with respect to the production rate

3   Model's Formulation

In the present work, it is considered a firm that has to select the amount of investment in vertical shifting or in flattening the specific energy consumption curve maximizing the NPV. Often the demand is uncertain, random and fluctuating; for that reason, the company has to face a wide interval of possible production rate. In this case, investment in flattening the specific energy consumption acquires greater relevance. Traditional capital budgeting investment decisions identify a profitable energy efficiency investment when the discounted sum of savings, S, is greater than the total investment cost, I. This net present value (NPV) provides an estimate of the net financial benefit provided to the organization if this investment is undertaken [12].

$$\max NPV = \sum_{i=1}^{n} \frac{S_i}{(1+\rho)^i} - \left(I_{shift} + I_{flat}\right) = \sum_{i=1}^{n} \frac{\left((c_{0,en} - c_{en}) \cdot D_i\right)}{(1+\rho)^i} - \left(I_{shift} + I_{flat}\right)$$

(3)

where

$$c_{en} = SEC \cdot p_e \tag{4}$$

$$a = a_0 - \delta_{a,shift} \ln\left(I_{shift}\right) - \delta_{a,flat} \ln\left(I_{flat}\right) \tag{5}$$

$$b = b_0 - \delta_{b,flat} \cdot \ln\left(I_{flat}\right) \tag{6}$$

Savings, S_i, are introduced by the reduction of the specific energy consumption and thus by the reduction of the energy cost of the production (Eq. 3). The subscript i identifies the year considered and it varies from 1 to n, which is the lifetime of the investment. In a first step, it has been considered the scenario where demand rate is constant (Scenario 1) evaluating the optimal investment decision for a given input value of the production rate. Then, in a second step, it has been modelled the demand rate and, thus, the production rate with a probability distribution (Scenario 2), defined in the assumption. Table 1 summarizes the demand modelling and the investment decisions of each considered scenario:

Table 1. Scenarios

Name	Demand	Investment decisions
Scenario 1.1	Constant	Vertical shifting
Scenario 1.2	Constant	Flattening
Scenario 2.1	Stochastic distribution	Vertical shifting
Scenario 2.2	Stochastic distribution	Flattening

3.1   Scenario 1.1

In Scenario 1.1, the demand is constant and the only investment considered is the vertical shifting of the specific energy consumption (I_{shift}). It is possible to study the function and its derivatives in order to evaluate the convexity of the NPV function in I_{shift} and to find the optimal value of I_{shift}^*, that is:

$$\frac{\partial NPV}{\partial I_{shift}} = 0 \Rightarrow I_{shift}^* = Dp_e\delta_{a,shift}\sum_{i=1}^{n}\frac{1}{(1+\rho)^i} \tag{7}$$

3.2   Scenario 1.2

In Scenario 1.2, the demand is still constant as the previous scenario; however, the only investment considered is the flattening of the specific energy consumption (I_{flat}) and the optimal value of I_{shift}^* is:

$$\frac{\partial NPV}{\partial I_{flat}} = 0 \Rightarrow I_{flat}^* = Dp_e\left(\delta_{a,flat} - \delta_{b,flat}P\right)\sum_{i=1}^{n}\frac{1}{(1+\rho)^i} \tag{8}$$

4   Numerical Study

In the present section two examples are presented: in the first, general investment alternatives which impact the entire production plant are considered; while, in the second, the subject of the study is related to a particular sub-system. Example 1 illustrates the results of the models in a specific sector and compares the behaviour of the different scenarios. The parameters used in Scenario 1 are the following: D = 1500 units/year, P_{max} = 2000 units/year, n = 10 year, ρ = 4 %, p_e = 0.25 €/kWh, a_0 = 10, b_0 = 0.001, $\delta_{a,shift}$ = 0.04, $\delta_{a,flat}$ = 0.2, $\delta_{b,flat}$ = 0.0001. After a first insight in Scenario 1, in Scenario 2 we assumed that the demand is modelled with a uniform distribution with parameters (750, 1750); while the other parameters are the same. The numerical example, for a given production rate (Scenario 1) and for the uniform distribution (Scenario 2), leads to the following results (Table 2):

Table 2. Results of the numerical example

		Scenario 1.1	Scenario 1.2	Scenario 2.1	Scenario 2.2
I_{shift}	[€]	121.66	–	101.49	–
I_{flat}	[€]	–	152.08	–	189.97
SEC	[kWh/unit]	8.31	8.25	8.56	8.36
NPV	[€]	462.47	612.03	367.38	719.53
PB	[year]	2.79	2.71	2.86	2.79

As can be observed in Table 2, both the investments result convenient (NPV > 0) and generates energy cost savings. In particular, Scenario 1.2 (i.e. the scenario in which the investment in flattening is considered) leads to a better result reducing the specific energy consumption of about 3 % with respect to the as – is scenario, i.e. without any kind of investment, in which the SEC was 8.5 kWh/unit, and leading to a NPV greater than the one with investment in vertical shifting; while the payback period is almost equal. An interesting value of the production rate is the one in which both the optimal investments leads to the same specific energy consumption ($P^\circ = 1617$ units): at that value, the investments are equally affordable. If the production rate is lower, the investment in flattening the SEC curve is advantageous; on the contrary, if the production rate is greater, the more convenient investment is the one in vertical shifting (Fig. 4).

As it has been previously said, in real context demand is subject to variability and uncertainty (Scenario 2). Thus, the value of D is not a fixed value but it is better defined with a stochastic distribution. It is interesting to observe how the optimal investment's amounts change whereas the demand rate can uniformly vary in a range of value. Every demand rate has a particular probability of occurrence and that probability is used as the weight in the determination of the total savings and, consequently, in the determination of the NPV. The uncertainty in the demand rate still leads to attractive NPV in both the scenario and the payback is still in-between 2–3 years; however, the invested amount, the reduction of the specific energy consumption and the impact on the savings change because of the introduction of a probability distribution.

In Example 2, it has been performed a study on two specific investment options. In order to reach an higher global energy efficiency and, consequently, a lower SEC, several alternatives exist: e.g. if we consider the energy consumption of a fan, it is possible to replace the motor with a more efficient one (IE 3 against IE 1) leading to a vertical shift to lower SEC, or to manage the intermittent production introducing an inverter technology which flats the SEC curve. These two options are characterized by a given cost for the investment: i.e., for a nominal power of 110 kW (400 V - 3 ph), the cost of the investments can be estimated as € 8,000 and € 6,500, respectively (source: www.inverterdrive.com). A simulation has been performed in order to understand which of the different solution fits better with different load factor profiles, LF (Fig. 5).

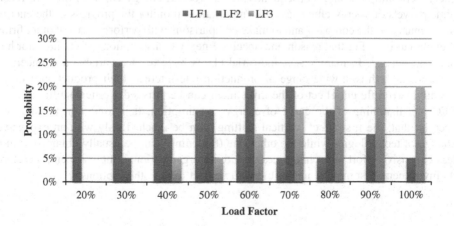

Fig. 5. Different load factors considered in the simulation

The results of the simulation conducted are represented in Fig. 6.

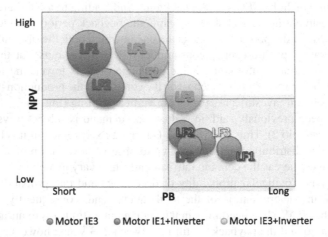

Fig. 6. Comparison between different investment solutions

It is possible to observe that the return of both investments strongly depend on the specific load factor corresponding to the variable production rate, which follows the market demand. In particular, to higher load factor (LF3) correspond higher success of the replacement of the motor, while the result of the installation of the inverter alone shows lower NPV that the former, but for LF1 and LF2 the latter shows quicker PB.

5   Conclusions

Energy efficiency in the industrial sector has emerged as one of the most significant manufacturing decision option and is gaining increasingly relevance because of the great energy consumption and, consequently, of the related energy costs. In order to reach higher levels of energy efficiency, it is important to monitor the progress of the energy performance of the company and to make comparisons with performances of other firms (benchmarking). For that reason, the Specific Energy Consumption (SEC) indicator has been introduced. In many cases, industrial plants have to face variable and uncertain demands and, thus, a wide range of production rate interests their production. Consequently, two different effect of the investment can be pursued: vertical shifting of the SEC and flattening of the curve of energy consumption. It is important to take into account that, the first effect (vertical shifting) can be reached only with an expensive change of technologies while the other one (flattening) can be usually obtained with a less expensive effort on technologies or with an organizational improvement, therefore its investment cost may be negligible with respect to the other options.

In the present work, the aim was to identify the more suitable investment in energy efficiency for different profile and variability of the demand and, thus, for different range of interest of the production rate.

From the analyses carried out, it is possible to observe that, in the lifetime considered, both the subcategories of investment (vertical shifting and flattening) result convenient (positive NPV) and generate energy cost savings. In particular, in the first example proposed, the scenario in which the investment in flattening is considered leads to the best results leading to a NPV greater than the one with investment in flattening. As it has been previously said, in real context demand is subject to variability and uncertainty (Scenario 2). Thus, the value of D is not a fixed value but it is better defined with a stochastic distribution and, for that reason, it has been also evaluate the optimal investments' amount considering that every demand rate has a certain probability of occurrence. Finally, another example has been performed analyzing a specific application in a variable load factor context.

References

1. IEA. World energy investment outlook (2014)
2. U.S. Energy Information Administration. How much energy is consumed in the world by each sector? (2014). http://www.eia.gov/tools/faqs/faq.cfm?id=447&t=1
3. Zhao, Y., Ke, J., Ni, C.C., McNeil, M., Khanna, N.Z., Zhou, N., Li, Q.: A comparative study of energy consumption and efficiency of Japanese and Chinese manufacturing industry. Energy Policy **70**, 45–56 (2014)
4. BP p.l.c. Energy Outlook 2035 (2014)
5. Hoque, M.A., Goyal, S.K.: A heuristic solution procedure for an integrated inventory system under controllable lead-time with equal or unequal sized batch shipments between a vendor and a buyer. Int. J. Prod. Econ. **102**(2), 217–225 (2006)
6. Fysikopoulos, A., Papacharalampopoulos, A., Pastras, G., Stavropoulos, P., Chryssolouris, G.: Energy efficiency of manufacturing processes: a critical review. Procedia CIRP **7**, 628–633 (2013)
7. Müller, E., Poller, R., Hopf, H., Krones, M.: Enabling energy management for planning energy-efficient factories. Procedia CIRP **7**, 622–627 (2013)
8. Bunse, K., Vodicka, M., Schönsleben, P., Brülhart, M., Ernst, F.O.: Integrating energy efficiency performance in production management – gap analysis between industrial needs and scientific literature. J. Clean. Prod. **19**(6–7), 667–679 (2011)
9. Wang, D., Li, S., Sueyoshi, T.: DEA environmental assessment on U.S. Industrial sectors: Investment for improvement in operational and environmental performance to attain corporate sustainability. Energy Econ. **45**, 254–267 (2014)
10. IEA. Assessing Measures of Energy Efficiency Performance and their Application in Industry, February 2008
11. Faccio, M., Gamberi, M.: Energy saving in case of intermittent production by retrofitting service plant systems through inverter technology: a feasibility study. Int. J. Prod. Res. **52**(2), 462–481 (2014)
12. Jackson, J.: Promoting energy efficiency investments with risk management decision tools. Energy Policy **38**(8), 3865–3873 (2010)

13. Beaumont, N.J., Tinch, R.: Abatement cost curves: a viable management tool for enabling the achievement of win-win waste reduction strategies? J. Environ. Manage. **71**(3), 207–215 (2004)
14. Porteus, E.L.: Investing in reduced setups in the EOQ model. Manage. Sci. **31**(8), 998–1010 (1985)
15. Zanoni, S., Mazzoldi, L., Zavanella, L.E., Jaber, M.Y.: A joint economic lot size model with price and environmentally sensitive demand. Prod. Manuf. Res. **2**(1), 341–354 (2014)

Analysis of Manual Work with 3D Cameras

Martin Benter[✉] and Hermann Lödding

Hamburg University of Technology, Hamburg, Germany
{m.benter,loedding}@tuhh.de

Abstract. This paper presents a low-cost and low-effort approach to analyze labor productivity with 3D cameras. The developed methodology tracks the movement of employees in assembly operations. The collected data is then analyzed with a methodology that is based on the primary-secondary analysis.

Keywords: Labor productivity · 3d cameras · Primary-secondary analysis

1 Introduction

The production costs of manufacturing companies are an important factor when facing international competition. Labor costs make up a vital proportion of the production costs when the production is characterized by a high amount of manual processes and high wages. Labor productivity is the main objective for controlling labor costs. Its analysis allows finding areas of improvement and appropriate measures to increase productivity. Classical work analyses such as the MTM system or the REFA systematics require expert knowledge and induce relatively high costs for the execution of the analysis. Small and medium-sized companies often have neither the knowledge about the methodologies nor the capacity to analyze the labor productivity in depth.

This paper presents a low-cost and low-effort approach to analyze labor productivity with 3D cameras. The developed methodology tracks the movement of employees in assembly operations. The collected data is then analyzed with a methodology that is based on the primary-secondary analysis.

2 Productivity Analysis

2.1 Analyzing Labor Productivity

Productivity is defined as the ratio between the output and the input of a system. In manufacturing areas, the output consists of the produced goods and is often measured in units. The input consists of the resources that were necessary to create the output. Resources are for example mechanical and human work. The ratio between the created output and the particular input is the respective partial productivity [1].

The labor productivity of a manufacturing area is thus the relation between the output of produced goods and the staff working time as input. As the output of a production is determined by the market, usually the paid working time is analyzed to investigate labor productivity.

© IFIP International Federation for Information Processing 2015
S. Umeda et al. (Eds.): APMS 2015, Part I, IFIP AICT 459, pp. 715–722, 2015.
DOI: 10.1007/978-3-319-22756-6_87

The assessment of actual working times can be performed by dividing the paid working time into work steps and measuring the times for these individual steps [2]. Instead of using measured actual times, some methods use predetermined times. Basic idea of these methods is to divide work processes in small work steps to which then times are assigned based on defined influencing factors [2]. Known representatives are MTM [3] or the work factor method [4].

2.2 Primary-Secondary Analysis

The primary-secondary analysis is a method developed by Lotter [5] to analyze the labor productivity of assembly processes. Basic principle is the distinction between primary processes (PP) and secondary processes (SP). This is similar to the Lean Management classification of value adding and non-value adding times [6]. According to Lotter, all efforts that add value are primary processes. For assembly operations, the most important examples are joining processes. Efforts that do not add value, such as the transportation of parts, are secondary processes.

Based on that, Lotter defines the efficiency (E) as the ratio between the duration of all the primary processes and the total duration. The efficiency equals one if the work task only consists of primary processes and is smaller than one if secondary processes occur. Figure 1 shows a graphical representation of the efficiency.

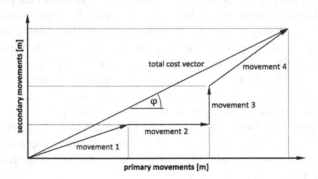

Fig. 1. Graphical representation of the economic efficiency

The abscissa shows the amount of primary processes and the ordinate the secondary processes. Movements that only consist of primary movements are drawn horizontally (movement 2) and movements that do not add value are drawn vertically (movement 3). The graphical addition of the processes results in the total cost vector of the analysis with the slope φ. The reduction of this angle corresponds to an increase in economic efficiency.

If the definition of primary and secondary processes is applied strictly, only joining movements are primary processes, while all other movements do not contribute directly to the customer satisfaction and are therefore secondary processes. However, this definition would imply that the proportion of primary processes would be minimal and the economic efficiency would be of little relevance. Lotter therefore proposes to classify necessary movements up to a defined minimum length as primary processes even if they do not add value.

3   The Microsoft Kinect as a 3D Camera

Motion capturing methods recognize, track and digitalize human movements for further processing [7]. The methods can be distinguished by the used type of sensors. Optical methods usually consist of a transmitter that emits infrared light, which is reflected by the analyzed object to the receiver. Depending on the mode of operation, markers are used as reflectors [7]. The tracking method of the Microsoft Kinect belongs to the non-marker-based systems [8], which means that the natural reflection of the body is used. This has the advantage that the user does not have to wear any devices, which might disturb him or her from the work.

Microsoft developed the Kinect for the gaming console Xbox as an inexpensive motion control. Microsoft also published a software development kit (SDK), a collection of tools and documentation, for non-commercial applications. The SDK includes the functionality to recognize human persons from the coordinates that the infrared camera collected. This way, the relevant joints of a person and their coordinates can be identified. The Kinect 1 detects 20 body joints while the updated Kinect 2, which was released in 2014 [8], detects 26 points. If joints and corresponding limbs are represented graphically, a skeleton image is created, that supports motion capture.

The Kinect is capable to identify the joints of the body and to record their coordinates. Velocity and acceleration of the joints are not measured but can be calculated from the coordinates. A deficit in applying the Kinect for productivity analyses is that it cannot identify stopping points between two movements. Furthermore, it is necessary to combine these stopping points to stopping areas to identify joining or material areas. Another difficulty in carrying out a primary-secondary analysis is the distinction between primary and secondary processes. Therefore, a productivity analysis, such as the primary-secondary analysis, is still very time consuming with the Microsoft Kinect and only executable by experts.

4   Data Collection

This chapter describes how the recorded data is prepared for productivity analysis. Section 4.1 describes the experimental set-up. Section 4.2 shows which raw data is recorded and what data can be derived directly. Section 4.3 describes how the stopping points can be determined and Sect. 4.4 describes how stopping areas can be deduced.

4.1   Experimental Set-up

To demonstrate the modified primary-secondary analysis with the Kinect, we recorded an exemplary assembly task. Figure 2 shows the experimental set-up. In this task, the recorded worker assembled small plastic tractors for 20 min. Each tractor consists of four parts, which are located in four material boxes. The recorded joint was the right hand. The worker used this hand to pick up materials from the boxes one, two and three and the left hand for box four. The distance between Kinect and the worker was three meters.

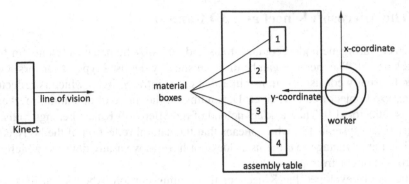

Fig. 2. Experimental set-up

4.2 Coordinate Tracking

To carry out the analysis, firstly the joint coordinates are read out. This is done with a rate of 30 frames per second. Thus, the data collection corresponds to a work sampling with a very high number of recordings. The following data is read for each joint:

- x-, y- and z-coordinate
- the tracking status of the joints: the information if the joint was identified or not.

If the joint is identified correctly, the coordinates can be used for the further analysis. The coordinates of the right hand joint are displayed graphically in Fig. 3 Left. The velocity and the acceleration can be calculated using the following equations.

$$v_{x,n} = \frac{\Delta x}{\Delta t} = \frac{x_n - x_{n-1}}{t_n - t_{n-1}} \tag{1}$$

x_n: x-coordinate at recording n
$v_{x,n}$: velocity at recording n

$$a_{x,n} = \frac{\Delta v}{\Delta t} = \frac{v_{x,n} - v_{x,n-1}}{t_n - t_{n-1}} \tag{2}$$

t_n: time of recording n
$a_{s,n}$: acceleration at recording n

Velocities and accelerations for the other directions can be determined in the same way.

4.3 Determination of Stopping Points

The coordinates, velocities and accelerations can be used to determine stopping points. They are defined as times, at which a joint stops between two movements. Since the Kinect does not deliver them automatically, algorithms were designed to determine these times:

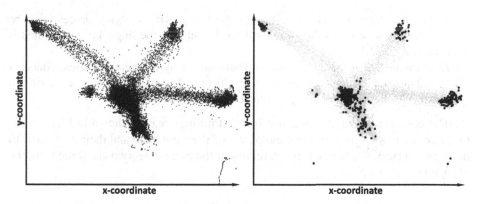

Fig. 3. Left: Right hand coordinates; Right: Right hand stopping points

1. *Velocity falls below a limit:* This algorithm checks whether the velocity of a joint falls below a predefined value for a certain period. This option is particularly suitable for processes in which longer stops dominate. This recognition algorithm fails when the performed movements are very fast.
2. *Sign change of acceleration:* This algorithm checks whether the sign of the acceleration changes from negative to positive over a certain period. This option is suitable for processes, where only short stops are performed, for example button pressing. There are problems with this algorithm if the movement gets slower and then accelerates again, but no stop occurs. Then, a false stop may be detected. This problem can be mitigated by combining this algorithm with the first one (adding a velocity limit).
3. *Change of movement direction:* This algorithm checks whether the motion vector of a joint changes by a defined angle over a certain period. This option is of great value when most movements are non-stop. This option is less suitable when stops are performed without changing the direction of the movement.

The combined use of the three algorithms leads to a good detection of stopping points as shown in Fig. 3 Right, in which the stopping points are marked black.

4.4   Cluster Analysis to Determine Stopping Areas

During manual activities such as assembly operations, many stopping points occur. The points have to be combined to stopping areas to allow meaningful interpretations. Thus, the next step is a cluster analysis to identify the stopping areas. In this approach, a hierarchical cluster analysis is performed which consists of three steps [9]:

1. *Determining the similarities:* A variety of distance measures exists to measure the similarity. For scale properties such as the x-, y- and z-coordinates of the stopping points, the Euclidean distance measure is commonly used [9].
2. *Selecting a fusion algorithm:* In this step, objects with small distances are merged. We used an agglomerative technique that starts with each object representing a single

cluster and then merges these clusters gradually. This merging process can be performed with different fusion algorithms. In our case the single linkage method is used [10].

3. *Determining the number of clusters:* There are many different statistical concepts that determine the optimal number of clusters. For this approach, a maximum distance is defined when merging clusters [9].

The outcome of the cluster analysis are stopping areas as shown in Fig. 4 Left. One can see in the figure all the breakpoints of the right hand and their allocation to different clusters. Cluster G, F and A represent the boxes one, two and three from the experimental set-up.

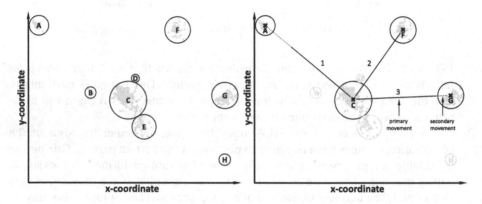

Fig. 4. Left: Determined stopping areas; Right: Movements

5 Primary-Secondary Analysis Using 3D Cameras

This chapter shows how the primary-secondary analysis can be performed by using the Microsoft Kinect. The analysis determines, which activities add value and which do not. The approach is divided into three steps. First, the joining point is determined from the stopping areas derived in Sect. 4.3. Subsequently, non-relevant movements are identified. The last step is the classification of the relevant movements in primary and secondary movements.

In the primary-secondary analysis by Lotter, the user determines the joining point and the primary range is set based on that point [5]. Alternatively, the joining point can be automatically identified. The Cluster analysis results in a number of stopping areas. In most cases, the stopping area with the most stopping points will also be the joining area. To make sure the right area is selected, the user still has the option to choose the joining area manually. In Fig. 4 Left stopping area C is the selected joining point. The middle of this joining area then will be used as the joining point for the further investigations. This option has the advantage that in contrast to the first option, the determination is based on the recorded data. In addition, different joining points can be defined for both hands.

In the next step, an overview of movements that took place between the different stopping areas is created. The user now examines the movements. He decides whether the movements were relevant to the assembly task (relevant movement) or not (non-relevant movement). The latter movements are henceforward referred to as tertiary movements. The number and duration of these tertiary movements can be easily computed from the captured data and may be an important area for further improvements. In the experimental set-up only movements between the joining area (Cluster C) and the boxes (Cluster A, F, G) are classified as relevant movements.

In the primary-secondary analysis by Lotter the second important step for classification is to determine the nearest material box or stopping area to calculate the minimum level of movement. This minimum, which is necessary for the joining, has to be defined by the user [5]. Two additional options have been developed:

- **Nearest stopping area:** In this option, the nearest stopping area is determined (area F in Fig. 4 Left). The distance from the center of this area to the joining point is used as minimum level of movement (movement 2 in Fig. 4 Right). Prerequisite for this option is that the non-relevant movements were identified correctly before.
- **Determination by using ergonomic aspects:** This option is based on ergonomic aspects, which means biological data like arm length is used to determine a movement distance which can be done quickly without harm for the body. An example is the distance that the hand can cover without moving the upper arm and without having harmful or uncomfortable angles for the elbow joint.

For our analysis, we chose the first option. Following the determination of the minimum level of movement, the relevant movements are divided into primary and secondary parts according to the primary-secondary analysis. To visualize the results of that analyzes the average length and duration are calculated for every pair of stopping areas that form a relevant movement. Figure 4 Right shows the relevant movements and their primary and secondary parts. These movements now can be drawn into a vector diagram as introduced by Lotter (see Sect. 2.2). Figure 5 shows this result.

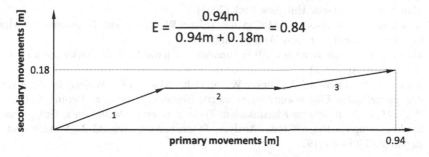

$$E = \frac{0.94m}{0.94m + 0.18m} = 0.84$$

Fig. 5. Graphical representation of the vector

6   Summary

This article presents an approach to analyze labor productivity using 3D cameras. The methodology developed is based on the primary-secondary analysis by Lotter. It divides the movements of a worker into primary, secondary and tertiary movements and thus shows potential for productivity improvement. In comparison to the classic primary-secondary analysis the presented approach offers the following advantages:

- **Recording of actual data:** The presented method does not assess the ideal, but the actual process, thus showing tertiary wastes in addition to the secondary ones.
- **Semi-Automated:** By using the Microsoft Kinect, the effort of recording the processes is significantly reduced.
- **Higher Accuracy:** The determination of the joining point from the stopping areas is based on real data and can be determined separately for both hands.
- **Visualization:** The graphical representation of the stopping areas and movements can help to directly determine incorrectly positioned parts.

Several aspects can further enhance the method. For example, additional body joints can be examined. In addition, the method could be used to reveal ergonomic potential.

References

1. Sumanth, D.J.: Productivity Engineering and Management: Productivity Measurement, Evaluation, Planning, and Improvement in Manufacturing and Service Organizations. McGraw-Hill, New York (1984)
2. REFA Datenermittlung. Methodenlehre der Betriebsorganisation, [15]. Hanser, München (1997)
3. Bokranz, R., Landau, K.: Produktivitätsmanagement von Arbeitssystemen: MTM-Handbuch. Schäffer-Poeschel, Stuttgart (2006)
4. Quick, J.H.: Das Work-Factor-System. Beuth, Berlin (1960)
5. Lotter, B., Baumgartner, P., Spath, D.: Primär-Sekundär-Analyse: Kundennutzenmessung und Kundennutzenorientierung im Unternehmen. expert-Verl., Renningen (2002)
6. Liker, J.K.: The Toyota Way: 14 Management Principles from the World's Greatest Manufacturer. McGraw-Hill, New York (2004)
7. Kitagawa, M., Windsor, B.: MoCap for Artists: Workflow and Techniques for Motion Capture. Elsevier/Focal Press, Amsterdam (2008)
8. Microsoft Kinect for Windows (2015). http://www.microsoft.com/en-us/kinectforwindows/. Accessed 20 April 2015
9. Backhaus, K., Erichson, B., Plinke, W., Schuchard-Ficher, C., Weiber, R.: Multivariate Analysemethoden: Eine anwendungsorientierte Einführung. Springer, Berlin (2011)
10. Bock, H.H.: Automatische Klassifikation: Theoret. u. prakt. Methoden z. Gruppierung u. Strukturierung von Daten (Cluster-Analyse). Studia mathematica, Bd. 24. Vandenhoeck und Ruprecht, Göttingen (1974)

Individuals' Perception of Which Materials are Most Important to Recycle

Marcus Bjelkemyr[1][✉], Sasha Shahbazi[1], Christina Jönsson[2], and Magnus Wiktorsson[1]

[1] School of Innovation, Design and Engineering, Mälardalen University, Eskilstuna, Sweden
{marcus.bjelkemyr,sasha.shahbazi,magnus.wiktorsson}@mdh.se
[2] Swerea IVF, Stockholm, Sweden
christina.jonsson@swerea.se

Abstract. In this study, we have asked respondents to rank ten different waste fractions that are both common in manufacturing industry and easily recognizable. The purpose of the study has been to clarify to what extent individuals are able to identify the waste fractions that are most important to recycle from an environmental perspective. The individuals' perception has then been correlated with a life cycle assessment of the ten materials. In addition, the respondents were also asked to rank the fractions according to cost.

The results show that metals are consistently considered most important to recycle, and plastics are commonly among the top five amongst the ten waste fractions together with glass. The cellulose based fractions, cotton, and compost are commonly rated low. In addition, there is a perceived correlation between the environmental and economic impact.

Keywords: Material efficiency · Waste management · Perceived recycling benefits

1 Introduction

Waste management in manufacturing companies is part semi-automatic and part manual. Generally, the direct materials that are machined are automatically transported to the correct waste bin and these are then emptied in larger containers. These materials are often metals, but some other materials may also occur. For these waste fractions the key is to keep them homogeneous and not contaminate them with materials that lower the quality of the fraction, and thereby the value.

Most other waste materials within a manufacturing company are handled manually by the employees. For larger or more valuable waste streams, there are commonly dedicated waste bins that are placed close to where that waste material is generated, and thereby become the easiest place to dispose the waste. However, not all locations where waste is generated can have a dedicated waste bin for each waste fraction because waste bins cost money, take up space, and add complexity to the waste management system. In these cases, the individual factory worker has to both identify the correct waste bin for that material, and estimate the value of transporting the waste to the correct bin, in comparison to throwing it in the closest possible waste bin. To make this choice, the

© IFIP International Federation for Information Processing 2015
S. Umeda et al. (Eds.): APMS 2015, Part I, IFIP AICT 459, pp. 723–729, 2015.
DOI: 10.1007/978-3-319-22756-6_88

individual has to compare her own additional effort with the perceived benefits for the individual, the company, and the environment.

For the company there is a potential economic gain associated with higher prices for more homogeneous waste fractions; however, this is rarely reflected on the individual level or even group level. Similarly, there is an environmental benefit of increased recycling, but this does not directly affect the individual that is making the choice. Regardless of the direct benefits for the individual, he or she will commonly put in the extra effort if the perceived economic or environmental benefits are high enough. It is therefore important to understand how individuals perceive different waste materials, and it is becoming even more important as consumption, manufacturing, and generated waste volumes increase drastically.

Population growth and increased wealth have caused material demand and energy consumption to increase significantly in the last 100 years. Total global material consumption has increased from 6 billion tons in 1900 to 60 billion tones in 2013, and it is estimated to reach 140 billion tons of key resources per year by 2050 [1]. The total generated waste from manufacturing activities in 2012 accounted for 270 million tons [2] and it is expected to increase by 10–20 % till 2020 in comparison to 2005 [3]. This means that the potential impact of industrial waste management improvements is significant.

The research questions in this study are: (1) do different individuals' perception of environmental impact and economic benefits correlate with each other, and (2) do the individuals' environmental perceptions correlate with the calculated benefits of recycling in comparison to incineration or landfill. The contribution from answering these questions is primarily related an increased understanding of which materials are perceived as more important to recycle than other materials. The results in this study are particularly interesting for the materials that are perceived differently by different individuals, and the materials that are perceived either more or less important than they actually are. These discrepancies can then be further analyzed and waste management efforts can be targeted more accurately.

2 Frame of Reference

Waste segregation and recycling behavior can be affected in many different ways. According to Maycox [7] the most important variables when changing recycling behavior are to understand why people act the way they do and what their attitudes towards recycling are. Public attitudes towards recycling and municipal solid waste management has been investigated in a multitude of contexts, e.g. [4–6]. Ajzen [10] clarifies the understanding of recycling behavior and stress that there are both positive and negative drivers; waste segregation and recycling behavior is first influenced by knowledge, infrastructure and proper opportunities, and secondly by aversion of physical recycling issues including time, space and inconvenience. In addition, the moral norm, personality, past experience, demographics, social pressure, convenience, and incentives may also have an impact on recycling and waste management, c.f. [7–9].

Homogenous quality of industrial waste is directly connected to the environmental actions and behaviors during operation [14]. Moreover, it is also directly connected to awareness, clear instructions, visualization, and that waste management is sufficiently convenient for the personnel. Among these, intuition and knowledge of operation in waste handling, segregation, and treatment are the key factors [11, 12].

Any system implementation and operation becomes easier if the decisions are intuitive, which is highly dependent on involvement of both environmental and operational perspectives [13], particularly when it comes to waste segregation. Even though the environmental coordinators and the engineers play crucial role in waste management, it is still the operators' task to segregate the waste. Hence, the operators' perception concerning environmental benefits of different waste fractions is important to improve waste management and material efficiency.

This research is based on the idea that individuals will make better waste management choices if they are able to perceive the environmental and economic benefits of recycling correctly. For this to be relevant there must be a significant difference between the benefits of recycling for different materials. In the graph below, CO_2 equivalent of the selected fractions have been assessed. The assessment has been gathered from a parallel study [15]; however, the data in the figure below should only be seen as indicative as individual estimates may differ depending on circumstance.

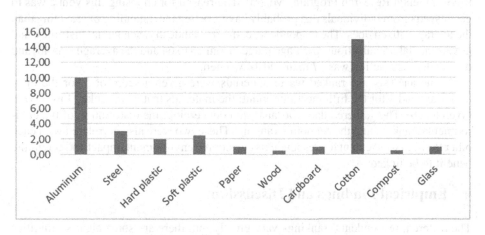

Fig. 1. CO_2 equivalent for the ten researched waste fractions.

3   Research Methodology

In the study, 31 respondents were presented with the picture below (Fig. 2), showing both a photograph and a descriptive term of ten selected waste fractions. These fractions were chosen because they are commonly available in manufacturing industry and/or easily recognizable for individuals without a manufacturing background. Of these ten materials, the respondents were asked to pick out the five materials that are most important to recycle and then rank them, first from an environmental point of view and then from an economic point of view.

Glass   Soft plastic   Steel   Paper   Wood

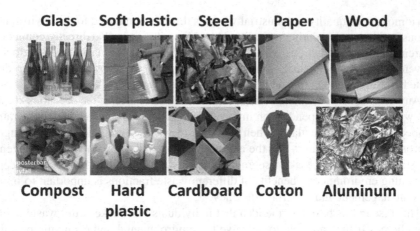

Compost   Hard   Cardboard Cotton Aluminum
plastic

Fig. 2. Ten waste materials that respondents were asked to rank.

The respondents were all participating in a workshop that was linked to a research program called Closing the Loop, funded by the Swedish Foundation for Strategic Environmental Research Program (Mistra). The reason for choosing this venue was to get answers from individuals that probably have a better understanding of recycling than the average citizen does. The respondents came from industry, academia, institutes, and governmental organizations; their age ranged from 23 to 64 and the average was 43; and the gender distribution was 17 men and 14 women.

In the analysis, the ranked waste materials were given a score of 5 for the most important and 1 for the fifth most important; the materials that were ranked lower were given a zero. The gathered data was analyzed concerning: the distribution of the environmental ranking and the economic ranking. These two were also correlated with each other to see to what extent the respondents considered environment impact and economic benefit to be linked.

4   Empirical Findings and Discussion

The different respondents' rankings vary greatly, but there are some clear similarities as well (Fig. 3). The respondents appear to group the different fractions, e.g. metals > glass > plastics > compost, cotton, and cellulose based fractions. This grouping is partly supported by the LCA analysis, but it also results in that some materials are ranked lower than they are, e.g. plastics. The variance is partly an effect of how the question was asked, but it also indicates that there is a significant uncertainty when it comes to recycling. This uncertainty reflects that the benefits of recycling specific materials are non-intuitive, and the knowledge level is low.

Even though the respondents' ranks vary, there are some materials that consistently rank among the five most important materials: aluminum (94 %), steel (97 %), glass (84 %), hard plastics (77 %), and soft plastics (%) (Fig. 4).

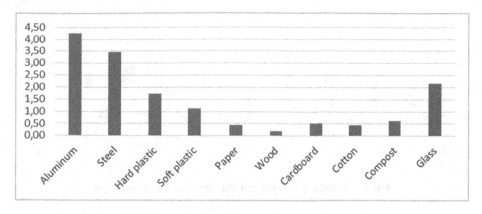

Fig. 3. Average rank for each material (5 = most important).

For some materials, there is a discrepancy between the environmental impact and the perceived environmental importance to recycle (cf. Figs. 1, 3 and 4). In the analysis of CO_2 equivalents, cotton had the highest value; however, only 16 % of the respondents had included cotton on their top-five list. As a contrast, glass was considered the third most important material by the respondents, but the environmental assessment indicates that has a significantly lower impact than hard and soft plastics.

The respondents' environmental and economic ranks differ, but only slightly (Fig. 5). This makes it difficult to draw any other conclusions than that the respondents include the economic variable when assessing environmental impact and vice versa.

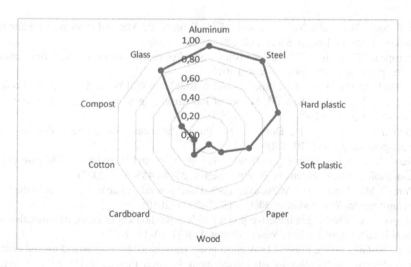

Fig. 4. Top five rankings of materials (%).

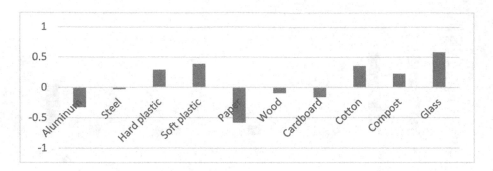

Fig. 5. Difference between environmental and economic rank

5   Conclusion and Future Study

The data and the analysis show individuals as a group have a good understanding of which materials are important to recycle. However, plastics are generally underestimated, and the rank of both glass and cotton do not correlate with the LCA analysis. There are several possible reasons for these discrepancies, e.g. direct vs. indirect material, recycling by households, and lack of material understanding.

The study also shows that there is very limited difference between the perceived environmental and economic impact. Further studies are needed to understand the underlying reasons behind the perceived importance of recycling, and how to affect the behavior or individuals. These studies need to look at diverse samples of individuals, e.g. different industries, regions, ages, and backgrounds.

References

1. Allwood, J.M., Ashby, M.F., Gutowski, T.G., Worrell, E.: Material efficiency: a white paper. Resour. Conserv. Recycl. **55**(3), 362–381 (2011)
2. European Commision Waste statistics. http://ec.europa.eu/eurostat/statistics-explained/index.php/Waste_statistics. Accessed 2015
3. Frostell, B.: The Future, Rest Products and Waste; How Will Waste Management Look Like in 2020? Ragn-Sells AB, KTH, School of Industrial Engineering and Management (ITM), Industrial Ecology (2006)
4. Leaman, J., Harvey, P., Durkacz, S.: Public attitudes towards recycling and waste management Ipsos MORI (2006)
5. Barr, S.: Factors influencing environmental attitudes and behaviors: a UK case study of household waste management. Environ. behav. **39**(4), 435–473 (2007)
6. Purcell, M., Magette, W.: Attitudes and behaviour towards waste management in the Dublin, Ireland region. Waste Manag. **30**(10), 1997–2006 (2010)
7. Maycox, A.: The village initiative project: achieving household waste minimisation in the rural locale. Chartered Inst. Wastes Manag. J. **4**(3), 10–17 (2003)
8. Barr, S., Gilg, A.W., Ford, N.J.: A conceptual framework for understanding and analysing attitudes towards household-waste management. Environ. Plan. A **33**(11), 2025–2048 (2001)

9. Tonglet, M., Phillips, P.S., Bates, M.P.: Determining the drivers for householder pro-environmental behaviour: waste minimisation compared to recycling. Resour. Conserv. Recycl. **42**(1), 27–48 (2004)
10. Ajzen, I.: The theory of planned behavior. Organ. Behav. Hum. Decis. Process. **50**(2), 179–211 (1991)
11. Oskamp, S., Harrington, M.J., Edwards, T.C., Sherwood, D.L., Okuda, S.M., Swanson, D.C.: Factors influencing household recycling behavior. Environ. behav. **23**(4), 494–519 (1991)
12. Barr, S., Gilg, A.W.: A conceptual framework for understanding and analyzing attitudes towards environmental behaviour. Geografiska Annaler: Ser. B, Hum. Geogr. **89**(4), 361–379 (2007)
13. Zhang, H.C., Kuo, T.C., Lu, H., Huang, S.H.: Environmentally conscious design and manufacturing: a state-of-the-art survey. J. Manuf. Syst. **16**(5), 352–371 (1997)
14. Kurdve, M., Shahbazi, S., Wendin, M., Bengtsson, C., Wiktorsson, M.: Waste flow mapping to improve sustainability of waste management: a case study approach. J. Cleaner Prod. **98**, 304–315 (2014)
15. Jönsson, C., Wilson, K.: LCA Memiman – Material efficiency in manufacturing, report (2015)

Formulation of Relationship
Between Productivity and Energy
Consumption in Manufacturing System

Takayuki Kobayashi[1(✉)], Makoto Yamaguchi[2], and Hironori Hibino[1]

[1] Tokyo University of Science, 2641 Yamazaki, Noda, Chiba, Japan
j7411048@ed.tus.ac.jp
[2] Akita University, 1-1 Tegatagakuen-Machi, Akita City, Akita, Japan

Abstract. In the industrial world, since the amount of energy to consume is very large, it is required to manage and reduce energy consumption while maintaining a high productivity. In order to approach the theoretical realization the production conditions that affect a productivity or energy consumption, we investigate the formulation of the relationship between energy consumption and production throughput, and verify it by using numerical simulation.

Keywords: Sustainable manufacturing system · Simulation · Productivity · Energy consumption · Mathematical formulation

1 Introduction

Recently, in various fields, reduction of energy consumption has been an important issue. [1–3] In particular, in the world of industrial, since the amount of energy to consume is very large, management of energy consumed is greatly required. It is necessary to reduce energy consumption while maintaining a high productivity. [3]

In the previous study, a simulation environment for sustainable manufacturing systems considering the productivity and energy consumption have been established, and an implementation for the simulation environment has been proposed [5, 6]. The state transition model for facility has been proposed and expressed by using a Unified Modelling Language (UML) model. A case study for a middle-scale semiconductor manufacturing line was carried out by using constructed simulation system. It has been found that the energy consumption per production throughput increase with decreasing lot size and, become a constant value with increasing lot size. This result has indicated that the number of times of setting-up increase with decreasing lot size. Since the energy is required for setting-up, energy consumption per production throughput becomes large.

However, in the manufacturing system, the theoretical realization the production conditions, such as lot size, failure rate, and so on that affect a productivity and energy consumption is not understood clearly. In this paper, therefore, we propose the formulation of the relationship between energy consumption and production throughput, and verify it by using numerical simulation system constructed in our previous report.

© IFIP International Federation for Information Processing 2015
S. Umeda et al. (Eds.): APMS 2015, Part I, IFIP AICT 459, pp. 730–737, 2015.
DOI: 10.1007/978-3-319-22756-6_89

2 Formalizing the Energy Consumption and Throughput

2.1   Energy Consumption Per Throughput, U

One of the most important indicators in the evaluation of productivity and energy consumption of manufacturing systems is energy consumption per production throughput (U). U is defined as

$$U = \frac{E}{P}. \tag{1}$$

Here, U is energy consumption per production throughput and the unit is [J/product], E is energy consumption and and the unit is [J], P is production throughput and the unit is [product]. An electric energy consumption per second is also defined electric power consumption e [W].

A line with n equipment which have m kinds of facility state is assumed in this study. An facility in line always belongs to some status during operating time (T), so the operating time of k-th facility (T^k) equal to T. The relation between T and the total of operating time of x state in k-th facility (T_x^k) is given by

$$T = T^k = \sum_{x}^{m} T_x^k. \tag{2}$$

The total electric energy consumption is given by

$$E = \sum_{k}^{n} E^k = \sum_{k}^{n} \sum_{x}^{m} e_x^k T_x^k, \tag{3}$$

where E^k is the total electric energy consumption of k-th facility, and e_x^k is electric power consumption of x state in k-th facility. Therefore, the energy consumption per production throughput can be written as

$$U = \sum_{k}^{n} U^k = \sum_{k}^{n} \frac{E^k}{P} = \sum_{k}^{n} \sum_{x}^{m} \frac{e_x^k T_x^k}{P}. \tag{4}$$

Here U^k is the energy consumption per production throughput in k-th facility. By using Eq. (4), U can be calculated by e_x^k, T_x^k and P. Figure 1 shows the summary of the relationship between E, P, T, U, e, and p.

2.2   Coefficient of Work in Process, q^k

In a line, a buffer is generally set up between facility. When some work exist in a buffer, production throughput in line and production throughput of each facility (P^k) is not same, that is,

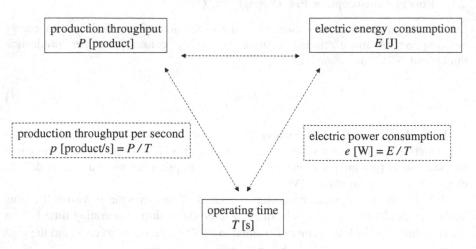

Fig. 1. Relationship between $E, P, T, U, e,$ and p.

$$P^k > P. \tag{5}$$

Here, coefficient of work in process (q^k) can be defined as

$$q^k \equiv \frac{P^k}{P}. \tag{6}$$

In the case of $P^k = P$, q^k equal 1. Usually, q^k increases as previous process, i.e.,

$$q^1 \geq \cdots \geq q^{k-1} \geq q^k \geq q^{k+1} \geq \cdots \geq q^n = 1. \tag{7}$$

2.3   Operating Time of State of x in K-th Facility, T_x^k

In this study, a state of running, setting-up, and idling will be discussed. The state of running, setting-up, and idling are described by x = r, s, and i, respectively.

In a running state in k-th facility, the production throughput per second (p_r^k) is the reciprocal of the cycle time (c_r^k). Production throughput in k-th facility (P_r^k) is calculated by multiplying T_r^k by $c_r^k = 1/p_r^k$. When the q_r^k is taken into account, T_r^k is obtained as

$$T_r^k = q^k \frac{P}{p_r^k}. \tag{8}$$

P divided by lot size (LS) is frequency of setting-up in k-th facility. The q_r^k and λ^k which is defended by the time required for a once setting-up are take into consideration, T_s^k obtained as

$$T_s^k = q^k \frac{P}{LS} \lambda^k. \tag{9}$$

It seems to be reasonable that T_s^k decrease with increasing LS.

Since a facility in line always belongs to some status during operation, so the operating time of k-th facility (T^k) equal to the sum of T_r^k, T_s^k and the operating time of idling state in k-th facility (T_i^k);

$$T^k = T_r^k + T_s^k + T_i^k. \tag{10}$$

As $T^k = T$,

$$
\begin{aligned}
T_i^k &= T - T_r^k - T_s^k \\
&= T - \frac{q^k}{p_r^k} P - \frac{q^k \lambda^k}{LS} P \\
&= P \left(\frac{T}{P} - \frac{q^k}{p_r^k} - \frac{q^k \lambda^k}{LS} \right) \\
&= P \left(\frac{1}{p} - \frac{q^k}{p_r^k} - \frac{q^k \lambda^k}{LS} \right).
\end{aligned}
\tag{11}
$$

Equations (9) (10) and (11) are substituted into Eq. (4), U^k is calculated as

$$
\begin{aligned}
U^k &= \frac{1}{P} \left(e_r^k T_r^k + e_s^k T_s^k + e_i^k T_i^k \right) \\
&= \frac{1}{P} \left(e_r^k \frac{q^k P}{p_r^k} + e_s^k \frac{q^k P}{p_r^k} + e_i^k P \left(\frac{1}{p} - \frac{q^k}{p_r^k} - \frac{q^k \lambda^k}{LS} \right) \right) \\
&= q^k \left(\frac{e_r^k}{p_r^k} + \frac{e_s^k \lambda^k}{LS} \right) + e_i^k \left(\frac{1}{p} - q^k \left(\frac{1}{p_r^k} + \frac{\lambda^k}{LS} \right) \right).
\end{aligned}
\tag{12}
$$

3 Simulation

The simulation system of manufacturing has already been developed using the Witness software which is a commercial discrete event simulator (Lanner). In this paper, a middle-scale semiconductor manufacturing line which consist of three facilities, the solder printing facility, the IC mounting facility (mounter facility), and the solder reflow facility is simulated. The three facilities were modelled in Witness using our proposed state transition model. The printing facility, the mounter facility, and the reflow facility

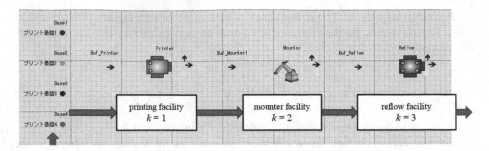

Fig. 2. Simulation model of the middle-scale semiconductor manufacturing line.

Table 1. Input data in simulation.

input data		Facility			
		printing $k=1$	mounter $k=2$	reflow $k=3$	
$1/p_r^k$	[s]	10	10	10	
e_r^k	[kW]	1.25	3.75	0.8*	*0.4 (rising), 1.2 (falling)
λ^k	[s]	120	120	-	
e_s^k	[kW]	3	1.5	-	
e_i^k	[kW]	0.2	0.2	0.8*	*0.4 (rising), 1.2 (falling)

are numbered to k = 1 to 3, respectively. Figure 2 show a simulation model of the middle-scale semiconductor manufacturing line. Table 1 shows the simulation input data. In contrast to simulation, input electric power consumption of running state and idle state in reflow facility (e_r^k and e_r^k) different between rising and falling of temperature in furnace, the average value is used in formulation as below. There are four types of lot sizes as 15, 30, 90, 360. The size of buffer between each facilities is big enough. The simulation period in this simulation is 40 h (5 day × 8 h).

4 Results and Discussion

Figure 3 show the relationship between electric energy consumption per production throughput and inverse of lot size. The opened circle in Fig. 3 indicate the simulation results of the electric energy consumption per production throughput of printing facility (U^1). Note that the linear correlation exists between the U^1 and inverse of lot size. In this

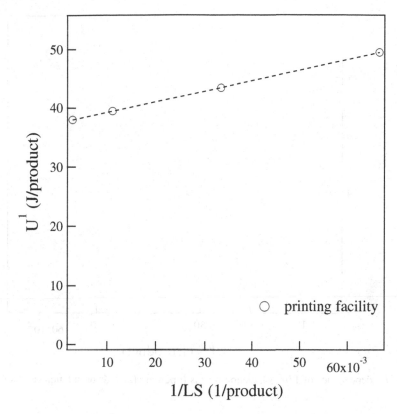

Fig. 3. *LS* dependence of U^1. Simulation results (open circle) and formulation results (dashed line)

simulation, since the cycle time of facilities is almost same, and the failure of facilities is not considered, the q^k can be considered as 1. Furthermore, the operating time of idling state in the printing facility is zero, because the size of buffer between each facilities is big enough. Taking these assumption into account, U^1 and p are given by

$$U^1 = \left(\frac{e_r^1}{p_r^1} + \frac{e_s^1 \lambda^1}{LS}\right), \tag{13}$$

$$\frac{1}{p} = \left(\frac{1}{p_r^1} + \frac{\lambda^1}{LS}\right), \tag{14}$$

respectively. The dashed line in Fig. 3 denotes calculated Eq. (13). The simulation results and formulation results are in reasonably good agreement. The opened circle and dashed line in Fig. 4 indicate the simulation results of production throughput and formulation results (Eq. (14)), respectively. Note that the results agrees well. We can obtain a relation between U^1 and p as

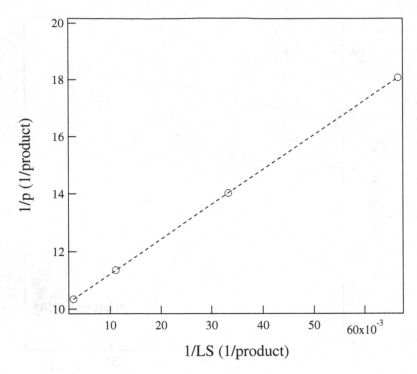

Fig. 4. *LS* dependence of $1/p$. Simulation results (open circle) and formulation results (dashed line)

$$U^1 = \frac{e_s^1}{p} + \frac{e_r^1}{p_r^1} - \frac{e_s^1}{p_r^1} \qquad (15)$$

from Eqs. (13) and (14). We can understand that energy consumption per production throughput decreases with an increase productivity.

5   Conclusion

In order to approach the theoretical realization the production conditions that affect a productivity or energy consumption, we investigated the formulation of the relationship between energy consumption and production throughput, and verified it by using numerical simulation. The simulation results and formulation results are in reasonably good agreement. The relation between lot size and energy consumption per production throughput, production throughput were understood. It is clearly shown that energy consumption per production throughput decreases with an increase productivity.

References

1. Göschel, A., Schieck, F., Schönherr, J.: Method for energy and resource balancing demonstrated as an example of the hot sheet metal production process. CIRP Ann.-Manuf. Technol. **61**(1), 399–402 (2012)
2. Fujitsu, Co., Green Monodukuri: RAGON. http://jp.fujitsu.com/about/csr/eco/services/energysaving/emdragon/ (Accessed 18-5-2012)
3. Nissan Motor Co., A case study of energy consumption per unit of production throughput. http://www.jsme.or.jp/publish/ronbun/JSME_Manual_20100730.pdf (Accessed 10-5-2011)
4. The Energy Conservation Center Japan, The revised energy conservation law. http://www.eccj.or.jp/law/pamph/outline_revision/new_outline2010.pdf (Accessed 25-4-2011)
5. Hibino, H., Sakuma, T., Yamaguchi, M.: Manufacturing system simulation for evaluation of productivity and energy consumption. J. Adv. Mech. Des. Syst. Manuf. **8**(2), 1–13 (2014)
6. Hibino, H., Sakuma, T., Yamaguchi, M.: Simulation for sustainable manufacturing system considering productivity and energy consumption. In: Grabot, B., Vallespir, B., Gomes, S., Bouras, A., Kiritsis, D. (eds.) Advances in Production Management Systems, Part II. IFIP AICT, vol. 439, pp. 310–318. Springer, Heidelberg (2014)

Author Index